# ESSENTIAL CROATIA

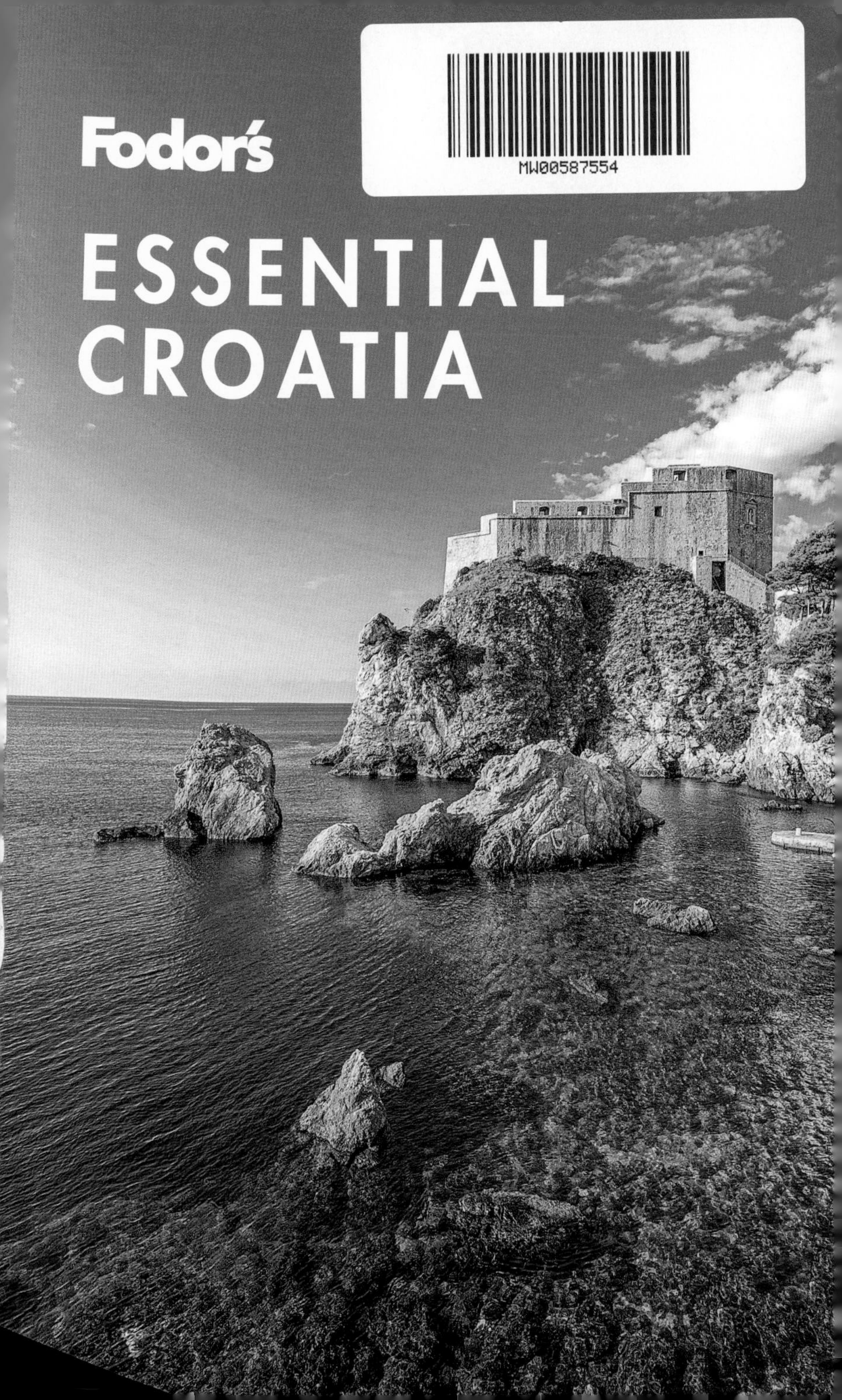

# Welcome to Croatia

Croatia's splendors extend from the deep-blue waters of the Adriatic coastline to the waterfall-laced mountains of the Dinaric Alps and throughout its medieval towns. From Dubrovnik's walled city, where baroque buildings are surrounded by centuries-old forts, to the lively islands of Brač and Hvar, this Central European country is an exciting blend of glamour and tradition. As you plan your upcoming travels to Croatia, please confirm that places are still open and let us know when we need to make updates by writing to us at editors@fodors.com.

## TOP REASONS TO GO

★ **History:** Visit Dubrovnik's walled Old Town and Diocletian's Palace in Split.

★ **Cool Cities:** Explore Zagreb's museums and café culture and Rovinj's old-city charm.

★ **Beaches:** From secluded hideaways to ocean-side party spots, each beach is unique.

★ **Natural Parks:** Plitvice Lakes, Brijuni Islands, and Mljet are just a few spots filled with gorgeous landscapes.

★ **Wine:** From Istria to Korčula, vineyards and wineries abound.

★ **Sailing:** Southern Dalmatia's dramatic coastline is a paradise for boating enthusiasts.

# Contents

## MAPS

Chapter 1



# EXPERIENCE CROATIA

# 20 ULTIMATE EXPERIENCES

Croatia offers terrific experiences that should be on every traveler's list. Here are Fodor's top picks for a memorable trip.

## 1 Dubrovnik

Few sights in the world are as impressive as the Pearl of the Adriatic. With its medieval walls rising from the glittering blue Adriatic Sea, Dubrovnik is Croatia's ultimate must-see destination. *(Ch. 3)*

## 2 Sailing

A 1,100-mile coastline studded with 1,244 stunning islands, emerald inlets, unspoiled beaches, and lively towns makes the country a paradise for sailing enthusiasts. *(Ch. 1)*

## 3 Diocletian's Palace, Split

Split's main attraction, the Roman emperor Diocletian's summer palace dates to the 3rd century AD and is one of the world's most impressive Roman ruins. *(Ch. 4)*

## 4 Hvar

Seaside Hvar Town is the country's nightlife capital, but beyond the glitz and glamour, the island is a wild paradise of olive groves, ancient vineyards, and lavender. *(Ch. 4)*

## 5 Seafood

Along the coast, look out for sea bream, sea bass, sardines, oysters, mussels, and octopus, often caught from the sea right beside your restaurant. *(Ch. 3–7)*

## 6 Plitvice National Park

One of eight national parks in the country, Plitvice National Park is a riot of color year-round, with 16 magnificent lakes connected by waterfalls. *(Ch. 8)*

## 7 Zagreb

With a thriving café culture, the country's best museums, great shopping, and plenty of green space, Zagreb offers the rare chance to experience a living European city without the crowds. *(Ch. 8)*

## 8 Wine

A tour of Croatia's four distinct wine-making regions involves centuries-old vineyards, millennia-long traditions, and a modern-day wine-making renaissance. *(Ch. 1–9)*

## 9 Café Culture

Coffee drinking is a favorite national pastime. Do it the local way: linger at a café, watch the world go by, and practice ordering a *bijela kava* ("white coffee"). *(Ch. 3–9)*

## 10 Beaches

Lovely pebble beaches abound in Croatia, but Zlatni Rat, a spit of land on Brač Island, is particularly stunning with its white sand, lush pine groves, and intensely blue water. *(Ch. 3–6)*

## 11 Biking

Exploring towns, islands, and the countryside by bike is both fun and smart. The inland region of Slavonia is made for cycling, with its flat roads, miles of bike lanes, and well-traveled routes. *(Ch. 9)*

## 12 Cultural Festivals

Folk festivals are enthusiastically celebrated by all ages, and they're a great way to experience the local life of a region through its traditional music, dance, and costume. *(Ch. 3–9)*

## 13 Vukovar

A visit to this Slavonian city is both a sobering reminder of the tragedies that unfolded here in the last half century and an inspiring vision of a city rebuilt. *(Ch. 9)*

## 14 Istria's Hill Towns

Perhaps the most perfect road trip in Croatia involves visiting medieval towns like Grožnjan and Motovun, sampling wine, olive oil, and truffles along the way. *(Ch. 7)*

## 15 Kvarner Bay Islands

Four of Croatia's largest, wildest islands—Cres, Rab, Krk, and Lošinj—offer dramatic views, diverse landscapes, sandy beaches, and excellent island-hopping opportunities. *(Ch. 6)*

## 16 Korčula

This pine-covered island is steeped in history, from its reputation as the birthplace of Marco Polo to the legendary sea battles that were waged along its shores. *(Ch. 3)*

## 17 Opatija Resorts

Genteel Opatija has been a resort town since the 1840s, fashionable among the high society who came to stay in its elegant spas and grand villas. *(Ch. 6)*

## 18 Baroque Architecture in Varaždin

A town of castles, ornate cemeteries, and thermal springs, Varaždin makes a wonderful day trip from Zagreb. *(Ch. 8)*

## 19 Kornati National Park

This archipelago with more than 100 uninhabited islands, islets, and reefs is a nautical paradise in Northern Dalmatia. *(Ch. 5)*

## 20 Roman Ruins in Pula

Pula boasts one of the largest and best-preserved ancient Roman arenas in the world; today, it makes a stunning backdrop to concerts and the annual Pula Film Festival. *(Ch. 7)*

# WHAT'S WHERE

**1 Dubrovnik and Southern Dalmatia.** Dubrovnik is Croatia's most popular destination and one of the world's most beautiful cities. If you need to escape the crowds, cruise to one of the nearby islands, head north to the Pelješac Peninsula, or south to the bucolic Konavle region.

**2 Split and Central Dalmatia.** With the remains of the 2,000-year old Diocletian's Palace that dominate its Old Town, Split makes a fascinating jumping-off point to the islands of Vis, Brač, and Hvar.

**3 Zadar and Northern Dalmatia.** Low-key Zadar offers a pleasant seaside atmosphere and easy access to four beautiful national parks.

**4 Kvarner Bay and the Northern Adriatic Islands.** Protected by mountain ranges on three sides, Kvarner enjoys a particularly mild climate, with Opatija, Rijeka, and nearby islands beckoning visitors to explore.

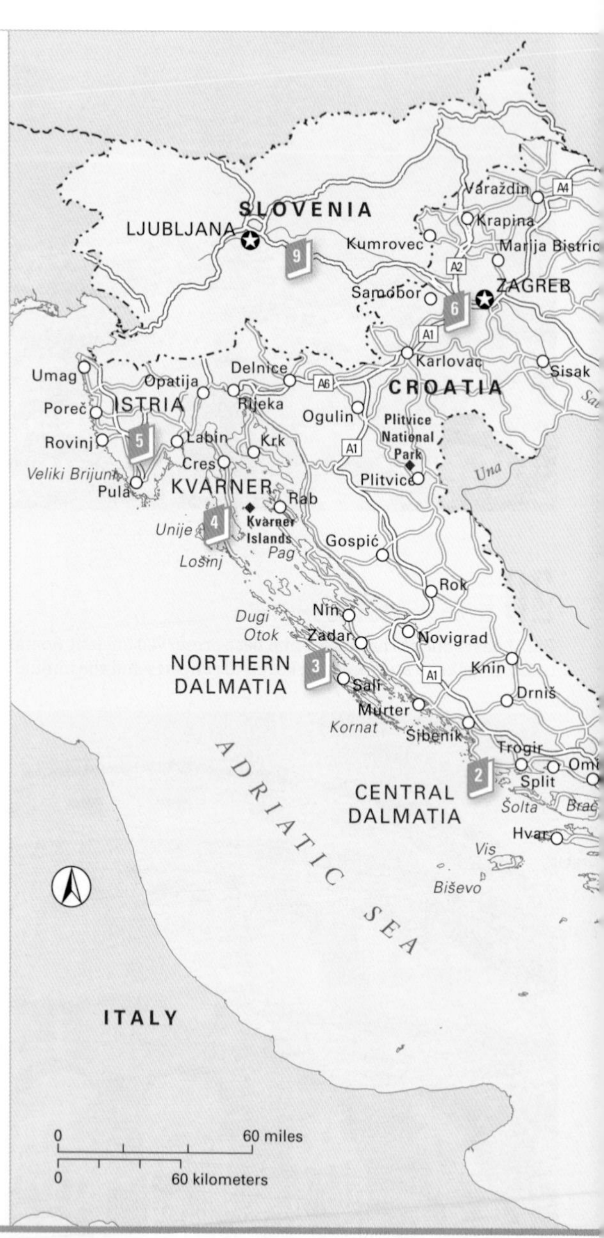

## FOLKLORE AND RELIGION

No matter how busy or how enmeshed with the rest of the continent it gets, Croatia retains a steadfast connection to its distinctive culture and traditions. Each region, sometimes each individual town, has its own traditional music, dance, costumes, and customs of which the local people are very proud. Folk festivals are enthusiastically celebrated by all ages, particularly those tied to religious holidays. After all, religion still plays a large part in everyday life (90% of the population identify as Catholic, while only 5% consider themselves nonreligious or atheist) and the major Catholic holidays like Easter and Christmas are cause for a great party all over the country. Feast Days for local saints—such as St. Blaise in Dubrovnik—are also widely celebrated, usually featuring performances from local folklore troupes.

## SPORTS

Another thing Croatians fervently believe in and celebrate is sports. For a relatively small country, Croatia has had enormous sporting success. Their football (that's soccer to the Americans) team made it to the semifinals of the World Cup in 1998—the first time they participated!—almost knocking out the hosts, and favorites to win, France. Fast-forward to 2018, when they squared off (and lost) against the same team, but this time in the final. In 2022, Croatia knocked out Brazil in a thriller of a match and eventually placed third in the tournament, losing to Argentina, the eventual champions. And it's not just football; Croatia can boast some of the best teams in the world at handball, water polo, and basketball, and they fare extremely well at many Olympic disciplines despite a smaller population and lower funding than many other countries.

## LOOKING AHEAD

Corruption in the public sector has not changed much since the country's Communist days, and it can be discouraging to try to start a business in Croatia. After the long-awaited accession into the European Union in 2013, many people, especially young Croats seeking a more secure life, left for places like Germany and Ireland. But there is hope for the future, as young entrepreneurs and people coming back to the country after years living abroad try to cut through the red tape to start new ventures. An influx of EU funds also means greater investment opportunities for people who successfully apply. Time will tell what the free movement of people and capital through Croatia will bring.

# What to Eat and Drink

### SEAFOOD

Fresh seafood is the star of most dishes served along the Adriatic Coast. The most typical dish is grilled fresh fish, such as sea bream, sea bass, scorpion fish, or John Dory. Don't leave without trying *crni rižot*, a risotto that gets its jet-black color from squid or cuttlefish ink.

### CURED MEATS AND CHEESES

Croatian meals often begin with a platter of local charcuterie and cheese. In Zagreb and Slavonia, you are likely to come across *kulen*, a pork sausage richly seasoned with pepper and paprika (leading to its bright red color). *Pršut*, a type of dry-cured ham, is very popular along the coast in Dalmatia and Istria; Dalmatians smoke and cure it longer and with more spices than the Istrians, and both leave it out to dry in the famous northeastern *bura* wind. That same wind is responsible for flavoring the country's most celebrated cheese, *Paški sir*; the bura sprinkles the entire island of Pag with salt water, flavoring the herbs (like fennel and sage) on which the sheep graze, making for a salty, dry, and crumbly cheese. Rounding out your charcuterie platter will likely be some type of *pašteta*, (a fish or meat pâté), a few olives, and perhaps marinated anchovies.

### BAKED GOODS

You can barely walk a block in a Croatian city, most notably Zagreb, without stumbling upon a bakery overflowing with everything from pizza to salty bread rolls and sausage rolls. The must-try is *burek*, a flaky phyllo pastry filled with either a type of cottage cheese, meat (the most traditional), or spinach, usually eaten for breakfast. Equally beloved is the humble *štrukli* (strudel), a finely-rolled dough filled with fresh cottage cheese which can be made sweet or savory, depending on the filling and whether or not you add powdered sugar; it is considered one of Croatia's national dishes, most typically eaten in Zagorje and Zagreb.

### TRUFFLES

The forests of inland Istria around Motovun are home to highly prized *tartufi* (truffles). The black truffle season conveniently peaks at the same time as the tourist season, from May until October, so it's relatively easy to find it on the menus of Istrian restaurants. The white truffle, on the other hand, grows in the winter months and may be harder to come by. The secretive flavorful truffles are rooted out in forests by specially trained dogs or pigs and incorporated into a variety of dishes, including *fuži s tartufima*, a simple dish of fresh fuži pasta and shaved white truffle.

### WINE

Croatia's wine-making renaissance continues with many France-, Napa Valley–, and Italy-educated winemakers returning to make the best of some truly exceptional terroirs. Croatian wine can be challenging to find at international wineshops—all the more reason to delve into these craftily revisited local vintages during your stay.

Wine

**SOUPS AND STEWS**
Each region has its own traditional soup or stew, served either as a starter or as a main course. It's often slow-cooked in a cast iron or copper pot, ideally outdoors over an open fire like the hunters and shepherds used to do. In Istria, the typical soup is *maneštra*, a take on Italian minestrone made with beans, dried meat, and corn. Dalmatia's most popular stew is *pašticada*, beef stewed in sweet or red wine and prunes, served alongside homemade gnocchi. The most typical Slavonian stew is *čobanac*, made with several types of meat from veal and wild game to beef and lots of paprika. All along the coast you can find a version of *brodet*, a hearty stew made with at least three different types of fish, while in Slavonia they enjoy *fiš paprikaš*, a spicy noodle soup made with a variety of freshwater fish.

**PEKA**
A traditional way of cooking meat (usually lamb or beef), seafood (usually octopus), or even bread is *ispod peke*, meaning "under the bell." The *peka*, a clay or wrought-iron cooking vessel, is buried under a pile of hot coals so that the meat, together with potatoes, carrots, rosemary, sage, and other Mediterranean herbs, stews slowly in its own juices until it falls off the bone. It's a must when visiting Dalmatia; advance notice is usually required to order it.

**DESSERTS**
The most common dessert in Croatia is *palačinke*, a thin pancake stuffed with Nutella or marmalade. *Fritule*, Dalmatia's brandy-spiked version of a doughnut hole, is made with lemon zest and raisins and sprinkled with powdered sugar; it's traditionally served at holidays. Candied almonds and fruit peels are common treats to end a meal in Southern Dalmatia, and *sladoled* (ice cream) is prevalent in all towns along the coast (try the dark chocolate).

**RAKIJA**
You won't be in Croatia long before you're introduced to your first taste of *rakija*, a distilled herbal or fruit spirit that makes up an important part of Croatian culture. All across the country, business deals are sealed, friendships are cemented, and journeys are begun to the clink of a few shot glasses of this fiery schnapps. It's used as a cure for everything, from a sore throat to a sea urchin sting. Croatians often brew rakija themselves at home, using everything from plums (*šljivovica*) to walnuts (*orahovica*) to herbs (*travarica*).

# What to Buy in Croatia

**HANDCRAFTED PAG LACE**
Handcrafted by women from the island of Pag since the 15th century, each of these intricate lace patterns is unique to the individual who crocheted it.

**WOODEN TOYS OF HRVATSKO ZAGORJE**
Dating back to the 19th century, these toys were traditionally carved by hand out of local wood (willow, beech, maple, and lime), painted in bright yellow, red, and blue patterns, and then passed down through generations.

**LAVENDER**
As soon as you arrive on the Croatian coast, particularly the island of Hvar, you will pick up the fresh scent of lavender. It is used in cooking, cosmetics, and even to treat sunburn and mosquito bites. You can buy all manner of lavender souvenirs, including sachets of the dried herb.

**CRAVATS**
In the 17th century, Croatian military uniforms featured patterned scarves knotted around the neck. French soldiers appreciated the style, introduced them to Parisian society with the name *cravat* (a play on the word "Croat"), and the rest is sartorial history. You can pick up an "original Croatian tie" in shops around the country, including the chain boutique Croata.

**ŠIBENIK BUTTON JEWELRY**
Originally part of the traditional folk costume worn by men in Šibenik, the Šibenik Button was proclaimed the most original Croatian souvenir in 2007. Originally made with silver, today you can find these intricate round buttons in different materials and sizes adorning earrings, rings, and other jewelry.

**OLIVE OIL**
Croatians have been making oil olive for two millennia, most notably in Istria, which has been named the top olive oil region in the world for several years running, as well as the islands of Cres, Krk, and Korčula. Croatian olive oil is distinctive for its bright green color and peppery flavor.

**LICITAR HEART**
These heart-shaped biscuits, handmade with honey dough and painted red with intricate swirls and hearts, have been given as romantic gifts since the 16th century. They are typical of Central Europe,

Licitar heart

particularly Zagreb, where they are used to decorate Christmas trees, including the thousands put up around the city during the Advent Market each December.

**ŠESTINE UMBRELLAS**
This bright red umbrella is a part of the traditional folk costume of the Šestine neighborhood in Zagreb. It has become the most famous emblem of Zagreb, thanks to its use as a sun shade by the vendors at the Dolac Market.

**BRAČ WHITE STONE**
Pure white stone has been excavated from quarries on the island of Brač since ancient times and has been used to build some of the most famous structures in the world. The center of stone masonry on the island is Pučišća, where students come to learn stone masonry at quarries that date back to the Romans. You can take a piece home with you in the form of candleholders, pestles and mortars, or sculptures.

**SAMOBOR CRYSTAL**
A worthwhile day trip from Zagreb, the quaint town of Samobor is known for two things: their exquisite cream cake and their crystalware. Hand-carved here using the same method since 1839, you can find beautifully crafted jugs, glasses, and vases in factories and shops around town.

**STON SEA SALT**
In the unassuming town of Ston on the Pelješac Peninsula, you'll find Europe's oldest salt pans, dating back 4,000 years. You can take a short tour to see how the tasty all-natural sea salt is still gathered using mostly ancient tools—sun, sea, and wind—and take home a small bag for yourself.

# Best Islands in Croatia

**VIS**
An off-the-beaten-path destination in Central Dalmatia, Vis has a wonderfully remote ambience, fragrant citrus orchards, and few tourists. Plan to spend a couple of days exploring the main town, ancient ruins, Renaissance churches, and the famous blue cave on nearby Biševo.

**BRAČ**
If you have time to visit only one island, Brač, off the coast of Split, is a good option. You'll find Zlatni Rat, touted as the most beautiful beach in Croatia; Vidova Gora, the highest peak in the Adriatic; and the alluring towns of Pučišća and Supetar, where you can buy souvenirs made of the famous white Brač stone.

**PAG**
With its barren expanses, wind-whipped jagged peaks, and the occasional patch of shrubs, Pag offers something totally unique to the rest of verdant Northern Dalmatia. Trek to the mysterious Pag Triangle and save lots of time to sample the country's most celebrated cheese, *P aški sir*.

**LASTOVO**
One of the most remote inhabited islands in the country, Lastovo has only one hotel and it takes several hours to reach by ferry from Split and Dubrovnik, so there are no day-trippers. Come to enjoy the walking trails, empty beaches, fresh shrimp on skewers, and solitude.

**MLJET**
Croatia's greenest island off the coast of Dubrovnik, Mljet is cloaked in dense pine forests, secret coves, and olive groves. One end of the island is encompassed by a national park with hiking and biking trails and two saltwater lakes, the other end is home to a beautiful sandy beach, and in the middle is the mythical Odysseus Cave.

**RAB**

With more than 30 sandy beaches, Rab, in Kvarner Bay, offers a respite from Croatia's typically rocky shores. For those who want to leave more than just their water shoes behind, Rab is also the birthplace—and still the hub—of naturism (nude beaches) in Croatia.

**KRK**

The varied terrain on Croatia's largest island means you can tour vineyards, traipse through pine forests, and test your acrophobia on the jaw-dropping limestone cliffs of Vrbnik—all before lunch.

**ZLARIN**

Home to just 300 permanent residents, Zlarin is an island of peace, quiet, and unspoiled splendor in the Šibenik archipelago. It has one lone village, with narrow lanes and old stone buildings, and is best known for the bright red coral that is harvested off the coast and turned into jewelry.

**HVAR**

Hvar is famous for its nightlife, so if you're looking to enjoy a bit of glitz and glamour, this is your place. Sun-splashed Hvar Town showcases a sparkling marina filled with yachts, trendy beach bars, and bumping nightclubs. Hvar Town also has heritage-rich landmarks, including the hilltop Fortica Spanish fortress.

**KORČULA**

With miles of perfect mountain biking roads; islets to discover by sail or motorboat; boutique wine, olive oil, and honey to sample; and a historical Old Town that is rivaled only by Dubrovnik itself in beauty, you could spend weeks on Korčula and never see it all.

# Croatia Sailing

With 1,777 km (around 1,100 miles) of coastline along the crystal clear Adriatic Sea and more than 1,000 islands, islets, cliffs, and reefs (about 50 of which are inhabited) dotted close to the mainland shore, Croatia is made for sailing and island-hopping. Along the way, there are picturesque coastal towns to visit and you won't have any problem finding a secluded cove to swim and snorkel in, even in the height of summer.

There are also three national parks on the sea: Brijuni National Park (a cluster of 14 verdant islands by the Istrian Peninsula), Kornati National Park (an archipelago of 89 islands in Northern Dalmatia), and Mljet National Park (a lush island adorned by Mediterranean greenery in Southern Dalmatia). Krka National Park (a spectacular series of waterfalls, winding rivers, and karst canyons in Central Dalmatia) can also be approached by sailboat; simply sail up the Šibenik Channel to Skradin Bay.

If you've got a week, a popular sailing route is from Split to Dubrovnik, stopping to explore the islands of Brač, Hvar, Korčula, Mljet, and the Elafiti Islands. If you have more time, you could start further north in Zadar and sail all the way down to Kotor in Montenegro. The yacht charter season runs from May through October, with the best month being September when the water is still warm, crowds are fewer, and yacht prices are reduced.

### SAILING 101

If you have sailing experience, you can go "bareboat" and charter a yacht to sail independently. By Croatian law at least one crew member needs to have an international sailing license considered valid by the Croatian Ministry of the Sea, Transport, and Infrastructure, plus a VHF radio certificate if one is not included in your license. To check whether your licenses are acceptable, head to the ministry's website. The coast is well-equipped to welcome sailors, with more than 50 marinas, roughly half of which are managed by **ACI (Adriatic Club International)**. In the summer, it is strongly advisable to arrive at the marina early in the afternoon to ensure a berth (around €25 to €50 per day), as they fill up quickly. You could also skip the marina altogether and moor in one of the country's many natural bays or islets.

If you have never sailed before or have little experience, then you will need a skipper, who generally does much more than navigate the boat; most are local and know the local waters, winds, history, the best secret coves for putting down anchor, and the best diving spots. Skippers cost around €100 per day, plus meals, which you are expected to provide.

The third option is sailing in a flotilla: a group of yachts, with people of mixed levels of sailing experience, led by a qualified expert. Or sign up for a sailing course, ranging from beginner to advanced; there are even courses for the whole family.

### CHARTER COMPANIES

Chartering a yacht or sailboat is not just for rich people; it's often comparable in price to a nice hotel, plus you have the option to self-cater and you don't have to worry about catching ferries or public transport. Some islands, such as the Kornati Islands, are only accessible by private boat so you'd end up booking a tour to visit them anyway. And having your morning coffee while you sail on the glassy sea, then pulling into a sparkling cove whenever you want to swim or snorkel is priceless.

There are dozens of charter companies operating tens of thousands of boats of all sizes. As a rough guide to pricing, in the summer 2023 high season, Sail Croatia offered a private yacht tour on a 2015 six-berth for €5,200 per week, including a skipper, fuel, and airport transfers. The price to charter the same yacht independently was €2,800.

The high season runs from May through October, with demand and prices peaking in July and August. Summer on the Croatian coast is typically hot, dry, and sunny, with windier periods usually happening on the polar ends of the high season. An experienced skipper, who knows which areas of the sea tend to be windy and which are calm, will be able to cater to your wishes, whether you want to crank it up a notch and go diagonal or just take it easy and smooth sail. During peak season, many charter rentals begin at 5 pm Saturday and end at 9 am the following Saturday, but times and lengths can vary depending on the company and your needs.

**Activity Yachting** The sailing programs offered by U.K.-based Activity Yachting operate along the roughly 160-km (100-mile) stretch of coastline between Split and Zadar. Flotilla holidays (with or without an educational "Learn to Sail" program, during which you can get your own skipper certification) are available, along with bareboat rentals. The company offers an array of sailboats and catamarans ranging in size from 30 to 55 feet. ☎ *1243/641–304 in U.K.* 🌐 *www.activityyachting.com.*

**Adriatic Nautical Academy** Based in the town of Jezera on the island of Murter in Central Dalmatia, the Adriatic Nautical Academy (ANA) is an international sailing school and certified RYA training center. ANA's offerings include basic sailing courses, advanced sailing lessons, and leisure sailing for those who just want to kick their feet up and enjoy the views. 🌐 *anasail.com/en.*

**Euromarine** With bases in Pula, Split, and Dubrovnik, Euromarine charters more than 100 sailing boats, motorboats, and catamarans. You can choose from bareboat, skippered, and crewed options. ☎ *1/555–2222* 🌐 *www.charter.euromarine.com.hr.*

**Nautilus** This company charters bareboat, skippered, and crewed yachts, catamarans, and motorboats at beautiful bases in Pula, Zadar, Biograd, Trogir, Split, and Dubrovnik. Flotilla sailing is also available from Trogir and Dubrovnik. ☎ *1/732–867445 in U.K.* 🌐 *www.nautilusyachting.com.*

**Sail Croatia** One of the best-known sailing companies around the coast, Sail Croatia offers cruises and yachts with diverse itinerary options to suit everyone. You can pick from party, adventure, relaxation, or luxury-focused experiences. While itineraries are flexible, departures are generally from Split. Boats can also be chartered on a bareboat, skippered, or crewed basis. ✉ *Split* ☎ *929/205–6952 in U.S.* 🌐 *www.sail-croatia.com.*

**Ultra Sailing** Founded by former members of the Croatian Olympic Team who now work as instructors, Ultra Sailing offers a variety of courses, with a main school office and base in the ACI Marina Split. The company also offers yacht charters from Pula, Trogir, Split, and Dubrovnik, plus an organized regatta center in Kaštela. ✉ *Split* ☎ *021/398–578* 🌐 *www.ultra-sailing.hr.*

# Wine in Croatia

You will be forgiven if you haven't heard of Croatian wine. Not much of it is exported to other countries, and it doesn't receive much international fanfare. To put it mildly, the last couple of centuries have been bad for the wine business in Croatia; the insect pest phylloxera, war, and crippling economic policies ravaged the industry and put it generations behind its European neighbors.

But a wine renaissance is now occurring here; blessed with a unique mineral-rich terroir ideal for grape-growing, four distinct wine-making regions, and more than 125 indigenous grapes, Croatian wines are once again winning awards and garnering attention.

## CROATIAN WINE TODAY

Most wineries are family-owned small-batch affairs, but that is changing. After Croatia joined the EU in 2013, there was an influx of money, technology, and ideas into the country. Many who left have come back to reclaim their family land and revive their wine-making traditions, bringing with them new techniques and skills picked up from their time living abroad.

With a huge number of tourists to satisfy—plus a big wine-loving local population—Croatia still imports more than it exports, which is why it's not easy to find Croatian wine abroad. That's what makes a visit to Croatia so interesting for wine lovers; you'll try wines that you've never tried before and can't get elsewhere, all in historical and beautiful settings with passionate young winemakers who are eager to share their stories.

## WHAT TO DRINK AND WHERE

There are four main wine-making regions in Croatia:

Istria is Croatia's best-known and most celebrated wine-making region with its most sophisticated wineries. The limestone- and terra-cotta-rich terroir produces Malvazija Istarska, Croatia's second most planted white varietal, as well as red teran.

The Croatian Uplands, encompassing Zagorje and Međimurje, are located north of Zagreb in central Croatia. This is the newest and least developed of the four wine regions, but it's one of the areas to watch for locals in the know. It's known for cool-climate wines, including Pinot Blanc, Riesling, Chardonnay, Pinot Noir, and its most famous varietal: white *pušipel*.

Slavonia is Croatia's largest wine-making region by volume. This flat region is known as much for its vineyards as for its forests full of Slavonian oak, which is renowned for its use in the manufacture of wine barrels worldwide. Almost 70% of wine produced in Croatia is white, and the most-planted varietal is Graševina, which thrives here. Another must-try in Slavonia is Traminac from Ilok, which was served at the coronation of Queen Elizabeth II.

Dalmatia and the islands have a mild dry climate with limestone soil and the country's longest history of wine-making, particularly on the islands. The mighty Plavac Mali grape thrives on the steep slopes of the Pelješac Peninsula overlooking the island Korčula, where the sun is reflected onto it from the sea, the limestone, and the sky, resulting in two full-bodied high-alcohol wines, Dingač and Postup, which were Croatia's first two appellations.

# Kids and Families

Croatia is an ideal place to travel with children. Local folks, from elderly people to young teens, adore kids and will rush to help if they see that your family needs assistance. As one of the safest countries on the continent, the only thing you have to worry about is stepping on a sea urchin at the beach (so bring water shoes). When traveling around, distances between towns are short, so you're never stuck in the car or on public transport for long. Most restaurants welcome little ones and have kid-friendly options on the menu, while pizzerias, markets, and bakeries are plentiful, so you can always grab a quick bite to stave off hunger.

**Where to Stay.** Private accommodations, villas, or self-catering apartments are a great option when traveling with kids. They can fit the whole family and you'll have handy facilities such as a kitchen, laundry, separate bedrooms and bathrooms, more room to play, and sometimes even a private pool. They are often located in more residential neighborhoods, so you won't have to worry about noise and you can get a feel for the local way of life (and maybe even make friends with a few local kids and parents). For nature-loving families, there are many campsites along the Adriatic, where accommodations range from tents to bungalows with all the modern amenities. If you want to treat yourselves to a hotel or resort, there are many excellent options with water parks, pools, kids' clubs, and playgrounds on-site.

**Natural Attractions.** The crystal clear Adriatic is an instant magnet for almost any little one; up and down the coast you'll be able to try family-friendly activities such as kayaking, windsurfing, paddleboarding, and tubing. Most Croatian beaches are rocky or pebbly, but there are a few sandy beaches scattered around, which are easier on little feet; Rab is a great choice with 30 sandy beaches, or further south, opt for Saplunara Beach on Mljet, Lumbarda on Korčula, or Šunj Beach on Lopud. If you're in Dubrovnik, don't miss Lokrum, where you can wander through old botanical gardens looking for peacocks and bunnies. Croatian national parks are also great areas to spend a day hiking, climbing, and admiring nature; Brijuni National Park in Istria might be particularly interesting, with its history of dinosaurs and the exotic animals at its safari park, while Plitvice and Krka national parks are a delight for all ages. Caves are another surefire way to ignite young imaginations; Biserujka Cave on Krk is a fun one.

**Cities.** Croatian cities are safe, walkable, and compact, making them very easy to maneuver with kids. Even the capital and largest city in the country, Zagreb, is extremely child-friendly; there's a funicular to shuttle you between the Upper and Lower Towns, interactive museums (the Museum of Illusions is a fun one), the biggest and best playgrounds in the country, and a myriad of parks to wander. Zadar is another interesting city for kids, with its unique Sea Organ and Greeting to the Sun. If you're around Šibenik in June and July, the International Children's Festival takes over the streets for two weeks, with workshops, games, concerts, and performances geared toward kids. The Old Towns in cities like Dubrovnik and Split are car-free, so you can let them run around without worry—just beware that most Old Towns are full of cobblestones, steps, and few accessible features; if you are traveling with a baby, it's recommended to bring a carrier or sling when you head out to explore.

# What to Watch and Read

### *GAME OF THRONES*

The series that changed it all for Dubrovnik, or as some fans know it better, King's Landing. The popular HBO show was partially filmed in Dubrovnik and nearby sites for seven seasons, and though some CGI was used, the walled city is remarkably distinguishable in many scenes.

### *STAR WARS: THE FORCE AWAKENS*

Dubrovnik made a short but memorable appearance as the city Canto Bight in this 2017 installment of the popular franchise.

### *MAMMA MIA! HERE WE GO AGAIN*

In the 2018 sequel to the original hit *Mamma Mia!*, the Dalmatian island of Vis stands in for the Greek island where the film is set.

### *BLACK LAMB AND GREY FALCON* BY REBECCA WEST

One of the most detailed and evocative books about pre–World War II Yugoslavia, this highly-regarded travel narrative, published in 1941 when Yugoslavia was under Nazi occupation, details West's six-week journey with her husband through the region four years earlier.

### *CROATIA: A NATION FORGED BY WAR* BY MARCUS TANNER

Published in 2001, this book provides an intriguing journalistic account of Croatian history, from its medieval origins and the creation and breakup of Yugoslavia to a firsthand account of the war in the 1990s and the tentative peace that followed.

### *HOW WE SURVIVED COMMUNISM AND EVEN LAUGHED* BY SLAVENKA DRAKULIĆ

Slavenka Drakulić is a Croatian journalist who has written extensively about the issues facing her country, including this collection of essays about her life during and after communism.

### *THE HOTEL TITO* BY IVANA BODROŽIĆ

This funny and insightful autobiography recounts the author's experiences as a refugee from Vukovar during the Homeland War.

Chapter 2

# TRAVEL SMART



Updated by
Andrea MacDonald

**★ CAPITAL:**
Zagreb

**POPULATION:**
4,029,164

**LANGUAGE:**
Croatian

**$ CURRENCY:**
Euro (€)

**COUNTRY CODE:**
385

**⚠ EMERGENCIES:**
112

**DRIVING:**
On the right

**ELECTRICITY:**
200V/50 cycles; electrical plugs have two round prongs

**TIME:**
Six hours ahead of New York

**WEB RESOURCES:**
croatia.hr

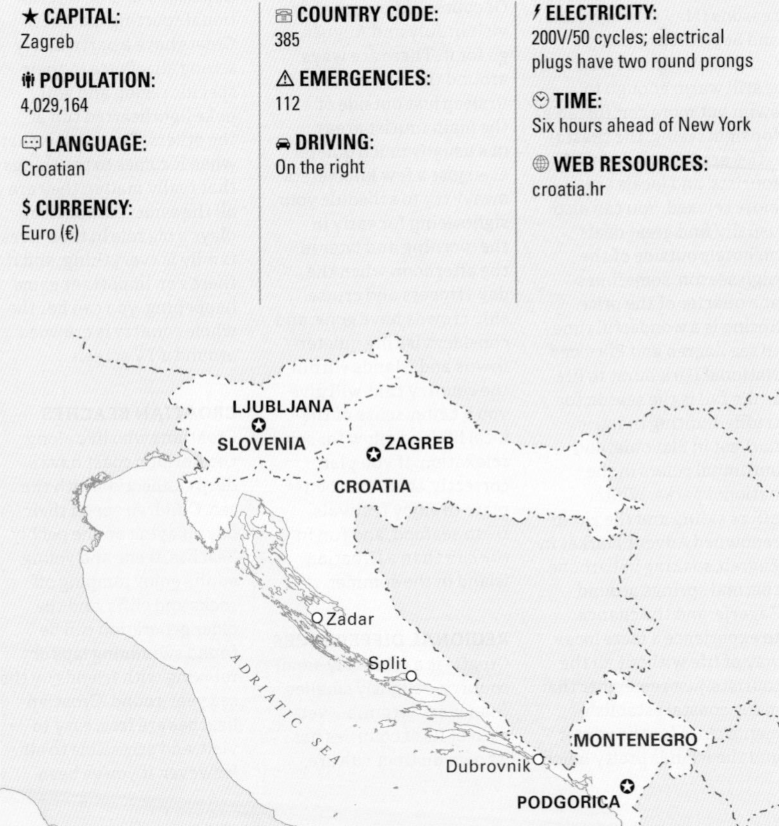

# Know Before You Go

A beautiful and diverse country, Croatia can be overwhelming for a first-time visitor. Here are some key tips to help you navigate your trip, whether it's your first time visiting or your twentieth.

## WHEN TO GO

Although most famous for its summertime activities along the Adriatic coast, the best time to visit Croatia is actually the shoulder seasons (May through June and September through October), when the weather is still warm enough to swim but more comfortable for sightseeing, the coastal cities aren't crowded with tourists, and locals are more relaxed. You can also usually find great deals on hotels outside of the high season, sometimes at a quarter of the price. Spring is a wonderful time to see Zagreb and Plitvice National Park burst to life, while fall is the season for truffle-hunting in Istria, harvest in Slavonia, and autumnal colors in the national parks. Winter offers skiing and the world-renowned Advent Market in Zagreb, soaking in baroque thermal springs around Zagorje, and the chance to experience a more local way of life without all the tourists; just remember that many coastal establishments close for the winter and the islands pretty much shut down, so if you plan a winter trip to the coast you'll want to stick to the larger cities like Dubrovnik, Split, and Zadar.

Of course, if you can only visit in July and August, go for it. There are ways around the crowds: try to sleep just outside of the main tourist areas (it's usually much quieter even just a few kilometers away); try to schedule your sightseeing for early in the morning and later in the afternoon when the day-trippers and cruise ship crowds have gone; and consider visiting quieter towns and islands within the country that will give you a better sense of the local life and allow for some relaxation. If you plan correctly, there's no better place to enjoy festivals, fresh seafood, and fun in the sun than a Croatian island in the summer.

## REGIONAL DIFFERENCES

Croatia is a relatively small country—slightly smaller than West Virginia—yet each of its 21 counties has its own distinct culture, traditions, and personality that reflect its history and geography. Istria, for example, has been ruled by the Roman Empire, the Venetian Empire, and was actually part of Italy right up until the end of World War II, resulting in a strong Italian influence on everything from its cuisine and its Roman ruins to the fact that most of the region is still bilingual. Inland, you'll notice a prominent Austro-Hungarian influence on the wine, cuisine, and architecture, stemming from centuries under Habsburg rule. Though extremely proud of the country as a whole (especially during international sporting matches), Croats have a particularly strong allegiance to their specific region and will poke lighthearted fun at the others. The truth is that when it comes to the things that really matter, they are all the same: Catholicism plays a big role in their lives; family is everything; and if there's an important game happening, you can bet the whole country is crowded around a TV screen.

## CROATIAN BEACHES

Croatians who live along the Adriatic coast have a deep connection with the sea. Children spend their days playing on the pebbly beaches, teens and young adults enjoy jumping off rocks and cliffs, and the older generation can be found swimming laps or relaxing with friends by the sea year-round. Croatian beaches are free, easy to visit, and accessible to all. However, if you've been dreaming about lounging on a sandy beach, you might be surprised to learn that there are only a handful in the entire country; most are pebbly, and some involve just a simple ladder leading straight into the sea from the rocks. The whole coast is a beach and you can jump in from nearly anywhere; just make sure to pack water shoes, and beware of sea urchins attached to the rocks—you can usually spot their round, spiky black form from a distance, but sometimes they are hidden.

Croatia has also been one of the pioneers in "naturism"; nude beaches, campsites, and even nude sailing charters abound in certain parts of the coast (mainly Istria), and hundreds of thousands come here each year to enjoy some fun in the sun *au naturel*. Naturism in Croatia began in 1936, when British King Edward VII and Wallis Simpson went skinny-dipping on the island of Rab. That beach became one of Europe's first official nude beaches, and since then, a thriving culture has taken root, mainly among European enthusiasts, especially Germans and Austrians. Croatians themselves don't make up the bulk of the clientele at these beaches, but they graciously make visitors feel welcome.

## COFFEE CULTURE

Croatians love to meet, chat, and have business meetings over coffee. They never order their *kava* to take-away; they always sit for at least a few minutes to enjoy. Coffee here is affordable (usually less than €2 for a cappuccino), delicious, and sitting in one of the many café-bars offers a great immersion into the local culture. If you like your coffee strong, order an espresso; if you prefer something milkier, practice ordering a *bijela kava* ("white coffee"). Be aware that smoking is still permitted in many establishments, so a seat outside on the terrace might be more comfortable.

## HOLIDAYS

In Croatia, national holidays include the following: January 1 (New Year's Day); January 6 (Epiphany); Easter Sunday and Monday; May 1 (May Day); Corpus Christi (40 days after Easter); June 22 (Anti-Fascist Day); June 25 (Statehood Day); August 5 (National Thanksgiving Day); August 15 (Assumption), October 8 (Independence Day); November 1 (All Saints' Day); and December 25 and 26 (Christmas).

## STAYING CONNECTED

Free Wi-Fi is prevalent throughout Croatian cities, but make sure you have a decent amount of phone data as well, because you will need to be connected in many different situations. The most important app to download prior to your trip is WhatsApp, which will be the primary mode of communication with many different contacts, whether it's receiving check-in details from your accommodation host, organizing the meeting point with your tour guide, or even confirming details with your rental car company. A local SIM card will also come in handy if you have to contact someone by phone or text; you can buy a local SIM card at the airport or visit a Tisak kiosk in any town around Croatia. Otherwise make sure you're part of an international plan with your phone company; most major ones now offer relatively affordable plans of a certain fee per day (usually around $10) to use your phone just like you would at home.

# Getting Here and Around

##  Air

There is now a direct flight between New York and Dubrovnik that operates through the summer months. Otherwise, travelers from the United States must fly into another European hub first—the best options are London, Munich, Frankfurt, Paris, or Vienna—and then transfer to a flight to Croatia with the national carrier, Croatia Airlines, or low-cost airlines such as easyJet, Ryanair, or Wizz Air; just keep in mind that they have stringent baggage limits, offer few free in-flight services, and you'll likely have to reclaim and recheck your bags at the airport, so make sure to leave plenty of time between flights.

Italy is another great choice for a stopover because there are many direct flights, as well as buses and ferries, connecting onward to Croatia. If you're planning to visit Istria or Kvarner, consider a flight to nearby Venice (2½ hours to Rijeka by car) or Trieste (1½ hours by car). If you're going to Dalmatia, you can take an overnight ferry across the Adriatic from Ancona to Split or from Bari to Dubrovnik.

Internal flights within Croatia are well-priced and may save you time if you want to cover some ground. You can fly from Zagreb to Dubrovnik, for example, for under $100, which is comparable in price to taking the bus or renting a car but much quicker. Airports are easy to maneuver and close to the cities, with well-organized and user-friendly ground transportation, making domestic air travel an efficient and affordable option.

### AIRPORTS

There are eight international airports in Croatia: Zagreb (ZAG), Dubrovnik (DBV), Osijek (OSI), Pula (PUY), Rijeka (RJK), Split (SPU), Zadar (ZAD), and Brač (BWK). You can fly direct to all of them from certain international destinations, although in winter most international flights go to Zagreb.

## Boat and Ferry

Several companies operate ferries between Italy and Croatia throughout the summer, the largest being the national carrier Jadrolinija. If traveling with a vehicle, you have three options: large car ferries between Ancona and Split (11 hours) or Zadar (9 hours), or down the coast between Bari and Dubrovnik (11 hours). Up the coast, there are high-speed passenger ferries connecting Venice and Trieste with various ports in Istria, including Rovinj, Pula, and Poreč, as well as Zadar and the islands of Rab, Pag, and Lošinj; journey time is 1–6 hours, depending on the route.

Within Croatia, regular car and passenger ferries connect all islands to the mainland and to each other, making island-hopping an easy and fun way to get around. Keep in mind that local ferries are quick and cheap for foot passengers (you can usually show up at the port, buy a ticket, and jump onboard), whereas those traveling with a car should buy a ticket in advance and still might end up waiting awhile for a spot in high season. Croatia Ferries (🌐 *www.croatiaferries.com*) is a great resource for domestic and international ferry timetables and specific route information.

## Bus

Bus travel in Croatia is inexpensive, efficient, and a great way to travel long distances. You can reach even the smallest towns by public bus, while larger cities are connected by regular, comfortable, and usually air-conditioned coaches. On most routes you can purchase a ticket at the station or from the driver, but for the major routes (between Zagreb and the coast or between Dubrovnik and Split), it's safer to buy tickets at least a few days in advance. Seating is assigned if you book in advance but not if you buy your ticket on the spot; however, apart from fully booked buses, seat allocations are not usually adhered to. Carry some coins in case you have to pay to put luggage in the hold or for the washroom at the station.

GetByBus is an excellent resource for checking routes and timetables and buying tickets in advance. **FlixBus** is a German bus company that operates many routes within Croatia and from abroad, which can easily be booked online and combined with international bus passes.

##  Car

Traveling by car is by far the best way to get around Croatia, whether you're on a tour, with a driver, or behind the wheel yourself. You don't need a car within big cities, as public transport is very efficient, traffic can be bad (especially in Dubrovnik), and many medieval city centers are pedestrian-only. However, driving allows you to travel easily between cities and to explore destinations along the way that aren't well served by public transport. The only time car travel isn't advisable is when going to the islands, as waiting to board a car ferry can add hours to your itinerary in the high season—plus parking on the islands is usually limited. However, once you're on the island, it's not a bad idea to rent a car or scooter for the day to venture further afield.

### GASOLINE

Most gas stations are open daily from 6 am to 8 pm; from June through September, many stations are open until 10 pm. In the bigger cities and on main international roads, stations offer 24-hour service. All pumps sell Eurosuper 95, Eurosuper 98, and Eurodiesel. Payment is made inside the gas station; there are no automatic payment options at the pump.

### PARKING

Most towns mark parking spaces with a blue line and a sign denoting time restrictions. Buy a ticket at the closest parking machine and leave it in the front window; make sure to carry coins because not all parking machines take bills or cards. The historic centers of walled towns along the coast and on the islands (Split, Trogir, Hvar Town, Korčula, and Dubrovnik) are completely closed to traffic, putting heavy pressure on the number of parking spaces outside the fortifications (and since parking is limited, it is also expensive).

### ROAD CONDITIONS

Motorways that connect most major cities are safe, quick, and well-maintained with plenty of rest stops. All motorways, which are marked with an A preceding the road number, have tolls which can be paid by cash or card; you'll take the ticket at the beginning of the toll road and pay at the end depending on where you exit.

On the islands, roads are often narrow, twisty, and unevenly maintained, so make sure to check the route in advance to make sure you're comfortable with it if driving. During winter, driving through the inland regions of Gorski Kotar and Lika is occasionally made hazardous by heavy snow.

Roads around Slavonia are typically flat, well-marked, and well-maintained.

### RULES OF THE ROAD

Croatians drive on the right and follow rules similar to those in other European countries. Speed limits are 50 kph (30 mph) in urban areas, 90 kph (55 mph) on main roads, and 130 kph (80 mph) on motorways. Seatbelts are compulsory.

# Getting Here and Around

The permitted blood-alcohol limit is 0.05%; drunk driving is punishable and can lead to severe fines. Talking on the phone while driving is prohibited unless the driver is using a hands-free device.

### DRIVING TIMES

The A1 Highway connects Zagreb to Rijeka (2 hours, 159 km/99 miles), Zadar (3 hours, 285 km/177 miles), and Split (4 hours, 407 km/253 miles). When driving to Dubrovnik (6 hours, 599 km/372 miles) from Split, you'll cross the Pelješac Bridge, cutting across the Pelješac Peninsula before returning to the mainland coastal road.

### CAR RENTALS

Renting a car is quite affordable in Croatia, sometimes as little as €5 a day (excluding extras such as child seats, GPS, and insurance). Book online in advance for the best rates. A valid driver's license is all you need to rent a car. The minimum age is usually 23 years old, and some companies also have maximum ages; be sure to inquire when making your arrangements.

If you intend to visit neighboring countries, be sure to ask about restrictions on crossing borders. Also, when you reserve your car ask about drop-off charges (if you're planning to pick up the car in one city and leave it in another) and any surcharges for additional drivers, driving to the islands, or beyond a specific distance; all of these things can add substantially to your costs. Request car seats and extras such as GPS when you book. Finally, make sure that a confirmed reservation guarantees you a car; agencies sometimes overbook, particularly for busy weekends and holiday periods.

## Cruise

Dubrovnik, Split, Hvar, and Korčula are common port calls for eastern Mediterranean cruises. Large cruise ships are somewhat controversial in Croatia because they have been pinpointed as a cause of overtourism, especially in Dubrovnik. Since 2019, regulations have been in place to limit the number of cruise ships that can dock at the port of Dubrovnik on any given day.

You might consider a small-ship cruise company, which can help reduce the pressure on small islands and towns and allow you to see the destinations in a more intimate way. If you do visit as part of a large cruise itinerary, you can still support the local economy by booking shore excursions in advance with local tour operators and frequenting local restaurants, shops, and cafés.

## Train

The train is a great option for getting to Croatia from abroad, with direct international connections to Zagreb from Austria, Germany, Hungary, Slovenia, and Switzerland. However, within Croatia, there is a limited rail network and trains are typically slower than buses. Train travel is a viable option if you're traveling around the north or east to Slavonia. If you're going to Istria, you can only travel as far as Rijeka before switching to a bus. When heading to Dalmatia, you can travel by train as far as Split (including a popular overnight train from Zagreb).

# Essentials

## Dining

The first thing to know about dining in Croatia is that Croatian people prefer to eat their main meals at home and meet their friends later for a drink, which is why you'll find many more café-bars (which serve only beverages) than restaurants, particularly in smaller towns. Younger people are a bit more interested in dining out, but you won't often see the older generation eating at a restaurant unless they're celebrating a special occasion. Restaurants are also increasingly expensive for local people, so if they do grab a quick bite to eat, it's often at a bakery or fast-food joint. Therefore, many restaurants are geared toward visitors, which is why so many of the best ones in the country are found in hotels, including half of all the spots with Michelin stars.

That doesn't mean that there is a shortage of great places to try traditional Croatian cuisine; on the contrary, the dining scene gets better each year, with passionate young chefs putting a modern twist on the recipes they grew up with. Generally speaking, fresh fish dominates along the coast and hearty meat dishes, soups, and stews rule the interior. That said, one of the most popular dishes in Dalmatia is lamb *peka*, cooked in a clay vessel buried in hot coals, while many of the must-try dishes inland are made with river fish. Like most of Croatian culture, its cuisine differs from region to region. In Istria, you'll eat Italian-influenced *fuži* (traditional Istrian pasta), *maneštra* (Istrian vegetable stew), truffles, asparagus, and lots of great pizza, while inland there is more of an Austro-Hungarian influence, most notable in the stews, *štrukli* (strudel), and the paprika added liberally to many dishes.

You'll find a few different terms used for dining establishments around the country. A *restoran* can be anything from a five-star restaurant to a sushi bar, is usually found in the bigger cities, and often caters to tourists. A *konoba* is typically family-owned and serves more traditional dishes and homemade food.

### MEALS AND MEALTIMES

As the working day begins early (with some offices opening at 7:30 am on weekdays), you'll find cafés open early as well. Eating breakfast in a restaurant is not typical, so if you need to find something to eat before lunch, head to a bakery. Lunch is usually served between noon and 3 in restaurants, and dinner is most often served after 7 pm. In the height of the tourist season along the coast, restaurants may stay open later (after 10 pm) to handle the volume.

*Marenda* (also known as *gablec* around Zagreb) is an important custom around the country. Served between breakfast and lunch, from around 11 am to 2 pm, it is as much about gathering with friends in the konoba as it is about eating. Dishes are rustic, often eaten with a spoon—tripe, *pašta fažol* (Dalmatian beans with pasta), and *polpeta u šugu* (meatballs with sauce) are typical examples and are often cheaper than lunch or dinner.

### RESERVATIONS

Regardless of where you are, it's a good idea to make a reservation if you really want to eat at a particular restaurant. Large parties should always call ahead to check the restaurant's reservation policy.

## Health

EU citizens have reciprocal agreements with Croatia, entitling them to free health care, while citizens from outside the EU have to pay in accordance with listed prices; expect to pay around €30 in cash for an emergency room visit. Most doctors speak English and the quality of health care, including dental work, is generally excellent and much more affordable than in the United States.

Water is safe to drink throughout Croatia, which should help with the main health issue most people seek attention for here: heatstroke. Sunscreen is also widely available at pharmacies and grocery stories; on long sunny days, make sure to reapply often.

### OVER-THE-COUNTER REMEDIES

Over-the-counter medications are sold in pharmacies, which are open until 6 or 7 pm on weekdays and 1 or 2 pm on Saturdays. In each town there is usually a 24-hour *ljekarna* (pharmacy) for emergencies. Most European pharmacists speak a word or two of English, but you're better off asking for a remedy by its medical name (e.g., ibuprofen) than its brand name (e.g., Advil). Pharmacies don't have a lot of open shelf space for goods, so you might have to ask the pharmacist for what you need.

## Lodging

You can find any type of accommodation you like in Croatia: five-star hotels, hostels, family-friendly resorts, more than 500 campsites, boutique wineries, and even lighthouses. In Zagreb and certain towns around Dalmatia and Istria, standards (and prices) are high, while in less-visited areas such as Slavonia there might not be as many choices but you can always find something suitable, reasonably priced, and often family-owned.

On the coast, prices are at their highest in July and August and hotels are often fully booked far in advance. Outside of the summer, you can find excellent bargains for properties that might be out of your budget otherwise—another good reason to consider traveling in the off-season. While there aren't many international chain hotels in Croatia, you'll find that many establishments in a specific region will fall under the umbrella of one company (for example, Adriatic Luxury Hotels owns several of the best hotels around Southern Dalmatia, while in Istria, Maistra does). This doesn't mean that they are cookie-cutter; on the contrary, they have usually been refurbished to enhance the property's unique character.

All foreign guests have to pay a tourist tax for each night they stay in a hotel or private accommodation. It's a negligible amount, around €1 per night depending on the hotel category and the season, and it's most often just added to your bill. Booking directly with the property will usually get you the best deal, but it's a good idea to check online for any offers on other booking sites.

### APARTMENT AND VILLA RENTALS

Until a decade or so ago, the best way to find local accommodation was to show up at the bus station, where a local person would wait with faded photos of their room for rent. In recent years the number of private beds has skyrocketed, as they are a great source of extra income for local people; you can now find everything from a single bed in a family home to a deluxe condo. They vary greatly in size, standard, and amenities, but are generally a safe and unique way to stay in a quiet neighborhood, save money, self-cater, and interact with locals.

Private villas are also very popular in Istria and Dalmatia; they're more expensive because it's a whole house, usually with a pool, and the amenities are high-standard. If you're traveling in a group there might not be such a big price difference, especially when you consider the extra amenities that are usually included.

Stays longer than seven nights usually get a discounted rate. Check Airbnb or VRBO for deals or contact local booking agencies, such as Dominium Travel in Southern Dalmatia or Croatia Villas for assistance.

## Safety

Croatia is one of the safest countries in Europe; violent crime is very rare and there are no particular local scams that visitors should be aware of. Take the normal precautions: be on guard for pick-pockets in crowded markets and don't wander alone down dark streets at night.

This probably won't be an issue that affects you, but it's worth noting: there are still thousands of unexploded land-mines in Croatia. Almost all of them are in forests far from tourist centers, but if you come across an image of a white skull on an inverted red triangle or some variation, usually with the word MINE, stop hiking and call 112 for help.

## Tipping

When eating out in Croatia, if you have enjoyed your meal and are satisfied with the service, it is customary to leave a 10% to 15% tip. It is not necessary to tip baristas, bartenders, or taxi drivers (although it will always be appreciated). Tour guides do receive a tip. For bellhops at hotels, €1 per bag will be appreciated; housekeepers at hotels should also get at least €2 a day.

## Visitor Information

The first place to start planning your trip to Croatia (after this book, of course) is the Croatian National Tourist Board's web-site. In addition to a general overview of the culture and history of the country, it has lots of practical information on accommodations, travel agencies, and events. Then you can consult regional tourist board websites to narrow your trip focus even further.

## Visas

Starting in mid-2025, Croatia and other European Union countries will imple-ment an electronic visa waiver program designed for foreign visitors to the EU from countries that don't require a visa to visit. If you are a citizen of one of these 60 or so non-EU countries (this includes the United States and the Unit-ed Kingdom), this means you will now have to "pre-register" your trip through a simple online process that costs €7; this pre-registration covers multiple trips of up to 90 days in any 180-day period and lasts three years or until your passport expires—whichever comes first. Visit the official ETIAS website at 🌐 *travel-europe.europa.eu/etias_en* to apply. The vast majority of applications should be approved within minutes, but it's still smart to not book flights or hotels until your application is approved. For more information, visit 🌐 *www.etias.com*. Just note that the program's implementation has been delayed several times, so be sure to confirm in advance that ETIAS registration is required at the time of your trip.

# Helpful Phrases

### BASICS

| | | |
|---|---|---|
| Hello | Zdravo/Halo | zdr**ah**-voh/**ha**-lo |
| Yes/No | Da/Ne | dah/neh |
| Please | Molim | **moh**-leem |
| Thank you | Hvala | hv**ah**-lah |
| You're welcome | Nema na čemu/ molim | nema na ch**e**moo/ **moh**-leem |
| I'm Sorry (apology) | Žao mi je | jh**ao** mee yeh |
| Sorry (Excuse me) | Oprostite | oh-**pro**-stee-teh |
| Good morning | Dobro jutro | d**oh**-bro **yoo**-tro |
| Good day | Dobar dan | d**oh**-bar dan |
| Good evening | Dobro veče | d**oh**-bro **ve**-che |
| Goodbye | Doviđenja | doh-vee-**jen**-ya |
| Mr. (Sir) | Gospodin | gos-**poh**-deen |
| Mrs. | Gospođa | **gos**-poh-ja |
| Miss | Gospođica | **gos**-poh-jee-tsa |
| Pleased to meet you | Drago mi je | drago-mee-yeh |
| How are you? | Kako ste? | **ka**-ko steh |

### NUMBERS

| | | |
|---|---|---|
| one-half | pola | **po**-la |
| one | jedan | **yeh**-dan |
| two | dva | dvah |
| three | tri | tree |
| four | četiri | **cheh**-tee-ree |
| five | pet | pet |
| six | šest | she**st** |
| seven | sedam | **seh**-dam |
| eight | osam | **oh**-sam |
| nine | devet | **deh**-vet |
| ten | deset | **deh**-set |
| eleven | dedanaest | yeh-**dana**-est |
| twelve | dvanaest | dv**a**na-est |
| thirteen | trinaest | **treen**a-est |
| fourteen | četrnaest | cheh-**ter**na-est |
| fifteen | petnaest | **pet**na-est |
| sixteen | šesnaest | **shes**na-est |
| seventeen | sedamnaest | seh-**dam**na-est |
| eighteen | osamnaest | oh-**sam**na-est |
| nineteen | devetnaest | deh-**vet**na-est |
| twenty | dvadeset | **dva**-deh-set |
| twenty-one | dvadeset jedan | **dva**-deh-set **yeh**-dan |
| thirty | trideset | **tree**-deh-set |
| forty | četrdeset | cheh-ter **deh**-set |
| fifty | pedeset | peh-**deh**-set |
| sixty | šezdeset | shez-**deh**-set |
| seventy | sedamdeset | seh-dam-**deh**-set |
| eighty | osamdeset | oh-sam-**deh**-set |
| ninety | devedeset | deh-veh-**deh**-set |
| one hundred | sto | stoh |
| one thousand | tisuća | **tee**-soo-chah |
| one million | milijun | mee-**lee**-yoon |

### COLORS

| | | |
|---|---|---|
| black | crn | tsern |
| blue | plav | plav |
| brown | smeđ | smej |
| green | zelen | **ze**-len |
| orange | narančast | **na**-ran-chast |
| red | crven | **tser**-ven |
| white | bijel | bee-ell |
| yellow | žut | jhoot |

### DAYS

| | | |
|---|---|---|
| Sunday | nedjelja | **ned**-yelya |
| Monday | ponedjeljak | poh-**ned**-yelyak |
| Tuesday | utorak | **oo**-torak |
| Wednesday | srijeda | sree-**yed**-ah |
| Thursday | četvrtak | chet-**ver**-tak |
| Friday | petak | **peh**-tak |
| Saturday | subota | **soo**-bota |

### MONTHS

| | | |
|---|---|---|
| January | siječanj | see-**yeh**-chan |
| February | veljača | **vel**-ya-cha |
| March | ožujak | **oh**-jhoo-yak |
| April | travanj | **tra**-van |
| May | svibanj | **svee**-ban |
| June | lipanj | **lee**-pan |
| July | srpanj | **ser**-pan |
| August | kolovoz | **koh**-loh-voz |
| September | rujan | **roo**-yan |
| October | listopad | **lee**-sto-pad |
| November | studeni | **stoo**-den-ee |
| December | prosinac | **pro**-see-nats |

### USEFUL PHRASES

| | | |
|---|---|---|
| Do you speak English? | Govorite li engleski? | **goh**-vo-ree-teh lee **Eng**-les-kee |
| I don't speak Croatian | Ne govorim Hrvatski | neh **goh**-vo-reem **Her**-vat-skee |
| I don't understand. | Ne razumijem | Neh rah-**zoo**-mee-yem |
| I don't know. | Ne znam | ne znam |
| I understand. | Razumijem | rah-**zoo**-mee-yem |
| I'm American. | Ja sam Amerikanac/ Americanka | ya sam ameree-**ka**-nats/ ameree-**kan**-ka |
| I'm British. | Ja sam Britanac/ Britanka | ya sam Bree-**tan**-ats/ Bree-**tan**-ka |
| What's your name? | Kako se zovete? | **ka**-ko seh **zo**-veh-teh |
| My name is ... | Zovem se... | **zo**-vem seh |
| What time is it? | Koliko je sati? | **ko**-lee-ko yeh **sa**-tee |
| How? | Kako? | **ka**-ko |

| | | |
|---|---|---|
| When? | Kada? | **ka**-da |
| Yesterday | Jučer | **yoo**-cher |
| Today | Danas | **dah**-nas |
| Tomorrow | Sutra | **soo**-tra |
| This morning | Jutros | **yoo**-tros |
| This afternoon | Danas poslije podne | **dah**-nas **pos**-lee-yeh **pod**-neh |
| Tonight | Večeras | vech-**air**-as |
| What? | Što? | shto |
| What is it? | Što je? | shto yeh |
| Why? | Zašto? | **za**-shto |
| Who? | Tko? | tko |
| Where is ... | Gdje je... | gd-yeh yeh |
| ... the train station? | ...željeznički kolodvor? | **jhel**-yez-neetch-kee **ko**-lod-vor |
| ... the subway station? | ...podzemna željeznica? | **pod**-zem-na **jhel**-yez-neetsa |
| ... the bus stop? | ...autobusna postaja? | **a**-ooto-busna **po**-sta-ya |
| ... the airport? | ...zračna luka? | **zra**-chna **loo**-ka |
| ... the post office? | ...pošta? | **po**-shta |
| ... the bank? | ...banka? | **ban**-ka |
| ... the hotel? | ...hotel? | **ho**-tel |
| ... the museum? | ...muzej? | **moo**-zay |
| ... the hospital? | ...bolnica? | **bol**-neetsa |
| ... the elevator? | ...dizalo? | **dee**-zalo |
| Where are the restrooms? | Gdje su zahodi? | gd-yeh soo **za**-hod-ee |
| Here/there | Ovdje/tamo | **ov**-dyeh/**ta**-mo |
| Left/right | Lijevo/Desno | lee-**yeh**-voh/ **deh**-sno |
| Is it near/far? | Je li blizu/daleko? | yeh lee **blee**-zoo/ **dah**-lecko |
| I'd like ... | Želio/Željela bih... | **jhel**-eeo/**jhel**-yell-ah bee |
| ... a room | ...soba | **so**-ba |
| ... the key | ...ključ | klyooch |
| ... a newspaper | ...novine | **no**-vee-neh |
| ... a stamp | ...marka | **mar**-ka |
| I'd like to buy ... | Želio/Željela bih kupiti | jhel-eeo/**jhel**-yell-ah bee **koo**-pee-tee |
| ... a city map | ...karta grada | **kar**ta **gra**-da |
| ... a road map | ...autokarta | **ah**-ooto-karta |
| ... a magazine | ...magazin | **mah**-ga-zeen |
| ... envelopes | ...koverta | ko-**ver**-ta |
| ... writing paper | ...papir za pisanje | **pa**-peer za pee-**san**-yeh |
| ... a postcard | ...razglednica | **raz**-gled-neetsa |
| ... a ticket | ...karta | **kar**-ta |
| How much is it? | Koliko je to? | **koh**-lee-ko |
| It's expensive/ cheap | Skupo/Jeftino je | **skoo**-po/**yef**-teeno yeh |
| A little/a lot | Malo/mnogo | **ma**-lo/mn-**oh**-goh |
| More/less | Više/manje | **vee**-shay/ **man**-yeh |
| Enough/too (much) | Dovoljno/previše | **do**-vol-eeno/ **preh**-vee-sheh |
| I am ill/sick | Osjećam se bolesno | **os**-yecham seh **bo**-lesno |
| Call a doctor | Zovite liječnika | **zoh**-vee-teh lee-**yech**-neeka |
| Help! | Upomoć! | **oo**-po-moch |
| Stop! | Prestani! | **pre**-stan-ee |

### DINING OUT

| | | |
|---|---|---|
| A bottle of ... | Boca... | **bo**-tsa |
| A cup of ... | Šalica ... | **sha**-leetsa |
| A glass of ... | Čaša.... | **cha**-sha |
| Beer | Pivo | **pee**-voh |
| Bill/check | Račun | **rah**-chun |
| Bread | Kruh | krooh |
| Breakfast | Doručak | **doh**-roo-chak |
| Butter | Maslac | **mas**-lats |
| Cocktail/aperatif | Koktel | **kok**-tel |
| Coffee | Kava | **ka**-va |
| Dinner | Večera | **ve**-cher-ah |
| Fixed-price menu | Meni | **me**-nee |
| Fork | Vilica | **vee**-leetsa |
| I am a vegetarian/I don't eat meat | Jja sam vegetari-janac/Ne jedem meso | ya sam vegetaree-**yan**-ats/neh **yeh**-dem **meh**-so |
| I cannot eat ... | Ne mogu jesti... | neh **mo**-goo **yeh**-stee |
| I'd like to order ... | Želio bih naručiti | **jhel**-ee-oh bee nah-**roo**-chee-tee |
| Is service included? | Je li napojnica uključena? | yeh lee **nah**-poy-neetsa ook-lee-**oo**-chen-ah |
| I'm hungry/thirsty | Gladan/žedan sam | **gla**-dan/**jhe**--dan sam |
| It's good/bad | Dobro je/to je loše | **doh**-bro yeh/toh yeh **lo**-sheh |
| It's hot/cold | To je vruće/hladno | toh yeh **vroo**-cheh/ **hlad**-no |
| Knife | Nož | nojh |
| Lunch | Ručak | **roo**-chak |
| Menu | Jelovnik | yeh-**lov**-neek |
| Napkin | Salveta | sal-**vet**-ah |
| Pepper | Bbiber | **bee**-ber |
| Plate | Tanjur | tan-**yoor** |
| Please give me ... | Možete li mi dati... | **mo**-jhe-teh lee mee **dah**-tee |
| Salt | Sol | sol |
| Spoon | Žlica | **jhlee**-tsa |
| Tea | Čaj | chy |
| Water | Voda | **voh**-da |
| Wine | Vino | **vee**-no |

# Great Itineraries

## 10 Days in Dubrovnik, Southern Dalmatia, and Montenegro

Dubrovnik is the perfect starting point for excursions to the wine and gastronomic pleasures of the Pelješac Peninsula, Korčula, and Montenegro. Dubrovnik has an international airport with direct flights from New York in the summer, and it is also well connected to all European hubs.

### DAYS 1 AND 2: DUBROVNIK

If arriving by sea or air, you'll see one of the most spectacular fortified cities in the world. From this view, you can tell why Dubrovnik (formerly Ragusa) was once the master of all Dalmatia. Check into your hotel and relax until around 4 pm; most of the day-trippers have departed by then, making it the best time to explore the Old Town. If you arrive early enough, book a walking tour (Sights and Bites is a good choice) to get the lay of the land and a few local tips, which will come in handy for the rest of your stay. Otherwise just take a walk through the old streets, check out a museum or two, and have dinner on an outdoor terrace, then stroll along the Stradun after dark, popping into a wine bar or grabbing an ice cream along the way.

The following day, get an early start to walk the city walls before it gets too hot. Aim to finish by noon (the walk takes around two hours) and then head straight to the beach or one of the Buža bars to refresh with a swim. Grab lunch in the Old Town—Azur is a great daytime spot away from the crowds—or catch a ferry out to peaceful Lokrum Island. Spend the rest of the day back at your hotel pool, grab a drink at a beach bar, or if you still have energy, head to the top of Mt. Srđ on the cable car to watch the sunset over the city.

### DAY 3: THE PELJEŠAC PENINSULA

Pick up your rental car early and drive straight out of town. Stop to admire the gardens at Trsteno along the way before reaching the Pelješac Peninsula. Just before you arrive at Mali Ston, there is a small shack called Oysters Antonio on the right-hand side of the road: pull over and order a couple of oysters with lemon, which are harvested right there in the channel and shucked right in front of you. Indulge in more fresh shellfish at one of the lovely waterfront restaurants in Mali Ston; if it's not too hot, take a walk on the defensive walls that stretch between Mali Ston and Ston or take a tour of the famed salt pans. There's one 60-km (37-mile) road that leads from Mali Ston all the way across the Peninsula to Orebić, and along the way you can stop off at family-owned wineries to sample the goods. Spend the night in Orebić, perhaps organizing a wine tasting and dinner at beautiful Korta Katarina Winery, or take the short 15-minute ferry ride across to Korčula.

### DAYS 4 AND 5: KORČULA

Relax and enjoy two full days on Korčula. If you have a car, you can drive around to explore the island's secluded coves, rural villages, rustic restaurants, and charming wineries. If you've come by passenger ferry, you can rent a mountain bike, speedboat, or arrange a sightseeing tour of the island. If you want to check out one more island, take a day trip from Korčula to Mljet, returning to Korčula Town for dinner and, if you're there on the right day, you can watch a performance of the traditional Moreška sword dance.

## DAY 6: PERAST, MONTENEGRO

Take the morning ferry back to Dubrovnik and head straight down the coast by car or bus to the sparkling Bay of Kotor in Montenegro. Plan on spending your first night in the charming waterfront village of Perast, which is best known for a pair of tiny islets, each topped with a church, or continue all the way to Kotor.

## DAY 7: KOTOR, MONTENEGRO

The UNESCO World Heritage town of Kotor sits on Europe's most southerly *ria* (a coastal inlet commonly confused with a fjord). Spend the day exploring its churches, markets, and wandering the Old Town's labyrinth of winding cobbled streets. Have lunch in one of the splendid marble piazzas, and don't miss hiking up to St. John's Fortress, following the medieval walls for breathtaking views.

## DAYS 8–10: CAVTAT

Return to Croatia to spend your final two nights in the lovely town of Cavtat. From here you can organize a day trip to the Elafiti Islands, Lokrum Island, or check out the rural agritourism properties around the Konavle region. Dubrovnik is just 45 minutes up the coast, so you can head into town one last time or just hang out and enjoy your final couple of days beside the sea.

### Tips

- This itinerary is best done by car, allowing you the freedom to stop at wineries, oyster shacks, and beaches along the way. You can pick up a rental car at the airport and drive to your hotel in Dubrovnik if your hotel has parking, but you won't need the car to get around Dubrovnik (local parking and traffic are notoriously bad). If your hotel doesn't have parking, plan to pick up your rental car on the day you leave the city and drive straight out. Drop the car off again in Dubrovnik and take public transport to Cavtat for the final two nights, or drop the car off at the airport when you leave.
- There are excellent organized tour options in this region, so if neither a car rental nor public transport suits you, consider basing yourself in Dubrovnik, Korčula, and/or Cavtat and taking day trips from there.

# Great Itineraries

## Island Hopping and National Parks in Central and Northern Dalmatia

If you want to immerse yourself in the natural landscapes of Croatia, this itinerary will take you to three national parks and several strikingly diverse islands, with a couple of ancient towns thrown in for good measure.

### DAY 1: SPLIT

Though many people use Split as the jumping-off point for nearby islands, it's definitely worth spending at least one day exploring the Meštrović Gallery and the Archaeological Museum, strolling the waterfront Riva, and getting lost in the streets of Diocletian's Palace. In the early evening, sit in the Palace's open peristyle and admire the Imperial quarters, the Cathedral of St. Domnius, and the Egyptian sphinx before having dinner.

### DAYS 2 AND 3: ISLAND HOPPING

The three closest islands to Split have very different vibes, so choose your getaway based on what type of vacation you're looking for. Brač, home to the famous Zlatni Rat beach, is best for families and wholesome seaside fun. Hvar is known for the beach clubs and nightlife of its main settlement, Hvar Town—although you'll find lavender fields, wineries, and peaceful Old Towns beyond the glitz and glamour. And if you're looking to get away from it all, Vis, a former Yugoslavian military base, is the least developed of all the islands and offers a wonderful respite from the crowds.

### Tips

- Avoid taking a car to the islands, as car ferries can involve a long wait and you won't need one once you arrive. Arrange to pick up your car in Split on Day 4 and head straight out of town.
- Try to schedule car trips on weekdays, as the roads—particularly the A1 highway—can get busy on weekends.
- Both Split and Zadar have international airports, so you can start this itinerary from either one.
- Bring an umbrella or waterproof jacket in case of summer showers near the Velebit Mountains.

### DAY 4: SPLIT TO ZADAR

Take a morning ferry back to Split and from there make your way up the stunning coastline, stopping off at Trogir, Primošten, or Šibenik along the way. Spend the night in Šibenik, from which you can organize a day trip to Kornati National Park, the largest archipelago in the Adriatic with more than 100 privately owned islands. Alternatively, head straight to Zadar for the evening and organize day trips to the islands from there.

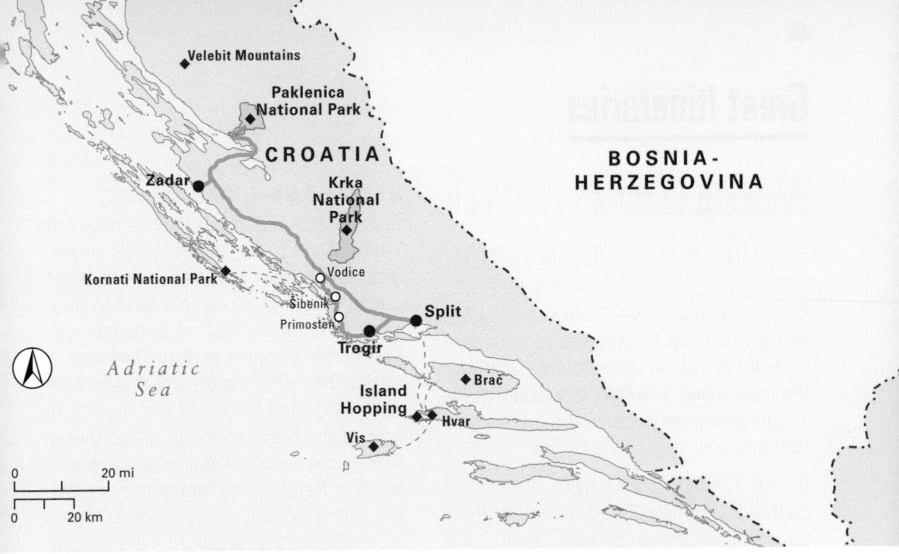


## DAYS 5 AND 6: ZADAR AND PAKLENICA NATIONAL PARK

Zadar has fast emerged as one of Croatia's top tourist destinations, and for good reason. Its Old Town is bustling and beautiful, with marble pedestrian streets, Roman ruins, medieval churches, palaces, and museums. Be sure to visit the St. Donatus Church, a massive cylindrical structure that is one of the largest early Byzantine churches in Croatia, and don't miss the Sea Organ and the Greeting to the Sun.

From Zadar, there are several worthwhile day trips to keep you busy for a few days. Drive or take a bus to neighboring Nin to see the former seat of the Dalmatian royal family as well as a quaint little salt museum. Head out island-hopping to Kornati National Park or venture to Paklenica National Park, a rugged limestone canyon in the Velebit Mountains that offers great hiking and the ultimate challenge for cliff climbers.

## DAY 7: KRKA NATIONAL PARK, TROGIR, AND SPLIT

Leaving Zadar, stop along the way at Krka National Park, which challenges Plitvice National Park with its cascading waters and amazing turquoise waterfalls. Head back to Split in time for sunset along the Riva and a final dinner near Diocletian's Palace.

# Great Itineraries

## Western Croatia in a Week: Zagreb, Istria, and Kvarner

If you only have a week but want to get a sense of all that Croatia has to offer, this itinerary is a good place to start. You'll get the mountains, seaside, city, countryside, a stunning national park, and a first-class Roman ruin.

### DAYS 1 AND 2: ZAGREB

Zagreb is a compact easygoing city that begs to be explored on foot. Upon arrival head to Ban Jelačić Square, the center of town. Grab a drink on the pedestrian street Ulica Ivana Tkalčića, do some shopping along Ilica (Zagreb's modern high street), and have dinner at one of the city's excellent restaurants. The following day, start your morning with a visit to the Cathedral and Dolac Market, then take the funicular to the Upper Town to explore the museums; the Croatian Historical Museum and the Museum of Broken Relationships are both worth a visit. Have dinner in the Upper Town or soak up a bit more of the evening atmosphere in the café-bars of the Lower Town.

### DAY 3: PLITVICE NATIONAL PARK

Get an early start the next morning, and pick up your rental car and head south toward Plitvice National Park. A UNESCO World Heritage site, this is one of Croatia's most popular tourist sites; no matter what time of year you visit, the colors here are spectacular and you'll spend hours admiringly wandering the trails. Spend the night in either of the nearby towns, Mukinje or Jezerce, both a nice walking distance from the park.

### DAYS 4 AND 5: RAB ISLAND

Enjoy the journey from Plitvice down the Velebit Mountains, the country's largest mountain range, to the eastern Kvarner coast, where you'll catch a ferry to Rab, one of the bay's most beautiful islands. The northeastern side of the island is mostly barren while the southwestern side is covered by one of the last oak forests of the Mediterranean. Once there, take in the sights of the medieval stone town of Rab or head straight to one of the island's many sandy beaches. Spend a couple of days relaxing on the beach, take in the sights of Rab, or take a ferry to the island of Krk and enjoy the cliff-top town of Valbiska, home of Žlahtina white wine.

### DAY 6: OPATIJA

Take the ferry from Rab or the bridge from Krk to Opatija. Check into one of the atmospheric turn-of-the-century hotels for a little slice of nostalgia, then head out for a stroll along the 12-km (7½-mile) promenade that zigzags along the sea. Sleep in Opatija or catch a ferry to the islands of Cres or Lošinj.

### DAY 7: PULA

From Opatija or Lošinj head south or west, respectively, to Pula and spend the morning exploring its incredible amphitheater, one of the best-preserved sites in the Roman world. After lunch, take a boat to the Brijuni Islands for the afternoon to visit the Tito-designed zoo and tropical gardens. Stay in Pula for the night or drive the short distance to Rovinj.

### DAYS 8 AND 9: ROVINJ AND POREČ

Spend a couple of days exploring the limestone architecture and Venetian houses of Rovinj and soaking up the delights of Istria. Drive or take a day tour to Poreč, stopping at some of the many fine wineries along the way and, depending on the season, making lots of time to eat dishes with fresh asparagus or truffles; if you visit in the fall, head out truffle hunting to see if you can find one yourself.

### DAY 10: MOTOVUN AND ZAGREB

Head back to Zagreb via the Istrian interior. Drive east toward Pazin, stopping in the medieval hill towns of Motovun and Grožnjan for lunch and breathtaking views. These villages are in the heart of truffle country, so keep your eyes open for some fresh goods to bring home. Continue northeast toward Zagreb, possibly stopping at the mountain town of Fužine for its famous cherry strudel and views of Lake Bajer.

## Tips

- This itinerary can be done by bus, but it is easier with a car. The main highway connecting Zagreb to Istria (the A6) is well maintained and offers beautiful views of Gorski Kotar. Tolls can be paid in cash or by card.
- Consider planning your visit to Plitvice on a weekday, when travel on the main highway between Zagreb and Zadar is lighter and the park is quieter.
- The closest ferry crossing from Opatija to Cres and Lošinj is at Brestova in Istria. If you plan to take your car in the height of summer, count on a wait.

# On the Calendar

## January

**The Night of Museums.** It gets cold all around Croatia in January (there might even be enough snow to ski in Zagreb), and many establishments along the coast close. But on the last Friday of the month, most of the country's top museums and galleries come alive again to offer free entrance from 6 pm to 1 am. The event, which has increased from 6 participating museums in Zagreb when it started in 2005 to more than 200 institutions (and counting), is a fun way for visitors and locals alike to spend the night exploring new spots around various cities. 🌐 *nocmuzeja.hr*

## February

**Rijeka Carnival.** Of all the Carnivals celebrated across the country, the biggest and best is this one. Held from mid-January to early February, it attracts hundreds of thousands of revelers who come to enjoy the costumes, street parties, masked balls, and parades. 🌐 *rijecki-karneval.hr*

**The Feast of St. Blaise.** Down the coast, Dubrovnik celebrates the feast day of its patron saint, St. Blaise, every February 3, an event that has been commemorated since the year 972. The festivities kick off on February 2 with the release of white doves in front of the Church of St. Blaise and the raising of the saint's flag, then on February 3 the day starts with a solemn mass followed by a procession carrying St. Blaise's relics down the Stradun. A gun salute ends the official proceedings but the festivities continue throughout the day. People come from all over to pay homage, often dressed in the traditional folk costumes of their region.

## March

**Oyster Festival.** The arrival of spring heralds a soft start to the season along the Croatian coast. For two days in March, the small towns of Ston and Mali Ston on the Pelješac Peninsula celebrate the Feast of St. Joseph with this festival. You can enjoy Dalmatian music along the waterfront and taste the renowned oysters at their very best, as well as sample Pelješac wines and other local products. 🌐 *www.ston.hr*

**International Flower Festival.** Held in Split, this event livens up the cellars of Diocletian's Palace and the Riva with floral arrangements as florists compete for best display. 🌐 *visitsplit.com*

## April

**Biennale.** April is a lovely time to visit Zagreb, when the parks will be in full bloom and the city hosts this international festival of contemporary music. It's attended by the heavy hitters of the classical world, as well as groundbreaking pioneers. 🌐 *www.mbz.hr*

## May

**Vinistra Fair.** May is one of the most ideal months to visit Croatia, including Istria, and is when Poreč hosts this three-day event where more than 80 winemakers and wine lovers gather at an exhibition hall to learn about wine-making and sample the latest vintages. 🌐 *vinistra.hr*

## June

**Hideout.** Croatia hosts some of the top dance music festivals in the world, and the season kicks off in June on the island of Pag with this five-day party on Zrce Beach. *hideoutfestival.com*

**Half New Year.** Korčula celebrates Half New Year on June 30, with a masquerade parade followed by music, dancing, and fireworks on the streets of its medieval Old Town.

## July and August

**Dubrovnik Summer Festival.** Croatia's most prestigious cultural event, the Dubrovnik Summer Festival features drama, ballet, concerts, and opera, all performed on open-air stages within Old Town. *www.dubrovnik-festival.hr*

**Pula Film Festival.** There are several international film festivals that take place in impressive locations across the country; the Pula Film Festival is the original, where films are screened against the stunning backdrop of the Roman Arena. *pulafilmfestival.hr*

**Split Summer Festival.** This festival hosts opera, theater, and dance events within the walls of Diocletian's Palace. *www.splitsko-ljeto.hr*

**Ultra Europe.** The largest of the dance music festivals in Croata, Ultra Europe takes place over three days in Split, drawing some of the top names in the EDM world. *ultraeurope.com*

## September

**Epidaurus Festival.** This event brings a variety of concerts, mostly classical and jazz, as well as an excellent selection of hands-on workshops, to the town of Cavtat. *epidaurusfestival.com*

**Varaždin Baroque Evenings.** Up north, Varaždin Baroque Evenings see eminent soloists and orchestras from Croatia and abroad perform Baroque music recitals in the city's most beautiful churches. *vbv.hr*

## October

**Zigante Truffle Days.** The tourist season has slowed down but October is high season for the elusive white truffle in Istria, and it is celebrated during the town's Truffle Fair. The fair takes place across nine weekends from September through November in the Motovun Forest, where you can attend culinary workshops, watch demonstrations of truffle hunting, and sample truffles and other Istrian delicacies. *sajamtartufa.com*

## November

**Martinje (St. Martin's Day).** By November, the weather has turned cold, the ferries to the islands have largely stopped running, and the coastal towns are starting to shut down for the season. In Zagorje, Martinje on November 11 sees the blessing of the season's new wine, accompanied by a hearty goose feast and endless toasts.

## December

**Advent Market.** Christmas and New Year are heartily celebrated across the country; the showstopper is Zagreb's Advent Market, heralded as the best Christmas market in Europe many times over. For the entire month of December, the capital dazzles with thousands of Christmas lights, ice-skating rinks, outdoor concerts, food stalls, and, of course, mulled wine. *www.adventzagreb.hr*

# Best Tours in Croatia

The best tours have a few things in common: they show you a side of the country you might not have seen otherwise, they offer the expertise of a local guide with the freedom to make some new discoveries on your own, and they introduce you to like-minded travelers who might become friends. Whether you're in Croatia for food, wine, biking, hiking, history, or *Game of Thrones,* here are some of your best options.

**Backroads.** Cycling tours are extremely popular in Croatia, and this company that combines island-hopping and cycling is one of the originals. It's suitable for couples, friends, families, and solo travelers. 🌐 *www.backroads.com.*

**Culinary Croatia.** Run by the folks from Secret Dalmatia, Culinary Croatia focuses on cooking classes, wine tours, and personalized foodie experiences of Dalmatia and Istria. 🌐 *www.culinary-croatia.com.*

**Exodus Travels.** With 500 itineraries across 90 countries, Exodus is one of the largest and best international travel companies for active travelers. They organize sustainable cycling, walking, and trekking tours of Croatia and the Balkans for travelers ages 12 and up. 🌐 *www.exodustravels.com.*

**Free Spirit Tours.** This young, enthusiastic Croatian company offers daily free walking tours in Dubrovnik, Rovinj, Pula, Split, Zadar, and Zagreb. They also offer great-value private day tours all around Croatia and to neighboring countries, as well as curated multiday trips. 🌐 *freespirittours.eu.*

**Intrepid Travel.** This well-respected Australian company comes with a strong emphasis on sustainable travel around the world. They specialize in small-group tours and cover a wide range of activities in Croatia, from sailing and cycling the islands to visiting the inland national parks, and they are one of the few companies that include Slavonia on their itineraries. They use local guides and focus on authentic off-the-beaten-track experiences. 🌐 *www.intrepidtravel.com.*

**Secret Dalmatia.** One of the originals, Croatia-based Secret Dalmatia excels at creating bespoke tours of Dalmatia, specializing in off-the-beaten-track destinations and a premium personalized experience. 🌐 *www.secretdalmatia.com.*

**Tasteful Croatian Journeys.** Specializing in tailor-made luxury itineraries and experiences, this American company was one of the pioneers in Croatia travel when it started nearly three decades ago. They can help put together five-star curated itineraries, as well as organize luxury yacht charters and villa rentals. 🌐 *visitcroatia.com.*

**Tureta Travel.** This boutique Zagreb-based company specializes in tailor-made tours to all corners of Croatia. 🌐 *www.tureta-travel.com.*

**Zagreb Bites.** This company offers a fun fresh way to explore the capital and surrounding area through its food, craft beer, and wine scenes. They also organize guided food tours of Zagreb's Advent Market. 🌐 *zagrebites.com.*

## Did You Know?

Within Krka National Park, the Krka River forms seven travertine waterfalls; a travertine waterfall is made of limestone formed by geothermally heated hot springs.

# Contacts

## Air

**AIRPORT CONTACTS Dubrovnik Airport.** ✉ *Cilipi* ☎ *020/773–100* 🌐 *www.airport-dubrovnik.hr.* **Osijek Airport.** ☎ *031/284–611* 🌐 *osijek-airport.hr.* **Pula Airport.** ☎ *052/550–926* 🌐 *airport-pula.hr.* **Rijeka Airport.** ☎ *099/525–8911* 🌐 *www.rijeka-airport.hr.* **Split Airport.** ☎ *021/203–589* 🌐 *www.split-airport.hr.* **Zadar Airport.** ☎ *060/355–355* 🌐 *www.zadar-airport.hr.* **Zagreb Airport.** ☎ *060/320–320* 🌐 *www.zagreb-airport.hr.*

## Boat and Ferry

**CONTACTS Croatia Ferries.** 🌐 *www.croatia-ferries.com.* **Jadrolinija.** ☎ *051/666–111* 🌐 *www.jadrolinija.hr.* **SNAV.** ☎ *081/428–5555* 🌐 *www.snav.it.* **Venezia Lines.** ☎ *052/422–896* 🌐 *www.venezialines.com.*

## Bus

**CONTACTS FlixBus.** 🌐 *www.flixbus.com.* **GetByBus.** 🌐 *getbybus.com.*

## Lodging

**CROATIA SPECIALISTS Croatian Villas.** 🌐 *www.croatianvillas.com.* **Dominium Accommodation and Tours.** ☎ *095/131–3142* 🌐 *bookdubrovnik.com.*

## Visitor Information

**CONTACTS Croatia National Tourist Board.** 🌐 *croatia.hr.* **Dalmatia Region.** 🌐 *www.dalmatia.hr.* **Istria Region.** 🌐 *www.istra.hr.* **Kvarner Region.** 🌐 *www.kvarner.hr.* **Zagreb.** 🌐 *www.infozagreb.hr.*

Chapter 3

# DUBROVNIK AND SOUTHERN DALMATIA



Updated by
Andrea MacDonald

| Sights | Restaurants | Hotels | Shopping | Nightlife |
|---|---|---|---|---|
| ★★★★★ | ★★★★★ | ★★★★★ | ★★★★☆ | ★★★★☆ |

# WELCOME TO DUBROVNIK AND SOUTHERN DALMATIA

## TOP REASONS TO GO

★ **Pearl of the Adriatic:** Walk the entire circuit of Dubrovnik's medieval city walls, which date back to the 13th century. Then take the cable car up Mt. Srđ for the postcard-perfect views of the walls, the Old Town, and the sea together in all their glory.

★ **Wine and oysters:** Feast on fresh oysters straight from the sea paired with local wine at a waterfront restaurant on the Pelješac Peninsula's Mali Ston. The oysters are justifiably famous and served year-round.

★ **Sword dancing:** Watch an incredibly entertaining, centuries-old sword dance in Korčula Town, the stunning walled city where Marco Polo was reputedly born.

★ **Secluded swimming:** Swim in the pristine lakes of Mljet National Park, surrounded by dense pine forests, then kayak out to the Benedictine monastery on an island in the middle of the lake.

★ **Chilling out:** Spend a day hiking, biking, or just lounging on the sun-drenched Elafiti Islands.

Occupying the tail end of Croatia before it trails off into Montenegro and the Bay of Kotor, Southern Dalmatia is bordered to the east by Bosnia and Herzegovina and to the west by the Adriatic Sea. At the very tip is the region of Konavle, where you'll find the airport and the seaside resort town of Cavtat. Dubrovnik is 22 km (13½ miles) up the coast; a further 54 km (34 miles) northwest is Mali Ston, the gateway to the Pelješac Peninsula. Orebić bookends the peninsula on the other side and is the jumping-off point for 15-minute ferry rides to the island of Korčula. From there, one can island-hop to Mljet, Šipan, and Lopud and back to Dubrovnik.

**1 Dubrovnik.** A historic walled city and Croatia's crown jewel.

**2 Elafiti Islands.** Laid-back islands that make great day trips from Dubrovnik.

3 **Cavtat.** An easygoing seaside retreat.

4 **The Pelješac Peninsula.** Fresh oysters, local wine, and secluded beaches.

5 **Korčula.** The alleged birthplace of Marco Polo.

6 **Mljet.** A beautiful island that is home to a gorgeous national park.

# Any region would be lucky to have just one sight as majestic as Dubrovnik. In Southern Dalmatia, the walled city is only the beginning.

Head south to pine-scented hiking trails in Cavtat, or up the coast to a garden full of exotic trees in Trsteno. Tour an ancient salt factory and feast on world-class oysters and superb red wine on the Pelješac Peninsula, then head out to sea to explore Marco Polo's birthplace on Korčula and Odysseus's mythical cave on Mljet. Along the way, you'll find some of the best windsurfing and sailing in Europe, kayak trips to citrus- and sage-covered islands, fresh seafood, centuries-old houses, millennia-old caves—and always, everywhere, that big blue sea.

The highlight of Southern Dalmatia is undoubtedly the stunning walled city of Dubrovnik, a rich and powerful independent republic that exerted its economic and cultural influence over almost the entire region from 1358 to 1808. Today it is one of Croatia's most sophisticated and upmarket destinations, as well as one of the world's most beautiful cities.

Dubrovnik is busy in the high season, so after a day or two of exploring, you might want to shift your attention to the towns and islands around it, which have remained remarkably untouched by mass tourism. Moving down the Adriatic coast you come to bucolic Konavle, the breadbasket of the region and a wonderful place to get a glimpse of rural life. The gateway to Konavle is Cavtat, a town founded by the ancient Greeks as Epidaurus and renamed Epidaurum once the Romans took over. Dubrovnik was actually founded by residents fleeing Epidaurum in the 7th century after the town was destroyed by Avars and Slavs. Today's Cavtat is a cheerful holiday resort with a palm-lined seaside promenade and a laid-back vibe.

That laid-back vibe actually has a name in Dalmatia: *fjaka*. It means "the sweetness of doing nothing," and the perfect place to experience this is on the Elafiti Islands. Just an hour away from Dubrovnik by boat, these three tiny islands were historically the favorite summer retreat for citizens of the Republic of Dubrovnik; today there's not much more to do on them than swim all day, eat fresh fish, admire the old stone houses, and maybe have an ice cream.

Back on the mainland, northwest of Dubrovnik, one arrives at the Pelješac Peninsula, the epitome of a hidden gem and the perfect place for a road trip. The main towns here are Mali Ston, known for its oysters, salt pans, and 14th-century walls, and Orebić, a low-key town with a lovely beach and water-sports facilities backed by a majestic hillside monastery. In the middle are sparkling coves and wineries producing full-bodied red wines from the Plavac Mali grape. From Orebić there are regular ferry crossings to Korčula, one of the most sophisticated of the Croatian islands, with dark pine trees, olive groves, vineyards, and a walled city that rivals Dubrovnik in beauty. Alternatively, the sparsely populated island of Mljet offers little in the way of architectural sites, but it is a haven for nature lovers with coniferous forests, lagoons, sandy beaches, and two emerald-green saltwater lakes in Mljet National Park.

# Planning

## When to Go

Southern Dalmatia works for half the year and sleeps for the other as much of the region shuts down through the winter, including the ferries to the islands. Dubrovnik is the exception, where sightseeing is just as important as swimming, so even in winter you will find some restaurants and attractions still open, plus serious deals on accommodation and a chance to tune in to the local way of life. Beware that while it rarely snows in the region, it does get quite cold and windy.

The best times to visit are the shoulder seasons: May through June and September through October. The days are still sunny and warm enough to swim but not too hot for sightseeing, there are fewer crowds, and the locals are more relaxed.

July and August are when everything happens at full speed; the prices are high, the hotels are fully booked, the harbors are full of boats, and the small streets are full of people. The payoff of a summer visit is that you're guaranteed hot sunny weather and plenty of festivals and entertainment. If you plan to visit during this period, make sure to book accommodations in advance and make dinner reservations a day or two ahead.

## Getting Here and Around

### AIR

Southern Dalmatia is served by Dubrovnik Airport (DBV) at Čilipi, 18 km (11 miles) southeast of Dubrovnik or just 5 km (3 miles) from Cavtat.

Throughout the summer, there are regular direct flights between Dubrovnik and New York, as well as many European cities. Most direct flights don't operate in the winter, but it's possible to fly directly to Istanbul all year. The national carrier, Croatia Airlines, operates direct flights between Dubrovnik and Zagreb year-round as well.

The Platanus shuttle bus travels several times per day between the airport and the main bus station in Gruž (€10 one-way; €14 return). The shuttle leaves the airport about 30 minutes after every flight and makes one stop near the Ploče Gate, so if you're staying in the Old Town that's where you should get off. The trip back to the airport is usually scheduled to leave the main bus station two hours before flight departure times, stopping along the way at the bus stop beside the entrance to the cable car. Check the website for exact timing, as it changes daily.

**AIRPORT CONTACTS Dubrovnik Airport.** ✉ *Cilipi* ☎ *020/773–100* 🌐 *www.airport-dubrovnik.hr.*

**AIRPORT TRANSFER CONTACTS Platanus Shuttle Bus.** ✉ *Ulica od Batale 2A, Dubrovnik* ☎ *020/358–516* 🌐 *platanus.hr.*

### BOAT AND FERRY

The national carrier, Jadrolinija, runs a once-weekly car ferry service between Bari (Italy) and Dubrovnik during the summer (€80; 10 hours). Throughout the summer, there are also several Jadrolinija passenger ferries per day from Dubrovnik to the Elafiti Islands of Koločep and Lopud (€5; 1 hour), as well as car ferries that stop in Mljet and Korčula before moving on to Split (€50; 5 hours).

Krilo's faster, more comfortable catamarans travel twice daily between Split and Dubrovnik, stopping in Korčula and Mljet en route. You can also take a high-speed catamaran operated by TP Line that runs daily from Dubrovnik to Šipan, Mljet, Korčula, and Lastovo. In addition, there are five daily Jadrolinija ferries between Mljet and Prapratno on the Pelješac Peninsula.

Tickets can be purchased in advance or at the individual ferry companies' offices at the harbor in each destination.

**CONTACTS Jadrolinija.** ✉ *Obala Stjepana Radića 40, Dubrovnik* ☎ *020/418–000* 🌐 *www.jadrolinija.hr.* **Krilo (Kapetan Luka).** ☎ *021/645–476* 🌐 *www.krilo.hr.* **TP Line.** ✉ *Obala Ivana Pavla II, Gruž* ☎ *020/313–119* 🌐 *www.tp-line.hr.*

### BUS

There are regular buses between Dubrovnik and destinations all over mainland Croatia, including hourly buses to Split (€30; 4 hours). Within Southern Dalmatia, hourly buses run down the coast from Dubrovnik to Cavtat and less frequently up the coast to Ston and Orebić on the Pelješac Peninsula.

**CONTACTS Dubrovnik Bus Station.** ✉ *Obala Ivana Pavla II 44A, Gruž* ☎ *060/305–070* 🌐 *libertasdubrovnik.hr.*

### CAR

Driving to Southern Dalmatia got a lot easier in 2022 with the opening of the Pelješac Bridge. It stretches from Komarna on the mainland to Brijesta on the Pelješac Peninsula, connecting the region to the rest of the country without having to cross a small section of Bosnia and Herzegovina, where border controls could often add hours to a journey in the high season. Now a trip between Split and Dubrovnik that used to take five hours can be done in less than three.

While visiting Dubrovnik you are better off without a car, as parking can be expensive and hard to find and traffic is notoriously bad in the summer. The Elafiti Islands are mostly car-free, but you might consider renting a car to explore Korčula as it will allow you to see more of the island, plus you can take a road trip through the Pelješac Peninsula to get there. You'll also need a car to explore Konavle and Mljet, as they are not well-served by public transport.

### TAXI

There is regular and efficient taxi service in Southern Dalmatia, but you'll find that Uber is much cheaper. In Dubrovnik you need to catch the taxi from designated stands, where you'll see a posted list of authorized prices.

## Restaurants

The dining scene in Southern Dalmatia gets better every year, with local ingredients taking center stage. Fresh catch dominates most menus in the region; white fish, including sea bream, sea bass, and scorpion fish, are common and traditionally served with *blitva* (potatoes and Swiss chard). The most celebrated regional delicacies are the oysters from Mali Ston on the Pelješac Peninsula, which can be enjoyed in restaurants across the region—nothing beats eating them raw with just a slice of lemon beside the channel where they were grown. Speaking of shellfish, be sure to try mussels or scampi *buzara*-style, which is a method of cooking seafood in olive oil, wine, garlic, bread crumbs, and fresh herbs. Another traditional dish is *brodet,* a rustic slow-cooked stew made with at least three kinds of fish. Fresh prawns, scallops, tuna, lobster (particularly in Mljet), and octopus (often served as a salad) round out the seafood selection, and don't miss *crni rižot* (black risotto), which gets its jet-black color from cuttlefish or squid ink.

At least once during your stay, you should make the effort to try food prepared *ispod peke* ("under the bell"): a terra-cotta casserole dish, usually containing lamb, octopus, or both, is buried in embers over which the *peka* (metal dome) is placed to ensure a long slow cooking process—it usually needs to be ordered a day in advance. Another must-try for meat lovers is *pašticada,* a sweet, rich, slow-cooked beef dish typically served with gnocchi. *Šporki makaruli* ("dirty macaroni") is a typical Dubrovnik specialty that involves beef sautéed with onions in pork fat and served with macaroni in a tomato sauce.

The region's most traditional dessert is *rožata* (creamy custard pudding), although the sweet treats you'll find most often are dried fruits: figs, apricots, candied almonds, and *arancini* (candied orange or lemon peels). Most meals are washed down with a small glass of *rakija*, often made with carob, roses, honey, or herbs, or Prošek, a sweet local dessert wine.

While you can definitely eat very well in Dubrovnik, the most memorable dining experiences happen on the islands. Hire a boat and sail right up to your restaurant. Taste the olive oil from the grove down the road, and smell the wild rosemary, oregano, and basil. Order a platter of fresh fish, perfectly cooked, accompanied by a glass of wine overlooking the only vineyard in the world where that particular grape grows. Dining doesn't get any finer than that.

## Hotels

You can find lodging to suit any style in Southern Dalmatia, from campsites and private apartments to villas and Croatia's highest concentration of five-star hotels. Sleeping in Dubrovnik allows you to immerse yourself in the city; for a truly unique experience, stay in one of the historical palaces right in the Old Town. Luxury hotels in Dubrovnik are expensive, but the quality is very high and the sea views are spectacular, so if you can afford it, this is a place to splurge. If you are looking for a more relaxed vacation, consider booking a hotel in one of the nearby towns or islands and taking day trips into the city. Hotels outside of Dubrovnik are slightly cheaper, but the quality is just as high.

For most of the region, the high season runs from May to October, peaking in July and August, when prices rise significantly. Most hotels on the islands or smaller towns close from November to April. In Dubrovnik, however, many properties stay open through the winter and you can find excellent bargains; many hotels have indoor pools and spas, making them an excellent choice for a winter city break.

**★ Dominium Travel**
Private apartments and villas are a great option, particularly if you're traveling with kids. But with so many throughout the region, choosing the right one can be overwhelming, not to mention a little risky. Do yourself a favor and contact Dominium Travel; a young enthusiastic company that manages more than 500 private apartments in 20 destinations along the coast, they'll work to find the perfect accommodation to suit your budget and style, and they can also organize transfers and tours. ✉ *Petra Svačića 29, Pile* ☎ *095/131–3142* 🌐 *bookdubrovnik.com.*

⇨ *Restaurant and hotel reviews have been shortened. For full information, visit Fodors.com. Restaurant prices are the average cost of a main course at dinner or, if dinner is not served, at lunch. Hotel prices are the lowest cost of a standard double room in high season.*

### What It Costs in Euros (€)

| | $ | $$ | $$$ | $$$$ |
|---|---|---|---|---|
| **RESTAURANTS** | | | | |
| | under €15 | €15–€23 | €24–€32 | over €32 |
| **HOTELS** | | | | |
| | under €150 | €150–€250 | €251–€350 | over €350 |

## Tours

**Dubrovnik Day Tours**
**GUIDED TOURS** | The friendly locals who operate this company bring more than a decade's worth of guiding experience—plus a lifetime of living in Dubrovnik—to their great-value private tours. They operate wine and oyster excursions to

the Pelješac Peninsula, as well as day trips to Konavle, Bosnia and Herzegovina, and Montenegro. They also do walking tours around Dubrovnik, including a fun tour with swords and props. The three-hour Dubrovnik Panorama tour is highly recommended and includes a comprehensive city tour and then a drive up Mt. Srđ for the best viewpoint over the Old Town. ✉ *Obala Stjepana Radića 2, Dubrovnik* ☎ *098/175–1775* 🌐 *www.dubrovnikdaytours.net.*

**Piknik Dubrovnik**

**SELF-GUIDED TOURS** | For a unique foodie experience, order a Piknik. You'll get an insulated backpack thoughtfully stocked with gourmet Croatian goodies and advice on the best secret beaches, panoramic viewpoints, and hiking trails where you can enjoy it. The owner is available to organize proposals and special occasions and can help plan hiking itineraries throughout Dalmatia. Advance notice is required. 🌐 *www.piknikdubrovnik.com.*

**Secret Dalmatia**

**PRIVATE GUIDES** | One of the pioneers in custom-made tours in the region, Secret Dalmatia organizes upmarket itineraries around Southern Dalmatia and Montenegro with a focus on local experiences, food and wine tastings, and off-the-beaten-track destinations. Their super helpful and friendly team can organize private or small-group tours. 🌐 *www.secretdalmatia.com.*

## Visitor Information

**CONTACTS Cavtat-Konavle Tourist Office.** ✉ *Zidine 6, Cavtat* ☎ *020/479–025* 🌐 *visit.cavtat-konavle.com.* **Dubrovnik Tourist Office.** ✉ *Brsalje 5, Pile* ☎ *020/312–011* 🌐 *tzdubrovnik.hr.* **Korčula Tourist Office.** ✉ *Trg 19. travnja 1921. br. 40, Korcula* ☎ *020/715–701* 🌐 *www.visitkorcula.eu.* **Lopud Tourist Office.** ✉ *Obala Iva Kuljevana 12, Lopud* ☎ *020/322–322.* **Mljet Tourist Office.** ✉ *Sobra* ☎ *020/780–7992* 🌐 *www.mljet.hr.* **Orebić Tourist Office.** ✉ *Zrinsko-frankopanska 2, Orebic* ☎ *020/713–718* 🌐 *visitorebic-croatia.hr.* **Ston Tourist Office.** ✉ *Gundulićeva Poljana 1, Ston* ☎ *020/754–452* 🌐 *www.ston.hr.*

# Dubrovnik

Nothing can prepare you for your first sight of Dubrovnik's Old Town. Completely encircled by thick fortified walls with a maze of gleaming white streets within, it is truly one of the world's most beautiful cities. And it never gets old; whether you're admiring it from the top of Mt. Srđ, from a kayak out at sea, or standing in the middle of the Stradun looking around in awe, your imagination will run wild picturing what it looked like when the walls were built eight centuries ago, without any suburbs or highways around it—just this magnificent stone city rising out of the sea.

In the 7th century AD, residents of the Roman city Epidaurum (now Cavtat) fled the Avars and Slavs of the north and founded a new settlement on a small rocky island, which they named Laus, and later Ragusa (Dubrovnik's Latin name). On the mainland hillside opposite the island, the Slav settlement called Dubrovnik grew up. In the 12th century, the narrow channel separating the two settlements was filled in (now the main street through the Old Town, called the Stradun) and Ragusa and Dubrovnik became one, officially going with the Slavic name. The city was surrounded by defensive walls during the 13th century and reinforced with towers and bastions in the late 15th century.

From 1358 to 1808, the city thrived as a powerful and remarkably sophisticated independent republic, reaching its golden age during the 16th century. In 1667 many of its splendid Gothic and Renaissance buildings were destroyed by an earthquake. The defensive walls survived the disaster, and the city was rebuilt in Baroque style.

Dubrovnik lost its independence to Napoléon in 1808 and passed to Austria-Hungary in 1815. During the 20th century, as part of Yugoslavia, the city was a popular destination for European travelers, and in 1979 it was listed as a UNESCO World Heritage site. During the Homeland War in 1991, it came under heavy siege. Thanks to careful restoration, few traces of damage remain.

Naturally, as one of the world's most beautiful cities, it has also become one of the most popular. Over the past decade, the number of private accommodation units grew rapidly, on-location filming for the television series brought widespread attention, and an increasing number of cruise ships brought massive crowds into the walled city, negatively impacting not only the visitor experience but the quality of life for locals, many of whom simply moved out. In 2019, Dubrovnik saw its highest tourist numbers ever, and plans were put in place to address sustainability issues, including limiting the number of cruise ships that are allowed to dock in the city per day and installing cameras around the Old Town to monitor the number of people within. There was even talk of banning wheelie suitcases, although that turned out to be more of a suggestion than a rule. In 2020, the COVID-19 pandemic halted visits to Dubrovnik, which was devastating for an economy that relied so heavily on tourism. On the other hand, the pause allowed local officials time to reimagine their strategy and gave locals the chance to reclaim their city for a summer.

Dubrovnik is, after all, a small city, with just 40,000 residents, fewer than 2,000 of whom still live in the Old Town. Walk just a couple of blocks uphill from the Stradun and you'll see a much quieter side of the city, where locals go about their lives, hanging their laundry, bringing their children to school, gossiping outside their front doors. The challenge moving forward will be how to balance the massive number of people who want to visit the city every year (and the money that inevitably brings in) with maintaining the quality of life of the people who actually live there.

## GETTING HERE AND AROUND

There are regular bus routes between Dubrovnik and destinations all over mainland Croatia and beyond. The main bus station is located in Gruž, 20 minutes outside the Old Town.

Within Dubrovnik, regular buses connect all parts of the city but they're often very crowded; tickets can be purchased from the driver (make sure you have cash) or from red Tisak stands. The Old Town is car-free, but there are public bus stops and taxi stands outside the Pile Gate and beside the entrance to the cable car. If you're going to Lapad or Gruž, catch the bus from the Pile Gate. If you're going south to Cavtat or the airport, head to the cable car stop.

It's not advisable to bring a car to Dubrovnik because traffic is heavy and parking is very expensive. Some hotels do include parking, and there is a public parking garage on Zagrebačka Street near the Old Town where you'll find the most reasonable prices.

There are taxi ranks at the main bus station, at the airport, just outside the city walls at Pile Gate and Ploče Gate, in front of Gruž Harbor, and in Lapad. It isn't possible to hail a taxi on the street; you must go to the rank or call to order one.

Most large ferries depart from the main port in Gruž. There is also a smaller, more atmospheric old port just outside the walls in the Old Town; some charter boats dock there, and it's also where boats depart for Lokrum Island.

## TOURS

### ★ Dubrovnik Tourist Guide

**GUIDED TOURS** | Ivan Vuković Vuka is one of the most in-demand tour guides in Dubrovnik and is called upon whenever movie productions need a location scout or when news organizations, such as National Geographic or CNN, need someone to cover a story. Luckily for us, he also offers private daily walking tours of Dubrovnik, which are a charming mix of history, personal anecdotes, and local lore. Check out his Wannabe Croatian Tour, where you'll basically hang out with Ivan and meet the locals that he knows (he grew up here, so he knows everyone). ☎ *98/328–554* 🌐 *dubrovnik-tourist-guides.com.*

### Sights and Bites

**FOOD AND DRINK TOURS** | **FAMILY** | With small group sizes and a knowledgeable, entertaining local guide, Sights and Bites combines a traditional walking tour with a food crawl, teaching you the history of Dubrovnik while sampling its tastiest treats. Starting at the Onofrio Fountain and weaving through the city and out the Ploče Gate, the tour makes at least four stops for food and wine. It starts at 4 pm, when the restaurants are quiet, and finishes around 7 pm so you can get back to the hotel or to your next activity on time. The tour is fun, informative, and a great value, even more so because you won't need to eat lunch beforehand or dinner afterward. 🌐 *croatiafoodtour.com* 🎫 *€89.*

## FESTIVALS

### Dubrovnik Summer Festival

**FESTIVALS** | **FAMILY** | The city's cultural highlight is the annual Dubrovnik Summer Festival, which runs from mid-July to late August and attracts thousands of artists from around the world. A variety of open-air classical concerts, ballets, and plays are held at various venues within the walls, and the city becomes a riot of folklore, traditional dresses, midnight performances, and music. The most prestigious event of the festival is the performance of *Hamlet* at Fort Lovrijenac. Tickets can be purchased online or at the festival box office. ✉ *Od Sigurate 1, Stari Grad* ☎ *020/326–100* 🌐 *www.dubrovnik-festival.hr* 🎫 *Tickets from €13.*

### Dubrovnik Winter Festival

**FESTIVALS** | **FAMILY** | From the end of November until the first week of January, the Old Town makes a spectacular backdrop for the Dubrovnik Winter Festival. Expect all the trappings of a traditional European Christmas market, with mulled wine and rakija, wooden booths selling handmade goods and sugary delicacies, concerts, and a giant skating rink. The Winter Festival is a much more relaxed and local affair than the Summer Festival and is another way the city is trying to attract visitors to Dubrovnik in the off-season. ✉ *Dubrovnik* 🌐 *www.dubrovackizimskifestival.com.*

## Dubrovnik Pass

If you plan to do a bit of sightseeing, it's worth buying the Dubrovnik Pass, which includes entry to 10 cultural sights around town (including the city walls and Fort Lovrijenac), plus free public transportation. You can buy a pass for one day (€35), three days (€45), or seven days (€55). Purchase the card online at 🌐 *www.dubrovnikpass.com* or pick it up at any of the tourist offices around the city.

## Sights

There are three main neighborhoods where you will spend most of your time in Dubrovnik. All of the major historical sites lie in the Old Town (or Stari Grad) within the city walls, a compact car-free area. Lapad is located on a peninsula

A walk along Dubrovnik's city walls is one of the best ways to get a sense of the city.

about 4 km (2½ miles) west of the Old Town; it is the most family-friendly part of town, with the city's most accessible beach and many casual shops, hotels, and restaurants. Gruž is about 3½ km (2 miles) from the Old Town, and it's where you'll find the main bus and ferry stations, as well as the Red History Museum.

When planning your days, keep in mind that the Old Town can get very hot and busy in the morning and early afternoon, especially if there are several cruise ships in town. If you're an early bird, take a walk around the city walls first thing in the morning before the crowds arrive, then spend the afternoon relaxing at the beach or your hotel or take a boat trip to Lokrum Island. In the evening, return to the Old Town when the crowds have gone and take the cable car to the top of Mt. Srđ for incredible sunset views.

**Bell Tower**

**CLOCK** | All walks down the Stradun lead to one point: the Bell Tower. The centerpiece of Luža Square, this bright white structure from 1444 is one of the main symbols of the city, reaching 31 meters (102 feet) high and featuring a moon dial and the original bell from 1506. Look a little closer to see Dubrovnik's two favorite mascots tolling the hours on either side of the bell; known as Maro and Baro, the current figures are made of bronze, while the original wooden men are now found in the Rector's Palace. ✉ *Luža, Stari Grad.*

★ **City Walls** (*Gradske Zidine*)

**HISTORIC SIGHT** | **FAMILY** | Dubrovnik's city walls define the Old Town and are one of the world's most stunning architectural achievements. A walk along the top is the ultimate Dubrovnik must-do for the magnificent views of the sea outside the walls and the terra-cotta rooftops and gleaming white streets within. Most of the original construction took place during the 13th century, though the walls were further reinforced with towers and bastions over the next 400 years. The walls completely encircle the Old Town as part of a fortification system that also includes the **Pile Gate** (still the main

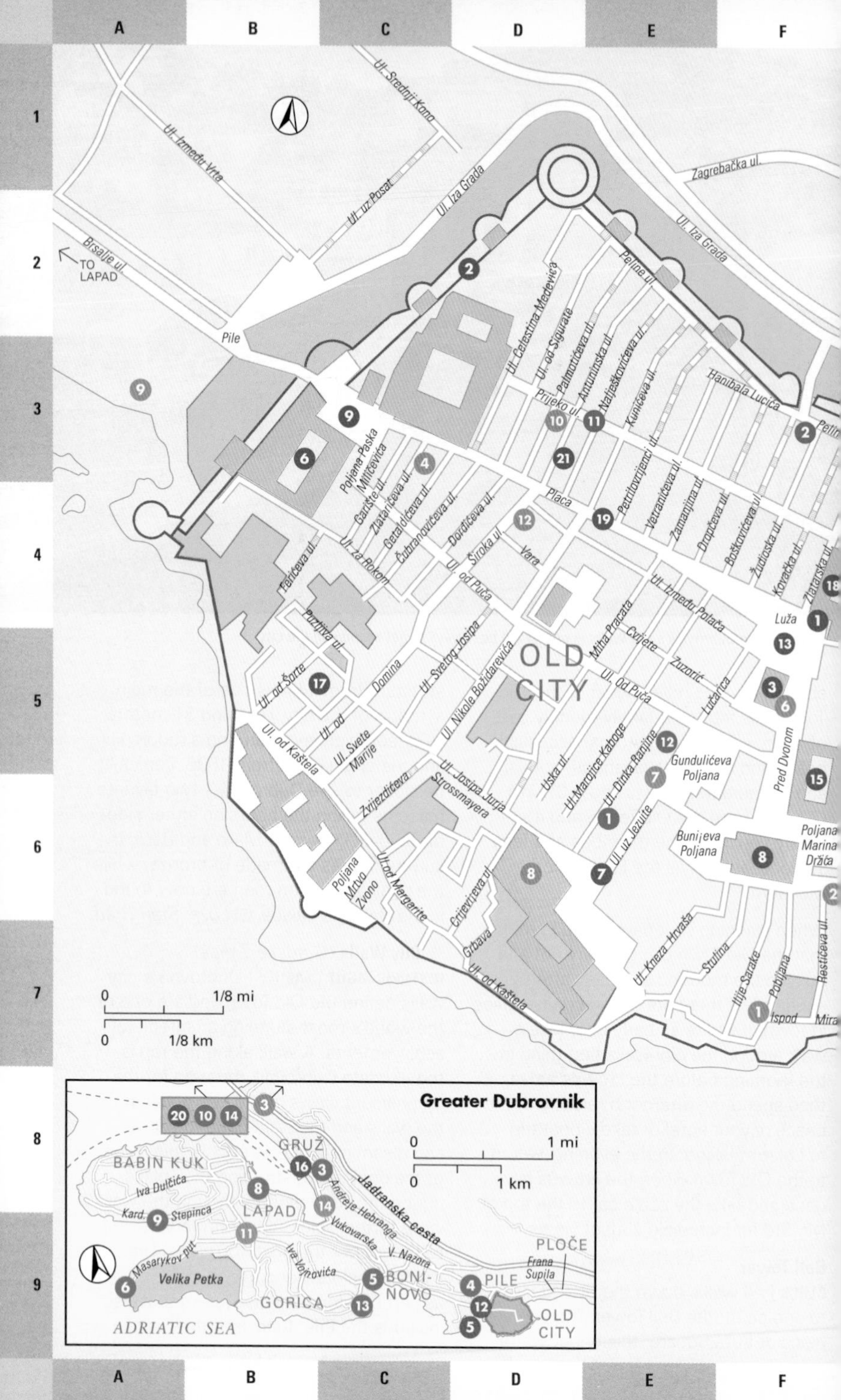

OLD CITY
Greater Dubrovnik
BABIN KUK
LAPAD
GRUŽ
GORICA
BONI-NOVO
PILE
PLOČE
OLD CITY
ADRIATIC SEA
Velika Petka
Jadranska cesta
TO LAPAD
Pile
Placa
Luža
Gundulićeva Poljana
Bunićeva Poljana
Poljana Marina Držića
Pred Dvorom

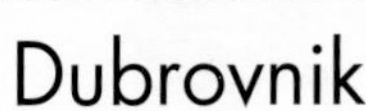


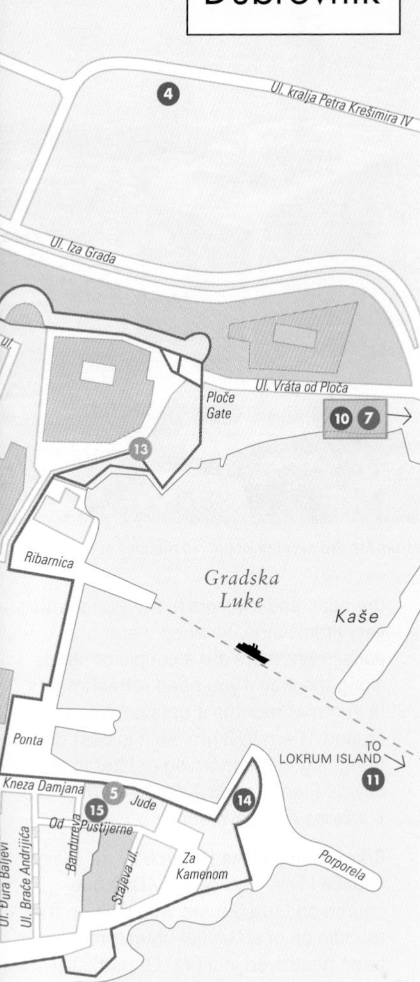


## Sights ▼

1 Bell Tower ................ F4
2 City Walls ................ D2
3 Crkva Svetog Vlaha...... F5
4 Dubrovnik Cable Car ... H2
5 Fort Lovrijenac .......... D9
6 Franciscan Monastery............... B3
7 Jesuit Steps ............. D6
8 Katedrala Velika Gospe ............. F6
9 Large Onofrio Fountain................... C3
10 Lazareti ....................I4
11 Lokrum Island ............. I6
12 Love Stories Museum ................. D9
13 Orlando's Column........ F5
14 Maritime Museum...... H6
15 Rector's Palace .......... F5
16 Red History Museum... B8
17 Rupe Ethnographic Museum .................. C5
18 Sponza Palace .......... F4
19 Stradun .................. E4
20 Trsteno Arboretum ..... A8
21 War Photo Limited...... D3

## Restaurants ▼

1 Azur ....................... F7
2 Bota Šare Oyster & Sushi Bar ................. F6
3 Fat Bastard Smokehouse & BBQ ... B8
4 Gelateria Dubrovnik..... C3
5 Gianni ..................... G6
6 Gradska Kavana ......... F5
7 Kamenice................. E5
8 Kopun .................... D6
9 Nautika Restaurant..... A3
10 Nishta ................... D3
11 Pantarul.................. B9
12 Proto ..................... D4
13 Restaurant 360 .......... H4
14 Urban & Veggie.......... C8

## Hotels ▼

1 Amoret Apartments .... D6
2 Apartments Paviša ...... F3
3 Berkeley Hotel & Spa ... C8
4 Hilton Imperial Dubrovnik................ D9
5 Hotel Bellevue ........... C9
6 Hotel Dubrovnik Palace.................... A9
7 Hotel Excelsior............ I4
8 Hotel Kazbek ............ B8
9 Hotel More .............. A9
10 Hotel Osmoliš ........... B8
11 Prijeko Palace............ E3
12 The Pucić Palace........ E5
13 Rixos Libertas ........... C9
14 Sun Gardens ............ B8
15 Van Bloemen Apartments.............. G6

The Dubrovnik Cable Car gives you a bird's-eye view from Mt. Srđ over the iconic red rooftops of the city.

entrance into the Old Town) and **Ploče Gate** (the main entrance coming from the east); both have drawbridges that used to be raised each night so no one could come in or out—the keys were given to the Rector. There are also six fortresses, including freestanding **Fort Lovrijenac** to the west and **Minčeta Tower** to the north (the highest point in the Old Town). On average, the walls are 80 feet high and 2 km (1¼ miles) long, 10 feet thick on the seaward side, and 20 feet thick on the inland side. The inland walls are thicker because when they were constructed, the largest threat came from the Turks who might attack from that direction. (Ironically they got the direction right, but not the source: it was Napoléon, attacking from the inland fortress atop Mt. Srđ, who finally conquered the Republic.)

The entire circuit takes a couple of hours. Tickets can be purchased at the main entrance inside the Pile or Ploče Gate or at a quieter entrance beside the Maritime Museum. Note that the walk can be strenuous, especially in the heat, and involves many stairs with very little shade, so bring water and sunscreen; there are a couple of shops along the way if you need refreshments. In summer months it gets crowded from around 11 am to 3 pm, so it is best done first thing in the morning or later in the day. ✉ *Stari Grad* ☎ *020/638–800* 🎫 *€35 (includes Fort Lovrijenac).*

**Crkva Svetog Vlaha** (*Church of St. Blaise*)
**CHURCH** | This 18th-century Baroque church on Luža Square was built on the foundation of an earlier church that had been destroyed in a fire. Of particular note is the silver statue on the high altar of St. Blaise holding a model of Dubrovnik, which was the only thing that survived the fire. It is paraded around town each year on February 3, the Day of St. Blaise. ✉ *Luža 3, Stari Grad.*

★ **Dubrovnik Cable Car**
**VIEWPOINT** | **FAMILY** | Originally built in 1969 and reopened in 2010 after being destroyed in the siege, this is one of the top experiences in Dubrovnik. The ultramodern cable car whisks you up to

the top of Mt. Srđ for the best view over the Old Town, Lokrum, and the Elafiti Islands. You can also join an hour-long buggy tour of the area, go for a hike, have a cocktail at the smart Panorama Restaurant, or just grab a seat and enjoy the view. At the top you'll also find the Imperial Fort, built between 1806 and 1812 by Napoléon during his short rule of the city and now home to the Homeland War Museum.

To reach the cable car, follow the signs from the Pile or Ploče Gate along the outside of the wall or climb the steps from the Stradun toward the mountain and exit via the Buža Gate. Buses from Gruž will drop you off right outside the entrance, where tickets can be purchased. If possible, try and plan your visit for sunset, when the views are magnificent and the line is shorter. ✉ *Lower Station, Kralja Petra Krešimira IV, Ploce* ☎ *020/414–355* 🌐 *www.dubrovnikcablecar.com* 🎫 *€15 one-way, €27 round-trip* 🕒 *Closed Jan. and Feb.*

**Fort Lovrijenac**

**HISTORIC SIGHT** | The only freestanding part of Dubrovnik's fortification system, this impressive tower stands on a 37-meter-high sheer rock overlooking the sea outside the Pile Gate. Construction began sometime in the 11th century; the story goes that the Venetians planned to build a fortress atop the rock from which to conquer Dubrovnik, but the Republic learned of their plans and beat them to it. The seaward walls are 12 meters thick while the walls facing Dubrovnik are only 60 centimeters thick, so that in the event the fortress was captured it could easily be destroyed from within the city walls. Above the entrance a Latin enscription reads: "*Non bene pro toto libertas venditur auro*"—"Freedom is not sold for all the gold in the world." The fortress makes a particularly memorable venue during the Dubrovnik Summer Festival, when it is the setting for *Hamlet*, and it is also recognizable to fans as the Red Keep. ✉ *Od Tabakarije 29, Stari Grad* 🎫 *€15; included with City Walls ticket.*

**Franciscan Monastery** (*Franjevačka samostan*)

**HISTORIC SIGHT** | Built in 1317 in Romanesque-Gothic style, this solid-stone Franciscan monastery on the Stradun has a delightful cloistered garden; a 17th-century library that contains more than 20,000 books; a small museum; and its chief claim to fame, a pharmacy that was founded in 1318, making it one of the oldest in Europe. Much of the original church was destroyed in the earthquake of 1667; the striking *Pietà*, located atop the door on the Stradun and sculpted by local masters Petar and Leonard Andrijic, was one of the only things that survived. In the Treasury, a painting shows what Dubrovnik looked like before the disastrous earthquake. Ivan Gundulić, the Republic's most prominent poet, is buried in the monastery. **■ TIP→ Watch for locals and tourists jumping up on a small gargoyle's head attached to the outer wall of the monastery along the Stradun. Legend has it that if you can stand on the head facing the wall and take off your shirt without falling down, you will find love. Give it a shot, but it's harder than it looks.** ✉ *Placa 2, Stari Grad* ☎ *020/321–410* 🎫 *€6.*

**Jesuit Steps**

**HISTORIC SIGHT** | Find this monumental Baroque staircase, Dubrovnik's very own version of the Spanish Steps, at the south side of Gundulićeva Poljana. At the top is the lovely Jesuit Church of St. Ignatius of Loyola, built between 1699 and 1725. This staircase will be particularly familiar to fans as the steps from Cersei's walk of shame scene. ✉ *Poljana Ruđera Boškovića 6, Stari Grad* 🎫 *Free.*

**Katedrala Velika Gospe** (*Assumption of the Virgin Mary Cathedral*)

**CHURCH** | Legend says that when Richard the Lionheart was shipwrecked on Lokrum Island, he vowed to show his thanks to God for saving his life by building a cathedral on the spot; locals

*Game of Thrones* fans love flocking to the Jesuit Steps to snap a photo where Queen Cersei did her walk of shame.

convinced him to move his plans to Dubrovnik instead. The present structure was completed in 1713 in Baroque style after the original was destroyed in the 1667 earthquake. The interior contains a number of notable paintings, including a large polyptych above the main altar depicting the Assumption of the Virgin Mary, attributed to Titian. The treasury displays 138 gold and silver reliquaries, including the skull of St. Blaise in the form of a bejeweled Byzantine crown and an arm and leg of the saint, likewise encased in decorated gold plating. ✉ *Držićeva Poljana, Stari Grad* 🎫 *Free.*

**Large Onofrio Fountain**

**FOUNTAIN** | Built between 1438 and 1440, the Large Onofrio Fountain is one of Dubrovnik's most iconic sites and popular meeting points, and it's the first thing you'll see upon entering through the Pile Gate. The 16-sided stone fountain is topped by a large dome and was designed by architect Onofrio di Giordano della Cava. Along with the Small Onofrio Fountain at the other end of the Stradun, it was part of a complex water-supply system designed to bring water into the Old Town from a well 12 km (7½ miles) away. It originally had more sculptures, but they were damaged during the earthquake in 1667; the 16 that remain spout water that is still cold and drinkable. ✉ *Pred Dvorom, Stari Grad.*

**Lazareti**

**HISTORIC DISTRICT** | A series of interconnected medieval buildings located just outside the Ploče Gate, these were the original quarantine stations where traders had to spend 40 days (*quaranta giorni* in Italian, hence the word "quarantine") before they could enter Dubrovnik to ensure they didn't bring any diseases with them. Because the Republic was involved in so much trade with other countries, they were always at risk of catching serious diseases, such as the plague or cholera, which were killing thousands of people across Europe and Asia at the time. In 1377, the first quarantine stations were built on remote Dalmatian islands (first fully outdoors, then in

## Game of Thrones

Perhaps no film setting is as evocative as Dubrovnik, or as fans know it better, King's Landing. For seven of its eight seasons, the popular HBO show was filmed in the walled city, on Lokrum Island (where you'll find a small museum and the "original" Iron Throne), and in Trsteno Arboretum. Many locals have great stories about their experiences with the show, including tales of cast members winding up on their hostel's couch after a big night out or the lengths the production went to to protect the secrecy of the final season. Some CGI was used in the show, but there are many sites around town that will be immediately recognizable to fans, including Fort Lovrijenac, the Jesuit Steps, and the abandoned Hotel Belvedere, which was the setting for the battle between Oberyn and The Mountain. There are many tours to choose from, most of which follow a similar structure: a walking tour of the main filming spots where the guide holds up a still shot of the scene so you can compare the set to reality. More broadly appealing are tours that combine details of Dubrovnik history with the stories and legends of King's Landing. A great option is Dubrovnik Day Tours (🌐 *www.dubrovnikdaytours.net*), which offers a fun tour experience with real swords and props.



small wooden stations so they could be burned easily if disease was detected). In 1647, construction was completed on the lazarettos, which were strategically located on the road that led to Dubrovnik from the south and right next to the main port. The quarantine requirement was finally abolished in 1872. Lazareti is now a sleepy area that's home to a couple of restaurants, art galleries, and shops. ✉ *Ploce.*

### ★ Lokrum Island

**ISLAND** | **FAMILY** | Some of Dubrovnik's most natural and peaceful beaches can be found on Lokrum, the island just off Dubrovnik's Old Town. It's a wonderful place to spend a day spotting peacocks (a Habsburg legacy), feeding wild rabbits, or just enjoying the fresh air among the pines.

Tiny Lokrum has swirled with legend and mystery ever since Richard the Lionheart was supposedly cast ashore there in 1191 upon returning from the Crusades. The story goes that when the Benedictine monks who owned the island at the time were expelled to make room for aristocrats in the 19th century, they left behind a curse on any future owners of the land, including Habsburg Emperor Maximilian I, who was executed in Mexico just eight years after he turned the monastery into his summer residence. To this day, it is considered bad luck to stay overnight on the island, though many a pair of romantics have tried.

Lush and fertile, Lokrum is home to the ruins of the abandoned 11th-century monastery, which is set among exotic botanical gardens. At the top of the island is a star-shaped fortress built by Napoléon's troops during French occupation and later used by the Austrian army. Footpaths leads down to the rocky shoreline, past the "dead sea" lake, where there are cliffs to jump from, coves to bathe in, and a small stretch of coast reserved for nudists. You can also visit a small museum with the original Iron Throne (Lokrum was one of many filming locations around town).

To reach Lokrum, take a taxi-boat from the Old Port (€7); tickets can be purchased at the tourist information center beneath the Bell Tower on the Stradun. Boats run every half hour from April through November, and the ride takes approximately 15 minutes. ✉ *Dubrovnik ⊕ 1 km (½ mile) from Old Port* 🌐 *www.lokrum.hr* 🎫 *€27* ⏲ *Closed Nov.–Apr.*

**★ Love Stories Museum**

**OTHER MUSEUM** | A counterpart to the Museum of Broken Relationships in Zagreb—except with happier endings—this delightful museum a short walk outside the Pile Gate is a simple life-affirming celebration of romance spread over four floors. Each room has a different theme, from Croatia-specific tales and local lore to celebrity love stories to an exhibit about the movies and series filmed in Dubrovnik (yes, is represented). The top floors are perhaps the most moving, with items sent in from real people and notes scribbled on heart-shaped Post-its tacked all over the "love wall." ✉ *Od Tabakarije 2, Pile* ☎ *095/3555–145* 🌐 *lovestoriesmuseum.com* 🎫 *€9.*

**Maritime Museum** (*Pomorski Muzej*)

**OTHER MUSEUM** | Above the aquarium, located on the first and second floors of St. John's Fortress, this museum's exhibits illustrate how rich and powerful Dubrovnik became one of the world's most important seafaring cities. On display are intricately detailed models of ships as well as engine-room equipment, sailors' uniforms, paintings, and maps. ✉ *St. John's Fortress, Kneza Damjana Jude 2, Stari Grad* ☎ *020/323–904* 🎫 *€20* ⏲ *Closed Wed.*

**Orlando's Column**

**MONUMENT** | Dating back to 1418, Orlando's Column, located at the end of the Stradun and serving as a popular meeting point, is dedicated to legendary 8th-century knight Roland, who is said to have saved Dubrovnik from a Saracen attack near Lokrum. The white-stone column has become a symbol of freedom for the city, and the white Libertas flag is traditionally flown from the top during important events, such as the opening ceremony of the Dubrovnik Summer Festival. ✉ *Luža, Stari Grad.*

**Rector's Palace** (*Knežev Dvor*)

**HISTORY MUSEUM** | One of the most significant buildings along the Croatian coast, this was the administrative center of the Dubrovnik Republic. It's where the Grand Council and Senate held their meetings and the chief citizen, the Rector, lived and did business during his one-month term. It also held a courtroom, prisons, meeting halls, and a gunpowder room, which exploded twice in the 15th century. The explosions, plus the earthquake of 1667, required the building to be reconstructed over the years in varying Baroque, Renaissance, and Gothic styles. The palace is now home to the Cultural History Museum, containing exhibits that give a picture of life in Dubrovnik from early days until the fall of the Republic. ✉ *Pred Dvorom 3, Stari Grad* ☎ *020/321–422* 🌐 *www.dumus.hr* 🎫 *€15.*

**★ Red History Museum**

**HISTORY MUSEUM** | Located in an industrial factory in Gruž, the Red History Museum tells the story of the rise and fall of communism in Croatia. Founded by a young group of entrepreneurs in 2019, among them a designer, a historian, and a couple who worked on film sets, it is a fun and fresh museum designed to be touched and explored. Taking a steadfastly neutral approach, the exhibits focus largely on everyday life under communism, from the clothing of the era to kitchen sets to sex education, with historical information weaved effortlessly throughout the colorful displays. ✉ *Svetog Križa 3, Gruž* ☎ *528–7744* 🌐 *www.redhistorymuseum.com* 🎫 *€9.*

**Rupe Ethnographic Museum**

**HISTORY MUSEUM** | This charming museum is worth the visit for both the building itself (built in 1590, it was used as a grain storage during the time of the Republic),

Old Town's main street, the Stradun, is lined with historic buildings like the Rector's Palace.

as well as the collection of 6,000 heritage pieces from around Croatia and neighboring countries, including tools, folk costumes, lace, and other handiwork. *Rupe* means "holes," which refers to the underground grain storage pits carved out of tufa below the building. ✉ *Od Rupa 3, Stari Grad* ☎ *020/323–056* 🌐 *www.dumus.hr* 🎫 *€8* ⏲ *Closed Tues.*

**Sponza Palace**

**HISTORIC SIGHT** | The original location where all trade goods coming into Dubrovnik went to be taxed, this 16th-century Gothic-Renaissance palace has served as the city's mint, an arsenal, and eventually a place for the Republic's most educated citizens to discuss cultural matters called the Academy of the Learned. It now contains the city's archives, as well as the occasional art exhibit; the shady arcaded interior is a lovely spot to escape the heat and crowds.

Turn left as you enter to find the Memorial Room for the Defenders of Dubrovnik, a heart-wrenching little gallery with photographs of those who died defending the city, along with remnants of the flag that once flew atop Mount Srđ. ✉ *Placa bb, Stari Grad* ☎ *020/321–032* 🎫 *Free.*

★ **Stradun** (*Placa*)

**STREET** | The Placa, commonly referred to as the Stradun, is the main street and the beating heart of Dubrovnik's Old Town. Stretching 300 meters from the Pile Gate to Luža Square and the Bell Tower, it was once the shallow sea channel separating the island of Laus from the mainland; although it was filled in during the 12th century, it continued to divide the city socially for several centuries, with the nobility living in the area to the south and commoners living on the hillside to the north. Today, the Stradun is the best people-watching promenade in town, with enough cafés, *gelaterias*, and boutiques to keep you busy for days. ✉ *Stari Grad.*

**Trsteno Arboretum**

**GARDEN** | Within the grounds of a small Renaissance villa, 14 km (9 miles) up the coast from Dubrovnik, Trsteno Arboretum

## Dubrovnik Under Siege

From November 1991 to May 1992, Dubrovnik was intermittently shelled by the Yugoslav army stationed on the rugged hills behind the city. Electricity and water supplies were cut off, and the local population took refuge in basements, surviving on a slowly diminishing quantity of food, fuel, and medical supplies. The city's massive medieval fortifications stood up well to the assault, though none of Dubrovnik's main monuments were targeted—apparently the Yugoslav army wanted to capture the city intact. Extensive media coverage whipped up a storm of international criticism over the wanton bombing of this historic city, which effectively turned world opinion against Belgrade and in favor of granting Croatia diplomatic recognition. Once hostilities ceased, the cleanup and rebuilding began. During the second half of the 1990s, money poured in from all over the world for the restoration and today, thanks to the work of highly skilled craftspeople, barely any traces of war damage remain. But there is still a subtle reminder of the damage wrought upon 68% of the buildings in the Old Town. Look closer at the clay roof tiles when you're walking the city walls: the brighter orange tiles are new, and the faded tiles are the originals.

was originally established during the 16th century by the noble Gučetić family and has been continuously developed over the centuries, acquiring Renaissance and Baroque additions along the way. Today, it is filled with hundreds of exotic species of trees and shrubs, most of which were brought home by local sailors from distant voyages. An original aqueduct is still in use, and a beautiful Baroque fountain of Neptune and two nymphs dates from 1736. Buses run regularly to Trsteno from Dubrovnik (€3; 30 minutes), and it makes a great stopover on the way to the Pelješac Peninsula.

For something a little different, organize a cooking class with Katja at her house within the grounds of the Arboretum. Katja's family has lived there for four generations, and together you will prepare a feast that might include black risotto, peka, or pašticada. The price includes admission to the arboretum, and Katja will also take you on a walking tour of the grounds. The cooking class can be booked through Culinary Croatia (*www.culinary-croatia.com*). *Potok 20, Trsteno 020/751–019 €7.*

**War Photo Limited**

**ART GALLERY** | Shocking and impressive, this modern gallery run by New Zealand photojournalist Wade Goddard, who drove from London to Croatia in 1992 to document the war and never left, devotes two floors to war photojournalism. The permanent exhibition showcases photos and video from former Yugoslavia, while recent exhibitions have been dedicated to conflicts in Ukraine, Myanmar, and Vietnam. It's a sobering, illuminating, and extremely worthwhile gallery. *Antuninska 6, Stari Grad 020/322–166 www.warphotoltd.com €10 Closed Nov.–Mar.*

## Restaurants

**★ Azur**

**$$** | **ASIAN** | One of the perennial top choices in Dubrovnik, Azur has a fun fresh vibe and an outstanding menu of Asian-inspired dishes that burst with flavor; favorites include pork belly tacos and Szechuan chili-garlic prawns. With its two shady terraces high up in the Old Town, just beneath the city walls, Azur provides a welcome retreat from the heat and crowds. **Known for:** Mediterranean-Asian fusion dishes; well-priced high-quality food; quiet location under the city walls. $ *Average main: €21* ✉ *Pobijana 10, Stari Grad* ☎ *020/324–806* 🌐 *www.azurvision.com.*

**Bota Šare Oyster & Sushi Bar**

**$$ | JAPANESE** | Using the best local bluefin tuna, shrimp, and shellfish, Bota Šare turns its fresh catches into beautifully presented sushi, sashimi, carpaccio, and tartare. The spot is owned by the Šare family of fishermen who operate some of the best seafood restaurants in the region, including Mali Ston, making this the ideal place to try the famous Mali Ston oysters (if raw oysters make you squeamish, try them tempura-style). **Known for:** first sushi restaurant in Dubrovnik; Japanese spin on local ingredients; shady location near Cathedral. $ *Average main: €16* ✉ *Đura Baglivija 1, Stari Grad* ☎ *020/324–034* 🌐 *www.bota-sare.hr.*

**Fat Bastard Smokehouse & BBQ**

**$$ | BARBECUE** | This spot has two unique elements that make it stand out among Dubrovnik restaurants: first, it's a BBQ restaurant in a seafood-centric town; second, it's located not by the sea but rather by the aquamarine Ombla River, right where it meets the mountain—a beautiful place not seen by most tourists. With funky artwork on the walls and a breezy terrace right over the river, along with an excellent selection of local craft beers and generous sharing platters, it's worth the trek out of the Old Town to find this hidden gem. **Known for:** meat-centric menu of burgers, ribs, wings, and taquitos; riverside location; funky interior design. $ *Average main: €16* ✉ *Gornji Rožat 1a , Dubrovnik* ☎ *099/340–5656* 🌐 *www.fatbastardsmokehouse.com* ⏲ *Closed Mon.*

**Gelateria Dubrovnik**

**$ | ICE CREAM | FAMILY** | In a city full of ice cream shops, family-run Gelateria Dubrovnik is the original. There's a reason why there's always a line out the door—and it's not just because they give free cones to local kids. **Known for:** long-standing institution since 1968; the most popular ice cream shop in town; friendly, gregarious service. $ *Average main: €3* ✉ *Placa 17, Dubrovnik* ☎ *099/771–5143* 🌐 *gelateria-dubrovnik.business.site.*

★ **Gianni**

**$ | ICE CREAM** | When the former pastry chef at Restaurant 360 opens his own artisanal ice cream and cake shop in Dubrovnik, you know it's going to be good; Gianni serves up the best scratch-made gelato in town, incorporating natural ingredients and some unusual flavors such as curry and chili alongside traditional favorites like pistachio and chocolate. Don't let the high-caliber credentials intimidate you—this little hole in the wall in the Old Town, located behind the Old Port, is as casual as it gets, with a few outdoor tables where you can hang out and make friends over ice cream, exquisite cakes, and great coffee. **Known for:** homemade natural gelato; laid-back location in the Old Town; renowned pastry chef. $ *Average main: €4* ✉ *Kneza Damjana Jude bb, Stari Grad* ☎ *095/3926–323* 🌐 *gianni-dubrovnik.com.*

**Gradska Kavana**

**$ | CAFÉ** | Occupying the ornate Arsenal building on Luža Square, Gradska Kavana remains Dubrovnik's favorite meeting place for morning coffee and cake, breakfast, or an evening aperitif. The grand café has an ample summer terrace and is a perfect spot for people-watching and admiring the sites that surround it, including Rector's Palace, Sponza Palace, and the Cathedral. **Known for:** best people-watching in town; long-standing local favorite for coffee and cake; prime Old Town location. $ *Average main: €10* ✉ *Pred Dvorom 1, Stari Grad*

Old Town is filled with charming restaurants where you can dine outside right on the cobblestones.

☎ *020/321–202* 🌐 *www.nautikarestaurants.com.*

**Kamenice**

$ | **SEAFOOD** | Overlooking the morning market and pigeons of Gundulić Square, Kamenice is a local institution popular for the fresh oysters for which it is named, plus generous platters of *girice* (small fried fish) and *pržene lignje* (fried squid). It's cheap and cheerful, offers unbeatable value for the location, and is much-loved by locals and tourists alike. **Known for:** cheap prices and large portions; Dubrovnik institution; great fried fish and black risotto. [$] *Average main: €10* ✉ *Gundulićeva Poljana 8, Stari Grad* ☎ *020/323–682.*

★ **Kopun**

$$$ | **MEDITERRANEAN** | The name of this eatery refers to *capon*, the rooster cooked in a bitter orange sauce that was a delicacy during the time of the Republic; it's just one of the classic Dubrovnik recipes that this charming local favorite has chosen to reinvent. The mission here is to take the most traditional Croatian dishes and put a modern spin on them, like their mouthwatering take on the typical brodet fish stew. **Known for:** classic Dubrovnik dishes with a modern aesthetic; expertly curated wine list; peaceful location at the top of the Jesuit Steps. [$] *Average main: €26* ✉ *Poljana Ruđera Boškovića 7, Stari Grad* ☎ *020/323–969* 🌐 *www.restaurantkopun.com.*

**Nautika Restaurant**

$$$$ | **SEAFOOD** | Occupying the beautifully restored 19th-century Nautical Academy building just outside the Pile Gate, Nautika has a solid reputation as Dubrovnik's finest restaurant. With an unrivaled view over Fort Lovrijenac from its two terraces, plus an exceptional seasonal menu showcasing the best local ingredients (particularly dishes featuring lobster from Vis or Adriatic shrimp), it's a reliable choice for a formal meal. **Known for:** long-standing Dubrovnik institution; five- or seven-course tasting menus available; romantic seaside terraces overlooking Fort Lovrijenac. [$] *Average main: €60* ✉ *Brsalje 3, Pile* ☎ *020/442–526* 🌐 *www.*

*nautikarestaurants.com* ⏲ *Closed Oct.–Mar.*

**Nishta**

$$ | **VEGETARIAN** | Specializing in vegan fare, this playful eatery on Prijeko Street has just a dozen tables and is deservedly popular; for years it was the only vegan option in town. Their menu changes regularly, but you can expect Indian-inspired dishes, different soups and salads, falafel, and freshly made desserts. **Known for:** Dubrovnik's original vegan restaurant; one of the best restaurants on busy Prijeko Street; fun vibe. [$] *Average main: €15* ✉ *Prijeko bb, Stari Grad* ☎ *020/322–088* 🌐 *www.nishtarestaurant.com.*

★ **Pantarul**

$$ | **MEDITERRANEAN** | **FAMILY** | A little off the beaten track in Lapad but worth the trek, this bistro is a love letter to the gastronomy of Dubrovnik; even the name means "fork" in the local dialect. The menu changes weekly but there are a few mainstays like sea bream, foie gras, and super tender ox cheek, all accompanied by fresh local produce from nearby farms. **Known for:** traditional Dubrovnik comfort food; local favorite; family-run restaurant with a welcoming vibe. [$] *Average main: €23* ✉ *Kralja Tomislava 1, Lapad* ☎ *020/333–486* 🌐 *www.pantarul.com* ⏲ *Closed Mon.*

**Proto**

$$$$ | **SEAFOOD** | Located right in the heart of the Old Town, Proto dates back to 1886 and most locals will respectfully acknowledge that it's still one of the best in town. It has hosted everyone from King Edward VIII and Wallis Simpson to modern-day celebs and sports figures who come to try its menu of premium local seafood and reliably prepared Dalmatian dishes. **Known for:** cool history; fine dining in the center of the Old Town; excellent seafood platter for two. [$] *Average main: €39* ✉ *Široka 1, Stari Grad* ☎ *020/323–234* 🌐 *www.esculaprestaurants.com.*

★ **Restaurant 360**

$$$$ | **MEDITERRANEAN** | With its location right on the city walls and romantic views over the Old Port, not to mention the extraordinary five-course tasting menu from Dubrovnik-born-and-bred chef Marijo Curić, Michelin-starred Restaurant 360 offers an unparalleled fine dining experience. The exquisite tasting menu is a culinary adventure that will surprise and delight you with its sophistication and simplicity in equal measures; settle in for a few hours to savor the view and enjoy the ride. **Known for:** first Michelin star in Dubrovnik; location in St. John's Fortress with panoramic views; fantastic tasting menu. [$] *Average main: €108* ✉ *Svetog Dominika bb, Stari Grad* ☎ *020/322–222* 🌐 *360dubrovnik.com* ⏲ *Closed Mon. and Oct.–Apr.; no lunch.*

**Urban & Veggie**

$ | **VEGETARIAN** | This colorful bistro in Gruž features local produce from farms around Southern Dalmatia on its plant-based menu and makes a great spot to fuel up before or after a long journey. Dishes change with the season but perennial highlights include Mac 'n Tease gnocchi (gnocchi with truffle "cheese" sauce) and marinated seitan. **Known for:** one of the only vegan options in Dalmatia; location just down the road from main ferry and bus terminals; great smoothies and coffees. [$] *Average main: €12* ✉ *Obala Stjepana Radića 13, Gruž* ☎ *095/326–2568* 🌐 *urbanveggie.restaurant.*

## Hotels

**Amoret Apartments**

$$ | **APARTMENT** | **FAMILY** | Located in four restored 16th-century stone buildings near the Cathedral in the heart of the Old Town, these tastefully furnished apartments, with heavy antiques and traditional decor, are an excellent value. **Pros:** perfect Old Town location; atmospheric rooms with antique furniture; inexpensive by Dubrovnik standards. **Cons:** rooms can be noisy at night; no common

spaces or extra amenities; no owners or staff on-site. *Rooms from: €150* *Dinka Ranjine 5, Stari Grad* *091/9194–868* *14 apartments* *Free Breakfast.*

**Apartments Paviša**

**$$ | APARTMENT |** These five well-established apartments, equipped with kitchenettes, televisions, simple furniture, and basic but comfortable decor, are some of the best budget finds in the Old Town. **Pros:** friendly service from owner Pero; excellent value for money; central Old Town locations. **Cons:** up several flights of steps from the Stradun; room decor is dated; basic amenities. *Rooms from: €160* *Žudioska 19, Stari Grad* *098/427–399* *No credit cards* *5 apartments* *No Meals.*

**Berkeley Hotel & Spa**

**$$$ | HOTEL |** Located on a quiet street just a five-minute walk from Gruž Harbor, this welcoming hotel run by a Croatian-Australian family is one of the best value properties in town and makes a comfortable and convenient base for exploring Dubrovnik and the surrounding areas. **Pros:** excellent cooked-to-order breakfast; great value for money; well-priced spa on-site. **Cons:** distance from Old Town; slightly isolated location; restaurant is not open for dinner. *Rooms from: €265* *Andrije Hebranga 116A, Gruž* *020/494–160* *www.berkeleyhotel.hr* *Closed Jan. and Feb.* *25 rooms* *Free Breakfast.*

**Hilton Imperial Dubrovnik**

**$$$$ | HOTEL |** The Grand Hotel Imperial was Dubrovnik's first modern hotel when it opened in 1897, and through the years it has played a part in the city's most memorable events, attracting high-class visitors from Viennese counts to King Edward VII and Wallis Simpson, who danced in the garden in 1936. **Pros:** great location close to Pile Gate; tranquil, spacious, and stylish rooms; hip indoor and outdoor common spaces. **Cons:** decor is slightly generic; area outside hotel can get very busy; small pool. *Rooms from: €450* *Marijana Blažića 2, Pile* *020/320–320* *www.hilton.com/en/hotels/dbvhihi-hilton-imperial-dubrovnik* *149 rooms* *Free Breakfast.*

**★ Hotel Bellevue**

**$$$$ | HOTEL |** Perched up on a steep cliff overlooking a rocky beach just under a mile from the Old Town, boutique Hotel Bellevue is a luxury property with both style and soul, thanks to the dedicated staff devoted to customer service. **Pros:** cliff-top location overlooking the sea; chic interiors; excellent dining. **Cons:** expensive; not in Old Town; not all rooms have balconies. *Rooms from: €640* *Pera Čingrije 7, Dubrovnik* *020/330–000* *www.adriaticluxuryhotels.com/hotel-bellevue-dubrovnik* *94 rooms* *Free Breakfast.*

**Hotel Dubrovnik Palace**

**$$$$ | HOTEL |** Located at a secluded tip of the Lapad peninsula, this vast five-star hotel is a destination in itself with a private rocky beach, indoor and outdoor pools, a spa, tennis courts, a PADI dive shop, and four on-site restaurants. **Pros:** every room comes with a balcony with magnificent sea view; large indoor and outdoor pools overlooking the sea; excellent on-site dining options (don't miss the truffle risotto at Maslina Tavern). **Cons:** distance from the rest of the city; vast building with somewhat impersonal service; common spaces and breakfast room can feel crowded. *Rooms from: €460* *Masarykov Put 20, Lapad* *020/300–300* *www.adriaticluxuryhotels.com/hotel-dubrovnik-palace* *308 rooms* *Free Breakfast.*

**Hotel Excelsior**

**$$$$ | HOTEL |** On the coastal road east of the center, this iconic hotel was the first five-star property in Dubrovnik, dating back to 1913—everyone from Queen Elizabeth II to Francis Ford Coppola has come to stay. **Pros:** seafront location with incredible views of the Old Town; luxurious indoor pool, sauna, and spa; most rooms have sea views and balconies or terraces. **Cons:** large and somewhat impersonal; distance from the Old Town; very expensive. *Rooms from: €710 Frane Supila 12, Ploce 020/300–300 www.adriaticluxuryhotels.com/hotel-excelsior-dubrovnik 158 rooms Free Breakfast.*

**★ Hotel Kazbek**

**$$$ | HOTEL** | The boutique Hotel Kazbek, located in the 16th-century home of a noble Dubrovnik family, offers five-star luxury on an intimate scale, with rooms individually decorated in classic Dubrovnik style, receptionists who know your name, and a peaceful courtyard pool that you'll never want to leave. **Pros:** personalized service; luxurious decor; beautiful pool. **Cons:** not many other services in the immediate vicinity; never-ending construction on the road out front; bus or taxi is necessary to reach Old Town. *Rooms from: €305 Lapadska Obala 25, Lapad 020/362–999 www.kazbekdubrovnik.com Closed Nov.–Apr. 13 rooms Free Breakfast.*

**Hotel More**

**$$ | HOTEL** | Rising from a seaside walkway up a forested cliff just a few minutes walk from the beaches and restaurants of Lapad, this affordable five-star property boasts a peaceful seaside location, superb sunbathing and swimming right off the rocks, and the city's most unique venue for a cocktail. **Pros:** great swimming spots; excellent breakfast included; most affordable of the five-star hotels in Dubrovnik. **Cons:** hotel layout is very confusing; you'll spend a lot of time trying to work out the elevators; distance from Old Town. *Rooms from: €230 Kardinala Stepinca 33, Lapad 020/494–200 hotel-more.hr 85 rooms Free Breakfast.*

**Hotel Osmoliš**

**$$ | HOTEL** | Perched on a wild remote hill surrounded by olive trees, bougainvillea, and Mediterranean plants in a hamlet near Brsečine, 17 km (10 miles) up the coast from Dubrovnik, you'll find one of the sleekest boutique hotels in the region. **Pros:** indoor and outdoor pool and spa on-site; short walk to the beach; stylish and comfortable design. **Cons:** distance from Dubrovnik; no other services nearby; car or public transport necessary. *Rooms from: €185 Brdari 2D, Dubrovnik 020/301–530 osmolis.hr Closed Oct.–May 28 rooms Free Breakfast.*

**Prijeko Palace**

**$$$ | HOTEL** | This fantastical property in the center of the Old Town merges an impeccably restored 15th-century palace with a modern art gallery; each room was created by a different artist with explosions of color and photography, Murano chandeliers, collages, lavish prints, and everything draped in silk. **Pros:** central location in the Old Town; breakfast included at excellent Stara Loza restaurant; unique experience for art and history lovers. **Cons:** design aesthetic is not for everyone; rooms can be noisy at night; no pool or spa facilities. *Rooms from: €320 Prijeko 22, Stari Grad 020/321–145 www.prijekopalace.com Closed Nov.–Mar. 9 rooms Free Breakfast.*

**★ The Pucić Palace**

**$$$$ | HOTEL** | Occupying a beautifully restored 17th-century Renaissance-style palace on Gundulić Square, The Pucić Palace stands out for the warm personal service you'll receive; returning here after a busy day in the city really feels like a welcome home. **Pros:** prime location in the Old Town; warm service; unique chance to stay in a historic palace. **Cons:** very expensive; rooms can get noisy; no pool or spa. *Rooms from: €500 Od Puča 1, Stari Grad 020/326–222 thepucicpalace.com 18 rooms Free Breakfast.*

**Rixos Libertas**

**$$$$ | RESORT** | This large five-star property spills down a rugged cliff between Lapad and the Old Town, and it makes excellent use of its space with three restaurants, libraries to browse, Ping-Pong and pool tables, a huge outdoor pool and sundeck beside the private beach, and a fantastic spa that includes a full-size Turkish hammam, salt room, and even an igloo. **Pros:** large comfortable space with many amenities; one of the best spas in town; excellent choice for a winter stay, with heavy discounts and great indoor facilities. **Cons:** huge layout means a lot of walking; lacks a distinctly Croatian vibe; not many services in the immediate vicinity. *Rooms from: €361* *Liechtensteinov Put 3, Lapad* *020/200–000* *www.rixos.com* *310 rooms* *Free Breakfast.*

**★ Sun Gardens**

**$$ | RESORT | FAMILY** | Set on 54 acres of sprawling gardens in Orašac—a tiny settlement 11 km (7 miles) up the coast from Dubrovnik—Sun Gardens is the best value resort in the region and a rare property that manages to never feel overwhelming despite its large size. **Pros:** wide range of activities and amenities for the whole family; top-notch spa facilities; three seafront pools and a long private beach. **Cons:** distance from Dubrovnik; isolated location; some rooms only have partial sea views. *Rooms from: €250* *Na Moru 1, Dubrovnik* *020/361–500* *www.dubrovniksungardens.com* *Closed Oct.–Apr.* *201 rooms* *Free Breakfast.*

**★ Van Bloemen Apartments**

**$ | APARTMENT** | These eclectic apartments are the best budget choice in the Old Town, just steps away from the Cathedral and the Old Port, with high ceilings, well-stocked kitchenettes, colorful furniture, and books and relics collected from all around the world. **Pros:** central location in Old Town; excellent value for money; friendly and super helpful owners. **Cons:** space can feel cluttered; rooms can be noisy at night; no breakfast. *Rooms from: €105* *Bandureva 1, Stari Grad* *020/323–433* *www.vanbloemen.com* *4 apartments* *No Meals.*

# Nightlife

## BARS

**Banje Beach Club**

**DANCE CLUBS** | Located on the only sandy beach near the Old Town, Banje Beach Club is a chilled-out lounge bar and restaurant by day where you can relax on plush couches and beach beds, and a sleek dance club by night. You can't beat watching the sunset over the city from the terrace, and dancing on the sand with a view of the city walls is a great way to spend a Dubrovnik evening. You'll find it a five-minute walk east of the Ploče Gate. *Frana Supila 10b, Banje Beach* *099/314–6485* *www.banjebeach.com.*

**Beach Bar Dodo**

**BARS** | Built into a cliff overlooking local favorite Šulić Beach and just a 10-minute walk outside Pile Gate, this is the most chill of the beach bars around the city. With its reclaimed wood decor, swings as seats around the bar, and access to the sea where you can swim between sips, it's a rustic place for a light lunch or a sundowner. *Od Kolorine, Pile* *99/689–8495* *dododubrovnik.com.*

**★ Buža**

**BARS** | Walking through an 800-year-old wall to find a secret swimming spot across the sea from a cursed island sounds like a fairy tale, but in Dubrovnik such places actually exist—and there are two of them. One of the Buža (hole-in-the-wall) bars is marked by a wooden sign pointing toward "cold drinks." The other has no signage at all; you just walk through a doorway in the city walls. With tables arranged on a series of terraces built into the rocks and jazzy soundtracks to go along with stunning vistas, both bars make a great place to stop for a drink or a swim; you can jump right off the rocks in front of the bar. Beware that both spots can get very busy in the summer; mornings are the best time to visit. ✉ *Stari Grad* ✣ *The only bars on the sea side of the city walls—look for "cold drinks" sign.*

**★ Cave Bar More**
**BARS** | When the Hotel More was being built, a piece of machinery fell through the ground; it was only then that an 8,000-year-old cave was discovered underneath. It has been carefully converted into a three-story bar, with twinkling lights and stalactites, making it an unforgettable setting for a coffee or cocktail. Outside, just a short walk along the peaceful promenade from the beach in Lapad, the multilevel terrace with easy access to the sea is the perfect spot for a swim. ✉ *Nika i Meda Pucića 13, Lapad* ☏ *020/494–200* 🌐 *cavebar-more.com.*

**Dubrovnik Beer Company**
**BREWPUBS** | Dubrovnik's leading craft brewery, Dubrovnik Beer Company produces four main beers: an IPA, a milk stout, a lager, and a pale ale. Located in a former salt storage building in Gruž, it's a popular hangout for both locals and tourists, with regular concerts, pub quizzes, and other events taking place. Hour-long brewery tours, which include samples and snacks, are offered daily. ✉ *Obala Pape Ivana Pavla II 15, Gruž* ☏ *095/356–9620* 🌐 *www.dubrovackapivovara.hr.*

**D'Vino Wine Bar**
**WINE BARS** | A cozy candlelit wine bar that spills onto the street outside in summer, D'Vino is a great place to spend an evening, chatting and people-watching on the steps with the fun knowledgeable staff. They have an impressive selection of 60 wines by the glass and bottle, including many Croatian options, plus tasting menus and wine flights accompanied by gourmet cheese and antipasto platters. ✉ *Palmotićeva 4A, Stari Grad* ☏ *020/321–130* 🌐 *www.dvino.net.*

## Performing Arts

### FILM

**Kino Slavica**
**FILM** | **FAMILY** | Watch a movie outdoors with either the city walls or the Adriatic Sea as your backdrop at Dubrovnik's two open-air cinemas, which show predominantly English-language films in their original versions nightly throughout the summer. Kino Slavica is located in a walled garden on the main road between the Old Town and Lapad, while Kino Jadran is right in the Old Town, completely hidden from sight. ✉ *Branitelja Dubrovnika 42, Pile* ☏ *020/638–640* 🌐 *www.kinematografi.org* 🎟 *€7.*

## Shopping

**Deša Pro**
**CRAFTS** | Founded in 2012, the Deša Association seeks to employ women over 40, women with disabilities, and other socially excluded people by selling their homemade products online and out of this small shop in Lazareti. Items rotate regularly but typically include local delicacies, handicrafts, cosmetics, and textiles. ✉ *Frana Supila 8, Ploce* ☏ *20/420–145* 🌐 *webshop.desapro.hr.*

**Dubrovačka Kuća**
**SOUVENIRS** | This tastefully decorated shop near the Ploče Gate stocks a fine selection of regional Croatian wines and sweets, rakija, olive oil, and handmade jewelry, plus works of art by contemporary local artists on the upper two levels. ✉ *Svetog Dominika bb, Stari Grad* ☏ *020/322–092.*

**Dubrovnik Treasures**
**JEWELRY & WATCHES** | You'll find this lovely oasis of a shop just steps from the bustling Pile Gate. The jewelry is handmade by a local artist who uses quality sterling silver, coral, and semiprecious stones to turn traditional designs into beautiful modern pieces. ✉ *Celestina Medovića 2, Stari Grad* ☏ 🌐 *www.dubrovniktreasures.com.*

★ **Life According to Kawa**

**SOUVENIRS** | Everything in this well-curated shop just outside the Ploče Gate is local, artisanal, and fun, from jewelry and clothing to cards, homeware, craft beer, and wine. There is also a small co-working space and a fully-stocked room for international grocery items that are hard to find elsewhere in town. Pop in for some shopping, or just hang out on the couch with a local Cogito-brand coffee and chat with the staff who are happy to share tips and help plan out your stay. ✉ *Hvarska 2, Ploce* ☎ *020/670–730* 🌐 *kawa.life.*

★ **Open Markets**

**MARKET** | There are two open markets in Dubrovnik where you can get a wonderful glimpse into local life as well as pick up a few goodies. In the Old Town, the morning market in Gundulić Square brims with local delicacies such as dried figs, liqueurs, and candied fruit and almonds. Plan your visit for noon to see the local man who feeds the pigeons—it's quite the spectacle to see hundreds of pigeons flock to the square in anticipation. Across town at the Gruž Market, local people arrive every morning from around 6 am to pick up fresh produce, fish, and flowers; it's sometimes easy to forget that Dubrovnik is a living working city, but this market and the café-bars around it are an excellent reminder. ✉ *Dubrovnik.*

**Suveniri Bačan**

**CRAFTS** | The streets of the Old Town are filled with women selling hand-stitched embroidery and needlecraft products created using traditional methods and materials. The best storefront is Bačan, which sells decorative fabric in a variety of sizes and designs, all inspired by traditional Croatian folk costumes. The store is run by a husband-and-wife team, with the wife handcrafting all the items sold in the store. ✉ *Prijeko 6, Stari Grad* ☎ *20/321–121* 🌐 *www.facebook.com/souvenirs.bachan.*

**Terra Croatica**

**SOUVENIRS** | Located one street away from the Stradun in the Old Town, this "gastro and gift shop" is your best bet for stocking up on authentic Croatian souvenirs (they even have a certification to prove it). Items include local jams (look out for traditional fig and bitter orange flavors), honey, salt from Ston, olive oil, wine, and truffles. They also have a selection of artwork, ceramics, items made from white Brač stone, cosmetics, and lavender. ✉ *Od Puča 17, Stari Grad* 🌐 *www.terracroaticadubrovnik.com.*

## Activities

### BEACHES

Closest to the Old Town, **Banje Beach** is a sandy beach just beyond the Ploče Gate with a beach bar and fantastic views of the walled city. For more family-friendly beaches, head to the beach in **Lapad,** where kids can enjoy water sports and the whole family can explore the many shops and restaurants nearby. A 20-minute walk east brings you to **Sveti Jakov Beach**, a bright-white sliver that can be reached by boat or by walking down a steep staircase. The most natural and peaceful beaches lie on the island of **Lokrum,** popular with rock-jumpers and nudists. For the most unique Dubrovnik experience, head to local favorite **Šulić Beach** for a swim in the shadow of Fort Lovrijenac.

### SEA KAYAKING

★ **Adriatic Kayak Tours**

**KAYAKING** | **FAMILY** | There is literally a sea full of kayaking companies in Dubrovnik, but the best is Adriatic Kayak Tours. Besides introductory half-day tours around Zaton Bay, they offer full-day trips, some of which include biking and hiking components, to the Elafiti Islands and even farther to the Konavle region and Montenegro. ✉ *Zrinsko Frankopanska 6, Ploce* ☎ *020/312–770* 🌐 *www.adriatickayaktours.com.*

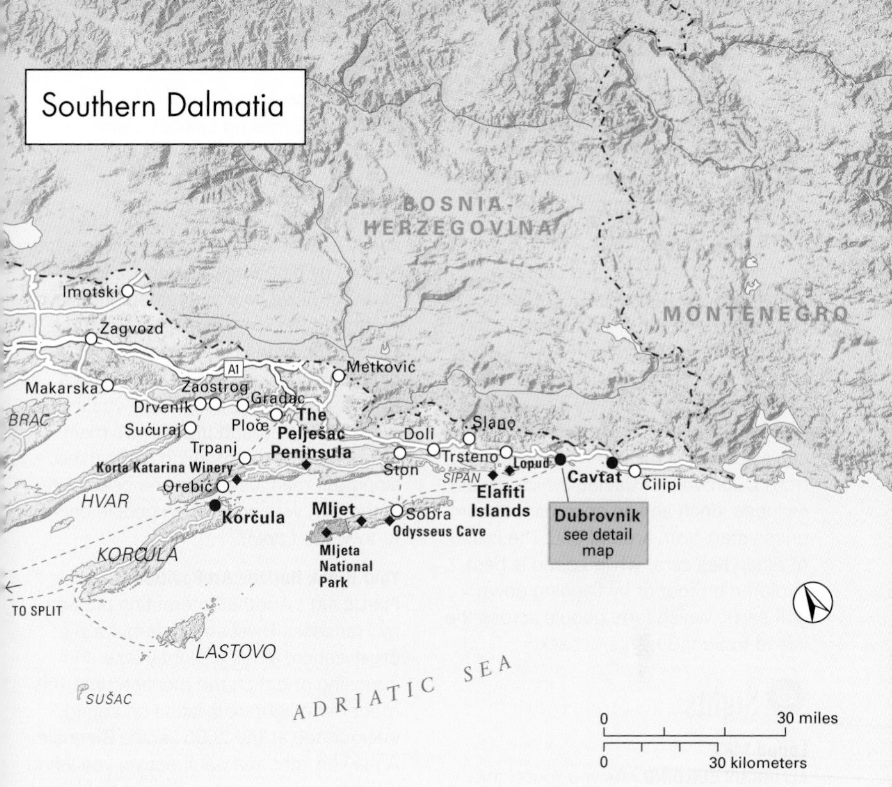


# Elafiti Islands

*Lopud is 7 nautical miles northwest of Dubrovnik. Šipan is 15 nautical miles northwest of Dubrovnik.*

Dotting the sea just a few miles offshore from Dubrovnik, the lush laid-back Elafiti Islands are waiting to provide a retreat when you're ready to escape the city. Historically, the 13 tiny islets have always been closely tied to Dubrovnik; the local aristocracy kept summer villas here, which are now scattered in various states of ruin around the islands. Today only the three larger ones—Koločep, Lopud, and Šipan—are inhabited, with a total population of around 1,000.

Lopud is best equipped to host visitors. With one main promenade made up of old stone houses built around a sheltered bay, plus a handful of shops and a couple of excellent restaurants, it makes a perfect place to unwind for a day or two of swimming, hiking, and riding golf carts (the island is car-free) along the herb-scented paths that crisscross the island. The main sights are a 15th-century Franciscan monastery that has been converted into a luxury villa; the 16th-century Fortress Sutvrac, located on the highest point of the island; the ruins of 30 chapels built during the golden age of the Republic; and family-friendly Šunj, one of Croatia's rare sandy beaches. There is a sense of faded grandeur on Lopud, but that only adds to its charm.

Šipan is the largest of the three islands and the only one with cars, although the best way to experience it is to ride a bicycle along the 5-kilometer-long (3-mile-long) road between the two main settlements (Suđurađ and Šipanska Luka), passing through olive groves and vineyards along the way. If it's a slower pace of life you're after, Šipan is most likely to be your favorite.

### GETTING HERE AND AROUND

Jadrolinija runs four or five passenger ferries per day between Gruž Port in Dubrovnik and the Elafiti Islands, stopping at Koločep (30 minutes; €4.91) and Lopud (1 hour; €4.91). Šipan is connected to Dubrovnik and Mljet by a once-daily TP Line ferry (45 minutes; €5.70). You can also book a full-day Three Island Tour from Dubrovnik or Cavtat, which usually includes lunch and an open bar onboard; prices start from around €60. The island of Šipan has cars, while Lopud is best explored on foot or by flagging down golf carts, which ferry people across the island to Šunj Beach and back.

## Sights

**Lopud 1483**

**RELIGIOUS BUILDING** | As you round the bend onto Lopud by sea, the first thing you'll notice is the imposing Franciscan monastery on the tip of the island. Dating back to 1483, it was abandoned and remained empty for 200 years before being rescued by Francesca Thyssen-Bornemisza, creator of the Thyssen-Bornemisza Art Contemporary Foundation (TBA21). After a meticulous 20-year refurbishment, the property has been converted into a luxury villa and private art gallery. It manages to retain the contemplative atmosphere of the monastery, with an infusion of furniture and art—everything from the Old Masters to modern photography—from the Thyssen-Bornemisza family's private collection, which at one point was second only to the collection of the Queen of England. The entire property, which sleeps 10 people, can be rented; if €10,000 per night is a bit out of budget, tours of the monastery can be arranged when the villa is not otherwise occupied. ✉ *Franciscan Monastery of Our Lady of the Cave (Gospa od Špilice), Dubrovnik* 🌐 *www.lopud1483.com.*

**★ Šunj Beach**

**BEACH** | **FAMILY** | One of Croatia's best sandy beaches, this swath of white sand backed by pine forests, with a couple of unobtrusive bars and restaurants, is worth the 2½ km (1½ mile) trek across Lopud. The path is quite hilly in both directions, so you might want to hail a golf cart to get there or back—you'll see them driving around the island's main promenade in the morning and parked along the road just above the beach later in the day, waiting to bring people back to town. ✉ *Lopud.*

**Your Black Horizon Art Pavilion**

**PUBLIC ART** | Another interesting project by Francesca Thyssen-Bornemisza's organization, albeit a slightly less imposing one than the monastery, is this modern art light installation on Lopud, inaugurated at the 2005 Venice Biennale. A play on light and perspective, you'll find it hidden away in the middle of the island. It's free to enter and only takes a few minutes to check out. ✉ *Lopud* 🌐 *tba21.org/lopud* ⏲ *Closed Oct.–May.*

## Restaurants

**★ BOWA**

**$$$$** | **SEAFOOD** | For the ultimate exclusive island dining experience, head to BOWA ("best of what's around"), nestled on its own secluded beach on Šipan with chic cabanas right over the water and a shady dining terrace right beside the beach. Choose between a three- or four-course menu (€90 or €120) or splurge on the seven-course tasting menu with wine pairing (€290); the seafood-centric dishes change regularly but favorites include bluefish tuna tartare, swordfish sashimi, oysters from Ston, and perfectly grilled white fish. **Known for:** expertly prepared fresh seafood; exclusive dining on a private beach; owned by same family as the Bota Šare empire. $ *Average main: €90* ✉ *Pakljena 3, Šipan* ☎ *091/636–6111* 🌐 *bowa-dubrovnik.com* ⏲ *Closed Oct.–May.*

**Konoba Kod Marka**

**$$ | SEAFOOD** | With a prime location overlooking the harbor in Šipanska Luka and sensational sunset views, Kod Marka is renowned among sailors and yacht guests as one of the best seafood restaurants and hidden gems in the region. There's no official menu—you just grab a seat on the terrace, order a glass of wine, and enjoy whatever the chef has prepared that day. **Known for:** local favorite; seaside location; four-course seafood menu. $ *Average main: €20* ✉ *Šipanska Luka, Lopud* ☎ *020/758–007* ⏲ *Closed Oct.–May.*

**La Villa Restaurant**

**$$$$ | MEDITERRANEAN** | Located in a stone villa on the Lopud waterfront, La Villa offers an immaculate dining experience with friendly service and a great local wine list. Expect beautiful dishes made with premium ingredients such as scallops, foie gras, langoustines, and lobster tail. **Known for:** seaside location with large shady terrace; sophisticated dishes with top-notch ingredients; friendly professional service. $ *Average main: €35* ✉ *Obala Iva Kuljevana 33, Lopud* ☎ *099/222–5115* ⏲ *Closed Oct.–May.*

**Restoran Obala**

**$$$ | SEAFOOD** | This smart restaurant has offered fine dining on Lopud's seafront promenade since 1939, with idyllic sunset views across the bay and wonderfully formal waiters. The house specialty is *školjke na buzaru* (mixed shellfish cooked in wine and garlic), and they also do a superb prawn and truffle risotto. **Known for:** long-standing family-owned institution; seaside location; formal service. $ *Average main: €28* ✉ *Obala Iva Kuljevana 18, Lopud* ☎ *098/512–725* 🌐 *www.obalalopud.com* ⏲ *Closed Nov.–Apr.*

## Hotels

**Hotel Božica**

**$ | HOTEL** | One of the most welcoming, peaceful, and relaxing hotels in the region, Hotel Božica on Šipan makes a great base for exploring the Elafiti Islands and beyond. **Pros:** private beach; close to ferry dock; wonderful pool. **Cons:** rooms are a little small; not many services nearby; on-site restaurant is expensive. $ *Rooms from: €125* ✉ *Suđurađ 13 1D, Šipan* ☎ *020/325–400* 🌐 *hotel-bozica.hr* ⏲ *Closed Oct.–Apr.* *33 rooms* *Free Breakfast.*

★ **Lafodia Sea Resort**

**$$ | HOTEL | FAMILY** | This solid lodging option rises from a perfect pebble beach up a hillside overlooking the stunning bay of Lopud. **Pros:** beach location with luxurious gazebos and beach beds; excellent spa facilities; one of the best values in the region. **Cons:** room decor feels a bit dated; distance from the ferry; day-trip boats from Dubrovnik dock just outside. $ *Rooms from: €215* ✉ *Obala Iva Kuljevana 35, Lopud* ☎ *020/450–300* 🌐 *www.lafodiahotel.com* ⏲ *Closed Oct.–May* *156 rooms* *Free Breakfast.*

# Cavtat

*17 km (10½ miles) southeast of Dubrovnik.*

While Dubrovnik's streets are being polished under the shoes of thousands of visitors per day, Cavtat's pine-covered trails seem comparatively tourist-free. There are secluded swimming spots, quiet walking paths, and park benches waiting for you to sit and enjoy the beauty and tranquility that you came to Croatia to find.

Founded by the ancient Greeks as Epidaurus, then taken by the Romans and renamed Epidaurum, the original settlement on the site of Cavtat was subsequently destroyed by tribes of

The seaside resort of Cavtat is filled with pine-shaded paths and lacks Dubrovnik's tourists.

Avars and Slavs in the early 7th century. The Romans fleeing Epidaurum founded Dubrovnik.

Cavtat developed even further during the 15th century under the Republic of Dubrovnik. Today, the medieval stone buildings of the Old Town occupy a small peninsula with a natural bay to each side. A palm-lined promenade with open-air cafés, shops, and restaurants curves around the main bay, while the second bay is overlooked by a beach backed by several socialist-era hotels. A shaded trail wraps around the peninsula, with a couple of beach bars and lounge chairs set up right on the rocks—if you look closely, you can see Dubrovnik's Old Town in the distance.

### GETTING HERE AND AROUND

Bus #10 departs from Gruž bus station in Dubrovnik and the cable car stop every half hour (€4.50 one-way; 40 minutes). Once in Cavtat, all sights are within walking distance.

A particularly scenic way to travel from Cavtat to Dubrovnik is by boat (€20 round-trip; 45 minutes), which will drop you off in Dubrovnik's Old Harbor. The boat departs hourly from 8:30 am to 11 pm and also stops in Mlini, Srebreno, and Plat (€20 round-trip; 20 minutes) and Lokrum (€20 round-trip; 45 minutes). Tickets can be purchased in advance from travel agency booths set up along both bays.

## Sights

**Kuća Bukovac** (*Vlaho Bukovac Home*)
**ART GALLERY** | The former home of local son Vlaho Bukovac (1855–1922), one of Croatia's greatest artists, has been beautifully converted into a gallery of his life and work. The two floors feature more than 200 works of art, including self-portraits and oil paintings from the periods he spent in Paris, Zagreb, Prague, and Cavtat. There's also period furniture and personal items. The stone house itself is a lovely example of typical 18th-century architecture; the east wing is covered

in murals that Bukovac painted as a gift to his father when he was 16 years old. ✉ *Bukovćeva 5, Cavtat* ☎ *020/478–646* 🌐 *www.migk.hr* 🎫 *€5.*

**Mauzolej Obitelji Račić** (*Račić Mausoleum*)

**CEMETERY** | The peaceful St. Rocco Cemetery sits atop the highest point of the peninsula overlooking the city and surrounding area. Its centerpiece is the mausoleum, sculpted from white Brač stone by beloved Croatian sculptor Ivan Meštrović for the Račić family in 1921. It is octagonal in plan, and the main entrance is guarded by two art nouveau caryatids. ✉ *Kvaternikova Ulica, Cavtat* ✥ *On the highest point of the peninsula* 🌐 *www.migk.hr* 🎫 *€4* ⏲ *Closed Sun.*

## Restaurants

★ **Bugenvila**

**$$** | **MEDITERRANEAN** | One of the brightest culinary stars in the region, Bugenvila is vibrant in every sense, from the flowers climbing the sides of the terrace to the happy patrons tucking into fresh meals that burst with flavor. The menu changes regularly but you can expect surprising and delightful dishes made with fine local ingredients: think green apple dumplings, raw king scallop in strawberry consommé, or lobster bisque paired with grilled wild boar cheeks and parsnip purée. **Known for:** local ingredients turned into beautiful dishes; waterfront location in the center of Cavtat; excellent value three-course lunch menu. [$] *Average main: €20* ✉ *Obala Ante Starčevića 9, Cavtat* ☎ *020/479–949* 🌐 *www.bugenvila.online* ⏲ *Closed Nov.–Mar.*

**Konoba Kolona**

**$$** | **SEAFOOD** | Located one street behind Tiha Bay, Konoba Kolona is a firm favorite for seafood among locals; the owner is also the fisherman and the cook, so you know you're in good hands. It has two large covered terraces, plus indoor seating and reasonable prices for popular dishes such as lobster by the kilo, mussels *buzara* (in tomato and white wine sauce), and octopus carpaccio. **Known for:** fresh seafood; popularity with locals; friendly service. [$] *Average main: €18* ✉ *Put Tihe 2, Cavtat* ☎ *020/478–787.*

## Hotels

★ **Castelletto**

**$** | **B&B/INN** | **FAMILY** | Located in a quiet neighborhood a short walk up the hill from the center of Cavtat, family-run Castelletto, with its bougainvillea-strewn terraces, cheerful rooms, and laid-back vibe, is a perfect place to unwind and soak up a bit of local life. **Pros:** very friendly owners; full buffet breakfast; pool, sauna, and bar on-site. **Cons:** 10-minute uphill walk from town center; dated decor; not much to do in the immediate vicinity. [$] *Rooms from: €95* ✉ *Jurja Dalmatinca 9, Cavtat* ☎ *099/2275–160* 🌐 *www.dubrovnikexperience.com* ⏲ *Closed Nov.–Mar.* 🛏 *13 rooms* 🍽 *Free Breakfast.*

**Hotel Cavtat**

**$$** | **HOTEL** | **FAMILY** | This spot offers a pleasant and comfortable stay right in the center of town. **Pros:** close to beach and center of town; on-site spa and rooftop infinity pool; made-to-order breakfast in waterfront restaurant. **Cons:** hotel layout can be confusing; pool area can get full; some rooms have no views. [$] *Rooms from: €250* ✉ *Iznad Tiha 8, Cavtat* ☎ *020/202–000* 🌐 *www.hotel-cavtat.hr* ⏲ *Closed Nov.–Apr.* 🛏 *140 rooms* 🍽 *Free Breakfast.*

**Hotel Croatia**

**$$$** | **HOTEL** | Sprawling across its own rocky pine-studded peninsula, with quiet walking trails weaving through the property, this vast hotel offers guests the chance to find their own place in the sun or shade, seemingly miles away from the rest of the world. **Pros:** gorgeous rocky beaches and large pool; five restaurants on-site; lovely spa and sauna. **Cons:** large property with an impersonal atmosphere;

distance from center of town; expensive by Cavtat standards. *Rooms from: €310* *Frankopanska 10, Cavtat* *020/475–555* *www.adriaticluxuryhotels.com/hotel-croatia-dubrovnik-cavtat* *Closed Nov.–Mar.* *487 rooms* *Free Breakfast.*

**★ Hotel Supetar**

**$$$$** | **HOTEL** | On the seafront promenade overlooking the harbor, this hotel in a 1920s-era stone villa is one of the freshest and most stylish boutique properties in the region. **Pros:** warm personalized service; central location on the waterfront; gorgeous terrace and pool. **Cons:** front rooms can be noisy; no parking on-site; often fully booked. *Rooms from: €400* *Obala Ante Starčevića 27, Cavtat* *020/479–833* *www.adriaticluxuryhotels.com/hotel-supetar-dubrovnik-cavtat* *Closed Nov.–Mar.* *16 rooms* *Free Breakfast.*

## Shopping

**Škatulica**

**SOUVENIRS** | Find this little treasure trove tucked away in an old stone storage building on the promenade. Items come from all over Croatia but the majority are handmade in Southern Dalmatia. You'll find wine, liqueurs, their own candied almonds and arancini, plus items made with Brač stone, jewelry, artwork, and natural cosmetics. Between the lovely interior and the friendly owner Nives, this is a perfect place to pick up great quality, well-priced gifts and souvenirs. *Obala Ante Starčevića 36, Cavtat* *099/2356–442* *skatulica.weebly.com.*

## Activities

East of the center, near **Uvala Tiha** (Tiha Bay), is where you'll find the large hotels and family-friendly beaches. Take a walk around the shady promenade that wraps around the peninsula to find smaller beaches and more peaceful spots to swim.

### DIVING

**Epidaurum Diving and Water Sports Center**

**DIVING & SNORKELING** | There are some excellent underwater sights around Cavtat, including shipwrecks and amforas (very old pottery). The center organizes certification and dive trips, as well as Jet-Skiing, parasailing, and other types of water fun. *Šetalište Žal 31, Cavtat* *098/427–550* *epidaurum.com.*

# The Pelješac Peninsula

*54 km (34 miles) northwest of Dubrovnik; 2 nautical miles from Korčula.*

The Pelješac Peninsula is Southern Dalmatia at its best. You know that red wine you've been drinking since you got to Dalmatia? It comes from the vineyards here. Those secret beaches you've been trying to find? The peninsula is surrounded by them. And those famous oysters you've been eating in Dubrovnik? They pull them out of the channel right in front of you in Mali Ston and serve them with a slice of lemon. A wild unexplored region full of secluded coves, stone villages, vineyards, and breathtaking views, Pelješac is a rare undiscovered gem just an hour away from Dubrovnik.

There are two main towns that make a great base from which to explore the peninsula. **Mali Ston** is the first town you come to when driving from Dubrovnik, famous for its fortified walls, salt pans, and oysters. On the other end of the peninsula, the resort town of **Orebić** straggles along the coast, facing across a narrow sea channel to the island of Korčula. Historically, the town spent several centuries under the Republic of Dubrovnik, supplying many able seamen to the Republic's merchant navy. Today, you can see a string of villas and their gardens overlooking the coastal promenade, built by wealthy local sea captains.

### GETTING HERE AND AROUND

The Pelješac Peninsula is 65 km (50 miles) in length, with one main road stretching from Mali Ston at one end to the small seaside town of Lovište at the other. Public buses drive this route daily in both directions, but they are not frequent; the best way to explore the peninsula is by car, which will allow you to visit wineries, villages, and beaches off the main road. The much-celebrated Pelješac Bridge and a network of new roads opened in 2022, connecting Komarna on the mainland to Brijesta on the Pelješac Peninsula. This made traveling here from the rest of the country much easier, as it eliminated the need to pass through a section of Bosnia and Herzegovina, where border checkpoints often added hours to the journey.

A passenger and car ferry connects Orebić with Korčula (around €3 for foot passengers, €18 for cars; 15 minutes) and another connects Prapratno with the island of Mljet (around €4 for foot passengers, €20 for cars; 45 minutes).

There are many companies offering day trips from Dubrovnik to Pelješac that usually stop for oysters and visit a couple of wineries; Secret Dalmatia and Dubrovnik Day Tours are two of the best.

## Sights

**Franjevački Samostan** (*Franciscan Monastery of Our Lady of the Angels*)
**RELIGIOUS BUILDING** | Perched 492 feet up the hill above Orebić is this modest 15th-century Franciscan monastery. During the heyday of the Dubrovnik Republic, the Pelješac Peninsula was under Dubrovnik's control, while just across the channel Korčula was ruled by their archrival, Venice. From their privileged vantage point on the hill, the Franciscan monks could spy upon their island neighbors, under strict orders to send a message to Dubrovnik if trouble looked likely. The monastery is also home to the Our Lady of the Angels icon that was said to protect captains on their voyages; when they passed under the monastery on their way home they would sound their sirens in greeting and the monks would ring the church bells in return. Today it's a welcoming retreat, with a lovely cloister and a small museum displaying scale models of the ships that local sea captains sailed across the oceans. You can also walk around the cemetery, where gray marble tombstones shaded by cypress trees mark the final resting places of many a local seafarer. It's worth the strenuous 40-minute hike from the center of Orebić (or the easier 5-minute drive) for the spectacular views across the channel to Korčula. ✉ *Celestinov Put bb, Orebic* ☎ *020/713–075* 🎫 *Free.*

★ **Korta Katarina Winery**
**WINERY** | Perched on a hill overlooking Trstenica Beach, award-winning Korta Katarina is a sophisticated venue to try Pelješac wines and the most accessible winery from Orebić. *Korta* is the name for the typical courtyards outside sea captains' homes around town, while *Katarina* is the daughter of the American couple, Lee and Penny Anderson, who traveled to Croatia in 2001, fell in love with it, and opened the winery. A winery tour, tasting, and optional food pairings, which range from gourmet tapas to a divine five-course pairing menu, can be arranged in advance. For an immersive winery experience, the five-star Villa Korta Katerina next door, a Relais & Chateaux member, has eight luxury rooms available to rent. ✉ *Trg Bana Josipa Jelačića 3, Orebic* ☎ *099/492–5830* 🌐 *www.kortakatarinawinery.com* 🎫 *€25 for wine tasting and tour.*

★ **Solana Ston** (*Salt Pans*)
**OTHER ATTRACTION** | There are records of salt being collected by Romans in this area dating back to 167 B.C, but it was the Republic of Dubrovnik that fully recognized the economic potential of the salt pans. In 1333, they founded the

# Wines of Pelješac

The Pelješac Peninsula is a rare Southern Dalmatian region that relies not only on tourism but also agriculture, thanks mainly to the vineyards producing two types of red wine from the hearty Plavac Mali grape: **Postup** and **Dingač.** Both are full-bodied but Dingač is particularly robust, with an alcohol content that can reach as high as 17.6%, owing to the conditions of its terroir. The grapes are grown on the 45-degree Dingač Slope, with the sun reflecting on the vines from three different surfaces—the sky, the sea, and the white karst stone—which increases the sugar content and makes for a stronger wine. Working conditions on the slope are notoriously difficult; prior to 1976, when local winemakers excavated a 400 meter long tunnel by hand to make the area more accessible, donkeys were used to help carry harvested grapes over the mountain and into the wineries. The donkey found on some bottles of Dingač is a symbol of the hearty stubborn vine that reaches its full potential in this very limited region. In 1961, Dingač became the first protected wine region in Croatia, followed by Postup.

There are many family-owned wineries along the peninsula where you can sample and buy wine. An organized tour will take in three or four, or if you're driving yourself, you might consider the following route. Coming from Dubrovnik, make your first stop at **Vinarija Miloš** (🌐 *www.milos.hr*) near Ston, renowned for its award-winning stagnum wines and family atmosphere. Next up is the village of Trstenik, where California wine lovers might recognize the name Mike Grgich, who was born in Dalmatia but gained fame in the Napa Valley; his winery, **Grgić Vina** (🌐 *www.grgic-vina.com*), is one of the most sophisticated on the peninsula. Next, you'll reach the village of Potomje, where you'll find a cluster of wineries; one of the best is **Matuško** (🌐 *matusko-vina.hr*). Just beyond Potomje is **Vinarija Bartulović** (🌐 *www.vinarijabartulovic.hr*). The Bartulović family has been making wine on Pelješac for nearly 500 years, and today it's the young energetic winemaker Mario who will tell you all about the winemaking process, his experiences on the Dingač Slopes, and his family's traditions. This winery is especially popular with visitors thanks to its authentic Dalmatian konoba, located in the former wine cellar, where you can combine wine tasting with a meal (call ahead to reserve). Return to Potomje and drive through the Dingač Tunnel; the slopes are on the other side. Continue along the coastal road for spectacular sea views, and make your final stop of the day at **Korta Katerina** (🌐 *www.kortakatarina.com*) in Orebić, where you can have a luscious wine and food pairing.

From the city walls of Ston, you can get a glimpse of the town's famous salt pans.

towns of Ston and Mali Ston and built a fortified wall to protect them. Eventually sea salt became the Republic's most valuable product, generating a third of its wealth. You can tour the massive salt pans—the oldest in Europe—to learn about the ancient collecting process, still in use today: the pans fill with seawater, which evaporates in the sun, and the salt that remains is shoveled out. If the salt pans are closed when you arrive, ask at Vila Koruna restaurant in Mali Ston (whose owners also operate the salt pans) about organizing a tour. You can buy small souvenir bags of sea salt around Mali Ston, which make an excellent culinary gift from the region. ✉ *Pelješki Put 1, Ston* ☎ *020/754–027* 🌐 *www.solanaston.hr* 🎫 *€2.60* ⏲ *Closed Oct.–Apr.*

### ★ Ston Walls

**HISTORIC SIGHT** | In order to protect the enormously valuable Ston salt pans, in 1333 the Republic of Dubrovnik built a 7-km (4½-mile) fortified wall (purportedly second in length only to the Great Wall of China), effectively controlling land access to the peninsula. The stretch of wall that remains is 5½ km (3½ miles) long, and you can walk atop it from Ston to Mali Ston, which takes about 40 minutes and offers incredible views of the channel and the salt pans. It's a strenuous walk, so good shoes and a moderate level of fitness are recommended. ✉ *Ston* ✣ *Follow signs to the entrance from Ston or Mali Ston* 🎫 *€10.*

## Restaurants

### Bota Šare Mali Ston

**$$$** | **SEAFOOD** | Occupying a 14th-century salt warehouse, Bota Šare (owned by the Šare family of fishermen who own some of the best seafood restaurants from Dubrovnik to Zagreb) is known for its menu of outstanding locally caught seafood. Order the fish platter for two to try a selection of the best catch of the day, and ask about boarding a boat to try oysters right from the channel where they are caught. **Known for:** best place to try Mali Ston oysters; owned by local family of fishermen; excellent fish platters.

Average main: €25 Mali Ston, Ston 020/754–482 www.bota-sare.hr.

**Croccantino**

$ | **DESSERTS** | **FAMILY** | If you have to wait to board the ferry from Orebić to Korčula, you'll be relieved to find Croccantino just around the corner from the port. This fun, colorful little café right along the waterfront promenade serves exquisite homemade gelato, artisan cakes and cupcakes, and excellent smoothies, coffee, and milkshakes. **Known for:** homemade gelato and cakes; waterfront location; great people- and boat-watching from the terrace. *Average main: €3 Obala Pomoraca 30, Orebic 020/714–416.*

**Estravaganca**

$$$ | **SEAFOOD** | **FAMILY** | The epitome of a hidden gem, there is no menu or prices at Estravaganca, just a chalkboard with the catch of the day and the owner who will rush out to grab your boat ropes, show you to your table, bring out the fish for you to choose from, then light the fire and grill it right in front of you. Most days there are mussels and oysters kept in the sea and pulled out just minutes before they're put on your plate; same goes for the crab and lobster, which is then cooked in a spicy *buzara* sauce with homemade pasta. **Known for:** fresh seafood pulled out of the sea and cooked in front of you; reachable by a steep narrow road or by boat; secluded location right on the beach. *Average main: €25 Lovište 098/944–7099 www.estravaganca.com No credit cards No dinner.*

**Kapetanova Kuća**

$$$ | **SEAFOOD** | Known throughout Croatia, this long-standing favorite helmed by chef Lidija Kralj has been synonymous with Ston and fresh oysters for more than 45 years. Located in an old stone home on the Mali Ston waterfront and slightly more upscale than other nearby restaurants, people come from far and wide to feast on the shellfish here, as well as the plentiful black risotto and unusual *stonski makaruli*, a cake made from pasta, nuts, sugar, and cinnamon, unique to Ston. **Known for:** local oysters, mussels, and clams; excellent black risotto; nationally celebrated female chef. *Average main: €30 Obala dr. Ante Starčevića 9, Mali Ston, Ston 020/754–264 www.ostrea.hr.*

**Stari Kapetan**

$$ | **SEAFOOD** | Designed to look like an actual ship with a life-size captain at the helm, this restaurant outside the classy Boutique Hotel Adriatic is one of the best in town. Try the seafood platter for two, with tuna steak, grilled squid, mussels, scampi, and extraordinary sea bream, plus a glass of Plavac Mali from the family's own vineyards. **Known for:** fresh local seafood platter; alfresco seaside dining; fun design. *Average main: €16 Šetalište Kneza Domagoja 8, Orebic 020/714–488 www.hoteladriaticorebic.com.*

## Hotels

**Aminess Grand Azur Hotel**

$ | **RESORT** | **FAMILY** | Set on a pebbly beach a 10-minute walk from the center of Orebić, this resort is a perfect base for the whole family. **Pros:** perfect for families with children; beachfront location; excellent value for all-inclusive package. **Cons:** can be hectic in the high season; spaces can get crowded; distance from center of town. *Rooms from: €120 Kralja Petra Kresimira IV 107, Orebic 052/858–600 www.aminess.com/en/aminess-grand-azur-hotel Closed Nov.–Apr. 185 rooms All-Inclusive.*

★ **Boutique Hotel Adriatic**

$$ | **HOTEL** | Locals are proud of their seafaring history in Orebić, but the Mikulić family has gone the extra mile and turned their boutique hotel—one of the most elegant, charming, and classy hotels on Pelješac—into an unofficial seafaring museum. **Pros:** beautifully restored rooms with stone walls; close to town

## Mali Ston Oysters

Ston is renowned throughout Croatia and beyond for the oysters grown in Mali Ston Bay. Their high quality is due to the perfect brackish conditions of the bay; salty seawater mixes with the fresh mineral-laden water that flows in from the nearby Neretva River. Oysters have been farmed here since Roman times and were appreciated by nobles from the Republic of Dubrovnik to the Habsburgs. But as famous as they are, oyster farming in Ston is still a small-scale operation; only a handful of local families have permits. While you can try them in the best restaurants around Dalmatia, nothing beats an oyster straight out of the bay with just a slice of lemon and a glass of wine to wash it down. Mali Ston has several great restaurants—foremost among them being Bota Šare—plus a handful of oyster stands along the road for a quick taste (check out Oysters Antonio, right off the main road at the entrance heading into town). They are said to be at their best in March, around the time of the Oyster Festival celebrating the feast of St. Joseph, where you can try oysters, wine, and other local products alongside concerts and folk festivals in Ston and Mali Ston.

center and beach; excellent restaurant on-site. **Cons:** often fully booked; no elevator; unique decor is not for everyone. *$ Rooms from: €185 ✉ Šetalište Kneza Domagoja 8, Orebic ☎ 020/714–488 🌐 www.hoteladriaticorebic.com 6 rooms 🍽 Free Breakfast ☞ No children allowed.*

**Vila Koruna**

$ | **HOTEL** | A prime location right beside the city walls makes up for the basic facilities at this family-run hotel. **Pros:** practical affordable base for Mali Ston; friendly staff; good restaurant right beside the water. **Cons:** basic rooms and facilities; rooms can get hot in summer; no elevator. *$ Rooms from: €75 ✉ Mali Ston, Ston ☎ 020/754–999 🌐 www.vila-koruna.hr 6 rooms 🍽 Free Breakfast.*

## Activities

### BEACHES

There are wild beaches and coves all around the Pelješac Peninsula, almost all of which need to be reached via private transport. The most accessible beach is **Trstenica**, a family-friendly 1½-km (1-mile) stretch of sand and pebbles in Orebić just below Korta Katerina winery. Just a few kilometers up the road, **Viganj** is regarded as one of the top windsurfing locations in Croatia and beyond. It hosts the Croatian surfing championship annually and has held both the European and world championships as well. Closer to Ston, there is a lovely pebble beach in **Prapratno**, where you can also catch a ferry to Mljet.

### WINDSURFING

**Water Donkey Windsurfing & Kitesurfing Center**

**WINDSURFING** | You can rent windsurfing and kitesurfing equipment and take lessons from the friendly staff here in Viganj. They also rent kayaks, bikes, and stand-up paddleboards. *✉ Ponta Beach, Viganj ☎ 091/152–0258 🌐 www.windsurfing-kitesurfing-viganj.com.*

# Korčula

*49 nautical miles northwest of Dubrovnik; 57 nautical miles southeast of Split.*

Southern Dalmatia's largest island, Korčula is quietly emerging as the most sophisticated and alluring island in the region. First settled by the ancient Greeks around 4 BC —who named it *Kerkyra Melaina*, or "Black Corfu," for its dark Aleppo pine trees—it spent several periods under Venetian rule between the 10th and 18th centuries, much to the frustration of Dubrovnik, which considered the Italian city-state its archrival. Venetian influence can still be seen in **Korčula Town**, one of the best preserved medieval island towns in the Mediterranean and where most of the island's main historical sights are located. It is known today for its traditional sword dances and its main—though disputed—claim to fame as the birthplace of Marco Polo.

Beyond the capital, the island is made up of stone villages, miles of mountainous roads perfect for biking, secluded beaches, and boutique wine, honey, and olive oil producers. Just 4 km (2½ miles) above Korčula Town you'll find **Žrnovo**, one of the oldest settlements on the island, where you can hike to see several 14th-century stone churches and a selection of lovely family-run restaurants where they still hand-roll a traditional pasta called *Žrnovski makaruni*. **Lumbarda**, 6 km (4 miles) southeast of Korčula Town with around 1,000 inhabitants, is where you'll find the nearest family-friendly beaches and a handful of wineries producing white wine from the indigenous grk grape. The other main wine-producing centers of **Čara** and **Smokvica**, where you can taste the native white varietal Pošip, are farther inland, as is the smallest and oldest settlement on the island, picturesque **Pupnat**. To the west is the port town of **Vela Luka**, where you'll find beautiful beaches, and lovely **Proizd**, one of the many islets of the Korčula Archipelago.

## GETTING HERE AND AROUND

Jadrolinija, Krilo, and TP Line operate car ferries and catamarans five or six times daily to Korčula from Dubrovnik, which stop in Mljet along the way and carry on to Hvar, Brač, and Split (prices range from €10 to €25 and the trips take around 2 to 2½ hours). TP Line also operates a catamaran from Dubrovnik to Lastovo, stopping at Korčula, Šipan, and Mljet along the way. The ferry will drop you off at the Korčula Town harbor, just outside the walls. If traveling by car or bus, you'll drive across the Pelješac Peninsula to board a ferry at Orebić for an hourly 15-minute crossing to Dominče, just a 5-minute drive from Korčula Town (car tickets cost around €15, foot passengers around €3). Keep in mind that if you're traveling with a car in the high season, you might have to wait hours for a space on the ferry, whereas if you're traveling by foot, you'll be able to buy a ticket and jump right on. On the other end of the island, ferries depart from Vela Luka to Hvar, Split, and Lastovo.

Korčula's Old Town is car-free and compact. The rest of the island is well connected by public buses and taxis, although it's much easier to explore off the beaten track with a car. The main bus station is located near the harbor, just outside the Old Town.

To visit the islands around the archipelago, catch a hop-on, hop-off water taxi from the harbor near the Old Town or Lumbarda or rent your own speedboat.

## TOURS

**Korčula Outdoor**

**ADVENTURE TOURS** | For active tours around the island, this company will take you mountain-biking, kayaking, rock-climbing, and sailing to secret beaches, wineries, and the more hidden corners of Korčula. ✉ *Put Svetog Antuna 4, Korcula*

☎ *091/6224–566* ⊕ *www.korcula-outdoor.com.*

**Korkyra Info**

**GUIDED TOURS** | This travel agency with an office just outside the Old Town organizes shuttle buses to and from Dubrovnik Airport (€50), as well as tours and excursions around Korčula and the islands, Dubrovnik, and Pelješac. They also offer car, boat, bike, and scooter rentals. ✉ *Trg Petra Šegedina 3A, Korcula* ☎ *091/571–4355* ⊕ *korkyra.info.*

## Sights

★ **Grad Korčula** (*Korčula Town*)

**TOWN** | Korčula Town is often called "mini-Dubrovnik" for the high fortified walls that surround its stone streets and the circular fortresses jutting out into the sparkling sea. But to constantly compare it to Dubrovnik is to sell it short; Korčula Town is an architectural achievement in its own right and one of the most stunning locations along the Adriatic Coast.

Within tiny Korčula Town, you'll find a treasure trove of Gothic and Renaissance churches, palaces, and piazzas. These important buildings, as well as the town's fortified walls and towers, were mostly built by the Venetians who ruled the town between the 13th and 15th centuries, the island's golden age. One of the most interesting aspects—and the main physical difference between Korčula and Dubrovnik—is the design of its streets, which are laid out in a fishbone pattern. The main road stretches right through the town like a spine; the streets on the western side are straight to allow a breeze to circulate in summer, while the streets on the eastern side are curved to prevent cold northeastern winds from whistling unimpeded through town in the winter ("medieval air-conditioning" as the tour guides like to say). The other main difference is that while Dubrovnik's Old Town heaves with visitors throughout the summer, Korčula Town is car-free, compact, and relaxed. You can spend a pleasant few hours browsing through its myriad boutiques, then settle in at one of the excellent restaurants along the periphery of town to admire the views of the Adriatic and the Pelješac Peninsula beyond. ✉ *Grad Korčula, Korcula.*

**Gradski Muzej Korčula** (*Town Museum*)

**HISTORY MUSEUM** | Located in a 16th-century stone palace on the main square, this charming museum contains items from all eras of the island's history, from Neolithic stone knives to vessels excavated from Greek and Roman shipwrecks to wooden ship models built in the 1960s. Don't miss the replica of the Lumbarda Psephisma, a striking 4th-century-BC stone tablet that details the establishment of a Greek colony in Lumbarda. There are also quirky objects in the original kitchen in the attic, such as gadgets for making macaroni and kneading bread. ✉ *Trg Svetog Marka, Korcula* ☎ *020/711–420* ⊕ *gradskimuzej-korcula.hr* 🎟 *€6* ⏲ *Closed Sun.*

**Katedrala Svetog Marka** (*St. Mark's Cathedral*)

**RELIGIOUS BUILDING** | On the main square, the splendid 15th-century Gothic-Renaissance cathedral, built by several generations of celebrated local stonemasons, is one of the most important buildings on the island. Enter through the beautifully carved Romanesque main portal, which is guarded by Adam and Eve standing underneath twin lions. Inside the cathedral, there are two paintings by Tintoretto. Be sure to climb the bell tower next door; it's steep and awkward, but worthwhile for the views. ✉ *Trg Svetog Marka, Korcula* ⊕ *gradskimuzej-korcula.hr* 🎟 *€3; bell tower €5* ⏲ *Closed Sun.*

**Kopnena Vrata** (*Land Gate*)

**NOTABLE BUILDING** | The main entrance into the Old Town, the Land Gate is topped by the 15th-century Revelin Tower, housing an exhibition connected with the Moreška sword dance and offering panoramic views. Like the other towers

The sword dancers of Korčula are the island's most famous sight.

around town, it features a winged lion—the symbol of Venice—and the seal of the Rector of Korčula, as well as a plaque commemorating the coronation of the first Croatian king, Tomislav. Walk up the grand steps to enter the Old Town; the main thoroughfare starts on the other side of the gate and leads all the way to the Berim Tower on the other end of town. ✉ *Kopnena Vrata, Korcula* 🎫 *€3* ⏲ *Closed Nov.–May.*

**Kuća Marka Pola** (*Marco Polo House*)
**NOTABLE BUILDING** | A couple of blocks east of the main square is the place where legendary 13th-century explorer Marco Polo is said to have been born while Korčula was part of the Venetian Empire. The house itself is nearly in ruins but the tower next door is open, offering great views over the Old Town. At the time of writing, the finishing touches were being put on a new museum celebrating the explorer's life. ✉ *Ulica Depolo, Korcula* 🌐 *gradskimuzej-korcula.hr.*

## Restaurants

**Aterina**
**$$ | MEDITERRANEAN** | Follow the scent of fresh basil to Aterina, a playful restaurant occupying a square on the periphery of the Old Town, with views to the palm-lined promenade and sea below. Order the "small plate" to try a sample of each of the tapas-style starters including cheese, smoked ham, anchovies, and marinated vegetables. **Known for:** fresh light fare that highlights local ingredients; extensive Korčula-focused wine list; breezy Old Town location. 💲 *Average main: €18* ✉ *Trg Korčulanskih Klesara i Kipara 2, Korcula* ☎ *091/986–1856* 🌐 *www.facebook.com/aterinakorcula* ⏲ *Closed Oct.–June.*

★ **Eko Škoj**
**$$ | MEDITERRANEAN** | Head to the hills around Žrnovo to this tiny stone konoba, rustically strung with lavender and bouquets of elderflower, and feast on whatever the Marović family has dreamed up for lunch. No matter what the dish of

the day, you can be sure it'll be seasonal, local, homemade, and delicious. **Known for:** homemade organic lunch menu; family-run rural agritourism; reservations mandatory for lunch. *Average main: €20 Žrnovo 96, Prvo Selo, Korcula 099/685–6301 www.eko-skoj.hr No dinner.*

**KIWI**

$ | **ICE CREAM** | **FAMILY** | European food rule number one: if you see locals lining up for ice cream, get in that line. That's certainly the case with KIWI, the island's oldest ice cream shop; grab a seat outside to try traditional pastries such as *klašuni* (walnut pastries) and *cukarini* (handmade biscuits), as well as muffins, strudels, and homemade ice cream that does Korčula's Italian heritage proud. **Known for:** best ice cream on the island; central location just outside Korčula town walls; local institution. *Average main: €3 Biline 16, Korcula 99/801–5100 slasticarna-kiwi.business.site No credit cards.*

**Konoba Belin**

$$ | **MEDITERRANEAN** | **FAMILY** | For such a small village, Žrnovo is home to a surprising number of great restaurants, most located in old stone homes and run by the families who own them. Konoba Belin is one of the originals and the best, where you'll linger for a few hours over platters of grilled seafood or the local delicacy Žrnovski makaruni; call ahead to arrange a lesson on how to roll macaroni. **Known for:** great place to try Žrnovski makaruni; cash-only policy; welcoming atmosphere. *Average main: €16 Žrnovo 50, Korcula 091/503–9258 No credit cards Closed Sept.–May. No lunch.*

★ **Konoba Feral**

$$ | **SEAFOOD** | **FAMILY** | The village of Lumbarda is known for two things: beaches and Grk wine, and you can enjoy them both at this beachside konoba. You'll tuck into uber-fresh octopus and other catches of the day right beside the beach while sipping Grk made by the charming local brothers who own the restaurant. **Known for:** fresh seafood; family atmosphere; seaside location. *Average main: €16 Lumbarda 63, Lumbarda 020/712–090 Closed Oct.–May.*

★ **Konoba Mate**

$$ | **MEDITERRANEAN** | **FAMILY** | In the courtyard of an old stone cottage in the tiny village of Pupnat (34 km [21 miles] west of Korčula Town), this welcoming restaurant is worth the effort to get there, thanks to its gourmet fare prepared from the family's own farm. The menu changes seasonally, but look out for the house specialty: a platter of homemade *pršut* (prosciutto), goat's cheese, olives, and eggplant pâté. **Known for:** organic vegetables from family garden; excellent value for high-quality food; traditional meals with a twist. *Average main: €20 Pupnat 28, Korcula 020/717–109 www.konobamate.com Closed Sun. and Oct.–Apr. No lunch.*

**LD Restaurant**

$$$$ | **MEDITERRANEAN** | Head chef Marko Gajski's menu here elevates exclusively seasonal Croatian produce—think wild asparagus in spring, strawberries in the summer, truffles and root vegetables in the fall—and local seafood such as lobster, Ston oysters, and scorpion fish into fine-dining creations. With an outdoor seating area stretching along the Old Town's fortified wall and panoramic views of the Pelješac Peninsula and the archipelago, you can enjoy your meal while admiring the very terroir from which it was gathered. **Known for:** one Michelin star; excellent chef's tasting menu available; panoramic views from outdoor tables. *Average main: €115 Don Pavla Poše 1–6, Korcula 020/601–726 www.ldrestaurant.com Closed Oct.–June.*

## Hotels

**Aminess Lume**
**$ | RESORT** | Situated in the middle of the island near the peaceful village of Brna, this resort 32 km (20 miles) southwest of Korčula Town is a perfect base for mountain biking to pristine beaches and viewpoints, visiting wineries in nearby Smokvica, or just lying on a lounger and gazing at the sea. **Pros:** peaceful beachfront resort; great base from which to explore the island; excellent value half-board package. **Cons:** distance from Korčula Town and the ferry terminals; not many facilities nearby; access to a car is necessary. *Rooms from: €110 Brna 400, Korcula 020/798–030 www.aminess.com/en/aminess-lume-hotel Closed Oct.–Apr. 82 rooms Free Breakfast.*

**Korčula Heritage Hotel**
**$$ | HOTEL** | Exuding old-fashioned charm, this became the island's first hotel when it opened in 1912 and has hosted the likes of Jackie Kennedy, Sophia Loren, and Wallis Simpson. **Pros:** central location on Korčula Town harborfront; fabulous terrace bar; historical Korčula landmark. **Cons:** decor feels a little dated; front rooms can be noisy; limited facilities. *Rooms from: €190 Obala dr. Franje Tuđmana 5, Korcula 052/858–600 www.aminess.com/en/aminess-korcula-heritage-hotel Closed Jan.–Mar. 20 rooms Free Breakfast.*

**★ Korčula Waterfront Accommodation**
**$ | APARTMENT** | Located in a quiet bay a 10-minute walk from Korčula Town, with a large private dock perfect for sunbathing and impromptu barbecues, these homey well-equipped rooms are run by Paulina and Antonio, the most helpful couple you could hope to meet on holiday. **Pros:** helpful and friendly hosts; quiet location with private dock for swimming; excellent value for money. **Cons:** no breakfast; few shops or other facilities nearby; distance from the Old Town. *Rooms from: €80 Šetalište Tina Ujevića 33, Korcula 098/937–0463 Closed Nov.-Apr. 4 rooms No Meals.*

**★ Lešić Dimitri Palace**
**$$$$ | HOTEL** | A cluster of stone buildings seamlessly woven into the fabric of the Old Town, this 18th-century palace has been thoughtfully restored into six luxury residences, each its own unique creation that pays subtle homage to stops along Marco Polo's silk route. **Pros:** unique high-end design in each room; central location in the Old Town; free breakfast at on-site Michelin-starred restaurant. **Cons:** very expensive; no pool; no common areas. *Rooms from: €525 Don Pavla Poše 1–6, Korcula 020/715–560 www.ldpalace.com Closed Nov.–Apr. 6 rooms Free Breakfast.*

## Nightlife

### BARS

**Cocktail Bar Massimo**
**BARS** | Surely among the world's most impressive venues, Cocktail Bar Massimo is located inside one of the turrets of the fortified town walls and offers wonderful sunset views over the peninsula. Drinks are raised up the turret on a pulley, and you have to climb a steep ladder to get to the top. *Šetalište Petra Kanavelića, Korcula 099/214–4568.*

## Performing Arts

### DANCE

**★ Moreška**
**FOLK/TRADITIONAL DANCE** | For an incredibly entertaining cultural show that the whole family will enjoy, catch a performance of the Moreška, a colorful medieval sword dance—using real swords—that has been performed in Korčula for more than 400 years. The word *Moreška* means "Moorish" and is said to celebrate the victory of the Christians over the Moors in Spain, told through the story of a clash between the Black King and the White

King over a young maiden. The dance itself is not native to Croatia and was once performed in many Mediterranean countries, but the tradition has disappeared elsewhere and nowadays only remains here. The hour-long performance involves traditional a cappella singing, a live brass band, and the energetic sword dance, performed only by males from local families. Performances take place at 9 pm Monday and Thursday in July and August and Thursday in May, June, September and October. They happen on an open-air stage just outside the city walls next to the Land Gate, with a spectacular performance held on July 29, the feast day of Korčula's protector, St. Theodore. ✉ *Kopnena Vrata, Korcula* 🌐 *www.moreska.hr* 🎫 *€20.*

## FESTIVALS

### Korkyra Baroque Festival

**MUSIC FESTIVALS** | This 10-day Baroque music festival takes place in September in venues across Korčula Town, including the Cathedral and the atrium of City Hall. Established in 2012, it has become one of the most important festivals on the island, attracting musicians and visitors from around the world. ✉ *Korcula* ☎ *099/319–5427* 🌐 *korkyrabaroque.com.*

# Shopping

One of the pleasures of a visit to Korčula Town is wandering the old streets, particularly the main thoroughfare through town, and browsing the renowned boutiques for artwork, items made from local white stone, and handmade jewelry. Elsewhere on the island, Korčula's wealth of homemade products, such as olive oil, honey, and wine, can be purchased right where they are made (and you can usually sample the goods first).

### Cukarin

**FOOD** | **FAMILY** | This long-standing family-run shop is renowned for its five different types of traditional pastries, including delicious handmade cukarin biscuits and klašun. They use local ingredients such as rose brandy, lemon, orange zest, carob, and almonds, and there are several gluten-free options. ✉ *Trg Hrvatska Bratske Zajednice bb, Korcula* ☎ *020/711–055* 🌐 *cukarin.hr.*

### Galerija Vapor

**ART GALLERIES** | Funky jewelry, colorful sculptures, and paintings with pop-art twists by more than 60 contemporary Croatian artists adorn the walls of this cavernous gallery inside the Sea Gate. ✉ *Kula Morska Vrata, Korcula.*

### Manina

**OTHER SPECIALTY STORE** | This little treasure trove on the main thoroughfare through town is run by a charming brother and sister, Miro and Ivana, and is well-stocked with art, fabulous clothing, and jewelry from local and Croatian designers. ✉ *Ulica Svetog Roka 7, Korcula* 🌐 *manina-jewelrystore.business.site.*

### Spot Shopping Mall

**MALL** | The largest shopping center near Korčula Town is located up the hill, about a 15-minute walk from the main bus station. Inside you'll find a large Tommy supermarket and a couple of other shops, but the main reason to visit is the spacious terrace of the Kavana No. 1 restaurant. Come for a coffee or casual lunch and stay for one of the best views overlooking Korčula Town from above. ✉ *Ulica Ante Starčevića 6, Korcula* ☎ *020/400–557.*

# Activities

## BEACHES

The sea around Korčula is so clean and clear that you can swim anywhere (and the locals do). The closest beach for a quick swim is **Banje,** a busy, family-friendly beach about a 10-minute walk east of the town walls where you can enjoy all manner of water sports. The best beaches near Korčula Town are 6 km (4 miles) away in the village of Lumbarda: sandy **Vela Przina,** 2 km (1 mile) south of Lumbarda, and smooth-white-stoned **Bilin Žal,** a short distance east.

Further away, **Pupnatska Luka,** 15 km (9 miles) southwest of Korčula Town, is a perfect wedge of shingle beach backed by steep hills where you can have lunch or a cold drink at the very inviting Beach Bar Mate, owned by the same family who runs Konoba Mate. **Vaja Beach,** near the lovely limestone fishing village of Račišće 13 km (8 miles) away, is a secret bay that involves a steep downhill hike, but you're rewarded with an isolated, perfect white pebble beach.

Of course, being an island surrounded by little islets, the best way to enjoy the sea around Korčula is by taking a boat into the archipelago. The three most popular islets to visit from Korčula Town are **Badija**, the largest in the archipelago, with walking trails and a 14th-century Franciscan monastery; **Stupe**, where you can spend the day sipping cocktails at flashy Moro Beach Bar; and **Vrnik**, where you can see Roman-era stone quarries. Rent your own boat or take one of the island-hopper water taxis, which depart hourly from the Korčula Town harbor; the whole route takes 1 hour (15 minutes between islands) and you can jump on and off as many times as you like (tickets €30). Check out **Korčula Boating** (🌐 *www.korculaboating.com*) for more details.

# Mljet

*18 nautical miles west of Dubrovnik.*

Mljet is the southernmost of the Dalmatian islands and one of the most peaceful and natural. It is a long thin island—37 km (23 miles) long and an average of 3 km (2 miles) wide—of steep rocky slopes and dense pine forests, more than a third of which is contained within Mljet National Park. There is one main road that runs the length of the island from the national park in the west to the sandy beaches and lagoons in the east, winding through olive groves and sleepy stone towns along the way. For such a small island with only 1,100 inhabitants, it makes two historically significant claims to fame. The first is it being the biblical island of Melita, where the apostle Paul was shipwrecked. The second is being home to the cave where the Greek legend Odysseus spent seven years with the nymph Calypso. Whether either claim is true is up for debate (most biblical scholars recognize Melita as modern-day Malta), but what is undebatable is that Mljet has a magic that pulls people in and, like Odysseus, you will not want to leave.

## GETTING HERE AND AROUND

Sobra is the main port on the island and the most convenient for Saplunara Beach, while Polače and Pomena are closer to the national park. TP Line and Kapetan Luka operate ferries between Dubrovnik and Pomena three times daily in the high season (€18 one-way; 1 hour 20 minutes), as well as between Korčula and Pomena (€15; 40 minutes). TP Line also operates a once-daily ferry from Dubrovnik to Polače (€10.35; 1 hour 40 minutes). Jadrolinija, TP Line, and Kapetan Luka each operate daily passenger ferries from Dubrovnik to Sobra (€6.50; 1 hour 20 minutes), while Jadrolinija operates a car ferry to Sobra from the port of Prapratno on the Pelješac Peninsula (€20; 45 minutes).

Once on Mljet, an infrequent public bus travels from each end of the island to Sobra once a day; if you want to cruise around to different points across the island, you'll need a car or scooter, which can be rented in the main settlements. If you are short on time, consider taking an organized day trip to the island from Dubrovnik or Korčula, which will bring you to the national park and may include lunch onboard.

A gorgeous national park covers the entire western part of the island of Mljet.

## Sights

### ★ Mljet National Park (*Nacionalni Park Mljeta*)

**NATIONAL PARK | FAMILY** | Most people come to Mljet to visit the peaceful national park that covers the entire western part of the island and encompasses the towns of Pomena and Polače. It has miles of dense pine forests, shady biking and walking trails, and two interconnected bright-blue saltwater lakes, **Malo jezero** (Little Lake) and **Veliko jezero** (Big Lake). The Benedictine monks who owned the island from 1191 to 1410 dug a transport channel to the coast through the lakes, which turned them from freshwater to saltwater. In the middle of Veliko Jezero is the **Isle of St. Mary**, with its charming 12th-century monastery, now a small restaurant. You can reach the Isle of St. Mary by boat or kayak from the small bridge, Mali Most. Mountain bikes are also available to rent at Mali Most or from Hotel Odisej in Pomena. The section of the park that includes the lakes and the monastery is ticketed; park entrances are within walking distance from the ports in Polače or Pomena. Malo jezero is a short walk from the entrance in Pomena. ✉ *Pristanište 2, Govedari* ☎ *020/744–041* 🌐 *np-mljet.hr* 🎫 *June–Sept. €25; Oct.–Dec., €15; Jan.–May €9 (includes entrance to the park and boat trip to Isle of St. Mary).*

### ★ Odysseus Cave

**CAVE** | There are idyllic swimming spots all around Mljet, but the village of Babino Polje in the center of the island is home to the most magical of all. Greek legend has it that when the hero Odysseus was shipwrecked off the island known as Ogygia, he swam into a cave where he was met by a nymph called Calypso; he was so bewitched that he stayed with her for the next seven years. The cave is tricky to reach so there are never any crowds, which adds to its mystique.

You can get there directly by boat or, if you're traveling by road, park at the Tommy market in Babino Polje and follow the signs through the olive groves on foot. The walk takes around an hour and includes a steep downhill section and uneven rocks, so make sure to wear decent shoes and bring water. Once you arrive, you can jump off the rocks and swim through a short tunnel into the cave; aim to arrive around noon, when the sun is high and the water is aquamarine. There is a makeshift café perched on the rocks above the cave; there may or may not be someone working there, but it makes a great place to stop for a break. ✉ *Babino Polje.*

## Restaurants

**★ Ante's Place**
**$$$ | SEAFOOD | FAMILY** | Located on the breezy seaside terrace at PineTree Boutique Apartments (and run by the same family), the food at Ante's Place is so good you'll likely eat all of your meals there while on Mljet. It's the best place to try traditional Dalmatian dishes, from lamb or octopus cooked peka-style to plentiful seafood platters and divine lobster spaghetti. **Known for:** peaceful seaside location; great place to order peka; family-run business. $ *Average main: €25* ✉ *Saplunara 17, Mljet* ☎ *99/591–0024* 🌐 *pinetreemljet.com* ⏲ *Closed Oct.–May.*

## Hotels

**Hotel Odisej**
**$ | HOTEL** | Located in the village of Pomena, just a 15-minute walk from the lakes, the Odisej's main appeal is its proximity to the national park. **Pros:** seafront location; best option for national park; only official hotel on Mljet. **Cons:** large and rather impersonal; food is disappointing; decor is tired. $ *Rooms from: €125* ✉ *Pomena 16, Pomena* ☎ *020/362–111* 🌐 *www.adriaticluxuryhotels.com/hotel-odisej-dubrovnik-mljet* ⏲ *Closed Nov.–Mar.* *157 rooms* *Free Breakfast.*

**★ PineTree Boutique Apartments**
**$$ | HOTEL | FAMILY** | This wonderful property just steps from sandy Saplunara Beach is relaxation at its best, thanks to its light, airy, and spacious rooms, infinity pool, and superb restaurant. **Pros:** owners and staff who feel like family; lovely infinity pool; close to the beach. **Cons:** not many services nearby; far from the national park; car or taxi necessary to reach other parts of the island. $ *Rooms from: €175* ✉ *Saplunara 17, Mljet* ☎ *098/266–007* 🌐 *www.pinetreemljet.com* ⏲ *Closed Oct.–May* *12 rooms* *Free Breakfast.*

## Activities

### BEACHES

One of Croatia's few sandy beaches, **Saplunara** lies at the southeastern tip of the island. All of Mljet is peaceful, but Saplunara is where you go to really get away from it all. It remains relatively wild and untended, and you will find several seasonal restaurants and beach bars in the tiny nearby settlement of the same name, including PineTree Boutique Apartments and Ante's Place. A car is recommended for a stay here.

Within the national park, the two saltwater lakes are even warmer than the sea, sheltered, and make a perfect place to swim and kayak.

### DIVING

**Aquatica Mljet**
**DIVING & SNORKELING** | Jacques Cousteau once called Mljet one of the best diving destinations in the world, and divers will love the reefs, wrecks, and caves around the island. This outfitter in Pomena will show you some of the best spots. ✉ *Pomena bb* ☎ *098/479–916* 🌐 *www.aquatica-mljet.hr.*

Chapter 4

# SPLIT AND CENTRAL DALMATIA



Updated by
Lara Rasin

Sights
★★★★★

Restaurants
★★★☆☆

Hotels
★★★☆☆

Shopping
★★☆☆☆

Nightlife
★★★★★

# WELCOME TO SPLIT AND CENTRAL DALMATIA

## TOP REASONS TO GO

★ **Roman splendor:** In Split, explore Diocletian's Palace, a massive historical complex with ruins dating back to Roman rule in the 3rd century AD. Take a tour in the early morning before the day's buzz drowns out the voices of the past.

★ **Island hopping:** Hire a taxi boat or a one-day sailing charter for a sojourn on one of Central Dalmatia's most enchanting islands, Hvar, with its lavender fields and olive tree groves.

★ **Hiking and swimming:** Plunge into the clear waters of Sutivan on Brač after climbing to Vidova gora or walking the Dolce Vita Trail through the island's vineyards.

★ **Sailing adventures:** Sail into Komiža Harbor on Vis Island aboard a yacht, perhaps having visited Modra špilja (the Blue Cave) on the nearby islet of Biševo.

★ **Natural beauty:** Climb Mt. Biokovo at sunrise, take a moonlight swim on the Tučepi coastline, and be awed by the Makarska Riviera's mountain views.

Split is the main jumping-off point for exploring all of Dalmatia, not just Central Dalmatia. From Split, it is easy to take a bus, boat, train, or rental car in any direction to see everything Dalmatia offers, on and off the beaten path. Directly south of Split is the island of Brač, easily accessible by ferry in about an hour. Southeast of Split are beautiful Omiš and the Cetina River Valley, and to the west is the ancient walled city of Trogir, reachable by car in 30 minutes or by taxi boat in up to an hour. Southeast toward Dubrovnik is the Makarska Riviera, with its string of hidden cove beaches that begins about one hour by car from Split. In the opposite direction lies magnificent Krka National Park, a one-hour scenic drive from Split.

1 **Split.** An ancient city, home to Diocletian's Palace, that also has excellent seafood restaurants.

2 **Šibenik.** A cobblestoned city home to the UNESCO-protected Cathedral of St. James.

3 **Prvić.** A charming island dotted with secret swimming coves.

4 **Krka National Park.** A national park with a stunning collection of turquoise waterfalls.

5 **Trogir.** A historic city founded as a Greek colony in the 3rd century BC, punctuated by stone buildings and known for its medieval Old Town.

6 **Omiš and the Cetina River Valley.** A beautiful town where one of the country's prettiest rivers meets the Adriatic Sea.

7 **Brač.** A gorgeous island with historic gems like a hidden 16th-century monastery reachable only by foot.

8 **Hvar.** One of the Adriatic's most popular islands, with a happening party scene and cultural wonders to boot.

**9 Vis.** An untouched island with a craggy cave-dotted coastline popular with yachters.

**10 Makarska.** A buzzing and beautiful seaside town.

**11 Lastovo.** An off-the-beaten-track island with scenic hiking opportunities galore.

Central Dalmatia's untamed natural beauty encompasses rocky coastal beaches, steep mountains, and a Mediterranean terrain dotted by olive groves, vineyards, and clusters of wild herb. The wonder elicited by these landscapes is matched only by the area's unique culture and lifestyle, evident everywhere from the larger city of Split to small towns.

Here, you can take in everything from ancient ruins and Renaissance-era architectural masterpieces to the exciting entertainment, buzzing art, and cutting-edge gastro scenes of today. For many, the one-of-a-kind journey around Central Dalmatia begins from Croatia's second-largest city and Dalmatia's de facto capital, Split.

Since the mid-2010s, Split has blossomed into one of the Mediterranean's most popular coastal hot spots. The layers of history contained within its Old Town walls (including the UNESCO-listed Diocletian's Palace) are worth more than a quick walk-through and a few photos. Take your time as you stroll through the city's labyrinth-like stone streets. While you're in town, channel your inner Dalmatian by going *laganini*—laid-back and without rushing—as you savor each bite of fresh seafood and enjoy each sip of sun-ripened local wine.

From Split you can hop on a ferry or catamaran to one of the nearby islands that offer paradise just two hours or less away. Split is also the region's main base for boat charter companies operating routes throughout the Adriatic. A 60-minute drive up the coast, northwest of Split, you'll find the stunning city of Šibenik, home to the UNESCO-designated Gothic-Renaissance Cathedral of St. James. Šibenik, with its medieval-era Old Town and grand fortresses of St. Michael and St. Nicholas, is more than worthy of a couple days of your time. The city also makes a splendid base for visiting the nearby cascading waterfalls of Krka National Park and the peaceful riverside town of Skradin.

On the way back from Šibenik toward Split is the historic city of Trogir. The city's Old Town is a remarkable conglomeration of Roman, Greek, and Venetian ancient stone architecture and culture all contained on a tiny island that residents call their living museum. South from Split, a 30-minute drive down the coast brings you to Omiš and the mouth of the Cetina River. The river forms a steep-sided valley, renowned as an adventure sport hub with activities from rafting to rock climbing.

What makes Central Dalmatia even more special are its islands. Brač, one of the nearest to Split and often recognized for its famous Zlatni Rat (Golden Cape) Beach, is an island of exceptional beauty and enchanting traditions, including a world-renowned stonemasonry school. South of Brač rises the island of Hvar, home to one of Central Dalmatia's most exclusive party destinations, Hvar Town. Venetian-style buildings ring three sides of the Hvar Town harbor and its magnificent main square, home to the Renaissance-era Cathedral of St. Stephen. The proud hilltop Fortica to the left of the main square beckons visitors to take in the view from higher ground.

Even farther out to sea lies wild windswept Vis, an oasis for lovers of the outdoors. It has two major settlements, Vis Town and Komiža, the latter making the best starting point for a day trip to Modra špilja (Blue Cave) on the islet of Biševo. Back on the mainland, a two-hour drive down the coast south of Split brings you to Makarska, a bustling seaside city built around a bay filled with fishing boats and backed by the rugged silhouette of the Biokovo Mountain Range. Biokovo's St. George Peak, soaring about 5,780 feet, is the third highest in Croatia and offers stunning views over the entire region.

Lastovo, Croatia's most distant inhabited island, remains firmly off the beaten track. Although it is geographically part of Southern Dalmatia, Lastovo's only public ferry and catamaran services to and from the mainland connect to Split.

# Planning

## When to Go

High season runs from July through August, when tourists from all over the world flock to the region and temperatures average from the mid-80s to the mid-90s Fahrenheit. Split Airport is connected to more than 70 locations during this time, and dozens of airlines have scheduled flights into Split, making it one of Croatia's most accessible destinations. In high season, prices can rise significantly, restaurant visits may require reservations, main beaches can be crowded, and it can be difficult to find a place to sleep if you haven't reserved in advance. Because of all this, local tourism ramps things up even more to provide the best experiences for guests: museums and churches have extended hours, open-air bars and clubs bring nightlife to the fore, and numerous cultural festivals host performances starring international musicians, dancers, and actors.

Low season runs from November through April, when some hotels and restaurants close completely. Exceptions during these slower months are around Christmas and the New Year, when Advent markets pop up with food stands and live music galore, among other events organized to celebrate the holidays. The weather can be unreliable during this time, but if you're lucky, you can find yourself drinking morning coffee in the sunshine below a deep blue sky against a backdrop of snowcapped mountains.

However, many people tout mid-season, May through June and September through October, as the best time to visit the region. During these periods you'll miss the largest crowds, the weather is most often sunny and dry, and the sea is usually warm enough for swimming. Most of the region's hotels and restaurants will be open, but at a pace slow enough to lend an air of true relaxation.

## Getting Here and Around

### AIR

Split is served by Split Airport (SPU) at Kaštela, 25 km (16 miles) northwest of the city center. This small airport, opened in 1966 and renovated over the years, is Croatia's second busiest after Zagreb. The island of Brač is served by Brač Airport (BWK) at Gornji Humac, 13 km (8 miles) northeast of Bol. Pleso Transport is a shuttle service that takes passengers to and from Split Airport and the main Split bus station. A one-way ticket is €8 and the trip takes around 30 minutes. Daily shuttle departures from the bus station generally run between 5 am and 8:30 pm, and from the airport between 7:20 am and 11:30 pm. Shuttles depart every 30–80 minutes.

Croatia's national carrier, Croatia Airlines, operates domestic flights from Split to Zagreb and Osijek in summer. During high season, Croatia Airlines also flies directly between Split and Amsterdam, Athens, Berlin, Bucharest, Copenhagen, Dublin, Dusseldorf, Frankfurt, London (LHR and LGW), Lyon, Milan, Munich, Oslo, Paris, Prague, Rome, Skopje, Stockholm, Vienna, and Zurich. Through summer, Croatia Airlines flies nonstop from the island of Brač to Zagreb, too. Several major international carriers fly to Split, along with low-budget operators such as easyJet, Eurowings, Jet2, Ryanair, and Wizz Air. Flights and timetables are subject to change, so it's best to double-check all booking details directly with airlines.

**AIRPORT CONTACTS Split Airport.** ✉ *Cesta dr. Franje Tuđmana 1270, Kaštel Štafilic* ☎ *021/203–589* 🌐 *www.split-airport.hr.* **Brač Airport.** ✉ *Gornji Humac 145, Supetar* ☎ *021/559–701* 🌐 *www.airport-brac.hr.*

**AIRPORT TRANSFER CONTACTS**
**Pleso Transport.** (*Pleso Prijevoz*) ✉ *Split* ☎ *099/711–8889 Pleso Customer Service for Split* 🌐 *plesoprijevoz.hr.*

## BOAT AND FERRY

From June through September, Jadrolinija, Croatia's largest boat transport company, usually runs services multiple times a week to Ancona, Italy (journey time between 9 and 12 hours), and Bari, Italy (journey time about 10 hours). Outside of the high season, service frequency can be reduced. From April to October, Italian company SNAV runs services between Ancona and Split multiple times a week as well. Departure times vary by month and day of travel. The journey time is between 9 and 12 hours in either direction.

In addition, Jadrolinija operates domestic coastal routes that run across Central and Southern Dalmatia. Split has direct connections with Vis (journey time approximately 2½ hours), Stari Grad on Hvar (journey time approximately 2 hours), Hvar Town on Hvar (journey time approximately 75 minutes), and Supetar on Brač (journey time approximately 1 hour). From Sumartin on Brač, there's a daily year-round (excluding some holidays) line with Makarska as well. Most Jadrolinija routes offer car transport, too. Croatian ferry company Krilo also connects Split with domestic coastal destinations, including a direct route to Hvar Town (journey time approximately 50 minutes). Purchase your ticket online in advance whenever possible—especially during the high season, when waiting until the last minute could mean waiting an extra day to travel—and arrive early. Also check the terms of your purchase to see if the ticket is valid all day or only for a specific departure time.

**CONTACTS Jadrolinija.** ✉ *Gat Svetog Duje bb, Split* ☎ *072/303–337 Jadrolinija call center* 🌐 *www.jadrolinija.hr.* **Krilo.** ✉ *Poljička cesta Suhi Potok 28, Jesenice* ☎ *021/645–476* 🌐 *www.krilo.hr.* **SNAV.** ✉ *Split* ☎ *081/428–5555 customer service* 🌐 *www.snav.it.*

## BUS

International buses arrive daily or weekly to Split from Berlin, Budapest, Frankfurt, Graz, Ljubljana, Milan, Mostar, Munich, Paris, Sarajevo, Stuttgart, Trieste, and Vienna, among other cities. Timetables are subject to change, so before planning your trip, check with the Split bus station directly.

Split has regular bus connections to destinations all over Croatia. There are approximately 40 buses per day to Zagreb, 20 to Zadar, 15 to Dubrovnik, and 5 to Rijeka. Some buses traveling south to Dubrovnik stop at Makarska en route; others going north to Zadar stop at Šibenik, with possible additional stops along the way depending on the time and bus company. Regular local buses also run multiple times a day to Trogir and down the coast to Omiš. Timetable information is available from the Split bus station or from its website. Note that the Zagreb bus station's website (🌐 *www.akz.hr*) can be easier to navigate and contains timetables for buses all over Croatia.

**CONTACTS Split Bus Station.** ✉ *Obala Kneza Domagoja 12, Split* ☎ *060/327–777* 🌐 *www.ak-split.hr.*

### CAR

You can certainly enjoy the delights of Split and the nearby islands of Brač, Hvar, and Vis without a car. However, you may wish to rent a vehicle for more flexibility in driving up the coast to Šibenik and Krka National Park or down to Omiš and Makarska, although these destinations are well served by buses. Car rental prices vary, and you will probably pay less if you rent from a local company that's not part of an international chain. If you drive one-way (say, from Split to Dubrovnik), there is often an additional drop-off charge, but it depends on the type of car and the number of days you are renting.

Renting a car once you arrive on the islands is an affordable option to see the entire island at your own pace. While on the islands, you can also rent a convertible VW Beetle, scooter, van, motorized tuk tuk (a three-wheeled vehicle), or beach buggy for the day and explore in style at your own pace. Rapidus has a fleet of quirky cars that can be picked up and dropped off in Hvar Town, Stari Grad, Jelsa, and Vrboska on Hvar.

**CONTACTS Rapidus Rent-a-Car.** ✉ *Dubrovačka 61, Split* ☎ *095/922–9884* 🌐 *www.rapidus.hr.*

### TAXI

In Split the main taxi ranks lie at each end of the Riva seafront promenade (Obala hrvatskog narodnog preporoda), in front of the *glavni pazar* (main open-air market), and in front of Hotel Bellevue. Taxis also wait outside the Split train station. They can be requested by phone, and Uber and Bolt ride-hailing services are available in Split as well.

### TRAIN

There are multiple day and night trains daily between Split and Zagreb (journey time between five and nine hours).
In addition, multiple trains travel daily between Split and Šibenik (journey time between one and five hours).

**CONTACTS Split Train Station.** ✉ *Obala Kneza Domagoja 8, Split* ☎ *060/333–444 Croatian Railways general information hotline* 🌐 *www.hzpp.hr/en.*

## Restaurants

Generally, eateries fall into two main categories here: you can eat in a *restoran* (restaurant) or *konoba* (tavern). Restaurants are more formal affairs, often offering Croatian cuisine and a choice of international dishes. In contrast, a *konoba* usually serves typical local dishes; many offer an authentic *marenda* (an affordable lunch special), often consisting of fish, vegetables, and a glass of wine. However, some taverns have started to give the traditional more of a modern flair.

Central Dalmatian specialties are mainly seafood-based. Catching fish and other seafood allowed centuries of Dalmatians to survive in this relatively rugged, not-so-fertile terrain. Dalmatia's loving relationship with the sea and its gifts is also visible in music, with many local love songs dedicated to the sea itself. Listening to a few songs by renowned singer and composer Oliver Dragojević (1947–2018), a Split native, with their blend of jazz and traditional *klapa* (traditional a cappella singing), will illustrate the passion for the Adriatic that is deliciously reflected in local cuisine. Meticulously prepared dishes such as *rižot* (risotto)—especially the kind with fresh squid ink—and *brodet* (fish stewed in a rich tomato, onion, and wine sauce) are menu mainstays.

Fish are often divided into two categories: "white" fish, including *brancin* (sea bass) and *kovač* (John Dory), are more expensive, while "blue" fish, including *srdele* (sardines) and *skuša* (mackerel), are cheaper. In restaurants, fresh fish is often priced by the kilogram, so costs can vary dramatically depending on how big your fish is.

A popular trend is eating at a charming Dalmatian wine bar, featuring delicious local wines, cheeses, and prosciutto. Some offer a wide selection of tapas, and all are eager to educate their clientele about the wines and provide suggestions on pairings.

## Hotels

Central Dalmatia's best and most expensive hotels are in Split and in Hvar Town on the island of Hvar. The region has options to suit all needs and budgets, including big-name upscale hotels, smaller boutique luxury hotels, and exclusive private villas. Many visitors prefer to rent a private room or apartment, a choice that offers value for money, more direct contact with locals, and (if you are lucky) an authentic stone cottage or apartment with a terrace and a blissful sea view. The high season runs from Easter to late October and peaks during July and August, when prices rise significantly and it may be difficult to find a place to sleep if you have not booked in advance. Prices have gone up year-round, especially in the larger cities, following Croatia's switch to the euro from the kuna on January 1, 2023.

⇨ *Restaurant and hotel reviews have been shortened. For full information, visit Fodors.com. Restaurant prices are the average cost of a main course at dinner or, if dinner is not served, at lunch. Hotel prices are the lowest cost of a standard double room in high season.*

### What It Costs in Euros (€)

| | $ | $$ | $$$ | $$$$ |
|---|---|---|---|---|
| **RESTAURANTS** | under €15 | €15–€23 | €24–€32 | over €32 |
| **HOTELS** | under €150 | €150–€250 | €251–€350 | over €350 |

## Tours

### ★ Secret Dalmatia

**CULTURAL TOURS | FAMILY** | These luxury tours are the best choice for adventurous foodies who want to experience Dalmatia's cultural heritage in an authentic way. The company offers culinary tours, sailing, and biking trips that showcase great food, wine, and chefs, as well as Croatia's blue seas, rolling hills, and forests in the hinterlands. Top-notch accommodation and transportation are arranged, too. ✉ *Split* ☎ *091/567–1604* 🌐 *www.secretdalmatia.com* 🎟 *Day tours from €150; individualized multiday tours from €800 per day.*

### Portal Day Tours

**GUIDED TOURS** | The company specializes in nature and cultural tours, both in and around Central Dalmatia. Destinations include national parks (Plitvice and Krka) and islands (Hvar and Brač), as well as city centers (Split and Trogir). ✉ *Obala Bana Berislavića 3, Trogir* ☎ *021/885–016* split-excursions.com *From €36 per person for national park day tours; €450 per group for private boat tours.*

## Visitor Information

**CONTACTS Bol Tourist Board.** *Porat Bolskih Pomoraca bb, Bol 021/635–638 www.bol.hr/en.* **Hvar Tourist Board.** *Trg Svetog Stjepana 42, Hvar 021/741–059 visithvar.hr.* **Lastovo Tourist Board.** *Pjevor 7, Lastovo 020/801–018 tz-lastovo.hr/en.* **Makarska Tourist Board.** *Franjevački Put 2A, Makarska 021/612–002 makarska-info.hr.* **Šibenik Tourist Board.** *Fausta Vrančića 18, Šibenik 022/212–075 www.sibenik-tourism.hr.* **Split Tourist Board.** *Obala Hrvatskog Narodnog Preporoda 9, Split 021/348–600 visitsplit.com.* **Trogir Tourist Board.** *Trg Ivana Pavla II/1, Trogir 021/885–628 www.visittrogir.hr.* **Vis Tourist Board.** *Šetalište Stare Isse 5, Vis Town 021/717–017 www.tz-vis.hr/en/.*

# Split

*230 km (143 miles) north of Dubrovnik.*

Split's ancient core and its centuries of history are spectacular, reflecting a heritage that dates back to prehistoric times and across the pre-Roman Illyrian period. The very heart of the city lies within the walls of Roman emperor Diocletian's palace, which was built in the 3rd century AD. Diocletian, born in the nearby Roman settlement of Salona around 245, achieved a successful career as a soldier and became emperor at the age of 40. Around 295, he ordered a vast palace complex to be built in his native Dalmatia, and when it was completed he stepped down from the throne and retired to his beloved homeland. Upon his death, he was laid to rest in an octagonal mausoleum, around which Split's magnificent cathedral was built.

Centuries later, Eurasian nomads migrated from the north, clashing with local inhabitants around the 7th century. Some locals found refuge within the palace walls. Over the years, the palace complex and its vast imperial apartments were divided up and expanded into living quarters. During the 10th century, Croatia got its first king, and the area developed into an important urban center for the new kingdom. By the 11th century, the small original settlement had expanded beyond the ancient walls.

From the 15th through 19th centuries, Split saw Venetian and Habsburg rule. In the early Middle Ages, the city became one of the Adriatic's main trading ports and blossomed, producing splendid Renaissance buildings, art, and literature. This was a time of great literary figures such as Marko Marulić (1450–1524), author of epic poem *Judita*, who is known as the father of Croatian literature. During the 19th century, an overland connection to Central Europe was established by the construction of the Split–Zagreb–Vienna railway line. The turn of the 20th century was an era of Split-native art masters such as sculptor Ivan Rendić (1849–1932) and Postimpressionist painter Emanuel Vidović (1870–1953), known for his depictions of landscapes around Split. The renowned Ivan Meštrović (1883–1962) spent time studying and creating art in Split during this time, too.

After World War II, Split faced a period of rapid urban expansion; industrialization accelerated, and the growing suburbs sprouted high-rise apartment blocks. Culture, though, continued to flourish, with *klapa*-style jazz great Oliver Dragojević (1947–2018) and funk mastermind Dino Dvornik (1964–2008), as well as the genesis of iconic bands such as pop group Magazin and rockers Daleka Obala (meaning "Distant Shore"). Today, the historic center of Split is included on UNESCO's list of World Heritage sites.

### GETTING HERE AND AROUND

Central Dalmatia's coastal capital is easy to get around and offers ferries to popular tourist spots, like the islands of Brač and Hvar. Local buses are available to visit nearby towns like Šibenik and Trogir.

## Sights

★ **Cathedral of St. Domnius** (*Katedrala sv. Duje*)

**CHURCH** | The main body of this cathedral is the 3rd-century-AD octagonal mausoleum designed as a shrine to Emperor Diocletian, and a peek inside and a trek up to the bell tower are well worth the views. During the 7th century, refugees from Salona converted the space into an early Christian church. Its interior contains a hexagonal Romanesque stone pulpit from the 13th century with rich carvings, and the elegant, 200-foot-tall Romanesque-Gothic bell tower was constructed and reconstructed in stages between the 13th and 20th centuries. Climb to the top of the bell tower (sometimes closed in winter and during bad weather) for a spectacular view of the entire palace, Split, and the surrounding Adriatic Sea. ✉ *Kraj Svetog Duje 3, Grad* 🌐 *visitsplit.com/en/527/cathedral-of-saint-domnius* 🎫 *€5 for cathedral; €7 for bell tower.*

**Crikvine-Kaštilac**

**ART MUSEUM** | The small chapel of this museum contains a magnificent collection of 20th-century sculptor Ivan Meštrović's work, produced over 40 years, that depicts the life of Christ in a series of bas-relief wood carvings that many consider among his finest work. Viewing the entire series should not be rushed, and it's worth visiting in conjunction with his other works in the Meštrović Gallery, a five-minute walk away. ✉ *Šetalište Ivana Meštrovicá 39, Meje* ☎ *021/340–800* 🌐 *mestrovic.hr* 🎫 *€12, includes entrance to Meštrović Gallery* ⏲ *Closed Mon.*

### Save with SplitCard

If you are staying in Split for more than five nights during summer or two nights during winter, be sure to pick up your SplitCard (no cost). It gives you free entry to certain museums and galleries and reduced rates at other establishments, including some museums, restaurants, and cafés. Just ask the staff at your hotel or go to the nearest Tourist Information Center to pick one up.

★ **Diocletian's Palace** (*Dioklecijanova palača*)

**CASTLE/PALACE** | The home of Split's thriving Old Town, Diocletian's Palace is a marvelous maze of restaurants, cafés, shops, and boutiques, as well as stunning ancient structures. The palace dates back to the late 3rd century AD and originally served as both a luxurious villa and a Roman garrison. Its rectangular shape has two main streets—Dioklecijanova Ulica, which runs north to south, and Poljana Kraljice Jelene, which runs east to west—that divide the palace complex into four quarters. Each of its four walls has a main gate, the largest and most important being the northern Zlatna vrata (Golden Gate), which once opened onto the road to the Roman settlement of Salona. The entrance from the western wall was the Željezna vrata (Iron Gate), and the entrance through the eastern wall was the Srebrena vrata (Silver Gate). The Mjedena vrata (Bronze Gate) on the southern wall directly faces the sea and likely served as an entryway for sailors who docked by it during Roman times. More than 1,000 people still live within the walls, though the number is diminishing as the area becomes more tourism-focused. **TIP→ Hire an experienced**

Split's Old Town is actually located within the historic walls of Diocletian's Palace.

**private guide who can give you a walking tour in the early morning to experience the history of the palace walls without the crowds.** ✉ *Dioklecijanova 1, Grad* 🌐 *visitsplit.com/en/448/diocletian-palace.*

**Ethnographic Museum** (*Etnografski muzej*)
**HISTORY MUSEUM** | Occupying a splendid location within the walls of Diocletian's Palace, this museum displays traditional Dalmatian folk costumes and local antique furniture, among other objects that give visitors a look into everyday life in historic Dalmatia. ✉ *Iza Vestibula 4, Grad* ☎ *021/344–161* 🌐 *etnografski-muzej-split.hr* 🎫 *€3, free with Split-Card* 🕓 *Closed Sun.*

**Golden Gate** (*Zlatna vrata*)
**HISTORIC SIGHT** | Formerly the main entrance into Diocletian's Palace, the northern Golden Gate is the most visited of the palace's four gates, and just outside it stands Ivan Meštrović's gigantic bronze statue of Grgur Ninski (Bishop Gregory of Nin). During the 10th century, the bishop campaigned for the use of the Slav language in the Croatian Church, as opposed to Latin, and found himself at odds with Rome. This statue was created in 1929 and first placed on the nearby Peristil, then moved here in 1954. Note the big toe on the left foot, which is considered to be a good luck charm and has been worn gold and smooth through years of rubbing. ✉ *Dioklecijanova 7, Grad.*

**Marjan** (*Marjan Hill*)
**CITY PARK** | Situated on a 3½-km-long (2-mile-long) peninsula covered with pine trees and Mediterranean shrubs, 178-meter (584-foot) Marjan Hill has been a protected nature park since 1964. It's known as the "lungs of the city" because of all its greenery and the fact that locals flock to it on weekends as a nearby recreational area. Stunning views await at the top, with rocky beach areas circling the peninsula. Paths crisscrossing the grounds are suitable for biking and jogging. Eight small churches also dot Marjan Hill, including St. Jerome (sv. Jeronim), which was built in the 15th century into a rock face and includes

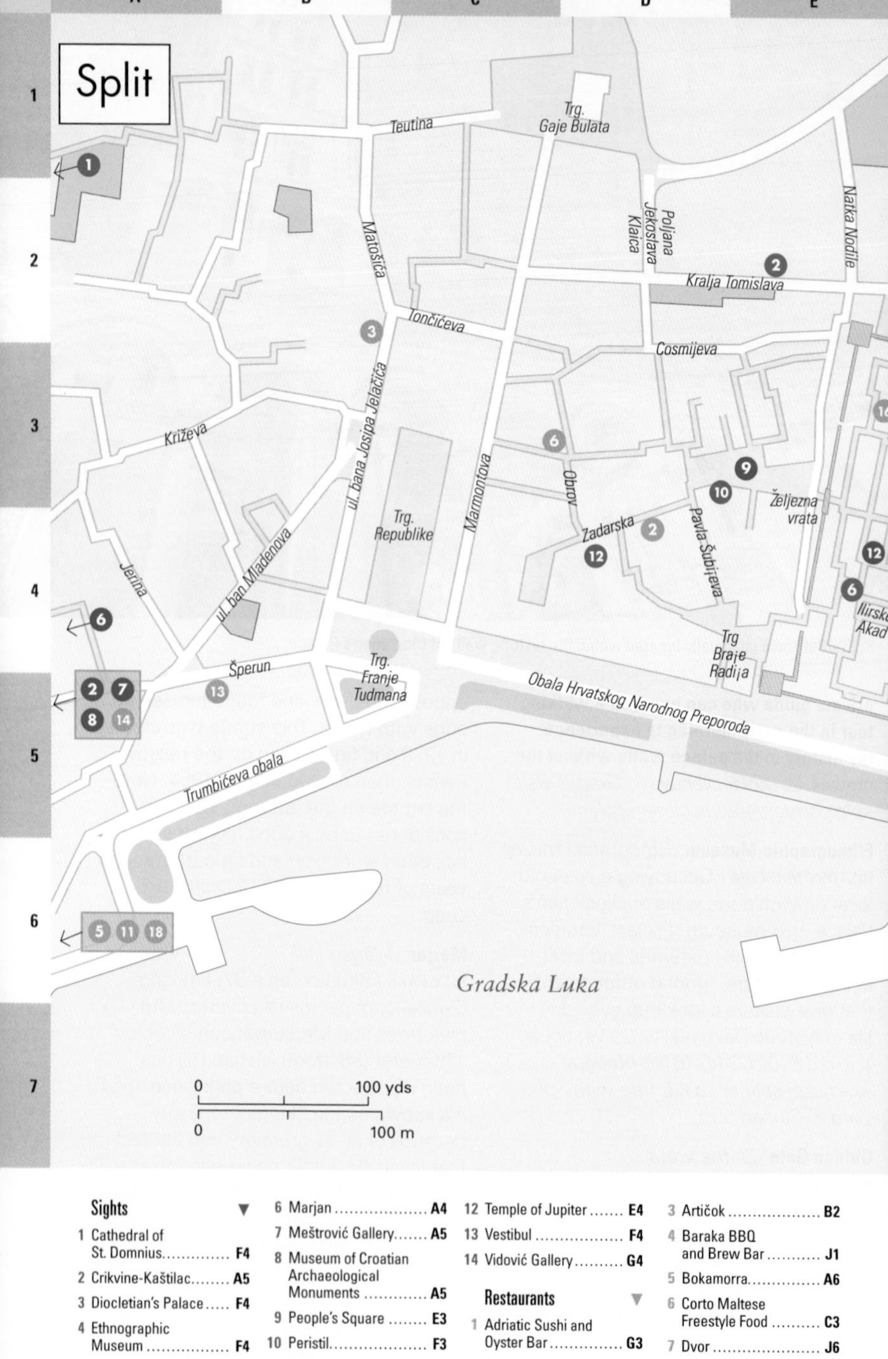


**Sights**

1 Cathedral of St. Domnius .......... F4
2 Crikvine-Kaštilac .......... A5
3 Diocletian's Palace .......... F4
4 Ethnographic Museum .......... F4
5 Golden Gate .......... F3
6 Marjan .......... A4
7 Meštrović Gallery .......... A5
8 Museum of Croatian Archaeological Monuments .......... A5
9 People's Square .......... E3
10 Peristil .......... F3
11 Salona .......... J1
12 Temple of Jupiter .......... E4
13 Vestibul .......... F4
14 Vidović Gallery .......... G4

**Restaurants**

1 Adriatic Sushi and Oyster Bar .......... G3
2 Apetit .......... D4
3 Artičok .......... B2
4 Baraka BBQ and Brew Bar .......... J1
5 Bokamorra .......... A6
6 Corto Maltese Freestyle Food .......... C3
7 Dvor .......... J6
8 Kadena .......... J6

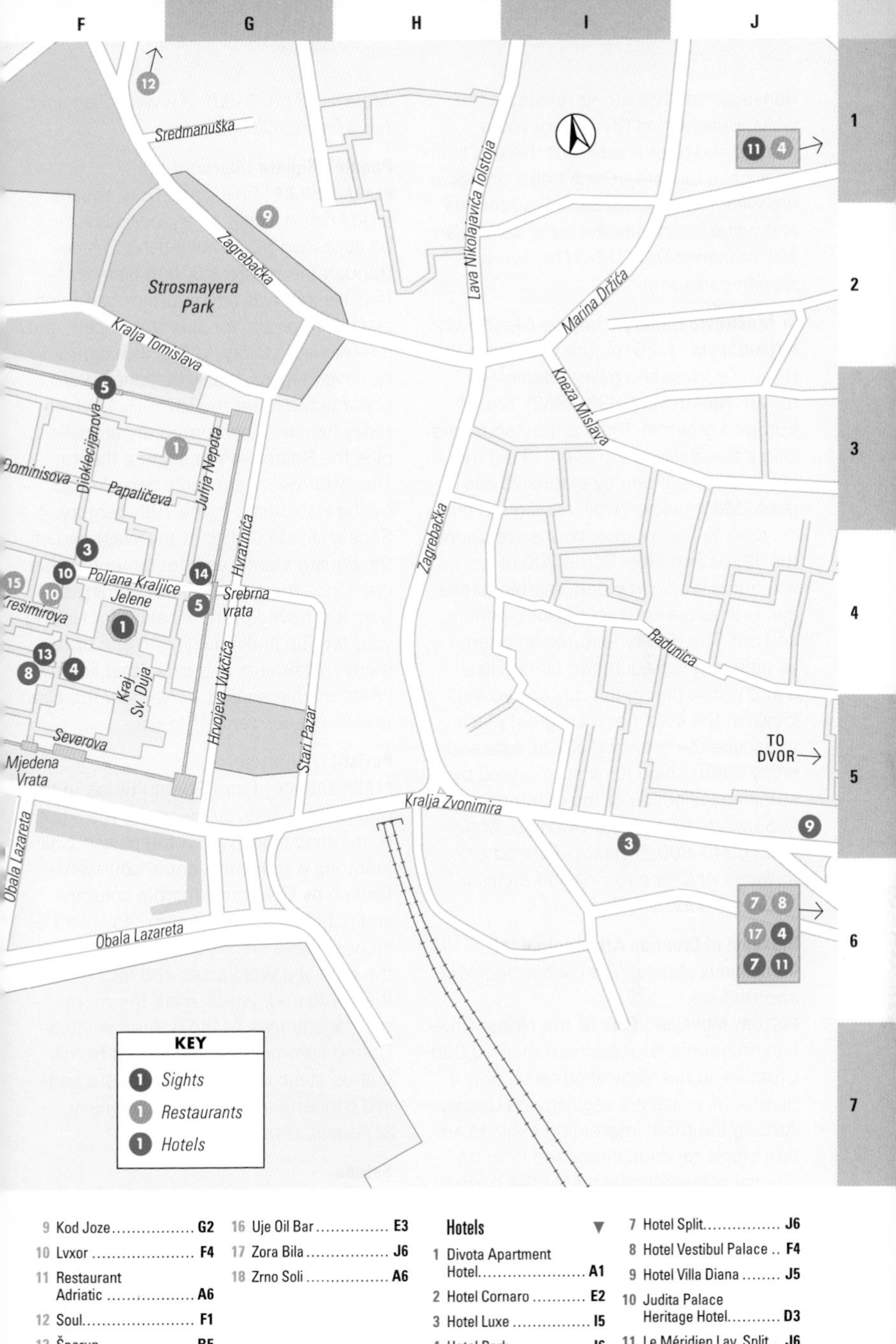


9 Kod Joze ................ G2
10 Lvxor .................... F4
11 Restaurant Adriatic ................. A6
12 Soul...................... F1
13 Šperun .................. B5
14 Teraca Vidilica .......... A5
15 To Je Tako ............... F4
16 Uje Oil Bar .............. E3
17 Zora Bila ................ J6
18 Zrno Soli ................ A6

**Hotels**

1 Divota Apartment Hotel..................... A1
2 Hotel Cornaro .......... E2
3 Hotel Luxe ............... I5
4 Hotel Park .............. J6
5 Hotel Peristil............ G4
6 Hotel Slavija ............ E4
7 Hotel Split............... J6
8 Hotel Vestibul Palace .. F4
9 Hotel Villa Diana ....... J5
10 Judita Palace Heritage Hotel.......... D3
11 Le Méridien Lav, Split .. J6
12 Marmont Heritage Hotel.......... D4

Renaissance-style stone reliefs on the walls. Beaches on Marjan are more relaxed and offer shade, but there is limited access for cars, which helps preserve the wilderness of the park. Bike rentals and water sports are available. ✉ *Marjan Hill, Marjan* ☎ *021/314–311* 🌐 *www.marjan-parksuma.hr.*

★ **Meštrović Gallery** (*Galerija Meštrović*)
**ART MUSEUM** | A 25-minute walk from the Riva, this must-see gallery dedicated to Ivan Meštrović (1883–1962), one of Europe's greatest 20th-century sculptors, is in a tranquil location overlooking the sea and surrounded by extensive gardens. Meštrović originally designed this building as his summer residence during the 1920s and '30s. Some 200 of his sculptural works in wood, marble, stone, and bronze are on display, both indoors and out. The gallery features an open-air café that is frequented by families and children during the day and young locals in the evening. It's a great place to escape the crowded city streets and enjoy a refreshing drink surrounded by a stunning collection of the master's work. ✉ *Šetalište Ivana Meštrovicá 46, Meje* ☎ *021/340–800* 🌐 *mestrovic.hr* 🎫 *€12, includes entrance to Crikvine-Kaštilac* 🕒 *Closed Mon.*

**Museum of Croatian Archaeological Monuments** (*Muzej hrvatskih arheološki spomenika*)
**HISTORY MUSEUM** | One of the oldest Croatian museums houses more than 20,000 Croatian archaeological artifacts, only a quarter of which are regularly on display. Among the most interesting exhibits are fine stone carvings decorated with traditional plaitwork designs. In the garden are several *stećci,* medieval monolithic tombstones. The museum also conducts archaeological excavations in the southern Croatian regions between the Cetina and Zrmanja rivers and has a large collection of cultural and historical guidebooks on early medieval monuments in Croatia. ✉ *Šetalište Ivana Meštrovića 18, Meje* ☎ *021/323–901* 🌐 *www.mhas-split.hr* 🎫 *Free* 🕒 *Closed Sun.*

**People's Square** (*Narodni trg*)
**PLAZA/SQUARE** | Split's main city square (also known locally as a *pjaca*) can be accessed from Diocletian's Palace through the western or Iron Gate. Historically this was an important gathering place for Splićani (people from Split), and it remains so today. In the 15th century, several major public buildings were constructed here: the Town Hall, which today houses a contemporary art gallery, plus the Rector's Palace and a theater. The latter two were sadly demolished by the Habsburgs in the 19th century. A Secessionist building at the west end of the square stands as a testament to that era. Once the city center of administration, it is now a prime location for kicking your feet up and indulging in one of the many restaurants and cafés that line the white marble square. ✉ *Narodni Trg, Grad* 🌐 *visitsplit.com/en/515/pjaca.*

**Peristil** (*Peristyle*)
**PLAZA/SQUARE** | From Roman times to the present day, this has been the main public meeting place within the palace walls, featuring a spacious central courtyard flanked by Corinthian marble columns and richly ornamented cornices linked by arches. There are six columns each on the east and west sides and four more at the south end, which mark the monumental entrance to the domed Vestibul. During summer, two costumed Roman guards stand watch on the square and live concerts take place occasionally. ✉ *Peristil, Grad.*

**Salona**
**RUINS** | The impressive ruins of the Roman city of Salona, Croatia's largest archaeological park, attract history buffs and anyone interested in seeing the ruins of an ancient forum, temples, towers, and a monumental amphitheater. It can take around an hour to stroll around the fully walkable (if less than perfectly maintained) site if you stop to

take photos—and you will. If you visit in summer, bring water and a sun hat, as little shade is offered, though this allows for striking unobstructed views of the surrounding mountains. The sprawling grounds, which grew into the largest city in Dalmatia after Romans captured an existing settlement in the 1st century BC, are said to be the birthplace of Emperor Diocletian. Salona was a powerful city until around AD 614, when Avar and Slav tribes moved in from the north and took over, forcing most of the city's inhabitants (about 60,000 in its heyday) southwest, where they founded Spalato, today's Split. The site is run by a branch of the Split Archaeological Museum. Salona is 8 km (5 miles) northeast of Split's center, about a 20-minute drive, near the modern town of Solin. Alternatively, the trip takes 30 minutes by bus, with buses departing every 30–60 minutes from the National Theater. ✉ *Don Frane Bulića 58, Solin* ☎ *021/212–900* 🌐 *www.armus.hr* 🎫 *€8* ⏲ *Closed Sun. and Nov.–Mar.*

**Temple of Jupiter** (*Jupiterov hram*)
**RELIGIOUS BUILDING** | Constructed as a place to worship the Roman god Jupiter under Emperor Diocletian's rule, the temple was later converted into a baptistery by Christians. The entrance is guarded by a black granite sphinx, one of several Diocletian brought to the palace from Egypt and the only one with its head intact. Many of the imported sphinxes (you can see another within the Baptistery) were damaged or destroyed as Christianity became the dominant religion. Inside, beneath the coffered barrel vault and ornamented cornice, the 11th-century baptismal font is adorned with a stone relief showing a medieval Croatian king on his throne. Directly behind it stands a bronze statue of St. John the Baptist, a work by Ivan Meštrović. ✉ *Kraj Svetog Ivana 2, Grad* 🌐 *visitsplit.com/en/526/temple-of-jupiter* 🎫 *€8, includes the Cathedral of St. Domnius.*

**Vestibul**
**NOTABLE BUILDING** | The cupola of this domed space would once have been decorated with marble and mosaics, but today there's only a round hole in the top of the dome, though it produces a stunning effect: picture the dark interior, the blue sky or a starlit night above and the tip of the cathedral's bell tower framed in the opening. The Vestibul is at the southern end of the Peristil. ✉ *Vestibul, Grad* 🌐 *visitsplit.com/en/525/vestibule.*

**Vidović Gallery** (*Galerija Vidović*)
**ART MUSEUM** | Emanuel Vidović (1870–1953) is acknowledged as one of Split's greatest painters, and in this gallery, you can see his original works as well as a reconstruction of his atelier. One section presents Vidović's paintings of Split landscapes, allowing you to experience the region through an artist's eyes. ✉ *Poljana Kraljice Jelene 1, Grad* ☎ *021/360–171* 🌐 *www.mgs.hr* 🎫 *€5* ⏲ *Closed Mon.*

## Beaches

**Bačvice Beach**
**BEACH** | **FAMILY** | The largest beach area in Split, a 10-minute walk east of the Old Town, has a shallow swimming area and is one of the few sandy beaches on the Dalmatian coast. If you don't mind the crowds, you can rent beach chairs and umbrellas, and you can also enjoy a string of cafés and bars along this stretch of coast. **Amenities:** food and drink; parking (fee); toilets. **Best for:** swimming. ✉ *Plaža Bačvice, Bacvica* 🎫 *Free.*

**Bene Beach**
**BEACH** | At this quieter rocky cove west of Split's Old Town, on the north side of Marjan Hill and a 20-minute drive from Diocletian's Palace, you can engage in a number of sports such as kayaking or tennis (there are courts). Bene is one of a string of beaches and coves dotting the Marjan Hill peninsula. **Amenities:** food and drink; showers; water sports. **Best**

**for:** swimming; walking. ✉ *Bene Beach, Marjan* 🎟 *Free.*

## Restaurants

### Adriatic Sushi and Oyster Bar

**$$$ | JAPANESE FUSION** | Some of the mainstays on this restaurant's menu come directly from the Adriatic Sea, and many of the ingredients are sourced from across the Croatian mainland. Located within the palace walls, this relaxed spot requires turning a few corners to find it but the food and setting are worth the hunt. **Known for:** local truffles; sea-to-table dishes made from daily catch; good Croatian wine list for sushi pairings. $ *Average main: €25* ✉ *Carrarina Poljana 4, Grad* ☎ *099/360–7777* 🌐 *adriatic-sushi.com.*

### Apetit

**$$ | MEDITERRANEAN** | Small and low-key, this modern clean-lined restaurant is tucked away on the second floor of a 15th-century palazzo just off the main square. It's known for traditional Adriatic dishes made with fresh, locally sourced, and high-quality ingredients. **Known for:** delicious tuna and squid; homemade tagliatelle; romantic setting in the city center. $ *Average main: €19* ✉ *Pavla Šubića 2, Grad* ☎ *021/332–549* 🌐 *www.apetit-split.hr.*

### Artičok

**$ | MODERN EUROPEAN** | This funky restaurant serves exciting food with well-selected ingredients and offers a pretty rooftop on which to enjoy it all. The name doesn't just mean "artichoke" in Croatian: it's also a literal blend of "art" and *čok* (a nibble) because guests can enjoy both a fabulous visual experience—whether dining inside or alfresco—and fun modern bites. **Known for:** Croatian classics with modern flair; super-fresh natural ingredients for breakfast, lunch, and dinner; hip art-oriented decor. $ *Average main: €14* ✉ *Trg Bana Josipa Jelačića 3, Split* ☎ *021/819–324* 🌐 *www.facebook.com/articoksplit.*

### Baraka BBQ and Brew Bar

**$ | BARBECUE** | Residents of Split favor this spot for its tasty barbecue, live rock and blues concerts, and—not least—its distance from the busy Old Town. If you need a break from seafood and crowds, stroll 15 minutes from the Diocletian's Palace complex to Baraka ("barracks") and sway to the music as you wash down delightfully smoky eats with regional craft beer. **Known for:** casual sit-down restaurant with live music every day except Sunday; BBQ platters for sharing; underground local vibe. $ *Average main: €11* ✉ *Vukovarska 35C, Gripe, Split* ☎ *095/222–9091* 🌐 *www.facebook.com/baraka.split* ⏲ *No lunch.*

### Bokamorra (*Bokamorra Pizzaurant & Cocktails*)

**$ | PIZZA** | For a fun atmosphere where you can let loose (often to a live DJ's tunes) as you watch your pizza being made in the open kitchen, head here. This pizzeria offers a menu covering the classics as well as unique options, and staff can recommend one (or a few) of the restaurant's signature cocktails to accompany your pizza of choice. **Known for:** music brings in younger crowds; distinctive house cocktails, served individually or in buckets; colorful cheerful space. $ *Average main: €13* ✉ *Obala Ante Trumbića 16, Split* ☎ *099/417–7191* 🌐 *www.facebook.com/bokamorra.*

### Corto Maltese Freestyle Food

**$$ | MEDITERRANEAN | FAMILY** | Decorated with a bit of the wit and themes from the beloved Italian comic strip about Corto Maltese, a seafaring adventurer, this lively restaurant offers traditional Croatian ingredients explained on a funny irreverent menu. The chef prepares the dishes in an open kitchen, and both the kitchen staff and waitstaff are engaging and eager to offer recommendations. **Known for:** vegetarian, pescatarian, and gluten-free options; healthy cooking techniques; exposed-brick interior and outdoor seating available. $ *Average main:*

*€20 ✉ Obrov 7, Split ☎ 021/587–201 🌐 www.facebook.com/corto.maltese.freestylefood.*

**Dvor**

**$$$ | MEDITERRANEAN** | Located in a quiet area a few miles out of town, Dvor offers up a superior rendition of Croatian seafood and professional service. Alfesco tables have outstanding views, and there's an outdoor grill as well as parking, which is a luxury in Split. **Known for:** stunning garden seating looking onto the sea; fresh Mediterranean fare with meat and seafood options; wine list with local and international options. *$ Average main: €25 ✉ Put Firula 14, Split ☎ 021/571–513 🌐 www.facebook.com/dvor.split.*

**Kadena**

**$$$$ | MEDITERRANEAN** | A seven-minute drive from the Old Town, Kadena serves Mediterranean seafood and meat dishes with a contemporary twist in a modern space. Don't miss Dalmatia's trademark *salata od hobotnice* (octopus salad) as an appetizer, and enjoy pairings with the rich wine list, full of local and global liquid treasures. **Known for:** new takes on traditional Dalmatian fare; views of the sea and boat docks; less noise and hubbub here than in the center. *$ Average main: €40 ✉ Ivana pl. Zajca 4, Split ☎ 021/389–400 🌐 restorankadena.com/en.*

**Kod Joze**

**$$ | MEDITERRANEAN** | Relaxed and romantic, this typical Dalmatian restaurant has exposed stone walls and heavy wooden furniture. With fewer frills than some of Split's more modern eateries, it stays true to tradition, offering the classic fare expected from an authentic spot. **Known for:** one of the oldest konobas in Split; good mix of seafood and meat mains; central location but a bit tricky to find. *$ Average main: €15 ✉ Sredmanuška 4, Manuš ☎ 021/347–397.*

**Lvxor**

**$$ | ECLECTIC** | This morning-to-night restaurant is the perfect place to sit over coffee or a glass of local wine and absorb the 2,000 years of magnificent architecture surrounding you in the Old Town. Pop in for an omelet in the morning to fuel up for the day, enjoying your surroundings before the streets fill up with crowds. **Known for:** up-close views of Diocletian's Palace; local and international options for various palates; people-watching and occasional live music. *$ Average main: €19 ✉ Kraj Svetog Ivana 11, Grad ☎ 021/341–082 🌐 lvxor.hr/en.*

**Restaurant Adriatic**

**$$$ | SEAFOOD** | Above the ACI Marina and at the foot of Marjan Hill, this mostly seafood restaurant has a light and airy, minimalist interior, as well as a summer terrace. In the spirit of slow food, the kitchen gives great care to fresh seasonal ingredients and presentation. **Known for:** fabulous sea views of yachts sailing in and out of port; classic Croatian fine dining with fish and meat options; previously owned by a local celebrity. *$ Average main: €25 ✉ Sustipanski Put 2, Zvoncac ☎ 021/398–560 🌐 www.restaurantadriatic.com.*

**Soul**

**$ | ECLECTIC** | Serving tasty tapas, brunch, and breakfast, Soul is a sweet place to pop into when you get tired of meandering through the Old Town. A five-minute walk from the Peristil, this affordable spot is loved by locals and offers dining in a courtyard between stone buildings or in a suavely decorated interior with wood paneling and records as wall art. **Known for:** location on a peaceful side street next to the center; international dishes with gluten-free options; live music some nights. *$ Average main: €8 ✉ Livanjska 18, Manuš ☎ 099/672–1241 🌐 soulsplit.info ⏲ Closed Sun.*

**Šperun**

**$$ | SEAFOOD** | This cozy restaurant has become popular because of its reasonably priced menu and quaint atmosphere. The Italo-Dalmatian menu features pasta dishes, seafood risottos, and old-fashioned local fish specialties such as *škampi na buzaru* (scampi in red sauce) and *pečene srdele s blitvom* (grilled sardines with chard). **Known for:** classic and basic Croatian fare; hearty fish stew for lunch; small dining room. *Average main: €15 Šperun 3, Varoš 021/346–999.*

**Teraca Vidilica**

$ | **CAFÉ** | This lounge-style café terrace is known for breathtaking views of the city and sea. Besides a full menu with soups and salads, as well as pasta, fish, and meat mains, they're open for coffee starting at 8 am—convenient if you need to wet your whistle after trekking up Marjan Hill. **Known for:** good spot for drinks; desserts to serve as post-Marjan hike sweet treats; nice place for a sunset dinner. *Average main: €14 Prilaz Vladimira Nazora 1, Marjan 095/583–3334.*

**To Je Tako**

$ | **MEXICAN** | Located in a narrow back alley, this cozy little space attracts a young fun crowd with its Dalmatian takes on Mexican and Latin American street food. It offers good food and great prices for lunch and dinner (along with brunch on the weekend), with some gluten-free options. **Known for:** must pay in cash; tasty margaritas otherwise not easily findable in Croatia; delicious tacos and empanadas. *Average main: €11 Kraj Svetog Ivana 5, Grad 021/553–021 www.tojetakosplit.com Closed Mon.*

**Uje Oil Bar**

$$ | **MEDITERRANEAN** | Stop in at Uje and sample some of the region's best olive oil, as well as a choice selection of Croatian cheese, prosciutto, and wine. This quaint back-alley tapas bar bases its menu on delicious olive oil, changes meals according to season, and sources many ingredients from local organic family farms. **Known for:** olive oils for sale by the bottle; good place to try a variety of small dishes; travelers' favorite in Old Town, so can get busy. *Average main: €22 Dominisova 6, Grad 095/200–8009 www.oilbar.hr.*

★ **Zora Bila**

$$ | **MEDITERRANEAN** | Two of the area's most beloved chefs, married couple Sandra and Dane Tahirović, spearhead the restaurant. Their haute edgy takes on classic Adriatic cuisine can be enjoyed with a sea view on the outdoor terrace. **Known for:** modern creative seafood and veggie pairings; closed between lunch and dinner; local classics accented with international flavors, such as cocoa and curry. *Average main: €20 Šetaliste Petra Preradovića 2, Split 021/782–711 zorabila.com.*

**Zrno Soli**

$$$$ | **MEDITERRANEAN** | Located right on the ACI Marina in Split, *Zrno Soli* means "grain of salt." This sophisticated spot serves elegantly presented fare—both fish and some meat options—including tasting menus with the freshest seafood options that can (and should) be accentuated with wine. **Known for:** great location for on-boat visitors; lovely views of ACI Marina; sommelier on hand to recommend wine and fish pairings. *Average main: €40 Uvala Baluni 8, Zvoncac 021/399–333 www.zrnosoli.hr.*

## Hotels

★ **Divota Apartment Hotel**

$$$ | **B&B/INN** | **FAMILY** | Set in a row of sun-bleached stone houses in the charming neighborhood of Veli Varoš, these beautifully renovated apartments and rooms have been lovingly reimagined to create a clean, bright, modern accommodation that preserves historic elements, like the steep tiled roofs and tiny shuttered windows. **Pros:** spa and yoga sessions; green and serene private garden on-site; peaceful location just northwest of Old Town. **Cons:** apartments are close together; free parking not available; bathrooms in some rooms are small. *Rooms from: €350 Plinarska 75,*

*Varoš ☎ 021/782–700 🌐 divota.hr 29 rooms 🍽 Free Breakfast.*

**Hotel Cornaro**

$$$$ | **HOTEL** | This sleek five-star hotel—offering rooms both functional and sophisticated, with wooden floors, earth-tone fabrics, and spacious bathrooms—is a short walk from the city's car-free center and close to all the main attractions. **Pros:** hearty buffet breakfast; spa and rooftop bar; tablets and smart TVs in rooms. **Cons:** parking is expensive; pricier food and drinks on-site; some rooms can be a little noisy. *$ Rooms from: €600 ✉ Sinjska 6 and Kralja Tomislava 9, Grad ☎ 021/644–200 🌐 cornarohotel.com 156 rooms 🍽 Free Breakfast.*

**Hotel Luxe**

$$$$ | **HOTEL** | **FAMILY** | Located just outside the palace walls and close to the port, this contemporary boutique hotel makes a great base for exploring Split and has spunkily designed rooms that are both sleek and well-insulated from the cacophony of the city. **Pros:** nearby free parking; well-organized and functional fitness and wellness area; generous breakfast buffet. **Cons:** no lunch and dinner on-site; some rooms on first floor have no sea view; not in a quiet neighborhood. *$ Rooms from: €500 ✉ Kralja Zvonimira 6, Grad ☎ 021/314–444 🌐 www.hotelluxesplit.com 30 rooms 🍽 Free Breakfast.*

**Hotel Park**

$$$$ | **HOTEL** | Smart and reliable, this five-star hotel in a 1921 building lies 10 minutes east of the city walls, overlooking Bačvice Bay. The rooms are modern and neatly furnished, and a pleasant restaurant terrace with palms offers views over the sea. **Pros:** close to both Old Town and beach; a sea view in some rooms; breakfast served on a lovely open-air terrace. **Cons:** pool and fitness center could be larger; small rooms feel a bit tight; parking can be difficult. *$ Rooms from: €400 ✉ Hatzeov Perivoj 3, Bacvica ☎ 021/406–400 🌐 www.hotelpark-split.hr 72 rooms 🍽 Free Breakfast.*

**Hotel Peristil**

$$ | **HOTEL** | One of only a handful of hotels within the palace walls, the comparatively affordable Peristil is located right behind the cathedral and just inside the Silver Gate, the city gate leading to the open-air market. **Pros:** budget-friendly compared to nearby hotels; hard-to-beat location; open-air restaurant terrace. **Cons:** smaller, less modern rooms; nearby parking difficult; limited facilities. *$ Rooms from: €250 ✉ Poljana Kraljice Jelene 5, Grad ☎ 021/329–070 🌐 hotelperistil.com 12 rooms 🍽 Free Breakfast.*

**Hotel Slavija**

$$$$ | **HOTEL** | Split's longest continuously operating hotel since it opened in 1900, Slavija occupies a historic building within the walls of Diocletian's Palace that offers affordable, basic, but comfortable rooms. **Pros:** building dates back to 16th century; varied nightlife options nearby; super-central location. **Cons:** some rooms can feel small; parking is not convenient; bar noise can get loud, especially during high season. *$ Rooms from: €400 ✉ Buvinina 2, Grad ☎ 021/323–840 🌐 www.hotelslavija.hr 25 rooms 🍽 Free Breakfast.*

**Hotel Split**

$$$ | **HOTEL** | Located on the outskirts of the city, this nearly net-zero-emission hotel offers guests comfortable modern rooms with sea views, as well as a private beach and an on-site restaurant. **Pros:** private beach has clear water; restaurant showcasing Mediterranean flavors; away from the city center's noise. **Cons:** on-site parking is on the pricier side; beach chairs for extra fee; 20-minute drive from the Old Town. *$ Rooms from: €280 ✉ Strožanačka 20, Podstrana ☎ 099/800–2000 🌐 www.hotelsplit.com 45 rooms 🍽 Free Breakfast.*

★ **Hotel Vestibul Palace**

$$$$ | **B&B/INN** | This intimate Old Town standout located directly within Diocletian's Palace features interiors that

have been carefully renovated to expose Roman stone and brickwork, along with more modern minimalist design details. **Pros:** cool history and standout architecture; superb concierge service; doesn't get more central than this. **Cons:** expensive for most of the season and often fully booked; rooms in two buildings (stay in main one versus annex); not great if you have trouble with stairs. *Rooms from: €630* *Iza Vestibula 4, Grad* *0800/048–2314* *vestibulpalace.com/en* *11 rooms* *Free Breakfast.*

**Hotel Villa Diana**

$$$ | **B&B/INN** | **FAMILY** | Just east of the Old Town, this hotel is a traditional Dalmatian stone building with green wooden shutters and guest rooms rustically decorated with wood and metal elements. **Pros:** five-minute walk from Diocletian's Palace; more affordable alternative to nearby larger, more expensive hotels; intimate setting that provides individual attention. **Cons:** often fully booked; located on a busy road leading into Split; parking costs extra. *Rooms from: €270* *Kuzmanićeva 3, Radunica* *021/482–460* *www.villadiana.hr* *6 rooms* *Free Breakfast.*

**★ Judita Palace Heritage Hotel**

$$$$ | **B&B/INN** | Only a couple steps away from Diocletian's Palace in a historical building, this is quite possibly the best lodging in the city with its rooftop terrace, library, bar, and a great view of the main Split square. **Pros:** deeply comfortable spacious rooms; unbeatable location; friendly and professional service. **Cons:** the hotel is small, so it's often full; parking not included; in the pedestrian-only area of Split, so can be hard to get to with baggage. *Rooms from: €500* *Narodni Trg 4, Grad* *021/420–220* *juditapalace.com* *11 rooms* *Free Breakfast.*

**Le Méridien Lav, Split**

$$$$ | **RESORT** | **FAMILY** | A world unto its own and set in landscaped gardens with a half mile of beach, this vast self-contained complex was Split's first five-star hotel, offering guests water-skiing, windsurfing, tennis courts, a luxurious spa and wellness center, an indoor pool, and an outdoor infinity pool overlooking the sea. **Pros:** beautifully designed modern interior; excellent sports facilities; rooms have floor-to-ceiling windows. **Cons:** 15-minute drive from the center of Split; meetings held here can lend to crowded feel; may seem too large and impersonal for some. *Rooms from: €450* *Grljevačka 2A, Podstrana* *021/500–500* *www.marriott.com/en-us/hotels/spumd-le-meridien-lav-split/overview* *378 rooms* *Free Breakfast.*

**Marmont Heritage Hotel**

$$$$ | **HOTEL** | Beautifully refurbished, this 15th-century stone building in the heart of the city offers guests a quiet retreat from the hustle and bustle of the Old Town. **Pros:** perfect base for walking the Old Town; rooftop terrace with a view; classic decor in earth tones and whites. **Cons:** no parking nearby; some rooms have unattractive views of adjacent walls or windows; rooms can feel small. *Rooms from: €500* *Zadarska 13, Grad* *021/308–060* *dlhv.hr* *21 rooms* *Free Breakfast.*

## Nightlife

### BARS

**Academia Club Ghetto**

**BARS** | With a colorful bohemian interior and a courtyard garden lit with flaming torches, Academia pulls in the cool, young, artsy crowd. It hosts occasional exhibitions and concerts. *Dosud 10, Grad* *021/346–879* *www.facebook.com/academiaclubghetto.*

**Charlie's Bar**

**BARS** | Twenty- and thirty-something travelers looking for a good time favor this boozy backpacker bar set within Diocletian's Palace. Big drinks-in-a-bucket, loud tunes, fun-loving staff, and cool hand-painted murals on the walls have people lined up at the door some nights. ✉ *Petra Kružića 5, Grad* ☎ *098/217–836* 🌐 *www.facebook.com/charliesbarsplit.*

★ **Marvlvs Library Jazz Bar**

**WINE BARS** | The name of this snazzy spot isn't a play on the word "marvelous," though the wine bar definitely is that; it's named after Marko Marulić, one of Split's most famous Renaissance-era writers. Conceptualized by Croatian-Argentinian poet Tin Bojanić and offering a delicious wine list, free library, and fantastic live music (think violins and acoustic guitars), Marvlvs is one of the coolest, artsiest, and twangiest places in town. ✉ *Papalićeva 4, Grad* 🌐 *www.facebook.com/marvlvs.*

**Teak**

**BARS** | Close to the Golden Gate, this small café-bar with an exposed-stone-work-and-wood interior is popular with highbrow locals who come here to leaf through the piles of international newspapers and magazines. It also has tables outside in summer for sipping your coffee, wine, or cocktail. ✉ *Majstora Jurja 11, Grad* ☎ *021/782–010.*

### CLUBS AND DISCOS

**Club 305 A.D.**

**DANCE CLUBS** | One of Split's most happening clubs offers all the party-hard requisites: a big dance floor, strobe lights, and blasting speakers—right within the Old Town. The name refers to the year construction of Diocletian's Palace was most likely finished. Open every night, it plays a mix of techno, pop, and hip-hop. Crozzies club-to-club crawl, run by Croatian-Australians and a favorite among young travelers, also kicks off from here every night before heading to Vanilla. ✉ *Trogirska 7, Grad* ☎ *091/305–3059* 🌐 *www.instagram.com/club_305_ad.*

**Mistral Beach Club**

**GATHERING PLACES** | Part of the Radisson Blu Resort & Spa, trendy Mistral is open to the public as well. Guests can rent sun chairs, cabanas, or VIP lounges here to relax and sunbathe, grab a cocktail and a bite to eat, and let loose to DJ entertainment. Live dancers are often present, too. The club closes at sunset, but the buzzy vibe drawing crowds of twenty- to forty-somethings is that of a club that replaced strobe lights with the sun's rays. ✉ *Šetalište Pape Ivana Pavla 2, Trstenik, Split* ☎ *021/303–030* 🌐 *mistralbeachclub.com.*

**Vanilla**

**DANCE CLUBS** | This veteran of Split's party scene, located about a 25-minute walk from the center of town near the public pools, often puts on concerts by big names in the regional music scene. It's also a trendy place for fans of all sorts of music from international hip-hop and techno to turbofolk and Croatian pop. ✉ *Mediteranskih Igara 21, Split* ☎ *099/831–3050* 🌐 *www.club-vanilla.hr.*

## Performing Arts

### FESTIVALS

**Split Summer Festival** (*Splitsko ljeto*)

**CULTURAL FESTIVALS** | Usually running annually from mid-July to mid-August, the festival includes a variety of open-air operas, classical music concerts, and dance and theatrical performances. Experience two highlights in one, as shows are held in gorgeous venues across the city, such as the Meštrović Gallery, Peristil, and a church on Marjan Hill. **TIP→ Tickets can be purchased online or from the theater box office. Book your accommodations in advance, as hotels fill up and rates go up during the festival.** ✉ *Croatian National Theater Split, Trg Gaje Bulata 1, Grad* ☎ *021/306–908 for ticket sales* 🌐 *www.splitsko-ljeto.hr/en.*

### FILM

★ **Bačvice Open-Air Cinema** (*Ljetno kino Bačvice*)

**FILM** | **FAMILY** | At this idyllic open-air summer cinema, first opened in 1956 in the woods above Bačvice Bay, films are projected among the pine trees as boats glide across the bay and crickets chirp in the background. Popcorn and drinks can be bought on-site, and the movies shown include major Hollywood pictures, Croatian movies, independent films, and kids' flicks. Check the schedule on the website, as some movies are not available with English subtitles. *Šetalište Petra Preradovića 6, Bacvica www.kinomediteran.hr.*

## Shopping

**Art Studio Naranča**

**ART GALLERIES** | Founded in 1983, family-run Naranča (the word means "orange") is a design studio showcasing and selling work by local artists. Here you'll find everything from graphic art and paintings to books and small handicrafts. *Majstora Jurja 5, Varoš 021/344–118 www.facebook.com/studionaranca.*

★ **City Marketplaces**

**MARKET** | Split is home to a marvelous array of open-air marketplaces selling all sorts of goods. Souvenir seekers beeline to the basements of Diocletian's Palace, full of stands selling jewelry, wood carvings, and other creative artisan handicrafts. Don't miss the expansive Pazar, also known as the City Marketplace or the Gradska tržnica, which sells everything from vegetables to clothes. The portion that stretches across Hrvojeva Street all along the eastern wall of Diocletian's Palace is known as Hrvojeva Street Market. Split's fish market (Ribarnica) on pedestrian Marmontova Street is also known as one of the best in the country.

★ **Croata Museum Concept Store**

**MIXED CLOTHING** | Located right on Peristil, Croata carries a wide range of specially designed and beautifully handcrafted ties. You'll learn about the history of the tie (which was invented in Croatia), too, because this concept store doubles as a museum. It also sells scarves and shawls for women. *Krešimirova 11, Grad 021/346–336 www.croata.hr.*

**Jaman Art**

**ART GALLERIES** | Danijel Jaman, a Croatian academic painter, showcases his vibrant work in this art-gallery-cum-shop in the Old Town. His fun, often pop culture–inspired prints are available for purchase as phone cases, posters, and other little souvenirs or as full-size original paintings. *Dobrić 14, Grad 098/322–719 www.jaman-art.com.*

**Kraš**

**CHOCOLATE** | One of Croatia's most famous brands creates delicious treats that can appease even the sweetest sweet tooth. The company has been producing high-quality chocolate, wafers, cocoa, and other goodies since 1911. One of the most popular gifts to give in Croatia is a Kraš Bajadera, a chocolate box comprised of gold-wrapped nutty nougat. *Martinjski Prolaz 1, Grad 021/346–138 www.kras.hr/en.*

**Vinoteka Terra**

**WINE/SPIRITS** | In this stone cellar close to Bačvice Bay, you can taste Croatian regional wines, accompanied by savory appetizers, before purchasing bottles. It also offers truffle products, olive oils, and a range of artistically designed wooden boxes for packing. *Prilaz Braće Kaliterna 6, Bacvica 021/314–800 www.vinoteka.hr.*

## Activities

### SAILING

Well connected to the rest of Europe by air, land, and sea—and within just a few hours' sailing of several of the Adriatic's most beautiful islands—Split is a major hub of the yacht-charter business in Dalmatia.

**ACI Marina Split**

**SAILING** | The 348-berth ACI Marina, southwest of the city center, stays open all year and is a base for dozens of

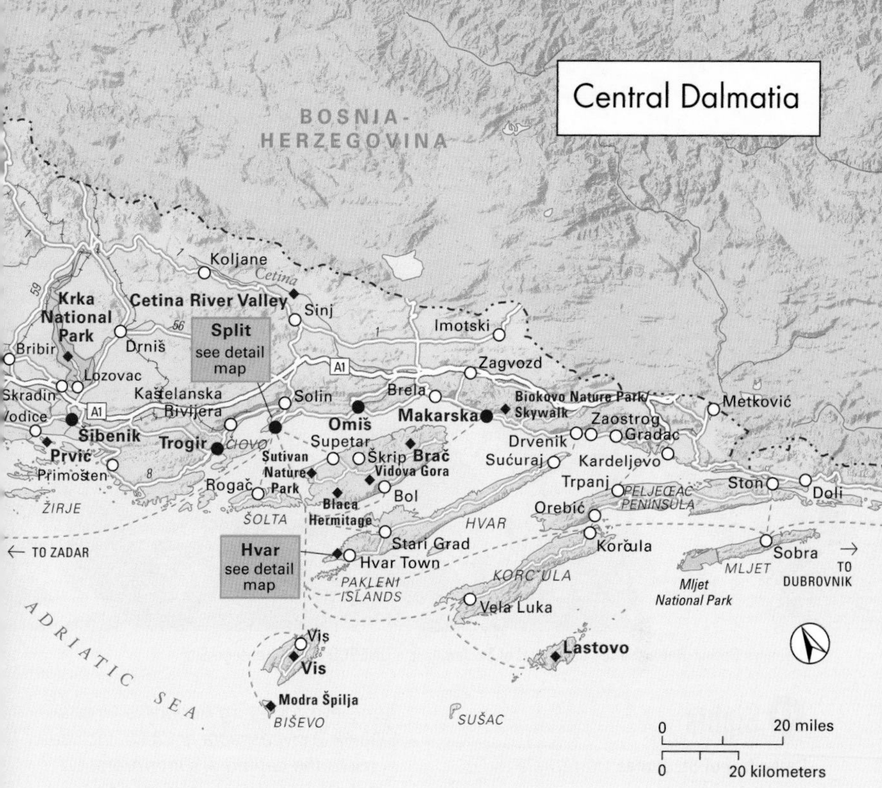


charter companies organizing sailing on the Adriatic. Prices for berth rental and amenities can be found on the website. The marina also features wonderful views of the Old Town and the surrounding Adriatic. ✉ *Uvala Baluni 8, Zvoncac* ☎ *098/398–850* 🌐 *aci-marinas.com.*

# Šibenik

*75 km (47 miles) northwest of Split.*

The trademark of Šibenik is its Gothic-Renaissance cathedral, built of pale-gray Dalmatian stone and designated a UNESCO World Heritage site, which stands on a raised piazza close to the seafront promenade. From here a network of narrow cobbled streets leads through the medieval quarter of tightly packed, terra-cotta-roof houses, and up to the ruins of a 16th-century hilltop fortress. The city is worth at least a day of exploring, if only to get lost wandering through its time-smoothed cobblestone streets and admiring its medieval architecture. More underrated—and therefore more peaceful—than some larger coastal towns, Šibenik is the perfect location for a romantic and peaceful getaway. It also makes a fantastic base for visiting the nearby waterfalls of Krka National Park. Sports fans may appreciate that NBA player Dražen Petrović (1964–1993), who played for the Portland Trail Blazers and New Jersey Nets, was born here.

### GETTING HERE AND AROUND

Šibenik is a one-hour drive from Split. Buses, which depart from Split for Šibenik every one to four hours, are another option. The narrow cobblestone streets of the city's Old Town are easily walkable.

Šibenik's Gothic-Renaissance Cathedral of St. James is a UNESCO World Heritage Site.

## Sights

**Cathedral of St. James** (*Katedrala sv. Jakova*)

**CHURCH** | Šibenik's most famous piece of architecture, the Cathedral of St. James was built in several distinct stages and styles between 1431 and 1535, and it's been a UNESCO World Heritage site since 2000. The lower level is the work of Venetian architects who contributed the finely carved Venetian-Gothic portals, whereas the rest of the building follows plans drawn up by local architect Juraj Dalmatinac, who proposed the Renaissance cupola. Note the frieze running around the outer wall, with 74 faces carved in stone from the island of Brač. One of the cathedral's highlights, the tiny baptistery with minutely chiseled stone decorations was designed by Dalmatinac but executed by Andrija Aleši. Admission includes entry to the worthwhile interpretation center Civitas Sacra, which has an interactive exhibition of sacral treasures and art. It's a three-minute walk from the cathedral in the Galbiani Palace (✉ *Kralja Tomislava 10*). ✉ *Trg Republike Hrvatske, Šibenik* 🌐 *civitassacra.hr* 🎫 *€5, includes entry to the cathedral's interpretation center* 🕒 *Interpretation center closed Sun.*

**Fortress of St. Michael** (*Tvrđava sv. Mihovila*)

**HISTORIC SIGHT** | This fortress dating back to the 11th century guards the city below from atop a steep rocky hill. Re-fortified over the years, it was once the city's main point of defense. A climb to the top grants you vistas of the sea, surrounding islands, and the medieval town. On occasion, special events and concerts are held on an open-air stage in the fortress. ✉ *Zagrađe 21, Šibenik* 🌐 *www.tvrdja-va-kulture.hr/en* 🎫 *€10.*

**Fortress of St. Nicholas** (*Tvrđava sv. Nikole*)

**HISTORIC SIGHT** | Standing at the entrance of Šibenik's St. Anthony's Channel, the Fortress of St. Nicholas sits on the islet of Ljuljevac and is an imposing Renaissance-era Venetian-style building. Constructed in 1540, the fortress was added to the UNESCO World Heritage list in 2017. It is definitely worth a visit from land—or better yet, from the sea via kayak. ✉ *Šibenik* 🌐 *www.kanal-svetog-ante.com/en* 🎫 *€21, includes entry and boat transfer.*

**Vinoplod Winery** (*Vinoplod vinarija*)
**WINERY** | The recipient of many awards for its bottles of the famous Babić wine variety—today a symbol of Primošten, Šibenik, and all of Croatia—Vinoplod Winery can be contacted for tours and tastings. ✉ *Velimira Škorpika 2, Šibenik* ☎ *022/334–011* 🌐 *www.vinoplod-vinarija.hr.*

## Restaurants

**Konoba Nostalgija**
**$$ | MEDITERRANEAN** | This excellent spot gives traditional Dalmatian meals a modern and creative twist atypical for a konoba in Dalmatia. Nostalgija (meaning "nostalgia") also provides a drink menu with local wines and craft beer, as well as cocktails based on Croatian classics such as rakija. **Known for:** owners source ingredients from local market; alfresco dining on the terrace; wines local to Šibenik. $ *Average main: €20* ✉ *Biskupa Foska 11, Šibenik* ☎ *022/661–269* 🌐 *www.facebook.com/konobanostalgija* 🕒 *Closed Sun. No lunch.*

★ **Pelegrini**
**$$$$ | MEDITERRANEAN** | A carefully restored 14th-century palazzo opposite the historic Cathedral of St. James is home to this magnificent award-winning restaurant. The seasonal six-course prix-fixe tasting menu (there is no à la carte option) features traditional Dalmatian cuisine that is innovatively prepared and beautifully presented, with exquisite flavor being the restaurant's guiding principle. **Known for:** thoughtful wine list; stunning courtyard seating; private on-boat fine dining by request. $ *Average main: €185* ✉ *Jurja Dalmatinca 1, Šibenik* ☎ *022/213–701* 🌐 *pelegrini.hr/en* 🕒 *Closed Sun. No lunch.*

## Hotels

**Agroturizam Kalpić**
**$ | B&B/INN | FAMILY** | Experience the peacefulness of the Croatian countryside at the Kalpić family estate while exploring both Šibenik and nearby Krka National Park. **Pros:** shady garden for kids to play; nice break from the city; traditional dishes from the restaurant. **Cons:** must have a car to reach it; too rural for city folk; nightlife options a bit far away. $ *Rooms from: €120* ✉ *Kalpići 4, Lozovac* ☎ *091/584–5520* 🌐 *kalpic.com* 🛏 *14 rooms* 🍽 *Free Breakfast.*

**Hotel Bellevue**
**$$ | HOTEL** | Sitting on the city waterfront, right next to the historic center, this modern four-star hotel offers a range of elegant rooms and suites. **Pros:** most rooms have sea or city views; pool, sauna, and fitness room; tasty breakfast with vegetarian options. **Cons:** parking fee not included and spaces can be tight; waterfront but a 10-minute walk from a beach; central location can mean some noisiness. $ *Rooms from: €210* ✉ *Obala Hrvatske Mornarice 1, Šibenik* ☎ *022/646–400* 🌐 *www.bellevuehotel.hr* 🛏 *48 rooms* 🍽 *Free Breakfast.*

## Nightlife

**Azimut**
**DANCE CLUBS** | On the city's waterfront, Azimut is an underground bar within the otherwise mostly peaceful walls of historic Šibenik. Its focus is on alternative music, covering genres from rock to techno (often live) all night. With a spacious dance floor and a number of courtyard tables, this hidden gem also offers delicious cocktails. ✉ *Obala Palih Omladinaca 2, Šibenik* 🌐 *www.facebook.com/Azimut.sibenik.*

### En Vogue Beach Club

**COCKTAIL LOUNGES** | While you can stay at the adjacent Amadria Park Jure Resort (Amadria Park Hotels owns the club), people like to visit this beach club just to party poolside and seaside at the same time. The pool complex is right next to the sea and dotted with bars, restaurants, and snack stands, all of which you can enjoy while you dip your feet in the water. Though it closes at 9 pm, En Vogue has a true party vibe. It's a 15-minute drive outside of the city center. ✉ *Hoteli Solaris 86, Šibenik* ☎ *022/362–963* 🌐 *www.amadriapark.com/attraction/en-vogue-beach-club.*

# Prvić

*4½ nautical miles west of Šibenik by ferry.*

Beyond Šibenik Bay lie the splendidly scattered islands of the Šibenik Archipelago, five of which—Zlarin, Prvić, Kaprije, Obonjan, and Žirje—are accessible by ferry from Šibenik and can provide a quick taste of island life. The nearest, Zlarin and Prvić, can be visited as day trips, but if you intend to stay overnight, Prvić is the better equipped, with a lovely small hotel, rooms to rent, and about half a dozen rustic eateries. Tiny car-free Prvić is just 3 km (2 miles) long and has a year-round population of around 200. Its two main villages, Prvić Luka and Šepurine, are made up of centuries-old traditional stone cottages (built from the UNESCO-designated art of dry-stone walling) and connected by a lovely footpath leading through a stand of pine trees that takes about 15 minutes to walk. Though some locals work in Šibenik, others still make a living on the island by cultivating figs, olives, and vines and by fishing. There are no large overcrowded beaches, but plenty of small secluded pebble coves with crystal clear water are perfect for swimming.

### GETTING HERE AND AROUND

Through high season, five to eight daily ferries depart from Šibenik, with frequency depending on the day; Sundays and holidays have fewer. Two routes are available and also vary depending on the day, so check timetables on the ferry website or directly at a ticket booth. Generally a ride from Šibenik to Zlarin takes around 30 minutes, to Prvić Luka around 45 minutes, to Prvić Šepurine one hour, and to Vodice 70 minutes. Routes then return to Šibenik, doing the same journey in reverse. Alternatively, you can take a water taxi from the Šibenik seafront to Prvić Luka for a hefty charge that can exceed €100; the ferry charges around €5.

## Sights

### Faust Vrančić Memorial Center

**HISTORY MUSEUM** | Born in Šibenik, Faust Vrančić (1551–1617) was an inventor, polymath, philosopher, and lexicographer whose legacy is examined in this modern museum in Prvić Luka. He is thought to have invented the first functional parachute, outlining it in a drawing titled "Homo Volans–Flying Man" in his book of inventions *Machinae Novae* (*New Machines*). Born well-off, Vrančić spent summers in his family mansion on Prvić, where he also escaped to avoid the plague that hit Šibenik several times during this period. He passed away in Venice, but he was buried on Prvić according to his wishes. ✉ *Ulica I 1A, Prvic* ☎ *091/524–0739* 🌐 *mc-faustvrancic.com* 🎟 *€5* ⏲ *Closed Sun. May, June, Sept., and weekends Oct.–Apr.*

## Restaurants

### ★ Maslina

**$$** | **MEDITERRANEAN** | On the waterfront of Prvić Harbor, Maslina ("Olive") is an authentic *konoba* with a pretty tree-covered stone patio that is surrounded by fairy lights and looks out onto the sea.

You can try all of the classics here, from fresh-caught shellfish to hearty Dalmatian stews. **Known for:** cozy inviting atmosphere; natural decor of greenery and stones; outstanding oysters and mussels. *Average main: €15 Ulica II br. 1, Prvic 091/736–3377 www.facebook.com/konobamaslina No lunch.*

## Hotels

**Hotel Maestral**

**$ | HOTEL | FAMILY** | This 19th-century stone building on the seafront in Prvić Luka was once the village school, and after a careful restoration it reopened as a boutique hotel with rooms that have wooden floors, modern minimalist furniture, and some exposed stone walls. **Pros:** delightful peaceful island location; small enough that guests receive individual attention; good restaurant on the harbor. **Cons:** if you miss the ferry, you could end up stranded; often fully booked; limited nightlife possibilities. *Rooms from: €100 Ulica IX br. 1, Prvic 022/448–300 www.hotelmaestral.com/en 16 rooms Free Breakfast.*

## Activities

### SWIMMING

**Swim Trek**

**SWIMMING** | This Britain-based agency has a pretty straightforward motto: "Ferries are for wimps—let's swim." The company offers a challenging and unusual one-week holiday, including swimming around the islands of the Šibenik Archipelago. Participants cover an average of 3 km (almost 2 miles) per day, including the stretch between the islands of Zlarin and Prvić. Overnight accommodation is in the Hotel Maestral in Prvić Luka. *1273/739–713 in U.K. www.swimtrek.com From €1,280 for all-inclusive trip.*

# Krka National Park

*20 km (12 miles) north of Šibenik.*

The Krka River cuts its way through a gorge shaded by limestone cliffs and dense woodland, tumbling down toward the Adriatic in a series of spectacular pools and waterfalls. The most beautiful stretch has been designated as Krka National Park.

### GETTING HERE AND AROUND

Drive from Šibenik to the town of Skradin, then take a 25-minute boat ride up the Krka River on a national park ferry. Alternatively, skip the boat ride and hike your way past the waterfalls.

## Sights

★ **Krka National Park** (*Nacionalni park Krka*)

**NATIONAL PARK | FAMILY** | A series of seven waterfalls are the main attraction here, the most spectacular being Skradinski buk, where 17 cascades of water fall 40 meters (131 feet) into an emerald-green pool. Moving upriver, a trail of wooden walkways and bridges crisscrosses its way through the woods and along the river to the Roški slap (waterfall), passing by the tiny island of Visovac, home to a Franciscan monastery that can be visited by boat. On the islet, there is also an old mill with a museum that demonstrates the different ways the mill was used centuries ago. From here, it's easier to understand how the power of these waters inspired Nikola Tesla, whose boyhood home is not far from the national park. In 1895 the first hydroelectric plant became operational here, only two days after Tesla's hydroelectric plant on Niagara Falls. This made the residents of Skradin the first Eastern European citizens to have electricity.

More than 860 species of plant life have been identified throughout the park, and more than 200 bird species live there,

Within Krka National Park is the island of Visovac, home to a Franciscan monastery.

making it one of Europe's most valuable ornithological areas. Something many visitors miss is a hawk training center, where you can observe birds of prey being trained by ornithological experts. For bird enthusiasts there is also the Gudućа Nature Reserve, where various species are closely studied and can be observed from boats. The Krka National Park office is located in Šibenik. For more active travelers, there is a 8½-km (5-mile) hiking trail, going Sitnice–Roški slap–Oziđana Cave, that takes about 2½ hours and has educational panels along the way explaining plant and animal life, geological phenomena, and historic sites.

Of the five entrances into the park, the easiest and most impressive route of arrival is to drive from Šibenik to the town of Skradin, then take a 25-minute boat ride up the Krka River on a national park ferry (included in the price of entry). The ferry will bring you to the park entrance close to the Skradinski buk waterfall, and from there you can get off and take a walk along the wooden bridges and explore the park further. **TIP→ Note that swimming is not allowed in the park.** There are several restaurants and snack bars, plus wooden tables and benches for picnics. For a full meal, your best bet is to return to Skradin, a town that dates back to Roman times and is well worth a look. ✉ *Lozovac* ☎ *022/201–777* 🌐 *www.np-krka.hr* 🎫 *€40 June–Sept.; €20 Oct.; €7 Nov.–Dec.; €6.65 Jan.–Mar.; €15 Apr.–May.*

## Restaurants

**Cantinetta**

**$$ | MEDITERRANEAN | FAMILY** | Hidden away in Skradin Bay, in a quiet location where the fresh waters from Krka National Park flow into the sea, Cantinetta is recognized among local residents as one of Skradin's best places to eat. Having grown from a humble family konoba to a serious culinary destination, this restaurant takes great pride in its well-preserved old recipes, passed on from generation to generation. **Known for:** pretty courtyard under stone walls and brick arches; excellent veal risotto (order in advance); meals can take a while to cook. $ *Average main: €18* ✉ *Aleja Skradinskih Svilara 7, Skradin* ☎ *091/150–6434* 🌐 *cantinetta.hr/en.*

**Zlatne Školjke**

$$ | **SEAFOOD** | **FAMILY** | This restaurant in a natural stone building is a favorite among the yachting crowd, in part because of its location near the ACI Marina Skradin. It's aptly named *Zlatne školjke,* which means "golden shells," because of the plethora of shellfish farms nearby. **Known for:** super fresh shellfish, from oysters to scampi; terrace overlooking the water; Skradin specialties such as almond cake. $ *Average main: €20* ✉ *Grgura Ninskog 9, Skradin* ☎ *022/771–022* 🌐 *www.facebook.com/ZlatneSkoljke.*

## Hotels

**Hotel Bonaca**

$$ | **HOTEL** | The second hotel to open in Skradin, the four-star Bonaca offers rooms with modern neutral-hued decor, an outdoor pool, and a sunbathing terrace. **Pros:** vistas of the picturesque town harbor; rooms with balconies; most modern hotel in town. **Cons:** small breakfast space; restaurant is separate from hotel building; one of the area's pricer lodgings. $ *Rooms from: €230* ✉ *Zagrađe 21, Skradin* ☎ *022/661–284* 🌐 *www.facebook.com/villabonacaskradin* *12 rooms* *Free Breakfast.*

**Hotel Skradinski Buk**

$ | **HOTEL** | **FAMILY** | Friendly and family-run, this simple hotel in a refurbished stone town house in the center of Skradin was the first hotel in town. **Pros:** in a pretty village close to Krka National Park; parking on the hotel grounds; solid breakfast options. **Cons:** basic old-school design; limited nightlife in Skradin; prices can spike during high season. $ *Rooms from: €140* ✉ *Burinovac 2, Skradin* ☎ *022/771–771* 🌐 *www.facebook.com/hotelskradinskibuk.hr* *29 rooms* *Free Breakfast.*

# Trogir

*27 km (17 miles) west of Split.*

On a small island no more than a few city blocks in length, the beautifully preserved medieval Old Town of Trogir is connected to the mainland by one bridge and to the outlying island of Čiovo by a second. The settlement dates back to the 3rd century BC, when it was colonized by ancient Greek seafarers who named it Tragurion. It later flourished as a Roman port. With the fall of the Western Roman Empire, it became part of Byzantium and then followed the shifting rulers of the Adriatic. In 1420, the Venetians moved in, staying until 1797. Today, it's a UNESCO World Heritage site, surviving principally from tourism.

You can explore Trogir's enchanting Old Town in about an hour on foot. A labyrinth of narrow cobbled streets centers on Narodni trg, the main square, where the most notable buildings are located, including the 15th-century loggia and clock tower, the Venetian-Gothic Ćipiko Palace, and the Cathedral of St. Lawrence, with its elegant bell tower. The south-facing seafront promenade is lined with cafés, ice-cream parlors, and restaurants, and there are several small old-fashioned hotels that offer a reasonable alternative to accommodations in Split. Note that because the city center spans just under 16 acres, it can feel extra crowded in high season.

### GETTING HERE AND AROUND

It can be more convenient and affordable to take a short boat ride from Split to Trogir if visiting for a day, as parking is limited and expensive during high season. Bura Line (🌐 *buraline.com*) offers several departures each way daily during high season.

★ **Cathedral of St. Lawrence** (*Katedrala sv. Lovre*)
**CHURCH | FAMILY** | In this remarkable example of Romanesque architecture, whose first construction dates back to the early 13th century, the most striking detail is the main (west) portal, adorned with a superb Romanesque sculpture by the Croatian master known as Radovan. The great door, flanked by a pair of imperious lions that form pedestals for figures of Adam and Eve, is framed by a fascinating series illustrating the daily life of peasants in a kind of medieval comic strip. In the dimly lit Romanesque interior, the 15th-century chapel of St. John Orsini (Sveti Ivan Orsini) of Trogir features statues of saints and apostles in niches facing the sarcophagus, on which lies the figure of St. John. The bell tower, built in successive stages—the first two stories Gothic, the third Renaissance—offers stunning views across the ancient rooftops. Note that tickets can't be purchased online. **TIP→ Be sure to also look down as you stroll through and gaze at the amazing structures at eye level and below—the marble sculptures and checkerboard floors make for a memorable view.** ✉ *Trg Ivana Pavla II, Trogir* ☎ *021/885–628 Trogir Tourist Board* 🎫 *€5, includes bell tower.*

**Trogirska Riva**
**PROMENADE** | Trogir's *riva* (waterfront walkway) is not as expansive or bustling as Split's, but it's worth a leisurely stroll that takes about five minutes—or longer, if you detour into one of the restaurants or cafés dotting the promenade. Flanked by palm trees and the city walls on one side and the sea on the other—with Čiovo Island peeking out between cruise ships and yachts across the bay—Trogir's riva leads up to to the 15th-century Venetian Kamerlengo Fortress, which can be climbed for a seagull's-eye view of the city. ✉ *Trg Ivana Pavla II, Trogir.*

**Calebotta**
**$$ | MEDITERRANEAN** | Retreat to a quiet closed-in courtyard just a minute away from the main square and allow the Calebotta family to wow you with their first-class service and menu of fresh ingredients. The Dalmatian menu can seem long, so feel free to ask your waiter for recommendations. **Known for:** a century ago, the space housed the area's first movie theater; menu has both international and Dalmatian fish and meat options; secluded courtyard garden. $ *Average main: €22* ✉ *Gradska 23, Trogir* ☎ *091/625–3102* 🌐 *calebotta.com.*

**Konoba TRS**
**$$$ | MEDITERRANEAN** | With a tremendous sense of style, family-owned TRS combines traditional food with modern ingredients that are freshly sourced from the owner's family farm in a nearby village. The unusual combinations are a welcome change and still subtle enough to allow the strength of the traditional Dalmatian food to dominate. **Known for:** well-balanced menu of hearty meat, lighter fish, and a range of seafood; local specialty ingredients such as sheep's cheese and sea urchins; excellent Adriatic fish. $ *Average main: €28* ✉ *Matije Gupca 14, Trogir* ☎ *021/796–956* 🌐 *www.konoba-trs.com.*

**Olive**
**$$$ | MEDITERRANEAN | FAMILY** | Based in an elegant stone building in the Old Town, this welcoming family-run restaurant (formerly called Vanjaka) serves Dalmatian specialties. Sit outside on the open-air terrace, or take a table in the intimate air-conditioned dining room. **Known for:** traditional tastes but modern presentation; alfresco dining with view of Cathedral of St. Lawrence; good cocktails and local wines. $ *Average main: €26* ✉ *Radovanov Trg 9, Trogir* ☎ *097/615–1044* 🌐 *www.facebook.com/restaurant.olive.trogir* ⏲ *Closed Sun.*

## Hotels

**Domus Maritima**

$$ | **B&B/INN** | This small, chic, family-run bed-and-breakfast in a beautifully renovated 400-year-old villa is perfectly located a few minutes' walk from the center of bustling Trogir and just across the street from the ACI Marina Trogir. **Pros:** relaxing Mediterranean garden; free parking nearby; some rooms have sea views or balconies. **Cons:** modern style may not appeal to those who want traditional decor; noisy at night during summer; rooms on the small side. *Rooms from: €150 ✉ Put Cumbrijana 10, Trogir ☎ 091/513–7802 🌐 domusmaritima.com 9 rooms No Meals.*

**Hotel Fontana**

$ | **HOTEL** | Located in the Old Town and overlooking the Trogir Channel, the hotel is in an old stone building that's been refurbished into a small family-run hotel above a popular restaurant. **Pros:** on seafront promenade; more affordable alternative to other lodgings nearby; arranges airport transfers (at cost). **Cons:** rooms tend to be small; basic, somewhat outdated furnishings; surrounding cafés get noisy at night. *Rooms from: €110 ✉ Obrov 1, Trogir ☎ 021/885–744 14 rooms Free Breakfast.*

**Hotel Pašike**

$$ | **B&B/INN** | Inherited and restored antique furniture fills this charming hotel in a typical Dalmatian stone building in the heart of the Old Town. **Pros:** lovely Old Town location; free airport transfers; good restaurant with occasional live Dalmatian music. **Cons:** some rooms are dark; no elevator; parking is paid and must be reserved in advance. *Rooms from: €150 ✉ Splitska 4, Trogir ☎ 021/885–185 🌐 hotelpasike.com 14 rooms Free Breakfast.*

**Hotel Vila Sikaa**

$$ | **B&B/INN** | This historical villa on Čiovo Island has been converted into a small family-run hotel with wood-floor rooms, some with a sea view and whirlpool tub. **Pros:** seafront location with great views of Trogir's Old Town; welcoming atmosphere; beautiful 18th-century building. **Cons:** front rooms can be noisy (from loud music and motorbikes); basic furnishings in rooms; parking can be difficult on island. *Rooms from: €150 ✉ Obala Kralja Zvonimira 13, Trogir ☎ 021/789–240 🌐 www.vila-sikaa-r.com 10 rooms Free Breakfast.*

**Tragos**

$ | **HOTEL** | Occupying an 18th-century Baroque palace in the heart of the Old Town, Tragos has simply furnished modern rooms, decorated in warm hues of cream, yellow, and orange; each has a spacious tiled bathroom. **Pros:** one-minute walk from Cathedral of St. Lawrence; friendly and helpful staff; good restaurant with hearty food. **Cons:** rooms can be noisy from downstairs restaurant; no elevator means luggage must be carried; parking can be challenging. *Rooms from: €110 ✉ Budislavićeva 3, Trogir ☎ 021/884–729 🌐 www.tragos.hr 12 rooms Free Breakfast.*

# Omiš and the Cetina River Valley

*28 km (17½ miles) southeast of Split.*

An easy day trip from Split, Omiš is a pleasant seaside town with a colorful open-air market and a conglomeration of old stone houses backed by a hilltop medieval fortress. What also makes it special is its location at the mouth of a dramatic gorge where the Cetina River meets the Adriatic Sea. The river carves a spectacular canyon with the fertile green Cetina River Valley at the bottom, surrounded by sheer limestone cliffs. Tumbling its way down toward the sea over a series of rapids, the river is a popular and challenging site for rafting and rock climbing. An asphalt road follows the course of the river upstream from Omiš, leading to a few pleasant waterside restaurants. Omiš is the location of the annual Festival of Dalmatian Klapa, which attracts singers of the UNESCO-protected music style from all over Croatia.

### GETTING HERE AND AROUND

Omiš is an easy day trip from Split by rental car or bus, with multiple buses running between the cities daily.

## Sights

### ★ Mila Gojsalić Statue

**PUBLIC ART** | Located at a stunning viewpoint, this statue by Ivan Meštrović honors legendary 16th-century heroine Mila Gojsalić, born in Poljice at a time when Croatia faced Ottoman attacks. Myth says she seduced an Ottoman general and then set fire to his camp after he fell asleep. Per legend, she perished in the fire or evaded capture by jumping to her death from the cliffside where the statue now stands. The site, a still relatively well-kept secret, offers awe-inspiring views of the town and the mouth of the Cetina River. It's an eight-minute drive north from Omiš center via an uphill road with four hairpin turns; going by car is safer than the 80-minute hike up the road. Parking is limited. ✉ *Omiš* 🎫 *Free.*

## Restaurants

### Radmanove Mlinice

**$ | EASTERN EUROPEAN | FAMILY** | The restaurant in this renovated 18th-century water mill is well-known for miles around for its Dalmatian and grill dishes, served at tables under trees in a pretty riverside garden. It lies 6 km (4 miles) from Omiš, up the Cetina River Valley. **Known for:** classic Croatian cuisine; management can organize outdoor excursions; payment is cash only. [$] *Average main: €14* ✉ *Omiš* ✣ *Cetina River Valley regional road, in the direction of Zadvarje* ☎ *091/188–8808* 🌐 *mlinice.com* ⏲ *Closed Oct.–Apr.*

### Restoran Kaštil Slanica

**$$ | MEDITERRANEAN** | Seafood and freshwater fish specialties, as well as traditional Croatian peka, are offered at this restaurant with a large riverside terrace and an indoor dining space. Both the main and dessert menus are long, so ask your waiter for a traditional recommendation depending on your mood. **Known for:** traditionally prepared regional dishes; long menu of main courses and desserts; lovely views of the Cetina River. [$] *Average main: €16* ✉ *Podašpilje, Omiš* ☎ *099/314–6220* 🌐 *kastil-slanica.hr.*

## Hotels

### ★ Hotel Villa Dvor

**$$ | HOTEL | FAMILY** | Built into a sheer cliff face overlooking the Cetina River, Villa Dvor has comfortable rooms offering sea, mountain, or river views. **Pros:** stunning view across river to Old Town and sea; eco-friendly ethos; breakfast served on terrace. **Cons:** location and view outshine the hotel itself; limited nightlife; somewhat old-fashioned decor. [$] *Rooms from: €180* ✉ *Mosorska Cesta 13, Omiš* ☎ *021/863–444* 🌐 *www.hotel-villadvor.hr* *23 rooms* 🍽 *Free Breakfast.*

## Performing Arts

### FESTIVALS

### Dalmatian Klapa Festival

**MUSIC FESTIVALS** | Klapa singing, an integral part of Dalmatian—and Croatian—culture, is widely celebrated all summer long with festivals devoted specifically to the cherished musical tradition. The Dalmatian Klapa Festival in Omiš, usually held for several weeks between June and July, brings together the best klapa performers from the region. Performances are staged in the parish church and on the main square, where you can enjoy the UNESCO-protected melodies alfresco. ✉ *Omiš* ☎ *021/861–015* 🌐 *fdk.hr.*

## The Pirates of Omiš

Most people connect historical pirates with what has been called the "golden age" of piracy, which took place in the 17th and 18th centuries across the Atlantic Ocean and Caribbean Sea. But few know that several centuries before piracy's most famous era—the inspiration for today's pop culture pirate stereotypes— swashbucklers were active on the Adriatic Sea, and the city of Omiš was their home base.

The Adriatic's pirates marauded from Split to Dubrovnik between the 12th and 15th centuries, forcing passing boats to pay a fee or engage in open battle on the sea. At their head were princes from the noble Kačić family of Omiš. Few ships could hold out against "Omiš Arrows," as the boats of the pirates were known. They were shallow-drafted so they could sail in and out of the city on the Cetina River, allowing the pirates to easily overtake their victims, including merchant ships from powerful cities such as Split, Dubrovnik, and Venice—and even papal galleys. (The latter resulted in Pope Honorius III leading a crusade against Omiš in 1221, which the crusaders lost.) The Omiš pirates weren't defeated until 1444, when the Venetian army finally succeeded after a 24-year effort to stop the oceanic outlaws. Today an annual pirate battle reenactment in the waters of Omiš takes place each August.



## Activities

The Cetina River Valley is a destination for adventure sports lovers of all kinds, from white-water rafters to rock climbers, who appreciate getting their adrenaline rush with a side of sheer natural beauty. Several adventure-tour companies arrange trips through the limestone cliffs of the canyon, leaving from both Split and Omiš.

**Active Holidays**

**WATER SPORTS** | The company offers ziplining, rafting, canyoneering, canoeing, and rock climbing in the Cetina River Valley, as well as windsurfing and sea kayaking off the coast at Omiš. They can assist with other sightseeing excursions and lodgings on request as well. ✉ *Knezova Kačića 2, Omiš* ☎ *021/861–829* 🌐 *www.activeholidays-croatia.com* 🎫 *From €35 rafting per person; €65 zipline per person; €120 quad safari per person.*

# Brač

*9 nautical miles south of Split by ferry.*

Well-connected to Split by ferry and catamaran services, the island of Brač is the perfect offshore escape. While it's a delightful day trip, it's easy to see why opting to stay a few nights is a no-brainer as soon as you step foot here. The island's charms include craggy seascapes, rosy bougainvillea crawling over sun-drenched stone houses, and calming cricket songs ringing out from the pine trees. Despite its proximity to the mainland, the slow pace of island life pervades many of Brač's attractions. While you're on the island, try a walking tour through the Dolce Vita Trail to see, touch, and taste where the country's best olive oil comes from. Or hook up with one of the many outdoor-adventure-sports companies for heart-pumping kayaking, climbing, windsurfing, or sailing. Although the famous Zlatni Rat (Golden Cape) Beach, a prime windsurfing spot, can seem a bit

Blaca Hermitage was built by monks who also grew vineyards and olive groves in the area.

overcrowded, exploring the island's more hidden sides like Bobovisće or Sutivan will reveal some of the most crystal clear water in the entire Adriatic.

### GETTING HERE AND AROUND

Several towns on Brač are easily accessible by ferry, catamaran, and boat. To get there, hop on a direct ferry from either Split to Supetar (a 50-minute ride) or Makarska to Sumartin (a 1-hour ride). Indirect options are also available, from Split to Milna on Brač and then further to other islands (Hvar and Vis), or from Split to Bol on Brač and then Hvar. Once you arrive, catch a bus between towns or, better yet, rent a bike and explore Brač via cycling trail. In 2021, Bol debuted two interactive Bike Storytelling Trails that are a superb way to experience the island up close and at your own pace.

## Sights

★ **Blaca Hermitage** (*Pustinja blaca*)
**HISTORIC SIGHT** | Built into a cliff face overlooking the sea by Glagolitic monks fleeing Ottoman invaders in the 16th century, the Blaca Hermitage is one of Brač's most serene sights. From the bay below the complex, it's a 2-km (1-mile) hike uphill and well off the beaten path, as it's only reachable by foot. Experiencing the hike helps you understand the monks' toil in constructing the site without modern amenities. You can also arrive by car from Nerežišća across Dragovode (now a ghost town) and then walk about 30 minutes up to the monastery. Either way, don hiking shoes and bring water, especially in summer. The monks also grew rich vineyards and lush olive groves, despite the wild and arid landscape. Inside, the fine collection of period furniture includes a piano and telescope that belonged to Father Nikola Miličević (1887–1963), Blaca's last hermit and an avid astronomer. In its heyday, the hermitage had a printing press, a school, and an observatory. Monks no longer liver here; today, it functions as a museum, where a guided tour is worth the expense. ✉ *Pustinja blaca, Brac*

☎ *091/516–4671* 🌐 *www.czk-brac.hr* 🎫 *€7* ⏲ *Closed Mon.*

**Branislav Dešković Art Gallery** (*Galerija Branislav Dešković*)
**ART MUSEUM | FAMILY** | In a fine Baroque building on the seafront, the gallery displays more than 300 paintings and sculptures by big-name 20th-century Croatian artists who drew inspiration from the sea and landscapes of Dalmatia. The intimate gallery was named after Brač-born sculptor Branislav Dešković (1883–1939), whose works are on display along with those of Ivan Meštrović, Ivan Rendić, and others. ✉ *Bolskih Pomoraca 7, Bol* ☎ *091/635–2700* 🌐 *www.czk-brac.hr* 🎫 *€4* ⏲ *Closed Mon.*

**Dominican Monastery** (*Dominikanski samostan*)
**RELIGIOUS BUILDING** | Founded in 1475, the Dominican monastery on the western edge of Bol has beautiful gardens overlooking the sea. The monastery church is home to a valuable 16th-century painting by Tintoretto, and the small on-site museum displays ancient Greek coins and amphorae found on the nearby islands of Hvar and Vis. In addition to maintaining the museum and church, the monastery's priests actively study and carry out the Dominican mission throughout Croatia and Europe. ✉ *Anđelka Rabadana 4, Bol* ☎ *021/778–000* 🌐 *www.dominikanci.hr/samostani/hrvatska/bol* 🎫 *€4.*

**Island of Brač Museum, Škrip** (*Muzej otoka Brača, Škrip*)
**HISTORY MUSEUM** | This is the island's regional museum, located within its oldest settlement, called Škrip. *Škrip* comes from the Latin *scrupus*, referring to large sharp stones. The area was inhabited by the ancient Illyrians around 1400 BC and later by a Roman community. Today the museum displays artifacts from both of these eras and much more. ✉ *Škrip, Pjaca 15, Brac* ☎ *091/637–0920* 🌐 *www.czk-brac.hr* 🎫 *€4.*

**Sutivan Nature Park** (*Park prirode Sutivan*)
**CITY PARK | FAMILY** | After you've spent a few days swimming and lying on the beach, this park is a great place for an afternoon picnic with kids. A small animal park shelters a wide variety of domestic animals including ducks, pigs, goats, turtles, peacocks, parrots, and cows. There are even donkeys that kids can pet and ride. The park is about 3 km (2 miles) from Sutivan toward Mlin and has a large playground, a barbecue area, a restaurant with produce from the on-site garden, and a botanical garden with a fountain, as well as an amphitheater for performances and events. ✉ *Krtine bb, Sutivan* ☎ *098/133–7345* 🌐 *moj-otok.com/wp/parkprirodesutivan* 🎫 *Free.*

**Vidova Gora**
**MOUNTAIN** | The town of Bol is backed by the highest peak on all the Croatian islands, Vidova gora, and from here, at a height of 778 meters (2,552 feet) above sea level, the Adriatic Sea and the islands of Hvar and Vis spread out before you like a map. It's possible to reach the top following a clearly marked footpath from Bol, but be sure to wear good hiking boots, take plenty of water, and expect to walk at least 2½ hours to reach the summit. Alternatively, rent a mountain bike from Big Blue Sport and cycle up—note that you need to be pretty fit to face the challenge by bike or by foot. **TIP→ If you have a headlamp and are relatively fit, wake early and hike up before sunrise, or go in the late afternoon and watch the sun set.** ✉ *Bol* ⊕ *4 km (2½ miles) north of the town center.*

## Beaches

**Lovrečina**
**BEACH | FAMILY** | This sandy beach sits in a cove on Brač's northern coast, offering a more low-key alternative to Zlatni rat that's worth a visit for its clear waters and views of the Dinaric Alps on the mainland. Crickets chirp from the surrounding pines, which also offer

shade from the sun. Above the beach are ruins from the 5th-century Basilica of St. Lawrence, which pilgrims visit on August 10, the saint's feast day. The beach is a 10-minute drive (about an hour walk) east of Postira following the main road, which turns to dirt for the last few miles. **Amenities:** food and drink; toilets. **Best for:** snorkeling; solitude; swimming; walking. ✉ *Plaža Lovrečina, Brac* ☎ *021/632–966 Postira Tourist Board* 🌐 *www.postira.hr/en.*

★ **Zlatni Rat** (*Golden Horn*)
**BEACH | FAMILY** | The obvious spot for swimming and sunning here is the glorious Zlatni Rat (Golden Cape or Golden Horn) Beach, complete with a café and snack bar, plus sun beds and parasols. Paddleboats and Jet Skis can be rented through peak season, when the beach can get crowded. Regular taxi-boats run from the Old Town harbor to Zlatni rat; walking distance is 20 minutes. **Amenities**: food and drink; showers; toilets; water sports. **Best for**: snorkeling; sunrise; sunset; swimming; windsurfing. ✉ *Bol* 🌐 *www.bol.hr/experience-bol/zlatni-rat-en1204.*

## Restaurants

### Kaštil Gospodnetić

**$$ | MEDITERRANEAN** | Sitting above the village of Dol, this family-run agritourism estate offers amazing vistas of the steep valley all the way to the sea. Inside, guests can step back in time with a tour through the 19th-century building before sitting down to a farm-fresh home-cooked meal. **Known for:** slow-cooked peka dishes can be ordered in advance; standout estate in a tiny village; lunch is by reservation only. 💲 *Average main: €20* ✉ *Dol bb, Dol* ☎ *091/799–7182* 🌐 *konobadol.com* ⏲ *Closed Nov.–Apr.; May and Oct. visits by reservation only.*

### Konoba Kopačina

**$$ | MEDITERRANEAN | FAMILY** | It is hard to spend more than a day on the island of Brač without giving in to the succulent aromas of roasted lamb, and many people claim this is the best place to enjoy the island delicacy. Farms on Brač take care to have their sheep feed only on their mother's milk and wild herbs, like the rosemary and sage that thrive on the rocky terrain. **Known for:** family-run tavern in small town; range of lamb specialties using much of the animal; Brač-grown wines. 💲 *Average main: €18* ✉ *Donji Humac 7, Donji Humac* ☎ *021/647–707* 🌐 *kopacina.com.*

### Konoba Toni

**$ | MEDITERRANEAN** | Family-owned Toni, in a typical Dalmatian house with a stone exterior and green window shutters, reflects the local vibe including the menu's ingredients and the staff's warm hospitality. Grilled fish, spit-roasted lamb and peka-cooked meals await diners, to be enjoyed on wooden tables in a stone interior or outside on a lovely terrace covered with grapevines. **Known for:** true-to-Brač food such as hrapaćuša cake; homemade local wine; authentically simple decor. 💲 *Average main: €13* ✉ *Dol 51,*

## Brač Stone

The island of Brač is well-known for its fine white stone, quarried across the island but particularly represented in the village of Pučišća on the north coast, which is still home to a prestigious stonemasonry school. For centuries, Brač stone has been used for world-famous buildings, including Diocletian's Palace in Split and the Cathedral of St. James in Šibenik. There are rumors that the island even lent its stone to the U.S. White House and the parliament building in Budapest. Today, prized Brač stone is used by sculptors and for the reconstruction of historic monuments.

*Dol ☎ 021/632–693 🌐 www.instagram.com/konobatoni.*

**Konoba Žiža**

**$$ | MEDITERRANEAN | FAMILY** | This konoba south of Supetar offers meals local to Brač and the wider Dalmatia region, along with a stunning outdoor terrace that looks out onto the sea. As a family-run business tucked away in a rural olive-grove-enveloped area, Žiža is a good choice for travelers seeking an authentic island experience. **Known for:** welcome drink of homemade brandy; locally grown produce and traditional cooking; one of the best views on the island. *$ Average main: €21 ✉ Donji Humac 136, Donji Humac ☎ 091/151–7128 🌐 www.facebook.com/KonobaZiza.*

## Coffee and Quick Bites

**Arguola**

**$ | SANDWICHES** | If you're looking for a quick bite for lunch on your way to the beach or after a late night out partying, this sandwich bar will do the trick. The salads and bread are made fresh and the portions are perfect. **Known for:** payment is cash only; super affordable and filling; late-night snacks. *$ Average main: €4 ✉ Vladimira Nazora 6, Bol ☎ 091/518–8295 ⏲ Closed Nov.–Apr.*

## Hotels

**Bluesun Hotel Borak**

**$$ | HOTEL | FAMILY** | Set amid pine trees on the path to Zlatni Rat Beach—and just a 10-minute walk from Bol's Old Town—this hotel occupies a modern, three-story white building with rooms renovated in 2022, and amenities include an outdoor pool and a gym, as well as a restaurant with a terrace. **Pros:** eight-minute walk from Zlatni rat; good sports facilities; family rooms available. **Cons:** large and slightly impersonal; popular with large tour groups; no hotel spa. *$ Rooms from: €220 ✉ Put Zlatnog Rata 42, Bol ☎ 01/384–4288 🌐 www.bluesunhotels.com/hotel-borak-bol-brac ⏲ Closed Nov.–Apr. 137 rooms 🍽 Free Breakfast.*

**Hotel Osam**

**$$ | HOTEL** | This sleek adults-only hotel with a rooftop bar, stylish rooms (most of which have a sea view), and a pool offers something not found in many places on Brač: an urban-style island retreat. **Pros:** excellent buffet breakfast and restaurant; convenient location in center of Supetar; unique former schoolhouse building. **Cons:** rooms are not soundproof; indoor-outdoor pool is small; some more modern rooms lack traditional charm. *$ Rooms from: €180 ✉ Vlačica 3, Supetar ☎ 021/552–0333 🌐 www.hotel-osam.com 27 rooms 🍽 Free Breakfast.*

**★ Villa Giardino Heritage Boutique Hotel**

**$$ | B&B/INN** | Just a five-minute walk from the harbor, this small hotel with strikingly designed rooms is set in a white stone building with large blue-shuttered windows and airy curtains. **Pros:** attentive staff; Mediterranean-style seclusion yet centrally located; breakfast served in lovely garden. **Cons:** often fully booked; limited facilities compared to large hotel; some rooms and bathrooms could be larger. *$ Rooms from: €220 ✉ Novi Put 2, Bol ☎ 021/635–900 🌐 www.villagiardinobol.com ⏲ Closed Nov.–Apr. 15 rooms 🍽 Free Breakfast.*

## Activities

### ADVENTURE TOURS

**Aldura Sport**

**HIKING & WALKING | FAMILY** | If you want to explore the island of Brač with local outdoor enthusiasts committed to preserving the traditions and beauty of the island, the experts at Aldura Sport have you covered. From beginner to experienced adventurers, everyone will enjoy the company's unparalleled excursions and tours including walking, sailing, biking, kayaking, and hiking. *✉ Porat bb, Sutivan ☎ 098/423–689 🌐 www.aldura-sport.hr 🎫 From €40 for guided* *adventure tours; from €5 for bikes and other equipment rentals.*

### WATER SPORTS

**Big Blue Sport**

**WATER SPORTS** | **FAMILY** | Besides windsurfing and scuba-diving training, this well-established local company rents equipment including stand-up paddleboards, sea kayaks, and mountain bikes. ✉ *Bolskih Pomoraca 15, Bol* ☎ *091/635–0401* 🌐 *www.bigbluesport.com* 🎫 *From €25 for windsurf rental; from €15 for kayak rental.*

# Hvar

*23 nautical miles south of Split by ferry.*

Hvar bills itself as the "sunniest island in the Adriatic," and it even has the figures to back up this claim—an annual average of 2,760 hours of sunshine with a maximum of two foggy days a year. Croatia's fourth-largest island is beloved by many, from families and avid foodies to international celebrities and yachters. Hvar is both the name of the island and the name of the capital (Hvar Town), which sits near the island's western tip. Hvar Town rises like an amphitheater from its harbor, backed by a hilltop fortress and protected from the open sea by a scattering of small islands known as Pakleni otoci ("hellish islands," although paradise islands would be a more fitting name). Partiers and explorers from all over the world flock to Hvar Town en masse, so expect it to be crowded and expensive through peak season. Celebrity visitors have included King Abdullah of Jordan and his wife, Queen Rania; Italian clothing entrepreneur Luciano Benetton; Prince Harry of England; Beyoncé and her husband Jay Z; and many, many more.

### GETTING HERE AND AROUND

The easiest way to reach Hvar Town is to catch a morning or midafternoon Jadrolinija catamaran from Split. Depending on the route, the catamaran either stops at Hvar Town (23 nautical miles) and goes back to Split, or continues on to the Southern Dalmatian islands of Korčula and Lastovo. Alternatively, take an early morning Jadrolinija ferry from Split to Stari Grad (23 nautical miles) if that's your destination, or continue from Stari Grad and catch a local bus across the island to Hvar Town. Note that there is no car ferry direct to Hvar Town from Split; you must take the ferry to Stari Grad.

##  Sights

★ **Fortica Fortress** (*Španjola*)

**VIEWPOINT** | During the 25-minute climb to see the breathtaking views from this 16th-century hilltop fortress, a symbol of Hvar Town, you get to take in the aromatic Mediterranean plant garden. Once you've made it to the top, you can explore the fortress's stone walls and behold the city below, along with the sea and islands stretching over the horizon as far as the eye can see. ✉ *Fortica Fortress, Hvar* 🎫 *€10 for entry; free for exterior and viewpoint.*

**Franciscan Monastery** (*Franjevački samostan*)

**RELIGIOUS BUILDING** | **FAMILY** | A short walk east of town, along the quay past the Arsenal, lies Hvar Town's Franciscan monastery. Within its walls, a pretty 15th-century Renaissance cloister leads to the former refectory, now housing a small museum with several notable artworks, including a beautiful fresco of the Last Supper. The grounds outside make a relaxing place for a stroll among centuries-old cypress trees. ✉ *Šetalište Put Križa bb, Hvar* ☎ *021/741–059 Hvar Tourist Board* 🎫 *€10.*

**Jelsa**

**TOWN** | **FAMILY** | On the northern coast of the island, Hvar's third main town is often overlooked, but that makes it all the more delightful once you do discover this more peaceful alternative to Hvar Town. Jelsa has many structures from the Renaissance and Baroque periods, though St. Mary's Church dates back to the early 1300s. A tower built by the ancient Greeks overlooks the harbor; it dates to the 3rd or 4th century BC. About 1 km (½ mile) east of the modern town is the older Grad, with the original fortified area that was protected by Galešnik, a fortress that now stands in ruins. The small town is surrounded by a thick forest of pine trees, several resorts, and many swimmable beaches—including some the island's most popular nude beaches. Jelsa is also famous for its annual Za križen procession, a 500-year-old, UNESCO-protected Easter tradition during which a shoeless cross-bearer and a crowd embark on a 25-km (16-mile) overnight walk. Chosen locals can be on the waiting list to carry the cross for decades, as it's considered a significant honor. ✉ *20 km (13 miles) east of Hvar Town, Hvar* ☎ *021/761–017 Jelsa Tourist Board* 🌐 *visitjelsa.hr.*

**Kazalište** (*Theater*)
**NOTABLE BUILDING** | Located on the upper floor of the Arsenal, the Kazalište opened in 1612, making it the oldest institution of its kind in Croatia and one of the first in Europe. Hvar Town's theater is still open for shorts today. The Arsenal building, where Venetian ships en route to East Asia once docked for repairs, dates back to the 13th century but was reconstructed after damage during a Turkish invasion in 1571. It reopened in 2019 following renovations. Note that tickets must be purchased in person. ✉ *Trg sv. Stjepana, Hvar* ☎ *021/741–059 Hvar Tourist Board* 🌐 *visithvar.hr* 🎫 *€10 for the Arsenal and theater* 🕒 *Closed Nov.–Apr.*

**Plančić Brothers Winery** (*Vinarija Braća Plančić*)
**WINERY** | On the beautiful vineyard-strewn island of Hvar you can visit the winery where the Plančić family has been producing a variety of top-quality wines, including rosé and dessert wines, as well as local rakija, since 1919. Look out for Bogdanuša (dry white wine) or Ivan Dolac (a select red). Call the winery for information about tours and tastings. ✉ *Vrbanj 191, Vrbanj* ☎ *091/973–2025* 🌐 *www.facebook.com/vinaplancic.*

**Plenković Winery**
**WINERY** | This award-winning winery on the island of Hvar—along with its restaurant Bilo Idro and on-site hotel—are well worth a visit. The Zlatan Plavac (a dry red) made by Zlatan Plenković has continually won prestigious awards at local and international wine fairs since the early 1990s. Call ahead for information about winery visits. ✉ *Bilo Idro, Put Veleg Kamika 1, Sveta Nedilja, Stari Grad* ☎ *021/745–709* 🌐 *zlatanotok.hr.*

★ **Stari Grad**
**TOWN | FAMILY** | As its name suggests, Stari Grad, or Old Town, is among Europe's first towns. Founded in the 4th century BC, this is the site of the original Greek settlement on Hvar, then known as Pharos. While much of the attraction in Stari Grad focuses on its ancient history, the city is still very much alive, especially during the summer. It features a beautiful walkable riviera and forest path, as well as a number of cultural attractions, such as the 15th-century Dominican Monastery of St. Peter the Martyr. The town is about 23 km (14 miles) east of Hvar Town. ✉ *Stari Grad* ☎ *021/765–763 Stari Grad Tourist Board* 🌐 *www.visit-stari-grad.com.*

**Tvrdalj**
**HISTORIC HOME** | Stari Grad's *tvrdalj*, or fortress, is the palace of renowned Renaissance-era local poet Petar Hektorović (1487–1572). The Tvrdalj was later renovated in 18th-century Baroque style, and a partial restoration was completed in the 19th century. Hektorović originally attempted to create a "model universe" to be embodied in his home. To that end, a large fish pond on-site is stocked with gray mullet, as it was in the poet's own time, representing the sea; above the fish pond in a tower is a dovecote,

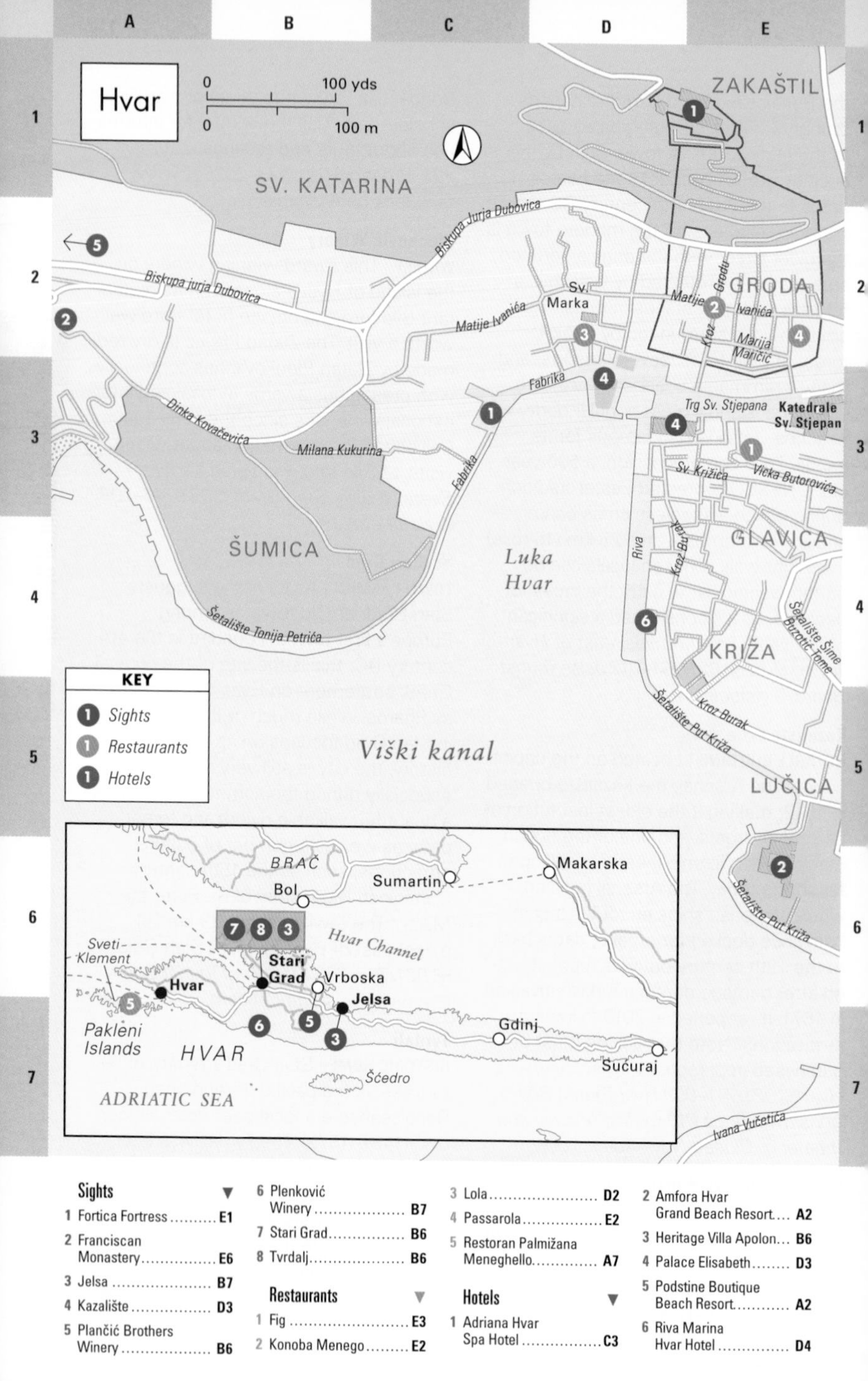


## Sights

1 Fortica Fortress .......... E1
2 Franciscan Monastery .......... E6
3 Jelsa .......... B7
4 Kazalište .......... D3
5 Plančić Brothers Winery .......... B6
6 Plenković Winery .......... B7
7 Stari Grad .......... B6
8 Tvrdalj .......... B6

## Restaurants

1 Fig .......... E3
2 Konoba Menego .......... E2
3 Lola .......... D2
4 Passarola .......... E2
5 Restoran Palmižana Meneghello .......... A7

## Hotels

1 Adriana Hvar Spa Hotel .......... C3
2 Amfora Hvar Grand Beach Resort .......... A2
3 Heritage Villa Apolon .......... B6
4 Palace Elisabeth .......... D3
5 Podstine Boutique Beach Resort .......... A2
6 Riva Marina Hvar Hotel .......... D4

representing the air. Ivy was allowed to cover the walls to tie the home to the land. Quotations from Hektorović's striking poetry are inscribed on many walls. *Trg Tvrdalj Petra Hektorovića, Priko bb, Stari Grad 021/765–068 www.visit-stari-grad.com €4 Closed Nov.–Apr., unless arranged in advance with tourist board.*

## Restaurants

**Fig**

$ | **ECLECTIC** | Tucked in a pretty stone alleyway, this restaurant just a three-minute walk east of the Hvar Town harbor regularly draws lines of people (reservations aren't possible, so be prepared for a wait). There's a small dimly lit interior, but the dark wooden tables outside are the best place to enjoy the affordable and healthy breakfast, brunch, lunch, and dinner options, catered to international tastes with less focus on local flavors. **Known for:** friendly and energetic staff; delicious vegetarian choices; super-central location. *Average main: €13 Ivana Frane Biundovića 3, Hvar figrestaurants.com Closed Nov.–Apr.*

**★ Konoba Menego**

$$ | **MEDITERRANEAN** | **FAMILY** | Candlelit tables and *pršut* (prosciutto) hanging from the raftered ceiling add to the atmosphere of this authentic stone-walled tavern on the steps between the main square and the fortress. Come here to share platters of locally produced, cold Dalmatian specialties such as *kožji sir* (goat cheese), *salata od hobotnice* (octopus salad), and *masline* (olives) or feast on wild boar and traditional *pašticada* (beef stew). Before leaving, round off your meal with *pijane smokve* (literally "drunken figs," figs marinated in brandy) and be sure to check out the world atlas, where guests sign on the pages of their hometowns. **Known for:** "drunken" (brandy-marinated) figs; no reservations, so waits are possible; payment is cash only. *Average main: €16 Kroz Grodu 26, Hvar 021/717–411 www.menego.hr Closed Dec.–Mar.*

### Wine in Central Dalmatia

Some of Croatia's best wines are born of the sun and salty air of Hvar. On the south coast, the steep, rugged, seaward-facing slopes between the villages of Sveta Nedilja and Ivan Dolac focus on full-bodied reds, made predominantly from the Plavac Mali grape. In contrast, the vineyards in the flat valley between Stari Grad and Jelsa on the north side produce mostly whites, such as the greenish-yellow Bogdanuša.

**Lola**

$$ | **MEDITERRANEAN** | When you're ready for a change from traditional Croatian food, this upbeat fun restaurant-bar adjacent to Hvar Town's harbor serves meals from various global cuisines as well as delicious cocktails. Make a reservation ahead of time if you're arriving for dinner, as the music turns up and the crowds roll in when the sun goes down; Lola stays open late. **Known for:** one of most popular places in town; payment is cash only; street-food favorites. *Average main: €17 Sveti Marak 8, Hvar 099/688–5057 www.instagram.com/lolabarhvar Closed Nov.–Apr.*

**Passarola**

$$$ | **MEDITERRANEAN** | Great care is taken to select and focus on the best local fresh ingredients at this sophisticated restaurant, tucked away in a picturesque courtyard off the main square of Hvar Town. The wine list is impressive and includes local standouts and a wide international selection. **Known for:** traditional

Hvar's Stari Grad is a frequent entryway for those arriving to the island via boat.

dishes from clams to grilled fish; cool presentation and delicious flavors; alfresco dining on the terrace. *Average main: €30* *Dr. Mate Miličića 10, Hvar* *021/383–6357* *www.instagram.com/passarola.hvar* *Closed Nov.–Apr.*

**Restoran Palmižana Meneghello**

$$$ | **SEAFOOD** | On the tiny island of Sveti Klement, a 20-minute taxi-boat ride from Hvar Town (or dock your sailboat in nearby ACI Marina), this terrace restaurant is backed by a romantic wilderness of Mediterranean flora and offers stunning views over the open sea. Besides wonderfully fresh seafood, dishes showcase local ingredients such as sheep's cheese, olives, and beef. **Known for:** upscale Croatian dishes; collection of colorful modern Croatian art; run by family who select or catch ingredients themselves. *Average main: €25* *Palmižana 8A, Vinogradišće Uvala, Sveti Klement* *091/478–3111* *www.palmizana.com* *Closed Nov.–Mar.*

## Hotels

**Adriana Hvar Spa Hotel**

$$$$ | **HOTEL** | This well-appointed hotel has a rooftop pool and sophisticated cocktail bar, affording stunning views of the sea and Old Town, and a chic ground-floor restaurant serving Mediterranean cuisine on the harborfront. **Pros:** prime location on seafront promenade; delicious breakfast with a view of the docks; high-end spa for post-sightseeing massages. **Cons:** among Hvar Town's more expensive hotels; proximity to harbor means noise possible at night; interior slightly dated. *Rooms from: €500* *Obala Fabrika 28, Hvar* *021/750–555* *www.suncanihvar.com* *62 rooms* *Free Breakfast.*

**Amfora Hvar Grand Beach Resort**

$$$ | **RESORT** | **FAMILY** | Sitting in its own bay with a pinewood backdrop, this colossal modern white structure is a peaceful 10-minute walk along the coastal path from the center of Hvar Town. **Pros:** great outdoor pool with swim-up

bar; varied breakfast served overlooking Hvar Town harbor; easy access to nearby public beach. **Cons:** inconsistent service; large and somewhat impersonal; some rooms have better facilities than others. *Rooms from: €320 Biskupa Jurja Dubokovica 5, Hvar 021/750–300 www.suncanihvar.com 324 rooms Free Breakfast.*

**Heritage Villa Apolon**

**$$ | B&B/INN | FAMILY |** Freshly renovated, this boutique villa with rooms and suites offers guests a sophisticated taste of times past in an intimate island setting. **Pros:** all but one room has a sea view; intimate and personal service; reasonable prices compared to similar luxury accommodation on Hvar. **Cons:** restaurant due to reopen in summer 2024; no official hotel parking lot; harbor noise can drift into rooms. *Rooms from: €250 Šetalište Don Šime Ljubića 7, Stari Grad 091/177–8320 www.apolon.hr/en Closed Nov.–Apr. 8 rooms Free Breakfast.*

**Palace Elisabeth**

**$$$$ | HOTEL | FAMILY |** Commanding a prime site on the edge of the main square and overlooking the harbor, the Palace was built in the 19th century, claiming the title of Hvar's first five-star hotel—and first hotel ever—but it now includes plenty of modern amenities. **Pros:** doesn't get more central than this in Hvar Town; room upgrades possible if there is space; more luxurious than other five-star hotels in region. **Cons:** fitness facilities could be better; pool is indoors so no sunbathing possible; can be noisier during high season. *Rooms from: €560 Trg Svetog Stjepana 5, Hvar 021/750–400 www.suncanihvar.com Closed Nov.–Apr. 44 rooms Free Breakfast.*

**Podstine Boutique Beach Resort**

**$$$$ | HOTEL |** With peaceful rooms—most with sea views, balconies, and spacious bathrooms—this family-run boutique resort lies on the coast, a 20-minute walk west of the center of Hvar Town. **Pros:** seafront location above small rocky private beach; terraced gardens with palm and lemon trees; spa and outdoor pool. **Cons:** far from Old Town; basic rooms and bathrooms (especially in the annex building); economy rooms have no sea view. *Rooms from: €400 Put Podstina 11, Hvar 021/740–400 www.podstine.com Closed Nov.–Apr. 50 rooms Free Breakfast.*

**★ Riva Marina Hvar Hotel**

**$$$$ | HOTEL |** Located on the palm-lined Hvar Town waterfront, opposite the ferry landing station, the hotel was renovated in 2022 with a sleek Mediterranean look that favors white, blue, and earth tones. **Pros:** prime location on seafront promenade; sea views from some rooms; excellent bar and restaurant. **Cons:** no free parking; in no-car zone, so walking to the hotel is required; rooms could be bigger, and some lack sea views. *Rooms from: €430 Obala Riva 27, Hvar 021/750–100 www.suncanihvar.com 50 rooms Free Breakfast.*

## Nightlife

Hvar Town is one of the hottest party destinations for the young and well-to-do. This phenomenon has led to crowding and rowdiness during the high season, which can be off-putting for those looking to enjoy the island's natural and traditional attractions. But those looking for a good time are sure to find it here: several stylish cocktail bars and clubs cater to the annual influx of summer visitors, including those who arrive with Yacht Week and the Ultra Music Festival that starts in Split and celebrates its last night with a beach party on Hvar. For those seeking a more serene experience, there are a number of elegant evening events, and staying in one of the island's other lovely towns with a more peaceful ambience is always an option.

## BARS AND CLUBS

### ★ BackLane

**BARS** | Whipping up what are arguably the best cocktails on the island, this craft bar sits four minutes southwest of Hvar Town's main square in a beautiful stone alleyway location. The expert mixologists cover the classics, offer signature blends, and cater to guest requests, using natural ingredients and high-class liquor brands. It's closed October through April. ✉ *Kroz Burak 31, Hvar* 🌐 *www.backlane-hvar.com.*

### ★ Carpe Diem Beach

**DANCE CLUBS** | A legendary beach club popular with twenty-somethings, this has been Hvar Town's top party destination for years. Go during the day at no entrance fee for a more relaxed vibe, great views, and the best people-watching. The serious partying starts around 5 pm and continues until early morning. To reach this club on Stipanska, a small island off the coast of Hvar, you can simply catch a taxi-boat (about €10; at night the transfer is included in the club entrance price) from the harbor next to the Hvar-side Carpe Diem Bar, which also has parties. A good selection of food is available at the on-site restaurant, with sushi being served until 9 pm. The club is closed October through May. ✉ *Carpe Diem Hvar, Stipanska, Hvar* ☎ *099/446–8468* 🌐 *beach.cdhvar.com.*

### Hula Hula

**DANCE CLUBS** | Built into the rocks overlooking the sea, this wooden beach bar attracts bathers throughout the day with its chill music, lounge chairs, VIP tables, and massages. Many stay for the sunset as the beach club transforms into a dance party with DJ music and cocktails. Even Beyoncé has been spotted here. Note that reservations are only possible on-site, and payment is cash only. ✉ *Petrićevo Šetalište 10, Hvar* ☎ *097/608–8002* 🌐 *www.hulahulahvar.com.*

# Performing Arts

## FESTIVALS

### Hvar Summer Festival

**ARTS FESTIVALS** | Classical music recitals in the cloisters of Hvar Town's Franciscan monastery have long been the highlight of the Hvar Summer Festival. Also look out for theater, folklore, and jazz at various open-air locations around town. The annual festival usually runs for one to several months sometime between June and September. ✉ *Hvar* ☎ *021/718–336* 🌐 *hvarsummerfestival.hr/en.*

# Activities

## BEACHES

Although there are several pretty beaches within walking distance of Hvar Town—the best-equipped being the pebble beach at the Amfora Hvar Grand Beach Resort, 10 minutes west of the main square—sun worshippers in the know head for the nearby **Pakleni otoci.** This group of islands can be reached by taxi-boats that depart regularly (every hour in peak season, from 8 to 8) from the town harbor. The best-known and best-served beaches are Sveti Jerolim (on the island of the same name, partially a nudist beach), Stipanska (on the island of Marinkovac, clothing-optional), and Palmižana (on the island of Sveti Klement, also clothing-optional).

## DIVING

### Diving Center Viking

**SCUBA DIVING** | The center offers scuba-diving courses at all levels for those with a taste for underwater adventure. The seabed is scattered with pieces of broken Greek amphorae, and the area's biggest underwater attraction is the Stambedar seawall, close to the Pakleni Islands, which is home to red and violet gorgonians. ✉ *Put Podstina 7, Hvar* ☎ *976/976–978* 🌐 *viking-diving.com* 🎟 *From €95 for diving courses.*

### SAILING

**Hvar Adventure**

**SAILING | FAMILY** | This multi-sport company arranges different kinds of one-day and longer sailing trips, as well as sea-kayaking tours from Hvar Town to the Pakleni Islands and hiking, cycling, rock climbing, and other activities. ✉ *Jurja Matijevića 20, Hvar* ☎ *091/228–0088* 🌐 *hvar-adventure.com* 🎟 *From €80 for group boat excursions; from €60 for group kayak excursions.*

★ **Sunburst Sailing**

**SAILING** | The 42-foot sailing yacht called *Nera*, based in Split, is available for fully catered day charters and evening cruises. ✉ *Hvar* ☎ *091/185–4559* 🌐 *www.sunburstsailing.com* 🎟 *From €85.*

### YOGA

**Suncokret Body & Soul Retreat**

**YOGA** | Founded by a New Yorker and her Dalmatia-born partner, Suncokret ("sunflower") offers holistic wellness retreats that combine yoga, nature walks, Reiki, life-path workshops, and excursions on Hvar. Guests are accommodated in private cottages in the village, and most courses last one week. Dol is 6 km (4 miles) from Stari Grad and 26 km (16 miles) from Hvar Town. ✉ *Gojava 7, Sveta Ana, Dol* ☎ *091/739–8717* 🌐 *www.suncokretdream.net* 🎟 *From €1,290 for a retreat.*

# Vis

*34 nautical miles southwest of Split by ferry.*

Closed to foreigners until 1989 due to its use as a military base, the distant island of Vis is relatively wild and unspoiled. Built around wide harbors, the main towns are popular among yachters, who appreciate the island's rugged nature, unpretentious fish restaurants, and excellent locally produced wine. The pretty fishing village of Komiža is 11 km (7 miles) west of Vis Town. Here you're just a 40-minute boat ride away from the Modra špilja (Blue Cave), often compared to the Blue Grotto on Italy's Capri.

### GETTING HERE AND AROUND

To get here from Split, you can take a direct 2½-hour Jadrolinija ferry ride to arrive in Vis Town, or you can stop in at your own pace if you're sailing. A multi-stop ferry route from Split also connects Vis Town with Hvar Town and Milna on Brač.

## Sights

★ **Modra Špilja** (*Blue Cave*)

**CAVE | FAMILY** | At this popular sight hidden away on the islet of Biševo (5 nautical miles southwest of Komiža), sunlight enters through the water, reflects off the seabed, and casts the interior in a fantastic shade of blue. The Blue Cave is 24 meters (78 feet) long and 12 meters (39 feet) wide, and throughout the summer, local fishermen and tour agencies take tourists—some of whom come from Split and Hvar by speedboat—into the caverns. It can be a long wait in summer when a line of small boats is waiting to enter the cave. Ask at the marina or the tourist information office (🌐 *www.tz-komiza.hr/home-eng*) to see who is offering trips. Sometimes, small boat operators will wait at the entrance of the cave for visitors arriving by sailboat and yacht (which are too large to enter the cave). ✉ *Biševo island* ☎ *021/713–849 Komiža Center for Nautical Tourism* 🌐 *www.komiza.hr/nauticki-centar* 🎟 *Entry to cave is €19 late June–mid-Sept.; €12 Apr.–late June and mid-Sept.–late Oct.; price does not include dock if you're sailing.*

## Restaurants

**Fabrika**

**$$ | ECLECTIC** | The cool atmosphere, bohemian furniture and decor, and original jewelry sold on-site all add up to a funky little place to go for a burger and a drink. The owners—a brother and

Vis is well known for its low-key vineyards and wineries.

sister team—are well-known Croatian singer Luka Nižetić (who won Croatian Master Chef in 2014) and fashion blogger Petra Nižetić Mastelić. **Known for:** great location on the Komiža Riva; good breakfast menu and vegetarian options; payment is cash only. *Average main: €19 ✉ Riva Svetoga Mikule 12, Komiža ☎ 021/713–155 🌐 www.fabrikavis.hr ⏲ Closed Oct.–Apr.*

**Jastožera**

**$$$ | SEAFOOD | FAMILY** | Conceptualized in 1883 and opened in 1902 as a lobster house, this cleverly converted restaurant has platforms with tables built out above the water, and guests arriving via sailboat can berth here for free. The house specialty is—as you may have guessed—lobster, which guests can choose from live cages in the sea. **Known for:** variety of takes on lobster dishes; fun waterfront dining, though somewhat pricey for what you get; wine list with many local and regional options. *Average main: €32 ✉ Gundulićeva 6, Komiža ☎ 099/670–7755 🌐 jastozera.eu ⏲ Closed Nov.–Mar.*

**★ Konoba & Bar Lola**

**$$ | MEDITERRANEAN | FAMILY** | A funky garden restaurant, this tavern offers something refreshingly different on the island of Vis, whether you dine in the bar area or alfresco in the main restaurant. The atmosphere is relaxed, the food is fresh, and most of the vegetables come from Lola's own garden on the mainland. **Known for:** romantic garden setting; impressive cocktails and desserts; bistro- and tapas-style offerings. *Average main: €17 ✉ Matije Gupca 12, Vis Town ☎ 095/563–3247 🌐 www.lolavis.com ⏲ Closed Nov.–Mar. No lunch.*

**Pojoda**

**$$$ | SEAFOOD | FAMILY** | In a modern glass-and-wood conservatory that looks onto a courtyard garden of orange and lemon trees, Pojoda makes for a popular spot among the sailing crowd that won't disappoint a food-savvy traveler either. During the summer, it can get crowded and service may be a bit inconsistent. **Known for:** fresh whole fish cooked on the grill; lovely seating amid Mediterranean greenery; reservations recommended in summer. *Average main: €30* *Don Cvjetka Marasovića 8, Vis Town* *021/711–575* *www.instagram.com/restaurant_pojoda* *Closed Nov.–Mar.*

## Hotels

**Hotel San Giorgio**
**$$$$** | **HOTEL** | In Vis Town, east of the ferry quay, this chic little hotel is hidden away between stone cottages on a quiet cobbled side street. **Pros:** yoga vacations offered; modern and comfortable rooms; good restaurant with a walled garden. **Cons:** only the deluxe suite has a terrace; often fully booked; 20-minute walk from ferry landing can be difficult for visitors with heavy luggage. *Rooms from: €400* *Petra Hektorovića 2, Vis Town* *021/607–630* *hotelsangiorgiovis.com* *10 rooms* *Free Breakfast.*

## Activities

### DIVING

**ISSA Diving Center**
**SCUBA DIVING** | Scuba-diving enthusiasts will find underwater attractions near Vis, including several caves, at least a half-dozen shipwrecks, and some spectacular coral reefs. Beginners and those with previous experience can contact this center for organized diving trips and training at all levels with expert instructors. The center is closed November through April. *Obala Pape Aleksandra III 29, Komiža* *098/924–3940* *scubadiving.hr* *From €20 for a dive; from €150 for a diving course.*

# Makarska

*67 km (42 miles) southeast of Split.*

Lined with palm trees and cheerful open-air cafés, this town's seafront promenade looks onto a protected bay dotted with wooden fishing boats. From here one enters the Old Town, a warren of stone buildings and cobbled streets surrounding the main square, which is backed by the parish church and a small open-air market off to one side. The atmosphere is relaxed and easygoing. The only drama you'll likely see is created by the limestone heights of Mt. Biokovo, which seems to alternate between protecting and threatening the town, depending on the color of the sky and the cloud formations that ride over its rugged peaks. Makarska is the center of the area known as the Makarska Riviera, a 60-km (37-mile) stretch of coastline from Brela to Gradac known for its beautiful Adriatic views.

### GETTING HERE AND AROUND

Makarska is reachable from Split by rental car or bus. Once you arrive, the cobblestone streets of the small bayside town are fully walkable and are best experienced on foot.

## Sights

**Biokovo Nature Park** (*Park Prirode Biokovo*)
**NATURE PRESERVE** | Behind Makarska, a large area of the rocky heights that form the majestic Mt. Biokovo has been designated as a nature park. Part of the Dinaric Alps, which run from Slovenia down to Montenegro, Biokovo abounds in rare indigenous plant species, and the mountain is primarily limestone with little green coverage. It's possible to reach the highest peak, Sveti Jure (1,762 meters, or 5,781 feet) in 5½ hours from Makarska. However, this is a strenuous hike, especially in summer, for which you will need good boots and plenty of water. Hiking the mountain on your own is not recommended; group excursions are a safer choice. The park has a few information centers, with one in Markarska (Franjevački Put 2A, generally closed October–April). Park entry includes the Skywalk, a glass-bottom walkway off the main road, which extends out from a cliff face. **TIP→ You must buy admission**

**tickets in advance on the website, though you can't purchase them more than five days before your visit. Don't wait until the last minute, as slots sell out.** ✉ *Makarska* ☎ *021/733–017* 🌐 *pp-biokovo.hr* 🎫 *€8, includes Skywalk* 🕑 *Closed Dec.–Mar.*

**Skywalk**

**VIEWPOINT** | This glass-bottom walkway in the Biolovo Nature Park, stretching out from a cliff face of the Biokovo Mountain Range, offers striking vistas of the Adriatic Sea and coastline. Opened in 2020, the Skywalk is 1,228 meters (more than 4,000 feet) above sea level and can be reached in 40 minutes by car from Makarska. The drive is 13 km (8 miles) up Biokovo Road from the entrance point by a relatively narrow road that includes hairpin bends. Park entry tickets include Skywalk and must be purchased ahead of time (maximum five days earlier) on the website. Don't wait until the last minute as slots are limited, and expect a wait to enter the Skywalk. ✉ *Tucepi* ☎ *023/733–017* 🌐 *pp-biokovo.hr/en/skywalk-biokovo* 🎫 *€8, park entrance fee (includes Skywalk)* 🕑 *Closed Nov.–Apr. and in case of bad weather.*

## Restaurants

**Hrpina**

**$$ | MEDITERRANEAN** | Located right on a beach on the Makarska Riviera, this casual restaurant is a great spot to fuel up on fresh seafood after a long day of swimming and sunbathing. If you time your dinner right, you can take in a sunset above the sea as you relax; you can make a reservation by phone and also check the seasonal closing, which depends on the number of customers. **Known for:** good mix of seafood and meat dishes; local wines; friendly service. 💲 *Average main: €22* ✉ *Put Cvitačke bb, Makarska* 🌐 *www.facebook.com/HrpinaMakarska* 🕑 *Generally closed Oct.–spring.*

★ **Jeny**

**$$$$ | EUROPEAN** | At one of the best fine-dining restaurants on the Makarska Riviera, it's clear that time and care have gone into creating the two tasting and wine-pairing menus. The expert food preparation—blending seafood and meat with locally grown and forage flavors like olives and broad beans—can match many of Croatia's most awarded restaurants. **Known for:** terrace overlooking Makarska Riviera has stunning sunset views; sophisticated wine list with a regional focus; cash-only, and diners must reserve in advance. 💲 *Average main: €195* ✉ *Čovići 1, Tucepi* ☎ *091/587–8078* 🌐 *www.restaurant-jeny.hr* 🕑 *Closed Oct.–May. No lunch.*

**Konoba Ranč**

**$$$ | MEDITERRANEAN | FAMILY** | Surrounded on all four sides by the shade of an olive grove, this restaurant is the perfect place to wind down after a day of sun and sightseeing. It's known for steak, lamb cooked peka-style, and fish prepared traditionally *na gradele* (on the grill). **Known for:** outdoor area for kids to run around; alfresco dining on hearty food; on-site apartments available. 💲 *Average main: €26* ✉ *Kamena 62, Tucepi* ☎ *021/623–563* 🌐 *www.ranc-tucepi.hr* 🕑 *Closed Oct. to mid- or late May. No lunch.*

## Hotels

★ **Boutique Hotel Marco Polo**

**$$ | B&B/INN** | With comfortable accommodations, fine food, and individualized excursions, this adults-only beachfront hotel stands out on the Makarska Riviera as a wonderful place for a summer holiday. **Pros:** excellent rooftop terrace; intimate relaxed atmosphere; devoted owners who provide personal touches, such as on-site wine tastings. **Cons:** not all rooms have a view; hard to find a spot on the beach; parking lot and outdoor pool can get crowded. 💲 *Rooms from: €220* ✉ *Obala 15, Gradac* ☎ *021/695–060* *hotel-marcopolo.com* *25 rooms* *Free Breakfast.*

**Hotel Biokovo**

**$$$** | **HOTEL** | In the center of Makarska, on the palm-lined seafront promenade, this old-fashioned hotel offers rooms with light pine floors accented by dark-color fabrics. **Pros:** central location a minute from the ferry port; friendly and helpful staff; pleasant café and decent restaurant. **Cons:** limited facilities; parking can be a problem; low-key furnishings might not impress lovers of chic decor. *Rooms from: €280* *Obala Kralja Tomislava 14, Makarska* *021/615–244* *www.sol.hr/hr/hotel-biokovo* *52 rooms* *Free Breakfast.*

## Activities

### BEACHES

The main town beach in Makarska, a lovely 1½-km (1-mile) stretch of pebbles backed by pine woods, lies northwest of the center and close to a string of big modern hotels. Alternatively, walk along the narrow coastal path southeast of town to find rocks and a series of secluded coves perfect for a swimming base. Beaches along the entire Makarska Riviera offer lovely Adriatic views, paired with the stunningly beautiful backdrop of the Biokovo Mountain Range. Several easily accessed islands are also nearby, offering an additional assortment of small-coved private beaches.

### DIVING

Local underwater attractions include a reef near Makarska, known as **Kraljev Gaj**, which is populated by sponges, coral, octopuses, and scorpionfish. Farther out from the coast you can visit the *Dubrovnik*, an old steamboat that sank in 1917.

**More Sub Makarska**

**SCUBA DIVING** | **FAMILY** | Scuba-diving enthusiasts, as well as complete beginners, can sign up for organized diving trips and training at all levels. Note that the company's office closes between 1 and 6 pm. *Kralja Petra Krešimira IV 43, Makarska* *095/515–6444* *more-sub-makarska.hr* *From €40 for a dive; from €400 for a PADI course.*

# Lastovo

*80 km (50 nautical miles) southeast of Split (daily ferry connections from Split, stopping at other islands in between).*

Lying far out to sea, Lastovo is an island of green fertile valleys and is practically self-sufficient: locally caught seafood—notably delicious lobster—and home-grown vegetables are the staple diet. The main settlement, Lastovo Town, is made up of stone houses built amphitheater-style into a hillside, crisscrossed by cobbled alleys and flights of steps; they're renowned for tall chimneys resembling minarets. The only other settlement on the island is the small port of Ubli, which is 10 km (6 miles) from Lastovo Town.

Few Croatians have visited Lastovo, though all will tell you it's beautiful. Like Vis, Lastovo was a Yugoslav military naval base during the Tito years and was closed to foreigners, so commercial tourism never reached the same levels it did in other places in Croatia. Today, there is still just one hotel, and it has been slow to catch up to the tourism standards of other islands. People may wish to stay in one of the apartments or rooms offered directly by locals via booking platforms.

### GETTING HERE AND AROUND

Although it is officially in Southern Dalmatia, Lastovo only has ferry links with Split in Central Dalmatia rather than Dubrovnik. To get to the idyllic island, take the Jadrolinija daily ferry service from Split to Ubli, stopping at Hvar Town and Vela Luka (on Korčula) en route.

## Restaurants

**Konoba Bačvara**

$ | **SEAFOOD** | Traditional home-cooked Dalmatian fare is served at this family-run eatery in an old stone building in Lastovo Town. Barbecued seafood predominates, and you'll also have the chance to try homegrown vegetables and local wine as part of a refreshing island escape. **Known for:** affordable meals with fresh ingredients; exposed stone interior; payment is cash only. *Average main: €14* *Počuvalo 14, Lastovo* *020/801–131* *konoba-bacvara.business.site* *Closed Nov.–May. No lunch.*

**Konoba Triton**

$$ | **SEAFOOD** | Widely acknowledged to be the best restaurant on the island, Triton is particularly popular with those traveling by sailboat, who can moor up on a small quay out front (at a cost) and feast on dishes like freshly caught fish with locally produced wine and olive oil; it opens at 3 pm. You'll find it in Zaklopatica, a north-facing bay 3 km (2 miles) west of Lastovo Town. **Known for:** outdoor tables for enjoying a good appetizer with a sea view; payment is cash only; several apartments upstairs can be rented. *Average main: €20* *Zaklopatica 15, Lastovo* *091/731–3122* *www.facebook.com/tritonlastovo* *Closed Nov.–Mar. No lunch.*

## Activities

### BEACHES

Lastovo has no shortage of phenomenal beaches, but the best ones might just be slightly offshore; see for yourself by heading to **Saplun,** one of the tiny unpopulated **Lastovnjaci Islands,** which are a short distance northeast of Lastovo and are served by taxi-boats through high season.

### DIVING

**Paradise Diving Center**

**SCUBA DIVING** | **FAMILY** | Just a five-minute boat ride from this scuba-diving center based in the Hotel Solitudo lies a reef of red, yellow, and violet gorgonias at a depth of 15 meters (49 feet). Farther afield, experienced divers can explore sea caves and sunken ships. **TIP→ Note that inquiries must be made in-person or on the phone.** *Hotel Solitudo, Pasadur bb, Lastovo* *091/233–3373, 020/805–179* *From €10 per day for equipment rental, €450 per lesson for beginner diving instruction* *Closed Oct.–May.*

Chapter 5

# ZADAR AND NORTHERN DALMATIA

Updated by
John Bills

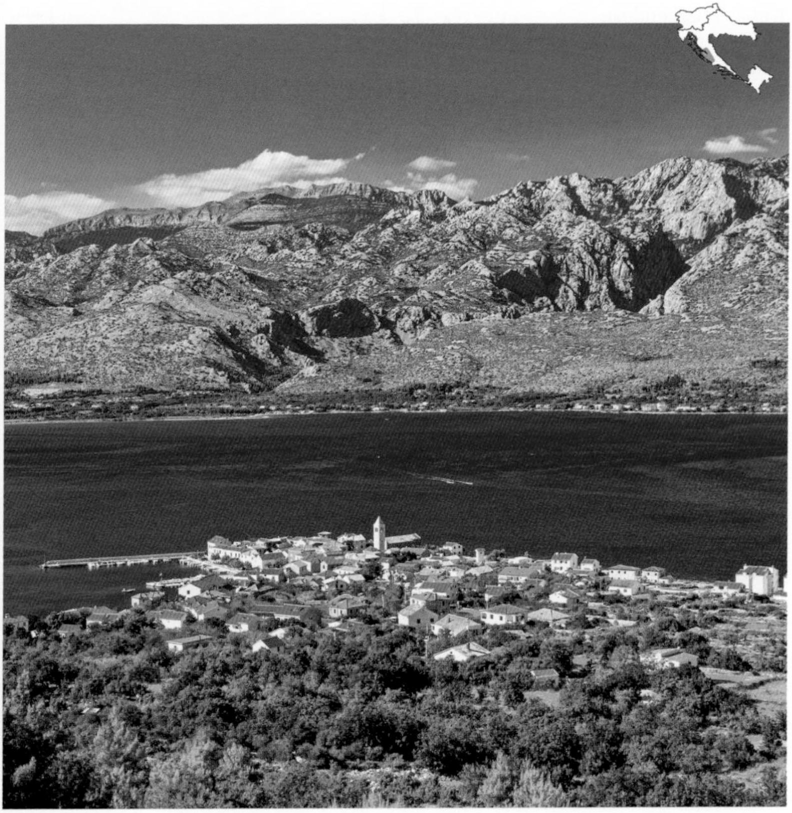

| Sights | Restaurants | Hotels | Shopping | Nightlife |
| --- | --- | --- | --- | --- |
| ★★★☆☆ | ★★☆☆☆ | ★★☆☆☆ | ★★☆☆☆ | ★★☆☆☆ |

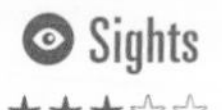

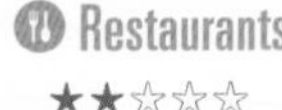

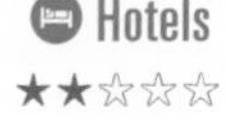

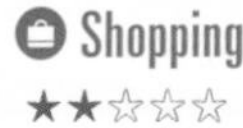

# WELCOME TO ZADAR AND NORTHERN DALMATIA

## TOP REASONS TO GO

★ **Zadar's historical center:** A history of trade and faith is embellished by a youthful populace and thrillingly innovative modern attractions.

★ **National and nature parks:** Croatia's natural beauty is at its most endearing here, thanks to the stunning landscapes of Telašćica Nature Park and Paklenica National Park.

★ **Island-hopping:** You'll find adventure and calm in equal measure, just off the Adriatic coast's northern reaches, from the peaceful Kornati Islands to fun-filled Pag, with its famous cheese and lace.

★ **Beaches:** Northern Dalmatia is a mecca for sun-worshippers of all shapes and sizes, especially those looking for something a little more down-to-earth.

Getting to Zadar is easiest by car. Be it on the A1 highway from Zagreb, down a winding coastal road from Rijeka, or from nearby Split—the roads are good, the views are stunning, and there are signs aplenty.

**1 Zadar.** The former capital of Dalmatia.

**2 Nin.** A peaceful town with rare sandy beaches.

**3 Sali and Telašćica Nature Park.** A charming fishing village that serves as the gateway to a lush nature park.

**4 Murter and the Kornati Islands.** The gateway to the largest archipelago in the Adriatic.

**5 Paklenica National Park.** A national park home to two fantastic gorges and other geological features.

**6 Pag.** An island famous for partying, cheese, and lace.

A1
E65
Brinje
Rakovica
Drežnik-Grad
Žuta Lokva
Plitvice Lakes National Park
Plitvice
Otočac
8
Starigrad
North Velebit National Park
Korenica
25
VELEBIT
Perušić
BOSNIA-HERZEGOVINA
Prizna
Gospić
Udbina
Karlobag
Medak
PAG
Pag
Paklenica National Park
Rok
Bruvno
Starigrad-Paklenica
Gračac
1
27
Nin
Posedarje
Obrovač
306
Novigrad
Zemunik
33
Zadar
UGLJAN
Sukošan
Benkovac
Knin
Zadar Archipelago
59
Biograd
PAŠMAN
Krka National Park
Sali
Vransko jezero
Bribir
Tkon
Telašćica Nature Park
Murter
Pirovac
Skradin
Drniš
KORNAT
Lozovac
Tijesno
Kornati National Park
Vodice
Šibenik
Primošten
30 miles
Split
30 kilometers
1
2
3
4
5
6

Safely protected from the northern Adriatic shore and continental Croatia by the imposing Velebit Mountains, Northern Dalmatia offers a whole new set of aesthetic and cultural values.

The islands get smaller and more abundant and the architecture, which varies between Roman, Venetian, Socialist, and modern influences, still carries the elegance of locally quarried limestone. Make Zadar, a fast-growing historical city, the focal point of your vacation, but do not overlook Nin and the islands, especially Kornati and Telašćica. Admirers of intact rough nature will revel in the beauty of Paklenica National Park.

Where exactly does Northern Dalmatia begin? Zadar may be the region's cultural and urban capital—it is, after all, the first sizable city you encounter in Dalmatia on your way south from Zagreb or Rijeka—but it is not where the region begins, either culturally or geographically. Look instead to the southern reaches of the Velebit Mountains, where that coastal range gives way to the flat sandy coastline of Nin and its environs. Practically speaking, though, you enter Dalmatia proper when you cross the long bright-red span of the Maslenica Bridge going south on the route from Zagreb to Zadar.

Though it's easy enough to drive on straight to Zadar, you won't regret stopping for a visit in Nin. While today it's an unassuming little town with well-preserved 17th-century architecture, more than 1,000 years ago—and for centuries afterward—it was one of the most important Croatian towns of all.

Much of the region is not on the mainland but instead comprises the Zadar Archipelago, including Pag, and, farther south, the Adriatic's largest archipelago, Kornati National Park. Farther inland, only miles from the coast is a sweeping expanse of countryside still visibly recovering from the Yugoslav war of the 1990s, where tourists rarely tread. Zadar, with its mix of Roman, Venetian, Communist-era, and modern architecture, has a bustling and beautiful historic center and is also the main point of access by ferry to the islands, including the beautiful Telašćica Nature Park.

## Planning

### When to Go

If you don't mind crowds, midsummer is a good time to visit Northern Dalmatia—when the Adriatic is at its optimal temperature for beachgoing and when you can also delight in the varied music, dance, and drama of the Zadar Summer Theatre (late June to early August), the Pag Summer Carnival (late July or early August), and Sali's annual Saljske užance, which features raucous horn-blown "donkey music" and donkey races (early August). However, if you don't mind missing out on midsummer culture and crowds, late spring to early autumn is preferable—when you can relax on relatively quiet beaches and enjoy discounts of up to 20% on accommodations relative to high season prices.

## Getting Here and Around

If you're driving or taking a bus from the north, you can stop for an excursion to Pag and Paklenica National Park before arriving in Zadar. The pretty little town of Nin is just 30 minutes north of Zadar and most easily done as a day trip (or even a half-day trip). Though many daily ferries can take you to the Zadar Archipelago, Sali (2 hours from Zadar by ferry) is an excellent place to base yourself for a night or two if you want to explore the outer reaches and have the best access to Telašćica Nature Park. A drive or bus trip to Murter will get you within a short boat ride of the spectacular Kornati National Park.

### AIR

Zadar's airport is in Zemunik Donji, 9 km (5½ miles) southeast of the city. Croatia Airlines, which offers service between Zadar and Zagreb as well as Paris and other European cities, runs buses (€4.65 one-way) between the airport, the city bus station, and the harbor near the ferry port on the Old Town's peninsula. The first bus leaves the city at 4 am, with the first departure from the airport leaving at 6:50 am.

### BOAT AND FERRY

Jadrolinija's local ferries (*trajektne linije*) and passenger boats (*brodske linije*) run daily routes that connect Zadar not only with the surrounding islands but also with Southern Dalmatia. The offices are by the Harbor Gate in the city walls, across from the ferry port. G&V Line Iadera also runs daily lines to Dugi Otok, Rava, Iž, Orebić, and others.

If you don't want to base yourself in Murter, you can take a cruise straight from the Borik Marina just outside Zadar all the way to Kornati National Park, that almost mythical archipelago even farther south. Zadar Archipelago's tours, which carry 14 passengers, will take you on a full-day journey (9 am to 6:30 pm) to the national park, including stops at Telašćica Nature Reserve, Vrulje Bay, Sali, and the islands of Mana and Levrnaka. Half-day tours are also available.

**CONTACTS Jadrolinija.** ✉ *Liburnska Obala 7, Zadar* ☎ *051/666–111* 🌐 *www.jadrolinija.hr.*

### BUS

Though sometimes crowded in midsummer, Zadar's bus station will almost certainly figure prominently in your travel plans unless you're driving or flying directly here. The trip to or from Zagreb takes around 3½ hours, and the one-way cost is between €15 and €18, depending on the company. Timetables are available at the station.

Getting to Nin from Zadar is easy by bus. The 30-minute trip follows the coastal road north; the fare is around €3 one-way, with buses running daily out of Zadar's station every 45 minutes or so. Be aware that FlixBus also runs between Zadar and Nin, but at a considerably higher price (€9).

Getting to Murter—to its tiny main square, Trg Rudina, which is where you're dropped off and picked up—from Zadar is certainly doable, if a bit complicated. There is a daily direct bus that takes 2 hours (€9), although these leave very early in the morning. Another option is to transfer either at Šibenik or at Vodice. Although the former option looks longer on the map, given the crowded confusion at Vodice's small station, Šibenik may be a less trying experience (and a surer way of getting a seat), even if it might take a bit longer; about 9 buses go on from Šibenik to Murter (via Vodice), versus 12 between Šibenik and Zadar. Travel time via Šibenik is 2½ hours or more (i.e., 90 minutes from Zadar to Šibenik, up to an hour of waiting time, then another 45 minutes to Murter via Vodice). The total cost is around €12 via Šibenik and around €11 if you go straight to Vodice (travel time is less than two hours, plus an even harder-to-predict wait time, because the bus from Šibenik might be contending with heavy traffic).

Numerous buses ply the one-hour route daily between Zadar and Starigrad for access to Paklenica National Park. The one-way cost to or from Starigrad—via the Zadar–Rijeka bus—is between €7 and €13, depending on the company. There are two stops in Starigrad; the national park information office is between the two, and the access road to the park is near the first stop (if you're coming from Zadar).

Around 10 buses daily drive the 1-hour route from Zadar to Pag Town, on Pag (€11).

Last but not least, the easiest way to get either from the bus station to Zadar's town center, or from the center to the Borik complex (with its beaches, hotels, and restaurants) on the northern outskirts, is by any of several user-friendly local buses. You can buy tickets at news kiosks for €1.60 (single ride); be sure to validate your ticket on boarding by inserting it into the stamping device. Once validated, tickets last 50 minutes.

**CONTACTS Zadar Bus Station.** ✉ *Ante Starčevića 1, Zadar* ☎ *023/316–915* 🌐 *liburnija-zadar.hr.*

### CAR

Zadar is the first major stop on the A1 highway between Zagreb and Dalmatia, which proceeds south toward Split. Barring traffic congestion, especially on weekends, the trip between Zagreb and Zadar is doable in 2½ hours. That said, you can also easily get to Zadar by bus—whether from Zagreb, Rijeka, or Split—and rent a car there if necessary. As the Zadar bus station can be a chaotic place at times, especially in midsummer, you might want to rent a car for some excursions—to Murter, for example, which otherwise involves a somewhat complicated time-consuming trip to or toward Šibenik with a transfer. But you'll be just fine without a car in and immediately around Zadar, as bus service is both good and affordable. To get to Pag by the Pag Bridge route, Pag Town (at the island's center) is within a 1-hour drive from Zadar. One good option is to spend two nights and take in Paklenica National Park, then drive another 25 minutes or so north along the coastal road toward Rab and Rijeka and take the ferry from the village of Prizna—roughly midway between Rijeka and Zadar, just south of Rab—to Žigljen in the north of the island (€3.32 per person, €14.86 for a car in midsummer); or do the same in reverse.

### TRAIN

Train travel in this region is next to nonexistent. Zadar has a train station but it has been out of use for several years, so it's better to use a bus or car to get around.

## Restaurants

Fresh seafood is the cuisine of choice in Northern Dalmatia, as it is elsewhere on Croatia's coast. Beyond standard coastal fare, look for Dalmatian specialties, including Pag Island lamb and *Paški sir* (Pag cheese); *pršut* (prosciutto) and*šokol* (smoked pork neck) from Posedarje; and sheep's cheese and peppery meat dishes from inner Dalmatia. And of course, there's Zadar's famous maraschino liqueur—compliments of the area's uniquely zesty cherry and the Maraska company, whose facility is just across the town's pedestrian bridge and whose brand name graces the bottles of the best maraschino.

## Hotels

As elsewhere along practically every populated area of the Croatian coast, package-hotel resorts are easy to find while top-notch pensions and intimate elegant small hotels are in short supply. However, a whole host of private rooms and apartments can be found, often for half the price of larger, more established accommodations, either through the local tourist information office or private travel agencies. And, as is the practice in other parts of Croatia, short stays (i.e., fewer than three days) often mean a surcharge of around 20%.

⇨ *Restaurant and hotel reviews have been shortened. For full information, visit Fodors.com. Restaurant prices are the average cost of a main course at dinner or, if dinner is not served, at lunch. Hotel prices are the lowest cost of a standard double room in high season.*

**What It Costs in Euros (€)**

| $ | $$ | $$$ | $$$$ |
|---|---|---|---|
| **RESTAURANTS** | | | |
| under €15 | €15–€23 | €24–€32 | over €32 |
| **HOTELS** | | | |
| under €150 | €150–€250 | €251–€350 | over €350 |

## Visitor Information

If there's no English speaker at the office you happen to contact, try the Zadar County Tourist Information office or the city of Zadar's corresponding office.

**CONTACTS Zadar Tourist Information.** ✉ *Jurja Barakovića 5, Zadar* ☎ *023/315–316* 🌐 *www.zadar.hr.*

## Zadar

*158 km (98 miles) northeast of Split.*

Dalmatia's capital for more than 1,000 years, Zadar is all too often passed over by travelers on their way to Split or Dubrovnik. What they miss out on is a city of more than 73,000 that is remarkably lovely and lively despite—and, in some measure, because of—its tumultuous history. The Old Town, separated from the rest of the city on a peninsula some 4 km (2½ miles) long and just 1,640 feet wide, is bustling and beautiful: the marble pedestrian streets are replete with Roman ruins, medieval churches, palaces, museums, archives, and libraries. Parts of the new town are comparatively dreary, a testament to what a world war followed by decades of communism, not to mention a civil war, can do to the architecture of a city that is 3,000 years old.

A settlement had already existed on the site of the present-day city for some 2,000 years when Rome finally conquered Zadar in the 1st century BC; the foundations of the Forum can be seen today. Before the Romans came, the Liburnians had made it a key center for trade with the Greeks and Romans for 800 years. In the 3rd century BC, the Romans began to seriously pester the Liburnians but required two centuries to bring the area under their control. During the Byzantine era, Zadar became the capital of Dalmatia, and this period saw the construction of its most famous church, the 9th-century St. Donat's Basilica. It remained the region's principal city through the ensuing centuries. The city then experienced successive onslaughts and occupations-—both long and short—by the Ostrogoths, the Croatian-Hungarian kings, the Venetians, the Turks, the Habsburgs, the French, the Habsburgs again, and finally the Italians before becoming part of Yugoslavia and, in 1991, the independent republic of Croatia.

Zadar was, for centuries, an Italian-speaking city, and Italian is still spoken widely, especially by older people. Indeed, it was ceded to Italy in 1921 under the Treaty of Rapallo (and reverted to its Italian name Zara). However, its occupation by the Germans in 1943 led to intense bombing by the Allies during World War II, which left most of the city in ruins. Zadar became part of Tito's Yugoslavia in 1947, prompting many Italian residents to leave. Zadar's more recent ravages occurred during a three-month siege by Serb forces and months more of bombardment during the Croatian-Serbian war between 1991 and 1995. But you'd be hard-pressed to find outward signs of this today in what is a city to behold.

### GETTING HERE AND AROUND

Zadar is the only sizable city in Northern Dalmatia and likely your first destination in the area. It has an international airport that connects it to Europe during the summer season (primarily via budget airlines) and to Zagreb and Pula year-round. You can also drive in via the A1 highway or the Adriatic Magistrala road, but a car will be of little use in the city itself, where narrow alleys are best explored on foot. There are ample regular bus lines from Zagreb, Rijeka, and Split, but be advised that the bus station is a 25-minute walk from the old city. Zadar's port is very busy, with lines serving local islands and an international line to Ancona, Italy.

### TOURS

**Malik Adventures**

**ADVENTURE TOURS** | **FAMILY** | Discover remote islands, sheltered coves, and steep cliffs only a short catamaran sail from Zadar with the energetic crew of Malik Adventures. The juxtaposition of intense adventure activities during the day with a night of slowly paced, exquisite local cuisine and island life may be the defining point of your vacation. This serene island is a rejuvenating break between touring cities. ✉ *Molat 40* ☎ *091/784–7547* 🌐 *malikadventures.com.*

**Secret Dalmatia**

**GUIDED TOURS** | Not the biggest, but certainly one of the best-organized companies, Secret Dalmatia specializes in showing you parts of Dalmatia that might not be on the tourist map. The owner, Alan, is very outgoing and reliable, and his team has Dalmatia well covered, from hidden little wineries to sailboats. Young and professional, their English is excellent. ✉ *Turanj 426* ☎ *091/567–1604* 🌐 *www.secretdalmatia.com.*

## Sights

**★ Archaeological Museum**

**HISTORY MUSEUM** | Founded in 1832, Zadar's Archaeological Museum is one of the oldest museums in this part of Europe. It occupies a plain but pleasant modern building beside the convent complex of Crkva svete Marije (St. Mary's Church). It is home to numerous artifacts from Zadar's past, from prehistoric times to the first Croatian settlements. The third floor focuses on ceramics, weaponry, and other items the seafaring Liburnians brought home from Greece and Italy, whereas the second floor covers the classical period, including a model of the Forum square as it would have looked back then. A smaller exhibit addresses the development of Christianity in Northern Dalmatia and contains rare artifacts from the invasion of the Goths. On the first floor, you'll find an exhibit focused on the early Middle Ages, taking you to the 12th century. ✉ *Trg Opatice Čike 1, Zadar* ☎ *023/250–516* 🌐 *amzd.hr* *€5* *Closed Sun. in Oct.–June.*

**BIBICh Winery**

**WINERY** | This winery, which operates a wine boutique in Zadar, produces wine both from native Dalmatian varieties, including Babić, Plavina, Lašina, and Debit, and nonnative grapes, including Grenache and Shiraz. The winery itself is located just outside of Skradin. ✉ *Zapadna Ulica 63, Plastovo* ☎ *091/323–5279* 🌐 *bibich.superbexperience.com* *Closed Mon.*

**Crkva Svete Marije** (*St. Mary's Church*)

**CHURCH** | Legend has it that a local noblewoman founded a Benedictine convent on this site in 1066 and the adjoining St. Mary's Church in 1091. Rebuilt in the 16th century, the church was supposed to incorporate a new Renaissance look into the remnants of its earlier style: its

St. Donatus Church is named after an Irish bishop who lived in the area in the early 800s.

rounded gables remained, continuing to express a particular Dalmatian touch. Early Romanesque frescoes are still evident amid the predominantly Baroque interior, and your eyes will discover 18th-century rococo above the original columns. Most noteworthy for modern-day visitors, however, is the adjoining convent complex, two wings of which house one of Zadar's most treasured museums. The Permanent Exhibition of Religious Art, whose highlight is commonly called "The Gold and Silver of Zadar," is a remarkable collection of work from centuries past by local gold- and silversmiths (including Italians and Venetians who lived here), from reliquaries for saints and crucifixes to vestments interwoven with gold and silver thread. ✉ *Poljana Opatice Čike, Zadar* 🌐 *benediktinke-zadar.com* 🎫 *€4 for museum.*

★ **Crkva Svetog Donata** (*St. Donatus Church*)

**CHURCH** | Zadar's star attraction, this massive cylindrical structure is the most monumental early Byzantine church in Croatia. Initially called the Church of the Holy Trinity, it was probably inspired by plans outlined in a book by the Byzantine emperor Constantine VII Porphyrogenitus, (*On Ruling the Empire*). Centuries later, it was rededicated to St. Donatus, the bishop here from 801 to 814. Legend has it that Donatus, an Irishman, was the one who had it built using stone from the adjacent Forum. The stark round interior features a circular center surrounded by an annular passageway; a sanctuary consisting of three apses attached to the lofty mantle of the church walls, set off from the center by two columns; and a gallery reached by a circular stairway. During the off-season (November to March), when the church is closed, someone at the Archaeological Museum next door may have a key to let you in. ✉ *Šimuna Kožičića Benje, Zadar* ☎ *023/250–613* 🌐 *amzd.hr* 🎫 *€3.50* 🕒 *Closed Nov.–Apr.*

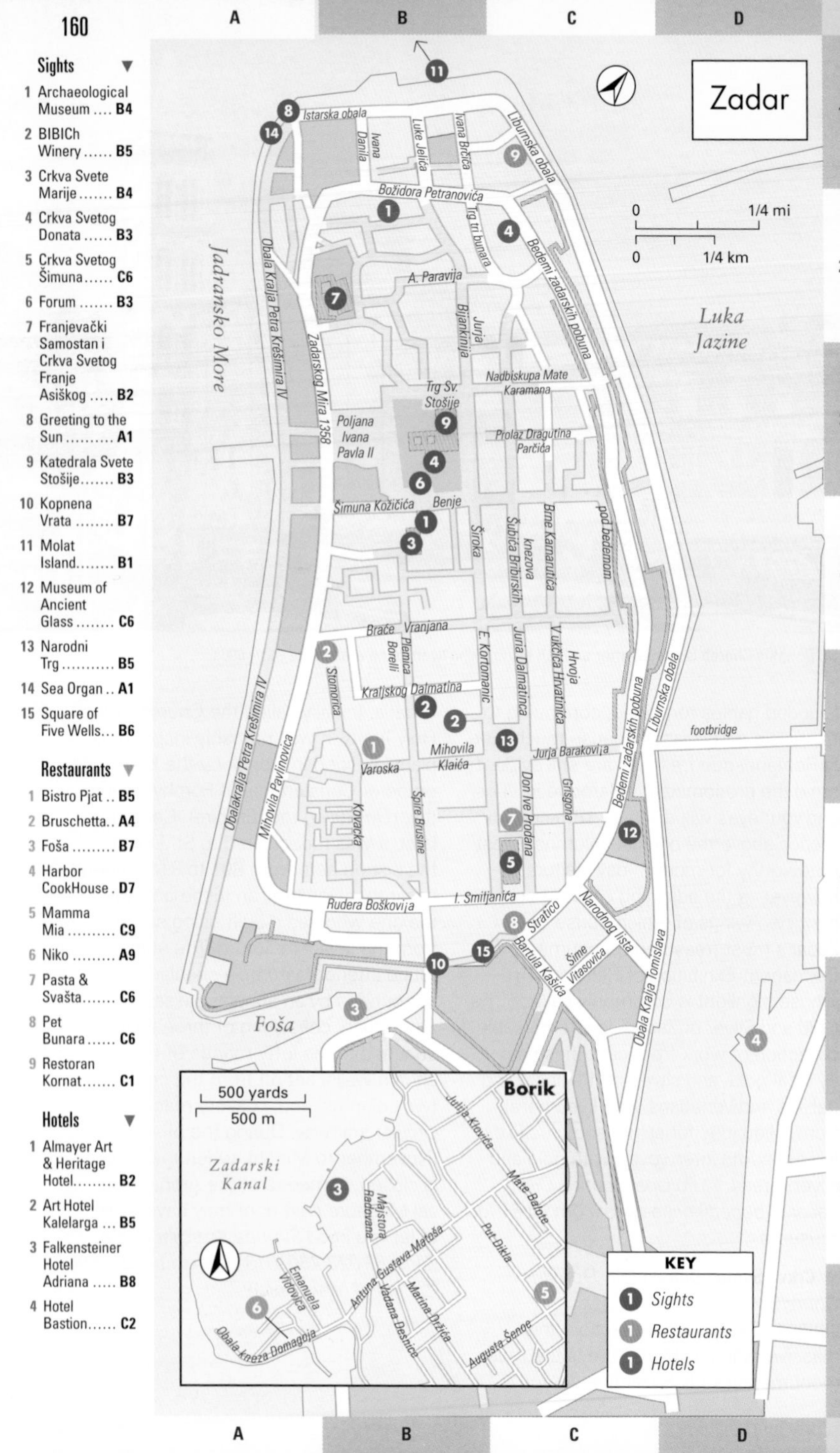
Sights
1 Archaeological Museum .... B4
2 BIBICh Winery ...... B5
3 Crkva Svete Marije ....... B4
4 Crkva Svetog Donata ...... B3
5 Crkva Svetog Šimuna ...... C6
6 Forum ....... B3
7 Franjevački Samostan i Crkva Svetog Franje Asiškog ..... B2
8 Greeting to the Sun .......... A1
9 Katedrala Svete Stošije....... B3
10 Kopnena Vrata ........ B7
11 Molat Island........ B1
12 Museum of Ancient Glass ........ C6
13 Narodni Trg........... B5
14 Sea Organ .. A1
15 Square of Five Wells... B6
Restaurants
1 Bistro Pjat .. B5
2 Bruschetta.. A4
3 Foša ......... B7
4 Harbor CookHouse . D7
5 Mamma Mia .......... C9
6 Niko ......... A9
7 Pasta & Svašta....... C6
8 Pet Bunara...... C6
9 Restoran Kornat....... C1
Hotels
1 Almayer Art & Heritage Hotel......... B2
2 Art Hotel Kalelarga ... B5
3 Falkensteiner Hotel Adriana ..... B8
4 Hotel Bastion...... C2
Zadar
0 1/4 mi
0 1/4 km
Jadransko More
Luka Jazine
Foša
Istarska obala
Ivana Dania
Luke Jelića
Ivana Brčića
Liburnska obala
Božidora Petranovića
Trg tri bunara
Bedemi zadarskih pobuna
Obala Kralja Petra Krešimira IV
A. Paravija
Jurja Bijankinija
Zadarskog Mira 1358
Nadbiskupa Mate Karamana
Trg Sv. Stošije
Poljana Ivana Pavla II
Prolaz Dragutina Parčića
Šimuna Kožičića
Benje
Široka
Šubića Bribirskih
knezova
Brne Karnarutića
pod bedemom
Braće Vranjana
Plemića Borelli
E. Kortomanic
Juria Dalmatinca
Vukčića Hrvatinića
Hrvoja
Stomorica
Kraljskog Dalmatina
Mihovila Klaića
Jurja Barakovića
footbridge
Varoska
Kovačka
Špire Brusine
Don Ive Prodana
Grisgona
Mihovila Pavlinovica
Obalakraljia Petra Krešimira IV
Rudera Boškovija
I. Smiljanića
Stratico
Narodnog lista
Šime Vitasovica
Bartula Kašića
Obala Kralja Tomislava
Borik
500 yards
500 m
Zadarski Kanal
Julija Klovića
Mate Balote
Majstora Radovana
Put Dikla
Antuna Gustava Matoša
Vadana Desnice
Marina Držića
Emanuela Vidovića
Obala kneza Domagoja
Augusta Šenoe
KEY
Sights
Restaurants
Hotels
A B C D
1 2 3 4 5 6 7 8 9

**Crkva Svetog Šimuna** (*St. Simeon's Church*)
**CHURCH** | Built in the 5th century as a three-nave basilica, St Simeon's Church was later reconstructed in Gothic style and again in Baroque style—however, the terra-cotta and white exterior pales when compared to some of the city's other churches. St. Simeon's Church is best known for housing the gilded silver sarcophagus of Zadar's most famous patron saint. The chest, which depicts intricately detailed scenes from St. Simeon's life and the city's history, was commissioned in 1381 by Elizabeth, wife of Croat-Hungarian King Ludwig I, and made by Francesco di Antonio da Sesto of Milan, one of Zadar's best silversmiths. As for St. Simeon, legend has it that his body wound up here while being transported from the Holy Land to Venice by a merchant who got caught in a storm, took refuge here, fell ill, and died—but not before drawing attention to the saintliness of the body he'd brought with him. Palm trees outside the church lend the site a pleasant Mediterranean touch. ✉ *Crkva Svetog Šime, Trg Petra Zoranića 7, Zadar* 🎫 *Free.*

**Forum**
**RUINS** | Established in the 1st century BC by the first emperor Augustus, the Roman Forum is, more than 2,000 years later, a vast empty space with some scattered ruins. However, since it was rediscovered in the 1930s and restored to its present condition in the 1960s, the Forum has been one of Zadar's most important public spaces. A raised area on the western flank indicates the site of a one-time temple dedicated to Jupiter, Juno, and Minerva. If you look closely, you will notice what remains of its altars that served as venues for blood sacrifices. The only surviving column was used in the Middle Ages as a "Pillar of Shame," to which wayward individuals were chained. Fragments of a second column were removed from the Forum in 1729 and put back together again near the Square of Five Wells, where the column still stands today. ✉ *Zeleni Trg, Zadar* 🎫 *Free.*

**Franjevački Samostan i Crkva Svetog Franje Asiškog** (*St. Francis Church & Franciscan Monastery*)
**CHURCH** | Dalmatia's oldest Gothic church, consecrated in 1280, is a stellar example of a so-called Gothic monastic church, characterized by a single nave with a raised shrine. Although the church underwent extensive reconstruction in the 18th century, behind the main altar is a shrine dating to 1672; inside the shrine, you can see choir stalls in the floral Gothic style that date to 1394. In 1358 a peace treaty was signed in this very sacristy under which the Venetian Republic ended centuries of attack and handed Zadar over to the protection of the Croat-Hungarian kingdom. From mid-October through March or April, the church may keep irregular hours. ✉ *Samostan Svetog Franje, Trg Svetog Frane 1, Zadar* ☎ *023/250–468.*

★ **Greeting to the Sun** (*Pozdrav Suncu*)
**PUBLIC ART** | The whimsically named The Greeting to the Sun is a 22-meter circle of multilayered glass plates set into the stone-paved waterfront. Under the glass, light-sensitive solar modules soak up the sun's energy during daylight hours, turning it into electrical energy. Just after sunset, it puts on an impressive light show, illuminating the waterfront in shades of blue, green, red, and yellow. It was installed in 2008 and was created by local architect Nikola Bašić, who also made the nearby sound art project, the Sea Organ. ✉ *Obala Kralja Petra Krešimira IV, Zadar* ✥ *Toward the western tip of the peninsula.*

**Katedrala Svete Stošije** (*St. Anastasia's Cathedral*)
**CHURCH** | From an earlier church, Dalmatia's largest basilica was shaped into its magnificent Romanesque form in the 12th and 13th centuries. However, it was damaged severely during World

War II and later reconstructed. The front portal is adorned with striking Gothic reliefs and a dedication to Archbishop Ivan from 1324. The interior includes not only a high spacious nave but also a Gothic stone ciborium from 1332 covering the 9th-century altar; intricately carved 15th-century choir stalls by the Venetian artist Matej Morozon; and, in the sacristy, an early Christian mosaic. St. Anastasia is buried in the altar's left apse; according to legend, she was the wife of a patrician in Rome but was eventually burned at the stake. Bishop Donatus of Zadar obtained the remains in 804 from Byzantine Emperor Nikephoros I. The late-19th-century belfry, separate from the main church building, offers a sweeping view to those who climb to the top for a fee, but even the 20 steps up to the ticket desk rewards you with a decent view of the square below. ✉ *Trg Svete Stošije 2, Zadar.*

**Kopnena Vrata** (*The Land Gate*)
**RUINS** | A walk around the walls of Zadar's Old Town is a walk around what was once the largest city-fortress in the Venetian Republic. One of the finest Venetian-era monuments in Dalmatia, the Land Gate was built in 1543 by the small Foša harbor as the main entrance to the city. It takes the form of a triumphal arch, with a large central passage for vehicles and two side entrances for pedestrians. It is decorated with reliefs of St. Chrysogonus (Zadar's foremost patron saint) on his horse and a winged lion (the symbol of the Venetian Republic). ✉ *Među Bedemima, Zadar.*

**Molat Island**
**ISLAND** | Many of Croatia's islands like to emphasize their serenity, but only one island gets the status of a true hermit heaven. Fewer than 200 people live on magnificent Molat, a verdant island covered in maquis and pine and a tranquil place that has fought for its survival over the centuries and lived to tell the tale. There isn't much to do on the island itself, but that is the point; this is an island for those searching for space and peace. One ferry heads this way daily from Zadar (sometimes two in summer, but there is no concrete schedule), with the journey taking an hour or so. Tickets are €3.50 in high season for foot passengers.

**Museum of Ancient Glass**
**OTHER MUSEUM** | Occupying the 19th-century Cosmacendi Palace on the edge of the Old Town, this museum displays one of the world's finest collections of Roman glassware outside Italy, with a vast array of ancient pieces unearthed from archaeological sites across Dalmatia. Highlights include the delicate vessels used by Roman ladies to store their perfumes, skin creams, essential oils, and sacred goblets used to celebrate Mass. ✉ *Poljana Zemaljskog Odbora 1, Zadar* ☎ *023/363–831* 🌐 *www.mas-zadar.hr* 🎫 *€6* 🕓 *Closed Sun. in Nov.–Apr.*

**Narodni Trg** (*People's Square*)
**PLAZA/SQUARE** | **FAMILY** | One of the Old Town's two main public spaces, the ever-bustling Narodni trg is home to the Gradska straža (City Sentinel), which was designed by a Venetian architect in late-Renaissance style with a large central clock tower. The sentinel's stone barrier and railing, complete with holes for cannons, were added later. This impressive tower once housed the ethnographic section of the National Museum and is today a venue for various regular cultural exhibits. ✉ *Narodni Trg, Zadar.*

★ **Sea Organ**
**PUBLIC ART** | Comprising 35 pipes under the quay stretching along a 230-foot stretch of Zadar's atmospheric Riva promenade, the Sea Organ yields a never-ending concert that delights one and all. Designed by architect Nikola Bašić with the help of other experts, the organ's sound resembles a whale song, but it is, in fact, the sea itself. It's hard not to be in awe as the sound of the sea undulates in rhythm and volume with the

Take a walk along Zadar's Riva promenade to hear the melodic tunes of the Sea Organ.

waves. ✉ *Obala Kralja Petra Krešimira IV, Zadar* ✣ *Toward the end of the western tip of the peninsula.*

**Square of Five Wells**

**PLAZA/SQUARE** | The square is the site of a large cistern built by the Venetians in the 1570s to help Zadar endure sieges by the Turks. The cistern has five wells that still look serviceable, even though they have long been sealed shut. Much later, in 1829, Baron Franz Ludwig von Welden, a passionate botanist, established a park above an adjacent pentagonal bastion built to keep the Turks at bay. ✉ *Trg Pet Bunara 1, Zadar.*

## Restaurants

**★ Bistro Pjat**

**$$** | **SEAFOOD** | For Zadar dining at its most convivial—and fish so fresh it practically dances off the plate—make a stop at Bistro Pjat. The menu changes daily depending on the catch, and the service here is tremendous. **Known for:** fresh catch menu; traditional atmosphere; charming service. $ *Average main: €18* ✉ *Stomorica 10, Zadar* ☎ *023/213–919* 🌐 *www.facebook.com/bistropjatzadar* ⏲ *Closed Sun.*

**Bruschetta**

**$$** | **MEDITERRANEAN** | With outdoor tables on a lovely terrace overlooking the sea in the Old Town, Bruschetta serves reasonably priced and well-presented Mediterranean cuisine. Popular with locals and visitors alike, it's primarily known for its pizzas and pasta dishes, but it also does excellent steaks, fresh fish, and an irresistible tiramisu. **Known for:** local seafood; view of the water; late-night eats. $ *Average main: €15* ✉ *Mihovila Pavlinovića 12, Zadar* ☎ *023/312–915* 🌐 *www.bruschetta.hr.*

**★ Foša**

**$$$$** | **SEAFOOD** | Boasting an appealing outdoor terrace overlooking a quiet little harbor, Foša combines age-old Dalmatian style with modern architectural design and gastronomy trends. Its old-world tastes give the kitchen foundation to create modern dishes with magnificent results. **Known for:** terrace views of the town walls; tasting menus; local tuna. $ *Average main: €70* ✉ *Kralja Dmitra Zvonimira 2, Zadar* ☎ *023/314–421* 🌐 *www.fosa.hr.*

**Harbor CookHouse**

$$$$ | **EUROPEAN** | Fantastic views and fashionable food are the main events at one of Zadar's finest business restaurants. The sunsets are almost as delicious as the food. **Known for:** friendly staff; top-notch international cuisine; the best sunsets in town. $ *Average main: €35* ✉ *Obala Kneza Branimira 6A, Zadar* ☎ *023/301–520* 🌐 *harbor.hr.*

**Mamma Mia**

$ | **PIZZA** | A popular place for locals and tourists, Mamma Mia serves delicious portions at fair prices and pizzas big enough to share (not that you'll want to). Pizza is the star here, with an impressive spread of toppings to choose from; if you're not a pizza fan, the daily specials always satisfy. **Known for:** oversized dishes; wood-fired pizza; good value. $ *Average main: €13* ✉ *Put Dikla 54, Zadar* ☎ *023/334–246* 🌐 *www.facebook.com/MammaMiaZadar.*

**Niko**

$$ | **MEDITERRANEAN** | Just across from a public beach and near the Borik resort complex, this distinguished restaurant has been serving up a delicious array of seafood, beef, veal, pork, and pasta dishes since 1963. You can choose between such lower-end fare as spaghetti with scampi or more expensive delights like scampi on the skewer. **Known for:** beachside location; historical ambience; something for everyone on the menu. $ *Average main: €18* ✉ *Obala Kneza Domagoja 9, Zadar* ☎ *023/337–880* 🌐 *hotel-niko.hr.*

**Pasta & Svašta**

$$ | **ITALIAN** | Charming and cozy (with limited but coveted seating), this tucked-away spot offers a consistently pleasant experience, especially on a clear night when you can sit in the courtyard, enjoying a tasty house wine that complements both the lighter fare and pasta plates. Knowledgeable servers will help you pair the fresh pasta and sauces; don't miss the pillowy gnocchi. **Known for:** local aperitifs; lovely courtyard; secluded location. $ *Average main: €15* ✉ *Poljana Šime Budinića 1, Zadar* ☎ *023/317–401.*

## Zadar's Cherry Liqueur

Zadar's famous maraschino cherry liqueur, one of the world's few liqueurs produced by distillation, is subtly sweet and robustly dry simultaneously. Look for bottles labeled Maraska, the Zadar company that produces this transparent spirit from the area's zesty sour cherries. It is typically enjoyed as either an aperitif or digestif.

★ **Pet Bunara**

$$$ | **MEDITERRANEAN** | For a break from the tourist bustle, head for Pet Bunara, a slow-food restaurant in a quiet little nook just off Trg pet bunara. The fare is creative and changes weekly, if not daily, according to the local produce available. **Known for:** secluded vibe; homemade fig jam; all local food. $ *Average main: €30* ✉ *Stratico 1, Zadar* ✣ *Near Trg Pet Bunara* ☎ *023/224–010* 🌐 *petbunara.hr.*

**Restoran Kornat**

$$$ | **SEAFOOD** | Just outside the city walls on the tip of the peninsula, and on the ground floor of a four-story concrete-box building, Kornat serves authentic first-rate cuisine with an emphasis on seafood—try the monkfish fillet with truffle sauce—plus a limited choice of hearty meat dishes. There's also an extensive wine list, from the best Croatian elixirs to the smoothest Shiraz. **Known for:** excellent seafood; wide-ranging wine

list; interesting desserts. [$] *Average main: €25* ✉ *Liburnska Obala 6, Zadar* ☎ *023/254–501* 🌐 *restaurant-kornat.hr.*

## Hotels

**Almayer Art & Heritage Hotel**
$$$ | **HOTEL** | Nestled into the historic Old Town, this family-owned boutique hotel in a 19th-century building preserves its historical character and has a modern, open, and artistic feel. **Pros:** beautiful interior and courtyard; green space; close to attractions and the beach. **Cons:** limited rooms, so often fully booked in high season; parking can be problematic; blankets on the small size. [$] *Rooms from: €350* ✉ *Braće Bersa 2, Zadar* ☎ *023/335–357* 🌐 *www.almayer.hr* *16 rooms* *Free Breakfast.*

★ **Art Hotel Kalelarga**
$$$ | **HOTEL** | Carefully curated modern furnishings create tremendous relief after a day of hustling through Zadar's narrow streets. **Pros:** excellent restaurant; one of the few hotels in the Old Town; good off-season packages. **Cons:** atmosphere can be stuffy; pricey; busy in summer. [$] *Rooms from: €260* ✉ *Majke Margarite 3, Zadar* ☎ *023/233–000* 🌐 *www.arthotel-kalelarga.com* *10 rooms* *Free Breakfast.*

**Falkensteiner Hotel Adriana**
$$ | **RESORT** | Flanked beachside by a grove of tall pines and encircled by a security fence (more to keep nonguests from enjoying the hotel's outdoor pool than for the sake of safety), this is an attractive place to stay even if the long narrow lobby does resemble an airport terminal. **Pros:** bright spacious rooms; lovely private beach; substantial discounts for stays of three nights or more. **Cons:** pricey; in a huge, somewhat characterless complex; not the best location. [$] *Rooms from: €160* ✉ *Majstora Radovana 7, Borik, Zadar* ☎ *023/206–300* 🌐 *www.falkensteiner.com* *48 rooms* *Free Breakfast.*

★ **Hotel Bastion**
$$ | **HOTEL** | Elegant, with artistic decoration and a refined ambience, Hotel Bastion offers a chic respite for travelers with a taste for sophistication. **Pros:** perhaps the best slow-food restaurant in the country; location in the Old Town; stylish interiors. **Cons:** small, so often fully booked in high season; Old Town is pedestrian-only and parking nearby can be problematic; guests pay to use the spa. [$] *Rooms from: €220* ✉ *Bedemi Zadarskih Pobuna 13, Zadar* ☎ *023/494–950* 🌐 *www.hotel-bastion.hr* *27 rooms* *Free Breakfast.*

## Nightlife

**Bamboo Caffe & Lounge Bar**
**BARS** | The big wooden deck clad with wooden benches, deck chairs, and grass umbrellas right on the beach certainly has its appeal. Bamboo Caffe & Lounge Bar overlooks the old city and outward to the islands. They know how to keep it simple, and their version of simple is pretty good. ✉ *Obala Kneza Domagoja 19, Zadar* 🌐 *www.beachbarbamboo.com.*

★ **Brlog**
**BARS** | Dalmatia hasn't wholly embraced the craft beer revolution (the abundance of great wine might be one reason), but there are plenty of great beers to be found here. Zadar's Brlog is top of the list, with several beers brewed by a fabulous team of fearless folks. They say that their beers are "crafted by stubbornness," but everything here is marvelously down-to-earth. The brewery's taproom is open through the summer months, with regular events posted on social media. ✉ *Andrije Hebranga 6, Zadar* ☎ *098/620–849* 🌐 *brlog.hr.*

**Deja Brew Pub**
**BARS** | The city's best beer selection blends well with the elegant surroundings of a Baroque palace, making for one of Zadar's most engaging nights out.

✉ *Borelli 8, Zadar* ☎ *098/331–392* 🌐 *deja-brew-pub-zadar.business.site.*

## Performing Arts

**Musical Evenings in Saint Donat**

**FESTIVALS** | Despite its name, this month-long series of classical music concerts and recitals, staged between early July and early August, is held in the Forum, St. Anastasia Cathedral, St. Donatus Church, and Marina Dalmacija, down the road in Bibinje. ✉ *Trg Petra Zoranića 1, Zadar* 🌐 *www.donat-festival.com.*

## Shopping

**Arsenal**

**WINE/SPIRITS** | Where the Venetians repaired their galleys in the 18th century is today a multipurpose cultural space that hosts art exhibitions and concerts, as well as a lounge bar, a restaurant, and a wineshop. ✉ *Trg Tri Bunara 1, Zadar* ☎ *023/253–821* 🌐 *arsenalzadar.com.*

## Activities

### BEACHES

Feel free to take a short dip off the quay in the Old Town—the most atmospheric place to do so being the Riva promenade and especially the tip of the peninsula directly over the Sea Organ, as nature's music accompanies your strokes. But for a more tranquil swim, head to the Kolovare district, just southeast of the Old Town, with its long stretch of park-flanked beach punctuated here and there by restaurants and cafés. There's also the resort complex in Borik, where relatively shallow waters and a sandy bottom may be more amenable to kids. Last but not least, by driving or taking a bus 30 minutes north along the coast, you can reach the famously sandy beaches of Zaton and Nin. For true peace and quiet, though, your best bet is an excursion by ferry and then on foot, by bicycle, or in a rental car out to some more isolated stretch of beach on an island of the Zadar Archipelago.

### BOATING

**Zadar Archipelago**

**BOATING** | This Zadar-based company runs day trips by boat from Zadar to the islands of Kornati National Park. All tours have a maximum of 12 travelers, allowing for a more individual approach rather than the general tourist offerings of uncomfortably packed boats. ✉ *Obala Kneza Trpimira 2, Zadar* ☎ *099/627–3333* 🌐 *zadar-archipelago.com.*

# Nin

*14 km (9 miles) northeast of Zadar.*

On a tiny 1,640-foot-wide island in a shallow sandy lagoon that affords a spectacular view of the Velebit Mountains to the northeast, Nin is connected to the mainland by two small bridges. The peaceful town of 1,700, a compact gem whose present-day size and unassuming attitude belie a turbulent history, is well worth a visit, whether on the way to Zadar or as a day trip from there—assuming that the beautiful sandy beaches stretching for miles around Nin don't inspire you to stay a bit longer.

Nin was a major settlement of the Liburnians, an Illyrian people who also settled Zadar hundreds of years before the Romans came, conquered, and named it Aenona. A vital harbor for centuries, it was the first seat of Croatia's royalty. It was also the region's episcopal see, whose bishop was responsible for converting all Croatian territory to Christianity. In 1382 the Venetians seized it and prospered from the trade in salt, livestock, and agriculture. However, the Venetian-Turkish wars eventually brought devastating onslaughts, including Nin's destruction in 1571; later, the Candian Wars of 1645–69 led to the decimation of Nin and the surrounding area yet again.

Aside from its historic buildings and monuments that testify to a rich past, Nin's draw also includes the only sandy beaches on this stretch of the Adriatic, not to mention the area's medicinal seaside mud. Since the sea here is shallow, water temperatures are warmer than in the rest of the Adriatic; moreover, the water is more saline, accounting for Nin's primary export—salt. But what would a Croatian coastal town be without the usual resort complex on its fringes? Zaton Holiday Resort is a 15-minute walk from the Old Town.

If you're coming from Zadar, soon before you reach Nin proper, look to your left (your right if headed back toward Zadar) to see the squat, stony 12th-century form of St. Nicholas's Church on a hillock out in the middle of a field, looking somewhat like a cake ornament with a lone Scotch pine at the foot of the little hill keeping it company. You can enter Nin via one of two small bridges—the most likely of the two being the charming pedestrian Donja most (Lower Bridge), only yards from the tourist information office, which provides a helpful map that folds small enough to fit in your palm. If you're coming by car, you can park in a lot on the right just beyond the office and then cross the bridge or find a semi-legal spot along the road roughly opposite the lot, which plenty of enterprising visitors prefer.

## GETTING HERE AND AROUND

The best way to Nin is a 15-km (9-mile) drive from Zadar, be it by car or on one of the regular buses. Once there, you can only get around on foot.

The small island of Nin holds only 1,700 residents.

## Sights

**Asseria**

**RUINS** | Close to Nin and situated 6 km (3¾ miles) east of Benkovac, near the village of Podgrađeare, lie the massive ruins of Asseria, an ancient city. First settled around 6 BC by Liburnians, who built it into one of their most important towns before the Romans came, Asseria—which is nearly 1,640 feet long and roughly a third as wide—was inhabited for more than 1,000 years before crumbling away along with the Roman Empire. ✉ *Village Podgrađe.*

**Crkva Svetog Anselma** (*St. Anselm's Church*)

**CHURCH** | The 18th-century Crkva svetog Anselma, dedicated to a 1st-century martyr believed to have been Nin's first bishop, was built on the site of Nin's former 9th-century cathedral, the first cathedral of the medieval Croatian principality. To the right of the altar is a 15th-century statue of the Madonna of Zečevo, inspired by the appearance of the Virgin Mary to a woman on a nearby island. Though the church is plain—the ceiling is adorned with only a lovely chandelier and a smoke detector—the foundations of the former cathedral are still much in evidence. Beside the church is the belfry, and next door is the treasury, which houses a stunning little collection of reliquaries containing various body parts of St. Anselmo. ✉ *Branimirova, Nin* ✥ *Near Višeslavov Trg* ☎ *098/509–307* 🎫 *Free.*

**Crkva Svetoga Križa** (*Church of the Holy Cross*)

**CHURCH** | Croatia's oldest church, the 8th-century Crkva svetog Križa is also known locally as the "world's smallest cathedral." Indeed, the simple, three-naved whitewashed structure—which has a solid cylindrical top and a few tall Romanesque windows (too high to peek inside)—has an unmistakable monumental quality to it even though it's no larger than a small house. There's little to see inside, though it is sometimes open, erratically, in summer; check with the tourist office or the Archaeological

Museum. ✉ *Petra Zoranića 8, Nin* 🎫 *Free.*

**Muzej Ninskih Starina** (*Archaeological Museum*)

**HISTORY MUSEUM** | Nin's shallow coast and centuries of sand deposits preserved numerous remains from prehistory to the Middle Ages under the sea. The Archaeological Museum has a rich collection for a town of this size, including replicas of two small late-11th-century fishing boats discovered only in 1966 and carefully removed from the sea in 1974. One of these boats has been completely reconstructed, the other only to the extent to which it had been preserved underwater. The main themes in each room are elucidated in clear English translations. ✉ *Trg Kraljevac 8, Nin* ☎ *023/250–542* 🎫 *€4.*

**Nin Saltworks**

**FACTORY** | Historically, Nin's riches came from an unlikely source: salt. Making the best of a rare geographical location with lots of sun, wind, and shallow sea basins, Nin Saltworks still produces salt in a traditional ecological way to this day. To commemorate salt's vast influence on the city's development, Nin opened a small but charming salt museum showing how this common table adornment was produced back in the day. While there, make sure to pick up a bag of *fleur du sel*, or "flower of salt," ultra-rich in minerals. You can take a tour led by a professional guide (offered on the hour) for a fee. ✉ *Ilirska Cesta 7, Nin* ☎ *023/264–021* 🌐 *www.solananin.hr* 🎫 *€5 for House of Salt; €10 for educational tour.*

**Konoba Bepo**

$$ | **MEDITERRANEAN** | **FAMILY** | Even if you are not staying at Zaton Holiday Resort, you might find yourself at Bepo in search of a good meal because Nin has few worthy alternatives. Bepo's charming atmosphere is lively, and the menu is a good representation of local Mediterranean fare. **Known for:** excellent regional olive oil; favorite with locals; traditional desserts. $ *Average main: €16* ✉ *Zaton Holiday Resort, Dražnikova 76T, Nin* ☎ *023/280–366* 🌐 *www.konoba-bepo.hr.*

**Zaton Holiday Resort**

$ | **RESORT** | Just 3 km (less than 2 miles) from Nin, the Zaton Holiday Resort is a one-size-fits-all holiday extravaganza perfect for anyone traveling with their family. **Pros:** sandy beach (a rarity in Croatia); wide-ranging entertainment offerings; relaxed resort atmosphere. **Cons:** decor is a bit old-fashioned; gets packed in summer; terrible Wi-Fi. $ *Rooms from: €100* ✉ *Dražnikova 78, Nin* ☎ *23/280–280* 🌐 *www.zaton.hr* *600 apartments, 374 mobile homes, 31 glamping lodges* 🍽 *No Meals.*

# Sali and Telašćica Nature Park

*Sali is approximately 30 km (19 miles) southwest of Zadar; Telašćica Nature Park is 10 km (6 miles) southeast of Sali.*

The largest and most westerly island of the Zadar Archipelago, Dugi Otok culminates at its southern end with a spectacular nature preserve in and around Telašćica Bay, the town of Sali being its ideal access point. Situated toward the southeastern tip of the 52-km-long (32-mile-long) island, which is no more than 4 km (2½ miles) wide, Sali is Dugi Otok's largest settlement—with around half of the island's 1,800 inhabitants, the rest of whom reside primarily in its 10 other villages—but it's a peaceful little place to arrive in after the 2-hour ferry ride from Zadar.

Telašćica Nature Park is surrounded by high vertical cliffs to the west, with lovely views to the east.

## GETTING HERE AND AROUND

Sali is on Dugi Otok and functions as a gateway to Telašćica Nature Park. You can get to Sali via the regular ferry line from Zadar to Dugi Otok or hop on one of many organized tours leaving from the area. Telašćica is a special treat, of course, for those chartering their own boat.

## Sights

### Sali

**TOWN** | Once an out-of-the-way fishing village, Sali draws tourists thanks to its location in and near such natural splendors. It is home to several old churches, including the 12th-century St. Mary's Church, whose Baroque altar was carved in Venice. Adding to the village's appeal is its annual Saljske užance (Donkey Festival) during the first full weekend in August, which includes an evening ritual during which lantern-lit boats enter Sali Harbor and there are donkey races and *tovareća muzika* (donkey music) produced by locals blowing or braying raucously into horns. Spending at least a night or two here can provide a relatively peaceful nature-filled respite from the rigors of tourism on the mainland or, for that matter, on more tourist-trodden reaches of the Zadar Archipelago. ✉ *Sali.*

### ★ Telašćica Nature Park

**NATIONAL PARK** | This nature park encompasses Telašćica Bay, which cuts 7 km (4½ miles) into the southern tip of Dugi Otok with an indented inner coastline that is a series of smaller bays and a handful of islands. Flanked by high vertical cliffs facing the open sea to the west and with low peaceful bays on the other side, it has a variety of vegetation. Relatively lush alpine forests and flower-filled fields, as well as vineyards, olive groves, and one-time cultivated fields give way as you move south to bare rocky ground of the sort that predominates on the Kornati Islands, whose northern boundary begins where Telašćica Nature Park ends.

Aside from Telašćica's other attractions, most of which are accessible only by boat, one of the park's key highlights—accessible by land on a 20-minute drive from Sali—is the salt lake Jezero mir, which formed when the sea filled a karst depression. Small boats (generally with 8–12 passengers) bound for both Telašćica Nature Park and the northern fringes of Kornati National Park leave the east side of Sali's harbor (i.e., where the Zadar ferry arrives) at approximately 11:15 each morning and return by 6 or 6:30 in the evening. Verify ferry times at 🌐 *www.croatiaferries.com.* The best way to arrange ferry passage is in person—by going to the harborside square near the post office around 8 pm on the day before you wish to leave, when boat captains gather there looking for passengers for the next day's excursion (which means at least a one-night stay in Sali). However, the tourist information office in Sali can put you in touch with operators by phone as well. ✉ *Put Danijela Grbina, Sali* ☎ *023/377–096* 🌐 *pp-telascica.hr.*

**Zadar Archipelago**

**ISLAND** | The Zadar Archipelago is so close and yet so far away: Ugljan and Pašman are just two of the myriad islands comprising the lacelike islands and are among the largest and the easiest to reach from Zadar. More than 15 ferries a day run the 5-km (3-mile) distance between Zadar and Ugljan, a 19-km-long (12-mile-long) island whose narrow width of just a couple of kilometers runs parallel to the mainland, with its midway point across from Zadar. From the ferry landing on Ugljan, your best bet may be to head north along the seafront for 10 minutes on foot to the heart of Preko, a fine access point to several worthwhile destinations (very) near and (not too) far. Going south will get you to the unassuming fishing village of Kali. From Preko's harbor, you can walk about 1 km (½ mile) farther north to a shallow bay locals like to swim in, or better yet, take a taxi-boat to Galevac, a charming wooded islet less than 100 yards from Preko that has not only splendid swimming but also a 15th-century Franciscan monastery set in a lush green park. And then there's the Tvrđava svetog Mihovila (Fortress of St. Michael), a 13th-century landmark atop a hill roughly an hour's walk west of town. Though mainly in ruins, the fortress offers spectacular views of nearby Zadar to the west and, on a cloudless day, the Italian coast.

Meanwhile, 10 km (6 miles) farther north is the quiet village of Ugljan, accessible from the ferry port by a handful of buses daily. For a somewhat sleepier island experience, hop aboard one of eight buses daily from Preko to the village of Pašman. You can eventually get to Tkon, Pašman Island's largest village, from which some 10 ferries daily can get you back to the mainland south of Zadar. ✉ *Zadar.*

## Restaurants

**Konoba Kod Sipe**

**$$ | EASTERN EUROPEAN** | If you want a hearty meal well above the tourist fray in Sali, you'll have to do some climbing (more than 100 steps!) to reach this rustic restaurant with tables on barrels, fishnets hanging from the ceiling's wooden beams, an enticing open hearth, and an outdoor terrace shaded by grapevines. Set in a village-like atmosphere that feels very off the beaten path, Konoba Kod Sipe serves everything from grilled calamari and pork chops to cuttlefish spaghetti. **Known for:** octopus under a baking lid; rustic barrel-themed decor; favorite with locals. $ *Average main: €20* ✉ *Sali* ☎ *099/741–3499* 🌐 *konoba-kod-sipe.business.site* 💳 *No credit cards.*

**Konoba Trapula**

**$$ | MEDITERRANEAN** | Located in the cool shade of a stone alleyway behind Sali's harbor, Konoba Trapula has the charm of a place you can find only by word of mouth, as well as delicious fresh seafood, such as *brudet* (seafood stew) and perfectly prepared tuna steak. The polished dark-wood tables and the nautical decor remind you of the restaurant's proximity to the sea. **Known for:** perfectly cooked seafood; nautical atmosphere; secluded location. $ *Average main: €15* ✉ *Sali II 74, Sali* ☎ *095/713–7297* 🌐 *konoba-trapula-sali.eatbu.hr.*

# Murter and the Kornati Islands

*70 km (44 miles) southeast of Zadar.*

Built near the ruins of the 1st-century Roman settlement of Colentum, Murter has that unmistakable tourism-driven hustle and bustle in midsummer that Sali doesn't—both because it is the crucial gateway to one of Croatia's chief offshore natural splendors, Kornati National Park, and because it is easily accessible by road from Zadar.

### GETTING HERE AND AROUND

Murter Island is serviced by regular ferries from the town of Tisno, a pretty place that straddles the peninsula and the mainland, halfway between Zadar and Šibenik. If you're visiting Kornati National Park only for a day, there are many daily boats leaving from Zadar (north of the park) and Vodice (south of the park).

## Sights

### ★ Kornati National Park

**NATIONAL PARK** | The largest archipelago in the Adriatic, Kornati National Park comprises more than 100 privately owned islands, primarily by residents of Murter, who purchased them more than a century ago from Zadar aristocrats. The new owners burned the forests to make room for sheep, which ate much of the remaining vegetation. Although anything but lush today, the islands' almost mythical beauty is ironically synonymous with their barrenness: their bone-white-to-ochre colors are a striking contrast to the azure sea.

However, owners do tend vineyards and orchards on some, and there are quite a few small buildings scattered about, mostly stone cottages—many of them on Kornat, which is by far the largest island, at 35 km (22 miles) long and less than a tenth as wide.

In 1980 the archipelago became a national park. It was reportedly during a visit to Kornati in 1936 that King Edward VIII of England decided between love for his throne and love for Wallis Simpson, the married woman who was to become his wife a year later. No public transport currently goes to Kornati, so visiting is only possible as part of an excursion or with a private boat, and tickets must be purchased beforehand. Pick up tickets from the official website or through the various tour groups in Zadar or Murter. The entrance ticket is included in the price of excursions departing from Zadar. ✉ *Zadar* ☎ *022/435–740* 🌐 *www.np-kornati.hr.*

### Murter

**TOWN** | However you go to Murter, you'll pass through Biograd-Na-Moru, a relatively big, bustling—but thoroughly tourist-trampled—town, where the resorts have long come to dominate what was once a charming place; Biograd-Na-Moru also serves as another access point for ferries to the Kornati Islands.

Murter, a town of 2,000 on the island of the same name that lies just off the mainland, is accessible by road from the main coastal route that runs south from Zadar toward Split. As important as tourism is to its present-day economy, boatbuilding has, not surprisingly, long been vital to Murter as well. This is not to mention its olive oil, which was once so famous that it made its way to the imperial table in Vienna. ✉ *Murter.*

## Restaurants

### Konoba Boba

$$$ | **MEDITERRANEAN** | **FAMILY** | Beyond its outstanding selection of seafood, Boba offers a variety of regional delicacies sure to please even picky diners. The outdoor terrace and shaded gardens provide a quiet respite, and while the restaurant is trendy, it doesn't feel crowded. **Known for:** popular among locals; diverse regional dishes; charming garden terrace. *Average main: €30* ✉ *Butina 22, Murter* ☎ *098/937–9181* 🌐 *www.konobaboba.hr* ⏲ *Closed Mon.*

### Tic Tac

$$$$ | **SEAFOOD** | At this elegant little restaurant near the main square, with tables lining the length of the narrow historic alleyway, you can begin with an appetizer such as mussels in wine sauce and move on to monkfish tail or grilled scampi—both in wine sauce. The chef likes putting seafood in wine sauce here to a gratifyingly delicious effect. **Known for:** historic location; seafood in wine sauce; delightful family backstory. *Average main: €40* ✉ *Hrokešina 5, Murter* ☎ *022/435–230* 🌐 *www.tictac-murter.com.*

## Activities

### DIVING

Kornati National Park is among Croatia's most popular diving destinations, with its shipwrecks, reefs, and underwater cliffs. You must dive with someone here and book your dive through a qualified center. The permit for diving in the park is €15, which includes the park entrance fee.

### Aquanaut Diving Center

**SCUBA DIVING** | This company offers a small menu of choice courses and excursions (to more than 100 sites) in the Kornati Islands. Nondiving companions are also welcome to join at a reduced fee. The company offers dolphin-watching tours, too. ✉ *Jurja Dalmatinca 1, Murter* ☎ *098/202–249* 🌐 *www.divingmurter.com.*

### Najada Diving

**SCUBA DIVING** | Offering supervised shore dives and half-day group excursions, Najada Diving has been a Murter institution for more than two decades. It features excursions to more than 30 sites. Among the highlights is a visit to the wreck of the World War II cargo ship *Francesca.* ✉ *Put Jersan 17, Murter* ☎ *098/137–1565* 🌐 *www.najada.com.*

# Paklenica National Park

*50 km (31 miles) northeast of Zadar.*

For mountain scenery at its most spectacular and mountain tourism at its most advanced, you need go no further from Zadar than Paklenica National Park.

## Sights

### ★ Paklenica National Park

**NATIONAL PARK** | The Velebit Mountains stretch along the Croatian coast for more than 100 km (62 miles), but nowhere do they pack in as much to see and do as in this relatively small, 96-square-km (37-square-mile) park at the southern terminus of the range. Here, less than an hour from Zadar is a wealth of extraordinary karst features—from fissures, crooks, and cliffs to pits and caves. The park comprises two limestone gorges, Velika Paklenica (which ends near the sea, at the park entrance in Starigrad) and Mala Paklenica, a few kilometers to the south; trails through the former gorge are better marked (and more tourist-trodden).

All that dry rockiness visible from the seaward side of the range turns resplendently green as you cross over the mountains to the landward side. Named after the sap of the black pine, *paklina,* which was used long ago to prime boats, the park is two-thirds forest, with beech and the indigenous black pine forming a crucial part of this picture; the remaining vegetation includes cliff-bound habitats featuring several types of bluebells and rocky areas abounding in sage and heather. The park is also home to 4,000 species of fauna, including butterflies that have long vanished elsewhere in Europe. It is also Croatia's only mainland nesting ground for the stately griffin vulture.

The park has more than 150 km (94 miles) of trails, from relatively easy ones leading from Velika Paklenica (from the entrance in Starigrad) to the 1,640-foot-long complex of caverns called Manita peć, to mountain huts situated strategically along the way to the Velebit's highest peaks, Vaganski vrh (5,768 feet) and Sveto brdo (5,751 feet). The most prominent of the park's immense and spectacular caves, Manita peć is accessible on foot from the park entrance in Starigrad; you can enter for €10, but remember to buy your ticket at the park entrance. Rock climbing is also a popular activity in the park. Meanwhile, mills and mountain villages scattered throughout Paklenica evoke the life of mountain folk from the not-too-distant past.

About a half mile down the park access road in Starigrad, you pass through the mostly abandoned hamlet of Marasovići, from which it's a few hundred yards more downhill to the small building where you buy your tickets and enter the park (from this point on, only on foot). From here, it's 45 minutes uphill to a side path to Anića kuk, a craggy peak, and from there it's not far to Manita peć. However, if you don't have the time or inclination for a substantial hike into the mountains, you will be happy to know that even the 45-minute walk to the entrance gate and back from the main road affords spectacular close-up views of the Velebit range's craggy ridgeline and the gorge entrance. Also, be forewarned that if you are looking to escape the crowds, you will be hard-pressed to do so here in midsummer unless you head well into the mountains or, perhaps, opt for the park's less frequented entrance at Mala Paklenica; more likely than not, you will be sharing the sublimities of nature with thousands of other seaside revelers taking a brief respite from the coast.

A further point of interest at the park is the Bunkers, an intricate system of underground shelters built by Marshal Tito in the early 1950s. With relations between Yugoslavia and the USSR then at their worst, Tito used the geographical benefits of the gorges to build a bomb shelter. All the work was done in complete secrecy, and very few people knew of the Bunkers. After Stalin's death, they were closed down and only reopened in 1991.

Although the park headquarters is on the main coastal road in the middle of Starigrad, fees are payable when you enter the park on the access road. Beyond the basic park admission and the supplemental fee to enter Manita peć, the park offers every possible service and presentation that might encourage you to part with your euros, from half-day group tours to presentations and more. ✉ *Dr. Franje Tuđmana 14A, Starigrad* ☎ *023/369–202* 🌐 *np-paklenica.hr* 🎫 *€10 entrance fee; €20 for 3-day pass.*

## Restaurants

**Restaurant Dinko**

**$ | MEDITERRANEAN** | With generous portions and a location just a short distance from Paklenica National Park, Restaurant Dinko is perfect for feeding hungry climbers, hikers, and park visitors. Dinko sticks to the basics, serving fresh seafood and traditional Croatian dishes in a rustic outdoor setting. **Known for:** neighboring national park; outdoor rustic atmosphere; knowledgeable staff. $ *Average main: €10* ✉ *Paklenicka 1, Starigrad* ☎ *091/512–9455* 🌐 *www.dinko-paklenica.com.*

**Hotel Rajna**
**$ | HOTEL** | On an isolated stretch of the main road just before you enter Starigrad from the south—and close to the national park access road—this friendly little hotel is a bit concrete-box-ish in appearance but offers not only a splendid view of the mountains to the east and clean, spacious (though not quite sparkling and modern) rooms, but also a restaurant with carefully prepared, scrumptious seafood fare. **Pros:** pleasantly isolated spot near park-access road; fine mountain views; good on-site dining. **Cons:** 15-minute walk from the village center; bland on the outside; rooms a tad worn. *Rooms from: €85* ✉ *Dr. Franje Tuđmana 105, Starigrad* ☎ *023/359–121* 🌐 *www.hotel-rajna.com* *10 rooms* *Free Breakfast.*

# Pag Island

*48 km (30 miles) northeast of Zadar.*

Telling an urbane resident of architecturally well-endowed Zadar that you are headed to Pag for a night or two will make them think you want to wallow on a sandy beach all day and party all night. Indeed, Pag has developed a reputation in recent years as a place to sunbathe and live it up rather than visit historical sites. The town of Novalja, in the north, has quite a summertime population of easy-livin' revelers. But to be fair, this narrow island—one of Croatia's longest, stretching 63 km (40 miles) north to south—has long been famous for other reasons, among them its cheese, salt, and, not least, its lace. Moreover, Pag Town, in particular, has an attractive historic center, a surprising contrast to its outskirts' modern resortish feel and distinct from the breathtaking natural barrenness of so much of the island.

Inaccessible for centuries except by sea, Pag saw a dramatic boost in tourism starting in 1968 with the completion of the Paškog mosta (Pag Bridge), which linked it with the mainland and the Zagreb–Split motorway. The first thing you'll notice on crossing over the bridge onto the island is that practically all vegetation disappears. You are on a moonlike landscape of whitewashed rocks scattered with clumps of green hanging on for dear life. But, sure enough, soon you'll also notice the sheep so instrumental in producing both Pag cheese—that strong, hard, Parmesan-like product that results from the sheep munching all day long on the island's salty herbs—and, yes, Pag lamb. Then, five minutes or so apart, pass through a couple of small villages and, finally, the vast salt flats stretching out along the road right before you pull into Pag Town.

### GETTING HERE AND AROUND

Pag is easiest to reach by car or bus from Zadar via the toll-free Pag Bridge. There are several inexpensive bus connections, with the journey lasting 50 minutes. If driving along the Magistrala from Rijeka, you will do well to take the ferry from Prizna, while nondrivers have the option of a daily fast boat connection from Rijeka to Novalja at the southern tip of the island.

**Crkva Sveta Marija** (*St. Mary's Church*)
**CHURCH** | This three-nave basilica's simple front is decorated with a Gothic portal, an appropriately lacelike Renaissance rosette, and unfinished figures of saints. A relief over the entrance depicts the Virgin Mary protecting the townsfolk of Pag. Begun in 1466 under Dalmatinac's direction, it was completed only decades after his death. Inside, note the elaborate 18th-century Baroque altars and the wood beams visible on the original stone walls. The church is open daily from 9 until noon and from 5

until 7 in the evening. ✉ *Glavni Trg, Jurja Dalmatinca 6, Pag.*

**Knežev Dvor** (*Duke's Palace*)
**HISTORIC HOME** | Across the square is the imposing Knežev dvor, with its magnificent richly detailed portal, a grand 15th-century edifice built to house the duke. Until the early 1990s, it housed a grocery store and a café; now it is a cultural and exhibition venue, hosting concerts, plays, and manifestations during the summer months. The upper floors have been converted into the City Hall. ✉ *Glavni Trg, Pag.*

**Stari Grad**
**NEIGHBORHOOD** | A mere 20-minute walk south of the present town center lies the ruins of the previous 9th-century town. You can wander around for free, taking in the Romanesque-style Crkva sveta Marija (St. Mary's Church), first mentioned in historical records in 1192; the ruins of a Franciscan monastery; and a legendary centuries-old well whose filling up with water after a drought was credited to the intervention of the Holy Virgin. On August 15, a procession of locals carries a statue of the Virgin Mary from here to the church on present-day Pag's main square. On September 8, they return. To get to Stari Grad, walk across the bridge and keep left on Put Starog Grada, the road that runs south along the bay. ✉ *Pag.*

## Restaurants

**Konoba Giardin**
**$$** | **EASTERN EUROPEAN** | This eatery has mastered the art of cooking with flame, producing delectably grilled entrées from a real wood fire nestled within a brick oven. Select a whole fish from the day's fresh catch, sold by the kilogram, or share a grill platter of mixed cuts of beef piled high atop potatoes and salads. **Known for:** flambé technique; live guitar music; local wine. $ *Average main: €18* ✉ *Vanđelje 1, Kolan* ☎ *023/698–007* 🌐 *konoba-giardin.metro.bar/?lang=en.*

## Pag Cheese

Thanks to its many sheep, Pag is known as the home of one of Croatia's most esteemed cheeses:*Paški sir* (Pag cheese). You can buy some for around €40 per kilogram or €5 for a decagram, which is a small piece indeed. If that sounds expensive, just try ordering a bit as an appetizer in a restaurant, where it's more than twice as much. You can easily find it on sale in private homes on some of the narrow streets off the main square. Celebrated local complements to the cheese include lamb, a herb brandy called *travarica,* and Pag prosciutto.

## Hotels

★ **Boškinac**
**$$$** | **B&B/INN** | Nestled amid vineyards and olive groves, elegant serenity awaits guests at Boškinac. **Pros:** phenomenal restaurant; great vineyard tour; luxurious everything. **Cons:** remote location; vehicle needed; overly formal staff. $ *Rooms from: €270* ✉ *Škopaljska 220, Novalja* ☎ *053/663–500* 🌐 *www.boskinac.com* *8 rooms* *Free Breakfast.*

## Performing Arts

### FESTIVALS

**Pag Carnival**
**FESTIVALS** | Featuring a range of music on and around the main square as well as dance and folk-song performances, Pag Carnival takes place immediately before Lent (which varies from year to year but is typically in February). There is also a shorter carnival held on the last weekend of July. See the tourist office website for specific dates. ✉ *Pag.*

## Did You Know?

Pag white lace is an integral part of many Croatian folk costumes worn during local festivals throughout the country.

## Pag Lace

There was a time when *paške čipke* was passed off abroad as Greek, Austrian, or Italian. Those days are long over. Today an officially recognized "authentic Croatian product" that is sometimes called "white gold," Pag lace is the iconic souvenir to take home from a visit to Pag—unless you are confident that a hulking block of Pag cheese won't spoil. An integral component of the colorful folk costumes locals wear during festivals, this celebrated white lace is featured most saliently as the huge peaked head ornaments ladies don on such occasions, which resemble fastidiously folded, ultra-starched white cloth napkins.

Originating in the ancient Greek city of Mycenae, the Pag lace-making tradition endured for centuries before being popularized far and wide as a Pag product beginning in the late 19th century. A lace-making school was founded in Pag Town in 1906, drawing orders from royalty from distant lands. In 1938, Pag lace-makers participated in the world exhibition in New York.

Pag lace differs from other types of lace in two key respects: a thin thread and exceptional durability. Using an ordinary mending needle against a solid background, and usually proceeding without a plan, the maker begins by creating a circle within which she (or he) makes tiny holes close together; the thread is then pulled through them. The completed lace has a starched quality and can even be washed without losing its firmness. It is best presented on a dark background and framed.

The process is painstaking, so Pag lace is not cheap: a typical small piece of around 20 centimeters in diameter costs at least €35 direct from a maker or double that from a shop.

**Pag Music Festivals**

**FESTIVALS** | An array of thrilling music festivals come to the island of Pag every summer. Some island festivals include Hideout Festival and Sonus Festival. ✉ *Pag.*

## Shopping

**Galerija Paške Čipke** (*Pag Lace Gallery*)

**FABRICS** | You needn't venture farther than the main square and surrounding narrow streets of Pag Town to find someone selling the famed Pag lace—whether an old lady or an equally enthusiastic child. Of course, you can also try Pag Town's very own Galerija paške čipke (call ahead to ensure it is open before visiting) or any local shops you will undoubtedly encounter near the main square. ✉ *Trg Kralja Petra Krešimira IV, Pag* ☎ *091/534–0176* 🌐 *tzgpag.hr/en/grad-i-otok-pag-en/kulturna-bastina/paska-cipka-en.*

## Activities

### BEACHES

Deciding where to swim once you reach Pag Town is a no-brainer; you can pick practically anywhere in the vast sheltered bay that stretches out from the short bridge in the town center. If you have kids, all that sand and shallow water is a real plus compared to Zadar and so many other stretches of Croatia's often deep rocky coast. Most of the 27 km (17 miles) of public beaches in the bay are accessible by car. For even better swimming—if that is possible—try heading north to Novalja and its environs.

Chapter 6

# KVARNER BAY AND THE NORTHERN ADRIATIC ISLANDS



Updated by
Melissa Paul

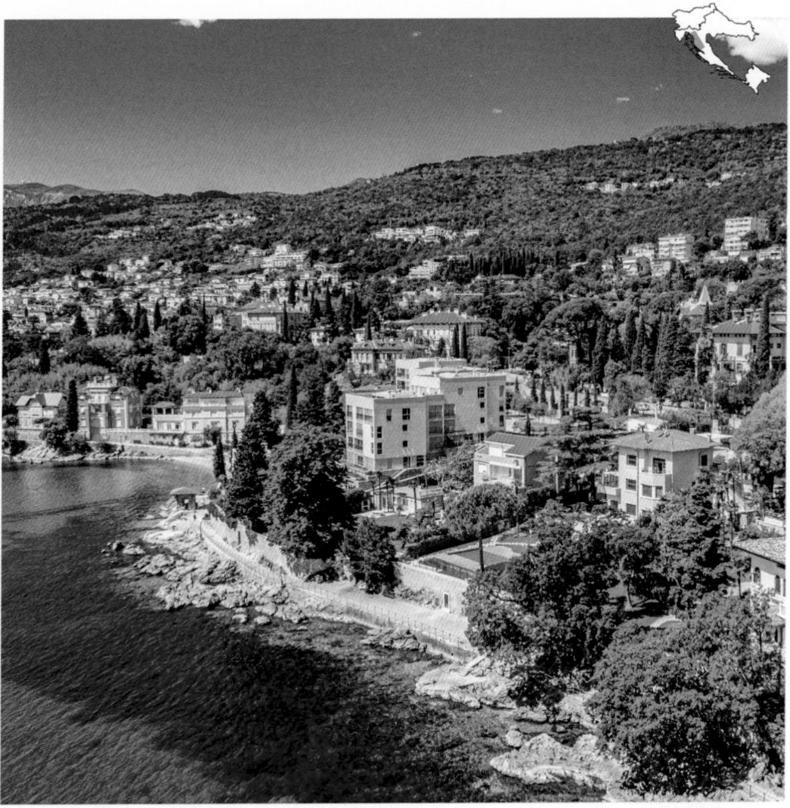

Sights ★★★☆☆ | Restaurants ★★☆☆☆ | Hotels ★★☆☆☆ | Shopping ★☆☆☆☆ | Nightlife ★☆☆☆☆

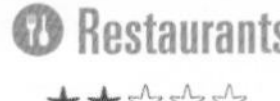

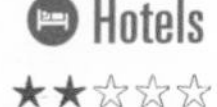

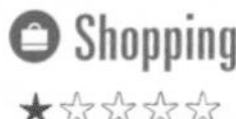

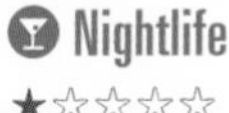

# WELCOME TO KVARNER BAY AND THE NORTHERN ADRIATIC ISLANDS

## TOP REASONS TO GO

★ **The ultimate waterfront path:** Opatija's Lungomare—an 11-km-long (7-mile-long) seafront promenade between Volosko and Lovran – is ideal for an early morning walk to awaken all your senses to the wonders of the Kvarner Bay.

★ **Beautiful beaches:** Take a taxi-boat or join one of the many daily excursions to the remote beaches below the hilltop village of Lubenice on Cres. The famed Sveti Ivan Beach is one of the prettiest in Croatia. Not far from it, at Žanja Beach, you can visit a sea cave.

★ **Towering views:** Climb to the top of the Great Bell Tower in Rab Town and take in the bird's-eye view of the perfectly preserved medieval square and all four church towers.

★ **Dive deeper into the blue:** Get acquainted with the Blue World Institute on Mali Losinj that protects 180 dolphins in Kvarner, then visit the museum dedicated to the thousands-of-years-old Greek statue discovered in the seabed in 1996.

The Kvarner region includes a stretch of Adriatic coast dotted with some of the largest Croatian islands. Croatia's main port city and Kvarner's administrative capital, Rijeka, is within two to five hours of European hubs like Munich, Milan, Vienna, Budapest, Zagreb, and Ljubljana. Due to its complex history, Rijeka is Croatia's most diverse city, and its liberal population has always been well-connected to Europe thanks to its industrial, transport, and migratory roots. The Habsburgs founded the seaside resort of Opatija in the mid-19th century as a medicinal wellness retreat for Viennese royalty. The regional airport is found on the island of Krk.

1 **Rijeka.** Croatia's first city to hold the European title of the Capital of Culture.

2 **Risnjak National Park.** A national park dedicated to the endangered bobcat that roams the nature reserve.

3 **Opatija.** A center for wellness and healing that attracts visitors year-round.

4 **Cres.** The longest of all Croatian islands, where the sheep roaming the rocky hillsides graze on wild herbs and produce the most succulent lamb chops.

5 **Lošinj.** The "isle of wellness" founded in the 12th century and dominated by the Osorčica Mountains.

6 **Krk.** Croatia's most popular and accessible island, connected to the mainland by a bridge.

7 **Delnice.** A mountainous region covered with hiking and biking trails that serves as a good base for exploring the mountains and rivers of Gorski Kotar.

8 **Rab.** A lush and romantic island with the only natural sand beaches in Croatia.

SLOVENIA
Risnjak National Park
Rupa
Buzet
Kastav
Opatija
Rijeka
Skrad
Delnice
Vrbovsko
ISTRIA
Lovran
Pazin
Mount Učka Nature Park
GORSKI KOTAR
Ogulin
Josipdol
Crikvenica
Novi Vinodolski
Žminj
Brestova
Porozina
Labin
Rabac
KRK
Krk
Valbiska
Baška
Senj
Brinje
Cres
Žuta Lokva
Valun
Lubenice
PRVIC
GOLI OTOK
Otočac
Pula
Medulin
Kvarner Gulf
Lopar
CRES
Starigrad
Rab
North Velebit National Park
Belej
Osor
Mišnjak
Jablanac
UNIJE
VELEBIT
ADRIATIC SEA
Stara Novalja
Prizna
LOŠINJ
Mali Lošinj
Žigljen
Veli Lošinj
Karlobag
PAG
Pag
0 20 miles
0 20 kilometers
TO ZADAR

Majestic scenery and natural diversity characterize the Kvarner region: the mainland is dominated by a stretch of coast backed by high-rising mountains, while some of the largest Croatian islands fill the heart of Kvarner Bay. Hike the wild Gorski Kotar Mountains, explore Krk on two wheels, beach-hop on the island of Cres, enjoy the mild climate and abundant vegetation of Lošinj, and experience the best of Croatian cuisine along the Opatija Riviera.

Kvarner Bay is a large deep bay with the Istrian peninsula to the north and Dalmatia to the south. Four major islands—Cres, Krk, Lošinj, and Rab—along with numerous smaller specks of land, fill the heart of the bay and can be viewed from the gentle resort towns strung around the coastal arc. This coastal strip's lush rolling hills wind their way around the gulf from Opatija. East of Rijeka, the scenic Magistrala coastal highway cuts into the solid rock of the foothills on its way to the southern tip of Croatia.

The wild Gorski Kotar mountain district is on the mainland northeast of Rijeka. Across the narrow range sits the inland part of Primorsko-goranska županija (Primorje–Gorski Kotar county), a region of small towns and thick forests that you pass through if you're traveling overland to Zagreb. You'll notice the entire northern stretch of the Croatian coast exhibits a strong Italian influence; yet thanks to centuries of control across the Adriatic, most mainland resorts developed during Habsburg rule. Robust and sophisticated Austro-Hungarian architecture and infrastructure predominate in these resort towns. In contrast, the islands tend toward Italy's cozier, less aspirational features. Dwellings are simpler, often of stone, and set in less geometric layouts.

Krk, entered via a short bridge from the eastern shore of the gulf region, reflects the mainland's arid nature more than its brethren. On Cres, the northern stretches are a twisted knot of forest peaks and rocky crags, while gentler cultivated slopes appear toward the center. Pine forests marching down to the shores provide welcome shade in the middle of the day. In the island's center, hollows have filled up to make freshwater lakes that provide the island's drinking water, counterbalancing the salty sea that licks at the land just a hill crest away. At the foot of Cres, a hop across a narrow stretch of the Adriatic brings you to Lošinj. This lush oasis owes much of its charm to the gardens and villas built here during the seafaring heyday of the 19th century. As you approach from the north, the silhouette of Rab resembles the humped back of a diving sea monster. The high north of the island is dry and barren, almost a desert of rock and scrub, whereas the lower southern part is lush and fertile.

# Planning

## When to Go

The Kvarner region gets very busy in high summer, so don't even dream of heading, for instance, to Opatija or Krk in August without accommodations lined up. Late May through early June and September are ideal times to visit, since you can expect good weather, warm seas, and open facilities. Early May and October are good if you're looking for peace, but remember that fewer tourist-related activities are on offer and you still need to book accommodations in advance. Rijeka and Opatija have increasingly become exciting places to visit during Carnival season from late January through February, a time of year referred to as the "fifth season."

## Getting Here and Around

### AIR

Rijeka Airport is in Omišalj on Krk, with regular bus service provided by Autotrans to downtown Rijeka and the beach towns on Krk and Mali Lošinj and Cres (though not to Rab). Ryanair serves the airport from London, Stockholm, and Brussels; Norwegian Air Shuttle from Oslo; Croatia Airlines from Munich; and Eurowings from Cologne, Berlin, and several other cities in Germany. The list of new destinations and airlines changes yearly, so always research before your trip.

**CONTACTS Rijeka Airport.** (*RJK*) ✉ *Hamec 1, Omišalj* ☎ *051/842–040* 🌐 *www.rijeka-airport.hr.*

### BOAT AND FERRY

The Jadrolinija ferries no longer travel between Dubrovnik and Rijeka, but they do run daily from Rijeka to the islands of Cres, Ilovik, Pag, Unije, Rab, and Susak. A ferry from Brestova (several miles down the road from Lovran) also connects to Cres and Lošinj. From June to September, as many as 13 ferries depart daily. Prices vary according to season, but expect to pay €5 a person during the summer; rates fall as much as 20% in the low season. Ferries also run between Valbiska on the island of Krk and Merag on Cres.

Every day in high season, G&V Line has a fast passenger boat that travels from Rijeka to Krk, Rab, Silba, and Zadar. Meanwhile, a catamaran service heads out to Rab at 5 pm and drops into the northern Dalmatian island of Pag about 2½ hours later. Tourist boats and water taxis offering transport on shorter stretches are also abundant at many resorts.

**CONTACTS Jadrolinija.** ✉ *Riječki Lukobran bb, Rijeka* ✣ *Inside the building about 100 meters opposite from where the ferry docks* ☎ *051/211–444* 🌐 *www.jadrolinija.hr.*

### BUS

There's a daily international bus service to Rijeka from Italy (Trieste), Slovenia (Ljubljana), Austria (Vienna), and Germany (Frankfurt, Munich, and Stuttgart). You can also reach destinations all over mainland Croatia from Rijeka. Timetable information is available at the Rijeka Bus Terminal. GetByBus, a Croatia-based company, offers instant online booking for many bus operators and lines in Croatia.

Buses travel from Rijeka to all the major towns on the mainland and the islands at least once daily. If you're traveling independently, you'll find that buses to the various islands are roughly scheduled to tie in with ferry services.

**CONTACTS Autotrans.** (*Arriva*) ✉ *Rijeka Bus Terminal, Trg Žabica 2, Rijeka* ☎ *060/888-666* 🌐 *www.arriva.com.hr.* **GetByBus.** ✉ *Trg Žabica 1, Rijeka* 🌐 *getbybus.com.* **Rijeka Bus Terminal.** ✉ *Trg Žabica 1, Rijeka* ☎ *060/888–666.*

### CAR

Although local buses and ferries are an excellent and low-stress method of touring the region, touring Kvarner by car does offer the opportunity to explore some of the smaller and more remote villages on the islands and up in the mountains. In addition, despite a poor safety record and heavy traffic in high season, few roads are more scenic than the Magistrala. A car is also useful if you leave Kvarner and head for Istria (passing through the Učka Tunnel). However, train and bus services to Zagreb, as well as bus service to Dalmatia, mean that a vehicle is not really essential for moving on to other areas.

### TRAIN

There are three trains daily from Rijeka to Zagreb (journey time is approximately 4 hours) and two trains daily to Ljubljana (2½ hours).

**CONTACTS Hrvatske Željeznice (Croatian Railways).** ☎ *060/333–444, 01/4724–026* 🌐 *www.hzpp.hr.* **Rijeka Train Station.** (*Rijeka Glavni kolodvor*) ✉ *Trg Kralja Tomislava 1, Rijeka* ☎ *051/211–304* 🌐 *rail.cc.*

## Restaurants

In recent years, the Kvarner area—and all of Croatia—has experienced a renaissance in food that has had a delightful influence on restaurant offerings. Many Croatian restaurants have taken a refreshing focus on high-quality locally grown foods woven with traditional dishes and lighter, more modern fare. At the same time, a growing population of young Croatian designers is having an increasingly visible influence on the design of spaces and furniture in many wineries and restaurants. You can look for this influence not only in the newer places but also on the menus, with management, and with the chefs driving this process. It is worth noting that while good fish lunches, pubs, and tapas-style eating are abundant in Rijeka, most of the higher-quality eateries are generally found outside the city limits.

The quintessential traditional Croatian eating establishment known as a *konoba* still holds solid ground as the defining place for a Croatian meal in this region. Ever-present in most seaside towns, these rustic fish restaurants are often operated by the brothers, uncles, or cousins of the fishermen, who spend the better part of the day either on the sea or in the small ports, sorting their fishnets.

While traveling in the Kvarner region, try the famed *Kvarnerski škampi* (Kvarner shrimp). Known for its size, light reddish color, thin and easy-to-peel shell, and delicate taste, this shrimp is best served independently (it should not be confused with the scampi often served with pasta or risotto dishes). In the mountainous region of Gorski Kotar, it is common to find hearty dishes like *jota,* a thick barley soup with sauerkraut, often served with cured meat. Frog legs, bear, wild boar, and wild mushrooms are common ingredients in stews prepared in mountainous regions. *Palenta* and homemade pasta like gnocchi are often served with meat stews and are a specialty of Gorski Kotar as well.

On Krk, try *šurlice,* the local version of pasta; handmade on a spindle, it's often served with wild game, meat goulash, or shaved black truffles. Lamb from Cres is prized for its delicate flavor, which results from the harsh summers and winters on the island and the wild herbs the sheep graze on. In Kvarner, *mrkač* is the local word for octopus (it's *hobotnica* in the rest of the country).

Krk is home to the most highly regarded wines from the region, with the dry white Vrbnićka žlahtina a strong candidate for best. *Rakija* (fruit and herb brandies) are the common end to a meal and the start of a long night.

## Hotels

Opatija, Krk, and Lošinj have a healthy selection of quality hotels that are usually part of a larger brand and managed as a group. Look for boutique-style and heritage villas owned and operated privately for a more personal experience. There is also an abundance of newly renovated homes and apartments equipped with swimming pools and other amenities available in most locations near the sea. Expect anything from a room in a block with a common kitchen to private homes with bikes and other sports equipment. Terraces and outdoor spaces are standard and range from a simple tiled slab with metal rails to a beautifully appointed perch shaded by a vine-covered trellis with an open grill for alfresco cooking. If you want to save money, consider renting a room in a private home. This arrangement rarely involves food, so you'll have to get up and out in the morning for your breakfast. Croats are a house-proud people, so generally, rented rooms are likely to be very clean and comfortable with private bathrooms. Your welcome will probably be very warm, with drinks—especially strong coffee—thrust under your nose when you step across the threshold. There's no better way to get a real feel for how Croats live.

⇨ *Restaurant and hotel reviews have been shortened. For full information, visit Fodors.com. Restaurant prices are the average cost of a main course at dinner or lunch if dinner is not served. Hotel prices are the lowest cost of a standard double room in the high season.*

### What It Costs in Euros (€)

| | $ | $$ | $$$ | $$$$ |
|---|---|---|---|---|
| **RESTAURANTS** | under €15 | €15–€23 | €24–€32 | over €32 |
| **HOTELS** | under €150 | €150–€250 | €251–€350 | over €350 |

## Visitor Information

Tourist information offices can help you with information about accommodations, activities, and excursions like diving, windsurfing, and sightseeing. Most offices give out maps and ferry schedules for free.

**CONTACTS Cres Tourist Information.** ✉ *Peškera 1, Cres Town* ☎ *051/571–535* 🌐 *www.visitcres.hr.* **Krk Tourist Information.** ✉ *Trg Svetog Kvirina 1, Krk Town* ☎ *051/221–359* 🌐 *krk.hr.* **Lošinj Tourist Information.** ✉ *Priko 42, Mali Lošinj* ☎ *051/231–884* 🌐 *www.visitlosinj.hr.* **Opatija Tourist Information.** ✉ *Maršala Tita 146, Opatija* ☎ *051/271–310* 🌐 *www.visitopatija.com.* **Rab Tourist Information.** ✉ *Trg Municipium Arba 8, Rab* ☎ *051/724–064* 🌐 *www.rab-visit.com.* **Rijeka Tourist Information.** ✉ *Korzo 14, Rijeka* ☎ *051/335–882* 🌐 *visitrijeka.hr.*

# Rijeka

*165 km (103 miles) southwest of Zagreb.*

Water is the essence of Kvarner, and the region's largest city expresses this simply. Whether in Croatian or Italian (Fiume) the translation of the name to English is the same: *river.* Although the history of Croatia's third city goes back to the days of Imperial Rome, modern Rijeka evolved under the rule of Austria-Hungary. The historic core retains vestiges of the old Habsburg monarchy from the time when Rijeka served as the empire's outlet to the Adriatic. During the 1960s, under Yugoslavia, the suburbs expanded rapidly. Rijeka is the country's largest port, with a huge shipyard, massive dry-dock facilities, refineries, and other heavy industries offering large-scale employment. Since the breakup of Yugoslavia, however, Rijeka's role as a shipping town has declined significantly, though local shipyards still repair many U.S. Navy ships and commercial cruisers.

At the city's core sits the Korzo, a pedestrian street of shops and cafés running parallel with the harbor, just to the south of where the land begins to rise toward the peaks of the mountains that back the bay. The high ground ensures that the suburbs stretch east and west, with little space to expand to the north. Rijeka is an important location in the region, offering key rail, road, and sea access into Istria, Slovenia, and Italy. As such, many regard Rijeka as a transit location rather than a holiday destination. That limited view continues to change each year, as more historical and cultural significance is recognized, such as Rijeka being awarded the prestigious title of European Capital of Culture 2020 for its "Port of Diversity" program.

Many visitors stay in the nearby seaside riviera of Opatija, and locals often head that way in their free time. Rijeka is a pleasant small city (approximately 130,000 people call it home), and this makes it one of the more authentically Croatian spots in the region in the summer. Those looking to avoid the hordes could do much worse than staying in Rijeka and using the excellent ferry network to explore the rest of Kvarner.

Rijeka is also the home port of Jadrolinija, the coast's major ferry company. Local ferries connect with all the Kvarner islands and will also take you farther afield.

### GETTING HERE AND AROUND

Rijeka is linked with Zagreb by the modern A6 motorway, which is clean, efficient, and fast, though tolls add up on the journey. To reach the Dalmatian coast from Rijeka via the larger highway, you must backtrack 75 km (47 miles) from the coast and get on the motorway heading south toward Split and Dubrovnik. Rijeka is also the start of the Jadranska Magistrala (the scenic coastal highway), which follows the coast south all the way to the Montenegro border.

## Sights

**City Market**

**MARKET | FAMILY** | Bursting with color and the busyness of an open-air green market, this is the natural starting point for getting acquainted with this port city. It is housed in three large halls, each distinct in its architecture and also in what is sold under its roofs. The most interesting of these halls is the art nouveau fish market, which includes crustacean sculptures on the walls and ceiling by Venetian artist Urbano Bottasso. Surrounding the market are many open-air stalls, mostly manned by women eager to sell their locally grown fresh fruits, vegetables, and other Croatian delicacies. Come early for coffee and people-watching in one of the many surrounding cafés, or come later and have an early lunch or prix-fixe *marenda* (mid-morning snack) in one of the nearby local eateries, where most offerings come fresh from the market.

**TIP→ Before you leave the market, take a stroll through the small formal park in front of the magnificent Croatian National Theatre, built by Viennese architects Fellner and Helmer in 1885.** ✉ *Vatroslava Lisinskog, Rijeka* ☎ *051/320–143* 🌐 *www.rijeka-plus.hr.*

Rijeka serves as the country's largest port, with many options for ferries and boat trips.

**Crkva Uznesenja Blažene Djevice Marije i Kosi Toranj** (*Church of St. Mary of the Assumption*)

**CHURCH | FAMILY** | Formerly the city's main church and dating back to the Middle Ages, St. Mary's is still known to locals as the "big church." However, many additions and changes now obscure much of the original architecture. The relatively recent updates have not imposed severe geometry, though: the bell tower remains leaning to one side by 40 centimeters or so. ✉ *Pavla Rittera Vitezovića 3, Rijeka* ☎ *051/214–177* 🌐 *bdm-uznesenja.org.*

**Guvernerova Palača** (*The Governor's Palace*)

**HISTORIC HOME | FAMILY** | High on a hill facing the Mediterranean sun and a short walk from the city's center, the Governor's Palace affords a grand view over the harbor. Built in 1893 by Hungarian architect Alajos Hauszmann, who also designed Budapest's castle and Palace of Justice, it was done in High Renaissance style and now houses several exhibits and cultural events. The large columned facade communicates the self-confidence of the robust Habsburg empire, as do the numerous statues placed throughout the green area surrounding the palace. The Maritime and Historical Museum of the Croatian Littoral, which investigates Kvarner's seafaring traditions and cultural heritage, is also housed here. After taking in one of the exhibits, enjoy the garden area surrounding the museum, which sometimes hosts an outdoor summer theater and beer garden. ✉ *Trg Riccarda Zanelle 1, Rijeka* ☎ *051/213–578* 🌐 *www.ppmhp.hr* 🎟 *€4.*

**Hrvatsko Narodno Kazalište Ivan Pleminiti Zajc** (*Croatian National Theatre Ivan Zajc*)

**PERFORMANCE VENUE | FAMILY** | Designed by specialist Viennese architects Fellner and Helmer, Rijeka's National Theatre opened in 1885. In high summer the theater plays host to a Festival of Summer Nights, held beneath wonderful ceiling paintings by Gustav Klimt and emerging from behind a stage curtain decorated by Croatian artist Oton Gliha. It's worth it to buy a ticket to a

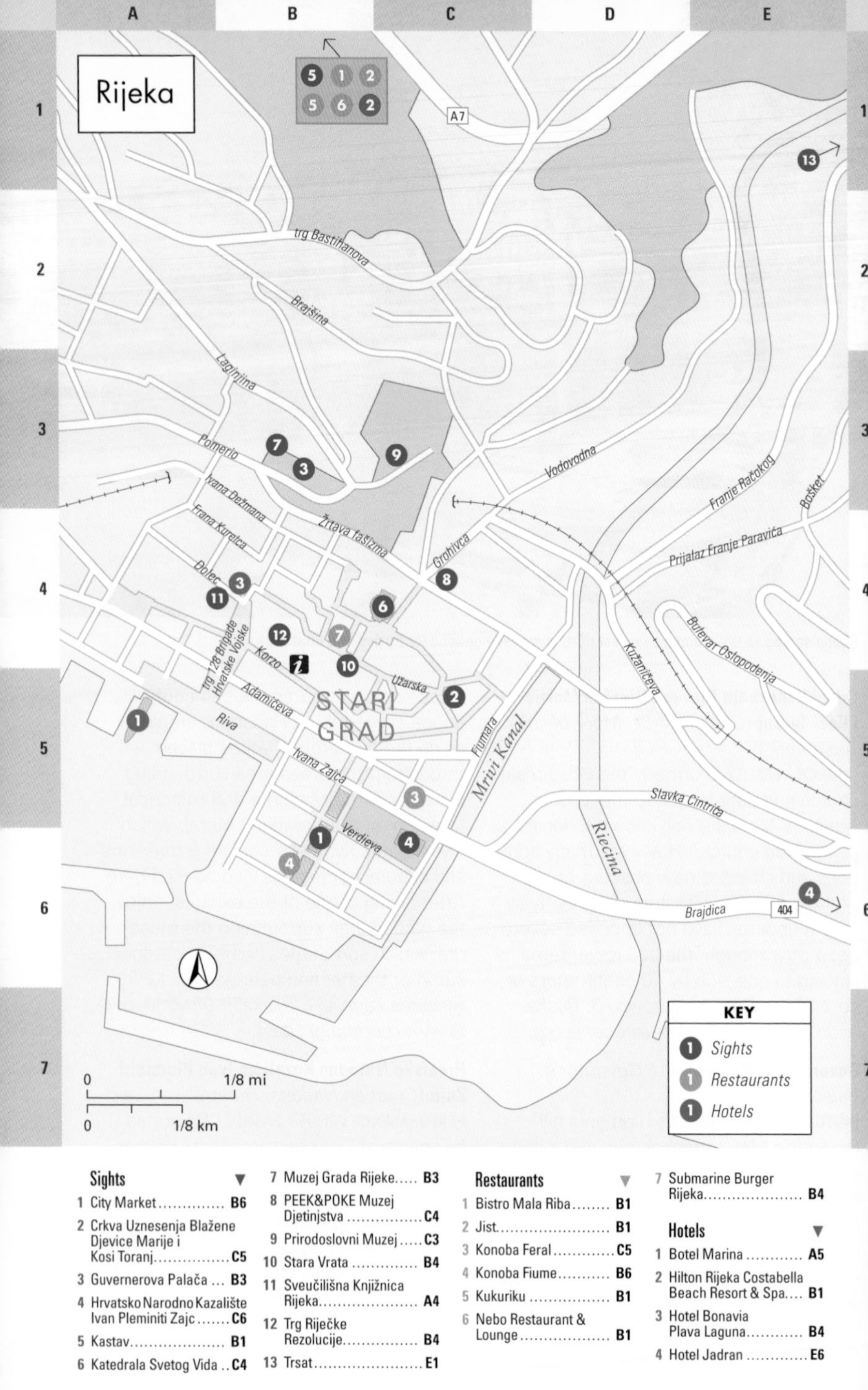


**Sights**

1 City Market .............. **B6**
2 Crkva Uznesenja Blažene Djevice Marije i Kosi Toranj ................ **C5**
3 Guvernerova Palača ... **B3**
4 Hrvatsko Narodno Kazalište Ivan Pleminiti Zajc ....... **C6**
5 Kastav .................... **B1**
6 Katedrala Svetog Vida .. **C4**
7 Muzej Grada Rijeke..... **B3**
8 PEEK&POKE Muzej Djetinjstva ................ **C4**
9 Prirodoslovni Muzej ..... **C3**
10 Stara Vrata ............. **B4**
11 Sveučilišna Knjižnica Rijeka..................... **A4**
12 Trg Riječke Rezolucije................ **B4**
13 Trsat....................... **E1**

**Restaurants**

1 Bistro Mala Riba ........ **B1**
2 Jist.......................... **B1**
3 Konoba Feral ............ **C5**
4 Konoba Fiume ........... **B6**
5 Kukuriku ................. **B1**
6 Nebo Restaurant & Lounge .................. **B1**
7 Submarine Burger Rijeka..................... **B4**

**Hotels**

1 Botel Marina ............ **A5**
2 Hilton Rijeka Costabella Beach Resort & Spa.... **B1**
3 Hotel Bonavia Plava Laguna............ **B4**
4 Hotel Jadran ............. **E6**

performance to experience Croatian culture and see the inside of the theater. ✉ *Verdijeva 1, Rijeka* ☎ *051/355–900* 🌐 *hnk-zajc.hr.*

★ **Kastav**

**TOWN | FAMILY** | A fine spot from which to admire the splendors of the Kvarner Bay, the Kastav—11 km (7 miles) northwest of Rijeka—was originally a medieval fortress comprising nine defensive towers. The old hilltop village sits at 1,200 feet and is still home to some 900 residents. The backside of the hilltop village is blanketed by a forest area with biking, hiking, and horseback riding trails leading from the loggia to the woods. The town is a popular venue for regular events throughout the year, from the monthly Zeleni Kastav organic green market to the summer Kastav Blues and Cultural Festival, the Bela Nedeja young white wine festival in October, and the traditional bell ringers during the Carnival season in February. Having been home to wealthy and powerful clans in the past, the tiny town has many splendid buildings from throughout the ages. E-bike rentals are available at the forest entrance. ✉ *Kastav* 🌐 *www.kastav-touristinfo.hr.*

**Katedrala Svetog Vida** (*St. Vitus's Cathedral*)

**CHURCH | FAMILY** | This Romanesque cathedral is unusual in this part of the world because of its rotunda and the semicircular apse behind the altar. Fine Baroque statues are sheltered by Baroque and Gothic construction. Founded by the Jesuits in 1638, the cathedral was named for Rijeka's patron saint. An 18th-century gallery was reportedly built to protect young novice monks from the tempting sights presented when the local lovelies attended services. You can find a cannonball in the wall at the main entrance, apparently fired from a British ship during the Napoleonic wars. The church is closed every day from noon to 3 pm. ✉ *Grivica 11, Rijeka* ☎ *051/330–879* 🌐 *visitrijeka.hr/katedrala-sv-vida.*

★ **Muzej Grada Rijeke** (*The Museum of the City of Rijeka*)

**HISTORY MUSEUM | FAMILY** | In a cube-shaped building on the grounds of the Governor's Palace, the museum has more than a dozen different permanent collections that capture the history of the city and the people who have left an indelible mark on it. The collections range from music to visual art and postage stamps, as well as cultural and scientific displays representative of the heritage of this historic port city. One of the most interesting is the Rijeka Torpedo Exhibit, the first of its kind in the world. ✉ *Trg Riccardo Zanella 1/1, Rijeka* ☎ *051/554–270* 🌐 *www.muzej-rijeka.hr* 🎫 *€8* 🕒 *Closed Mon.*

**PEEK&POKE Muzej Djetinjstva** (*Peek and Poke Computer Museum*)

**SCIENCE MUSEUM | FAMILY** | This museum was founded by computer enthusiasts interested in collecting vintage computers and technology from the early days of the technological revolution. The collection includes everything from LEGOs to computers, old game consoles, and calculators. A large part of the mission of the museum is to educate visitors in the areas of science and math as the foundation for understanding technology. The great thing about the museum is that they encourage visitors to peek and poke at the displays not only with their eyes but also with their hands and their minds (hence the name). ✉ *Ivana Grohovca 2, Rijeka* ☎ *091/780–5709, 051/562–100* 🌐 *www.peekpoke.hr* 🎫 *€7* 🕒 *Closed Sun. year-round and weekdays mid-Oct.–Apr. Closed Sat. May–mid-Oct.*

**Prirodoslovni Muzej** (*Natural History Museum*)

**HISTORY MUSEUM | FAMILY** | Exploring the geology and biology of the region at the Rijeka's Natural History Museum invariably involves holding a sizable chunk of marine life up to the eyes. The shark and ray display here is predictably popular, starring a brigade of stuffed sharks swimming in strict formation while suspended from the ceiling. A multimedia center based on an aquarium adds to the extensive collection of nonmammalian species, some 90,000 specimens in total, but also includes rocks, plants, and other less animated elements of the locality. The botanical garden contributes more exotic plants to the array from the museum's grounds. Considering the fearsome appearance of some of the more fascinating inhabitants of the museum, it may be worth considering putting off a visit here until the end of your stay on the coast, lest your imagination get the better of you while bathing on the beaches. ✉ *Lorenzov Prolaz 1, Rijeka* ☎ *051/553–669* 🌐 *www.prirodoslovni.com* 🎫 *€2.75.*

**Stara Vrata** (*The Roman Gate*)
**HISTORIC SIGHT** | This enormous stone arch—the oldest structure in the city—is an ancient town gate. Today it's partly engulfed by additions from more recent times, but it was from this site many centuries ago that the chain of mountain fortresses in the region was commanded by the Romans. These days, the Roman elite's enthusiasm for comfort is catered to with a handful of park benches amid what is left of the ancient walls and columns. ✉ *Stara Vrata, Rijeka.*

**Sveučilišna Knjižnica Rijeka** (*University Library*)
**LIBRARY** | **FAMILY** | The University Library now houses a permanent exhibition about the Glagolitic script. Stone tablets written in the ancient Slavic script, plus more than 120 other items, are permanently exhibited here. Books, paintings, masonry, and frescoes are also displayed. Call in advance to view the exhibition, which is open by appointment only for a small fee. ✉ *Dolac 1, Rijeka* ☎ *091/245-0007* 🌐 *svkri.uniri.hr* 🎫 *€3* ⏲ *Closed weekends.*

**Trg Riječke Rezolucije** (*Rijeka Resolution Square*)
**PLAZA/SQUARE** | In this historic square sits the city's former municipal palace, which was built in 1873 and was originally part of an Augustinian monastery. It connects to St. Jerome's Church and the Dominican monastery. The square is named for the resolution that was drawn up here in 1905 and contributed to the formation of Yugoslavia. The square's lemon-meringue buildings cluster around the foot of the city flagpole, erected on a high base in the 16th century and featuring a likeness of the city's patron saint, St. Vitus, holding a scale model of Rijeka protectively in his hand. Many outdoor events are staged here throughout the year. ✉ *Marina Držića, Rijeka.*

★ **Trsat** (*Trsat Castle*)
**CASTLE/PALACE** | **FAMILY** | The medieval castle was built on the foundations of a prehistoric fort. In the early 1800s, it was bought by an Austrian general of Irish descent, who converted it to include a Greek temple with Doric columns. Today it hosts a popular café, offering stunning views of the Kvarner Bay; throughout the summer, open-air theater performances and concerts take place. Across the street, the pilgrimage church of Sveta Marija (St. Mary) was constructed in 1453 to commemorate the Miracle of Trsat, when angels carrying the humble house of the Virgin Mary are said to have landed here. Although the angels later moved the house to Loreto in Italy, Trsat has remained a place of pilgrimage. The path up to Trsat from the city center takes you close to Titov trg, at a bridge across the Rječina. It passes through a stone gateway, then makes a long steep climb up 538 steps. Local Bus 2 will get you here, too. ✉ *Petra Zrinskog bb, Rijeka* ☎ *051/217–714 for the castle, 051/452–900 for the church* 🎫 *Church and castle admission are free; €2 for castle exhibits* ⏲ *No church visits during religious services.*

Medieval Trsat Castle is surrounded by nature and offers stunning views.

## Restaurants

**Bistro Mala Riba**

$$ | **SEAFOOD** | **FAMILY** | This cheerful bistro offers a delicious lineup of Kvarner-style tapas that are best enjoyed on the pleasant outdoor terrace. Seafood lovers will have a hard time choosing between menu items—including assorted fish crudo, sardines marinated in lemon juice, octopus salad, sea-snail salad, fried olives, barley, and squid stew—and will definitely find themselves coming back for more. **Known for:** Kvarner-style seafood tapas; bright and trendy atmosphere; friendly service. *Average main: €15 Ulica 43 Istarske Divizije 22A, Matulji, Opatija 051/277–945.*

**Jist**

$$ | **STEAKHOUSE** | **FAMILY** | This is the best—and perhaps the only—place to have steak in the entire Kvarner region. The high-quality and sophisticated menu offerings here are highly worthy of the extra effort it requires to find the restaurant. **Known for:** steak tartare; degustation menu with wine pairings; duck prosciutto salad. *Average main: €18 Siroli 27, Rijeka 051/374–597 jist.hr Closed Sun. and Mon.*

**Konoba Feral**

$ | **SEAFOOD** | **FAMILY** | Frequented by locals (especially at lunch), this excellent informal seafood restaurant lies on a side road conveniently close to the City Market. House specialties are *crni rižot* (cuttlefish-ink risotto), seafood tagliatelle, whole fish, and shellfish. **Known for:** affordable traditional dishes; popular with locals; cozy atmosphere. *Average main: €14 Matije Gupca 5B, Rijeka 051/212–274 www.konoba-feral.com Closed Sun. No dinner mid-Sept.–June.*

★ **Konoba Fiume**

$$ | **MEDITERRANEAN** | **FAMILY** | Tucked away in an alley right next to Rijeka's fish market, quaint Fiume fills with locals at lunchtime but closes early (by 6 pm). Unpretentious and friendly with a small streetside terrace, the tavern serves mostly seafood but also meat and pasta

dishes. **Known for:** friendly atmosphere; fresh seafood; affordable prices. $ *Average main: €18 ✉ Vatroslava Lisinskog 12, Rijeka ☎ 051/312–108 ⏲ Closed Sun.*

**Kukuriku**

$$ | **MEDITERRANEAN** | This restaurant is quaintly situated in the heart of the old city of Kastav, which sits on a hill that overlooks the entire Kvarner Bay. In the same family for over a century, it has walked off with many an award for select offerings from the inland cuisine of Croatia. **Known for:** terrace with quiant village views; great wine pairings; slow-food dining experience. $ *Average main: €20 ✉ Trg Lokvina 3, Kastav ☎ 051/691–519 🌐 kukuriku.hr ⏲ Closed Sun. and Mon.*

★ **Nebo Restaurant & Lounge**

$$$$ | **MODERN EUROPEAN** | With unbelievable panoramic views of the Kvarner Bay, this Michelin-starred restaurant within the Hilton Rijeka Costabella Beach Resort & Spa brings a whole new level of sophistication to the food and beverage scene in Rijeka. Chef Deni Srdoc creates tasting menus that feature traditional ingredients and regional specialties with a clever modern flair. **Known for:** sophisticated food; stunning sea views; elegant professional service. $ *Average main: €65 ✉ Hilton Rijeka Costabella Beach Resort & Spa, Opatijska 9, Rijeka ☎ 051/600–119 🌐 neborijeka.com ⏲ Closed Sun.*

★ **Submarine Burger Rijeka**

$ | **BURGER** | **FAMILY** | Tucked in a corner just off the main walking area, this family-friendly spot is a great place to come for a healthier burger. Try the homemade fries with shaved Grana Padano cheese and *tartufi* (truffle) sauce. **Known for:** sliders (trios of mini-versions of their most popular burgers); ice cream with cookies; giving back to local community. $ *Average main: €7 ✉ Marka Marulića 4, Rijeka ☎ 051/581–363 🌐 submarineburger.com.*

## Hotels

The selection of hotels in Rijeka reflects the city's humble status as a simple transit town, with more accommodations desired in nearby Kastav, Opatija, and on the island of Krk.

**Botel Marina**

$ | **HOTEL** | **FAMILY** | Docked at the pier in Rijeka, the first Croatian boat hotel is a cool place to stay, with 35 modern rooms, from doubles to dorms, all furnished with comfy beds and en-suite bathrooms. **Pros:** centrally located; unique concept; friendly staff. **Cons:** no elevators, so carrying luggage to the rooms on lower decks can be inconvenient; smallish rooms; location is on a noisy working harbor. $ *Rooms from: €107 ✉ Adamićev Gat, Rijeka ☎ 051/410–162 🌐 www.botel-marina.com 35 rooms No Meals.*

★ **Hilton Rijeka Costabella Beach Resort & Spa**

$$$$ | **RESORT** | **FAMILY** | This modern luxury hotel has a spectacular beachfront location between Rijeka and the Opatija Riviera. **Pros:** Michelin-starred restaurant on premises; beachfront location; beathtaking panoramic views. **Cons:** rooms could be quieter; more housekeepers needed; average food and beverage service at non-Michelin-starred eateries. $ *Rooms from: €400 ✉ Opatijska 9, Rijeka ☎ 051/600–100 🌐 www.hilton.com/en/hotels/rjkochi-hilton-rijeka-costabella-beach-resort-and-spa 194 rooms Free Breakfast.*

**Hotel Bonavia Plava Laguna**

$$ | **HOTEL** | In the city center, one block back from the Korzo, the Hotel Bonavia is a modern high-rise with comfortable rooms, specially-designed furnishings, and original oil paintings. **Pros:** spacious rooms; good service; excellent location. **Cons:** old-school furnishings; caters to business guests; can be noisy. $ *Rooms from: €185 ✉ Dolac 4, Rijeka*

051/357–980 www.plavalaguna.com 121 rooms Free Breakfast.

**Hotel Jadran**

$$ | **HOTEL** | A good 20-minute walk (or 10-minute bus ride) from central Rijeka, this pleasant hotel is situated right on the water with incomparable views of the Kvarner Bay. Modern and comfortable rooms have extra-large double beds and Wi-Fi. **Pros:** substantial breakfast; unfettered sea views; quiet residential location. **Cons:** outdated decor; difficult parking; 20-minute walk from the city. *Rooms from: €160 Šetalište XIII Divizije 46, Rijeka 051/216–600 www.jadran-hoteli.hr 69 rooms Free Breakfast.*

## Nightlife

### BARS

**Celtic Cafe Bard**

**PUBS** | Located on a small town square next to St. Vitus Cathedral, this cozy spot is a hangout spot for locals in their twenties and thirties and for beer lovers and coffee drinkers alike. It offers an excellent choice of Croatian and international beers in a friendly low-key atmosphere. Local bands are often featured on weekends, and occasionally you might hear some Irish music. *Trg Grivica 6B, Rijeka 091/511–4447.*

**King's Caffé Food Pub**

**PUBS** | This local café is on the main square near the Rijeka Central Market and Croatian National Theater, making it a fantastic spot for a pre-theater cocktail or post-opera snack. It also has delicious eggs Benedict and chia smoothie bowls for breakfast and juicy hamburgers and crispy fries for lunch. *Verdijeva 7B, Rijeka 051/561–916 www.facebook.com/KingsCaffeFoodRi.*

**Phanas Pub**

**PUBS** | The best party place in town, this nautically themed pub is like an old sailboat with its dark wood, long bar, and maritime decorations. Music ranges from acoustic and R&B to dance, and you can enjoy it until the wee hours on Friday and Saturday. *Ivana Zajca 9, Rijeka 099/344–3445.*

**River Pub**

**PUBS** | For those who might remember summer nights sitting on a terrace, drinking, dancing, chatting, and actually being able to hear what others are saying, the River Pub is the place to make it all come back. They have a regular pub quiz crowd on Wednesdays, too. *Frana Supila 12, Rijeka 051/324–673.*

## Performing Arts

### ART VENUES

**Palach**

**ARTS CENTERS** | The center of alternative and creative culture for youth in the city, Palach is a somewhat gritty urban space filled with exhibitions, workshops, performance, live music, and DJs, rotating on a regular basis. *Kružna 8, Rijeka 091/529–7158, 051/215–063.*

### FESTIVALS

★ **Rijeka Carnival**

**CULTURAL FESTIVALS** | **FAMILY** | Known as the "fifth season," Carnival lasts from the end of January until mid-February and awakens a specific kind of energy in the city only experienced during this time of year. The passion locals pour into *Karneval* cannot be compared to neighboring Venice's big-city sophistication, but celebrations here have a village feel and are closely linked to local traditions that are safeguarded in each particular town and passed down through generations. The excitement in the streets as the city is taken over by crazy antics, colorful costumes, and masquerading revelers who poke fun at local politics all make Rijeka a worthy winter destination. The season kicks off with the Carnival Queen Pageant and continues with weeks of fun activities and masked parties all over town, ending with the Children's Carnival

Parade and the International Carnival Parade. ✉ *Rijeka* 🌐 *visitrijeka.hr/karneval.*

**Rijeka's Summer Nights**

**FESTIVALS | FAMILY** | Beginning in late June, the four-week annual Rijeka's Summer Nights festival ensures that venues, streets, and squares are filled with cultural performances. Visitors can experience classical music and theater, as well as contemporary music and performance art. Most of the venues are outdoors under the stars; smaller venues are in the various small squares throughout the city and add a charming intimacy to the atmosphere. ✉ *Rijeka* 🌐 *www.rijeka.hr/en/themes-for-citizens/culture/manifestations/rijeka-summer-nights.*

**Summer on Gradina**

**ARTS FESTIVALS | FAMILY** | From mid-July to the beginning of September, *Ljeto na Gradini* brings theater plays, live concerts, craft fairs, conceptual art, and themed events to the Trsat Castle grounds. ✉ *Trsat Castle, Petar Zrinskog bb, Rijeka* ☎ *051/217–714* 🌐 *www.trsatskagradina.com.*

## Shopping

Appearance is of great importance to Croatians, and the local ladies will invariably be exhibiting style and glamour even as they sip coffee or shop for vegetables on any given weekday morning. To serve this fashion-conscious crowd, many hip little boutiques offer the latest styles in imported clothing and shoes (mostly from Italy and Germany). Prices are generally higher than what you'd pay in Italy, so unless you're caught short needing some posh clothes, it's better for your wallet to do your high-fashion shopping elsewhere. The Korzo, a pedestrian shopping street that snakes through the center of Rijeka, is the best place to go to browse. Modern multilevel shopping malls are also available at both ends of the city center.

Fresh local produce, fish, cheeses, olive oils, wines, and rakijas are the items that should be on your Kvarner shopping list. The best place to buy these is the City Market on Verdijeva. Although there are "professional" traders present, many of the stallholders are still locals who bring their home-produced wares to sell. Noisy and colorful, Rijeka's central market is the place to haggle over fresh produce, swap gossip, and, of course, drink coffee. Pick up a picnic lunch of cheeses, salads, fruit, and nuts here, then pop into one of the multitude of bakeries for freshly baked *burek* (cheese and meat pies) to complete the feast. Although a little tricky to transport, homemade olive oil, apple-cider vinegar, and rakija—usually sold in recycled bottles—are good buys as well. Smaller containers of dried herbal tea leaves and seasonings like rosemary and oregano are a good alternative if your luggage is already tightly packed.

**Mala Galerija Bruketa**

**CERAMICS** | This family art gallery was founded by sculptor Vladimir Bruketa, with more than 40 years of experience producing specific art objects using media such as ceramics, wood, and glass. The various sculptures, ceramics, and paintings are all produced by Croatian artists, including members of the Bruketa family. ✉ *Užarska 25, Rijeka* ☎ *051/335–403* 🌐 *mala-galerija.hr.*

**ZTC**

**MALL | FAMILY** | This mall right at the seafront is the favorite shopping destination of Rijeka residents. Shops include fashion brands like Benetton, H&M, and S'Oliver; Lush and L'Occitane cosmetics; and sport store Hervis. ✉ *Zvonimirova 3, Rijeka* ☎ *051/561–014* 🌐 *ztc.hr.*

Risnjak National Park is home to the mountain peak of Veliki Risnjak.

## Activities

### BEACHES

Since it serves as the country's largest port, there aren't too many beautiful beaches in the middle of Rijeka. However, you don't imagine locals stay here the whole summer without having a few spots they try to keep secret from the tourists, do you? Favorite beaches easily accessible from the city include **Bivio Cove,** near Kantrida to the west. In the opposite direction around the coast, **Uvala Žurkovo** at Kostrena is wonderful. Within the city itself, the popular place to swim is **Pećine** to the east, where you can swim off rocky beaches and admire the local villas.

### FISHING

The Croatian coast is well-known for its population of bluefin tuna, as well as bass, sea bream, sardines, anchovies, mackerel, shrimp, squid, and other shellfish.

**Ministry of Agriculture, Forestry & Water Management**

**FISHING** | You need a fishing license to hunt for any marine life using a line or gun. In Rijeka licenses are available from the local office of the Ministry of Agriculture, Forestry & Water Management or online through the ministry's website, which is in English. ✉ *Demetrova 3, Rijeka* ☎ *051/213–626* 🌐 *ribarstvo.mps.hr.*

# Risnjak National Park

*40 km (25 miles) northeast of Rijeka.*

The northern outpost of the forested and karst-peaked Gorski Kotar region, Veliki Risnjak is the major peak in this national park, peering over Rijeka from 5,013 feet. The thick pine-forest meadows are covered with wildflowers in the spring, and limestone peaks, crevices, and caves cover around 60 square km (25 square miles).

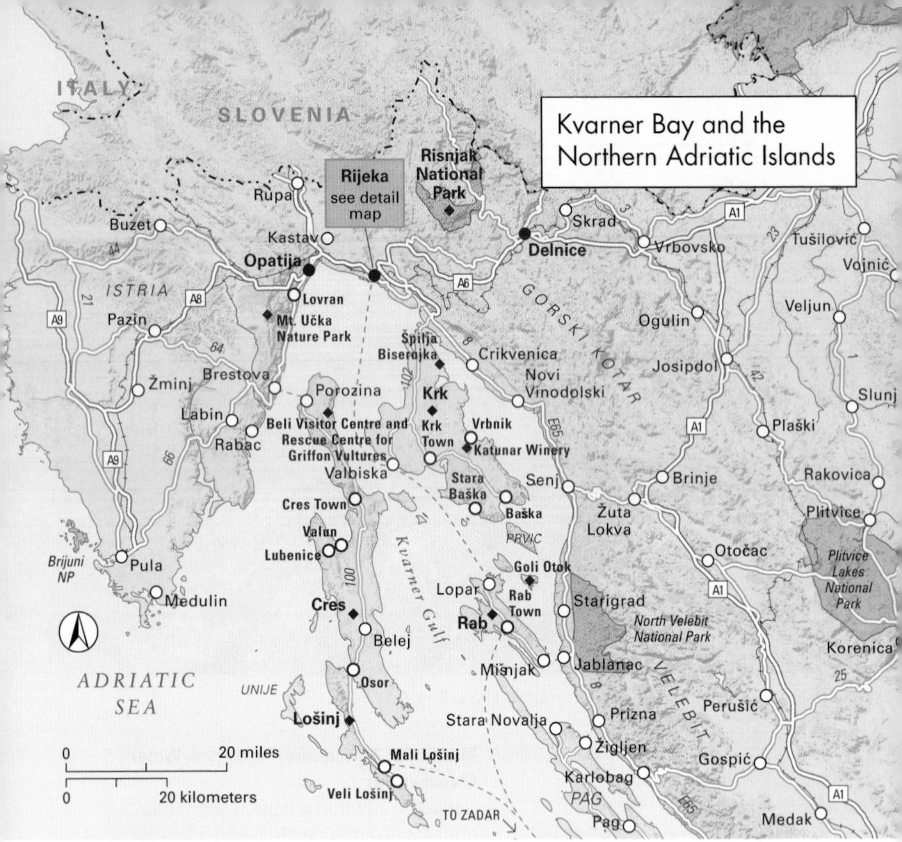

## Kvarner Bay and the Northern Adriatic Islands

## Sights

### ★ Risnjak National Park

**NATIONAL PARK** | Risnjak is a popular destination year-round. In winter you'll find a healthy contingent of snow aficionados desperately trying to avoid a trip up to Austria to sample the real thing. In summer, however, as the sun and the tourists beat down upon the coast, this is perhaps the best place to be. The cool mountain air—the average temperature in the region in July is around 16°C (60°F)—is a bonus to Risnjak's virtually unpopulated landscape.

You'll be free to commune with the locals, which include deer, bear, wildcat, and lynx (*ris*), from which the park takes its name. Geologic and botanical features are occasionally explained by English-language information points over which you may stumble on one of the more popular walking routes. Marked trails can occupy you for an hour's evening stroll to a full seven-day trek on the monstrous Rijeka Mountain Transversal from one side of Gorski Kotar to the other. Hiking huts are strung across the peaks to accommodate such ambitious expeditions. More information regarding these multiday hiking trips is available from the Croatian Mountaineering Association.

The park information office is in the village of Crni Lug, at the eastern entrance to the park. Near the park entrance is a guesthouse and restaurant, Pension NP Risnjak, open year-round. You can easily explore the gentler trails from either Rijeka or Delnice on day trips. Paths from the villages of Razloge and Kupari lead up to the source of the wild Kupa River, which can then be followed down the slopes through the "Valley of the Butterflies." ✉ *Bijela Vodica 48, Crni Lug* ☎ *051/836–133* 🌐 *www.np-risnjak.hr* 🎫 *€8* ⏲ *Information office closed Oct.–Apr.*

# Opatija

*15 km (9 miles) southwest of Rijeka.*

In the late 19th century, Opatija (Abbazia in Italian) was among the most elegant and fashionable resorts in Europe. Its history as a resort town dates from the 1840s, when villas were built for members of minor royalty. In 1873 the start of rail service from Vienna and Budapest, along with an aggressive publicity campaign, put Abbazia on the tourist map as a spa of the first magnitude. With the high mineral content of the seawater, iodine in the air, and an annual average of 2,230 hours of sunshine, it qualified as a top-rated climatic health resort and emerged as a favorite wintering spot for Central European nobility and high society.

A hint of the formality that gilded Opatija in its heyday still survives; the narrow pines and grand buildings remind one of the Italian lakes. This means that many visitors from all over Europe continue to head to the Opatija Riviera in the summer. At the same time, this stretch of coast has not gone unnoticed by the locals. Until recently, the town was a weekend haunt for some younger mobile Rijeka citizens. Thanks to these driving forces, the upmarket hotel guests still share the resort with some of the region's more upwardly mobile restaurants. However, their number is dwindling and the town's once admirable nightlife has packed up and headed back to the cooler parts of Rijeka, leaving Opatija to wealthy and more elderly visitors from the surrounding countries. These guests seem more eager to sip the waters than wine and spirits.

The main street, Maršala Tita, runs parallel to the coast for the length of the town, and you can go from one end of town to the other on foot in about half an hour, passing numerous terrace cafés along the way. The best seafood restaurants are in the neighboring fishing village of Volosko, a 15-minute walk along the seafront. The mild climate year-round and resulting subtropical vegetation, frequently sunny skies, and shelter from cold north winds provided by Mt. Učka give Opatija pleasant weather for much of the year. In summer, fresh sea breezes dispel any oppressive heat, making the city an ideal seaside resort.

## Sights

**Croatian Museum of Tourism** (*Villa Angiolina*)

**OTHER MUSEUM | FAMILY** | Visit this mini-museum to get a good understanding of Croatian (and particularly Opatija's) tourism in the 19th century. Set in the gorgeous pink Villa Angiolina and neighboring Swiss House, the museum's permanent collection includes postcards and photographs, souvenirs, and hotel inventory and equipment such as 19th-century hotel silverware and furniture. The villa's neoclassical design includes superb mosaic floors and frescoes. The park and green area in front of the museum are an attraction in and of themselves and a great place to make a small picnic on the grass. ✉ *Park Angiolina 1, Opatija* ☎ *051/603–636* 🌐 *www.hrmt.hr* 🎫 *€3 for Villa Angiolina; €5 for Villa Angiolina and Swiss House.*

★ **Lovran**

**TOWN** | Just 5 km (3 miles) southwest of Opatija, the lovely town of Lovran is home to good swimming coves, Habsburg villas, and paths up to Mt. Učka Nature Park. Massive chestnut trees dot the medieval town, giving shady relief from the sun on long summer days. If the crowds of Opatija leave you no place for peace and quiet,

When in Opatija, make sure you visit the nearby fishing village of Volosko and its excellent seafood eateries.

walk along the Lungomare through Ičići and Ika (or take Bus No. 32) to Lovran, where you can take in the sea air that lured Austrian royalty to winter here. If you find yourself on the Opatija Riviera in October, don't miss Lovran's Marunada (Chestnut Festival). ✉ *Lovran* ☎ *051/291–740* 🌐 *visitlovran.com.*

### ★ Lungomare

**PROMENADE** | If you enjoy walking by the sea, set off along the magnificent paved waterfront Lungomare. Built in 1889, this 12-km (7½-mile) path leads from the fishing village of Volosko through Opatija—passing in front of old hotels, parks, and gardens and around yacht basins—all the way past the villages of Ičići and Ika to Lovran. In the middle you'll find the popular town beach that fronts the center of Opatija. Close to many cafés, ice cream shops, and other essentials, the beach also has a couple of protected sections of water for safe swimming. ✉ *Obalno Šetalište Franza Josefa I, Opatija.*

### ★ Mt. Učka Nature Park

**MOUNTAIN** | **FAMILY** | From gentle hiking to mountain biking, climbing, and paragliding, all are available in the 160 square km (62 square miles) of Mt. Učka Nature Park, a series of peaks that help shelter the Liburnia Riviera (the official name for the stretch of coast centered on Opatija) and the islands from weather systems to the north. Hiking trails leading toward the summit of the Učka range start from all the resorts along the coast. A climb up to the fine stone lookout tower at the summit of the highest peak, Vojak (4,596 feet), can be well worth it, but it is not for the faint of heart nor inexperienced, out-of-shape hiking enthusiasts. On a clear day, the view offers a distant tour of the islands of Kvarner Bay, the Italian Alps, and perhaps even an indistinct view of Venice. Most routes up to the heights lead through the forest so that you can trek in summer without overheating. Along the way, you'll find natural springs to quench your thirst, ponds, tumbling waterfalls (in the wetter months), impressive natural stone columns, and several hundred caves. The local inhabitants include deer, wild boar, and bears in the park's northernmost sections. Humans have also been living in these hills for centuries, rearing cattle, farming, and working the forest; you'll come across numerous tiny villages and historical sites if you roam far enough. If you're running short on time, many mountain-biking tracks throughout the park offer the chance to expand your lungs on the way up and test your nerve rattling back down to the coast. There is also the possibility to drive to the top and take in the views from the stone tower. There is an information point with maps and souvenirs on the road leading to the summit called Poklon. At Poklon, hikers will find two great restaurants with accommodation and a mountain-hiking hut that sleeps 18. There's also a modern educational center. ✉ *Liganj 42, Lovran* ☎ *051/770–100* 🌐 *www.pp-ucka.hr* 🎫 *Free.*

**Park Angiolina**

**GARDEN | FAMILY** | The grounds of Park Angiolina are a wonderful spread of palm-punctuated lawns with a botanical garden. The vegetation is strikingly lush, including cacti, bamboo, and magnolias, plus neatly kept beds of colorful flowers and sweet-scented shrubs. Indeed, Opatija as a whole is a town saturated with botanical splendor. Iginio Scarpa, an aristocrat from Rijeka and the first settler in Opatija, began importing exotic plants and the tradition has survived into the present. The camellia is the symbol of the city. ✉ *Between Maršala Tita and the seafront, Opatija* 🌐 *www.visitopatija.com* 🎫 *Free.*

## Restaurants

**Draga di Lovrana**

**$$$$ | MODERN EUROPEAN** | Tucked in a forested green valley of the Učka mountains with a gorgeous view of the island of Cres, this boutique hotel is also the proud holder of the first Michelin-starred restaurant in the Kvarner Bay region. The peaceful nature of the restaurant's surroundings is enough reason to make the trek up from Lovran. **Known for:** first-class fine dining; tales that the hotel was once haunted; surroundings of wild beauty. 💲 *Average main: €60* ✉ *Lovranska Draga 1, Lovran* ☎ *051/294–166* 🌐 *www.dragadilovrana.hr* ⏲ *Closed Mon. and Tues.*

★ **Ganeum**

**$$ | CONTEMPORARY** | This casual fine-dining experience is as relaxed and intimate as it is an enjoyable gourmet meal. When choosing the tasting menu, it is not hard to detect the passion for quality that has been invested into the selection of the produce and the selection of wines. **Known for:** tasting menu; engaging and welcoming waitstaff; creative use of local products. 💲 *Average main: €15* ✉ *Stari Grad 5, Lovran* ☎ *051/294-444* 🌐 *www.facebook.com/ganeumlovran* ⏲ *Closed Jan.*

**Istranka**

**$$ | ITALIAN | FAMILY** | With a delightful covered terrace flanked by a twisting tree, this small restaurant is Opatija's best option for fresh simply prepared seafood like grilled octopus and scampi risotto. But Istranka is also a winner for those who are not fans of seafood: taking its influence from the neighboring region of Istria, the menu features *njoki,* gnocchi with local ham and cheese, and of course, other local dishes with famous Istrian truffles. **Known for:** traditional Istrian cuisine; affordable prices; friendly service. 💲 *Average main: €15* ✉ *Bože Milanovića 2, Opatija* ☎ *051/271–835* ⏲ *Closed Jan.*

**Konoba Tramerka**

**$$ | SEAFOOD | FAMILY** | Located in Volosko, just above the more famed Plavi Podrum, this small seafood tavern offers fresh creative seafood dishes in a cozy interior with exposed stone walls; a tiny street-side terrace has only a few tables. Locals rave about their bonito tartare, monkfish stew, and dirty calamari (baby calamari too small to be thoroughly cleaned before cooking, thus "dirty"). **Known for:** fish tapas; creative food; friendly atmosphere. *Average main: €18 Dr. Andrije Mohorovičića 15, Volosko 051/701–707 konoba-tramerka.eatbu.hr Closed Mon. and Jan.*

### ★ Konoba Valle Losca

$$ | **MEDITERRANEAN** | In the neighborly village of Volosko, where old stone houses are fixed precariously close to one another and give shape to the one road, this restaurant justifies spending an afternoon or evening in a setting that is not to be missed. The intimate artistic atmosphere tells you everything you need to know about the owners and how sincere they are about sharing good food, much of which is produced on their family farm in Istria. **Known for:** intimate communal dining experience; good food at a good price; homemade ice cream. *Average main: €20 Andrije Štangera 2, Volosko 095/580–3757 www.vallelosca.com Closed Mon.*

### Plavi Podrum

$$$ | **SEAFOOD** | This is an upscale, traditional fine-dining fish restaurant in Volosko. The owner has won some wine awards and has, accordingly, inflated the costs for dining here, which results in unusually high expectations from diners. **Known for:** tasting menus; excellent wine list; pasta with shrimp, peaches, and black truffles. *Average main: €28 Frana Supila 12, Volosko 051/701–223 www.plavipodrum.com Closed Jan.*

## Hotels

### ★ Bevanda

$$$ | **HOTEL** | With only 10 rooms—each with its own private view of the sea—this luxurious design hotel is one of Opatija's best. **Pros:** VIP saltwater pool; chic restaurant and lounge; offers concierge services. **Cons:** parking is tricky; not a place for families; pricey. *Rooms from: €280 Zert 8, Opatija Located in the marina behind the outdoor theater 051/493–888 www.bevanda.hr 10 rooms Free Breakfast.*

### Hotel Astoria by OHM Group

$ | **HOTEL** | The modern interior here is more South Beach than Austro-Hungarian grandeur, and with its coastal perks, the Astoria is justifiably popular with young international travelers. **Pros:** convenient location to beach and restaurants; big breakfasts; stylish decor. **Cons:** superior rooms are on the small side; not directly on the sea; difficult parking. *Rooms from: €145 Maršala Tita 174, Opatija 051/711–761 www.astoriadesignhotel.hr Closed Nov.–Apr. 50 rooms Free Breakfast.*

### Hotel Milenij

$$$ | **HOTEL** | On the coastal promenade, this bright pink luxury villa is part old and part new; rooms are furnished accordingly, with either Louis XV–style antiques heavily striped in silk or modern designer pieces. **Pros:** centrally located luxury hotel on the seafront; outdoor breakfast area overlooking the sea; excellent spa facilities. **Cons:** small outdoor pool with few lounge chairs; lack of parking spaces; most expensive coffee in Opatija. *Rooms from: €265 Maršala Tita 109, Opatija 051/202–000 www.milenijhoteli.hr 99 rooms Free Breakfast.*

### Liburnia Hotel Ambasador

$ | **HOTEL** | A 10-floor skyscraper may not look like the rest of the traditional Opatija Riviera, but this luxurious hotel is surprisingly elegant inside, with an airy lobby area and floor-to-ceiling windows overlooking the sea. **Pros:** gorgeous view from sea-facing rooms; luxurious pool area overlooking the beach; superior spa facilities. **Cons:** parking fees; hotel also caters to business travelers; only buffet-style dinners with half-board option. *Rooms from: €140 Feliksa Peršića 5, Opatija 051/710-444 for reservation center, 051/743–333 www.liburnia.hr/en/hotel-ambasador 200 rooms Free Breakfast.*

**Liburnia Hotel Kvarner**
**$$ | HOTEL** | The former summer residence of European royalty, Kvarner's oldest hotel first opened its doors to guests in 1884. **Pros:** Habsburg-era grandeur; spacious patio overlooking the sea; spa and fitness center included in price of the room. **Cons:** noise from wedding parties sometimes hosted in the Crystal Ballroom; limited parking; stuffy atmosphere. *$ Rooms from: €187 ✉ Pava Tomašica 2, Opatija ☎ 051/271–233, 051/710–444 for reservation center 🌐 www.liburnia.hr/en/hotel-kvarner ⏲ Closed Nov.–Apr. 58 rooms 🍽 Free Breakfast.*

## Nightlife

There was a time when folk from Rijeka used Opatija as their playground; then, the town offered superb nightlife options. These days, however, the big city along the coast is reclaiming its post as the cultural hot spot of the region, and Opatija has been busy transforming itself back into Central and Eastern Europe's health resort. The wealthy Italians and Austrians who dominate here enjoy nights out for live music, open-air movies, and regional theater.

**Colosseum Lounge & Beach Bar**
**DANCE CLUBS** | If there is nightlife to be found in Opatija, this is where it's at. The Colosseum has an actual disco and features DJs, dancers, and other performers with fun events geared toward a hip crowd. The club also has sun beds around a pool that looks out over the sea and is perfect for enjoying cocktails after salsa dancing. *✉ Maršala Tita 129, Opatija 🌐 www.opatija-colosseum.com.*

**Monokini**
**COCKTAIL LOUNGES** | Centrally located in Opatija, Monokini attracts a young crowd who enjoys lounging on the couches inside or on the glassed-in terrace as they listen to music and watch the passersby. You'll find good music, a young and mostly friendly staff, good drinks, cocktails, and a selection of teas—not to mention a friendly atmosphere with plenty of locals. Just be aware that it's cash-only. *✉ Maršala Tita 96, Opatija ☎ 051/703–888.*

## Performing Arts

**★ Gervais Center**
**ARTS CENTERS | FAMILY** | Since the 19th century, a live performance and musical theater has sat where the modern Gervais Center sits today. The theater started showing films at the beginning of the 20th century, until it officially became the city cinema in the 1950s. In 2012, the original building was demolished, then in 2017 the current contemporary performance house opened, offering a vibrant year-round schedule of regional musical theater, plays, concerts, opera, festivals, and movie screenings. *✉ Nikole Tesle 5, Opatija ☎ 051/588–460 🌐 www.festivalopatija.hr/centargervais.*

## Activities

Mt. Učka Nature Park, accessible from virtually any point along the coast, offers the easiest opportunity for active exploring, including mountain-biking and hiking trails up through the forested slopes.

**Marotti Watersport Center**
**WINDSURFING | FAMILY** | Marotti Watersport Center in Volosko is the best place in the region to learn to windsurf. There is a Tramontana wind that blows down from the mountains every morning in Volosko, creating the perfect conditions for both beginners and experts. The team at Marotti are as friendly and relaxed as they are experienced. They also offer team-building, stand-up paddleboarding tours, and equipment storage. *✉ Frana Supila 2, Opatija ☎ 099/662–9546 🌐 marottiwindsurfing.hr.*

# Cres

*Brestova is 30 km (18 miles) southwest of Opatija, then a 20-minute ferry ride to Cres.*

Twisting down the entire length of the Kvarner Bay on its western side is Cres, whose current claim to fame is that it is the largest of all Croatian islands. Neighboring Krk was awarded this distinction for many years, but recent recalculations have rectified a long-standing error. Cres has been known as one of the most unspoiled islands in the Adriatic for a long time. More difficult to get to than Krk and with a wilder and more rugged topography, Cres is quite frankly a delight. Its natural stretches are punctuated with olive groves and tiny towns and villages that remain authentic for the most part.

### GETTING HERE AND AROUND

Ferries to Cres take about 20 minutes, embarking from Brestova, which is on the mainland southwest of Opatija, to Porozina; another ferry goes from Valbiska on Krk to Merag, on the east side of Cres.

## Sights

### ★ Beli Visitor Centre and Rescue Centre for Griffon Vultures

**WILDLIFE REFUGE | FAMILY** | The northern end of Cres is mountainous and forested, harboring wildlife such as the rare griffin vulture. This rescue center helps protect and rescue these beasts, as well as preserve the environment and heritage of the island. The center houses rescued vultures before they are released back into the wild and includes educational info on the biodiversity and history of northern Cres, bird-watching, eco-trails, and volunteer opportunities. The naturalists that run the center are full of passion about their work and are excited teachers. Visit this center with your kids to learn more about these protected birds, then try to spot the griffins flying in their natural habitat around the cliffs of the island. From November to April, the center is open by appointment only, so call in advance during this period. ✉ *Beli 4, Beli* ☎ *095/506–1116, 051/352–400* 🌐 *belivisitorcentre.eu* 🎫 *Free (donations accepted)* 🕓 *Closed Sept.–May.*

### ★ Cres Town

**TOWN | FAMILY** | Tucked into a well-protected bay midway down the island, Cres Town is set around a lovely little fishing harbor, small but perfectly formed, with numerous Gothic and Renaissance churches, monasteries, and palaces. For the most part these are in the Old Town, which sits protected by winged Venetian lions atop three 16th-century gates, the only remains of a defensive wall. A small harbor (Mandrać), as well as a municipal loggia built in the 15th-century, remain the soul of the town.

The town beach, at Camp Kovačine, holds a Blue Flag award for cleanliness. To get there, follow the path around the harbor from the main road and keep going for at least 15 minutes along the promenade, where you'll find spots to jump into the water and the odd café or restaurant to keep you fueled. Although the seaside here is man-made, it somehow doesn't detract too much from the experience. ✉ *Cres Town* 🌐 *www.visitcres.hr.*

### ★ Lubenice

**TOWN** | One of the most tempting beaches on the island is on the western coast of Cres at the foot of a steep cliff, at the top of which is the tiny village of Lubenice, which offers great views out to sea and up the western coast. This picturesque collection of houses that surrounds the 15th-century Church of St. Anthony the Hermit has been clinging to its outcrop for around 4,000 years. The hamlet is popular among artsy types and hosts exhibitions and music performances in the summer. From the beach

On Cres, the small village of Lubenice is home to artists and music performances in the summer.

below, a short walk through vineyards will bring you to Žanja Cove, which has a blue grotto, a cave at water level that fills with brilliant blue light as strong sunlight filters through the azure water. ✉ *Lubenice* 🌐 *www.visitcres.hr.*

**Osor**

**TOWN** | At the southwestern tip of Cres is the town of Osor, whose strategic position on the channel between the islands of Cres and Lošinj ensured that wealth flowed into the town from trade ships. Famous for its garden sculptures, a wander through this well-preserved medieval town makes for a pleasant afternoon in an exceptionally tranquil location. There's even a cathedral, reflecting its former status, and many important archaeological sites have been discovered in the vicinity. ✉ *Osor* 🌐 *www.visitlosinj.hr.*

**Osor Archaeological Collection**

**HISTORY MUSEUM** | **FAMILY** | Housed in the former city hall near the cathedral, this museum contains one of the oldest archeological collections in Croatia, including artifacts from across the Roman empire. ✉ *Gradska vijecnica, Osor* ☎ *051/233–892* 🌐 *www.muzej.losinj.hr* 🎫 *€5* 🕒 *Closed Mon. in mid-June–Aug.; by reservation only Oct.–mid-May.*

**Valun**

**TOWN** | **FAMILY** | Across the bay from Cres, the village of Valun has a nice beach. The town's claim to fame is the Valun Tablet, a gravestone that is one of the oldest known examples of Glagolitic script. The tablet is now kept in the parish church, right on the waterfront. Get to Valun by car or by taking the wooden boat that sits just outside the Cres Harbor wall; it's easily spotted from the main square. ✉ *Valun.*

## Restaurants

**Konoba Belona**

**$** | **MEDITERRANEAN** | **FAMILY** | This family-run restaurant understands the true meaning of making guests feel welcome. Meals are freshly prepared in a classic

As the largest of the Croatian islands, Cres has some of its best beaches.

way that honors the treasures of Cres. **Known for:** pepper steak; pistachio semifreddo; away from the harbor crowds. *Average main: €12 Hrvatskih Branitelja 15, Cres Town 051/571–203 Closed Dec.–Mar.*

**Konoba Bonifačić**

$ | **MEDITERRANEAN** | The subtitle on the road signs reads *nonina kuhinja* (granny's cooking), and you were a spoiled child indeed if your grandma turned out dishes of this standard for you. The shady garden in the heart of ancient Osor is a perfect setting in which to enjoy the typical plates of the konoba: meat, seafood, pasta, and salads. **Known for:** lovely garden terrace; traditional Mediterranean dishes; idyllic location in Osor. *Average main: €12 Osor 64, Osor 051/237–413 www.jazon.hr Closed Oct.–Easter. No lunch.*

★ **Konoba Bukaleta**

$ | **MEDITERRANEAN** | Cres is famous for its lamb, and although the majority of restaurants have it on the menu, Bukaleta is *the* place for the best on the island. Located in the small village of Loznati, just 10 km (6 miles) south of Cres Town, Bukaleta has been run by the same family for more than 30 years. **Known for:** lamb 13 different ways; lamb slow-cooked in stone bread oven; traditional recipes passed down through generations. *Average main: €14 Loznati 9A, Loznati 051/571–606, 099/598–3970 Closed Oct.–Apr.*

**Konoba Hibernicia**

$ | **MEDITERRANEAN** | **FAMILY** | A nice little terrace right by the bell tower in the heart of the stone hilltop village of Lubenice is the perfect location for a light lunch of *pršut* (prosciutto), cheese, olives, and a glass of local wine. For a more hearty meal, order lamb-stew gnocchi or lamb liver with polenta, since lamb is a specialty on Cres. **Known for:** relaxed atmosphere; simple traditional food; not-so-friendly staff. *Average main: €12 Lubenice 17, Lubenice 051/525–040 No credit cards Closed Oct.–Apr.*

**Riva**

**$$ | SEAFOOD | FAMILY** | The colorful square on the edge of Cres Town Harbor is lined with many restaurants serving seafood, pasta, and risotto, and Riva is an excellent choice. Tables edge out onto the flagstones of the square, meaning the steady stream of strollers through the town will eye your plate with appreciative glances. **Known for:** fresh seafood; harbor-view terrace; dinner reservations necessary. *Average main: €18* *Riva Creskih Kapetana 13, Cres Town* *051/571–107* *Closed Nov.–Easter.*

Reflecting its splendid undeveloped nature, Cres offers very few hotels, though there are plenty of apartments and guest rooms available for rent on the island.

**Hotel Kimen**

**$ | HOTEL | FAMILY** | Tucked away in a shady pine forest just a stone's throw from the town beach and a 10-minute walk from the center, Kimen's four stories provide the only hotel accommodation in Cres Town. **Pros:** enviable position on an attractive cove; close to town center; kid- and dog-friendly. **Cons:** smallish rooms; a bit outdated; Wi-Fi not available in every room. *Rooms from: €130* *Melin I 16, Cres Town* *051/573–305* *www.hotel-kimen.com* *Closed mid-Oct.–Apr.* *128 rooms* *Free Breakfast.*

The half-dozen or so bars around the main harbor are great for casual drinking and chatting while you sit outside on balmy evenings listening to the clinking chains of boats. Head inside for quicker quaffing and shouting above Croatian high-energy pop music, where you'll share the space with German yachtsmen. If you're looking for livelier options, unfortunately you're on the wrong island.

### BIKING

**Camp Kovačine**

**BIKING | FAMILY** | The staff at Camp Kovačine, which is nicely set under shady pines and right on the main town beach, can rent you bikes and boats or organize diving trips, beach volleyball, and even paragliding. They have added a new pool and extended their season until the end of October (it's closed from November to March). *Melin I 20, Cres Town* *051/573–150 for sales office, 051/571–423 for front desk* *camp-kovacine.com.*

### DIVING

**Diving Cres**

**SCUBA DIVING | FAMILY** | If you prefer to explore beneath the waves, Diving Cres can be found at Camp Kovačine, about a 10-minute walk from the harbor. A single orientation dive can be tried for €69, or a ticket of 10 dives for €80. They also have a boat and rental equipment available in many sizes. The dive center is managed by a community of divers based in Germany and has been operating since 1996. *Camp Kovačine, Melin I 20, Cres Town* *051/571–706* *www.diving.de.*

## Lošinj

*55 km (35 miles) from Cres Town.*

As you approach the southern tip of Cres, you'll see the steep slopes of Mt. Osorčica on nearby Lošinj. Sheltered by the Alps to the north and Velebit to the east, the favorable island climate prompted the creation of a health resort here in 1892.

Blink and you might miss the bridge connecting Cres to Lošinj, unless you arrive when the span is raised to allow a ship through the narrow channel that splits the two islands. In fact, until Roman times, the two islands were one, connected near Osor. Mother Nature's inconsiderate arrangement did much to frustrate trade ships; entire vessels

The island of Lošinj has a past and present that are both very connected to the shipping industry.

would be hauled across the few feet of land that blocked the route here rather than sail around the southern tip of the archipelago. Eventually, some bright spark decided to cut the present-day channel, opening the shipping lanes. Lošinj is an elongated low-lying island covered with pine forests. Viewed from the hills of Cres, the slim green outline of the main island and its surrounding islets, with a backbone of hills in the middle, resembles a long frog splayed out in the water, basking in the sun and contrasting beautifully with the water. Lošinj's past and present are very much connected to the shipping industry. The sea captains who populated the towns of Veli and Mali Lošinj when the island reached its golden age in the 19th century are very much responsible for bringing exotic plant life here from around the world and for building the fine villas that have made this a colorful destination for vacationers, who contribute much more to the island's economy today. The smaller islands that make up the archipelago include Unije, Susak, and Ilovik—all of which are large enough to provide some lodging to visitors—and even smaller islands such as Vele and Male Srakane, Male Orjule, and Sveti Petar, which can be reached by tourist boats from the resorts on Lošinj.

## Sights

**Church of St. Anthony the Hermit**

**CHURCH** | The intimate harbor is the centerpiece of Veli Lošinj, at the entrance to which is the delightful Church of St. Anthony the Hermit, with a separate bell tower in pink and cream stone. Built on the site of a former church in 1774, the church has always had a congregation of seafarers, who have filled it with religious art and altars from spots such as Venice.
✉ *On the Veli Lošinj waterfront, Lošinj*
⏲ *Closed Sun. and Sept.–July.*

**★ Čikat Bay**

**BEACH** | **FAMILY** | The road that runs along the Mali Lošinj Harbor leads to Čikat Bay, a pine-covered area dotted with impressive Habsburg-era villas and pebbled beach coves. Nearby hotels and campsites, plus good parking, lots of cafés, and ice-cream stands make these beaches popular. There's a gracious promenade along the bay that's perfect for strolling, a windsurfing school for the adventurous, and paddleboat rentals. ✉ *Mali Lošinj.*

**Kula** (*The Tower*)

**MILITARY SIGHT | FAMILY** | Opposite the harbor, but now hidden by a row of houses, are the battlements of a defensive tower that dates back to the 15th century. The squat construction, known as The Tower, now houses a museum and an art gallery staging temporary exhibitions by notable Croatian artists. The permanent exhibition tracing the town's history includes a copy of a Greek statue of Apoxyomenos, which was discovered on the seabed in 1996. ✉ *Kaštel bb, Veli Lošinj* ☎ *051/236–594* 🌐 *www.muzej.losinj.hr* 🎫 *€5* 🕒 *Closed Mon. Easter–mid-Oct. and Sun. mid-Sept.–mid-Oct. and Easter–mid-June.*

★ **Lošinj Marine Education Centre/Blue World Institute**

**WILDLIFE REFUGE | FAMILY** | A community of around 180 bottlenose dolphins makes its home just off the coast of Lošinj, and the nonprofit Lošinj Marine Education Centre has made it its mission to protect the marine environment of the Adriatic Sea. The center has a few engaging displays that use various media forms that invite visitors to take a deeper look at the amazing blue world surrounding the island. You can even "adopt" your own dolphin; you can't take it home with you, of course, but for €35 you'll receive an adoption certificate, a photo of your adopted dolphin, membership for a year, and, of course, that warm fuzzy feeling of doing something good for the world. ✉ *Kaštel 24, Veli Lošinj* ☎ *051/604–666* 🌐 *www.blue-world.org* 🎫 *€5* 🕒 *Closed Sun. in May, June, and Sept. and weekends Oct.–Apr.*

**Mali Lošinj**

**TOWN | FAMILY** | With 8,000 inhabitants sheltered around an inlet, Mali Lošinj is the largest island settlement in the Adriatic. In the 19th century, Mali and Veli Lošinj experienced a golden age when many wealthy sea captains lived on the island. Brightening the waterfront, the mansions and villas they constructed contributed greatly to the town's appeal. There are a handful of churches to wander into and take in the sense of history and time that has been well preserved by the island's faithful. The 15th-century St. Martin's Church was the original centerpiece around which the town was built but is now a bit decrepit, though its ominous presence with a tall square tower and pointed top are hard to miss. At the base of the tower is a cemetery where the history of the town's past residents is collected. If you wish to dig a bit deeper, the Church of Our Little Lady (aka Church of the Nativity of Our Lord) houses many fine examples of religious art. ✉ *Mali Lošinj* 🌐 *www.visitlosinj.hr.*

**Miomirisni Otočki Vrt** (*Garden of Fine Scents*)

**GARDEN | FAMILY** | After a few days of dipping your toes in the water and basking in the sun, you might be itching for a diversionary outing. The Miomirisni otočki vrt is a pleasant place to spend the afternoon—rain or shine—sitting on the terrace admiring the sea of lavender on the hilltop. A donkey, a rabbit, and a small sheep delight visitors, especially children. A small shop in a wooden building sells organic products like soaps, marmalades, and, of course, lavender oil. ✉ *Bukovica 6, Mali Lošinj* ☎ *098/326–519* 🌐 *miomirisni-vrt.hr/en* 🎫 *Free* 🕒 *Closed Jan. and Feb.*

★ **Museum of Apoxyomenos**

**HISTORY MUSEUM | FAMILY** | This is an entire museum dedicated to telling the amazing story of a single ancient artifact found on the bottom of the sea near Mali Losinj in 1996. After six years of restoration,

## Slow Down: Islands of Lošinj

If life on the major islands is too hectic, knock your engine down to quarter-speed and head out to one of the tiny islands that pepper the seas around the coast of Lošinj. The island of **Unije** is by far the largest, managing to fit in a population of 90, although many are summer-only residents. The tiny town of the same name has a few restaurants settled around a large pebble bay, although exploring the northern coasts by foot or by boat should reveal many private swimming spots. **Ilovik** is the southernmost island of the group. Its nickname, "Island of Flowers," is accurate; oleanders and roses surround almost every home. Watch yachts at close quarters cutting through the channel between Ilovik and the islet of Sveti Petar, on which there was once a convent. The graveyard remains and burial processions by fishing boat still take place. Paržine, on the southeastern coast, has a large sandy beach.

If you're from New Jersey, you may have a good chance of being related to one of the 188 people living on **Susak** since many folks from here have settled in the Garden State. Susak is flung farther out into the sea than any of the other islands. While the rest of the Kvarner is composed of limestone karst, Susak consists entirely of sand, so its coast is gentler in elevation and indentation. Not wanting to be outdone, the population retains a distinctive character and culture. The only wheeled transport on the island is wheelbarrows.

the bronze statue, which is presumed to date back to the 1st or 2nd century BC, is an awesome piece of Greek work that is displayed in an artistic and mesmerizing way, making a remarkable impression of what may have happened when the statue fell into the ocean thousands of years ago (but also about the process of its restoration). The building itself is reason enough to buy a ticket and enjoy a guided tour (offered twice-daily at noon and 5 pm). ✉ *Riva Lošinjskih Kapetana 13, Mali Lošinj* ☎ *051/734–260* 🌐 *www.muzejapoksiomena.hr* 🎫 *€12 Nov.–Apr.; €15 May.–Oct.* ⏲ *Closed Mon.*

**★ Veli Lošinj**

**TOWN** | **FAMILY** | The sea captains of Veli Lošinj evidently preferred to escape the harsh working conditions of life on the sea while they were back on land, so they built their villas away from the waterfront, often surrounding themselves with gardens filled with exotic plants brought back from their travels. Archduke Karl Stephan built a winter residence in Veli Lošinj that is now a sanatorium surrounded by wonderful gardens, with a range of exotic plants and an arboretum. It's possible to spend the night in the sanatorium, even if you are healthy. A short walk beyond the main harbor is the quaint fishing cove of Rovenska. Beyond that, there's a pebble beach and several inviting restaurants. The breakwater was established by Archduke Maximilian I. ✉ *Veli Lošinj* 🌐 *www.visitlosinj.hr.*

### Restaurants

**Artatore/Kod Janje**

**$$$** | **MEDITERRANEAN** | **FAMILY** | Ten km (6 miles) north of Mali Lošinj, in the small village of Artatore, you'll find a restaurant of the same name, which locals also call *Kod Janje* (Chez Janje) and consider the best on the entire island. The seafood here is *à l'ordre du jour*; order the scampi in white wine with polenta, grilled fish, or lobster tagliatelle. **Known for:** a seafood lover's paradise; longevity: the place has been open for over 45 years; thick crab soup. $ *Average main: €26* ✉ *Artatore 132, Mali Lošinj* ☎ *098/536–477* ⊙ *Closed Nov.–Apr.*

★ **Baracuda**

$$ | **SEAFOOD** | Many of the yachts that line the harbor unload their human cargo at this small restaurant, which enjoys a big reputation for fresh fish dinners. Tuna carpaccio, shark on the grill, and lobster *na buzaru* (cooked with wine) are all great. **Known for:** fresh fish and seafood; great location on the marina; gets crowded so reservations are smart. $ *Average main: €18* ✉ *Priko 31, Mali Lošinj* ☎ *051/233–309* ⊙ *Closed Oct.–Apr.*

**Bora Bar**

$$ | **MEDITERRANEAN** | **FAMILY** | Creative Italian dishes like tuna carpaccio with celery root and truffles are what you'll find at this friendly restaurant in Rovenska Bay. The dynamic owners—part Croatian, part expat—bring a joie de vivre and an eclectic style to the place that attracts curious foodies to their tables. **Known for:** homemade pasta; truffle-infused dishes; homemade limoncello. $ *Average main: €18* ✉ *Rovenska 3, Veli Lošinj* ☎ *051/867–544* 🌐 *www.borabar.net* ⊙ *Closed Oct.–Apr.*

★ **Restaurant Matsunoki**

$$$ | **ASIAN FUSION** | This upscale restaurant combines the best of local organic ingredients with Japanese cooking techniques and tastes. As good as Mediterranean food is, it can often leave your taste buds yearning for something more exotic, and the chef here introduces a masterful Japanese style to the menu. **Known for:** Japanese dumplings stuffed with lamb, fennel, and carrot; smoked oysters with unagi sauce; excellent selection of sake. $ *Average main: €28* ✉ *Hotel Bellevue, Čikat 9, Lošinj* ☎ *051/679–0000* 🌐 *www.losinj-hotels.com/en/dining/restaurant-matsunoki.*

## Hotels

**Hotel Apoksiomen**

$$ | **HOTEL** | Named after a Greek statue recovered from the seabed near Mali Lošinj in 1999, this renovated villa turned modern boutique hotel imposes itself on the seafront close to the main square. **Pros:** stunning views; central location right on the water; delicious pastries in the café. **Cons:** rooms don't match the gorgeous hotel exterior; parking is off-site and pricey; can be noisy. $ *Rooms from: €185* ✉ *Riva Lošinjskih Kapetana 1, Mali Lošinj* ☎ *051/520–820* 🌐 *hotel-apoksiomen.hr* ⊙ *Closed Nov.–Apr.* *25 rooms* *Free Breakfast.*

**Vitality Hotel Punta**

$$ | **HOTEL** | The attractive colored blocks of this four-star property in Veli Lošinj line the seashore in a style that complements the island's traditional architecture surprisingly well. **Pros:** good on-site facilities, including excellent wellness center; near both the sea and the town of Veli Lošinj; stunning views from some rooms. **Cons:** pool is on the small side for the size of the hotel; large hotel complex can feel a bit impersonal; inconsistent service. $ *Rooms from: €175* ✉ *Šestavine 17, Veli Lošinj* ☎ *051/662–000* 🌐 *www.losinj-hotels.com/en/hotels-and-villas/hotel-punta* ⊙ *Closed Nov.–Mar.* *289 rooms* *Free Breakfast.*

## Nightlife

Both Mali and Vela Lošinj offer a healthy selection of bars, where you can sit outside on warm evenings, sip drinks, and chat. Those looking for brighter lights had better move on to Krk or the mainland.

## Activities

### BIKING

**Rent-A-Bike Junior** (*Rent-A-Bike Best Price*)

**BIKING** | **FAMILY** | You can rent bikes here for €5 per hour or €17 per day, though availability is limited (and you need to call ahead) from October through May. E-bikes are also available to rent from €15 per hour. The more days you rent, the better the price. ✉ *Velopin 15, Mali Lošinj* ☎ *099/409–9943* 🌐 *www.losinjbike.com.*

### DIVING AND SAILING

**SUBSEASON Scuba School**

**SCUBA DIVING | FAMILY** | SUBSEASON is run by Neno, an SSI diving instructor who is relaxed and experienced. The company has a dive boat and offers a range of courses for beginner, certification, or advanced instruction. Take a test dive for €65. ✉ *Del Conte 1, Mali Lošinj* ☎ *098/294–887* 🌐 *www.subseason.com.*

# Krk

*50 km (31 miles) southeast of Rijeka.*

Since Krk is one of the largest Croatian islands, hosts the regional airport, and is connected to the mainland by a bridge, it's no surprise that this robust island is one of the most developed in the country. The dusty edges and agricultural interior get very busy during the high season, and if you visit then, you will likely be in traffic jams along the snaking routes between the resort towns. Add the sight of the oil refinery on the mainland near the bridge and the terminal for tankers near Omišalj on the island's northern coast, and you may think twice about heading here. The sights aren't exactly what you'd call picturesque, but don't be put off so easily. Krk still offers many of the same delights found in the rest of the region: great beaches, interesting history, and pretty old towns. Although other islands may offer a slower pace, Krk compensates by offering more facilities and convenience. With numerous accommodation options and more entertainment, it may very well be the best choice for families with easily bored children in tow.

## Sights

**Baška**

**TOWN | FAMILY** | On the southern end of the island, this town has a great beach as well as the conveniences of civilization. However, this means that you must sometimes fight to find a spot in season. The 2-km (1-mile) beach is fronted by colorfully painted houses (and hotels at the southern end) and adorned with interesting nooks and stairways, all lending a fun and slightly eccentric air to the town. Cute backstreets behind the houses offer a selection of cozy cafés and a plethora of ice-cream shops. ✉ *Baška* 🌐 *www.tz-baska.hr.*

**Crkva Svete Lucije** (*Church of St. Lucy*)

**CHURCH | FAMILY** | Driving into Baška, you'll pass through Draga Bašćanska and then find yourself in Jurandvor. While on this road, take the chance to visit the Church of St. Lucy, which has achieved cultlike status since the discovery of the Glagolitic Baška Tablet on its grounds in 1851. ✉ *Jurandvor* ☎ *051/860–184* 🌐 *azjurandvor.com* 🎫 *€5* 🕓 *Closed Nov.–Apr.*

**Goli Otok**

**ISLAND | FAMILY** | If you like Communist history, consider a day trip to this uninhabited island that was a Yugoslav prison just off the coast of Rab. Goli Otok means "naked island," a name aptly given for the lack of vegetation and inhabitable conditions on the island. After Tito broke ranks with Stalin in 1948, the island became known as the place where Yugoslav political prisoners were confined. Men were incarcerated here while women were taken to nearby Sveti Grgur island. The treatment of these prisoners is wholly unknown, as very few prisoners lived to tell of their experiences, but a stone quarry indicates that prisoners were forced to do hard labor quarrying stone. Conditions on Goli Otok were harsh, with blistering temperatures in the summer and brutal *bura* winds ripping across the barren island in the

**Krk is one of the more developed of the Croatian islands, meaning activities and entertainment options abound.**

winter. Any mention of Goli Otok was strictly forbidden in Yugoslavia until after Tito's death. The prison was completely abandoned in 1989, but prison barracks remain there. You can make a short trip to this legendary gulag by taxi-boat with one of the many charter companies in Baška or Punat on Krk. ✉ *Rab.*

**Katunar Winery**

**WINERY** | At Katunar Winery on the island of Krk, you can sample the Žlatina varietal, which is indigenous to the island. Individual visits and group tours can be arranged to sample the dry white Žlahtina Katunar, the Černo Katunar (a dry red), or the "pearl wine" Biser Mora, a dessert wine produced from 100% žlahtina grapes. This dry white wine is famous around the world. ✉ *Sveta Nedilja, Krk Town* ☎ *051/857–393* 🌐 *www.katunar.hr* 💳 *€13 for tasting (includes 7 wines, cheese, olives, bread, and olive oil).*

**★ Krk Town**

**TOWN** | In terms of its importance and the pride of the 4,000 locals, the island's capital could perhaps even be called a city. It's not completely clear when the old city walls were first built, but the oldest mention of the walls dates back to the 1st century BC. The present-day walls, however, date mainly to the Middle Ages and have four gates. The seafront has a pleasant green area that takes you past cafés and a fish market, while the main square, Vela Placa, sits just behind the first row of houses. There's a beach underneath the town walls with a lovely view of the town.

The old town hall on Vela Placa was built in the 15th century. Its clock shows all 24 hours: daytime on the upper part, nighttime on the lower. Krk Town has two well-known visual anchors. The first is the imposing citadel that sits on Trg Kamplin. The bell tower of St. Quirinus is the other, with its angular onion dome typical of Krk. ✉ *Krk Town.*

**Špilja Biserujka** (*Biserujka Cave*)

**CAVE** | **FAMILY** | North of Vrbnik, near Rudine, this cave is only one of many caverns on Krk; however, it's the only one open to the public. The stalactites, stalagmites, and calcine pillars inside are lit for easier exploring. ✥ *½ km (⅓ mile) from Rudine* ☎ *098/211–630, 051/852–203* 🌐 *www.spilja-biserujka.com.hr* 🎫 *€5* ⏲ *Closed Nov.–Apr.* ☞ *Parking is about 500 feet from the entrance to the cave.*

### ★ Stara Baška

**TOWN** | **FAMILY** | If you're looking for a more secluded spot, head to this town that sits just above the beaches that trim a wide cove and peninsula. The road here is a single track through the tiny village, so you may find yourself performing intricate maneuvers in your car should you be unlucky enough to meet the water truck that keeps the village's houses supplied. Unless you arrive by boat, it is best to park in the first empty spot you see and walk into town or down the hill to the beach. ✉ *Stara Baška.*

### ★ Vrbnik

**TOWN** | **FAMILY** | This clifftop town on the northeast coast of the island offers majestic views of the Velebit Mountains and a bird's-eye view of the crystal clear waters far below. Clustered on a hilltop 157 feet above a small harbor, it's a mass of confusing winding streets. As you traverse the town on foot you will find many corners where long staircases suddenly arise due to the steep terrain. As one of the oldest settlements on Krk, Vrbnik can feel a little ramshackle, but this more lends to the charm than distracts from it. The fragrance of old wine barrels is ubiquitous on Vrbnik, and it is likely that they were once filled with Žlahtina, a local white wine that some claim is the best from the Kvarner region. The vineyards are just a short hop from town. ✉ *Vrbnik.*

## Restaurants

In the summer, you'll be sharing tables with busloads of tourists at many of Krk's best restaurants, all of which tend to be outside the capital city. Krk Town also has many restaurants serving delicious local and regional foods such as grilled fish, homemade pasta, and wood-fired pizza.

### ★ Nada

**$$** | **MEDITERRANEAN** | Many locals consider Nada's outdoor terrace the best place to enjoy a glass of crisp Žlahtina wine, island cheeses, seafood crudo, and homemade bread on a late summer afternoon. The sweeping views from its cliffside perch are magnificent and the homemade wines are refreshing. Just across the street, the main restaurant offers a sophisticated indoor seating area and a front terrace lined with traditional wooden tables. **Known for:** excellent seafood dishes; cheese platters, prosciutto, and wine; cliffside terrace ideal for aperitivo. 💲 *Average main: €22* ✉ *Glavača 22, Vrbnik* ☎ *051/857–065* 🌐 *www.nada-vrbnik.hr* ⏲ *Closed Nov.–Easter.*

### Pod Prevolt

**$** | **MEDITERRANEAN** | **FAMILY** | A small family-run tavern in the village of Milohnići, Pod Prevolt is a bit off the beaten path, but it's a place where you can get a real feel for the island's peaceful beauty and delicious traditional food. The traditional homemade Krk dishes include octopus with veggies baked in a wood-burning oven, dried octopus macaroni, homemade prosciutto and cheese, grilled and marinated fish, and the like. **Known for:** tiny interior; housemade charcuterie and cheeses; simple but delicious desserts. 💲 *Average main: €12* ✉ *Milohnići 21B, Malinska* ☎ *051/862–149* ⏲ *Closed Oct.–Apr.*

### ★ Rivica

**$$** | **SEAFOOD** | This classic seafood restaurant has a long tradition of superior service and sophisticated dishes but lacks much of the pretense usually attached to such accolades. This is not a restaurant that rests on its past laurels, as is clear from the modern menu additions like the Tuna 2F, a fresh-fusion cold starter tuna tartare with sashimi and chips, or the duck mousse with caramelized onions on toast. **Known for:** grilled lobster and crayfish; foie gras and duck fillet; warm professional staff. *Average main: €20* *Ribarska Obala 13, Njivice* *051/846–101* *rivica.hr* *Closed Dec.–Mar.*

**★ Žal**

$$ | **SEAFOOD** | **FAMILY** | If you ask locals where to go on Krk for incredible seafood in a scenic setting, you'll hear this restaurant recommended over and over again. Located right on the water in the small fishing village of Klimno (the north end of the island), this family-run establishment combines delicious traditional dishes like whole *brancin* (sea bass), slow-roasted *u soli* (under salt), and šurlice with Kvarner scampi with gorgeous seaside views. **Known for:** fresh whole fish; quayside setting perfect for sunset dining; traditional island specialties. *Average main: €22* *Klimno 44, Dobrinj* *051/853–142* *www.restaurant-zal.com.*

## Hotels

**Hotel Kanajt**

$$ | **HOTEL** | **FAMILY** | A 16th-century building that once served as a bishop's summer residence, this resort hotel is on a large expanse of land that is surrounded by palm, pine, and olive trees. **Pros:** location close to the marina; great spa facilities; open all year. **Cons:** good beaches are a bit away from the hotel; not all rooms have a balcony; rooms need a little updating. *Rooms from: €165* *Kanajt 5, Punat* *051/654–340* *www.kanajt.hr* *22 rooms* *Free Breakfast.*

**Hotel Pinia**

$$$ | **HOTEL** | **FAMILY** | Located in the small seaside village of Porat, just next to Malinska, this hotel is perfectly positioned close to the sea but also surrounded by greenery. **Pros:** great location by the sea; good on-site restaurant; spacious rooms. **Cons:** hotel beach can get very busy in July and August; Wi-Fi is weak; long walk to Malinska. *Rooms from: €279* *Porat 31, Malinska* *051/866–333* *www.hotel-pinia.hr* *Closed Nov.–Apr.* *45 rooms* *Free Breakfast.*

**Valamar Atrium Baška Residence**

$$ | **HOTEL** | **FAMILY** | On Baška Bay, just steps from the famous Vela Plaža Beach, the Atrium Residence has spacious luxurious rooms and apartments. **Pros:** seafront location; great beach views; spacious rooms. **Cons:** standard rooms have French balconies; parking located at the sister hotel, Corinthia; lack of in-hotel facilities (guests can use facilities of the nearby hotels). *Rooms from: €197* *Emila Geistlicha 39, Baška* *052/465–000* *www.valamar.com/en/apartments-baska/atrium-baska-residence* *Closed Oct.–Apr.* *64 rooms* *Free Breakfast.*

**Valamar Koralj Sunny Hotel**

$$ | **HOTEL** | **FAMILY** | For long days on the beach and all conveniences on tap, this hotel on the edge of Krk Town is a decent choice; half-board (breakfast and dinner) is included in all rates, though those who plan busy evenings may want to find somewhere closer to the center. **Pros:** great for families with kids in summer; good for couples off-season; peaceful location amid pine trees. **Cons:** small rooms; some rooms without balcony; better rooms quite pricey for the quality. *Rooms from: €150* *Vlade Tomašića 38, Krk Town* *052/465–000* *www.valamar.com/en/hotels-krk/valamar-koralj-romantic-hotel* *Closed Oct.–Apr.* *194 rooms* *Free Breakfast.*

## Nightlife

Krk Town and Baška are the places to head for relatively low-key drinks in the evening. The center of the capital and the stretch of town above the beach at Baška offer numerous bars with music and tables out under the stars. A firm family favorite, Krk is definitely not the place for cutting-edge nightlife. However, if you really can't live without getting your club fix, there are a couple of large venues offering house DJs. Note that clubs are open only in the summer.

**Cabana Bar**

**BARS** | With a stunning seaside position tucked on the far edge of the Aminess Camping Resort, this casual collection of outdoor living rooms serves tasty cocktails and light bites like caprese salads and tuna sandwiches. It's the perfect place to unwind after a long day on the beach or a rugged bike ride on the trails surrounding the entire Njivice area of Krk. ✉ *Primorska Cesta 41, Njivice* ☎ *051/846–720.*

**Cocktail Bar Volsonis**

**DANCE CLUBS** | One of the livelier nightspots in Krk Town, this bar has the appropriate, though somewhat mysterious, ruins of a wonderful sacrificial altar to love goddess Venus down in the basement. In fact, all of Volsonis is incorporated into a 2,000-year-old archaeological site that the owners, Maria Elena and Goran, found under the house. Electronic music plays on weekends in the underground Catacombs, or you can chill out with a glass of wine, beer, or coffee in the Secret Garden. The owners have expanded their offerings with a menu that includes breakfast and lunch offerings that use many ingredients from their garden. This is likely the only place to have a substantial breakfast. ✉ *Vela Placa 8, Krk Town* ☎ *051/880–249* 🌐 *www.volsonis.hr.*

## Shopping

**Stanic**

**OTHER SPECIALTY STORE** | This wonderful gallery is a comprehensive collection of works by local artists, as well as locally designed lamps, ceramics, mirrors, and other souvenirs. ✉ *Vela Placa 8, Krk Town* ☎ *051/220–052* 🌐 *www.helena.hr.*

## Activities

### BIKING

You can bike around the island for transportation or exercise.

**Cycling Union Krk**

**BIKING** | **FAMILY** | The best place to rent a bicycle or e-bike is at Cycling Union in Grad Krk or the marina in Punat. Make sure you call before you head over to pick up a bike to ensure they have the inventory available. ✉ *Omišaljska 16, Krk Town* ☎ *099/672–0424* 🌐 *cyclingunionkrk.com.*

### DIVING

**Dive Center Krk**

**SCUBA DIVING** | **FAMILY** | The most exciting sights in Kvarner Bay are the shipwrecks. At Dive Center Krk on the Bay of Punat, a full-day diving trip (two dives) sets you back about €65 plus the equipment rental, if you need it. ✉ *Dunat 50, Kornic* ☎ *051/867–303* 🌐 *www.dive-center-krk.com.*

### HIKING

There are many marked paths for walks and hiking in the area around Baška. For a longer hike, consider visiting the splendid remote villages at Vela and Mala Luka; take this path as part of a group, and be aware that the section of the trail through the canyon may flood if there's rain. For some nice hikes around Baška, consider the path from Baška to Mjesec Hill (5½ km [3 miles], 2 hours). Offering spectacular views over the bay, this easy route passes by St. John's Church, where you can take a breather while contemplating higher things. The route from Baška to Jurandvor (5 km [3 miles], 2 hours) takes you through the Baška Valley and leaves you with a visit to the Church of St. Lucy, home of the Baška Tablet. The short hike between Baška and Stara Baška will give you a little exercise; a delightful stretch of small quiet beaches is the reward for a short hike.

**Krk Tourist Office**
**HIKING & WALKING** | **FAMILY** | For more hiking information and maps, contact the Krk Tourist Office. ✉ *Vela Placa 1, Krk Town* ☎ *051/221–414* 🌐 *experiencekrk.com.*

## WATERSKIING

### ★ Wakeboard Cable Krk
**WATER SPORTS** | **FAMILY** | Always fancied spraying majestic jets of water across the aquamarine seas, but sorting out a boat and someone to drive seems too much trouble? Well, the answer lies with Cable Krk, on a calm bay just outside the resort of Punat, toward Krk Town. A large wooden pier with a bar and restaurant to entertain your companions is the gateway to a cableway, which is not much different than a drag-lift at a ski resort. The cable pulls you around a short course, with instructions on hand to help you get your sea legs. One hour costs €24, not including equipment. ✉ *Dunat, Prvo More on the Danube, Kornic* ☎ *091/262–7303* 🌐 *wakeboarder.hr.*

# Delnice

*50 km (31 miles) east of Rijeka.*

Delnice, which sits on the road between Rijeka and Zagreb, is a breath of fresh mountain air, especially in summer after leaving the crowded hot seaside. It makes a good base for exploring the mountains of the Gorski Kotar region that sit above Kvarner Bay. The region is covered with well-marked hiking and biking trails and mountain huts that offer refreshment and respite from the elements. Delnice is often blanketed in several feet of snow in winter, while cities along the sea are wet and gray. A full-size hockey rink, groomed cross-country ski trails, and popular sled-riding spots make this a weekend winter escape for locals. It's also a convenient stopover if you're taking the slow route back to Zagreb on your way back to the airport. Take a day or two to swap the brilliant blue of the sea for a few nights in the peaceful and wild green forests and rivers of Gorski Kotar.

## Restaurants

### ★ Eva
**$$** | **EUROPEAN** | **FAMILY** | This modern Alpine-style restaurant is a breath of fresh air, thanks to its contemporary versions of traditional favorites including goulash, bear stew, grilled venison steaks, and hunter's dumplings. All are served in an elegant contemporary setting in a lush green forest environment. **Known for:** modern takes on local game; forest setting; homemade strudel for dessert. Ⓢ *Average main: €22* ✉ *Gorski Raj 4, Lokve, Delnice* ☎ *051/270–500* 🌐 *eva-gorskiraj.hr* ⏲ *Closed Mon. and Tues.*

### Volta
**$** | **AUSTRIAN** | **FAMILY** | The small town of Fužine is very close to Delnice and is well-known for its pine-bordered lake, where you'll find this eatery. This is typical mountain food that includes lots of wild game like boar, bear, deer stew, and frog legs. **Known for:** horse and game meat; local crowd; hearty meals. Ⓢ *Average main: €12* ✉ *Franje Račkog 8, Fužine* ☎ *051/830–030* ⏲ *Closed Feb.*

## Hotels

### Mountain Center Petehovac
**$** | **B&B/INN** | **FAMILY** | Come to Petehovac to escape the city and be surrounded by nature. **Pros:** location in nature; good and very affordable food; views over the surrounding area. **Cons:** basic facilities; strict cancellation policy; weak Wi-Fi connection. Ⓢ *Rooms from: €40* ✉ *Polane 1A, Delnice* ☎ *051/814–901* 🌐 *petehovac.com.hr* *72 beds* *Free Breakfast.*

## Activities

### HIKING

Delnice is a good base for hiking around Risnjak and the Gorski Kotar range, which have many marked walking and hiking paths.

### RAFTING AND CANOEING

**Gorski Tok**

**WHITE-WATER RAFTING | FAMILY** | On a super hot summer day, the cool refreshing waters of the Kupa River are most welcome. Float down the river on a canoe or kayak expedition organized by Gorski Tok, depending on your skills and the water level. The company also runs canoe safari trips, in case the water level is low. ✉ *Kralja Tomislava 11, Brod na Kupi, Delnice* ☎ *098/177-2585* 🌐 *www.gorski-tok.hr.*

# Rab

*120 km (75 miles) southeast of Rijeka.*

Rab presents an utterly fascinating landscape. When you drive southward, down the Magistrala, you see that the island resembles the humped back of a diving sea monster. Once you've mounted this beast, via a short ferry ride from Stinica to Mišnjak, you travel along the center of its back, which is almost entirely bald to the north, letting all its hair hang out to the south. The high northern coast, which bears the brunt of the northern bura winds, is dry, rocky, and barren. Crouching below this crusty ledge, the southern half of the island could hardly differ more and has possibly the lushest terrain found on any Croatian island. Low green hills dip into the seas, while the ancient Dundo Forest grows so voraciously that it's almost impossible to walk in.

## Sights

Sitting on a narrow peninsula halfway up the island's southern coast, Rab Town, a compact, well-preserved medieval village, is best known for its distinctive skyline of four elegant bell towers and its many churches. Author Rebecca West, who traveled through Yugoslavia in the 1930s, called Rab Town "one of the most beautiful cities of the world" in her masterpiece, *Black Lamb and Grey Falcon.* Closed to traffic, the narrow cobbled streets of the Old Town, lined with Romanesque churches and patrician palaces, can be explored in an hour's stroll. The urban layout is simple: three longitudinal streets run parallel to the waterfront promenade and are linked by steep passages traversing the hillside. The lower street is Donja Ulica, the middle street Srednja Ulica, and the upper street Gornja Ulica.

**Komrčar Park**

**CITY PARK | FAMILY** | On the edge of town, the green expanse of Komrčar Park, laid out in the 19th century, offers avenues lined with pine trees for gentle strolling and access down to the sea. Although the Old Town and its immediate surroundings are Rab's chief treasures, this park is characteristic of the abundance of green areas on Rab that are conducive for escaping the sun on hot days or laying a blanket down under one of the big trees and taking a nap. ✉ *Northwest of the Old Town, just behind the seafront promenade, Obala Kralja Petra Krešimira IV, Rab.*

**Sveta Marija Velika** (*Cathedral of St. Mary*)

**CHURCH | FAMILY** | The Romanesque Sveta Marija Velika, built in the 12th century and consecrated by the pope in 1177, is the biggest church in Rab Town, and was built on the site of Roman ruins.

## Did You Know?

The oldest part of Rab Town is Kaldanac, the very tip of the narrow peninsula that juts into the sea. From here, the ancient city grew in the 15th century to include Varoš, farther north, and later was widened and fortified by walls during a brief Venetian rule.

However, the only way to visit is to attend one of the masses, which are posted on the announcement board outside. ✉ *Ivana Rabljanina, Rab* 🌐 *www.rab-visit.com.*

★ **Veli Zvonik** (*Great Bell Tower*)
**OTHER ATTRACTION** | The tallest and most beautiful of Rab's campaniles, the freestanding Veli Zvonik forms part of the former cathedral complex and dominates the southwest side of the peninsula. Built in the 12th century, it stands 85 feet high. A climb to the top is well worth the effort since it affords breathtaking views over the town and sea. ✉ *Gornja, Rab* *€3* ⏲ *Closed Oct.–May.*

## Restaurants

★ **Agatini Vrtovi**
**$$$** | **MEDITERRANEAN** | Quite possibly the most romantic restaurant in Rab Town, this spot has a garden terrace located right next to the ancient city walls. Soft intimate lighting and linen-topped tables accompany traditional Mediterranean cuisine served in a modern style. **Known for:** romantic garden setting; top-notch wine list; fresh local ingredients. [$] *Average main: €25* ✉ *Arbiana Luxury Boutique Hotel, Obala Kralja Petra Krešimira IV/12, Rab* ☎ *051/775–900* 🌐 *arbianahotel.com/agatini-vrtovi* ⏲ *Closed Oct.–Apr.*

★ **Konoba Rab**
**$$** | **MEDITERRANEAN** | **FAMILY** | Tucked away in a narrow side street between Srednja and Gornja in Rab Town, this konoba is warm and inviting, with exposed-stone walls, traditional decor, and rustic furniture. Grilled fish and meat are the house specialties, and the menu offers a good choice of pastas and risotto. **Known for:** welcoming staff and cozy atmosphere; traditional specialties slow cooked in the peka over the fire; excellent seafood dishes. [$] *Average main: €18* ✉ *Kneza Branimira 3, Rab* ☎ *051/725–666* ⏲ *Closed Nov. and Feb. No lunch Sun.*

**Konoba Santa Maria**
**$$** | **MEDITERRANEAN** | **FAMILY** | Although the medieval palace setting may feel a bit dramatic for some, others love sitting in this character-filled historic restaurant. You are perched in front of and upon massive wooden furniture in an old stone building in the heart of Old Town Rab. **Known for:** local seafood dishes; welcoming friendly service; medieval stone setting. [$] *Average main: €20* ✉ *Dinka Dokule 6, Rab* ☎ *051/724–196* ⏲ *Closed Nov.–Apr.*

★ **Kuća Rabske Torte**
**$** | **CAFÉ** | **FAMILY** | Tucked away in the Old Town, this charming café-museum has a wonderful courtyard that's ideal for chilling out and enjoying a lemonade after exploring Rab Town. Sit inside and watch as they prepare the famed *rabska torta*, a traditional Croatian cake made of ground almonds, maraschino liqueur, lemon, and orange peel. **Known for:** traditional recipes; great small bites and sweets; charming location. [$] *Average main: €12* ✉ *Stjepana Radića 5, Rab* ☎ *051/774–863* 🌐 *www.rabskatorta.com* ⏲ *Closed Nov.–Apr.*

**Restaurant More**
**$$** | **MEDITERRANEAN** | **FAMILY** | This family-owned restaurant has an amazing location with seating right on the quay, especially attractive for those arriving by boat. The fish served here is caught by the owner, so the phrase "catch of the day" really means something. **Known for:** lovely waterfront location; grilled shellfish; romantic setting. [$] *Average main: €16* ✉ *Supetarska Draga 321, Supetarska Draga* ☎ *051/776–202* 🌐 *www.more-rab.net* ⏲ *Closed Oct.–Apr.*

★ **Velum**
**$$** | **MEDITERRANEAN** | **FAMILY** | This family-owned restaurant offers regional and local Rab specialties, such as seafood risotto, homemade pasta with mussels and shrimp, seafood crudo, grilled meats, and locally caught fish. All are served

with a friendly welcoming attitude in a cool modern environment. **Known for:** perfect homemade chocolate cake for dessert; excellent grilled meat platter for two; local seafood dishes like grandma would make. *$ Average main: €20 ✉ Palit 71, Rab ☎ 051/774–855 🌐 www.velum.hr.*

## Hotels

Rab offers a variety of accommodation, from campgrounds on beaches to apartments and villa rentals to chic boutique hotels, family resorts, and grand adult-only hotels.

### ★ Arbiana Hotel

$$ | **HOTEL** | It's hard to imagine a more romantic setting than this harborside inn that sits in a perfectly restored medieval villa with balconies and a gorgeous garden overlooking the Rab Marina and the hills of Barbat in the distance. **Pros:** luxurious private setting; easy on-site parking; most rooms have beautiful sea views. **Cons:** no pool or private beach; not all rooms have balconies; can be noisy during concerts. *$ Rooms from: €215 ✉ Obala Kralja Petra Krešimira IV br.12, Rab ☎ 051/775–900 🌐 arbianahotel.com ⏲ Closed mid-Oct.–Apr. 28 rooms 🍽 Free Breakfast.*

### San Marino Sunny Resort by Valamar

$ | **HOTEL** | **FAMILY** | A complex of five hotels stretches across the peninsula at this family-friendly resort that surrounds the famous sandy Paradise Beach. **Pros:** access to Paradise Beach couldn't be better; good choice of on-site activities; free Wi-Fi. **Cons:** sprawling complex lacks personality; rooms are on the small side and lack luxuries; big and busy. *$ Rooms from: €82 ✉ Lopar 608, Lopar ☎ 051/667–700, 051/775–144 🌐 www.valamar.com/en/resorts-rab/san-marino-resort ⏲ Closed Oct.–May 495 rooms 🍽 Free Breakfast.*

### Valamar Collection Imperial

$$ | **ALL-INCLUSIVE** | Amid the greenery of Komrčar Park, this peaceful 1930s-era heritage hotel is a stone's throw from the center of Rab Town. **Pros:** centrally located but removed from the crowds; tennis, indoor and outdoor pool, and spa facilities; heritage hotel with beautiful harbor views. **Cons:** limited parking spaces in high season; double rooms a bit smallish; above a busy city park. *$ Rooms from: €150 ✉ M. de Dominisa 9, Rab ☎ 051/724–522 🌐 www.valamar.com/en/hotels-rab/imperial-grand-hotel ⏲ Closed Oct.–Apr. 136 rooms 🍽 Free Breakfast.*

### Valamar Padova Hotel

$$ | **HOTEL** | **FAMILY** | As one of Valamar's "Maro" hotels, the Padova has thought of everything regarding family-friendly vacations, including a free on-site professional babysitting service that gives parents with young children a chance to get away for a few hours. **Pros:** incredibly family-friendly; plenty of activities offered; walking distance to Rab town. **Cons:** family focus not for everyone; no à la carte restaurant for dinner; access to small public beach only. *$ Rooms from: €175 ✉ Banjol 322, Rab ☎ 051/724–544 🌐 www.valamar.com/en/hotels-rab/padova-hotel ⏲ Closed Oct.–Apr. 175 rooms 🍽 All-Inclusive.*

## Nightlife

For such a small town, Rab has surprisingly active nightlife in the summer if you are not looking for techno discos. Trg Municipium Arba on the waterfront is lined with bars and can get noisy as the night progresses. All-night house parties are found at Santos Beach Club on Pudarica Beach, 2 km (1 mile) from Barbat toward the ferry terminal.

**Conte Nero**

**BARS** | Whether you come for a coffee and slice of chocolate cake, to enjoy a fancy cocktail with friends, or to sample the homemade gelato, Conte Nero is the place to hang out in Rab Town. You can even order small snack plates of prosciutto and cheese, light pizzas, bruschetta, or tuna pâté to accompany your drinks. ✉ *Trg Municipium Arba 2, Rab* ☎ *051/670–207* 🌐 *www.contenero-rab.com.*

**Forum Bar**

**BARS** | A favorite among locals, this bar may be short on luxury, but not on entertainment, beers, and great cocktails. Forum is a hot spot that attracts all kinds of events and festival crowds, as well as anyone who loves drinks made with the best ingredients. Just note that it's cash-only. ✉ *Donja 9A, Rab* ☎ *098/960–1112.*

**San Antonio Club**

**DANCE CLUBS** | Those after a little glitz to show off their suntan can head to the center of Rab Town for cocktails, cool DJs, and lively dancing at the San Antonio Club. ✉ *Trg Municipium Arba 4, Rab* ☎ *098/282–945.*

## Activities

### DIVING

**Aqua Sport**

**SCUBA DIVING** | **FAMILY** | A single dive with this company costs about €35, including equipment; a full diving course costs €350. You can dive at various sites from their boat, and your nondiving companions are welcome to go along for the ride for €10 each. ✉ *Supetarska Draga 331, Supetarska Draga* ☎ *091/524–8141* 🌐 *aquasport.hr.*

### KAYAKING

**Sea Kayak Excursions**

**KAYAKING** | **FAMILY** | This family-owned business has been sharing the beauty of Rab with visitors for more than 15 years. All tours are guided and enjoyed from your kayak, whether you can join other tourists visiting the island or go as part of your own large group. They can even arrange for an all-weekend kayak tour complete with gourmet foods and local accommodations. You can also hire Jogi and his team to guide you on a week-long kayak trip around the Šibenik rivers. Of course, you can just rent kayaks and guide yourself around the islands, too. ✉ *Banjol 341, Rab* ☎ *099/322–7006 for daily tours and kayak rentals, 099/282–8628 for expeditions and tours* 🌐 *www.seakayak.hr.*

Chapter 7

# ISTRIA



Updated by
Melissa Paul

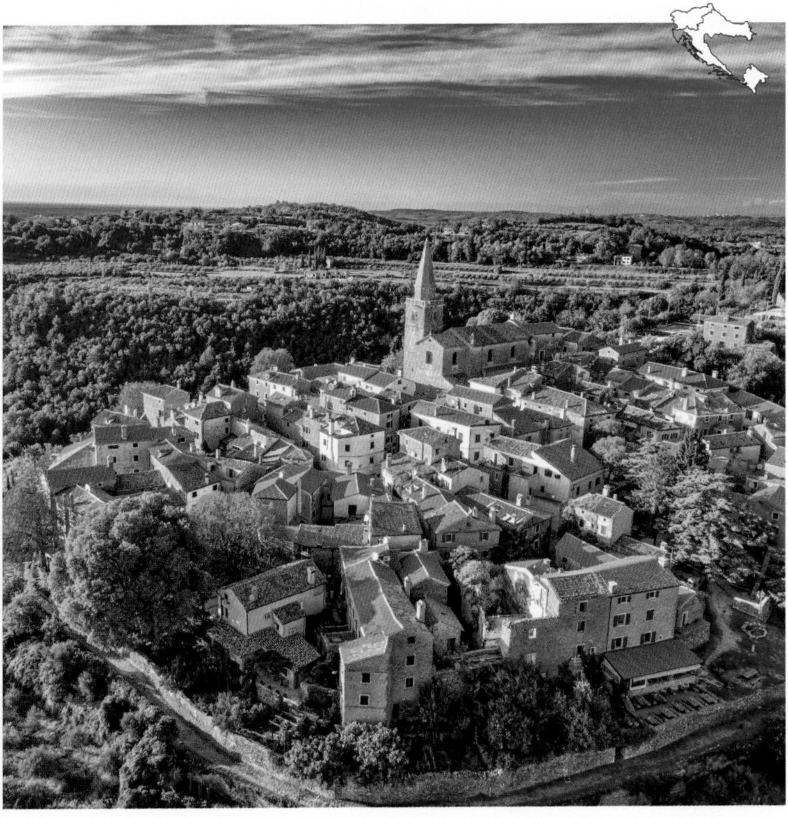

Sights ★★★☆☆ | Restaurants ★★★★★ | Hotels ★★★☆☆ | Shopping ★★★☆☆ | Nightlife ★★☆☆☆

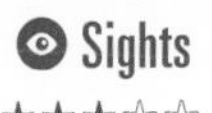

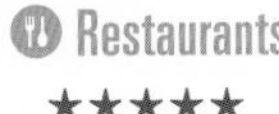

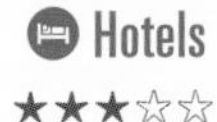

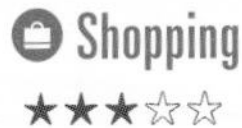

# WELCOME TO ISTRIA

## TOP REASONS TO GO

★ **Roman ruins:** Take a walk through the Roman area in Pula, where you will find one of the world's biggest and best-preserved amphitheaters (in fact, the sixth-largest in the world).

★ **Natural beauty:** Breathtaking beaches with crystal clear water, rolling vineyard-covered hills, and groves of ancient olive trees.

★ **Medieval hilltop towns:** A scenic drive through the medieval towns of Grožnjan, Oprtalj, and Motovun in the hilly interior is not to be missed; these are villages that time seems to have forgotten. Indulge in a wine or olive oil tasting at Kabola, Clai, or Chiavalon estates.

★ **Ancient churches:** Enjoy a tour of the amazing 6th-century Byzantine mosaics at St. Euphrasius Basilica in Poreč; St. Euphrasius is one of Europe's best-preserved early Christian churches.

★ **Gourmet delights:** Indulge in delicious olive oil, wind-cured prosciutto, fresh seafood, earthy truffles, and boutique wines.

Sandwiched between Italy, Slovenia, and inland Croatia, the Istrian Peninsula is located in the Northern Adriatic region, facing the Venetian lagoon to the west and Kvarner Bay to the southeast. Reaching Istria, Croatia's largest peninsula, is easy: many large European cities are less than five hours away. Pula has a seasonal airport, and airports in Venice, Trieste, Ljubljana, Rijeka, and Zagreb are all within a three-hour drive.

1 **Pula.** A former Roman colony and now Istria's main city.

2 **Vodnjan.** A quiet town devoted to producing excellent olive oil.

3 **Brijuni National Park.** A group of small islands that is now a stunning national park.

4 **Rovinj.** The cultural heart and soul of Istria.

5 **Poreč.** A one-time Roman fort and current charming red-roofed city.

6 **Novigrad.** A pretty fisherman's village with a charming Old Town.

7 **Umag.** One of Istria's more low-key coastal towns.

8 **Motovun.** The highest medieval hilltop town in Istria.

9 **Grožnjan.** A quaint hilltop town filled with art and music.

10 **Labin-Rabac.** The charming hilltop town of Labin with its sister seaside resort of Rabac.

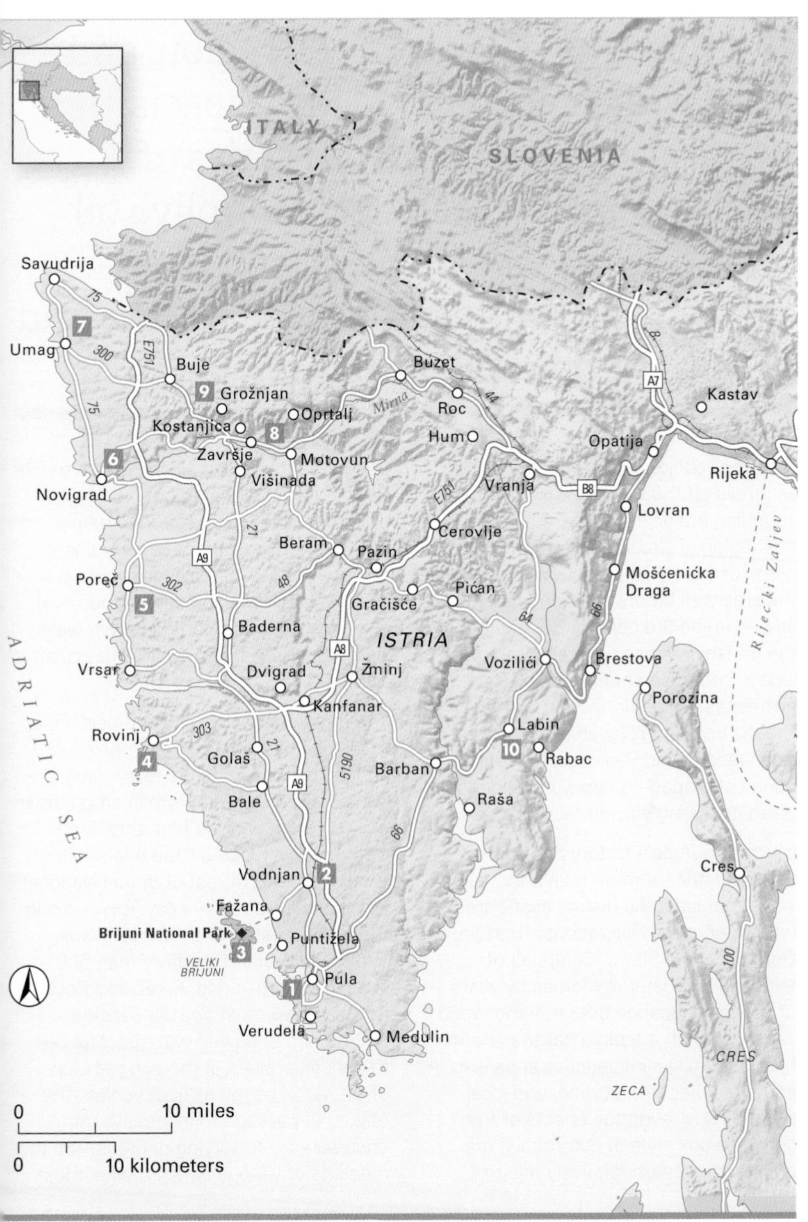
ITALY
SLOVENIA
Savudrija
Umag
Buje
Grožnjan
Buzet
Roc
Hum
Oprtalj
Kostanjica
Završje
Motovun
Višinada
Novigrad
Kastav
Opatija
Rijeka
Vranja
Lovran
Cerovlje
Beram
Pazin
Poreč
Gračišće
Pićan
Mošćenićka Draga
Baderna
ISTRIA
Vrsar
Dvigrad
Žminj
Vozilići
Brestova
Porozina
Kanfanar
Labin
Rabac
Rovinj
Golaš
Barban
Bale
Raša
ADRIATIC SEA
Riječki Zaljev
Vodnjan
Fažana
Brijuni National Park
VELIKI BRIJUNI
Puntižela
Pula
Verudela
Medulin
Cres
CRES
ZECA
0
10 miles
0
10 kilometers

Discover a thousand years of rich Istrian history in the hilltop fortresses, early Christian churches, Byzantine mosaics, and Baroque palaces of the region, and treat your taste buds to local specialties: white and black truffles (a series of festivals is dedicated to them), olive oil (many of the world's best), and wine (crisp fruity white Malvazija Istarska and light harmonious red Teran).

---

The word conjures something magical as it rolls off the tongue: *Istria*. Beyond sounding poetic, however, the name of this region of Croatia is derived from the name of the Illyrian people who occupied the area well before the Romans first arrived in the 3rd century BC—namely, the Istrians, whose chief architectural legacy comprised numerous hilltop fortresses. In the northwest corner of Croatia bordering Slovenia, the triangular-shaped Istrian Peninsula looks like a bunch of grapes—a happy coincidence, given its strong viticultural heritage.

Much of Europe's history has passed through Istria for more than a thousand years, not least the history associated with three great civilizations—Roman, Germanic, and Slavic. Centuries of Venetian rule, later reinforced by years of Italian occupation between the world wars, have left a sizable Italian minority here, and Italian influence is apparent in the architecture, cuisine, and local dialect. Here, even the effects of the concrete-box style of communist-era architecture seem relatively minimal compared to the overall sense of a much deeper past suggested by the rich mix of architectural styles—from a whole array of well-preserved Roman ruins to Romanesque basilicas; as well as breathtakingly well-preserved medieval towns, bell towers, fortified town walls, Baroque palaces, and Austro-Hungarian battlements.

The region's principal city and port, Pula, is on the southern tip of the peninsula and is best known for its remarkably preserved 1,900-year-old Roman amphitheater and Forum and the Triumphal Arch of the Sergii. Close by, the beautifully nurtured island retreat of Brijuni National Park can be visited in a day. Towns along the west coast have an unmistakable Venetian flavor left by more than 500 years of Venetian rule. Poreč and Rovinj, Croatia's two most popular seaside resorts, are endowed with graceful bell towers and reliefs of the winged Lion of St. Mark, patron saint of Venice. The effects of package tourism have long encroached—to varying degrees—on the outskirts of various Istrian towns, most notably Poreč and Vrsar. Rovinj, likewise brimming with tourists in high season, retains more of its ravishing historic beauty and redolence than almost any other town in Croatia. A side trip to the romantic hilltop towns of Motovun, Oprtalj, and Grožnjan will prove unforgettable, whether as a brief excursion from the sea in the warmer months or as a more substantial autumn journey. This inland area is particularly rich in truffles, mushrooms, grapes, and chestnuts; from mid-September to late October, these local delicacies are celebrated with a series of gastronomic festivals.

# Planning

## When to Go

If you are partial to the sun and the idea of swimming in the warm, clear aqua-blue waters of the Adriatic, and you don't mind crowds and a bit of extra expense, by all means, visit Istria in summer. Otherwise, this tourism-trampled region might be best for spring or fall (the water stays warm well into September), when you might save as much as 15% to 20% on lodging. The season in Istria for many restaurants and bars is Easter through the first week in November. While the region is always dramatically beautiful, you won't find much going on in the winter months.

## Getting Here and Around

### AIR

Croatia Airlines operates flights to Pula from Amsterdam, Frankfurt, Zadar, and Zagreb from April through October. Ryanair has service to Pula from London Stansted, Berlin, Brussels, and Vienna. Jet2.com flies from Leeds, Manchester, Edinburgh, Birmingham, and London Stansted to Pula from May until late September. Many other airlines fly into Pula, including British Airways, Lufthansa, easyJet, TUI, Edelweiss, SAS, People, Volotea, Transavia, Norwegian, Air Serbia, Eurowings, Aer Lingus, BRA, and Trade Air.

**CONTACTS Croatia Airlines.** ✉ *Pula Airport, Valtursko Polje 210, Ližnjan, Pula* ☎ *052/218–909* 🌐 *www.croatiaairlines.com.* **Jet2.com.** ✉ *Pula* 🌐 *www.jet2.com.* **Ryanair.** 🌐 *www.ryanair.com.*

### BOAT AND FERRY

From May through October, Venezia Lines runs a high-speed catamaran service from Venice to Rovinj, Pula, Poreč, and Umag. Tickets are available online.

**CONTACTS Venezia Lines.** ✉ *Zagrebačka 7, Poreč* ☎ *052/422–896* 🌐 *www.venezialines.com.*

### BUS

There are domestic connections all over mainland Croatia to and from Pula, Poreč, Labin, and Rovinj, as well as local services between these towns and smaller inland destinations such as Motovun and Vodnjan. International buses offer daily connections to Italy (Trieste) and Slovenia (Ljubljana, Koper, Piran, and Portorož). Bus stations in Pula, Rovinj, Labin, and Poreč are run by one bus company, Autotrans. Additionally, in summer, FlixBus, a German company offering low-cost bus travel throughout Europe, connects Istrian coastal towns with Germany (Munich), Italy (Venice, Padua, Brescia, Milano), and Austria (Villach, Vienna, Graz). Timetables are available at all bus stations. However, as elsewhere in Croatia, the sheer number of different companies offering bus service out of each station can be confusing; it's best to confirm at the information window what you might find posted on the wall.

**BUS CONTACTS Autotrans.** ☎ *072/660–660* 🌐 *www.arriva.com.hr/en-us/home.* **FlixBus.** 🌐 *global.flixbus.com/bus/croatia.*

**BUS STATIONS Poreč Bus Station.** ✉ *Karla Huguesa 2, Poreč* ☎ *052/432–153.* **Pula Bus Station.** ✉ *Trg I. Istarske Brigade 1, Pula* ☎ *052/356–532.* **Rovinj Bus Station.** ✉ *Trg na Lokvi 6, Rovinj* ☎ *060/888–611.*

### CAR

While visiting Pula, Rovinj, and Poreč, a car may be more of a hindrance than an asset: all three towns are served by good bus connections, and having your own vehicle only causes parking problems. The best way to see the Istrian interior and east coast towns, however, is by car. The "sight" to see is the countryside itself and the small villages that dot it, so renting a car even for a day will give you much more satisfaction than trying to arrange a bus trip to one or another hilltop town (and bus connections to the interior are infrequent or nonexistent). If you are traveling from Zagreb, you can rent a car there, but major agencies have offices in Pula. Other towns along the coast all have one or more local agencies that generally offer better rates than the major chains without sacrificing the quality of service; however, they may be less equipped than the major chains and have fewer cars on offer. Some, such as Vetura, also rent bicycles, e-bicycles, and mopeds. Lastly, remember that finding an available car on short notice in midsummer can be tricky, regardless of the agency involved, and most have manual transmissions.

**CONTACTS Europcar.** ✉ *Pula Airport, Valtursko Polje 210, Pula* ☎ *098/475–346* 🌐 *www.europcar.com/en/stations/croatia/pula-airport.* **Greenway Travel.** ✉ *Partizanska 5A, Poreč* ☎ *095/797–2222, 095/558–9000* 🌐 *www.greenway-travel.net.* **Interauto.** ✉ *Trgovačka 19, Umag* ☎ *091/206–0483, 052/743–111* 🌐 *www.inter-auto.hr.* **Sixt.** ✉ *Riva Mall, Rade Končara 1, Poreč* ☎ *095/438–2416* 🌐 *www.sixt.hr.* **Vetura Rent a Car.** ✉ *Pula Airport, Valtursko Polje 210, Pula* ☎ *091/494–9627* 🌐 *www.vetura-rentacar.com.*

### TRAIN

Istria is not well-connected to the rest of Croatia by rail—or to neighboring Slovenia and Italy. To get to Zagreb or Split by train, you must transit through Rijeka, partly by bus. But there is an excellent train between Pula and Pazin that locals love.

**CONTACT Pula Train Station.** ✉ *Kolodvorska 5, Pula* ☎ *052/541–982* 🌐 *www.hzpp.hr/en.*

## Restaurants

Food in Istria is more sophisticated and varied than in the rest of Croatia. Culinary tourism is one of the region's biggest draws, and you will get (for a price) a markedly better meal here than elsewhere in the country. The quaysides and old town squares have many touristy restaurants, and many new exceptional places have opened in recent years, helping to set the standard for the country's gastronomical identity. Istrian food today means fresh and simple seafood dishes, locally made *fuži* (egg noodles), elegant white or black truffle sauces and flavors, and earthy *pršut* (air-dried local prosciutto), alongside the familiar Italian staples of pizza and pasta. Seafood is usually grilled, baked in sea salt, or served *crudo* (raw) with a dash of local extra-virgin olive oil. Truffles are the superstars of the interior villages and work their way onto autumn menus in pasta, game dishes, grilled meats, frittatas, and on beds of homemade polenta. Keep your eyes peeled for traditional favorites like *supa,* a brew of red wine, sugar, olive oil, pepper, and warm, toasted bread; and *maneštra,* an Istrian bean soup, both popular in fall and winter. All these gourmet aspirations mean that dining in Istria can be costly relative to much of inland Croatia. For a quick and cheap, albeit greasy, lunch, you can always buy a *burek* (a cheese- or meat-filled pastry) in a bakery.

# Hotels

In Istria, as in most other reaches of the Croatian coast, it's a question of whether to stay at the big resorts on the beach, with a full range of services and activities available, or at smaller, sometimes family-run hotels and bed-and-breakfasts called *rezidenze*. Either way, booking ahead is imperative, as most places—big and small—book up fast for the summer months. Bear in mind that some smaller hotels and residences may impose a surcharge—usually 20%—for stays of fewer than three nights in high season, since they cater primarily to tourists who stay a week or two. Hotels listed here are geared toward travelers looking to stay fewer than seven nights in the same city.

### VILLA RENTALS

Villa rentals are extremely popular in Istria, where many properties—from one-bedroom apartments to houses for 16—offer a high standard of accommodation. The medieval villages of the hilly interior are scenic and offer sweeping (and almost uninterrupted) views of vineyards and olive groves. Hunkering down in a stone farmhouse and exploring the rest of the peninsula from there is a leisurely way to appreciate Istria. Istria is still not nearly as crowded as other parts of the Mediterranean, so you won't have to share your view with the hordes. Kompas Travel offers a collection of luxury villa rentals and holiday homes throughout Istria, as well as daytime excursions across the region and into other parts of Croatia, Slovenia, and Venice, Italy.

⇨ *Restaurant and hotel reviews have been shortened. For full information, visit Fodors.com. Restaurant prices are the average cost of a main course at dinner or, if dinner is not served, at lunch. Hotel prices are the lowest cost of a standard double room in high season.*

## What It Costs in Euros (€)

| | $ | $$ | $$$ | $$$$ |
|---|---|---|---|---|
| **RESTAURANTS** | | | | |
| | under €15 | €15–€23 | €24–32 | over €32 |
| **HOTELS** | | | | |
| | under €150 | €150–€250 | €251–€350 | over €350 |

# Tours

**Excursions Delfin**
**SPECIAL-INTEREST TOURS | FAMILY |** Known for its variety of water-based tours, Delfin offers daily boat tours to Lim Fjord (half- and full-day tours), panoramic boat tours of Rovinj and its archipelago, dolphin-watching cruises, and sunset boat excursions from Rovinj to Vrsar. They also provide free transfers between all tourist resorts and campsites in Rovinj and the boats. ✉ *Obala Vladimira Nazora, Rovinj* ☎ *091/514–2169* 🌐 *www.excursion-delfin.com.*

**Fiore Tours**
**BICYCLE TOURS | FAMILY |** This Poreč-based agency specializing in outdoor tourism—cycling, kayaking, and trekking—offers many fully guided and self-guided cycling and walking holidays in Istria, from half-day kayaking to weeklong explorations. Their eight-day tour starts in historic Poreč and leads you through the Istrian countryside and onto the coast. Daily distances range from 47 km to 70 km (30 to 43 miles). Fiore Tours arranges all accommodation and luggage transfers, and provides you with an itinerary. ✉ *Mate Vlašića 6, Poreč* ☎ *052/431–397* 🌐 *fiore-tours.com* 🎫 *From €80.*

**Kompas Travel**
**GUIDED TOURS |** In business since 1951, Kompas Travel is one of the largest excursion providers in Istria and offers a wide variety of tours, luxury villas, and holiday homes. They can arrange daily excursions

to Venice or Plitvice Lakes, as well as tours to inland Istria or Postojna Cave in Slovenia from either Poreč or Rovinj. ✉ *Obala M. Tita 16, Poreč* ☎ *052/451–100* 🌐 *kompas-travel.com.*

## Visitor Information

Although the various official tourist offices listed here can provide you with every bit of information imaginable, they generally leave the booking of rooms, villas, and excursions to private tourist agencies and hotels.

**CONTACTS** **Fažana Tourist Information.** ✉ *Titova Riva 2, Fažana* ☎ *052/383–727* 🌐 *www.infofazana.hr.* **Grožnjan Tourist Information.** ✉ *Umberta Gorjana 12, Grožnjan* ☎ *052/776–131, 052/776–064* 🌐 *www.tz-groznjan.hr.* **Istria Tourist Board.** ✉ *Pionirska 1A, Poreč* ☎ *052/880–088* 🌐 *www.istra.hr.* **Labin and Rabac Tourist Information.** ✉ *Aldo Negri 20, Labin* ☎ *052/855–560 for main office, 052/854–886* 🌐 *rabac-labin.com.* **Novigrad Tourist Information.** ✉ *Mandrač 29A, Novigrad* ☎ *052/757–075* 🌐 *coloursofistria.com.* **Poreč Tourist Information.** ✉ *Zagrebačka 9, Poreč* ☎ *052/451–293* 🌐 *www.myporec.com.* **Rovinj Tourist Information.** ✉ *Trg na Mostu 2, Rovinj* ☎ *052/811–566, 052/813–469* 🌐 *www.rovinj-tourism.com.* **Umag Tourist Information.** ✉ *Trgovačka 6, Umag* ☎ *052/741–363* 🌐 *coloursofistria.com.* **Vodnjan Tourist Information.** ✉ *Narodni Trg 10, Vodnjan* ☎ *052/511–700* 🌐 *www.vodnjandignano.com.*

# Pula

*270 km (168 miles) southwest of Zagreb.*

Now an industrial port town, Istria's chief administrative center (population 58,000), and a major tourist destination, Pula became a Roman colony in the 1st century BC. This came about a century after the decisive defeat by the Romans, in 177 BC, of the nearby Histrian stronghold of Nesactium, prompting the Histrian king Epulon to plunge a sword into his chest lest he fall into the hands of the victors, who indeed conquered all of Istria. Remains from Pula's ancient past have survived up to the present: as you drive in on the coastal route toward its choice setting on a bay near the southern tip of the Istrian Peninsula, the monumental Roman amphitheater blocks out the sky on your left. Under Venetian rule (1331–1797), Pula was architecturally neglected, even substantially dismantled. Many structures from the Roman era were pulled down, and stones and columns were carted across the sea to Italy for new buildings there. Pula's second great development period occurred in the late 19th century under the Habsburgs, when it served as the chief base for the Imperial Austro-Hungarian Navy. Today it's as much a working city as a tourist town, where Roman ruins and Austro-Hungarian architecture serve as the backdrop for the bustle of everyday life amid a bit of Communist-era soot and socialist realism. James Joyce lived here briefly in 1904–05, before fleeing what he dismissed as a cultural backwater for Trieste. Moreover, there are some outstanding restaurants and several pleasant family-run hotels, not to mention the nearby resort area of Verudela, where seaside tourism thrives in all its soothing sunny sameness.

### GETTING HERE AND AROUND

Pula is Istria's main entry point as it's home to the only regional airport for commercial flights, located just 9 km (5½ miles) from the town center. There is a shuttle bus from the airport to Pula's main bus station (located downtown) and also to the resort areas of Verudela, Medulin, and Puntižela. The best way to get around Pula is on foot. However, buses run every 20 to 30 minutes, depending on the line.

### VISITOR INFORMATION

**CONTACTS Pula Tourist Information.** ✉ *Forum 3, Pula* ☎ *052/219–197* 🌐 *www.pulainfo.hr.*

## Sights

Pula's compact commercial and administrative center is on a small semicircular protrusion of land in the Puljski Zaljev (Bay of Pula), which faces west into the Adriatic. Several ringlike streets radiate inward from the port, culminating in the small fortress-capped hill at the center of this semicircle. Most of the cultural and historical sights are along this web of streets to the south, west, and north of the hill, with the huge Roman amphitheater on the northeastern fringes of this zone (accessible via Giardini and then Istarska Ulica, on the landward side of the hill, a couple of blocks in from the bay); the bus station is another few minutes' walk from there. Meanwhile, a long walk (or a short drive) south of the city center are suburbs that culminate with the Verudela and Stoja peninsulas, home to bustling tourist resorts, beaches, some excellent restaurants, and a modern shopping mall.

**Aquarium Pula**

**AQUARIUM** | **FAMILY** | Located on the ground floor of the onetime Austro-Hungarian fortress in the resort area of Verudela, a few kilometers from the city center, the aquarium also serves as a sea turtle rescue center. Its 35 pools offer a colorful look at hundreds of sea creatures from the Adriatic's underwater world and include a touch pool with sea stars, sea urchins, crabs, and sea squirts. Climb to the roof of the fort for great vistas over Pula. ✉ *Verudela 33, Pula* ☎ *052/381–402* 🌐 *aquarium.hr* 🎫 *€20.*

★ **Arena** (*Roman Amphitheater*)
**RUINS** | Designed to accommodate 23,000 spectators, Pula's Arena is the sixth-largest building of its type in the world (after the Colosseum in Rome and similar arenas in Verona, Catania, Capua, and Arles). Construction was completed in the 1st century AD under the reign of Emperor Vespasian, and the Romans staged gladiator games here until such bloodthirsty sports were forbidden during the 5th century. It has remained more or less intact, except for the original tiers of stone seats and numerous columns that were hauled away for other buildings. Today it is used for summer concerts (by musicians including Sting, Robbie Williams, Imagine Dragons, and Jose Carreras), opera performances, and the annual film festival in mid-July. The underground halls house a museum with large wooden oil presses and amphorae. ✉ *Flavijevska bb, Pula* ☎ *052/351–300, 052/219–028* 🌐 *www.ami-pula.hr* 🎫 *€10.*

**Crkva Sveta Marije od Trstika** (*Chapel of St. Mary of Formosa*)
**CHURCH** | Once part of a magnificent basilica built in the 6th century by Bishop Maximilian of Istria, the humble stone Chapel of St. Mary of Formosa can be found between Sigirijeva Ulica and the port. Over the centuries, the chapel fell into ruin, especially during a 1242 fire at the time of the Venetian conquest of Pula. A large portion of its interior was shipped to Venice, where it was used in building the St. Mark's Library and the Sale delle Quattro Porte of the Doge's Palace. Usually closed to visitors, it's occasionally used as a gallery space, which will give you a chance to take a peek at the interior. ✉ *Between Sigirijeva ul and Flaciusova ul, Pula* ✥ *Left off Sigirijeva ul, 2 blocks before the Forum.*

**Floor Mosaic**
**RUINS** | The central scene of this large and lovely 3rd-century mosaic—which otherwise features geometric patterns, animals, and plants aplenty—is of the punishment of Dirce, who, according to Greek legend, lies under the enraged bull to whose horns she is about to be fastened. Once part of a Roman house, the mosaic was unearthed after World War II bombings.

**TIP→ The mosaic can be viewed for free by looking down through a grate beside an uninspiring apartment building a stone's throw from the Chapel of St. Mary of Formosa.** ✉ *Between Sergijevaca and Flaciusova, Pula* ✥ *Left off Sergijevaca, 2 blocks before the Forum.*

★ **Forum**
**PLAZA/SQUARE** | The Forum, the original central square, administrative hub, and marketplace of ancient and medieval Pula, is still the city's most important public meeting place after 2,000 years. Today, the Forum is a spacious square ringed with bustling cafés, shops, and restaurants. There were once three temples here, only one of which remains: the Temple of Augustus. Perfectly preserved, the Augustov Hram was built between 2 BC and AD 14. Next to it stands the Gradska Palača (Town Hall), which was erected during the 13th century using part of another Roman temple as the back wall. The arcades on three sides of the Forum square were added later, during the Renaissance. ✉ *Pula* ✥ *About 30 feet past Kapitolinski Trg from Kandlerova Promenade* 🌐 *www.ami-pula.hr* 🎫 *€2 for Augustov Hram* 🕒 *Augustov Hram closed Oct.–Apr.*

**Kaštel** (*Fortress*)
**MILITARY SIGHT | FAMILY** | Whether from the cathedral or elsewhere along Kandlerova Ulica, a walk up the hill will lead you within minutes to the 17th-century Venetian fortress, the Kaštel, that towers over Pula's city center and houses

Pula is home to Croatia's largest collection of Roman ruins.

the Historical and Maritime Museum of Istria. Built on the site of a pre-Roman fort, the preserved star-shaped fortress dates back to 1630 and has four bastions. Despite its 100,000 items of cultural, historical, political, military, and ethnographic character displayed across 18 collections, the museum is somewhat lackluster. However, it does carry the value-added benefit of allowing you to wander around its ramparts.

**TIP→ Simply walking around its perimeter offers fine views of the city's extensive shipyard below and, if you look to the north, the steeple of Vodnjan's church 12 km (7½ miles) away.** ✉ *Gradinski Uspon 6, Pula* ☎ *052/211–566* 🌐 *www.ppmi.hr* 🎫 *€6.*

**Katedrala Uznesenja Blažene Djevice Marije** (*Cathedral of the Assumption of the Blessed Virgin Mary*)

**CHURCH | FAMILY** | Built originally in the 4th century, the Cathedral of the Assumption of the Blessed Virgin Mary, Pula's star ecclesiastical attraction—more often called simply St. Mary's Cathedral—was transformed in the second half of the 5th century into a three-nave basilica. Extensive reconstruction began in the 16th century, with the adjacent bell tower constructed in the late 17th century from stones taken from the Arena. Note that the Roman-era mosaic on the floor of the central nave bears a 5th-century donor's inscription. ✉ *Kandlerova 27, Pula* 🌐 *www.zupa-uznesenja-marijina-pula.hr* 🕓 *Closed for tours and open by appointment only Oct.–Apr.*

**Malo Rimsko Kazalište (Small Roman Theater)**

**RUINS | FAMILY** | If you descend from the Kaštel along the eastern slope of the hill toward the Archaeological Museum and the Twin Gates, you will pass right through the ruins of the 1st-century Small Roman Theater. This 1,700-seat outdoor musical theater still hosts opera, classical, and jazz musical events. ✉ *Herculov Prolaz 1, Pula* ☎ *052/351–300* 🌐 *www.ami-pula.hr.*

The Forum has been Pula's central square for more than 2,000 years.

★ **Narodni Trg (Market Square)**
**MARKET | FAMILY** | For a lively and aromatic atmosphere in which to have a shot of espresso, buy a banana, or just wander about gazing at food stands, check out Pula's market square, Narodni trg. The Tržnica (City Market) sits in the center of the square. On one side of the stately two-story market building—whose iron-and-glass construction was state-of-the-art when it opened to great fanfare in 1903—you'll find outdoor fruit and vegetable stands on stone tables under red umbrellas and, on the other side, cafés and small boutiques. Inside the Tržnica itself you will find the fish market (downstairs), meat and poultry butchers, bakeries, cheesemongers, fresh pasta, and several fast-food eateries (second floor). ✉ *Narodni Trg 9, Pula* 🌐 *www.trznica-pula.hr.*

**Slavoluk Sergijevaca** (*Triumphal Arch of the Sergians*)
**RUINS** | Built by the Sergi family between 29 and 27 BC as a monument to three relatives who were great warriors, this striking monument features elaborate reliefs that even inspired Michelangelo to draw the arch during a 16th-century visit to Pula. The surrounding city gate and walls were removed in the 19th century to allow the city's expansion beyond the Old Town. Locals call it *Zlatna vrata*, or Golden Gate. ✉ *Between Giardini and Sergijevaca ulica, Pula.*

**Trapan Food & Wine Station**
**WINERY** | Don't miss a trip to Trapan Food & Wine Station in Šišan, less than 10 km (6 miles) from Pula. A visit to this trendy winery includes a wine tasting and tour, with a full gastronomy experience available to complement the wines offered. Popular labels to take home include Uroboros and Ponente, both white wines of 100% Malvazija Istarska, and Che, a sparkling wine of 100% Terrano. ✉ *Giordano Dobran 63, Šišan, Pula* ☎ *091/581–7281* 🌐 *trapanwines.com.*

## Restaurants

**Alla Becaccia**
$$ | EUROPEAN | FAMILY | Located in the village of Valbandon, close to Fažana, Alla Becaccia offers hearty meat dishes with an emphasis on game—the owner is a hunter. A huge fireplace dominates the dining room in the simple but tasteful interior, and the kitchen door is always open. **Known for:** meat and fish grilled on wood; wild game and steaks; quiet garden setting. *Average main: €20* *Pineta 25, Fažana* *052/520–753* *www.beccaccia.hr* *Closed Mon.*

**Farabuto**
$ | MEDITERRANEAN | FAMILY | In residential Pula, far from tourist attractions, Farabuto has a short menu of fresh and tasty seafood and just a few meat and vegetarian dishes, all based on what's available from Pula's green and fish markets. The modern and innovative cuisine is well presented in Farabuto's small cozy interior or on the terrace. **Known for:** local crowd; casual neighborhood vibe; fresh seafood crudo and homemade ravioli with Adriatic scampi. *Average main: €14* *Sisplac 15, Pula* *052/386–074* *www.farabuto.hr* *Closed Sun.*

**Jupiter**
$ | PIZZA | FAMILY | Located on a quiet street a couple of blocks from the Forum, this is Pula's premier place for casual budget-friendly Italian fare. Try any of its more than 20 types of wood-fired pizza, grilled meats like *ćevapi* (small minced-meat sausages), or a plate of homestyle pasta as you sip a glass of house red wine at one of the rustic wooden tables on the rear terrace. **Known for:** pizzas from a wood-burning oven; good value for money; summer crowds. *Average main: €9* *Castropola 42, Pula* *052/214–333* *www.instagram.com/jupiterpizzeria.*

**★ Konoba Batelina**
$$ | SEAFOOD | This quirky innovative restaurant is considered by many locals—and foodies around the world—to be the best seafood restaurant in Croatia. Run by a family of fishermen, Batelina is popular for its fresh-caught but totally delicious appetizers; specialties include fish tripe brodetto, scampi risotto, shark-liver pâté, bonito tartare, cuttlefish stew, and tuna carpaccio. **Known for:** owner David Skoko, one of the best chefs in Croatia; accepting cash only; being booked days in advance. *Average main: €20* *Čimulje 25, Pula* *052/573–767* *No credit cards* *Closed Dec. and Jan.*

**Trattoria Vodnjanka**
$ | ITALIAN | FAMILY | One of the few restaurants in downtown Pula offering honest and authentic Croatian dishes, no-frills Vodnjanka is a short walk from the farmers' market. Lunch is the best time to enjoy its flavorful unpretentious home-cooked dishes—a truly local experience that brings back the forgotten flavors of old times. **Known for:** a reasonably priced home-cooked meal; cash-only policy; small and cozy interior. *Average main: €11* *Dinka Vitezića 4, Pula* *098/175–7343* *No credit cards* *Closed Sun.*

## Coffee and Quick Bites

**Café Galerija Cvajner**
$ | CAFÉ | Stop at the chic but unpretentious Café Galerija Cvajner for morning coffee or an evening aperitif. Inside, contemporary art and minimalist boho-style furniture play off frescoes uncovered during restoration, and outdoor tables offer great views of the Forum square. **Known for:** outstanding location in ancient Roman square; art gallery interiors; indoor/outdoor seating. *Average main: €3* *Forum 2, Pula* *052/216–502.*

★ **Street Food Two**

$ | **MEDITERRANEAN** | **FAMILY** | This fast food shack offers some of the most mouth-watering food in Pula, from modern takes on Istrian favorites to vegan plates of international flavors not easily found in the city. The small menu changes often, but you may enjoy a vegan poke bowl, chicken burritos, shrimp risotto, gluten-free panko tofu, and endless delicious sandwiches, pasta, stews, and smoothies. **Known for:** high-class street food; very limited seating so come early for a table; central location near the market. *Average main: €12 ✉ Veronska 2A, Pula ☎ 052/203–236 🌐 www.two.hr.*

## Hotels

**Boutique Hotel Valsabbion**

$$$ | **HOTEL** | This stylish waterfront boutique hotel is in Pješčana Uvala, the posh seaside suburb just 3 km (2 miles) from Pula's city center. **Pros:** private beach; beautiful pool; stunning views of the bay. **Cons:** must drive to the city center; no elevator to higher floors; breakfast is additional fee. *Rooms from: €270 ✉ Pješčana Uvala IX/26, Pula ☎ 052/218–003 🌐 www.valsabbion.hr ⊙ Closed Jan.–Mar. 10 rooms No Meals.*

**D&A Center Apartments**

$$ | **APARTMENT** | **FAMILY** | These seven bright modern apartments and studios have Wi-Fi, flat-screen TVs, air-conditioning, and kitchenettes. **Pros:** convenient location in the middle of Old Town; modern and well-maintained rooms; continental breakfast included. **Cons:** distance from the beach; no views; no common areas. *Rooms from: €225 ✉ Giardini 3, Pula ☎ 099/489–6000 🌐 apartmani-pula.com/en/ 7 units Free Breakfast.*

★ **Grand Hotel Brioni, Radisson Collection**

$$$$ | **HOTEL** | The beachfront location and expansive sea views from every floor make this grand hotel a welcome addition to the Pula scene. **Pros:** spectacular sea views; walking distance to many beaches and the aquarium; several excellent restaurants on property. **Cons:** must drive to Old Town; no nightlife or dancing on property; crowds of tourists tend to surround the peaceful hotel. *Rooms from: €380 ✉ Verudela 16, Pula ☎ 052/378–700 🌐 www.grandhotelbrioni.com 227 rooms Free Breakfast.*

**Hotel Amfiteatar**

$$ | **B&B/INN** | **FAMILY** | This boutique hotel is in a converted three-story town house just two minutes from the Roman Arena and one block from the seafront and has rooms with smart minimalist furniture, free Wi–Fi, and spacious modern bathrooms. **Pros:** central location next to historic Roman ampitheater; good restaurant with open-air terrace and vegan dishes; private parking. **Cons:** "sea views" really mean "harbor views"; only one room has a balcony; top-floor rooms have only skylights (i.e., no windows). *Rooms from: €150 ✉ Amfiteatarska 6, Pula ☎ 052/375–600 🌐 hotelamfiteatar.com 18 rooms Free Breakfast.*

**Hotel Scaletta**

$ | **B&B/INN** | **FAMILY** | Ideally situated close to the Roman Arena, this small family-run boutique hotel occupies a tastefully refurbished old town house decorated in cheerful yellows and greens with simple modern furniture. **Pros:** friendly atmosphere; good central location; plenty of public parking nearby. **Cons:** popular but small, so books up quickly; no private parking; loud during concerts at the Arena. *Rooms from: €130 ✉ Flavijevska 26, Pula ☎ 052/541–599, 052/541–025 🌐 www.hotel-scaletta.com 12 rooms Free Breakfast.*

★ **Radisson Park Plaza Histria Pula**

$$$ | **HOTEL** | **FAMILY** | With its superb location at the tip of the Verudela Peninsula overlooking the marina and the sea, this large Radisson hotel has stylish modern rooms that are comfortable and well appointed with comfy beds, flat-screen TVs, Wi-Fi, and balconies. **Pros:** quiet seaside location; panoramic views from

## Shipwreck Diving in Croatia

On August 13, 1914, the *Baron Gautsch*, a passenger ferry owned by Austria's royal family, was on its way from Kotor to Trieste when it collided with an undersea mine and sank 12½ km (8 miles) from Rovinj, claiming more than 240 lives.

Following the long-standing tradition of diving to shipwrecks, of which Istria's coastal waters hold several good examples, more than 100 years later the *Baron Gautsch* is considered one of the most beautiful dive sites in the world. With its upper deck at a depth of 28 meters, its lower deck at 36 meters, and its bottom at 40 meters, the site—now home to plenty of flora and fauna, including a whole lot of lobsters—caters to advanced divers while stirring the imaginations of many others.

Croatia has more than 100 officially registered dive sites, from shipwrecks and caves to cliffs and coral reefs. Around 20 other shipwrecks off the Istrian coast make for popular dives. Near Novigrad lies the *Coriolanus*, a suspected British spy ship that sank in 1945 after hitting a mine. And then there are the warships *Giuseppe Dezza, Cesare Rossarol*, and *Flamingo* as well as the *Draga, Varese, Argo, Josephine*, and *John Gilmore*. Of course, Croatia's waters abound in shipwrecks well beyond Istria. For example, the waters off Krk are the resting place of the *Peltastis*, which sank in 1968 after smashing into rocks during a storm. At a depth of 16 to 32 meters, the ship is accessible to divers of all abilities.

For organized diving, you must be a member of a diving center or a diving association registered in Croatia for underwater activities. For individual diving, you have to get approval issued by the local Port Authority—local meaning that it has to be the one where you plan to dive, under its jurisdiction. The price for the approval or license is €320 and is valid for one year from the issue date. Also, better be safe than sorry—go straight to your local Port Authority to get the license and info on zones where diving is not allowed.

Although diving in Istria is possible year-round, optimal sea temperatures are from May to November. Locations must be marked by orange or red buoys or flags (and, at night, fitted with a yellow or white light visible from 300 meters). The maximum allowable diving depth when using a compressed-air cylinder is 40 meters. Diving is prohibited in protected areas, including Brijuni National Park and Krka National Park.

Dive centers can be found in all the major destinations in Istria, including Poreč, Rabac, Pula, and Rovinj.

some rooms; good in-room and on-site facilities. **Cons:** can feel overcrowded and impersonal; a bit of a hike from town; disappointing sea views from some rooms. *$ Rooms from: €280 ✉ Verudela 17, Pula ☎ 052/590–000 🌐 www.parkplazacroatia.hr ⊗ Closed Jan.–Mar. 368 rooms 🍴 Free Breakfast.*

**Ribarska Koliba Resort & Restaurant**
**$$** | **HOTEL** | **FAMILY** | Formerly a fisherman's cottage, this 100-year-old waterfront hotel in Verudela offers stylish hotel rooms, a posh penthouse apartment, a modern sauna, and an outdoor pool. **Pros:** excellent seafood restaurant on-site; rooftop lounge bar with great views; location right on the marina. **Cons:** long walking distance to the city center; some marina noise in the morning; small pool. *$ Rooms from: €235 ✉ Verudela 16, Pula ☎ 091/600–1269 🌐 www.ribarskakoliba.com 18 rooms 🍴 Free Breakfast.*

##  Nightlife

Club life in Pula tends to begin in early April and continue through late October or early November. Pubs and bars are open year-round, and you can always get a cocktail at a café bar.

**Beach Bar La Playa**
**BARS** | Just down the beach from Splendid Resort and a short walk through the forest, you'll find this casual waterfront bar and lounge. Tasty cocktails and cool live music can be found here on most summer nights. Three terraces and vibrant lighting mark this waterfront hot spot as the place to be after a long lazy day on the beach. *✉ Valsaline 29, Pula ☎ 099/315–7020 🌐 www.facebook.com/beachbarlaplayapula.*

★ **Bonaca Restauant & Lounge Bar**
**BARS** | Come here for the incredible views of the beaches below this almost floating restaurant bar. A modern, all-glass, multi-tiered venue, it offers excellent cocktails, tasty bites, live music, and space for group gatherings. But it's really the panoramic views of the sea, the sailboats gliding by, and the beachgoers just below that keep visitors coming back to this beautiful place. *✉ Verudela 11, Pula ☎ 091/633–3358 🌐 bonacapula.hr.*

**E&D Lounge Bar**
**BARS** | Set in a landscaped garden with a small swimming pool surrounded by stylish lounge chairs, E&D "Day and Night" Lounge Bar is the perfect place to hang during the day with a leisurely coffee or beer as you enjoy the views over the sea and beaches below. At night in summer, the lounge comes alive with DJ dance parties. During the height of the summer season, the bar also serves light Mediterranean dishes, ice cream, and other desserts. *✉ Verudela 22, Pula ☎ 052/213–404.*

**Ožujsko Pub**
**PUBS** | This industrial-style hot spot, located between a BMW dealership and a gas station on the busiest street in Pula, offers everything from hearty breakfasts and American-style pub fare to local craft beers and hip cocktails. It's also a year-round location for enjoying live music, comedians, and DJs and watching sports on the big-screen TVs. There's a large indoor space with a central bar and an even bigger covered terrace outside. *✉ Ante Dukića 1, Pula ☎ 052/825–693 🌐 ozujsko-pub-zaobilaznica.business.site.*

**Pietas Julia**
**DANCE CLUBS** | This large seafront lounge bar and dance club also features a coffee bar and pizzeria. This is the place to dance a night away in Pula, with DJs playing electronic, house, techno, and R&B music. A great selection of cocktails makes this sexy spot popular among Pula's hip crowd. *✉ Riva 20, Pula ☎ 091/181–1855 🌐 www.pietasjulia.com.*

## Performing Arts

Being the most prominent place in town, the Arena hosts a fair share of the city's marquee art and music performances and even select sporting events.

**Pula Film Festival**
**FESTIVALS | FAMILY** | Dating back to 1954, this annual film festival is the oldest Croatian film festival and occurs in mid-July, before the more well-known Motovun International Film Festival. Screenings occur in the Arena and feature Croatian and international works. ✉ *Kaštel 2, Pula* ☎ *052/393–321* 🌐 *pulafilmfestival.hr.*

**Visualia Festival**
**ARTS FESTIVALS** | As the first festival of light in Croatia, Visualia has installed a variety of light, technology, performance, and multimedia installations all over the city for almost a decade now, usually geared to a single theme. In one of the most popular displays, *Lighting Giants*, the illuminated cranes of Uljanik Shipyard struck a nerve and has become a consistent symbol of local pride. The Pulska Xica, a fun night run that starts at the Arena and passes the *Lighting Giants*, takes place during Visualia. ✉ *Gajeva 3, Pula* ☎ *099/233–8823* 🌐 *visualia-festival.com.*

## Shopping

Pula continues to grow as a shopping destination, with several modern multilevel malls, stores with quality goods from Istria, and Croatian delicacies, wines, crafts, and more. On Monday and Tuesday evenings in July and August (from 8 to 11), the Forum hosts an open-air fair of Istrian handicrafts. A walk through the Triumphal Arch of the Sergians onto bustling Sergijevaca Ulica will show you much of what the city has available, shopping-wise; the boutiques listed here are just a few of what's on offer. Most shops are closed on Sunday by law.

★ **Hižica**
**SOUVENIRS** | A curated collection of designer home accessories from architect and interior designers Ana Visković and Bernard and Sara Domniku is sold in this petite-but-stylish boutique. It sits right below their design studio and offices, all of which offer locally made hand-crafted decorative pieces that double as wonderful take-home souvenirs. ✉ *Veronska 6, Pula* ☎ *052/204–320* 🌐 *hizicadesignshop.com.*

★ **Pula Green Market (Tržnica)**
**MARKET** | Join locals at the Tržnica as they stock up on their daily fresh produce, locally sourced meats, fresh-caught fish, and domestic cheeses. Although open most of the day, it's best to experience the market like the locals do, early in the morning. A couple of highlights include the Jelenic charcuterie, which offers homemade traditional Istrian cured meats like cooked ham, prosciutto, and sausages, as well as Kumparicka Dairy, which produces unpasteurized, fresh, and aged (up to 30 months) goat cheeses. ✉ *Narodni Trg 9, Pula* ☎ *052/218–122* 🌐 *trznica-pula.hr.*

## Activities

Unlike some smaller towns farther up the coast like Rovinj, it can be a little more challenging to get that dip in the sea in between visits to cultural attractions in downtown Pula. But the good news is that the beaches aren't far away. A short drive or bus ride to the Verudela or Stoja resort areas, each around 4 km (2½ miles) south of downtown, will provide the clear water (and rocky shores) Croatia has in no short supply. You might also try the long stretch of relatively isolated beach between the two, on the Lungomare. If you have a car or a bicycle, this lovely little stretch of undeveloped coast is close to town and popular with locals as well as tourists. Head south about 2 km (1 mile) along the main road out of Pula and follow the signs to the right toward Stoja, a resort-cum-camping area. Once there, proceed left and then back north along the pine-fringed Lungomare as it makes its way to the Verudela resort area.

If you have a car at your disposal, drive 10 km (6 miles) southwest of central Pula to the Premantura Peninsula. The relatively remote shoreline there, at the very southern tip of Istria, is even more scenic, punctuated by cliffs, caves, and coves—and the crowds are mercifully thinner.

# Vodnjan

*12 km (7½ miles) north of Pula.*

Vodnjan may look a bit weathered at first glance, but there are five really good reasons to come here: its saintly mummies; its collection of award-winning olive oil producers; its quiet, narrow, centuries-old streets populated by Italian speakers; the more than 40 murals painted throughout the town; and the museum park devoted to the *kažun* traditional stone hut.

### GETTING HERE AND AROUND

Ten buses run daily between Pula and Vodnjan, at €2 each way, payable directly to the driver.

## Sights

**★ Chiavalon Olive Oil Mill and Tasting Room**

**OTHER ATTRACTION | FAMILY |** Sandi Chiavalon was barely 13 when he planted his first olive trees and decided to become an olive oil producer. Less than two decades later, Chiavalon's organic extra-virgin olive oil was chosen among the 15 best olive oils in the world by the prestigious Flos Olei. A visit to the Chiavalon tasting room is well worth a detour; book online one day in advance to arrange the tasting and farm tour, some of which are accompanied by delicious Istrian fare like cheese, prosciutto, and sausages. Make sure to take or ship home their oils and homemade tomato sauce and jams. ✉ *Salvela 50, Vodnjan* ☎ *052/655–050, 098/441–561* 🌐 *chiavalon.hr* 🕒 *Closed Sun.* *Reservations essential.*

**Crkva Svetog Blaža** (*St. Blaise's Church*)

**CHURCH | FAMILY |** From the tourist office on the main square, stroll down Ulica Castello to Crkva Svetog Blaža, an 18th-century structure built in the style of architect Palladio that not only has the highest campanile in all of Istria but is also the unlikely home of more than 370 relics, such as the mummies or mummified body parts of six saints impressively preserved without embalming. Among the best preserved are St. Nicolosa Bursa and Leon Bembo the Blessed. Nicolosa, whose relatively elastic skin and overall postmortem presentability make her one of the best-preserved human bodies in Europe, was born in Koper (Istria) in the 15th century and was a nun in Venice and elsewhere; she's the one with the garland of flowers still on her head. Leon Bembo the Blessed was a 12th-century Venetian priest tortured in religious riots while ambassador to Syria. And then there is St. Sebastian, a Roman-officer-turned-Christian who was whipped and strangled around AD 288 in Rome after initially surviving torture by arrows. This famous saint's head, spinal column, neck muscles, and related parts are on display here. As for St. Barbara, from 3rd-century Nicomeda (in present-day Turkey), only her leg remains; she so disagreed with her father's pagan slave-keeping lifestyle that he personally killed her with a sword. Admittance to the mummy room, behind the main altar, includes an English-language recording that sums up the saints' lives and roads to mummy-hood. Call to make an appointment to see the collection. ✉ *Župni Ured Svetog Blaža, Svetoga Roka 4, Vodnjan* ☎ *052/511–420* 🌐 *www.zupavodnjan.com* **€12** 🕒 *By appointment only. Closed Oct.–June.*

Kažun Park tells the story of the traditional structure known as a kažun.

### Kažun Park

**MUSEUM VILLAGE** | **FAMILY** | A *kažun* is a traditional, dry-stone round structure or hut built in ancient times, traditionally used as a shelter for farmers and shepherds in remote fields. There are still more than 3,000 of these huts in the vicinity of Vodnjan. Kažun Park, an outdoor museum, demonstrates the four stages of kažun construction, from its foundation, walls, and roof to its final appearance. To many citizens of Vodnjan, the kažun is a part of their identity and serves as the pride of the people and the theme of their inexhaustible inspirations. ✉ *Vodnjan* ✥ *Entrance right off the main roundabout to Vodnjan* ☎ *052/511–522* 🌐 *www.vodnjan.hr/hr/sto-posjetiti-u-vodnjanu-/park-kazuna*.

### Murals

**PUBLIC ART** | **FAMILY** | Once a year, artists from around the world come to the ancient town of Vodnjan for the Boombarstick and Street Art Festival. They leave behind old stone walls and historic buildings covered with intriguing murals and creative graffiti designs. Art-loving travelers will enjoy wandering the tiny streets of Vodnjan on the hunt for the more than 45 painted murals. ✉ *Vodnjan* ✥ *Murals can be found throughout the Old Town* ☎ *052/511–700*.

## Restaurants

### Vodnjanka

**$$** | **ITALIAN** | **FAMILY** | This restaurant is the place to go for the most mouthwatering homemade pasta dishes you can imagine, not least *fuži* with wild asparagus and prosciutto, which is simply unforgettable. The inner of two small rooms, with its six tables and framed family-style photographs, is positively homey, while the outer room features bizarre but fantastic wall art by sculptor/painter Lilia Batel. **Known for:** authentic Istrian cuisine; elegant-but-quirky decorations; rooftop terrace perfect for summer sunsets. 💲 *Average main: €20* ✉ *Istarska 22B, Vodnjan* ☎ *052/511–435* 🌐 *www.vodnjanka.com* ⏲ *Closed Jan. and Sun.*

In Brijuni National Park, you'll find many relics from the Roman and Byzantine eras.

## Hotels

**★ La Casa di Matiki**

**$ | B&B/INN | FAMILY |** Located in the countryside near the village of Žminj, La Casa di Matiki may not be a fully working farm, but you'll find donkeys, chickens, and three dogs here—you can even opt to sleep on hay in the converted barn, or in the more traditional apartments and cottage. **Pros:** peaceful location far from the crowds; excellent breakfast with homemade and homegrown products (extra charge); large swimming pool. **Cons:** remote location means a car is essential; no credit cards accepted; early wake-up call by rooster or donkey. *$ Rooms from: €120 ✉ Matiki 14, Žminj ☎ 098/299–040 🌐 www.matiki.com 💳 No credit cards 🛏 8 rooms 🍽 No Meals.*

# Brijuni National Park

*Ferry from Fažana is 15 km (9 miles) northwest of Pula.*

When Austrian industrialist Paul Kupelwieser set off for Brijuni by boat from Fažana in 1885, the archipelago had long been a haven for the Austro-Hungarian military and for malaria. Kupelwieser was to change all that. In 1893 he bought the 14 islands and islets, eradicated the disease with the help of doctors, and fashioned parks from Mediterranean scrub. Thus arose a vacation retreat par excellence—not for rich Romans, as had been the case here 17 centuries earlier, but for fin-de-siècle Viennese and other European high-society sorts. Archduke Franz Ferdinand summered here, as did such literary lights as Thomas Mann and Arthur Schnitzler; James Joyce came here to celebrate his 23rd birthday. Two world wars ensued, however, and the islands' fate grew cloudy as they changed hands—coming under Italian rule and, later, Yugoslavian. From 1949 to 1979, the largest island, Veliki Brijun, was the official summer residence of Marshal Josip Broz Tito, Yugoslavia's "president for life." Here he retreated to work, rest, and pursue his hobbies. World leaders, film and opera stars, artists, and writers were his frequent guests, and it was here that, together with President Gamal Abdel Nasser of Egypt and Prime Minister Jawaharlal Nehru of India, Tito forged the Brioni Declaration, uniting the so-called nonaligned nations (countries adhering to neither NATO nor the Warsaw Pact). The archipelago was designated a national park in 1983 and opened to the public.

## Sights

★ **Brijuni National Park** (*Nacionalni Park Brijuni*)
**NATIONAL PARK | FAMILY** | The Brijuni Islands are a group of 14 small islands developed in the late 19th century, once the summer home to Yugoslavian president Tito and now one of Croatia's national parks. You'll need to pass through Fažana to catch the boat that will take you to the islands, and pausing in the seaside town at one of its collections of touristy restaurants and charming cafés along its small harbor can be restorative. Fažana's main cultural attractions—all just a short walk from the harbor—are the 16th-century Church of Saints Kosmas and Damian and the smaller 14th-century Church of Our Lady of Mount Carmel, which you enter through an atmospheric loggia and whose ceiling features several layers of fascinating 15th-century Renaissance frescoes. But you are presumably here to visit the archipelago. Book tickets—whether by phone, at the box office, or directly on the Brijuni National Park website—at least one day in advance to reserve your seats on the boat. After the 15-minute national park ferry from Fažana, the entire tour of the park takes about four hours when using the tourist train (you can also rent golf carts or bikes). Your first view is of a low-lying island with a dense canopy of evergreens over blue waters. Ashore on Veliki Brijun, the largest island, a tourist train takes you past villas in the seaside forest and relics from the Roman and Byzantine eras. The Romans laid down the network of roads on this 6½-km-long (4-mile-long) island, and stretches of original Roman stonework remain. Rows of cypresses shade herds of deer and peacocks strut along pathways. The train stops at the Safari Park, a piece of Africa transplanted to the Adriatic; its zebras, Indian holy cattle, llamas, and elephants were all gifts from visitors from faraway lands. In the museum, an archaeological exhibition traces life on Brijuni through the centuries and a photography exhibition, "Tito on Brijuni," focuses on Tito and his fascinating guests.

**TIP→ The Brijuni Pocket Guide app gives you a self-guided tour by foot, bicycle, or electric car.** ✉ *Brionska 10, Fažana* ☎ *052/525–881, 052/525–882* 🌐 *www.np-brijuni.hr* 🎫 *€ 35* ⏲ *Closed Nov.–Apr.*

## Hotels

You can save money by booking a room in Fažana and taking a day trip or two to the islands.

**Heritage Hotel Chersin**
**$$ | HOTEL | FAMILY** | Set in a beautifully restored old house in the center of Fažana, Heritage Hotel Chersin is a small and cozy family-run hotel perfect for couples. **Pros:** wonderful location; lovely design and ambience; tasty on-site restaurant. **Cons:** wooden floors; some village noise; public parking only. 💲 *Rooms from: €160* ✉ *Piazza Grande 8, Fažana* ☎ *095/398–5350* 🌐 *www.hotel-chersin.com* ⏲ *Closed mid-Oct.–mid-Apr.* 🛏 *8 rooms* 🍽 *Free Breakfast.*

# Rovinj

*35 km (22 miles) northwest of Pula.*

It is hard to imagine how Rovinj could be more romantic than it is. In a fantastic setting, with centuries-old red-roofed houses clustered around the hill of a former island, Istria's cultural mecca is crowned by the monumental Baroque Crkva Svete Eufemije (Church of St. Euphemia), which has a typical Venetian bell tower topped by a gleaming bronze figure of St. Euphemia. Far below, a wide harbor crowded with pleasure boats is rimmed with bright awnings and colorful café umbrellas. Artists, writers, musicians, and actors have long gravitated to this ravishing place to carve out apartments in historic houses. Throughout the summer, the winding cobbled streets are crowded with vacationers from all reaches of the world. South of the harbor lies the beautiful nature park of Zlatni Rt, planted with avenues of cedars, oaks, and cypresses for strolling and offering numerous secluded coves for bathing.

### GETTING HERE AND AROUND

A shuttle bus runs from Pula Airport to Rovinj. Buses travel daily between Pula's bus station and Rovinj and between Zagreb and Rovinj. The town is easily reachable by car, but the best way to get around Rovinj is on foot, scooter, or by bicycle—due to stairs along almost all the steep streets, you are not permitted to cycle within the Old Town.

## Sights

**★ Crkva Svete Eufemije** (*Church of St. Euphemia*)

**CHURCH** | Inside this 18th-century Baroque church, the remains of Rovinj's patron saint are said to lie within a 6th-century sarcophagus. Born near Constantinople, Euphemia was martyred in her youth, on September 16 in AD 304, under the reign of Emperor Diocletian. The marble sarcophagus containing her remains mysteriously vanished in AD 800, when it was at risk of destruction by iconoclasts—and, legend has it, it somehow floated out to sea and washed up in faraway Rovinj. (Note the wall engraving just to the right of the entrance of St. Euphemia holding Rovinj in her arms.) On September 16 of each year many people gather to pray by her tomb. There is no better place to enjoy 360-degree sunset views of Rovinj than from the church bell tower. In summer, concerts and art shows take place in the piazza in front of the church. ✉ *Trg Svete Eufemije, Rovinj* ☎ *052/815–615* 🎟 *Free for church; €4 for campanile* ⏲ *No tours Nov.–May.*

**Dvigrad**

**TOWN** | When its residents abandoned Dvigrad's "two towns" suddenly in the mid-17th century—fleeing the combined misfortune of plague and attacks by Uskok raiders—and established nearby Kanfanar, surely they didn't foresee that more than three centuries later, tourists would delight in what they left behind. If exploring ruins is your (or your child's) thing, this is the place for you. Along an isolated road 23 km (14 miles) east of Rovinj, outside the sleepy town of Kanfanar (a short detour if you're headed north toward Poreč, Motovun, or Grožnjan), this huge maze of dirt paths surrounded by high stone walls makes for an adventuresome, imagination-stirring walk. Indeed, just enough restoration has been done to let your imagination "reconstruct" the rest: some of the walls are vine-covered, and much of the place is overgrown with vegetation. Nor is there a single explanatory sign in any language. All this combines to give you the sense that you are discovering this eerie ghost town of a fortress city, even if a few other tourists are also wandering about. The battlements are impressively intact, and toward the center of the fortress you will find the remains of St. Sophia's Church, replete with depressions in the ground that contained the crypts of very important persons. To get here, take the main road east out of Rovinj toward Kanfanar. Just before you cross the railroad tracks and enter Kanfanar, you'll see a sign pointing to Dvigrad, which is to your left; from the sign, the ruins are about 4 km (2½ miles) down an isolated scrub-lined road. A Medieval Fair takes place in May, complete with historical theater, music, jousting, food, and drinks. ✉ *Kanfanar* *Free.*

**Galerija Sveti Toma** (*St. Thomas Gallery*)
**ART GALLERY | FAMILY** | Today a public art gallery, St. Thomas was previously a small bright-yellow church dating to the Middle Ages but was rebuilt in 1722. It's on your way back down the hill from the main cathedral, and right after you pass by it, you will pass under a lovely arched hall some 50 feet long with a wood-beamed ceiling. On your left, you'll notice a small courtyard encircled by pastel-painted houses with green and blue shutters and colorful flowers in the window. St. Thomas is part of the Heritage Museum of Rovinj. ✉ *Bregovita, Rovinj* *www.muzej-rovinj.hr* *Free* *Closed Mon.–Tues. and Oct.–June.*

**Kuća o Batani** (*Batana Eco-museum*)
**OTHER MUSEUM | FAMILY** | Devoted to Rovinj's *batana* (traditional wooden boat), this small museum in a typical multistory house has a permanent exhibition of boats and fishing tools. It also hosts various cultural events and educational programs, and during the summer the museum organizes gourmet evenings on Tuesday and Thursday in a *spacio,* a typical Rovinj tavern or wine cellar. These start with a batana ride from the Mali mol around Rovinj's Old Town to the tavern, where guests taste typical dishes like salted anchovies or marinated sardines and local wine. ✉ *Obala Pina Budicina 2, Rovinj* ☎ *052/812–593* *www.batana.org* *€3* *Closed Mon.*

**Matošević**
**WINERY** | With vineyards in the northeast, Matošević Winery welcomes visitors for a tour and tasting at their top-notch cellars in Krunčići, near Sveti Lovreč, a village not far from Rovinj. Their Malvazijas Rubina and Alba bear international renown and are served at many Michelin-starred restaurants. ✉ *Krunčići 2, Kruncici* ☎ *052/448–558* *www.matosevic.com* *Closed Sun.*

**San Tommaso Winery**
**WINERY** | This small family-run winery in Golaš, a small village in Bale, just 17 km (10½ miles) south of Rovinj, is housed in a beautifully restored 150-year-old farmhouse with exposed stones and large wooden beams. The property features a wine cellar, a tasting room with a big open fireplace, and a small ethnographic museum displaying old family photos and equipment that once was used in the wine-making process in Istria. Don't let their Malvazija Istarska fool you–although the wine is fresh, easy to drink, and sweet, it is still 14% alcohol. They also produce a few reds, a rosé, and the sweet dessert, Muscat Žuti. If the owner, Janja, happens to be there, ask her to let you taste her raisin wine, which isn't for sale. You can also stay in the winery's modern pension. ✉ *Golaš 13, Bale* ☎ *098/309–594, 099/339–9640* *santommaso.hr* *Closed Mon., and Nov.–Apr.*

**Trg Maršala Tita**
**PLAZA/SQUARE** | Standing on the Old Town's main square, you can't help but notice the Balbi Arch, which at one time was the gate to Rovinj's fish market. Notice the Venetian lion with an open book (a symbol of acceptance of Venetian rule without a fight) and a Venetian head on one side and a Turkish head on the other, the symbolism of which hasn't yet been explained. A Latin epigraph is at the top between the two Balbi coats of arms. Also quite prominent on the square is the city's pinkish-orange watchtower, whose base houses the tourist agency. Although it looks Venetian, the tower was erected in 1907. That said, the winged-lion relief

on one side is from the 16th century. ✉ *Trg Maršala Tita, Rovinj.*

## ★ Agli Amici

**$$$$ | FRIULIAN** | Chef Emanuele Scarello of Udine, Italy, opened his second restaurant in Rovinj in 2021 during the pandemic, and three months later was awarded a Michelin star for its gastronomic excellence. There's no à la carte menu—only three tasting menus, each featuring thoughtful blends of Istrian, Godia (the Rovinj area), and Friuli flavors. **Known for:** clever interpretations of local foods; spectacular waterfront views; incredible dining experience that can last three hours. *$ Average main: €150 ✉ Šetalište Vijeća Europe 1–2, Rovinj ☎ 052/642–084 🌐 www.agliamici.it ⏲ Closed Mon.–Wed. No dinner weekends.*

## ★ Barba Danilo

**$$ | MEDITERRANEAN** | Don't let this restaurant's location in a campsite outside of town fool you: this fine-dining seafood restaurant is by far the best restaurant in Rovinj, and possibly in all of Istria. Forget the standard starter-main-dessert kind of meal and instead indulge in a variety of innovative cold and warm appetizers made with the freshest local ingredients. **Known for:** upscale dining experience; imaginative dishes; a variety of cold and warm seafood starters. *$ Average main: €22 ✉ Polari 5, Rovinj ☎ 052/830–002 🌐 barbadanilo.com ⏲ Closed Nov.–Apr.*

## ★ Bookeria

**$$ | MEDITERRANEAN | FAMILY** | Inventive Mediterranean food is served in an eye-catching, whimsically decorated garden dropped right on the stone square. You may not be seated on the sea but you'll feel the vibrant holiday vibe flowing from the minute you arrive. **Known for:** juicy burgers; hipster vibe and whimsical decor; friendly service. *$ Average main: €15 ✉ Trg G. Pignaton 7, Rovinj ☎ 052/817–399, 091/219–0007 🌐 bookeria-rovinj.com ⏲ Closed Oct.–Apr.*

## Giannino

**$$ | MEDITERRANEAN | FAMILY** | Tucked away on a small square in a residential area of the Old Town, Giannino is equally popular among locals and tourists for its fresh and delicious Mediterranean fare such as pan-fried squid with polenta, spicy boiled Adriatic shrimp, branzino *al forno* (baked slowly in the oven), cuttlefish ravioli, grilled rib eye with roasted potatoes, and tagliatelle with lobster. Starched white and blue checkered tablecloths make the place look classy, but the atmosphere is convivial and relaxed with friendly staff. **Known for:** fresh fish and seafood; run by the same family since 1972; charming location in the center. *$ Average main: €22 ✉ Augusta Ferrija 38, Rovinj ☎ 052/813–402 🌐 restoran-giannino.com ⏲ Closed Tues. and Nov.–Mar.*

## Maestral

**$$ | MEDITERRANEAN | FAMILY** | You won't find a bad seat at this outdoor seafront restaurant with fantastic views of the Old Town, particularly at sunset. An extensive menu, friendly staff, a laid-back vibe, and affordable prices draw crowds here all day. **Known for:** outstanding views; lots of crowds; fresh seafood dishes, including excellent fisherman's pie. *$ Average main: €20 ✉ Obala Vladimira Nazora 3, Rovinj ☎ 052/830–565 ⏲ Closed Oct.–Apr.*

## ★ Monte

**$$$$ | MEDITERRANEAN** | Dinner here promises upscale, out-of-this-world, creatively presented Italian-Istrian dishes served on a special garden terrace just below the famous St. Euphemia's Church. The menu changes often but usually includes *mare crudo,* an eye-popping feast of super-fresh seafood carpaccio, or try a bit of everything with a five- or seven-course tasting menu. **Known for:** reservations essential; multicourse tasting menus; exceptional wine pairings. *$ Average main: €45 ✉ Montalbano 75,*

*Rovinj ☏ 052/830–203 🌐 www.monte.hr ⏲ Closed mid-Oct.–Easter. No lunch.*

**Orca**
$$ | **MEDITERRANEAN** | **FAMILY** | Local, fresh, traditional food makes this restaurant on the outskirts of town a favorite among locals. Its location on the main road may not draw visitors in at first, but the food is excellent and a great value. **Known for:** tagliatelle with scampi and mushrooms; traditional restaurant with old-fashioned interior; big portions. *$ Average main: €22 ✉ Gripole 70, Rovinj ☏ 052/816–851 🌐 www.orca-rovinj.com ⏲ Closed Nov., and Tues. Oct.–May.*

**Pizzeria Da Sergio**
$ | **PIZZA** | **FAMILY** | With 50-plus varieties of delicious thin-crust pizzas, there's plenty to choose from at this conveniently located venue along the narrow road leading up to the main cathedral. Pizzas are all baked in a wood-burning oven and are so good locals come from all over Istria to get them. **Known for:** some of the best pizza in Istria; old Italian tavern atmosphere; cash-only policy. *$ Average main: €12 ✉ Grisia 11, Rovinj ☏ 052/816–949 No credit cards ⏲ Closed Mon. Nov.–Easter. No lunch Nov.–Easter.*

## Hotels

**★ Grand Park Hotel Rovinj**
$$$$ | **HOTEL** | **FAMILY** | Emerging from the fragrant pine forest, this hotel has an unbelievably perfect location on the waterfront opposite Sveta Katarina Island and the charming Old Town of Rovinj, an excellent restaurant, a top spa, and luxurious accommodations. **Pros:** spectacular location overlooking Old Town; great restaurants, including Michelin-starred restaurant Agli Amici; unique Istrian-inspired spa menu. **Cons:** shared beach with Katarina Hotel on island across; outdoor infinity pool can get crowded; some suites on lower floors do not have views. *$ Rooms from: €615 ✉ Smareglijeva 1A, Rovinj ☏ 052/800–250 🌐 www.maistra.com/grand-park-hotel-rovinj 209 rooms Free Breakfast.*

**Hotel Adriatic**
$$$ | **HOTEL** | Founded in 1912, this harborside boutique hotel is the oldest (still functioning) one in town, and is modern, artsy, and as cosmopolitan as anything in New York or London. **Pros:** first-class view of Old Town square and harbor; breakfast served on the terrace; sophisticated design. **Cons:** no spa facilities; off-site parking; neither direct beach nor swimming pool. *$ Rooms from: €350 ✉ Pino Budicin 16, Rovinj ☏ 052/803–510, 052/800–250 🌐 www.maistra.com/properties/hotel-adriatic 18 rooms Free Breakfast.*

**Hotel Angelo d'Oro**
$$ | **HOTEL** | Rovinj's first boutique heritage hotel is housed in a beautifully restored 16th-century building on a cobblestone street in the heart of the Old Town. **Pros:** beautiful Venetian building with wrought-iron and stone details; modern updates and recent renovations; secret courtyard garden for breakfast. **Cons:** some street noise; parking is outside Old Town; books up quickly. *$ Rooms from: €225 ✉ Vladimira Švalba 40, Rovinj ☏ 052/853–920 🌐 www.angelodoro.com 27 rooms Free Breakfast.*

**Hotel Lone**
$$$ | **HOTEL** | Superbly designed by an all-star Croatian team, the large Hotel Lone blends perfectly with its lush surroundings; rooms are modern, spacious, and comfortable, with sleek bathrooms and huge balconies. **Pros:** contemporary design; great balcony views; right on the beach in a wonderful forest park. **Cons:** pool is shared with nearby Eden Hotel; energy can feel a bit cold and distant; large hotel also caters to business travelers. *$ Rooms from: €335 ✉ Luje Adamovića 31, Rovinj ☏ 052/800–250 for reservation center, 052/632–000 🌐 www.maistra.com/properties/hotel-lone 248 rooms Free Breakfast.*

### Hotel Monte Mulini

$$$$ | **HOTEL** | **FAMILY** | Considered one of the top luxury hotels in Croatia, the Hotel Monte Mulini has a stunning location just a 20-minute walk from Rovinj's Old Town, in a landscaped park next to the nature park Zlatni rt and 164 feet from the sea. **Pros:** gorgeous location by the sea; within walking distance of town; spacious, elegantly appointed rooms. **Cons:** pricey; heated outdoor swimming pool sometimes too cold; not enough stools at the swim-up bar. *Rooms from: €465 ✉ Antonia Smareglie 3, Rovinj ☎ 052/636–000, 052/800–250 for reservation center ⊕ www.maistra.com/properties/hotel-monte-mulini ⊙ Closed Nov.–Easter 113 rooms Free Breakfast.*

### Island Hotel Katarina

$$ | **HOTEL** | **FAMILY** | Located on Sveta Katarina Island, just a 15-minute boat ride from the Old Town, Island Hotel Katarina is partly housed in an old family castle from the early 20th century with basic and outdated but spacious rooms, some with breathtaking views over the Old Town. **Pros:** surrounded by beautiful parks; stunning views; great amenities for families. **Cons:** dependent on a boat schedule; outdated decor in the rooms; pricey. *Rooms from: €177 ✉ Otok Katarina 1, Rovinj ☎ 052/800–250 ⊕ www.maistra.com/properties/island-hotel-katarina ⊙ Closed Oct.–May 120 rooms Free Breakfast.*

### Stancija 1904

$$ | **B&B/INN** | This lovingly restored turn-of-the-century villa 30 minutes east of Rovinj is an excellent place to stay—and a good example of what you're likely to find if you venture into the agritourism section of the Istria lodging scene. **Pros:** secluded property but still convenient to major tourist sites; friendly and dedicated owners; great homemade meals offered on-site for guests only. **Cons:** no swimming pool; car is essential; no spa. *Rooms from: €185 ✉ Smoljanci 2–3, Svetvincenat ☎ 052/560–022, 098/738–974 ⊕ www.stancija.com ⊙ Closed Oct.–Easter 3 rooms Free Breakfast.*

## Nightlife

### Caffe Bar Limbo

**BARS** | **FAMILY** | A small romantic café bar serving delicious cocktails, coffee, and craft beers, this intimate Bohemian-style spot is nestled down the steps of one of Rovinj's most charming streets. Cushions, pillows, coffee tables, candles, plants, and even cats create a character-filled experience that is quintessentially Rovinj. Your host for the evening will usually be the ever-welcoming Boris, a master mixologist excited to pour something you'll enjoy. *✉ Casale 22B, Rovinj ☎ 095/902–1064.*

### Havana Club

**BARS** | The Adriatic may not be quite as warm as the Caribbean, but at the Havana Club—a spacious tropical-themed cocktail bar/café right on the harbor—you can sip a piña colada or a *canchánchara* (rum, lime, and honey). There's a great selection of more than 100 Caribbean rums and premium gins plus nonalcoholic cocktails, as well as iced tea and coffee. Kick back and relax in a wicker chair under a bamboo umbrella while listening to reggae. That's not to mention the real Cuban cigars you can puff starting at €8. *✉ Obala Alda Negria 3, Rovinj ☎ 091/588–3470.*

### ★ Mediterraneo Bar

**BARS** | With a lovely terrace on the sea's edge, friendly staff at the ready but not hovering, a great selection of pretty cocktails, a relaxed atmosphere, and more affordable prices than similar bars nearby, Mediterraneo is popular among locals and visitors alike. Pass through the low archway and head down a staircase to the fun terrace with colorful tables, stone benches, and cushions for those willing to have a drink sitting on the rocks. Even dolphins occasionally visit. The owners of this atmospheric bar also offer charming Old Town accommodations. ✉ *Svetog Križa 24, Rovinj* 🌐 *mediterraneo-rovinj.eu.*

**Puntulina Restaurant & Wine Bar**
**WINE BARS** | Take the steps down to Puntulina's terrace, where you can enjoy a glass of Istrian or other Croatian wine in a pleasant atmosphere yards from the sea, with light pop music setting the tone, plus amazing sunsets. And, yes, you can take a few more steps down, if you wish, to the rocks and take a dip in the sea before or after being served—this is where Rovinj's free public swimming area begins. There's also an excellent seafood restaurant on the upper level, which offers the same gorgeous views in one of the most romantic settings in Rovinj. ✉ *Svetog Križa 38, Rovinj* ☎ *052/813–186* 🌐 *puntulina.eu.*

## Performing Arts

**★ Croatian Summer Salsa Festival**
**ARTS FESTIVALS** | **FAMILY** | During the last week of June, the Croatian Summer Salsa Festival offers eight days of dancing lessons in various town squares, gallery spaces, and even on the beach, as well as beach and pool parties, dance-life workshops, and best practices on how to DJ and emcee dance parties. International salsa experts and professional DJs entertain, inspire, and encourage more than 2,000 attendees. ✉ *Rovinj* 🌐 *www.crosalsafestival.com.*

**Rovinj Photodays**
**ARTS FESTIVALS** | **FAMILY** | Since 2008 Rovinj has hosted the largest photo festival and international competition of contemporary photography in southeastern Europe. Usually taking place during the first weekend in May, the festival activities include workshops, lectures, displays, presentations, gallery shows, and streets lined with artful and thought-provoking photography. ✉ *Rovinj* ☎ *099/200–6666, 051/301–182* 🌐 *photodays-rovinj.com.*

## Shopping

**House of Batana**
**SOUVENIRS** | **FAMILY** | Original souvenirs based on Rovinj's fishing heritage—including key chains, T-shirts, and replicas of its traditional vessel, the batana—can be bought at the House of Batana museum. Besides batana-inspired souvenirs, you can pick up a small recipe book with old, almost-forgotten recipes from Rovinj fishermen, also available in English. ✉ *Obala Pina Budicina 2, Rovinj* ☎ *052/812–593* 🌐 *www.batana.org.*

**★ Profumo di Rovigno**
**PERFUME** | The Salvi family offers an intoxicating array of unique perfumes, sachets, bath gels, lotions, soaps, diffusers, cotton throws, silk wraps, and home fragrances under their Profumo di Rovigno brand. All products at their tiny store on the main shopping street are inspired by the flora and fauna in the hills around Rovinj, including wild sage, lavender, roses, lemon balm, and other herbals. All are beautifully packaged in elegant bottles and boxes, perfect to bring home as gifts or mementos of your trip. ✉ *Carera 45–47, Rovinj* ☎ *052/813–419* 🌐 *www.profumodirovigno.com.*

## Activities

### SCUBA DIVING

As elsewhere along the coast, the Rovinj area has its share of places to kayak, boat, windsurf, Jet Ski, parasail, stand-up paddle, cycle, and deep-sea dive. Several diving centers will take you by boat for supervised dives to shipwrecks and other fascinating spots, not least the famous wreck of the *Baron Gautsch,* an Austrian passenger ferry that sank in 1914, just 9 nautical miles from Rovinj.

**Morski Puz Diving Center Rovinj**
**DIVING & SNORKELING** | Maddy and Jure are SSI-certified diving instructors offering diving instruction, from beginner to advanced, for both adults and children

(be sure to check out the very popular SSI Mermaid training course). They can also take you to dive sites off the shores of Rovinj and to local wrecks like the *Baron Gautsch* and the *Maona*, as well as to the underwater caves of Banjole. ✉ *Veštar 1, Rovinj* ☎ *097/671–2846* 🌐 *diving-rovinj.com* 🎫 *Starting at €15.*

# Poreč

*55 km (34 miles) northwest of Pula.*

A chic, bustling little city founded as a Roman *castrum* (fort) in the 2nd century BC and swarming with tourists more than 2,000 years later, Poreč may not be quite as lovely as Rovinj—few places are—nor does it enjoy the benefits of a hilltop panorama. Still, it comes with a pretty view of red-tiled roofs on a peninsula jutting out to sea. Within the historic center, the network of streets still follows the original urban layout. Dekumanova, the Roman *decumanus* (the main traverse street), has maintained its character as the principal thoroughfare. Today it is a worn flagstone passage lined with Romanesque and Gothic mansions and patrician palaces, some of which now house cafés and restaurants. Close by lies the magnificent UNESCO-listed Eufrazijeva Bazilika (St. Euphrasius Basilica), Istria's prime ecclesiastical attraction and one of the coast's major artistic showpieces. Although the town is small, Poreč has ample capacity for overnight stays, thanks to the vast hotel complexes of Plava and Zelena Laguna, situated along the pine-rimmed shoreline a short distance from the center. Although you can cover the main sights in two or three hours, Poreč surely merits a one-night stay—or more, if you take a day trip to a nearby attraction such as the Baredine Cave or the Limski Kanal.

### GETTING HERE AND AROUND

Getting to Poreč is easier straight from Pula than from Rovinj, as you simply take the main inland highway north for 42 km (26 miles), then follow the signs before turning west onto the secondary road that leads you another 13 km (8 miles) to Poreč—a 45-to-60-minute drive in all, depending on the traffic and how much pressure you apply to the pedal.

**CONTACTS Tourist Information Center Poreč.** ✉ *Zagrebačka 9, Poreč* ☎ *052/451–293* 🌐 *www.myporec.com.*

## Sights

### AgroLaguna Winery

**WINERY | FAMILY** | You can taste, experience, and shop all at this well-regarded value-oriented winery. The tasting room provides a sampling of their high-quality Istrian wines, olive oils, and cheeses. One white varietal, Malvazija, is well known throughout the Adriatic, dating back to the days of the Venetian city-states. Muškat Ottonel is another high-quality native variety. Small lovingly produced batches of *barrique* provide high-quality (red) wine that is well-regarded in restaurants and hotels across Croatia. You can also get guided tastings, cellar tours, wine roads, and vineyard tours, and the winery has the largest AgroLaguna single olive grove in Croatia. ✉ *Mate Vlašića 34, Poreč* ☎ *052/453–179, 091/442–1015* 🌐 *agrolaguna.hr.*

### Aquacolors Water Park Poreč

**WATER PARK | FAMILY** | Whether you're looking for an adrenaline-filled day or a relaxing one by the pool, Aquacolors Water Park has you covered. With 12 slides and over a full acre of pools, it's the largest water park in Croatia. A 61-meter-long (200-foot-long) looping slide rockets you down at high speed, while a 204-meter-long (⅓-mile-long) lazy river eases you along on an inflatable tube. The park offers endless hours of fun for the whole family and favorable pricing. There's even

St. Euphrasius Basilica is decorated with stunning mosaics.

an adult-only area with a high-tech bar. *Molindrio 18, Poreč* *052/219–671* *www.aquacolors.eu* *€36* *Closed Oct.–Apr.*

★ **Eufrazijeva Bazilika** (*St. Euphrasius Basilica*)

**CHURCH** | **FAMILY** | The magnificent Eufrazijeva Bazilika is among the most perfectly preserved early Christian churches in Europe, and as a UNESCO World Heritage site, one of the most important monuments of Byzantine art on the Adriatic. Built by Bishop Euphrasius in the middle of the 6th century, the basilica consists of a delightful atrium, a church decorated with stunning mosaics, and an octagonal baptistery. Added in the 17th century was a bell tower you can climb (for a modest fee) and a 17th-century Bishop's Palace, whose foundations date to the 6th century; the basement contains an exhibit of stone monuments and mosaics previously on the basilica floor. The church interior is dominated by biblical mosaics above, behind, and around the main apse. In the apsidal semidome, the Virgin holding the Christ child is seated in a celestial sphere on a golden throne, flanked by angels in flowing white robes. On the right side are three martyrs, the patrons of Poreč; the mosaic on the left shows Bishop Euphrasius holding a model of the church, slightly askew. High above the main apse, just below the beamed ceiling, Christ holds an open book while apostles approach on both sides. Other luminous, shimmeringly intense mosaics portray further ecclesiastical themes. *Eufrazijeva 22, Poreč* *052/451–784* *www.zupaporec.com/eufrazijeva-bazilika.html* *€18* *No tours Sun.*

★ **Jama Baredine** (*Baredine Cave*)

**CAVE** | **FAMILY** | Far from sun and sea though it may be, this cave has long been one of the Poreč area's top natural attractions. About 8 km (5 miles) northeast of town, near Nova Vas, this wonderful world of five limestone halls includes not only the miniature olm (known as the cave salamander) and insects but, of course, stalactites, stalagmites, and dripstone formations—from "curtains"

30 feet long to "statues" resembling the Virgin Mary, the Leaning Tower of Pisa, and the body of the 13th-century shepherdess Milka, who supposedly lost her way down here while looking for her lover Gabriel (who met the same fate). One of the halls includes a hatch some 70 yards deep that leads to underground lakes. Groups leave every half hour on a 40-minute guided tour. Those without car transport may wish to join an excursion to the cave from Poreč or another nearby town. ✉ *Tar-Gedići 55, Nova Vas* ☎ *098/224–350, 095/421–4210* 🌐 *baredine.com* 🎟 *€11* 🕐 *Tours by appointment only Nov.–Mar.*

**Limski Canal**

**BODY OF WATER** | **FAMILY** | The Limski *kanal* is a 13-km-long (8-mile-long) karst canyon, whose emerald-green waters are flanked by forested valley walls that rise gradually to more than 300 feet inland. The canyon was formed in the last Ice Age, and it is Istria's most fertile breeding area for mussels and oysters—hence, you'll find the excellent Viking seafood restaurant on-site. Tours are available from both Poreč and Rovinj, with various agencies and independent operators whose stands and boats are impossible to miss. A reservation a day or two in advance can't hurt, though, particularly in midsummer. Expect to pay approximately €25 for the four-hour tour or €50 for a daylong tour that includes a "fish picnic." You can also visit the canal on your own by car. And hiking enthusiasts can take a trail to the Romualdova Cave, which is open daily from June to September. ✉ *D21, Kruncici* ✥ *Halfway between Rovinj and Poreč.*

**Trg Marafor**

**PLAZA/SQUARE** | This square is located toward the tip of the peninsula and was the site of Poreč's Roman forum, whose original stonework is visible in spots amid the present-day pavement. Beside it is a park containing the ruins of Roman temples dedicated to the gods Mars and Neptune. It's still an important meeting place, so you will find a variety of cafés, restaurants, and shops around the square. ✉ *Poreč.*

**★ Vrsar**

**TOWN** | This pretty, waterfront medieval hilltop town just 10 km (6 miles) south of Poreč is situated near the Limski fjord's northern juncture with the sea (and yet another place you can catch a tour of the fjord). Famous since Roman times for its high-quality stone, which helped build Venice, Vrsar is home to the 12th-century Romanesque church Svete Marija od Mora (St. Mary of the Sea), which has three naves. In his memoirs, the Venetian adventurer Casanova fondly recalled the local Teran red wine. Additionally, Croatia's oldest and largest naturist/nudist resort, FKK Park Koversada, is just a couple miles south. 🌐 *infovrsar.com.*

## Beaches

Walk 10 minutes south of Poreč along the shore, past the marina, and you'll meet with the thoroughly swimmable, if typically rocky, pine-fringed beaches of the Brulo and Plava Laguna resort areas. Keep walking until you're about 5 km (3 miles) south, and you'll be right in the center of Zelena Laguna, which, though more concrete than rock, is one of the best-equipped tourist resorts on the Adriatic coast. Every day from May through September, two charming tourist trains (tiny open-walled buses) run hourly from 9 am to 11 pm between the town center and the resort and Hotel Luna to the north—costing you €3 but saving you the walk. Another option is the boat that runs between Zelena Laguna and the center daily May through September from 10 am to 11 pm, with stops at other resort areas. Tickets can be purchased on board.

## Restaurants

**Konoba Daniela**

$$ | **MEDITERRANEAN** | **FAMILY** | In the village of Veleniki, just a few miles from Poreč, this rustic family-run tavern has exposed stone walls, wooden beams, and an outdoor terrace in an enclosed courtyard. With its simple and honest food, friendly staff, and huge portions, Konoba Daniela offers excellent value for money. **Known for:** excellent steak tartare; many seafood options; popular with locals. *Average main: €22 Veleniki 15A, Veleniki 052/460–519 konobadaniela.com Closed mid-Feb.–mid-Mar.*

**Peterokutna Kula**

$$$ | **SEAFOOD** | A 15th-century pentagonal tower in the heart of the Old Town now holds a sophisticated restaurant on a series of floors and terraces, including the roof. House specialties include beautifully plated seafood crudo, sea urchin with cauliflower foam, homemade *pljukanci* pasta with skampi, and Istrian steak with tartufi. **Known for:** rooftop views; historic location; sophisticated menu. *Average main: €30 Dekumanova 1, Poreč 052/451–378, 091/303–5644 www.kula-porec.com.hr.*

**Pizzeria Nono**

$ | **PIZZA** | **FAMILY** | Right across the street from the main tourist office, the Nono is teeming with locals and tourists who go crazy over the scrumptious comfort-food fare. You'll find everything from wood-fired pizzas and fresh green salads to grilled squid and french fries, burgers, and *ćevapi* (regional sausages). **Known for:** affordable prices; streetside terrace; summer crowds. *Average main: €12 Zagrebačka 4, Poreč 052/453–088 Closed Mon., Oct.–Apr., and 1st 2 weeks in Nov.*

**★ Sveti Nikola Restaurant**

$$ | **CONTEMPORARY** | Those with a discriminating palate and a not-so-discriminating pocketbook should try this sparkling air-conditioned restaurant very close to the harbor. The menu offers such delicacies as grilled octopus, fish filet in scampi and scallops sauce, cream soup with local mushrooms, and beefsteak with tartufi sauce, but the elegant seafront terrace makes this the top fine-dining spot in Poreč. **Known for:** special-occasion dining; harbor-facing terrace; delicious seafood food. *Average main: €22 Obala Maršala Tita 23, Poreč 052/423–018 www.svnikola.com.*

**Tunaholic Fish Bar**

$ | **BURGER** | **FAMILY** | You won't be able to resist these mouthwatering fish and seafood burgers prepared with modern innovative appeal. Served from a bright and welcoming fast food store in fun branded materials, you can walk away with paper cones of fried local fish, trays of crispy squid and *pommes frites*, or tuna burgers oozing cabbage and spicy mayonnaise. **Known for:** tasty local fish shop; fast and friendly service; affordable prices. *Average main: €8 Svetog Eleuterija 6, Poreč 091/443–1235 www.tunaholicfishbar.com.*

## Coffee and Quick Bites

**★ Torre Rotonda Cocktail & Coffee Bar**

$ | **CAFÉ** | **FAMILY** | Do not be deterred by the cannon facing you as you enter the 15th-century stone tower that now houses the Torre Rotonda café and bar. Climb up the spiral staircase to a second floor with several intimate nooks, or go one more flight to the roof for an unbeatable outstanding view of Poreč and its harbor. **Known for:** spectacular views over Old Town and the marina; delicious Aperol spritz; lively atmosphere at night. *Average main: €6 Narodni Trg 3A, Poreč 098/255–731 www.torrerotonda.com Closed Oct.–Apr.*

## Hotels

**BO Hotel Palazzo**

$$ | **HOTEL** | Its outstanding location on the head of a small peninsula in Poreč's Old Town sets this historic hotel apart; built in 1910, it housed the very first hotel in town. **Pros:** excellent location; historical building with character; outdoor pool and spa. **Cons:** smallish rooms; lacks its own beach; can be noisy at night. *Rooms from: €245 Obala Maršala Tita 24, Poreč 052/858–800 www.bohotel.com/en/hotels/1/bo-hotel-porec Closed Nov.–Mar. 74 rooms Free Breakfast.*

**Hotel Park Plava Laguna**

$$$ | **RESORT** | **FAMILY** | The ideal family resort, the Park Plava allows each family member to choose what they most want to do: animation activities, beaches, sports, fine dining, or hanging out at the five on-property pools. **Pros:** many activities and programs for children; on the beach; close to Old Town. **Cons:** big and busy; not a romantic retreat; à la carte dining only for lunch. *Rooms from: €270 Špadići 15B, Poreč 052/415-500 www.plavalaguna.com Closed mid-Oct.–Mar 154 rooms All-Inclusive.*

**Korta Gira**

$ | **B&B/INN** | **FAMILY** | Only 5 km (3 miles) from downtown Poreč, this small B&B on a family farm feels like a world apart. **Pros:** quiet and relaxing, yet not far from Poreč; warm friendly hosts; homemade products at breakfast. **Cons:** car is essential; outside town; not a full-service hotel. *Rooms from: €125 Buići 8, Poreč 091/505–7747 3 rooms Free Breakfast.*

**★ Valamar Collection Isabella Island Resort**

$$$ | **RESORT** | **FAMILY** | Accommodations at this sprawling premium resort on car-free Sveti Nikola island (across the harbor from Old Town Poreč), include apartments, villas, and hotels. **Pros:** wonderful location on car-free island; five-minute boat ride to downtown; stylish accommodations. **Cons:** large resort; hectic at dinner when full; different service level at different properties. *Rooms from: €305 Sveti Nikola, Poreč 052/465–000 www.valamar.com/en/hotels-porec/valamar-isabella-island-resort Closed Oct.–May 334 rooms Free Breakfast.*

**Valamar Diamant Hotel & Residence**

$ | **HOTEL** | **FAMILY** | Located a mile south of Old Town Poreč in the Brulo neighborhood, this large hotel is surrounded by pine forest but still close to the sea and a favorite for travelers looking for an activity-rich vacation. **Pros:** superlative sports facilities; excellent buffet food with all dietary needs; modern, bright, and comfy rooms. **Cons:** 10-minute walk from Poreč; busy active environment; caters to business travelers, too. *Rooms from: €109 Brulo 1, Poreč 052/465–000 for reservation center, 052/400–000 www.valamar.com/en/hotels-porec/valamar-diamant-hotel-residence Closed Nov.–Mar. 246 rooms All-Inclusive.*

**Valamar Riviera Hotel & Residence**

$ | **HOTEL** | On the seafront promenade, where Poreč's oldest hotels are found, the Valamar Riviera is an adults-only hotel with a chic restaurant and comfortable, traditionally appointed rooms, most of which have sea views and balconies. **Pros:** located right in Old Town; private sand beach served by shuttle boat; popular restaurant with outdoor dining. **Cons:** noise from the promenade reaches the rooms; off-site parking reached by shuttle; occasional exhaust from yachts parked in front. *Rooms from: €147 Obala Maršala Tita 15, Poreč 052/465–000 for reservation center, 052/400–800 www.valamar.com/en/hotels-porec/valamar-riviera-hotel-residence Closed Oct.–Apr. 105 rooms Free Breakfast.*

## Nightlife

**★ Garaz Bar**

**BARS** | Whether you come for the cold-pressed juices and delicious espressos in the morning or choose to sit and enjoy the panoramic views of Old Town Poreč at sunset, the Garaz's friendly seaside location cannot be beaten. There's even a small pebble beach right in front of the café-bar for easy sea dipping in between cocktails. Parking isn't far off from this hidden gem, but it's best to stroll the waterfront promenade to and from the bar. ✉ *Nikole Tesla 13A, Poreč* ☎ *091/411–3828.*

**Villa Club Poreč**

**DANCE CLUBS** | Located near the marina, right by the beach, the Villa Club is a popular hangout with lounge chairs, wicker canopy beds, and lounge music during the day. Night brings DJs, theme parties, live bands playing dance music, and go-go dancers until dawn. ✉ *Rade Končara 4A, Poreč* ☎ *099/214–9004.*

## Performing Arts

**Street Art Festival**

**ARTS FESTIVALS** | **FAMILY** | In the third week of August, Poreč's annual Street Art Festival enlivens the Old Town's streets and squares with musical, theatrical, art, multimedia, and acrobatic events and street performances. ✉ *Poreč* ☎ *052/887–223* 🌐 *www.poup.hr.*

**★ Vinistra Wine Fair**

**FESTIVALS** | In May each year, at least 80 different Istrian winemakers exhibit their wines at Vinistra, a wine fair produced by the Association of Wine Growers and Winemakers of Istria. Local gourmet food producers, farmers, and restaurants also provide tastings cleverly paired with a variety of wines on offer. During this three-day festival, viticulture classes, seminars, presentations, and award ceremonies fill the schedule between sips. ✉ *Dvorana Žatika, Poreč* ☎ *052/621–698* 🌐 *vinistra.hr* 🎫 *€25 for ticket, €10 for a glass (refundable).*

## Activities

### DIVING

**Starfish Diving Center**

**SCUBA DIVING** | This diving outfitter offers aspiring or advanced divers daily diving tours to local shipwrecks, reefs, and caves. A four-day certification course is also available for those looking to improve their skills while on holiday in Istria. ✉ *Autokamp Porto Sole, Vrsar* ✥ *10 km (6 miles) south of Poreč* ☎ *098/335–506, 098/334–816* 🌐 *starfish.hr* 🎫 *From €20.*

# Novigrad

*15 km (9½ miles) northwest of Poreč.*

Imagine a mini Rovinj of sorts, not quite as well-preserved and without the hill. This is Novigrad—a pretty little peninsula town that was the seat of a bishopric for more than 1,300 years, from 520 to 1831, and, like Rovinj, was at one time an island (before being connected with the mainland in the 18th century). With its medieval structures still impressively intact and its Old Town wall, it merits a substantial visit and perhaps a one-night stay as you make your way up and down the coast or before heading inland toward the hilltop towns of Grožnjan and Motovun. At first glance, as you enter town on an uninspiring main road bordered by Communist-era concrete-box apartment buildings, you might wonder if it was worth coming this far. Continue and you'll arrive at a little gem: to your right is a pint-size protected harbor filled with boats, the Old Town is in front of you, and to your left is a peaceful park. The bustling harborside square has a few bars and restaurants. A nearby ice cream stand is manned by enterprising acrobatic young men who wow the crowds by hurling scoops 50 or more feet into

Novigrad greets you with its charming harbor and colorful houses.

the air to open-mouthed colleagues who then discreetly spit them into napkins, garnering much applause (and generating long lines). If you continue walking past the harbor on the left, you'll arrive at Vitriol, one of Istria's most popular sunset bars.

### GETTING HERE AND AROUND

There are daily buses from Pula to Novigrad. The town is also connected by bus with Zagreb, Rijeka, and Trieste. Novigrad is easily reachable by car, but the best way to get around town is on foot or by bicycle. The electric tourist train connects the resort complex to the south with Novigrad Harbor from June to September.

## Sights

The 13th-century Crkva Svetog Pelagija (Church of St. Pelagius), built on a 6th-century foundation and containing some elaborate Baroque artwork, stands near the tip of the peninsula with its towering late-19th-century campanile topped by a statue of St. Pelagius. As in Rovinj, the main church faces the sea.

On nearby Veliki Trg is Novigrad's pale-red city hall, topped by a watchtower and contrasting sharply with the yellow building beside it. Here and there, Gothic elements are evidence of the medieval architecture around town (e.g., two windows on a 15th-century building at Velika Ulica 33).

**Aquapark IstraLandia**

**WATER PARK | FAMILY** | The first water park in Istria opened in 2014, featuring 20 waterslides, including an almost 90-foot-high free-fall waterslide; family rafting in inflatable rafts; three pools, including a children's pool with a water castle, pirate ship, and several smaller slides; sand volleyball; and a badminton court. Direct buses from Poreč, Novigrad, and resort towns in between run throughout the day in July and August. ✉ *Nova Vas, Novigrad* ☎ *052/866–900* 🌐 *www.istralandia.hr* 🎫 *From €25* ⏲ *Closed Oct.–June.*

## Restaurants

**★ Damir & Ornella**
$$$$ | **SEAFOOD** | Tucked away on a quiet side street, this superb (and pricey) little family-run establishment is a secret wonder you may want to share only with your fellow gourmands who appreciate raw-fish specialties. You can also enjoy grilled seafood and gnocchi, although you don't go here for a simple plate of pasta, but instead to indulge in a four-course meal. **Known for:** Mediterranean-style sashimi; intimate atmosphere; advanced reservations needed. *Average main: €65 Zidine 5, Novigrad 052/758–134 damir-ornela.com Closed Nov. and Feb. No lunch Sept.–May.*

**Restaurant Marina**
$$$$ | **CONTEMPORARY** | On the first floor of what looks like a typical family house, this seafood restaurant has a surprisingly elegant and stylish interior. Husband-and-wife duo Marina and Davor don't have a fixed menu; offerings are recited by the young owner. **Known for:** innovative seafood dishes; multicourse tasting menus; great food and wine pairings. *Average main: €40 Svete Antona 38, Novigrad 099/812–1267, 052/726–691 Closed Tues., and Jan. and Feb.*

**★ Vecchio Mulino**
$ | **PIZZA** | **FAMILY** | The Old Mill pizzeria may look touristy—it is, after all, centrally located right by the harbor, and it is packed—but it's also good, and the raised terrace gives you the feeling of being a bit above the fray. This is the best place in town for pizza, spaghetti, salads, *čevapčići* (grilled Balkan sausages) and tiramisu. **Known for:** central location; large crowds; best casual Italian spot in town. *Average main: €12 Mlinska 8, Novigrad 052/647–451, 052/726–300.*

## Olive Oil in Istria

As you head to the northwestern corner of Istria, toward Umag or the interior hilltop towns, remember that you're driving through some of the region's most fertile olive oil territory. The tourist offices in Novigrad, Buje, and Umag can give you a map outlining an olive oil (and vineyard) route with directions to several production facilities that offer tastings and tours. Farther south in and around Vodnjan, you will also find a wonderful collection of award-winning olive oil farms to visit.

## Hotels

**Hotel Cittar**
$$ | **HOTEL** | The stone facade of this hotel is part of the medieval Old Town wall; inside, a glass-covered vestibule imaginatively separates the ancient wall from the modern hotel lobby. **Pros:** central location on the sea; free breakfast; good pool and sauna. **Cons:** modern minimalist interiors; limited parking near hotel; indoor pool is adults-only. *Rooms from: €165 Prolaz Venecija 1, Novigrad 052/757–737 www.cittar.hr Closed Dec. 14 rooms Free Breakfast.*

**Hotel San Rocco**
$$ | **HOTEL** | Nine km (6 miles) up the road from Novigrad in Brtonigla (on the road to Buje), Hotel San Rocco is a real change of pace from the coast: among rolling hills surrounded by olive trees and vineyards, this upscale boutique hotel makes an impressive entrée to the Istrian interior. **Pros:** good restaurant on-site; magnificent views; elegant rural relaxation close to town. **Cons:** you'll need a car; terrace is within earshot of

busy road; cute but simple local village to wander. $ *Rooms from: €185* ✉ *Srednja 2, Brtonigla–Verteneglio* ☎ *052/725–000* 🌐 *san-rocco.hr* ⏲ *Closed Nov.–Apr.* 🛏 *14 rooms* 🍽 *Free Breakfast.*

**Rivalmare Boutique Hotel**
**$$ | HOTEL** | With just 13 spacious contemporary rooms—some with lovely sea views and balcony—this boutique hotel is popular for its chic minimalist look, elegance, design furniture, and superb location right at the seafront. **Pros:** small and intimate; top location; on-site parking. **Cons:** no free parking; no swimming pool; extra charge for sun loungers at the beach. $ *Rooms from: €235* ✉ *Rivarela 19, Novigrad* ☎ *052/555–600* 🌐 *www.rivalmare.hr* ⏲ *Closed Dec.–Mar.* 🛏 *13 rooms* 🍽 *Free Breakfast.*

# Umag

*15 km (9 miles) northwest of Novigrad.*

Yet another onetime island, the peninsula town of Umag draws the fewest tourists of any of the major towns along Istria's western coast, even if it has more than its share of the usual beach resorts nearby. Perhaps it's the frustration with waiters who, while twiddling their thumbs in front of their restaurants, call out to every passing tourist, "Italiano? Deutsch? English?" and, less often, "Français?"

And yet Umag is a nice enough place to stroll for a couple hours if you are passing this way, even if you might not be moved to stay for the night. Although the town grew up under the rule of Rome, practically none of its ancient roots are apparent in what remains of the historic core, which dates to the Middle Ages.

### GETTING HERE AND AROUND

The best way to get to Umag is by car. Once here, the quaint historic town is best explored on foot.

## Sights

**Cuj Winery**
**WINERY | FAMILY** | The Cuj olive oils (and wines) are a true labor of love and passion. Owner Danijel Kraljevic—Cuj—will infuse you with both when you visit his wine and olive oil estate in the village of Farnažine near Umag. A beautifully restored, old stone building houses an olive mill, wine cellar, and tasting room with an open fireplace. He produces three single-sort extra-virgin olive oils—Buža, Črna, and Bjelica—and one multi-sort extra-virgin olive oil—Selekcija. Call in advance to arrange a visit. ✉ *Farnažine 6A, Umag* ☎ *091/2121–920, 098/219–277* 🌐 *www.cuj.hr* 🎫 *Tastings from €20* ⏲ *Closed Sun.*

★ **Kabola Winery**
**WINERY** | Near the small medieval hill town of Momjan, the Kabola Winery is a must-visit for wine and olive oil aficionados. This boutique winery offers tours of its wine cellar and small wine museum and full tastings in its picturesque traditional Istrian farmhouse. Vintners since 1891, the Markezic family produces only organic wines and extra-virgin olive oil. Their wines are wonderful, with their Malvazija Unica, Teran, and Dolce being some of the more popular. Their olive oil blends three kinds of olives: indigenous Istarska Bjelica mixed with Leccino and Pendolino. Fresh, well-rounded, and balanced, it marries perfectly with seafood, cheese, and salads. Call in advance to arrange a visit to sample their wares. ✉ *Kanedolo 90, Momjan* ☎ *099/720–7106, 052/779–208* 🌐 *kabola.hr* ⏲ *Closed Sun.*

★ **Kozlović Winery**
**WINERY** | At Gianfranco and Antonella Kozlović's stylish architecturally impressive winery, which complements the scenic countryside, you can enjoy an extensive wine tasting indoors or on their outdoor terrace overlooking the vineyard.

If you call ahead, you can enjoy a full tasting of wine and olive oil as you enjoy local cheeses and prosciutto. Next door is Stari Podrum, one of the best tavern restaurants in Istria. ✉ *Vale 78, Momjan* ☎ *052/779–177* 🌐 *www.kozlovic.hr* ⏲ *Closed Sun.*

**Moreno Coronica Winery**
**WINERY** | A family boutique winery in the northeast corner of the peninsula between Buje and Umag, Coronica produces some of Croatia's most delicious wines. A highlight is their Malvazija, a white grape native to Istria best enjoyed served with fish and seafood. The Gran Teran, a local variety of red wine, has been a gold medal winner at international wine competitions for many years. ✉ *Koreniki 86, Koreniki* ☎ *052/730–357* 🌐 *www.coronica.eu* ⏲ *Closed Sun.*

## Restaurants

**Tavern Nono**
**$$ | ITALIAN | FAMILY** | Extremely popular and always busy, Tavern Nono is located in Petrovija, just a mile east of Umag. This family-run tavern offers hearty Istrian seafood, meat, and pasta dishes in a cozy and friendly atmosphere. **Known for:** traditional Istrian food; kid-friendly dining with a playground and a small farm behind the restaurant; popularity among locals and tourists. [$] *Average main: €18* ✉ *Umaška 35, Petrovija, Umag* ☎ *052/740–160* 🌐 *konoba-nono.com* ⏲ *Closed Mon. Oct.–May.*

# Motovun

*38 km (24 miles) southeast of Umag, 30 km (19 miles) northeast of Poreč.*

It is an understatement to say that a day exploring the undulating green countryside and medieval hill towns of inland Istria makes a pleasant contrast to life on the coast. Motovun, for one, is a ravishing place. The king of Istria's medieval hilltop towns, with its double ring of defensive walls as well as towers and gates, may even evoke a scene straight from *The Lord of the Rings*. It's the perfect place to visit if you opt to travel inland for only a day or two. Be warned, though: the town sees lots of tour buses. That said, a walk around the ramparts offers views across the oak forests and vineyards of the Mirna Valley. On the town's main square stands a church built according to plans by Palladio. In late July, the famed Motovun Film Festival transforms the town into one of Croatia's liveliest (and most crowded) destinations for about five days.

### GETTING HERE AND AROUND

The best way to get to Motovun is by car; unless you are part of a bus tour, traveling here by local bus isn't a viable option. This small hilltop town is best explored on foot.

## Exploring Inland Istria

Istria's interior hilltop towns have been much celebrated in recent years, both for their stunning beauty and their gastronomical traditions. It's smart to rent a car, even for just one day, for a drive into the interior in the late afternoon, when fewer tour buses will likely be on the road. Aside from Motovun and Grožnjan, you'll find that Oprtalj, Roč, Hum, Buzet, Pican, and Gračišće are all picturesque villages with their medieval churches, old clock towers, culinary specialties, and small-town restaurants.

Istria is filled with medieval hill towns, and Motovun is one of the most charming.

## Restaurants

### ★ Konoba Tončić

$$ | **ITALIAN** | **FAMILY** | This rustic tavern with exposed stone walls, wooden beams, and a large open fireplace offers traditional hearty Istrian meat dishes. Located off the beaten path well past Oprtalj, the outdoor terrace has scenic views over the rolling hills, valley, and mountains in the background. **Known for:** delicious traditional Istrian food; charming but remote location; reservations are essential. *Average main: €20 ✉ Čabarnica 42, Zrenj ☎ 052/644–146 🌐 www.agroturizam-toncic.com No credit cards ⏲ Closed weekdays and July.*

### Mondo

$$ | **ITALIAN** | **FAMILY** | On a narrow cobblestone street just a few yards from the town's gate, this tavern is perhaps the best place to eat in town, with a truffle-centric menu and a breezy terrace perfect for alfresco dining. The menu screams truffles—almost every dish features them: homemade pasta, steaks, and even panna cotta desserts come with shaved black truffles on top. **Known for:** truffle-stuffed menu; rustic interior; charming location. *Average main: €20 ✉ Joakima Rakovca, Motovun ☎ 052/681–791 🌐 konoba-mondo.com ⏲ Closed Tues. and Jan.–Mar.*

### Restaurant Zigante

$$ | **EASTERN EUROPEAN** | **FAMILY** | This family-run restaurant/truffle shop is 3 km (2 miles) from Motovun and is not simply a gift shop filled with truffles, truffle products, olive oil, and wine (as with other branches in Motovun and Buzet). Here in their renovated villa, you can sit down for a delicious meal of gilthead carpaccio with white truffles (gilthead being a type of sea bream) or thin *palačinke* (crepes) filled with white-chocolate mousse and finely shaved black truffles. **Known for:** cozy elegant ambience; local products for sale; truffle-inspired menu. *Average main: €16 ✉ Livade 7, Livade ☎ 052/664–302 🌐 restaurantzigante.com.*

## Truffles in Istria

On November 2, 1999, in the village of Livade near Motovun, Giancarlo Zigante and his sharp-nosed dog unearthed a record-breaking 1.31-kilogram (2.89-pound) white truffle. What he foraged was the most delicious fungus you are likely to find.

Truffles grow underground, in a symbiotic relationship with the roots of oaks and certain other trees. As such, they cannot readily be seen. It is their scent that gives them away—a swoon-inducing scent. Sows were once the truffle hunter's favored companion, as truffles smell a lot like male hogs. (To be fair, the earthy aroma and pungent taste of truffles, which has also been likened to garlic, is prized by gourmands the world over.) These days, dogs are a truffle hunter's best friend.

Truffles are extremely rare. Most efforts to cultivate them domestically have failed because you first need to grow a forest full of trees whose roots are just right for truffles. Prices fluctuate, but the white truffle, prized for its superior scent—the "white diamond," it's often called—sells for up to $10,000 a pound. In addition to white truffles, Istria is also home to three sorts of black truffle, which sell for a mere $1,500 a pound.

In Istria truffles have been harvested since ancient times. Even Roman emperors and Austro-Hungarian aristocrats had a taste for truffles, not least because of the aphrodisiac qualities attributed to them. Truffles were once consumed and gathered like potatoes—that's how plentiful they were. That was in the 1800s. No longer, of course. Still, their fine shavings impart an unforgettable earthy aroma and an irresistibly pungent, vaguely garlicky taste to pastas, salads, omelets, beef specialties, sauces, and more.

Economics and truffle scarcity being what they are, the Istrian truffle has become a hot commodity indeed. These days, for example, much of what is sold by Italy as Italian white truffles actually comes from Croatia—not least from the moist woods around Motovun and Buzet, near the river Mirna.

**Karlić Tartufi.** The Karlić family has been truffle hunting for over half a century, and a visit to their estate in Paladini near Buzet is a must for aficionados of this rare fungus. The family offers truffle-hunting tours followed by truffle-inspired meals, and their shop sells a variety of truffle products, such as fresh and frozen black and white truffles and truffle-infused olive oil, honey, and various tapenades. ✉ *Paladini 14, Village Paladini, Buzet* ☎ *052/667–304* 🌐 *karlic-tartufi.hr.*

**Istriana Travel.** If you'd like to join a truffle hunt, reserve a spot on a truffle-hunting excursion that departs from the village of Vrh from April to December. Accompanied by an English-speaking guide, you'll meet a truffle hunter and his trained truffle-sniffing dogs at the hunter's house, spend 45 minutes hunting in the woods, and enjoy a light lunch or dinner made with the truffles you unearthed. ✉ *Vrh 46/3, Buzet* ☎ *091/541–2099* 🌐 *www.trufflehuntingcroatia.com* 🎫 *From €55.*

## Hotels

**Boutique Hotel Kaštel**
$$ | **HOTEL** | Nestled in a cloistered niche at the very top of the hilltop town sits this peaceful old-fashioned boutique hotel that makes an ideal retreat if you prefer quaint streets and rolling green hills to sea views and island escapes. **Pros:** quiet location; nice indoor pool and spa facilities; nice views over the Mirna River Valley from some rooms. **Cons:** uphill walk to the hotel; no car access or parking at hotel; some smaller rooms. *Rooms from: €156 Trg Andrea Antico 7, Motovun 052/681–607, 052/681–735 www.hotel-kastel-motovun.hr Closed Jan.–Apr. 33 rooms Free Breakfast.*

★ **Roxanich Wine & Heritage Hotel**
$$ | **HOTEL** | **FAMILY** | A communal wine cellar until 1990, this Hapsburg-era stone building today houses a sophisticated hotel and restaurant to complement the high-tech family-run winery below. **Pros:** impressive wine tastings and vineyard tours; stylish design; amazing location with breathtaking views. **Cons:** not for those who don't like wine; high beds can be challenging; long walk up to Old Town. *Rooms from: €185 Kanal 30, Motovun 052/205–700 www.roxanich.hr 32 rooms Free Breakfast.*

# Grožnjan

*18 km (11 miles) northeast of Motovun.*

Close to Motovun and a reasonable drive from Poreč, Novigrad, Rovinj, or Umag, Grožnjan is among Istria's preeminent and most beautiful hilltop towns. A Renaissance loggia adjoining the ancient town gate are must-see historical sites, but it's really wandering through the narrow rustic stone streets and perusing the many boutiques, galleries, and ateliers that make this town a favorite for locals and visitors. In 1358, after at least 250 years as a walled city, Grožnjan came under Venetian rule and remained so for more than 400 years. Though most of its population left after World War II, when decades of Italian rule ended and it officially became part of Yugoslavia, the government encouraged artists and musicians to settle here starting in the mid-1960s. This explains the number of art studios, painting and ceramic ateliers, and sculpture galleries you will encounter, as well as charming cafés with views of the sea or the Mirna River Valley. Many art, antique, and music festivals take place, including an international federation of young musicians that meets for training and workshops, presenting concerts beneath the stars throughout July and August.

## Oprtalj and Završje

As you near Grožnjan, you can take a small detour to the picturesque hilltop villages of Oprtalj and Završje. Take a stroll around Oprtalj's hushed little streets and central loggia, where the 15th-century Church of Sveti Juraj and 16th-century bell tower still stand. Just a bit farther, halfway between Oprtalj and Grožnjan, mystical Završje is almost deserted today. Large houses covered in creeping ivy, as well as the town gate, a leaning tower, and the remains of defensive walls, are witnesses to Završje's past glory.

### GETTING HERE AND AROUND

The best way to get to Grožnjan is by car, as no buses connect it to Pula or other coastal towns. Once you get there, this small hilltop town can only be explored on foot, with plenty of time to sit and enjoy the view from one of the cafés perched on the outside ring of the city walls.

## Restaurants

**San Servolo Steakhouse, Resort & Beer Spa**
$$ | **STEAKHOUSE** | It's always time for a cold one in this tavern and steak house tucked in the rolling hills between Buje and Grožnjan. The menu includes a tasty selection of six unfiltered and unpasteurized Istrian craft beers alongside an expansive menu of grilled meats and other hearty Istrian dishes. **Known for:** local craft beer; grilled meats; stunning views. *$ Average main: €22 ✉ Momjanska 7, Momjan ✣ Just outside Buje, 9 km (6 miles) northwest of Grožnjan ☎ 052/772–505 🌐 www.sanservoloresort.com ⏲ No lunch Mon. and Tues.*

**Stara Škola**
$$$$ | **MEDITERRANEAN** | This salvaged school is now a stylish multilevel restaurant offering guests a welcoming delicious experience. Whether you enjoy a cocktail and hors d'oeuvres on the rooftop terrace, gather at the community table in the lounge, or sit with friends for a multicourse tasting menu in the main dining room, you'll see the culinary staff puts great importance on sourcing ingredients from local farms and producers, even if that means picking the beets before they come to work. **Known for:** good selection of natural wines; beautiful views; locally sourced and thoughtful ingredients. *$ Average main: €65 ✉ Krasica 35, Buje, Grožnjan ☎ 052/770–870 🌐 www.staraskola.hr ⏲ Closed Mon.*

## Hotels

★ **Bolara 60 Guesthouse**
$ | **B&B/INN** | **FAMILY** | In a tiny village just below Grožnjan, you'll find Bolara 60, a lovingly restored 18th-century stone farmhouse surrounded by peaceful rolling hills, vineyards, and olive groves. **Pros:** welcoming attentive hosts; incredible homemade food; charming decor. **Cons:** shared bathrooms; 30-minute drive to the beach; healthy walk or ride uphill to town. *$ Rooms from: €105 ✉ Bolara 60, Grožnjan ☎ 099/447–3267 🌐 www.bolara60.com ⏲ Closed Dec.–Apr. 6 rooms Free Breakfast.*

★ **San Canzian Village & Hotel**
$$$$ | **HOTEL** | A luxurious boutique hotel has been created from several old houses found in the medieval village of Mužolini Donji, near Buje, Momjan, and Grožnjan. **Pros:** high-style interiors throughout; excellent restaurant with a knowledgeable sommelier; peaceful and restorative energy. **Cons:** more spa services needed; changing chefs; a drive to the beach. *$ Rooms from: €599 ✉ Mužolini Donji 7, Grožnjan ☎ 099/302–0000 🌐 san-canzian.hr ⏲ Closed Jan.–Mar. 24 rooms Free Breakfast.*

## Shopping

**Zigante Tartufi**
**FOOD** | Tourists visit the charming hilltop town of Grožnjan to enjoy its rustic beauty, arts and crafts, and music programs. There's enough tourism, in fact, to merit yet another outlet of the family-owned Zigante Tartufi chain. The shop sells locally unearthed truffles and everything truffle-related you can possibly imagine, as well as other local products from aromatic herb brandies to honey, dried porcini mushrooms, wine, and olive oil. The gourmet boutique is near the town's loggia. Just follow your nose. *✉ Ulica Gorjan 5, Grožnjan ☎ 052/776–099 🌐 zigantetartufi.hr.*

# Labin-Rabac

*44 km (28 miles) northeast of Pula.*

More travelers are exploring Istria's newest must-stay tourist destination, Labin-Rabac. Located on the eastern coast, these sister towns offer the perfect combination of a historic hilltop town (Labin) with a beachfront resort town (Rabac) just 4 km (2½ miles) below. Beautiful Blue Flag beaches are surrounded by lush green mountains that lend themselves to hiking and biking.

### GETTING HERE AND AROUND

There are 16 buses daily from Pula to Labin, from which you can easily reach Rabac by minibus or taxi. The best way to get around both Rabac and Labin is on foot. Electric tourist trains in Rabac run from one end of the coastal town to the other (in other words, from Maslinica Hotel to Girandella Resort) from mid-June to mid-September. Of course, having a rental car will allow you to move from town to town easily.

## Sights

### ★ Labin

**TOWN** | **FAMILY** | Perched in all its compact medieval redolence atop a hill a short drive or walk from the sea, Labin is Croatia's former coal-mining capital and the birthplace of Matthias Flacius Illyricus, a Reformation-era collaborator of Martin Luther. Its narrow historic streets are well deserving of a good walk—followed, if time allows, by a dip in the sea in Rabac. From Labin's endearing main square lined with cafés and boutiques to its 16th-century loggia and bastion, it's an easy stroll to Šetalište San Marco, a fountain-filled promenade with spectacular views of the sea. Walk to the end and take a sharp left up the steep cobblestone road to the onetime fortress, Fortica. At the top, you will enjoy sweeping panoramic views of Ucka Mountain, Cres and Losinj islands, Rabac, and the sea. As you go down the other side of the hill toward the main square, you will pass the Crkva Rođenja Blažene Djevice Marije (Church of the Birth of the Virgin Mary). With a facade featuring a 14th-century rose window and a 17th-century Venetian lion you will encounter elsewhere in Istria, the church is a mix of architectural styles dating back to a late 16th-century renovation, though its foundations may date to the 11th century. Working art studios, souvenir shops, museums, and galleries are dotted throughout Old Town Labin. The Labin Art Republika hosts art openings, live musical concerts, and an outdoor documentary film festival in July and August. ✉ *Labin* 🌐 *rabac-labin.com.*

### ★ Rabac

**TOWN** | **FAMILY** | With its beautiful aqua-blue bay and splendid natural surroundings down rocky cliffs that call to mind the Amalfi Coast, the seaside resort town of Rabac has transformed from a quiet 17th-century fishing village into one of the most popular tourist destinations in Istria. Perfectly situated just below Old Town Labin and equidistant from Opatija and Pula, Rabac offers an endless number of white pebble beaches and untouched nature ideal for hiking, biking, kayaking, windsurfing, fishing, diving, and snorkeling. Many hotels, resorts, boutique hotels, villas, apartments, and campgrounds host international tourists looking for family-friendly holiday experiences. Yet, despite its growing popularity, Rabac still manages to transmit the same casual coastal charm and welcoming spirit of the 17th-century village it once was. A bonus is having the medieval hilltop town of Labin just 10 minutes up the road, where its numerous chic restaurants, live music programs, art galleries, and historical sites further enrich your holiday. ✉ *Rabac* 🌐 *rabac-labin.com.*

## Restaurants

### Burra Bistro & Pizzeria

$ | **CAFÉ** | **FAMILY** | This casual upbeat eatery in Old Town Plomin, just 12 km (8 miles) north of Labin, is worth stopping at for a decadent burger, Asian stir-fry, spicy wings, steaming plate of pasta, or cheesy pizza. Order one of the many craft beers or sample a delicious homemade dessert (or three). **Known for:** cozy atmosphere; great desserts; delicious international comfort food. *Average main: €9 Plomin 1, Plomin, Labin 052/204–330 Closed Mon.*

### Due Fratelli

$$ | **MEDITERRANEAN** | **FAMILY** | When this family is not catching fish, they are preparing it at their well-regarded folksy restaurant with a cool, grapevine-shaded, family-friendly terrace. The menu offers fresh delicious seafood specialties like grilled squid, mussels *alla buzara*, and a good selection of grilled steaks and poultry dishes. **Known for:** fresh fish; traditional Istrian dishes; relaxed atmosphere. *Average main: €20 Montozi 6, Labin 052/853–577 restaurantduefratelli.com Closed Jan. and Mon. in Oct.–May.*

### ★ Pizzeria Rumore

$ | **ITALIAN** | **FAMILY** | At this popular and highly lauded pizzeria, Neapolitan-style pizzas are made in a gold-glazed brick oven made by Stefano Ferrara Forni in Naples. High-quality ingredients and strict adherence to Napolitana dough preparation—using only Maestro Santucci flour and letting the dough rest for 30 hours before baking—ensure you walk away ready to tell everyone you know about this pizza. **Known for:** traditional Neapolitan-style pizza; charming terrace on piazza with stunning views; fast friendly service. *Average main: €9 Šetalište San Marco bb, Labin 052/686–615 www.facebook.com/PizzeriaRumore Closed Mon.*

### Velo Kafe

$$ | **INTERNATIONAL** | **FAMILY** | Whether it be a coffee, homemade cake, or hand-crafted gelato enjoyed on the shady ground-floor terrace, a gourmet dinner on the first-floor balcony, or hearty Istrian comfort food in the cozy lower-level tavern, it's all to be found at this popular restaurant located in the heart of Old Town Labin on Titov Trg, Labin's main square. The locally inspired menu is extensive and includes specialties like nettle gnocchi with salmon, steak in black-truffle sauce, branzino al forno, and hand-rolled pasta with foraged mushrooms. **Known for:** three floors, three experiences (café, restaurant, and tavern); great location with large outdoor spaces; homemade cakes and gelato. *Average main: €18 Titov Trg 12, Labin 052/852–745 velokafe.com.*

### Vorichi Osteria Mediteraneo

$$ | **MEDITERRANEAN** | **FAMILY** | For those staying in or visiting Labin-Rabac, make sure to reserve a much-desired table at Vorichi Osteria in the little village of Orihi, between Barban and Svetivinčenat, just 22 km (14 miles) from Old Town Labin as you head towards Rovinj. This hidden culinary gem is serving up modern Mediterranean food in an open-air garden setting, with orders for dinner taken by Tamara, the owner, as she joins you for a glass of Malvazija wine or Aperol spritz. **Known for:** relaxed garden setting; freshest local ingredients; incredible wine selection. *Average main: €20 Orihi 58, Orihi, Labin 099/229–4300 vorichi.com Closed Mon. and Nov.–Apr.*

## Hotels

### Adoral Boutique Hotel

$$$ | **HOTEL** | This family-run hotel has an excellent location right across the seafront promenade just a few yards from the water, and its spacious, modern, and well-equipped rooms have balconies overlooking the sea. **Pros:** location right at the seafront; modern, stylish,

and spacious rooms; great for business travelers. **Cons:** only street parking; needs more on-site options for bar or food service; ground-floor rooms have only partial sea views. *Rooms from: €265* *Obala Maršala Tita 2A, Rabac* *052/535–840* *www.adoral-hotel.com* *15 rooms* *Free Breakfast.*

**Floria Glamping Garden**
$$$ | **RESORT** | **FAMILY** | A luxury glamping resort in the peaceful countryside overlooking the sea, Floria offers lush gardens, private pools, Jacuzzis, a large community pool, a wellness center, saunas, a cocktail bar, a gift store, and a restaurant. **Pros:** eco-friendly ethos with sustainable practices; beautiful natural surroundings; 15-minute walk from Old Town (and golf cart transport is also offered). **Cons:** restaurant doesn't offer dinner; parties and groups are not permitted; must drive to beaches. *Rooms from: €275* *Gondolići 2A, Labin* *091/1404–014, 052/404–603* *www.floria-glamping.com* *Closed Jan.* *8 glamping tents, 10 camping pitches* *Free Breakfast.*

**Girandella Valamar Collection Resort**
$$$ | **RESORT** | **FAMILY** | Offering three different sections (family hotel, adults-only hotel, and private villas) with shared facilities, this resort is 100 meters from the most beautiful blue-flag Istrian beaches. **Pros:** outstanding panoramic views of the sea; six restaurants on-site; extensive kids' programs and on-site babysitting. **Cons:** rooms can be small; a large resort that can seem impersonal; lots of kids in all but the adults-only section. *Rooms from: €285* *Girandella 7, Rabac* *052/465–000* *www.valamar.com/en/hotels-rabac/valamar-girandella-resort* *Closed Nov.–Apr.* *173 rooms* *Free Breakfast.*

★ **Hotel Peteani**
$$ | **HOTEL** | On the main road leading up to Labin's Old Town, this stylish boutique hotel offers fresh and playful designer interiors in a beautifully renovated palazzo with thoughtful facilities at the ready, such as saunas, steam baths, bicycles, and one of the absolute best restaurants in town. **Pros:** small and friendly family-owned hotel; free parking; excellent on-site restaurant. **Cons:** some traffic noise in street-facing rooms; short uphill walk to main square; in-house family activities are minimal. *Rooms from: €150* *Aldo Negri 9, Labin* *052/863–404* *www.hotel-peteani.hr* *14 rooms* *Free Breakfast.*

**Terra Residence**
$ | **B&B/INN** | For those desiring an apartment-like stay but with maid service and a shared lounge, dining room, and garden, the sophisticated Terra Residence is for you. **Pros:** romantic interiors; near restaurants and cafés in Old Town; quiet private location. **Cons:** no elevator, only stairs; rooms can seem dark; lots of couples and families make it not ideal for solo travelers. *Rooms from: €95* *Bože Štemberge 2, Labin* *095/911–8420* *www.terra-residence.hr* *8 rooms* *Free Breakfast.*

## Activities

**Diving Rabac**
**DIVING & SNORKELING** | **FAMILY** | This diving center offers shore dives, off-site island and wreck dives, and night diving starting from €20. Diving spots include the protected Girandella Reef and its stunning underwater scenery, the wreck of the *Lina* off the island of Cres, and the famous underwater rock arch. The center also offers diving courses, a two-hour discovery dive, and specialized courses for advanced divers. *Hotel Mimosa, Maslinica 3, Rabac* *098/192–4007* *www.diving.de.*

Chapter 8

# ZAGREB AND INLAND CROATIA



Updated by
Lara Rasin

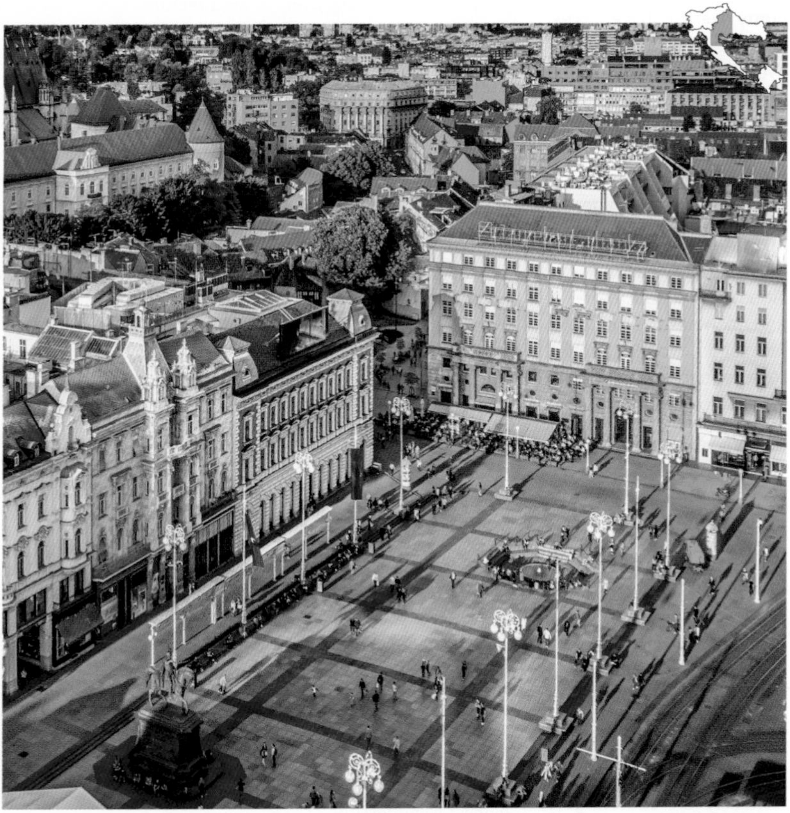

| Sights | Restaurants | Hotels | Shopping | Nightlife |
|---|---|---|---|---|
| ★★★★★ | ★★★★★ | ★★★☆☆ | ★★★★☆ | ★★☆☆☆ |

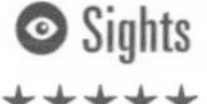

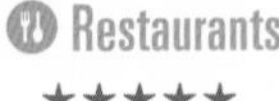

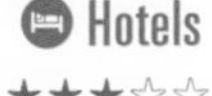

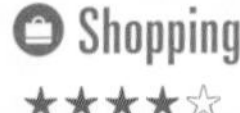

# WELCOME TO ZAGREB AND INLAND CROATIA

## TOP REASONS TO GO

★ **Walkable Zagreb:** With lovely parks, squares, museums, and churches at every corner, exploring the compact Old Town of Croatia's capital is an unforgettable experience.

★ **Sparkling waterfalls and pretty rivers:** Plitvice Lakes National Park, a UNESCO World Heritage site, is one of Croatia's most visited destinations, with more than 16 crystal clear turquoise lakes connected by waterfalls and cascades.

★ **Fairy-tale villages:** Idyllic countryside villages dot inland Croatia, and each has charming farmlands, wooden architecture, and ever-smoking cooking chimneys.

★ **Baroque beauty:** Cities like Čakovec and Varaždin offer some of the most beautiful and well-preserved Baroque architecture in this corner of the continent.

★ **Unique cuisine:** This region is a historical crossroads of cultures, with the cuisine to prove it. Here, you'll get everything from fresh seafood to hearty fare centering on meats and spices.

With the exception of the vast plains of Slavonia that stretch to the east, the rest of the inland region—with Zagreb as its approximate center—can be divided into two parts: north and south. To the north is the hilly castle-rich Krapina-Zagorje region, the smaller often-overlooked Međimurje region, and, just a tram and bus ride from the city center, the hiking trails and ski slopes of Sljeme. To the south is the mountainous route to the coast that includes Karlovac, a regional center; Croatia's most visited national park, Plitvice Lakes; and a second route along the less-traveled banks of the Sava River to Lonjsko Polje Nature Park, one of Europe's largest and best-preserved wetlands.

1 **Zagreb.** Croatia's capital city.

2 **Sljeme.** Mt. Medvednica's peak.

3 **Marija Bistrica.** A Catholic pilgrimage site.

4 **Veliki Tabor.** A medieval hilltop castle dating to the 15th century.

5 **Krapina.** An idyllic village, home to the biggest Neanderthal archeological site in the world.

6 **Trakošćan.** A hilltop castle dating to the 13th century, surrounded by a lake and walking trails.

7 **Varaždin.** A charming Baroque town.

8 **Čakovec and Međimurje.** A beautiful town and small region with pretty landscapes and interesting architecture.

9 **Samobor.** A pretty town known for its 13th-century castle ruins and delicious desserts.

10 **Karlovac.** An industrial city at the crossroads of three major rivers and home to one of Croatia's most popular brews.

11 **Plitvice Lakes National Park.** Croatia's first national park and a stunning collection of lakes and waterfalls.

12 **Sisak.** The biggest city in Sisak-Moslavina County, dotted with walkways, sculptures, and interesting architecture.

13 **Čigoč.** Home to a multitude of migrating storks and the beautiful Lonjsko Poje Nature Park.

14 **Jasenovac.** The site of Croatia's most notorious World War II labor camps.

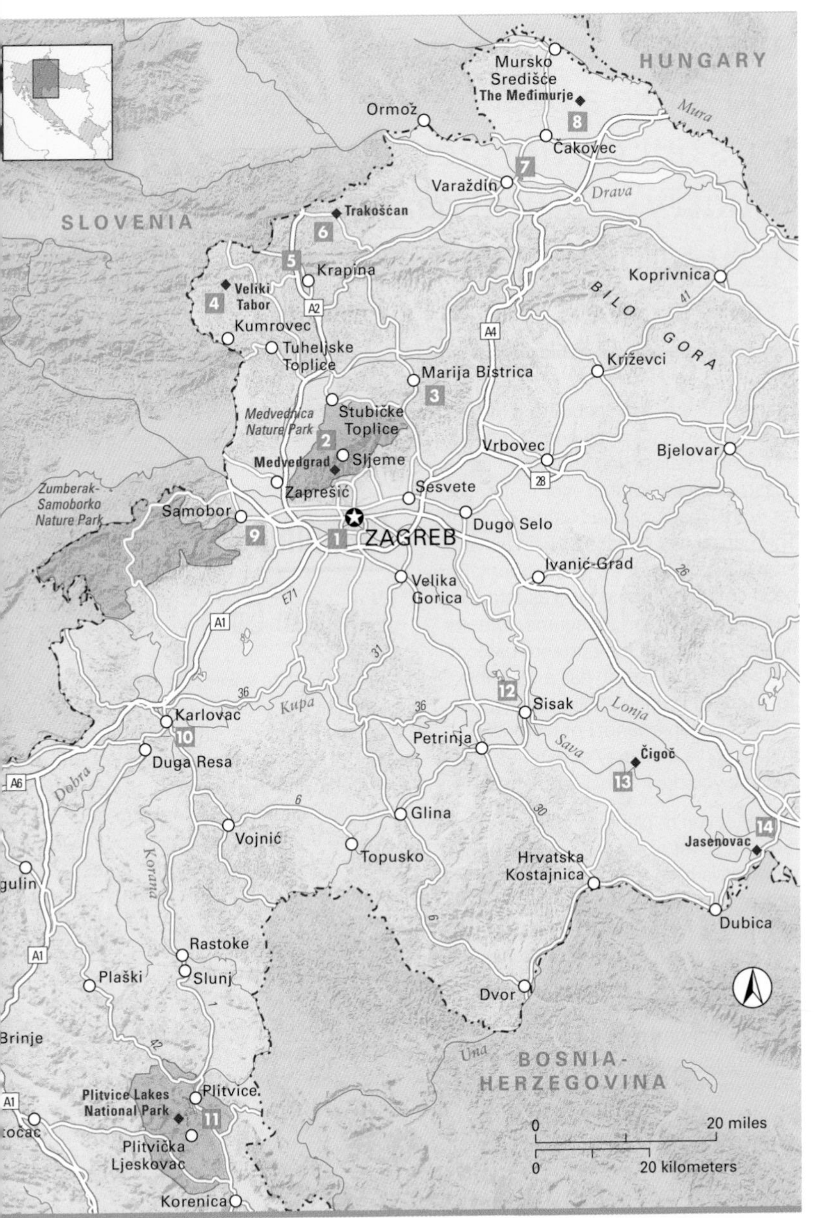
HUNGARY
Mursko Središće
The Međimurje
8
Ormož
Mura
Čakovec
7
Varaždin
Drava
SLOVENIA
Trakošćan
6
5
Krapina
Koprivnica
Veliki Tabor
4
A2
BILO GORA
41
A4
Kumrovec
Tuheljske Toplice
Križevci
Marija Bistrica
3
Medvednica Nature Park
Stubičke Toplice
2
Vrbovec
Bjelovar
Medvedgrad
Sljeme
28
Žumberak-Samoborko Nature Park
Zaprešić
Sesvete
Samobor
ZAGREB
Dugo Selo
9
1
Ivanić-Grad
26
Velika Gorica
E71
A1
31
36
12
Sisak
Karlovac
Kupa
36
Lonja
10
Petrinja
Sava
Čigoč
13
Duga Resa
A6
Dobra
6
Glina
30
14
Vojnić
Jasenovac
Korana
Topusko
Hrvatska Kostajnica
gulin
Dubica
6
Rastoke
A1
Plaški
Slunj
Dvor
1
Brinje
42
Una
BOSNIA-HERZEGOVINA
Plitvice Lakes National Park
Plitvice
A1
11
0
20 miles
ločac
Plitvička Ljeskovac
0
20 kilometers
Korenica

Zagreb has become a full-fledged hot spot for tourism, thanks to its year-round festivals, world-class cuisine, and historical architecture. Travelers who still make a beeline to the coast will miss out on the fact that much of the country's natural beauty and cultural heritage is rooted in places well inland from the sea.

Unless you arrive overland from Slovenia, by boat from Italy, or by one of the air routes that deliver you straight to the coast, chances are that your first encounter with Croatia will be beautiful Zagreb. This capital city, Croatia's business and financial hub, features an eminently European coffee culture as well as attractive parks, squares, and museums. With its historic center on the northern bank of the Sava River, Zagreb has a walkable Old Town full of inviting public spaces, grand architecture in a variety of historical styles, and a rich array of eateries that will lure you down small side streets.

Whether you're planning on hightailing it to the coast or staying inland, spend a few days here to explore the urban capital's historic center and pastoral environs. Even if you've already been lucky enough to explore the region, there are always more secret surprises waiting to be discovered. Zagreb and its bucolic environs have inspired many a mysterious legend—some more frightful, some more fairy-tale—from the Witch of Grič, penned into a seven-part series by renowned author Marija Jurić Zagorka (1873–1957; also Croatia's first female journalist), to the Black Queen, an evil ruler who is supposed to have once lived in medieval Medvedgrad Castle overlooking Zagreb.

## Planning

### When to Go

Zagreb and its environs are well worth a visit at any time of year, with each season bringing a different type of delight. Winter means skiing on Sljeme and enjoying the lively Zagreb Advent Market—continuously voted best or among the best Christmas markets in Europe. Spring kicks off hiking season, with plenty of treks and blooming greenery waiting all throughout the region. Summertime in Zagreb is a special affair, when festivals pop up in almost every neighborhood, from big-name music fests to smaller-scale art and food events. Fall means foggy days made colorful by the foliage waiting to be explored around inland Croatia's hills, one of the prettiest areas being the Žumberak Mountains near Samobor.

No matter the time of year, there's never a shortage of things to do in Zagreb. Music, art, and food festivals take place across the city all year long. Outdoor activities—from hiking on Sljeme and jogging on the Sava riverbanks to kayaking on Jarun Lake—are at your fingertips. Between that and a vibrant nightlife scene, consisting of everything from buzzing clubs to underground live gigs, as well as hard-to-beat museums and cultural outings, this is a city you're not likely to be bored in, even if you're just sipping coffee in a café and people-watching.

## Getting Here and Around

### AIR

Franjo Tuđman Airport Zagreb (ZAG) is actually located in the city of Velika Gorica, 17 km (10 miles) southeast of Zagreb's center. Croatia's busiest airport is relatively small but features several small eateries and a modern design.

There are no direct flights between the United States and Zagreb, but more than 20 airlines, including Croatia Airlines and several major European carriers, connect Zagreb with the rest of the world. Croatia Airlines usually operates at least two direct flights daily to Split (45 minutes), two direct flights daily to Dubrovnik (55 minutes), one direct flight several times a week to Osijek (45 minutes), and one direct flight several times a week to Pula (40 minutes). Internationally, there are usually regular flights to Frankfurt (1 hour 25 minutes), Paris (1 hour 50 minutes), London (2 hours 15 minutes), Barcelona (2 hours 10 minutes), and more.

A shuttle bus runs from the airport to the main bus station, and vice versa. Daily shuttle departures from the bus station generally run between 4 am and 8:30 pm, and from the airport between 6 am and 9 pm. Shuttles generally depart every 30 minutes. A one-way ticket costs €8, and the trip takes 35 minutes. By taxi, Uber, or Bolt expect to pay €15 to €35 from the airport; the trip will be slightly faster and will take you directly to your destination.

**AIRPORT CONTACTS Zagreb International Airport.** (*Franjo Tuđman Airport Zagreb*) ✉ *Rudolfa Fizira 21, Velika Gorica* ☎ *01/456–2170 for general information, 01/456–2229 for lost luggage* 🌐 *www.zagreb-airport.hr/en.*

**AIRPORT TRANSFER CONTACTS Pleso Transfer.** (*Pleso prijevoz*) ✉ *Avenija Marina Držića 4, Zagreb* ☎ *01/633–1982* 🌐 *plesoprijevoz.hr.*

### BUS

Frequent coach services to destinations all over mainland Croatia depart from the capital. The travel time is around 5 to 6 hours for direct lines from Zagreb to Split (and costs €20–€35) and between 9 and 12 hours from Zagreb to Dubrovnik (costing €30–€60). There are also daily international bus lines to Slovenia (Ljubljana), Serbia (Belgrade), Austria (Graz and Vienna), Germany (Munich, Stuttgart, Frankfurt, Dortmund, and Düsseldorf), Italy (Trieste, Verona, and Milan), Switzerland (Zurich), and more. Timetable information is available from the main bus station (Autobusni Kolodvor Zagreb) online or in-person. The station is a 25-minute walk from the main square.

Samobor is an hour-long bus ride from Zagreb; about 50 buses run between Zagreb and Samobor daily. The fare is around €5 each way. Samobor and other cities around Zagreb have smaller bus stations, from which walking to the city centers is usually easy.

About 40 buses run daily between Zagreb and Karlovac in around an hour and for a one-way fare of around €5–€8.

There are around 25 buses from Zagreb to Varaždin daily, with a travel time of around 90 minutes and a one-way ticket cost of €5–€12.

About 20 buses depart daily from Zagreb to Sisak, with a travel time under an hour and an approximate €4–€6 cost for a one-way ticket.

There are around 20 buses from Zagreb to Plitvice Lakes National Park, with a fare of around €10–€16 one-way. Some buses between Zagreb and Split will stop at both entrances to the park.

Zagreb and Marija Bistrica are connected with about 20 buses daily, at a one-way price of €4–€6. Just under 10 buses connect Zagreb with Čakovec, taking around 2 hours and costing about €12–€14 in one direction. There is usually one daily bus in the afternoon that connects Zagreb with Krapina at a fare of around €7–€8.

**CONTACTS Varaždin Bus Station.** ✉ *Zrinskih i Frankopana bb, Varaždin* ☎ *060/300–300.* **Zagreb Bus Station.** (*Autobusni kolodvor Zagreb*) ✉ *Avenija Marina Držića 4, Trnje, Zagreb* ☎ *072/500–400* 🌐 *www.akz.hr/en.*

### CAR

Rental prices vary, and you will probably pay less if you rent from a local company. You can find economy cars from €50 per day, SUVs from €60, and luxury cars from €160. If you drive one-way (say, from Zagreb to Dubrovnik), there is often an additional drop-off charge, but it depends on the type of car and the number of days you are renting. While staying in the capital, you are better off without a car, but if you wish to venture out—for example, to visit the nearby hills of Zagorje or go farther afield to the Međimurje region—a vehicle is helpful unless you want to take a bus or taxi to a different attraction each day.

### TAXI

You can find taxi ranks in front of the bus and train stations, near Trg Bana Jelačića, and often in front of large hotels. Several companies are available, including Eko Taxi, Radio Taxi 1717, and Taxi Cammeo. It is also possible to order a taxi, or ask your hotel to order one for you. All drivers are bound by law to run a meter—but this doesn't necessarily mean they will unless you ask—and the price can vary from €1 for a fixed start fee and from €.66 per kilometer. You can also order Uber and Bolt within the city, as well as to and from the airport. Most drivers do not charge for luggage.

**CONTACTS Eko Taxi.** ✉ *Vodovodna 20A, Zagreb* ☎ *01/549–9474* 🌐 *www.ekotaxi.hr/en.* **Radio Taxi 1717.** ✉ *Božidara Magovca 55, Zagreb* ☎ *1717* 🌐 *taxi1717.hr/en.* **Taxi Cammeo.** ✉ *Damira Tomljanovića Gavrana 13, Zagreb* ☎ *01/121–2211* 🌐 *cammeo.hr/en.*

### TRAIN

Zagreb's main train station (known as Glavni Kolodvor) lies in the Lower Town, a 10-minute walk south from Trg Bana Jelačića. There are regular international trains to and from Budapest (Hungary), Belgrade (Serbia), Ljubljana and Maribor (Slovenia), Munich (Germany), Vienna (Austria), Venice (Italy), Zürich (Switzerland), and beyond via easy connecting routes. From Zagreb there are multiple trains daily to Split in Dalmatia (6–9 hours for €15–€16, one-way) and to Osijek in Slavonia (5–6 hours for €15–€18). Trains also connect Zagreb to nearer cities such as Karlovac (10–20 trains daily, under one hour for €5–€7, one-way), Sisak (10–20 trains daily, under one hour for €4–€6), Varaždin (one 2½-hour train daily for around €8), and Čakovec (one 2½-hour train daily for around €8); however, these are less popular than buses with travelers and sometimes less reliable.

**CONTACTS Čakovec Train Station.** ✉ *Kolodvorska 2, Cakovec* ☎ *060/333–444 for information hotline.* **Croatian Railways.** (*Hrvatske željeznice*) ✉ *Strojarska 11, Donji Grad* ☎ *060/333–444* 🌐 *www.hzpp.hr/en.* **Karlovac Train Station.** ✉ *Vilima Reinera 3, Karlovac* ☎ *060/333–444 for information hotline.* **Varaždin Train Station.** ✉ *Kolodvorska 17, Varaždin* ☎ *060/333–444 for information hotline.* **Zagreb Train Station.** ✉ *Trg Kralja Tomislava 12, Donji Grad* ☎ *060/333–444 for information hotline.*

## Restaurants

Due to Zagreb's proximity to the coast (under two hours at the closest point), fresh Adriatic fish fill up the city's marketplaces—and restaurants—daily. There are seafood restaurants in the other large inland towns, too, though the offerings might be a bit less varied. Each inland region has its own delicious specialties, with many focused on roasted or fried meats accompanied by fresh salad and vegetable side dishes. For example, Zagorje is famous for *patka s mlincima* (duck with *mlinci*, thin pieces of flatbread soaked in oil), while the Plitvice Lakes area is known for meaty dishes with wild game.

Various types of cuisine converge in Croatia's heartland. The influence of Austria to the northwest and Hungary to the northeast is evident in the form of hearty soups and stews like *varivo* (a thick broth with vegetables) and *gulaš* (the Croatian version of Hungarian goulash). Many restaurants also serve Italian-influenced pasta and pizza with added Croatian twists like Istrian truffles or Slavonian sausage. Other options include Turkish-influenced grilled meats such as *ćevapi* (seasoned minced meat links, often served with raw onions and pepper relish called *ajvar*), which are generally lower in price than more elaborate main courses. Don't miss out on rich appetizers and desserts either. Doubling as both are the Zagorje region's famous *štrukli* (baked dough filled and topped with cheese)—served either baked or boiled, and salty or sweet. *Međimurska gibanica* (a triple-layer apple, sweet cheese, and poppy seed cake) is a must-try in Međimurje. Chocolate-, jam-, and sweet-cheese–filled *palačinke* (crepes) are on nearly every menu in the region, too. If you head to Varaždin or a smaller town, prices will drop somewhat.

## Hotels

In Zagreb hotels, rates of €150 or much more for a double room are not uncommon, though there are chic hostels and apartments for rent that are comfortable, modern, and more budget-friendly. Smaller towns and the countryside, as a whole, do still offer cheaper options than the capital, with affordable private rooms and agritourism-style accommodations aplenty.

⇨ *Restaurant and hotel reviews have been shortened. For full information, visit Fodors.com. Restaurant prices are the average cost of a main course at dinner or, if dinner is not served, at lunch. Hotel prices are the lowest cost of a standard double room in high season.*

**What It Costs in Euros (€)**

| $ | $$ | $$$ | $$$$ |
|---|---|---|---|
| **RESTAURANTS** | | | |
| under €15 | €15–€23 | €24–€32 | over €32 |
| **HOTELS** | | | |
| under €150 | €150–€250 | €251–€350 | over €350 |

## Tours

**Limitless Balkan**
**PRIVATE GUIDES** | This company organizes one-day and multiday private tours out of Zagreb (and other places in Croatia and the region), offering personalized or preset itineraries. Routes available include guided tours of Zagreb, trips to Slovenia and the Croatian coast, and tours of mainland Croatia to destinations including Plitvice Lakes, Varaždin, and the castles of northern Croatia. Private transfers (without a tour) between cities are also possible if you want to skip public transport or a car rental to get from the capital to your next destination. ☎ *098/873–488* 🌐 *www.limitlessbalkan.com* 🎫 *From*

*€100 for guided tours of Zagreb; from €350 for trips to other areas.*

### ★ Secret Zagreb

**GUIDED TOURS** | A tour with this company is a unique way to get to know Zagreb. Your tour guide will be founder Iva Silla, a passionate local who will show you around Zagreb while often engaging in games as you go, or a member of her awesome team. Tours include Sleeping Dragon and Other Legends, Badass Women of Zagreb, and the seasonal Zagreb Christmas Carol. Tours usually last two hours and can be organized for small private groups. "Quests" are also available in the form of self-guided or expert-guided tours, where movement around the city is spurred by riddle-solving. ✉ *Zagreb* ☎ *097/673–8738* 🌐 *secret-zagreb.com* 🎫 *Tours from €47 per 1–4-person group; guided "Quests" from €55 per 1–3-person group.*

### Segway City Tour Zagreb

**GUIDED TOURS** | For a state-of-the-art Segway tour experience year-round, try the 130-minute Zagreb All Around tour and ride through the main sights in the city center, including more than 20 sights, 7 parks, and fun facts along the way. Another option, the three-hour Leisure Tour, adds a detour to the Mirogoj Cemetery along with all of the Old Town's must-sees. ✉ *Zagreb* ☎ *095/903–4227* 🌐 *segwaycitytourzagreb.com* 🎫 *From €55.*

### ZET City Tours

**BUS TOURS** | The Zagreb Electric Tram Company (ZET), in cooperation with the Zagreb Tourist Board, provides open-top buses operating along three routes (red, green, and yellow) throughout the city. The red line (1-hour tour) operates within the narrow city center, with six stops along the route. The green line (1½-hour tour) includes the best-known green oases of Zagreb, with seven stops along the route. The yellow line (1½-hour tour) includes New Zagreb (city neighborhoods south of the Sava River), the Mirogoj Cemetery, and more. Tickets (a single ticket covers all three routes) are valid for 24 hours, which allows time to hop on and off and see most of Zagreb's most famous landmarks. The departure point is from Bakačeva on Kaptol. The red line departs at 10 am, noon, 2 pm, and 4 pm; the green line at noon and 3 pm; and the yellow line at 12:30 pm and 2:45 pm. Tickets are free for children under seven. You can purchase tickets from the tourist information office on the main square. ✉ *Zagreb* ☎ *01/365–1555* 🌐 *www.zet.hr/tourist-services/sightseeing-tour-buses/597* 🎫 *€9.29.*

## Visitor Information

**CONTACTS Čakovec Tourist Board.** ✉ *Kralja Tomislava 1, Cakovec* ☎ *040/313–319* 🌐 *www.visitcakovec.com.* **Croatian National Tourist Board.** ✉ *Iblerov Trg 10/IV, Zagreb* 🌐 *croatia.hr/en-gb.* **Karlovac Tourist Board.** ✉ *Petra Zrinskog 3, Karlovac* ☎ *047/615–115* 🌐 *visitkarlovac.hr.* **Krapina Tourist Board.** ✉ *Magistratska 28, Krapina* ☎ *049/371–330* 🌐 *www.tzg-krapina.hr/en.* **Marija Bistrica Tourist Board.** ✉ *Zagrebačka bb, Marija Bistrica* ☎ *049/468–380* 🌐 *www.tz-marija-bistrica.hr/en.* **Plitvice Lakes National Park Information Office.** ✉ *Trg Svetog Jurja 19, Plitvicka Jezera* ☎ *053/776–798 for tourist board office, 053/751–014 for information office* 🌐 *www.discoverplitvice.com.* **Samobor Tourist Board.** ✉ *Trg Kralja Tomislava 5, Samobor* ☎ *01/336–0004* 🌐 *www.samobor.hr/en.* **Sisak–Moslavina County Tourist Board.** ✉ *Rimska 28/II, Sisak* ☎ *044/540–163* 🌐 *turizam-smz.hr/en.* **Varaždin Tourist Board.** ✉ *Ivana Padovca 3, Varaždin* ☎ *042/210–987* 🌐 *visitvarazdin.hr/en.* **Zagreb Tourist Board.** ✉ *Trg Bana Jelačića, Donji Grad* ☎ *01/481–4051, 01/481–4052, 01/481–4054* 🌐 *www.infozagreb.hr.*

# Zagreb

The capital of Croatia, Zagreb (population around 800,000) draws visitors to its historic and walkable city center, museums, and a culinary scene that is one of the country's best. Modern Zagreb is divided into 17 city districts that span almost 700 square km (270 square miles). Each has a number of neat attractions; for example, Novi Zagreb encompasses Bundek Park and the Museum of Contemporary Art, Trešnjevka is home to Jarun Lake and the Technical Museum Nikola Tesla, and Podsljeme includes Mirogoj, often called the most beautiful cemetery in Europe. Zagreb's historic city center is divided into two distinct districts: Gornji Grad (Upper Town) and Donji Grad (Lower Town). Gornji Grad is made up of winding cobbled streets and terra-cotta rooftops, among which are some of the city's most famous sites such as St. Mark's Church and Square, the Strossmayer Promenade, and the Stone Gate. Donji Grad is where you'll find some of the city's most important 19th-century cultural institutions, including the National Theater and a number of museums, all in a walkable (or tram-able) distance. Anywhere in the city, you'll find top-notch restaurants and cafés.

The city straddles the north and south banks of the Sava River and is nestled below Mt. Medvednica. The area has a long history: excavations have not yet yielded signs of any Stone Age settlements, but archaeologists have found serpentine tools that point to the region first being an area of transit. Archaeological finds have confirmed that the area was definitely settled from the Neolithic Age on, being home to the intriguing Vučedol and Vinkovci cultures of the Bronze Age. The largest Neanderthal settlement in the world is located in Krapina; today, you can learn all about it at the on-site museum.

During the first millennium BC, the region saw a number of different inhabitants. First came the Hallstatt culture (proto-Illyrian tribes) and the La Tène culture (proto-Celtic tribes). The ancient Roman government captured much of present-day Croatia in the second century BC. Fourteen km (8½ miles) from the Zagreb center, you can visit Andautonia, an old Roman town that left well-preserved ruins. Slavic tribes descended into the area from the north, inhabiting it starting around the 7th century AD. In AD 925, King Tomislav became Croatia's first monarch.

One of Central Europe's oldest towns, the area of Zagreb was first documented as an official diocese in 1094. Two separate but adjacent towns once stood on the area of the city: Gradec (today the Upper Town) and Kaptol (today the Lower Town). Gradec was designated a free royal city by Croatian-Hungarian King Béla IV following Tatar attacks in 1242.

The capital and ruling seat of Croatia changed throughout the centuries. Zagreb was first mentioned as being the capital in 1557, but Varaždin served as the main city from 1767 to 1776 until a fire moved the government seat back to Zagreb. Kaptol and Gradec were put under a single city administration in 1850, officially becoming the city of Zagreb. The legendary Orient Express flourished during the late 1800s and early 1900s, when Zagreb was a main stop for passengers on the Paris-Venice-Istanbul line. Beautiful public buildings began popping up across the city, including the National Theater, the university, and various museums. Designed in a grand style and interspersed by wide tree-lined boulevards, parks, and gardens, these old buildings adorn the entire city center today.

Throughout the 20th century, Zagreb saw increasing industrialization coupled with urban expansion, and the high-rise suburb of Novi Zagreb was constructed south of the Sava. Today, Novi Zagreb is a bustling residential area home to Bundek Park and the Museum of Contemporary Art. From 1990 to 2000, Zagreb was, like the rest of the country, suffering and then recovering from the War of Independence. That also included a transition period from the communist government of the Socialist Federal Republic of Yugoslavia to a free-market economy and the parliamentary constitutional government of the Republic of Croatia.

Over the past couple decades, Zagreb has undergone an economic boom, highlighted by Croatia's entry into the European Union in 2013. Today, Zagreb is home to many international companies and an exciting local entrepreneurial scene.

### GETTING HERE AND AROUND

After arriving via any one of the numerous flights from Germany (Frankfurt, Munich), United Kingdom (London), France (Paris), Austria (Vienna), Hungary (Budapest), or elsewhere, the best way to get into the city is by taxi, Bolt, Uber, or the economical airport shuttle.

In Zagreb, an extensive network of city buses and trams—almost exclusively trams within the town center—runs 24 hours a day, with less frequent night service (which also offers fewer routes) starting around 11:50 pm and lasting until 4 am. Tickets for €.53 (€.80 if purchased on boarding) last in any direction for 30 minutes; €.93 (€1.33 if purchased on boarding) for 60 minutes in any direction; €1.33 (€1.99 if purchased on boarding) for 90 minutes in any direction; and €1.99 (same price if purchased before or upon boarding) for a night-service ride. Like night-service and 30- to 90-minute tickets, one-day tickets (€3.98) can be bought ahead at Tisak kiosks, iNovine kiosks, and ZET stores, or on-board from the driver. One-day tickets are valid until 4 am the next morning for an unlimited number of tram and bus rides during the day or night. Multiday tickets are available exclusively at ZET stores (three-day tickets are €9.29, seven-day tickets €19.91). As an alternative, you can buy the Zagreb Card for €20; this covers public transport within the city limits for 24 hours (for 72 hours, the cost is €26) and offers free entry to various museums and venues.

After you board the bus or tram, you must immediately purchase a ticket from the driver if you don't have one already and validate your ticket with a timestamp (little yellow machines in the first and last cars of each tram). If you are caught without a valid ticket, you will be fined a minimum of €66.36, which can be reduced by 50% if you pay on the spot.

# Gornji Grad (Upper Town)

The romantic hilltop area of Gornji Grad dates back to medieval times and is undoubtedly one of the loveliest parts of Zagreb, with plenty of top sights and museums. Because of ongoing renovations following a series of earthquakes in the area in 2020, St. Catherine's Church and Atelier Meštrović are closed, with no reopening date at the time of this writing. The interiors of St. Mark's Church and the Zagreb Cathedral are closed for the same reason, but they are included because their exteriors are particularly notable.

## Sights

★ **Croatian Museum of Naïve Art** (*Hrvatski muzej naivne umjetnosti*)

**ART MUSEUM** | The Naïve school of painting dates back to the 1930s, and the museum features more than 1,900 works of peasant artists who were largely self-taught. The Naïve movement in Croatia began in the village of Hlebine in Koprivnica-Križevci County, and canvases by one of its founders, the highly esteemed Ivan Generalić (1914–1992), dominate here, though there are also paintings, drawings, sculptures, and prints by other noted members of the movement, plus a section devoted to foreigners working along similar lines. The museum is on the second floor of the Raffay Palace. ✉ *Ćirilometodska 3, Gornji Grad* ☎ *01/485–1911* 🌐 *hmnu.hr* 🎟 *€5.50* ⏱ *Closed Sun.*

**Dolac Market**

**MARKET** | Farmers from the countryside set up stalls here daily, though the market is busiest on Saturday and Sunday mornings. On the upper level, fresh fruit and vegetables, along with flowers, traditional souvenirs, and artisan goods from honey to fresh juices are displayed on an open-air piazza. Goods are sold under the protective shade of oversized umbrellas with a distinctive red color, known as *Šestinski kišobrani* (much smaller versions form part of the traditional garb of Zagreb's Šestine region). Dairy products and meats are sold in an indoor market below. **TIP→ When you get tired of shopping, pop into one of the stylish eateries right by the market, such as Salo or Broom44, for delicious pastries, brunch, and some of the best coffee in town.** ✉ *Dolac 9, Gornji Grad* 🌐 *www.trznice-zg.hr.*

**Kamenita Vrata** (*Stone Gate*)

**RELIGIOUS BUILDING** | The original 13th-century city walls had four gates, of which only Kamenita vrata remains. Deep inside the dark passageway, locals stop to pray before a small shrine adorned with flickering candles. In 1731 a devastating fire consumed all the wooden elements of the gate. Legend says that only a painting of the Virgin and Child, which was found in the ashes, remained remarkably undamaged. The gate has since become a pilgrimage site, as can be seen from the numerous stone plaques reading *Hvala Majko Božja* (Thank you, Mother of God). ✉ *Kamenita 1, Gornji Grad* 🎟 *Free.*

**Klovićevi Dvori Gallery**

**ART MUSEUM** | Located off St. Catherine's Square, Croatia's largest art museum opened in 1982. International, local, classical, and modern art shows are regularly held in its three-story exhibition space, and concerts often take place in the gallery's beautiful atrium. **TIP→ Some of the city's best street art is hidden just behind the building as well.** ✉ *Jezuitski Trg 4, Gornji Grad* ☎ *01/485–1926* 🌐 *gkd.hr/en* 🎟 *From €4 per exhibition* ⏱ *Closed Mon.*

## The Zagreb Card

Sold both online and in several venues around town, the Zagreb Card (🌐 *zagrebcard.com*) offers unlimited travel on public transportation in the city and free entry to five museums (the Chocolate Museum, City Museum, Museum of Broken Relationships, Museum of Contemporary Art, and Technical Museum Nikola Tesla), as well as the Zagreb Zoo. It's valid for 24 or 72 hours (from the date and time stamped on the card) and costs €20 or €26.

**Lotrščak Tower** (*Kula Lotrščak*)

**VIEWPOINT** | Formerly the entrance to the fortified medieval town of Gradec, Kula Lotrščak now houses a multilevel gallery with occasional exhibits of contemporary art. Each day at noon, a small cannon is fired from the top of the tower in memory of the times when it was used to warn of the possibility of an Ottoman attack. You can climb the tower partway via a spiral wooden staircase for a look into the gallery rooms (which occupy several floors), or you can ascend all the way to the observation deck for splendid views of Zagreb and its environs. You can also take the 216-foot Zagreb Funicular (the world's shortest) straight to the tower. ✉ *Strossmayerovo Šetalište 9, Gornji Grad* ☎ *01/485–1926* 🌐 *gkd.hr/en/strongIotrscak-tower-strong* 🎟 *€3* ⏱ *Closed Mon.*

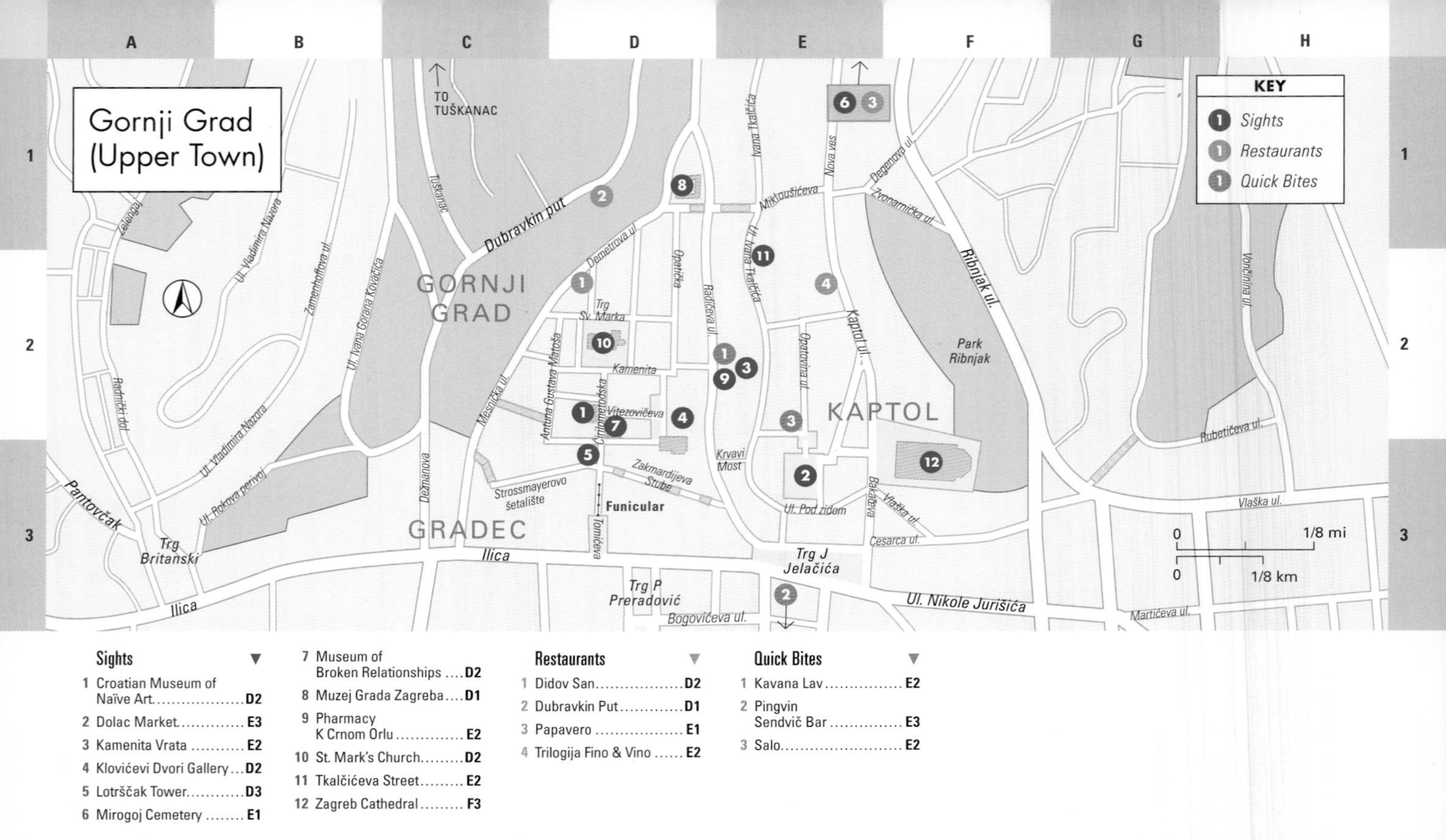


**Sights**

1 Croatian Museum of Naïve Art ........ D2
2 Dolac Market ........ E3
3 Kamenita Vrata ........ E2
4 Klovićevi Dvori Gallery ... D2
5 Lotrščak Tower ........ D3
6 Mirogoj Cemetery ........ E1
7 Museum of Broken Relationships .... D2
8 Muzej Grada Zagreba .... D1
9 Pharmacy K Crnom Orlu ........ E2
10 St. Mark's Church ........ D2
11 Tkalčićeva Street ........ E2
12 Zagreb Cathedral ........ F3

**Restaurants**

1 Didov San ........ D2
2 Dubravkin Put ........ D1
3 Papavero ........ E1
4 Trilogija Fino & Vino ...... E2

**Quick Bites**

1 Kavana Lav ........ E2
2 Pingvin Sendvič Bar ........ E3
3 Salo ........ E2

**Mirogoj Cemetery**

**CEMETERY** | Designed by architect Hermann Bollé and opened in 1872, Zagreb's most celebrated cemetery is set on a hillside north of downtown and features an imposing entrance: a long massive brick wall topped by a row of green cupolas. This parklike cemetery, marked by paths lined with horse chestnut trees and black marble graves, is the final resting place for those of many creeds, from Roman Catholic and Serbian Orthodox to Jewish and Muslim. This satisfying, if somber, outing can be had by catching Bus 106 or 226 on Kaptol, in front of the Zagreb Cathedral, and riding it about 10 minutes to the fifth stop, Arkade. On November 1, the cemetery is lit up by thousands of red candles for All Saints' Day, when people honor their relatives, as well as famous figures buried there such as Herman Bollé himself, renowned author August Šenoa (1838–1881), and basketball great Dražen Petrović (1964–1993). ✉ *Aleja Hermanna Bollea 27, Zagreb* 🌐 *www.gradskagroblja.hr/en* 🎫 *Free.*

★ **Museum of Broken Relationships** (*Muzej prekinutih veza*)

**OTHER MUSEUM** | The first museum of its kind in the world displays objects connected to love stories that didn't work out. The entire exhibition is made up of personal belongings donated by people from around the world who endured a failed relationship, and each exhibit is accompanied by a brief text, explaining the connection between the object and the relationship. Subtly illustrating the tragicomedy that is love, it is now one of Zagreb's most visited museums, and the collection has toured numerous locations in Asia, Africa, the United States, and Europe. The museum's collection is ever-expanding, and exhibits change regularly (only 15% of the collection is displayed in a year), which keeps visitors coming back for new stories. ✉ *Ćirilometodska 2, Gornji Grad* ☎ *01/485–1021* 🌐 *www.brokenships.com* 🎫 *€7.*

## Zagreb Funicular

If you're walking along Ilica from the main square, you might wonder about the best route up the hill to Lotrščak Tower and beyond to St. Mark's Church. Well, you can save yourself the steep hike by catching the 216-foot funicular. This cable railway runs every 10 minutes, 6:30 am to 10 pm, from short Tomićeva Ulica (just off Ilica) just a few hundred yards up the hillside. The one-way cost is €.66, and you can buy the ticket on-board. Lasting 64 seconds, it's the world's shortest funicular.

**Muzej Grada Zagreba** (*Zagreb City Museum*)

**HISTORY MUSEUM** | Well worth a visit for anyone interested in urban design, this museum traces the city's most important historical, economic, political, social, and cultural events from medieval times to the present day. Exhibits include detailed scale models of how the city has evolved, as well as sections devoted to the old trade guilds, domestic life, and sacred art. The museum also hosts a range of cool temporary exhibits year-round. ✉ *Opatička 20, Gornji Grad* ☎ *01/485–1361* 🌐 *www.mgz.hr/en* 🎫 *€5* 🕒 *Closed Mon.*

**Pharmacy K Crnom Orlu**

**STORE/MALL** | Zagreb's oldest pharmacy, K Crnom Orlu (meaning "to the black eagle") sits between the Stone Gate and St. Mark's Square. It dates back to 1355 and operates to this day, continuing to specialize in house-made tinctures. Local rumors say that pharmacist Nicolo Alighieri, great-grandson of Dante Alighieri, worked here while he lived in Zagreb. ✉ *Kamenita 9, Gornji Grad.*

The Museum of Broken Relationships contains artifacts donated from people around the world that tell the story of their failed love affairs.

★ **St. Mark's Church** (*Crkva svetog Marka*)
**CHURCH** | Nestled among the regal buildings of the Croatian parliament, the original church building was erected in the 13th century and was once the parish church of Gradec. The Baroque bell tower was added in the 17th century, and the steeply pitched roof—decorated in brilliant multicolor tiles arranged to depict the coats of arms of Zagreb on the right and the Kingdom of Croatia, Dalmatia, and Slavonia on the left—was added during reconstruction in the 19th century. It underwent another reconstruction in the first half of the 20th century. At that time, renowned painter Jozo Kljaković painted its walls, while the altar was decorated with works of famous sculptor Ivan Meštrović. **TIP→ At the time of this writing, the church's interior was closed for renovation, but the exterior is well worth a look.** ✉ *Trg Svetog Marka 5, Gornji Grad* ☎ *01/485–1611* 🌐 *zupa-svmarkaev.hr.*

**Tkalčićeva Street** (*Tkalčićeva*)
**STREET** | This street was once a stream until it was built over, but few people know that the water still flows beneath it. Today Tkalčićeva is a charming well-maintained pedestrian zone lined with 19th-century town houses. Many of these have been converted into popular cafés, bars, and restaurants at street level, attracting a huge cross section of locals and tourists from morning until late at night. ✉ *Ivana Tkalčića, Gornji Grad.*

★ **Zagreb Cathedral** (*Zagrebačka katedrala*)
**CHURCH** | Dedicated to the Assumption of Mary and to the kings St. Stephen and St. Ladislaus, this cathedral was built on the site of a former 12th-century cathedral destroyed by the Tatars in 1242. The present structure was constructed between the 13th and 16th centuries. The striking neo-Gothic facade was added by architect Hermann Bollé following the earthquake of 1880, its twin steeples being the identifying feature of the city's skyline. Behind the impressive main altar are crypts of Zagreb's archbishops and Croatian national heroes. The interior is imposing and inspires silent reflection.

Don't neglect the north wall, which bears an inscription of the Ten Commandments in 12th-century Glagolitic script. The cathedral's face is ever-changing, as its towers are being reconstructed again following the earthquake that hit Zagreb in 2020. **TIP→ At the time of this writing, the interior is closed for renovations.** *Kaptol 31, Gornji Grad 01/481–4727 www.zg-nadbiskupija.hr Free.*

## Restaurants

**Didov San**

**$$ | MEDITERRANEAN** | A two-minute walk north of St. Mark's Church, you'll find a fairly rare sight: a rustic *konoba* in Zagreb. Didov San (meaning Grandpa's Dream) offers fare usually more typical of the coast, such as grilled squid and *pašticada*, a Dalmatian beef stew. **Known for:** a taste of Dalmatia in Zagreb; filling portions; lengthy varied menu. *Average main: €19 Mletačka 11, Gornji Grad 091/484–2061 konoba-didovsan.com.*

**★ Dubravkin Put**

**$$$ | MEDITERRANEAN** | Nestled in a verdant dale in Tuškanac Park, a 15-minute walk from the center, in a low-rise building that might be mistaken for a ranch-style house, this prestigious fish restaurant specializes in creative Mediterranean fare. The dining room is light and airy, with candlelit tables, a wooden floor, potted plants, and colorful abstract art. **Known for:** quiet romantic location; amazing scratch-made desserts; high-end waitstaff and sommelier service. *Average main: €28 Dubravkin Put 2, Gornji Grad 01/483–4975 www.dubravkin-put.com Closed Sun.*

**Papavero**

**$ | PIZZA | FAMILY** | This restaurant with a rustic-style interior and a terrace is the love child of married dynamic duo Ana, from Slavonia, and Pasquale, from Italy. They use fresh ingredients from Italy and Croatia to make amazing pizza doughs and exciting topping combinations. **Known for:** great pizza with sourdough options available; peaceful location near Mt. Medvednica; pet-friendly policy. *Average main: €14 Mlinovi 85A, Gornji Grad 091/628–0008 papavero.hr Closed Mon.*

**Trilogija Fino & Vino**

**$$ | MEDITERRANEAN** | Superb food and friendly professional staff are hallmarks of this quaint unpretentious restaurant. The menu changes frequently, depending on the seasons and what's fresh at the morning market, but you can expect a variety of Mediterranean main courses, as well as a selection of wines that includes all of Croatia's best varieties. **Known for:** tapas with local ingredients; 4-minute walk north of Zagreb Cathedral; great wine list for food pairings. *Average main: €24 Kaptol 10, Gornji Grad 01/484–5336 www.facebook.com/TrilogijaFinoiVinoKaptol.*

## Coffee and Quick Bites

**★ Kavana Lav**

**$ | CAFÉ** | Located in a 13th-century palace that is a protected cultural landmark, this café will make you feel as if you were sitting in an art gallery or perhaps the living room of a wealthy art-collecting uncle. Just up the hill (first right) from the Stone Gate, it is a perfect place to take a load off after the steep climb into Gornji Grad before heading on to seeing the parliament, Museum of Broken Relationships, and St. Mark's Church. If you're lucky, the weather will be fine and you'll find a seat on the charming outside terrace, perched atop the passage leading down to the Stone Gate. **Known for:** delicious cookies and cakes; good coffee and cocktails; charming stone terrace. *Average main: €6 Opatička 2, Gornji Grad 099/222–2075 kavanalav.com.*

**Pingvin Sendvič Bar**

**$ | SANDWICHES** | If you are looking for a quick and inexpensive lunch on the go, consider Pingvin, the city's first sandwich bar and extra popular as a post-party late-night snack joint. This stand, just a few minutes' walk from Trg Bana Jelačića, offers simple fare like grilled chicken sandwiches. **Known for:** basic super-affordable bites; beloved Zagreb spot since 1987; veggie burgers. 💲 *Average main: €6* ✉ *Nikole Tesle 7, Donji Grad* ☎ *01/481–1446* 🌐 *www.facebook.com/pingvin1987sb.*

### ★ Salo

**$ | CAFÉ** | White walls and light wooden furniture set off cool decor like big glass jars of flour in this small airy space on the north end of Dolac Market. With a name meaning "fat" (pork lard, specifically), this café-bakery serves up delicious freshly baked pastries such as *salenjaci* (a type of Croatian sweet croissant) using traditional Croatian baking ingredients with a modern twist, as well as some sweet and salty light brunch options and acclaimed Cogito-brand coffee. **Known for:** small tapas-like portions; arrive early for best selections (no reservations); ingredients sourced from small family-owned farms in Croatia. 💲 *Average main: €6* ✉ *Opatovina 13, Gornji Grad* 🌐 *www.instagram.com/salo_dolac* ⏲ *Closed Sun.–Tues. No dinner.*

## Nightlife

### Oliver Twist Pub

**PUBS** | Although in good weather practically all the patrons are seated out front (a prime position for people-watching on Tkalčićeva), inside is an English-style pub whose walls, on the upper floor, are decorated with memorabilia associated with different novels by Charles Dickens. It's a run-of-the-mill pub where the cool decor and prime location can outshine the rather basic menu options and service. ✉ *Ivana Tkalčića 60, Gornji Grad* ☎ *01/481–2206* 🌐 *www.facebook.com/olivertwistpubzagreb.*

## Performing Arts

### ★ The Courtyards (*Dvorišta*)

**MUSIC FESTIVALS** | At this annual local-favorite summer event that usually lasts a few weeks in July, some of Zagreb's most beautiful—and most secret—courtyards open their doors with music for guests. They include private historical villas, educational institutions such as the Institute of History, and government buildings. Each courtyard features live music (generally acoustic, jazz, or soft rock), finger food, fun drinks, and perfect vibes of laid-back fun. ✉ *Gornji Grad* 🌐 *www.facebook.com/dvorista.in.*

### Kaptol Boutique Cinema and Bar

**FILM** | Part of the Centar Kaptol shopping complex, this cinema and bar is wedged in an area with a serene parklike atmosphere a 10-minute walk north of the cathedral. Most foreign films (including those from the United States) are shown in their original language with Croatian subtitles. The cinema features a handful of showing rooms that are each uniquely designed, and grabbing a coffee or drink in the establishment's designer bar before or after your movie is a must. ✉ *Nova Ves 17, Gornji Grad* ☎ *01/639–6720* 🌐 *kaptolcinema.hr.*

### Strossventura

**ARTS FESTIVALS** | Embark on a journey toward the Strossmayer Promenade, next to the Lotrščak Tower, and you will see one of Zagreb's best entertainment projects. Stross, as the walkway is known, is arguably the most spirited spot in town, thanks to everything from abundant summer festivals to the much-awarded Advent in Zagreb offering concerts, exhibitions, and art workshops. There are also great wine, beer, and food stands year-round. ✉ *Strossmayerovo Šetalište, Gornji Grad* 🌐 *www.infozagreb.hr.*

### Tuškanac

**FESTIVALS** | Despite its location in a forested hilly area, Tuškanac is part of Zagreb, and over the summer, the 20th-century

Tkalčićeva Street is a pedestrian-only area of Zagreb that appeals to visitors and locals alike.

outdoor stage in this park transforms into an open-air movie theater airing a variety of flicks. It's also home to a number of festivals, including the fun Pop-Up Summer Garden, centered around cool seating, food, and drink stands. Tuškanac features some historical vacation villas once used by the city's aristocracy, and its great walking path amid the greenery is worth a stroll at any time. ✉ *Dubravkin Put bb, Gornji Grad* 🌐 *www.infozagreb.hr.*

## Shopping

★ **Bornstein Wine Bar** (*Vinoteka Bornstein*)
**WINE/SPIRITS** | Housed in a tastefully arranged, vaulted brick cellar, this shop and bar stocks a wide range of quality Croatian wines, olive oils, and truffle products. Wine can be enjoyed on-site as well. ✉ *Kaptol 19, Gornji Grad* ☎ *01/481–2361* 🌐 *www.bornstein.hr/en.*

# Donji Grad (Lower Town)

The Lower Town includes a succession of squares and parks laid out in a horseshoe shape (hence its nickname, the Green Horseshoe), all encircled by many of the city's stunning public buildings and cultural institutions and dotted by restaurants, bars, and stores. This part of the area's urban plan, which follows a grid pattern, was drawn up by architect Milan Lenuci (1849–1924). Open-air festivals of all sorts—from food to music and art—are common here. The most famous park in the Green Horseshoe is Zrinjevac, a grassy space with plane trees and a music pavilion that often hosts open-air concerts. North of the horseshoe are the bustling Ilica and the city's heart, Trg Bana Jelačića, the main square.

At the time of this writing, the Museum of Arts and Crafts and the Strossmayer Gallery of Old Masters were closed for renovations following the 2020 earthquakes, with no set reopening date. Check ahead if you want to visit them.

Zagreb's stately Croatian National Theater dates from 1895.

## Sights

**Archaeological Museum** (*Arheološki muzej*)

**HISTORY MUSEUM** | Museum exhibits here range all the way from prehistoric times to the Middle Ages. Pride of place is given to the Vučedol Dove, a three-legged ceramic dove found near Vukovar in Slavonia dating back to the 4th millennium BC, and a piece of linen bearing the longest known text in ancient Etruscan writing. The courtyard features a collection of stone relics from Roman times. The museum also runs the Archaeological Park Andautonia, an ancient Roman town with well-preserved ruins located in the modern-day village of Šćitarjevo, a 20-minute drive from Zagreb center. At the time of this writing, the museum sometimes offers temporary exhibitions on its first floor. The permanent collection and the rest of the museum building are currently closed for renovations, with no reopening date announced. **TIP→ Call ahead if you plan to visit to see what's happening.** ✉ *Trg Nikole Šubića Zrinskog 19, Donji Grad* ☎ *01/487–3000* 🌐 *www.amz.hr/en* *Admission varies by exhibition* ⏲ *Closed Sun. and Mon.*

**Ban Jelačić Square** (*Trg bana Jelačića*)

**PLAZA/SQUARE** | Buildings lining the city's main square date from 1827 onward and include several fine examples of Secessionist architecture. The centerpiece is an equestrian statue of Ban Josip Jelačić, the first Croatian viceroy, erected in 1866. Originally facing north toward Hungary, against which Jelačić waged war as a commander in the Austrian Imperial Army, the statue was dismantled after World War II by the communist government, only to be reinstalled in 1990, this time facing south. The square also features the Manduševac fountain, located to the east. ✉ *Donji Grad* ✣ *Between Ilica to the west, Praška to the south, and Jurišićeva to the east.*

**Botanički Vrt** (*Botanical Garden*)

**GARDEN** | Founded in 1889, Zagreb's Botanical Garden includes an arboretum with a regularly used exhibition space, a small artificial lake, and an ornamental bridge. Today, the garden has more than 5,000 species of plants and is run by the prestigious Faculty of Science of the University of Zagreb. **TIP→ Bring cash, as credit cards aren't accepted.** ✉ *Marulićev Trg 9A, Donji Grad* ☎ *01/489–8066* 🌐 *botanickivrt.biol.pmf.hr/en* 🎫 *€2* ⏲ *Closed Dec.–Mar.*

★ **Croatian National Theater in Zagreb** (*Hrvatsko narodno kazalište*)
**PERFORMANCE VENUE** | The building dates from 1895, when it was designed by the Viennese firm Hellmer and Fellner as part of preparations for a state visit by Emperor Franz Josef. In front of the theater, set deep in a round concrete basin, is Ivan Meštrović's eerily lifelike sculpture *Zdenac Života* (*Fountain of Life*) from 1912, which depicts four naked couples writhing uncomfortably in each other's arms around a small pool of water while one lone likewise naked gentleman stares meditatively into the pool. The only way to see the impressive stately interior of the theater is to attend a performance from its impressive show repertoire. Don your best clothes as the locals do and enjoy. ✉ *Trg Republike Hrvatske 15, Donji Grad* ☎ *01/488–8415* 🌐 *www.hnk.hr/en.*

**Maksimir Park**
**CITY PARK** | For a peaceful stroll in Zagreb's biggest (and southeastern Europe's oldest) public park, hop on a tram and head to Maksimir. A short ride east of the center of Zagreb (10 minutes on Tram 11 or 12 from Trg Bana Jelačića or 15 minutes on Tram 4 or 7 from the train station), this 44½-acre expanse of vine-covered forests and artificial lakes was a groundbreaker when it opened back in 1794. After getting off the tram, you walk forward a bit and enter on the left, through a gate opposite the city's main soccer stadium, aptly named Stadion Maksimir. A long wide promenade flanked by benches leads to Bellevue Pavilion (1843), perched atop a small hill and featuring a café. Do check out the Echo Pavilion (Paviljon jeka), built in the late 19th century in honor of the Greek nymph Echo. Stand in the middle and you can hear the whispers of anyone standing within the pavilion, as if they were right next to you. To your right along the way are some small lakes and, beyond, the city's modest zoo, Zoološki vrt Grada Zagreb, where admission is €4. To your left is a playground. One restaurant is located in the zoo, and two others are in the park outside it. ✉ *Maksimirski Perivoj 1, Zagreb* ☎ *01/232–0460* 🌐 *park-maksimir.hr* 🎫 *Free.*

**Mimara Museum** (*Muzej Mimara*)
**ART MUSEUM** | In a huge gray building, this vast private collection, including paintings, sculptures, ceramics, textiles, and rugs, was donated by Ante Topić Mimara (1898–1987), a Croatian who spent many years abroad where he made his fortune, supposedly as a merchant. On display are canvases attributed to such old masters as Raphael, Rembrandt, and Rubens, as well as more modern works by the likes of Manet, Degas, and Renoir and ancient artifacts including Egyptian glassware and Chinese porcelain. **TIP→ At the time of this writing, the museum was closed but hopes to reopen by early 2025 after renovations. Check before you go.** ✉ *Rooseveltov Trg 5, Donji Grad* ☎ *01/482–8100* 🌐 *www.mimara.hr.*

**Museum of Contemporary Art** (*Muzej suvremene umjetnosti*)
**ART MUSEUM** | Displaying works created since 1950 by Croatian and foreign artists, this museum is well worth a visit for anyone interested in modern art—the vast collection includes paintings, sculptures, graphic design, films, and videos. It lies outside the city center, south of the Sava River in Novi Zagreb. To get here, take Tram 6 (toward Sopot) or Tram 14 (toward Zapruđe) from the main square; journey time is approximately 30 minutes. ✉ *Avenija Dubrovnik 17, Novi Zagreb* ☎ *01/605–2700* 🌐 *www.msu.hr* 🎫 *€4–€10, depending on exhibitions* ⏲ *Closed Mon.*

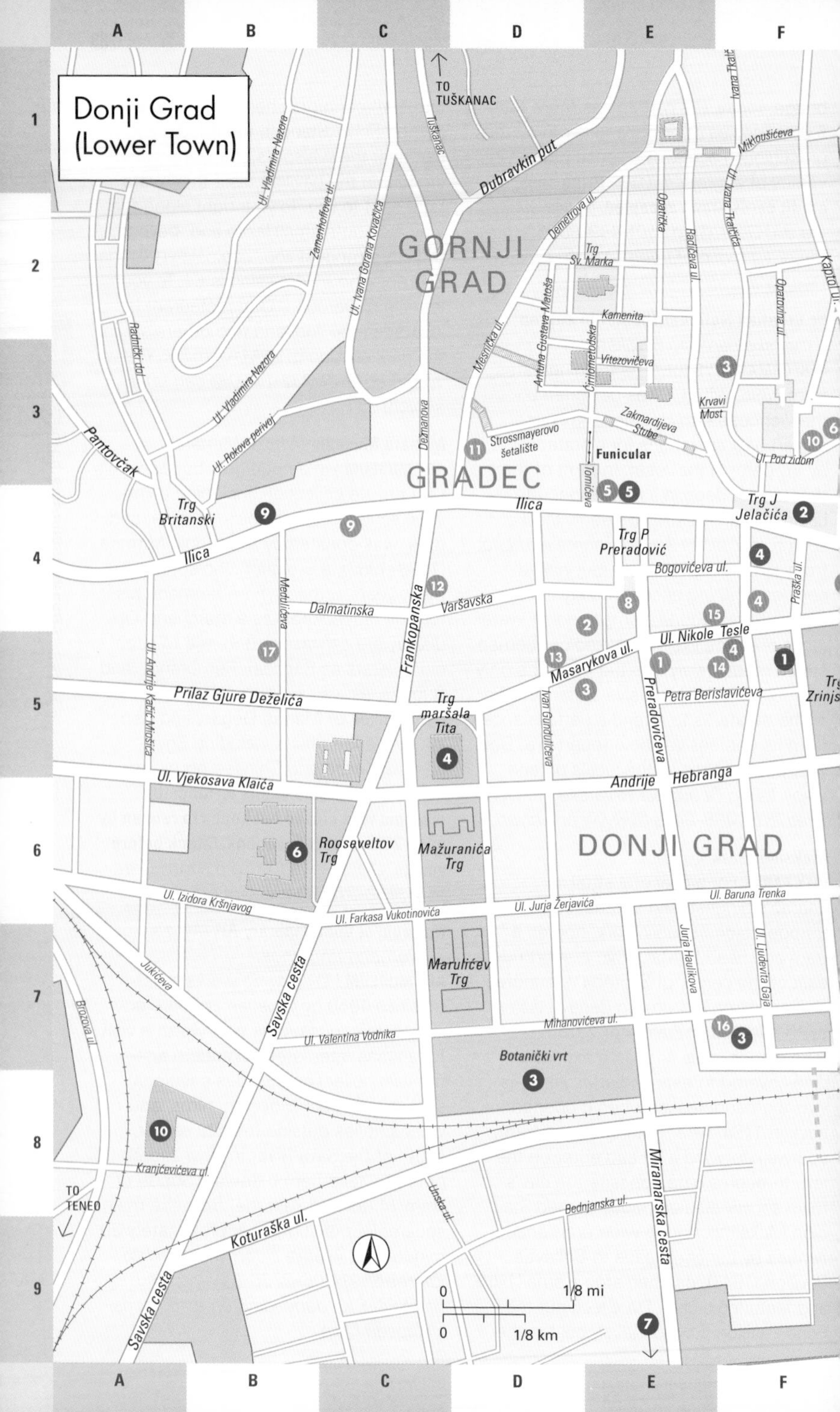

Donji Grad (Lower Town)
A
B
C
D
E
F
1
2
3
4
5
6
7
8
9
TO TUŠKANAC
Tuškanac
Dubravkin put
Ul. Vladimira Nazora
Zamenhoffova ul.
Ul. Ivana Gorana Kovačića
GORNJI GRAD
Demetrova ul.
Opatička
Radićeva ul.
Ul. Ivana Tkalčića
Miklošićeva
Trg Sv. Marka
Kamenita
Vitezovićeva
Mesnička ul.
Antuna Gustava Matoša
Ćirilometodska
Opatovina ul.
Kaptol ul.
Radnički dol
Ul. Vladimira Nazora
Ul. Rokova perivoj
Pantovčak
Dežmanova
Strossmayerovo šetalište
Zakmardijeva Stube
Krvavi Most
Funicular
Tomićeva
Ul. Pod zidom
GRADEC
Trg Britanski
Ilica
Ilica
Trg J Jelačića
Trg P Preradović
Bogovićeva ul.
Praška ul.
Medulićeva
Dalmatinska
Varšavska
Frankopanska
Ul. Nikole Tesle
Masarykova ul.
Petra Berislavićeva
Trg Zrinjs
Ul. Andrije Kačić Miošića
Prilaz Gjure Deželića
Trg maršala Tita
Ivan Gundulićeva
Preradovićeva
Ul. Vjekosava Klaića
Andrije Hebranga
Roosveltov Trg
Mažuranića Trg
DONJI GRAD
Ul. Izidora Kršnjavog
Ul. Farkasa Vukotinovića
Ul. Jurja Žerjavića
Ul. Baruna Trenka
Jukićeva
Savska cesta
Marulićev Trg
Jurja Haulikova
Ul. Ljudevita Gaja
Brozova ul.
Ul. Valentina Vodnika
Mihanovićeva ul.
Botanički vrt
Kranjčevićeva ul.
Miramarska cesta
TO TENEO
Unska ul.
Bednjanska ul.
Koturaška ul.
Savska cesta
0
1/8 mi
0
1/8 km

## Sights

1 Archaeological Museum ........ F5
2 Ban Jelačić Square ..... F4
3 Botanički Vrt ............ D8
4 Croatian National Theatre in Zagreb ........ C5
5 Maksimir Park ............. I5
6 Mimara Museum ....... B6
7 Museum of Contemporary Art ........ E9
8 Museum of Hangovers ............ H3
9 Museum of Illusions .... B4
10 Technical Museum Nikola Tesla ............ A8

## Restaurants

1 Arepera Maracay ........ E5
2 Basta .................... D4
3 Beštija .................... D5
4 Boban .................... F4
5 El Toro .................... I5
6 Gostionica Ficlek ........ F3
7 Kai Street Food Bar ...... F4
8 Namaste Bistro .......... E4
9 Pivnica Medvedgrad ............ C4
10 Pod Zidom Bistro ........ F3
11 Stari Fijaker .............. D3
12 Submarine ................ C4
13 Takenoko ................ D5
14 Theatrium by Filho ....... F5
15 Vinodol .................... E4
16 Zinfandel's Restaurant ................ F7
17 Zrno Bio Bistro .......... B5

## Quick Bites

1 Amélie .................... G3
2 Bread Club 2 ............ G3
3 The Cookie Factory ...... F3
4 Good Food ................ F5
5 Vincek .................... E4

## Hotels

1 Best Western Premier Hotel Astoria ........... G6
2 DoubleTree by Hilton Zagreb .............. I7
3 Esplanade Zagreb ....... F7
4 Hotel Dubrovnik .......... F4
5 Hotel Jägerhorn ......... E4
6 Hotel Vila Tina ............. I3
7 Le Premier ................. I5
8 Sheraton Zagreb Hotel .............. I6

**Museum of Hangovers** (*Musej Mamurluka*)
**OTHER MUSEUM** | Zagreb is home to several unique first-in-the-world museums, including this exhibition featuring more than 50 real-life stories related to drunkenness, submitted by people from all over the world, along with associated objects. Each visitor has the chance to win a free ticket by hitting a bull's-eye dartboard while wearing beer goggles. Most exhibits are comical, but some are educational and others are cautionary tales. Beer or wine can be purchased at the entrance to enjoy as you stroll through. ✉ *Vlaška 35, Donji Grad* ☎ *098/819–747* 🌐 *www.muzejmamurluka.com* 🎫 *€8.*

**Museum of Illusions** (*Musej iluzija*)
**OTHER MUSEUM** | **FAMILY** | In 2015, Roko Živković and Tomislav Pamuković founded this innovative museum of perception in Zagreb, and thanks to popular demand it has expanded to more than 40 locations in 25 countries across 4 continents. Including an antigravity room, mirror room, and many silly optical illusion exhibits, this museum will leave you laughing, curious about how visual perception works—and maybe even a bit dizzy. This is a fun visit for families as well. ✉ *Ilica 72, Donji Grad* ☎ *095/878–7107* 🌐 *muzejiluzija.com/en/home* 🎫 *€9.*

**Technical Museum Nikola Tesla** (*Tehnički muzej Nikola Tesla*)
**SCIENCE MUSEUM** | **FAMILY** | Situated within an industrial building, this museum is guaranteed to appeal to both children and adults interested in science. Try to visit in the afternoon on a weekday or in the late morning on the weekend, when a series of guided visits are offered. The highlight here is the demonstration of some of Nikola Tesla's inventions, scheduled weekdays at 3:30 pm and weekends at 11:30 am, but there's also the tour of a lifelike reconstruction of a coal mine at 3 pm on weekdays and 11 am on weekends. That's not to mention all the vehicles on display, as well as a fascinating historical exhibit of firefighting equipment with trucks, ladders, and hoses aplenty. The museum is in the Trešnjevka neighborhood. ✉ *Savska Cesta 18, Donji Grad* ☎ *01/484–4050* 🌐 *tmnt.hr* 🎫 *€4* 🕒 *Closed Mon.*

## Restaurants

**Arepera Maracay**
**$** | **SOUTH AMERICAN** | Founded by Ricardo Luque, singer in Zagreb-based Latin-jazz group Cubismo, this is a great spot to grab a bite of authentic Venezuelan street food—just choose among filling options for these cornmeal favorites, such as chicken, beef, pork, and cheese, and various sauces. Named after the founder's birthplace, Maracay, the restaurant is a six-minute walk southwest of the main square and features a small but cheerful interior with colorful tiles and murals. **Known for:** first and only Venezuelan restaurant in Croatia; affordable and delicious arepas, juices, and sides; food can tend to be salty. $ *Average main: €7* ✉ *Preradovićeva 9, Donji Grad* ☎ *01/234–5229* 🌐 *areperamaracay.com* 🕒 *Closed Mon.*

**Basta**
**$** | **PIZZA** | A five-minute walk from the main square, this lively restaurant is tucked into a pretty courtyard that's almost always full as local pizza lovers flock in for quality Neapolitan pies. The interior is stylish modern rustic, with wooden elements and furniture. **Known for:** certificate from the True Neapolitan Pizza Association of Italy; variety of pizza flavors for all palates; Neapolitan sandwiches, salads, and a long drinks list round out the offerings. $ *Average main: €13* ✉ *Varšavska 5, Donji Grad* ☎ *095/707–0003* 🌐 *basta.bar/zagreb.*

**Beštija**
**$$** | **EUROPEAN** | Carnivores, pescatarians, and vegetarians seeking tasty modern fare that draws from a range of cuisines will all find something to delight at

this stylishly decorated restaurant in a peaceful courtyard tucked away from the buzzing city center. Enjoy eating outside during the summer, and remember to leave room for something from the small-but-very-sweet dessert menu. **Known for:** fresh ingredients from Dolac Market; excellent value for the price; house-made juices and desserts. *Average main: €20 Masarykova 11/1, Donji Grad 091/922–8861 bistro-bestija.com.*

**Boban**

$$ | **EUROPEAN** | Just down the street from the Hotel Dubrovnik, Boban serves food not only at its street-level bar and dining room but also in its restaurant in the large vaulted cellar space below. Specializing in pasta dishes, it is extremely popular with locals, so be prepared to line up for a table or call ahead for a reservation. **Known for:** Italian influence in many dishes; house-made pastas, desserts, and bread; lively outdoor terrace for dining and people-watching. *Average main: €22 Gajeva 9, Donji Grad 01/481–1549 www.boban.hr.*

**El Toro**

$$ | **FUSION** | Under the expert guidance of chef Mario Mihelj, El Toro serves up delicious Latin American and Asian fusion fare. Choices from a variety of steak and roasted meats to seafood and veggie dishes are served in the restaurant's romantically low-lit interior, which blends matte black decor with wooden elements. **Known for:** good sushi menu; live music and DJ entertainment some nights; chic atmosphere in a quieter neighborhood. *Average main: €20 Fra Filipa Grabovca 1, Zagreb 099/613–2926 eltoro.hr Closed Mon.*

**★ Gostionica Ficlek**

$$ | **EUROPEAN** | A creation of the brilliant minds at Pod Zidom, this restaurant between the Zagreb Cathedral and Dolac Market is the city's first to serve only authentic Zagreb fare prepared in traditional ways (think pasta with cabbage, Zagreb-style meat cuts, and soups just like Croatian grandmas make them). The interior design is modern but also features old-school touches like classic masonry heater tiles. **Known for:** some seasonal specialties; terrace seats have views of cathedral; ingredients sourced from neighboring Dolac Market. *Average main: €20 Pod Zidom 5, Donji Grad 099/495–8909 www.facebook.com/gostionicaficlek.*

**Kai Street Food Bar**

$ | **FUSION** | Delicious fusion street food that draws on Asian and South American influences is the name of Kai's game. With a quaint but well-decorated interior space and a menu that is short and sweet, featuring five or six dishes at any given time, this is an intimate spot to enjoy creative takes on buns, noodles, sandwiches, and more. **Known for:** interior with handpainted murals; local craft beers, wines, and rakijas; friendly service. *Average main: €12 Jurišićeva 2a, Donji Grad www.facebook.com/kaistreetfoodbar Closed Sun. and Mon.*

**Namaste Bistro**

$ | **INDIAN** | The masters behind the delicious dishes at Namaste are a group of chefs hailing from various regions of India. Their love for the food is reflected in an extensive varied menu with masala dosas and other vegan options, as well as meaty choices such as duck vindaloo. **Known for:** authentic Indian cuisine, including delicious paneer options; owned by Indian family living in Croatia for 15 years; sister restaurant in quieter neighborhood southwest of center. *Average main: €11 Preradovićeva 2, Donji Grad 01/626–4458 www.namaste-bistro.com.*

**Pivnica Medvedgrad**

$ | **EASTERN EUROPEAN** | Best known for excellent beers brewed on the premises, all three of the Pivnica Medvedgrad locations serve up roast meats, goulash, and beans and sausage, accompanied by a range of salads. The Ilica location and its cavernous beer hall—replete with long wooden tables, high leather-backed chairs, and wood-beamed ceilings—is about a 10-minute walk west from the main square. **Known for:** Croatia's biggest craft brewery; generous rich meals; frequent live music nights at Ilica location. *Average main: €10 Ilica 49, Donji Grad 01/484–6922 pivovara-medved-grad.hr/en/pubs.*

### ★ Pod Zidom Bistro

**$$ | EASTERN EUROPEAN** | Wedged between the cathedral and the Dolac Market, this jazzy good-value bistro offers a creative take on classic Croatian dishes, making the most of the fresh ingredients at its doorstep. Keeping it close to traditional values, the emphasis is on meat and fish dishes but varies according to what is in season and available. **Known for:** farm-to-table fruits and vegetables; fresh organic meat; excellent selection of Croatian wines. *Average main: €23 Pod Zidom 5, Donji Grad 099/325–3600 podzidom.hr.*

### Stari Fijaker

**$ | EASTERN EUROPEAN** | This old-fashioned restaurant with vaulted ceilings, wood-paneled walls, and crisp white table linens was the first one in Croatia to earn the certificate of Croatian Authentic Cuisine. The menu features carefully presented traditional Croatian dishes not easy to find at other restaurants—especially those native to the Zagreb region—such as *Za gorska juha* (Zagorje-style potato soup with ham and mushrooms), *pečena teletina* (roast veal), and *punjene paprike* (stuffed peppers). **Known for:** popular spot, so reservations are recommended; eight-minute walk down Ilica from the main square; excellent service showcasing Croatian hospitality. *Average main: €12 Mesnička 6, Donji Grad 01/483–3829 starifijaker.hr.*

### Submarine

**$ | BURGER | FAMILY** | Popular demand has helped this fast-growing chain expand to 11 locations around Zagreb, including this one on Frankopanska near the main square and two other more central spots on Tkalčićeva and Bogovićeva. The restaurant offers a range of all-natural burgers with locally procured toppings, including tasty vegetarian options as well. **Known for:** great truffle fries; good value for fast-casual fare; voted Croatia's best restaurant in 2023 (by users of popular food-delivery app Wolt). *Average main: €11 Frankopanska 11, Donji Grad 01/483–1500 submarineburger.com.*

### Takenoko

**$$$ | JAPANESE** | The menu of this chic restaurant offers everything from sushi—both traditional Japanese rolls and American-style varieties—and teriyaki to wok dishes and specialties that merge Asian and European cuisine. Black chairs, black place mats, and cherry-tone wood floors set the scene in one of the glittery glass-walled spaces in this Lower Town hot spot. **Known for:** upscale vibe; long drink list, including sakes; some of the best sushi in town. *Average main: €32 Masarykova 22, Donji Grad 01/646–3385 www.takenoko.hr Closed Sun.*

### Theatrium by Filho

**$$ | EUROPEAN** | Sitting five minutes south of the main square by foot, this airy modern restaurant sits prettily in the atrium of Zagreb's Youth Theater. Chef Filip Horvat, who trained in Michelin-starred establishments, serves up various European cuisines with healthy ingredients, from Mediterranean seafood dishes to Austrian meat plates to pastas, all with his own creative touches. **Known for:** sounds of theater performances add to cool ambience; attractively presented food; fresh organic ingredients from Dolac Market. *Average main: €18 Nikole Tesle 7, Donji Grad 099/584–4652 theatrium.hr/en Closed Sun.*

### ★ Vinodol

**$$ | EASTERN EUROPEAN** | Both locals and tourists flock to this elegant spot a few blocks southwest of the main square when they hanker for excellent traditional meaty fare such as veal and lamb, pork with plum sauce, or, for starters (or dessert), melt-in-your-mouth štrukli. Enjoy all this in a spacious shaded courtyard or inside under brick-vaulted ceilings with low lighting that create the impression of a wine cellar even though you're not in a cellar at all. **Known for:** attractively plated dishes; Croatian art enhances decor; site has continuously been a restaurant since the 1940s. *Average main: €20* ✉ *Nikole Tesle 10, Donji Grad* ☎ *01/481–1427* 🌐 *vinodol-zg.hr.*

### ★ Zinfandel's Restaurant

$$$$ | **EUROPEAN** | Just inside the luxurious Esplanade Hotel, once a stop on the Orient Express, lies one of Zagreb's most elegant dining destinations, known for its formal yet comfortable atmosphere. Order from the tasting menu, where a sommelier selects wines to perfectly complement each dish, or experience the best of Croatian and international cuisine à la carte, with choices from Istrian truffle pasta to American-style steak. **Known for:** more than 200 wines available; weekly Sunday brunch event; first-class head chef Ana Grgić Tomić. *Average main: €45* ✉ *Antuna Mihanovića 1, Donji Grad* ☎ *01/456–6644* 🌐 *zinfandels.hr.*

### Zrno Bio Bistro

$ | **VEGETARIAN** | If you want to strengthen the body and nourish the spirit with seasonal organic fruits and vegetables in a vegan haven, walk a few blocks west from the main square to Zrno, which offers fresh vegetables, tofu, seitan, warm sourdough bread, biodynamic coffee, tea, juice, smoothies, and shakes. All ingredients are delivered each day directly from Croatia's first 100% organic farm of the same name. **Known for:** organic wine and beer choices from Croatia; variety of superfood drinks; cheerful and casual vegan environment. *Average main: €13* ✉ *Medulićeva 20, Donji Grad* ☎ *01/484–7540* 🌐 *zrnobiobistro.hr* ⏲ *Closed Sun.*

## Coffee and Quick Bites

### Amélie

$ | **CAFÉ** | For a cake and coffee experience that the French namesake of this cute little café would be proud of, pop into Amélie just down the hill from the Zagreb Cathedral. The wooden tables and cozy white interior give the place a charming, even slightly rustic feel, and the surprisingly varied selection of delectable cakes and pies will release all your caloric inhibitions. **Known for:** homemade everything; unique cakes for those with a sweet tooth; tasty quiches for those who prefer savory treats. *Average main: €6* ✉ *Vlaška 6, Donji Grad* ☎ *01/558–3360* 🌐 *www.slasticeamelie.com.*

### Bread Club 2

$ | **BAKERY** | Though it's conveniently nestled behind the Zagreb Cathedral, you'll still be able to smell the aromas of fresh-baked bread and warm pastries at this bakery from down the street. Pop in to see what's on the menu for the day, and then grab a seat on the outdoor terrace—there are heaters during the winter—and people-watch. **Known for:** house-made sourdough pastries and bread; one of five locations around town; internationally oriented selection. *Average main: €6* ✉ *Vlaška 27, Donji Grad* ☎ *01/655–1293* 🌐 *www.breadclub.eu.*

### The Cookie Factory

$ | **CAFÉ** | With an extensive selection of cookies, cupcakes, brownies, and cakes, this bakery and café with indoor and outdoor seating offers desserts both European-style and of the North American variety. Full-size cakes are available for sale and custom creations can be ordered as well, in case you're in town celebrating. **Known for:** cookies and brownies à la mode; buzzing atmosphere on Tkalčićeva Street; tailor-made cakes and dessert boxes. *Average main: €3* ✉ *Ivana Tkalčića 21, Donji Grad* ☎ *091/276–0016* 🌐 *www.cookiefactory.hr.*

**Good Food**

$ | **FAST FOOD** | **FAMILY** | At one of the city's few fast-food places, you can select from a range of decent salads and bowls, prepared right in front of you, as well as other light refreshing fare such as ciabatta sandwiches and vegetarian tortillas. Of course, this minichain (three locations in Zagreb) also serves the standbys of burgers and fries, in case you're hungering for more carbs and protein. **Known for:** quick bites in the center of town; healthier alternative to other fast-food joints; vegetarian options in salads, wraps, and burgers. *Average main: €8* *Nikole Tesle 7, Donji Grad* *goodfood.hr.*

★ **Vincek**

$ | **BAKERY** | **FAMILY** | Founded in 1977 by the Vincek family, this sweets shop regularly draws crowds lining up out the door and down Ilica Street. Dozens of ice cream flavors and sundaes are available, along with delicious cakes and desserts to be savored at the limited indoor tables in the slightly dark interior or, more often (tables fill up), taken out. **Known for:** first spot in town to offer the decadent creamy Zagreb kremšnita dessert; among city's best places for ice cream in summer; eight locations, including a gluten-free one near Ilica. *Average main: €4* *Ilica 18, Donji Grad* *01/483–3612* *www.vincek.com.hr* *Closed Sun.*

## Hotels

**Best Western Premier Hotel Astoria**

$$ | **HOTEL** | Less than five minutes by foot from the train station and 10 minutes from downtown, this hotel offers bright modern rooms with partly marble bathrooms that meet the chain's requirements of its Premier category. **Pros:** good location on a quiet side street between train station and main square; luxurious bathrooms with excellent amenities; free parking. **Cons:** smallish rooms; no fitness facilities or pool; shades that open when you enter the room may take some by surprise. *Rooms from: €170* *Petrinjska 71, Donji Grad* *01/480–8900* *www.bestwestern.com* *102 rooms* *Free Breakfast.*

**DoubleTree by Hilton Zagreb**

$ | **HOTEL** | A 12-minute drive from the historic city center, this hotel featuring comfortable carpeted rooms with dark wooden furniture (some rooms also have amazing city views) is well-suited to business travelers looking to stay in Zagreb's main business district near Radnička Cesta. **Pros:** excellent spa with Finnish sauna; spacious fitness center; pool with a panoramic view of the city and Mt. Medvednica. **Cons:** located on one of the city's busiest streets; chain ambience may not appeal to all; parking garage can be confusing. *Rooms from: €130* *Grada Vukovara 269A, Donji Grad* *01/600–1900* *www.hilton.com/en/hotels/zagcrdi-doubletree-zagreb* *152 rooms* *Free Breakfast.*

★ **Esplanade Zagreb**

$$ | **HOTEL** | Diagonally across from the train station, this beautiful hotel built in 1925 for travelers on the original Orient Express has retained and enhanced its elegance and luxury thanks to regular renovations. **Pros:** fascinating history combined with modern amenities like a spa; still the best hotel in Zagreb; terrace with lovely city views. **Cons:** pricey for the city; smallish lobby; formal atmosphere can be a bit stuffy. *Rooms from: €210* *Mihanovićeva 1, Donji Grad* *01/456–6666* *esplanade.hr* *208 rooms* *Free Breakfast.*

**Hotel Dubrovnik**

$$ | **HOTEL** | Claiming the most central location in the city, just off Trg Bana Jelačića, this hotel has been popular with business travelers and tourists since opening back in 1929. **Pros:** fitness center; some rooms offer amazing views of the Old Town; most rooms and bathrooms are spacious. **Cons:** noise can reach some rooms, especially during festivals; location outshines the hotel itself; somewhat outdated decor. *Rooms*

*from: €150 ✉ Gajeva 1, Donji Grad ☎ 01/486–3512 🌐 www.hotel-dubrovnik.hr ⇨ 214 rooms 🍴 Free Breakfast.*

**Hotel Jägerhorn**

$$ | **HOTEL** | Located at the far end of a shop-filled courtyard off Zagreb's busiest shopping street and just a minute's walk from Trg Bana Jelačića, this quaint hotel is the oldest in Zagreb and a perfect base for exploring the city. **Pros:** hotel courtyard serves as pretty stairway between Upper and Lower Town; staff goes the extra mile; historic café with great coffee. **Cons:** small, so often fully booked; basic interior means this isn't the trendiest hotel in town; no spa, gym, or pool. *$ Rooms from: €170 ✉ Ilica 14, Donji Grad ☎ 01/483–3877 🌐 www.hotel-jagerhorn.hr ⇨ 18 rooms 🍴 Free Breakfast.*

**Hotel Vila Tina**

$ | **HOTEL** | If you prefer a quiet environment and don't mind the somewhat tacky look of the lobby (pseudo-classical statuettes, anyone?), then this family-run hotel may be just for you. **Pros:** public transport options for efficient transport to center; near Maksimir Park and hiking opportunities in the hills; cozier than big hotels downtown. **Cons:** a 90-minute hike from the main square; few amenities in line with three-star level; outmoded decor. *$ Rooms from: €140 ✉ Bukovačka Cesta 213, Donji Grad ☎ 01/244–5204 🌐 hotelvilatina.hr ⇨ 14 rooms 🍴 Free Breakfast.*

**Le Premier**

$$ | **HOTEL** | Located on the doorstep of the Meštrović Pavilion, this boutique hotel in a former 20th-century palace features elegantly decorated modern rooms, a lobby with a crystal chandelier, and a spa. **Pros:** soothing white, beige, and light gold room decor; buffet breakfast served in inner courtyard; 10 minutes from main square and a minute from Meštrović Pavilion. **Cons:** proximity to tram tracks can cause noise and vibration in some rooms; parking not included; can be pricey. *$ Rooms from: €200 ✉ Kralja Držislava 5, Donji Grad ☎ 01/440–0880 🌐 www.lepremier.hr ⇨ 59 rooms 🍴 Free Breakfast.*

**Sheraton Zagreb Hotel**

$ | **HOTEL** | Located on a small side street in a somewhat nondescript part of the Lower Town, the six-story Sheraton has comfortable, classically decorated rooms favored by business travelers. **Pros:** quieter neighborhood well-connected to center with trams; good indoor pool, spa, gym, and sauna; tasty and varied breakfast. **Cons:** 15-minute walk from the main square; interior could use a more modern renovation; little sense of place. *$ Rooms from: €140 ✉ Kneza Borne 2, Donji Grad ☎ 01/455–3535 🌐 www.marriott.com/en-us/hotels/zagsi-sheraton-zagreb-hotel/overview ⇨ 335 rooms 🍴 Free Breakfast.*

## Nightlife

**Alcatraz**

**BARS** | With a lively combination of Zagreb students, partiers, and people looking for a chill night out, plus great drinks on the cheaper side and good music (usually rock), this bar can be a bit of a tight squeeze but is a favorite among both locals and visitors seeking to make friends in the city. *✉ Preradovićeva 12, Donji Grad ☎ 091/521–3703 🌐 www.night-club-alcatraz.com.*

**Aquarius Klub**

**DANCE CLUBS** | A chilled out coffee-and-cocktails café during the day, Aquarius becomes one of Zagreb's top clubs for dancing, especially for disco and techno music, by night. Works on display from local artists and designers complement the musical program. The club overlooks the beach at Malo Jezero, the smaller of the two interconnected lakes comprising Lake Jarun, 5 km (3 miles) from the city center. *✉ Aleja Matija Ljubeka 19, Jarun ☎ 091/364–0234 🌐 www.facebook.com/aquariusklub.*

**Bulldog Zagreb**

**BARS** | At night the bar vibes turn up at this café-cum-wine-bar and bistro, and you can often enjoy live stand-up (in English), as well as soul, rock, blues, and jazz performers. During the morning and afternoon, there's coffee sipping and people-watching. This popular split-level venue also has a lively summer terrace. ✉ *Bogovićeva 6, Donji Grad* ☎ *01/605–2320* 🌐 *www.facebook.com/BulldogZagreb.*

**MUSEUM Katran**

**DANCE CLUBS** | Croatian nightclubs are known for their lack of curfew, but this dance mecca takes that to the next level, bringing the party, and then the after-party, and then the after-after-party. The former warehouse factory sits on Radnička Street, about 15 minutes by car from the main square. The decor of exposed walls, graffiti, and pipe-lined ceilings testifies to its past. Four floors have different music, from rock and funk to rap and EDM. It's only open Friday and Saturday, and may close in summer. ✉ *Radnička Cesta 27, Donji Grad* 🌐 *www.facebook.com/MUSEUM.Katran* ⏲ *Closed Sun.–Thurs.*

**Old Pharmacy Pub**

**PUBS** | International sports fans of all kinds flock to this English-style pub, and its decor—such as a mirror behind the brass bar, pharmacy-related sepia photographs and vintage ads crowding the walls, and dark wood everywhere—perfectly matches the smoky atmosphere. (As at other bars and cafés in Croatia, indoor smoking is allowed.) Other than sports screenings, the pub regularly hosts acoustic rock bands and quiz nights. ✉ *Andrije Hebranga 11A, Donji Grad* ☎ *091/245–6183* 🌐 *www.facebook.com/oldpharmacypub.*

**★ Swanky Monkey Garden**

**BARS** | A trendy vintage bar in an industrial space (a former dry cleaning and textile dye factory) with exposed brick and lofty ceilings, this bar has outdoor seating on a beautiful terrace covered in lights, as well as a pool section in summer. Parties and music events are common here, the on-site hostel is rarely empty, and the adjacent restaurant (SOI) offers delicious Asian fusion fare to edge out Varionica craft beers, available in the bar. ✉ *Ilica 50, Donji Grad* 🌐 *www.facebook.com/swankymonkeygarden.*

## Performing Arts

**World Theatre Festival**

**ARTS FESTIVALS** | For one week in mid-September, this festival brings theater companies from all over the world to Zagreb for one or more performances each evening at various theatrical venues about town, mostly in the Lower Town. ✉ *Zagreb* ☎ *01/488–8401* 🌐 *www.facebook.com/FestivalSvjetskogKazalista.*

**★ Zagreb International Folklore Festival**

**CULTURAL FESTIVALS** | Since 1966, this has become one of the world's best folklore festivals, showcasing traditional dance, song, and costume from all over Croatia and the world. Talented performing groups and eager audiences flock to Zagreb each summer to rejoice in folk shows at gorgeous venues such as Zrinjevac Park, Trg Bana Jelačića, and the European Square. The festival usually takes place over the course of a week in July and is accompanied by cultural programs in the city's museums. ✉ *Zagreb* ☎ *01/660–1626* 🌐 *msf.hr/en.*

## Shopping

**★ bio&bio**

**OTHER SPECIALTY STORE** | Owned by the Pejić family, all-organic and mostly vegan bio&bio offers shoppers fresh and shelf-stable food and drink sourced from chosen producers worldwide as well as the owners' Zrno Eko Estate (Croatia's oldest all-organic farm). There's also a range of all-natural beauty and household products, and a good selection of healthy-living books, as well as a small in-house café with items to go. The store is is the perfect place to buy a few healthy products to take home, then grab some organic berries, a bottle of organic wine, and a few vegan sandwiches and head to Zrinjevac Park (a seven-minute walk) for a picnic. ✉ *Oktagon 5, Donji Grad* ☎ *01/487–6577* 🌐 *www.biobio.hr.*

**★ Croata**

**OTHER ACCESSORIES** | Ties may not be the most original of gifts, but they are uniquely Croatian. During the 17th century, Croatian mercenaries who fought in France sported narrow silk neck scarfs, which soon became known to the French as cravats (from *hrvat,* meaning "Croatian person"). "Original Croatian ties" are sold here in presentation boxes, accompanied by a brief history of the tie. You can also find tasteful gifts for women, including scarves, shawls, and accessories. ✉ *Ilica 5, Donji Grad* ✣ *Within the Oktagon shopping arcade* ☎ *01/645–7052* 🌐 *www.croata.hr.*

**Croatia Records**

**MUSIC** | Carrying a good selection of Croatian and international pop and rock records, this is the brick-and-mortar of Croatia's largest and oldest music production house of the same name. The location moved from Bogovićeva (where it had been the oldest record shop in the region for 56 years) to Gundulićeva in 2021. ✉ *Gundulićeva 3, Donji Grad* ☎ *01/481–0886* 🌐 *crorec.net.*

**Ilica Street**

**OTHER SPECIALTY STORE** | Stretching over 5½ km (3½ miles), Zagreb's main street is a shopping mecca, as well as one of the city's longest roads and home to some of the most expensive apartments in town. Shoppers can browse small-scale and specialty stores—think clothing boutiques NAF NAF and LeiLou, fine jewelry hub Prahir, chocolate and chai shop La Chocolate, and antiquarian bookstore Antikvarijat—as well as big-name brands like MAC Cosmetics, Pandora, Mango, Nespresso, Zara, and more. ✉ *Donji Grad.*

**Kobali**

**HATS & GLOVES** | For more than 100 years, Kobali has been beautifying Zagreb with elegant women's hats made fully by hand, and the still-family-owned brand is influential on the local fashion scene and synonymous with first-class craftsmanship. A Kobali hat is a symbol of Zagreb in all its forms, whether it's a summer Panama model woven with light parasisal fibers (a natural straw made from sisal) or a winter style crafted from rabbit fur. ✉ *Trg Petra Preradovića 1, Donji Grad* ☎ *098/238–586* 🌐 *www.kobali.hr.*

**Zaks**

**JEWELRY & WATCHES** | This luxury Croatian jewelry brand was founded in 2008 and offers a variety of fine gold and silver accessories. Keep an eye out for items from the Heritage Collection, which blends modern with traditional elements, such as earrings inspired by UNESCO-protected Croatian lace patterns or a necklace showcasing spherical buttons native to Šibenik. This location is one of five stores in Zagreb; there are 17 in all around Croatia. ✉ *Trg Bana Jelačića 1, Donji Grad* ☎ *01/370–6009* 🌐 *zaks.hr.*

**Znanje**

**BOOKS** | The solid selection of English-language books includes plenty of guides and coffee-table books on Croatia, and this bookstore occasionally hosts book launches (accompanied by live music and small bites) by local authors. ✉ *Gajeva 1, Donji Grad* ☎ *01/557–7953* 🌐 *znanje.hr.*

# Sljeme

*5 km (3 miles) north of Zagreb.*

A favorite excursion on the outskirts of Zagreb is to the heights of Sljeme, the peak of Mt. Medvednica at 3,363 feet. Mt. Medvednica is, along with Medvedgrad Castle, one of several places in Zagreb named after *medvjedi* (bears). Although there are now no bears in sight, Sljeme and Mt. Medvednica were

On Sljeme, you'll find Medvedgrad Castle with a museum on-site.

once home to a large bear community. As Zagreb grew into a major city, bears migrated south to the yet-untamed regions of Gorski Kotar and Lika, where they number in the hundreds today.

### GETTING HERE AND AROUND

You can reach Sljeme by taking Tram 14 or 8 (direction: Mihaljevac) all the way to the terminal stop, where you should change to the bus to Sljeme (Tomislavov Dom). An alternative and scenic option is the Sljeme Cable Car (€9.95 one-way; weather permitting). There's free outdoor parking next to the cable car's lower station, which can also be reached from Mihaljevac by Tram 15, the shortest tram line in Zagreb.

## Sights

### Medvedgrad Castle

**CASTLE/PALACE** | On the southwest flank of Mt. Medvednica's summit proudly sits Medvedgrad Castle, Zagreb's guardian fortress and the inspiration for many legends. The original was built in the 13th century by Bishop Filip of Zagreb, but it was destroyed in an earthquake in 1590. Today, the renovated building houses an interactive family-friendly museum with exhibits on the castle's past as well as the surrounding nature; it's worth an hour or two of your time. You can also wander around the outside for free and take in great views of Zagreb. It's a one-hour trek to the fortress from the cable car, or you can reach it more directly by taking Bus 102 from Britanski Trg in central Zagreb (just off Ilica, a 20-minute walk west of Trg Bana Jelačića) to the Blue Church in Šestine and then hiking some 40 minutes uphill from there. Take trail No. 12, which is off the paved road past the church cemetery. ✉ *Medvedgrad, Himper 16, Gornji Grad* ☎ *01/458–6317* 🎫 *€6–€8, depending on the day* 🕑 *Closed Mon.*

### Sljeme

**MOUNTAIN** | Sljeme is a fantastic destination for hikers and mountain bikers alike (along with skiers in the winter), with more than 70 trails ranging in difficulty from easy and kid-friendly to challenging even for experts. Every Saturday and Sunday, the mountain gets busy as locals pour in to get their dose of greenery and outdoor activities. The peak of Mt. Medvednica is an ideal place for picnicking, but you may wish to save your appetite for dinner at one of the excellent restaurants (located in large mountain cabins) on the road home. Additional activities on Sljeme include Medvedgrad Castle, the Zrinski Mine (€3.30) that was mined for precious metals in the 16th and 17th centuries, and Veternica Cave (€5.30), once home to Neanderthals and today housing 18 bat species. Those wishing to overnight on Sljeme can choose from two hotels and 11 mountain lodges. ✉ *Sljeme, Gornji Grad* ☎ *01/458–6317* 🌐 *www.sljeme.hr* 🎫 *Free.*

## Restaurants

**Stari Puntijar**
$ | **EASTERN EUROPEAN** | On the road between Zagreb and Sljeme, this restaurant is renowned for game and traditional Zagreb dishes and desserts. The wine list is excellent, and the interior design is marked by trophies, hunting weapons, old paintings, and big chandeliers. **Known for:** game dishes with ingredients sourced from local hunters; old-world vibe; connected to hotel and small gastronomic museum. [$] *Average main: €13* ✉ *Gračanska Cesta 65, Medvešcak* ☎ *01/645–7900* 🌐 *hotelpuntijar.com.*

# Marija Bistrica

*40 km (25 miles) northeast of Zagreb.*

Marija Bistrica and its famous pilgrimage site is the perfect destination for those looking for a peaceful countryside getaway or day trip with few distractions. While there, you can sleep in a rural-style cabin or book a room at the Bluesun Hotel Kaj (*kaj* being a local way of saying "what"). Don't leave the town without trying some local štrukli —this dish originated in the hills around Zagreb, after all —and a glass of local wine.

### GETTING HERE AND AROUND

You can reach the village from the Zagreb Bus Station or drive, taking the A2 highway.

## Sights

**Pilgrimage Church of St. Mary of Bistrica** (*Hodočasnička Crkva Majke Božje Bistričke*)
**CHURCH** | Croatia's preeminent religious pilgrimage site is home to the Blessed Virgin of Bistrica, a black, wooden, 15th-century Gothic statue of the Holy Mother associated with miraculous powers (per legend, having survived the Turkish invasion and a subsequent fire) and set in the main altar. The church, which was proclaimed a Croatian shrine by the nation's parliament in 1715, was rebuilt in the neo-Renaissance style in the late 19th century; the shrine complex adjacent to the church was enlarged in time for a 1998 visit by Pope John Paul II. Behind the church is a huge amphitheater built for the pope's visit, and from there, you can climb up Kalvarija (Calvary Hill) to the Stations of the Cross, ornamented with sculptures by Croatian artists. ✉ *Župni Ured, Trg Pape Ivana Pavla II 32, Marija Bistrica* ☎ *049/469–156* 🌐 *www.svetiste-mbb.hr* 🎫 *Free.*

**Pilgrimage Pathways**
**TRAIL** | Follow in the footsteps of countless pilgrims by exploring Marija Bistrica's pathways, both in and outside of town. Marija Bistrica's surroundings (like much of Zagorje) are covered with beautiful hiking trails. Around the village, you'll find a number of interesting sights as you stroll. Check out more than 100 works at the grassroots-led sculpture park located close to Marija Bistrica's main square, visit the Hudek Gallery with art by academic sculptor Pavao Hudek, and see an exhibition on UNESCO-protected

*licitarstvo*, the Croatian art of decorating gingerbread biscuits. If you see a souvenir stand, a *licitarsko srce* (Licitar heart) makes a great decoration or Christmas tree ornament, and there's no better place to purchase one than in the region where the craft developed. ✉ *Marija Bistrica* ☎ *049/468–380* 🌐 *www.tz-marija-bistrica.hr/en.*

# Veliki Tabor

*52 km (32 miles) northwest of Marija Bistrica, 70 km (43 miles) north of Zagreb.*

On a lofty hilltop in a rural area of Zagorje stands the regal Veliki Tabor Castle. A visit to the castle grounds and a walk through the castle are a must, and all the better if you're in town during a multiday festival hosted at the castle. Guests wishing to stay a few days and explore the area will find a range of traditional restaurants, as well as hiking, walking, and biking pathways. Hotels nearby are sparse, but a handful of countryside tourism estates offering rentable rooms and apartments, with on-site restaurants usually available, can be found within 10 km (6 miles). Masnec Tourist Farm, Seoski Turizam Sumak, King of the Hill, and Villa Marija are the closest.

### GETTING HERE AND AROUND

Between four and nine buses daily will get you to the nearby village of Desinić from Zagreb's main bus station in two hours for €8.30 one-way, but after getting off you'll have a 3.5-km (2-mile) walk still ahead of you. So, as is true generally of site-hopping in the Zagorje region, a rental car is handy, giving you the opportunity to stay longer in the countryside after taking in Veliki Tabor.

## Sights

### ★ Veliki Tabor

**CASTLE/PALACE** | When you arrive here, the view from outside—with stretching vistas of the lush surrounding hills—is sure to stun you, but don't miss wandering around the interior of this impressive castle and learning about its past. Built in the late 15th or early 16th century, the castle had a turbulent history, including being home to nobles (such as the Ratkaj family), being abandoned, and being the site of the chilling legend of Veronika Desnička. The story goes that Veronika, a commoner, and Fridrik II, a count, fell in love, for which they were punished by his noble family. Fridrik is thought to have been locked in a tower in the castle, and Veronika immured in the walls (legend says you can still hear her voice calling out on windy nights). Today the castle hosts many musical, theater, and art events, including the annual Tabor Film Festival, which usually takes place over a week in July. ✉ *Košnički Hum 1, Desinic* ☎ *049/374–970* 🌐 *www.veliki-tabor.hr/en* 🎫 *€5.*

## Restaurants

### ★ Grešna Gorica

**$ | EASTERN EUROPEAN** | Visiting this rustic tavern is like stepping into a friend's home, although your friend's home is unlikely to have a stuffed fawn and a pair of *kuna*, the former national currency's namesake, on the wall. Local farmers supply all produce used here, and the menu features typical Zagorje dishes such as *purica s mlincima* (turkey with savory pastries). **Known for:** delicious štrukli; rustically decorated outdoor terrace under the treetops; great views onto Veliki Tabor Castle from the garden. $ *Average main: €13* ✉ *Taborgradska 35, Desinic* ☎ *049/343–001* 🌐 *www.gresna-gorica.com* ⏲ *Closed Mon.*

# Krapina

*20 km (12 miles) east of Veliki Tabor, 66 km (41 miles) north of Zagreb.*

Zagorje's quaint administrative and cultural center is on the tourism radar primarily as the home of *krapinski pračovjek* (Krapina Neanderthal). This is due to the 1899 discovery of the world's largest *homo Neanderthalensis* settlement, dating from 30,000–40,000 years ago, on a hillside a short walk from the town center. Indeed, this may be one of the few places in the world today where you can meet up with a family of such hominids—that is, with life-size statues of Neanderthals going about their daily business (hunting, exploring, tending fire) at the same spot where the discovery was made. Leading its excavation was Croatian paleoanthropologist Dragutin Gorjanović-Kramberger.

### GETTING HERE AND AROUND

Krapina is a 40-minute drive from Veliki Tabor or a 50-minute drive from Zagreb. On weekdays, there's a bus once a day from Zagreb that takes 80 minutes.

★ **Krapina Neanderthal Museum** (*Muzej krapinskih neandertalaca*)

**HISTORY MUSEUM** | The Krapina Neanderthal Museum is located near Hušnjakovo Hill, the world-famous archaeological site of the Krapina Neanderthals, and its architecture evokes the habitat of these prehistoric people. Displays provide insight into who these early Neanderthals were, how they lived, and more broadly into the region's geology and history. ✉ *Šetalište Vilibalda Sluge bb, Krapina* ☎ *049/371–491* 🌐 *mkn.mhz.hr* *€10* *Closed Mon.*

**Vuglec Breg**

**$$$** | **EUROPEAN** | This combined restaurant, winery, and villa is a 15-minute drive south of Krapina and offers wine tastings, traditional Zagorje food (duck with mlinci, anyone?), and unbeatable views of the vineyard-carpeted hills. A straw-covered terrace, open hearth, and classic dark wooden elements complete the ambience, and there's also a "picnic bar" where visitors can recline on the grass in lawn chairs as they sip on house-made wine. **Known for:** dishes made from local grandmas' recipes with family farm ingredients; awarded wines (regular and sparkling) such as Vuglec Extra Brut; lodging also available here. $ *Average main: €26* ✉ *Škarićevo 151, Krapina* ☎ *049/345–015* 🌐 *www.vuglec-breg.hr.*

# Trakošćan

*41 km (25½ miles) west of Varaždin, 36 km (22 miles) northeast of Veliki Tabor.*

Perched resplendently several hundred feet above the parking lot where the tour buses come and go, the hilltop Trakošćan Castle is set amid beautifully landscaped grounds and overlooks a lovely lake circled by a hiking trail. Rooms and apartments on rural estates in the surrounding hills are available to guests who wish to sleep over, but day trips from Zagreb are also doable.

### GETTING HERE AND AROUND

The castle is 1 hour 15 minutes by car from the center of Zagreb, a drive that takes you between hills and partially through the scenic Krapina River Valley.

## Sights

★ **Trakošćan Castle** (*Dvor Trakošćan*)

**CASTLE/PALACE** | Croatia's most visited castle took on its present neo-Gothic appearance during the mid-19th century, compliments of Juraj VI Drašković, whose family had already owned the castle for some 300 years and would go on to live there until 1944. There has been a building here since the 14th

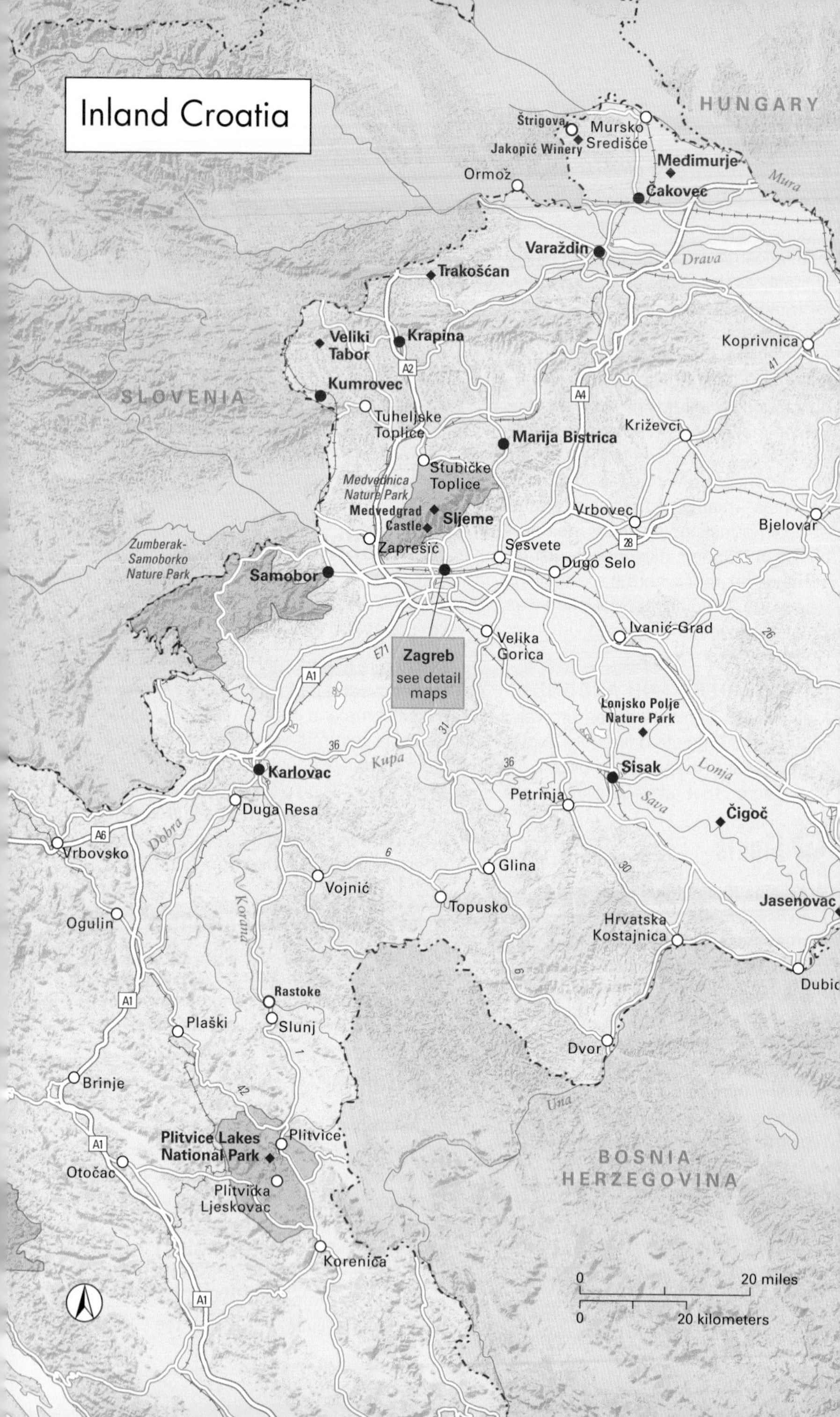
Inland Croatia
HUNGARY
Štrigova
Mursko Središće
Jakopić Winery
Međimurje
Mura
Ormož
Čakovec
Varaždin
Drava
Trakošćan
Veliki Tabor
Krapina
A2
Koprivnica
41
SLOVENIA
Kumrovec
A4
Tuheljske Toplice
Marija Bistrica
Križevci
Stubičke Toplice
Medvednica Nature Park
Medvedgrad Castle
Sljeme
Vrbovec
Bjelovar
Zumberak-Samoborko Nature Park
Zaprešić
Sesvete
28
Samobor
Dugo Selo
Velika Gorica
Ivanić-Grad
26
E71
Zagreb
see detail maps
A1
Lonjsko Polje Nature Park
31
36
Kupa
36
Karlovac
Sisak
Lonja
Petrinja
Sava
Duga Resa
Čigoč
A6
Vrbovsko
Dobra
6
Glina
Vojnić
30
Topusko
Korana
Ogulin
Jasenovac
Hrvatska Kostajnica
Dubic
A1
Rastoke
Plaški
Slunj
1
Dvor
Brinje
42
Una
Plitvice
Plitvice Lakes National Park
A1
BOSNIA-HERZEGOVINA
Otočac
Plitvička Ljeskovac
Korenica
0
20 miles
0
20 kilometers
A1

Trakošćan Castle is Croatia's most visited castle and is gorgeous inside and out.

century. The inside is as spectacular as the outside, with the wood-paneled rooms—a Baroque room, a rococo room, a neoclassical room, and so on—filled with period furnishings and family portraits, giving you some idea of how the wealthy local aristocracy once lived. A restaurant, café, and souvenir shop occupy the less extravagant Ministry of Culture–owned building at the foot of the hill. ✉ *Trakošćan 1, Bednja* ✣ *5 km (3 miles) northwest of the village of Bednja* ☎ *042/796–281* 🌐 *trakoscan.hr* 🎫 *€7.*

## Varaždin

*70 km (48 miles) northeast of Zagreb.*

Situated on a plain just south of the Drava River, Varaždin (population around 45,000) is the most beautifully preserved Baroque town in this corner of the continent. A vibrant commercial and cultural center, still basking in the glow of its trade-town heyday in the 18th century, Varaždin is richly adorned with extraordinary churches and the palaces of the aristocratic families who once lived here. It was Croatia's capital from 1756 until a devastating fire in 1776 prompted a move to Zagreb. First mentioned under the name Garestin in a document by the Hungarian-Croatian king Béla III from 1181, it was declared a free royal town by King András II of Hungary's Arpad dynasty in 1209 and went on to become an important economic, social, administrative, and military center. Near the heart of the city, in a park surrounded by grassy ramparts, the well-preserved castle is the main attraction. A short walk from the castle, on the outskirts of town, is one of Europe's loveliest cemeteries, with immense hedges trimmed and shaped around ornate memorials. Note that Varaždin's main churches are open only around an hour before and after mass, which is generally held several times daily, more often on weekends. The tourist information office can help you contact individual churches to arrange a look inside at other times; entry is free.

## GETTING HERE AND AROUND

After arriving in this charming city by bus from Zagreb, the best thing to do is to walk straight to the historical downtown, which will serve as your base for sightseeing and café-visiting.

**City Museum Varaždin** (*Gradski muzej Varaždin*)

**HISTORY MUSEUM | FAMILY** | Varaždin's city museum is composed of multiple departments, including Archaeology, History, Ethnography, and more, and is housed in three buildings: the Culture and History Department in the Stari Grad (Old Town) fortress; the Gallery of Old and Contemporary Masters in Sermage Palace, and the Entomology Collection in Herzer Palace. The latter is one of the museum's highlights, with a fascinating presentation of some 50,000 different insect specimens. ✉ *Šetalište Josipa Jurja Strossmayera 1, Varaždin* ☎ *042/658–750* 🌐 *www.gmv.hr/en* 🎫 *€5 for 1 of 3 museum buildings; €12 for 3 (Sermage Palace, Herzer Palace, Stari Grad/Old Town)* ⏲ *Closed Mon.*

**Franciscan Church** (*Franjevačka crkva*)

**CHURCH** | Consecrated in 1650 on the site of a medieval predecessor, this pale yellow church has the highest tower in Varaždin, at almost 180 feet tall. In front is a statue of 10th-century Croatian bishop Grgur Ninski, a replica of the original, which is in Split; another such replica can be seen in Nin. ✉ *Franjevački Trg 8, Varaždin* ☎ *042/210–987 for Varaždin Tourist Board.*

**Gallery of Old and Contemporary Masters** (*Galerija starih i novih majstora*)

**ART MUSEUM** | Housed in the striking 18th-century rococo Palača Sermage (Sermage Palace)—characterized by cinnamon-colored, black-framed geometric medallions decorating its facade and an impressive wrought-iron terrace—this gallery has a rich array of traditional paintings by Croatian and other European artists. It's part of the City Museum Varaždin. ✉ *Trg Miljenka Stančića 3, Varaždin* ☎ *042/658–754* 🌐 *www.gmv.hr/en* 🎫 *€5; €12 for 3 museum buildings (Sermage Palace, Herzer Palace, Stari Grad/Old Town)* ⏲ *Closed Mon.*

**Gradska Vijećnica** (*City Hall*)

**GOVERNMENT BUILDING** | This imposing landmark, one of Europe's oldest city halls, has been the seat of Varaždin's public administration since December 14, 1523. It was completely restored after the great fire of 1776. From May through October you can stop by on a Saturday morning between 11 and noon to watch the changing of the guard called Purgari (🌐 *www.varazdinska-garda.com*), a 250-year-old tradition that lives on. ✉ *Trg Kralja Tomislava 1, Varaždin* ☎ *099/335–5342 for City Hall, 042/402–500 for information on Purgari and changing of the guard* 🌐 *www.varazdin.hr.*

**Lisakova Kula** (*Lisak Tower*)

**NOTABLE BUILDING** | Built in the16th century, this tower is the only part of Varaždin's northern town wall that has been preserved. The wall formed part of the onetime city fortress, but most of it was razed in the early 19th century. It's from this spot that Ban Josip Jelačić (to whom Zagreb's main square is also dedicated) led 50,000 soldiers across the Drava in 1848, taking back Croatia's northernmost region of Međimurje from the Hungarian Kingdom. In 2022, during work on the tower, archaeological ruins of the ancient defense system around Varaždin were discovered. ✉ *Trg Bana Jelačića, Varaždin.*

**Parish Church of St. Nicholas** (*Župna crkva Sv. Nikole*)

**CHURCH** | Consecrated to Varaždin's patron saint in 1761 on the site of an older church, this Baroque structure is more attractive on the outside than the inside. Note the false yet imposing white columns in the facade, the red-tiled conical steeple, and the sculpture at the foot of the steeple of a firefighting St. Florian

Varaždin's Stari Grad was created as a defense fortification but today serves as a history museum.

pouring a bucket of water onto a church, presumably an allusion to the fire that devastated Varaždin in 1776. ✉ *Medpotoki 1, Varaždin* ☎ *042/212–412* 🌐 *www.zupa-sv-nikole-varazdin.hr.*

★ **Stari Grad** (*Stari Grad Castle and Fortress*)
**HISTORIC SIGHT** | Today a historic site and home to part of the City Museum, Varaždin's main attraction is the massive Stari Grad (Old Town), which assumed its present form in the 16th century as a state-of-the-art defense fortification against the Turks, complete with moats, dikes, and bastions with low round defense towers connected by galleries with openings for firearms. In the ensuing centuries it was often reconstructed by the families that owned it; for more than three centuries, until its 1925 purchase by the city, it belonged to the Erdödy clan. From the 12th century up until 1925, the castle served as the seat of the county prefect. You enter through the 16th-century tower gatehouse, which has a wooden drawbridge, to arrive in the internal courtyard with three levels of arcaded galleries. Indoors, there's an extensive display of antique furniture, with pieces laid out in chronological order and each room representing a specific period. Even if you don't go inside, do take a stroll around the perimeter along the path that takes you between the outer wall and a ditch that used to be the moat. ✉ *Strossmayerovo Šetalište 1, Varaždin* ☎ *042/658–754* 🌐 *www.gmv.hr/en* 🎫 *€5; €12 includes 3 museum buildings (Sermage Palace, Herzer Palace, Stari Grad/Old Town)* ⏲ *Closed Mon.*

**Ursuline Church of the Birth of Christ** (*Uršulinska crkva Rođenja Isusovog*)
**CHURCH** | This single-nave, pale-pink Baroque church with a particularly colorful late-Baroque altar was consecrated in 1712 by the Ursuline sisters, who came to Varaždin from Bratislava nine years earlier at the invitation of the Drašković family. Its charming, strikingly slender tower was added in 1726. ✉ *Uršulinska 3, Varaždin* ☎ *042/211–808* 🌐 *www.ursulinke.hr.*

★ **Varaždin Cemetery** (*Gradsko groblje*)
**CEMETERY** | Built in 1773 and thoroughly relandscaped in 1905 by Herman Haller, a self-taught landscape architect who revolutionized traditional notions of what graveyards should look like, Varaždin's City Cemetery is as pleasant a place for a restful stroll as can be. Replete with flower beds and rows of tall cedars and linden trees flanking ornate memorials, all laid out in geometric patterns, the cemetery sublimely manifests Haller's conviction that each plot should be a "serene, hidden place only hinting at its true purpose, with no clue as to whether its occupant is rich or poor, since all are tended equally, surrounded by every kind of flower … producing perfect harmony for the visitor." Haller, who ran the cemetery from 1905 to 1946, is buried here in a rather conspicuous mausoleum. You can reach the cemetery by walking about 10 minutes east of the castle along Hallerova Aleja. ✉ *Hallerova Aleja, Varaždin.*

**Varaždin City Market** (*Varaždinska Gradska tržnica*)
**MARKET** | Enjoy the smells of fresh fruits and vegetables, plus the friendly clamor of locals negotiating the best prices, with a stop at the City Market, open from around 7 am to 2 pm. The open-air marketplace also features a number of bakeries and meat and fish stores. ✉ *Gradska Tržnica, Augusta Šenoe 12, Varaždin* ☎ *042/320–956* 🌐 *www.varazdinskiplac.hr* 🕒 *Closed Sun.*

**Varaždin County Castle** (*Palača Varaždinske županije*)
**GOVERNMENT BUILDING** | The palace rivals City Hall (on nearby Trg Kralja Tomislava) in terms of sheer visual appeal, even if it is more than two centuries younger, what with its flamingo-pink facade and its location right across from the Franciscan Church. Opened in 1772, it boasted a late-Baroque pediment for four years only, until the fire of 1776 did away with that; the replacement was a triangular neoclassical one. Today regional authorities use the building, so the interior is generally off-limits to the public, but the outside is worth a look. ✉ *Franjevački Trg 7, Varaždin* ☎ *042/210–987* 🌐 *visitvarazdin.hr/en/palaces.*

## Restaurants

**Restoran Angelus**
**$$ | ITALIAN | FAMILY** | A five-minute walk from the center of town, Angelus is best known for decent pizza but has a huge menu with plenty of pastas and other meatier fare, not to mention a half-dozen creative salads and lots of beer. **Known for:** kind staff and warm atmosphere; pricier than nearby options; across the street from a peaceful shaded park. $ *Average main: €16* ✉ *Alojzija Stepinca 3, Varaždin* ☎ *042/303–868* 🌐 *angelus.hr.*

## Hotels

**Hotel Istra**
**$ | HOTEL** | One of the only accommodations in the heart of the city center, the Istra has simply furnished but sleek rooms with small windows that don't offer much of a view. **Pros:** near attractions, shops, and restaurants; all rooms have bathtubs; hotel has an elevator. **Cons:** hallways are hot in warm weather; service may be inconsistent; few frills. $ *Rooms from: €90* ✉ *Ivana Kukuljevića Sakcinskog 6, Varaždin* ☎ *042/659–659* 🌐 *www.istra-hotel.hr/en* *11 rooms* *Free Breakfast.*

**Hotel Varaždin**
**$ | HOTEL** | In business since 2007, this hotel in an early-20th-century building across from the train station has bright modern rooms. **Pros:** convenient if you come by train; attractive breakfast room with solid options; all rooms are nonsmoking. **Cons:** a 15-minute walk from the town center; small bathrooms; few frills and somewhat outdated decor. $ *Rooms from: €100* ✉ *Kolodvorska 19, Varaždin* ☎ *042/290–720* 🌐 *hotelvarazdin.com* *31 rooms* *Free Breakfast.*

**Pansion Garestin**

$ | **B&B/INN** | A short walk from the town center, this small hotel has simply furnished rooms with ocher carpeting, sturdy if scratched desks, and small windows under a pitched roof. **Pros:** reasonably priced for the location; comfy basic rooms; pleasant outdoor dining terrace. **Cons:** small bathrooms; few amenities, with interior in need of renovation; some rooms are smoking rooms. *Rooms from: €70 ✉ Zagrebačka 34, Varaždin ☎ 042/214–314 🌐 gastrocom-ugostiteljstvo.com/en/home-en 13 rooms Free Breakfast.*

**Pansion Maltar**

$ | **B&B/INN** | A short walk from the town center, this small guesthouse has clean, no-frills, but comfortable rooms that are quite acceptable for a short stay. **Pros:** good value and friendly service; has some rooms and apartments in other buildings; a five-minute walk to the town center. **Cons:** smoky café; modest decor; some rooms have twin beds only. *Rooms from: €88 ✉ Franca Prešerna 1, Varaždin ☎ 042/311–100 🌐 www.maltar.hr 18 rooms Free Breakfast.*

## Nightlife

**Rock Art Caffe**

**CAFÉS** | On Saturday, stop by this café, which draws in young party-lovers for dancing and DJ tunes below vaulted ceilings covered with LED lights. During the day, it's a peaceful café, ideal for enjoying coffee or beer on the outdoor terrace. *✉ Petra Preradovića 24, Varaždin 🌐 www.instagram.com/rockartcaffe.*

## Performing Arts

**Advent in Varaždin**

**FESTIVALS** | Throughout December, the town of Varaždin celebrates Advent, when the streets and squares come alive with the Christmas spirit. Ornaments and sweets are on sale, there's outdoor skating—and, yes, Santa Claus wanders about handing out gifts to kids. *✉ Varaždin ☎ 042/210–987 for Varaždin Tourist Board 🌐 www.adventuvarazdinu.com.*

**Špancirfest**

**FESTIVALS** | For 10 days, usually in late August, Špancirfest occupies various squares in the town center, featuring a colorful array of free open-air theatrical and acrobatic performances, live music from classical to rock, traditional and modern dance, arts-and-crafts exhibits, and more. *Špancir* is a local expression referring to a leisurely enjoyable stroll, so the event may be translated in tourist brochures as Street Walkers' Festival. *✉ Varaždin ☎ 042/210–987 🌐 www.spancirfest.com/en.*

**★ Varaždin Baroque Evenings**

**MUSIC FESTIVALS** | For several weeks, usually from September to October, this event takes the form of classical-music concerts in various churches, palaces, and other venues throughout town. This is one of the most important cultural events in northern Croatia, having been held in Varaždin and serving to continue the city's rich musical heritage since the mid-20th century. *✉ Varaždin ☎ 042/212–907 🌐 vbv.hr/en.*

# Čakovec and Međimurje

*15 km (9 miles) northeast of Varaždin.*

At the northernmost tip of Croatia, between the Drava River to the south and the Mura River to the north, the Međimurje region looks small on the map, but it possesses a distinctive character that makes it ripe for at least a day of exploration. Long off the radar of Croatia-bound visitors, Međimurje is also one of the country's newest up-and-coming inland tourist destinations: its largest town, Čakovec, is the most important cultural center between Varaždin and Hungary to the north (many Zagreb–Budapest trains stop there). Its many small villages are home to rich wine-making and embroidery traditions, and there is even a locally cherished spa town, Toplice Sveti Martin, in the very north, close to the Mura River.

Back in the 13th century, Count Dimitrius Chaky, court magistrate of the Croatian-Hungarian king Béla IV, had a wooden defense tower erected in the central part of Međimurje. The tower eventually became known as Čakov toranj (Chak's Tower). It was around this tower and other nearby fortifications that Čakovec saw a period of economic and cultural development under the influential Zrinski family, from the mid-16th century to the late 17th century. After a failed rebellion by the Zrinskis and the Frankopans against the Viennese court, the Viennese imperial army plundered the tower for building materials, and the last Zrinski died in 1691. A disastrous earthquake in 1738 saw the old Gothic architecture give way to the Baroque. Međimurje's last feudal proprietors were the Feštetić counts, who lived here from 1791 to 1923—a period during which the region came under the administrative control of Hungary, then Croatia, then Hungary once again (until 1918). Toward the close of the 19th century the region was linked inextricably to the railroad network of the Austro-Hungarian Empire, setting the stage for intense economic development. Today, the region hosts a number of festivals, the largest being Porcijunkulovo, during which Čakovec turns into an open-air food, drink, wine-tasting, and music festival.

## GETTING HERE AND AROUND

If you're arriving by bus from Zagreb, you're practically already in the city center. Walk a minute south from the bus station and begin experiencing the history all around you. The train station is a 5-minute drive or 20-minute walk northeast to the city center.

## Sights

**Jakopić Winery**

**WINERY** | Near the spa town of Sveti Martin in the Varaždin region, Jakopić Winery is operated by brothers Martin and Branimir Jakopić, who offer superb dining as well as several kinds of tastings of wines from the lush vineyards near the border with Slovenia. The first wine here was produced in 1908, and the winery is especially renowned for its Pušipel, a notable white wine variety indigenous to Međimurje. ✉ *Železna Gora 92, Štrigova* ☎ *040/851–300* 🌐 *vina-jakopic.hr* 🎫 *€12 for standard tasting* ⏲ *Closed Sun.*

**Štrigova**

**TOWN** | In a bucolic hilly setting near the Slovenian border, 15 km (9 miles) northwest of Čakovec, the village of Štrigova is best known as the largest producer of Međimurje wines. More than 20 wineries on a wine route through Štrigova and its surroundings offer tastings. It's also attractive for hiking and cycling routes (a lovely bike trail stretches from Međimurje to Hungary), the Mađerkin Breg viewpoint, the Church of St. Jerome, and three historic castles. A car or a bike is the preferred method of transport here, so that you can cruise the wine route and hit the highlights.

The first thing you're likely to notice about the Church of St. Jerome (Crkva Svetog Jeronima), which is perched on a hillside above the village center, is its yellow-and-white double steeple. Completed in 1749, the church is dedicated to the village's most famous son: St. Jerome (340–420), known for translating the Bible from Greek and Hebrew into Latin. Note the painting of a bearded St. Jerome on the facade, framed by two little windows made to look like red hearts. The church is also noted for its wall and ceiling frescoes by Baroque artist Ivan Ranger the Baptist (1700–1753). The building is usually closed, but you can call the local tourist board to arrange a look inside. ✉ *Štrigova* ☎ *040/851–325* 🌐 *www.strigova.info.*

**Trgovački Kasino** (*Commercial Casino*)
**NOTABLE BUILDING** | Čakovec's main square, Trg Republike, is a pretty Baroque affair, with a major highlight being the Trgovački Kasino. It's odd that the key gathering place of the town's early-20th-century bourgeois class should have survived the Communist era intact, but here it has stood since 1903, wearing its Hungarian art nouveau style very much on its sleeve: red brick interspersed with a white stucco background, squares and circles across the bottom, and curved lines formed by the brickwork working their way to the top. Back in its heyday, this was more than a casino in the gambling sense of the word: besides a card room and a game parlor, it housed a ladies' salon, a reading room, and a dance hall. The building was mostly a trade-union headquarters in the post–World War II era, and its interior is still off-limits to the public. To explore a bit further, just off Trg Republike is Trg Kralja Tomislava, the town's major pedestrian shopping street. ✉ *Trg Republike, Cakovec* ☎ *040/313–319 for Čakovec Tourist Board* 🌐 *www.visitcakovec.com.*

**Zrinski Castle** (*Stari grad Zrinskih*)
**CASTLE/PALACE** | Set in the middle of a large shaded park right beside the main square is Čakovec's key landmark, the massive four-story Stari Grad Zrinskih. Built in an Italian-Renaissance style over the course of a century, beginning around 1550 by Nikola Šubic Zrinski, it was the Zrinski family nest until the late 17th century. The fortress's foremost present-day attraction, the Muzej Međimurja (Museum of Međimurje), can be reached through the courtyard. If you overlook the inconsistent availability of English-language text, you will be treated on this floor to an intriguing life-size look at a year in the life of a peasant family, from season to season, as you proceed through the rooms. Move up a floor for a chronological display of the region's history from the Stone Age to the recent past. Also on this floor are individual rooms dedicated to the Zrinski family, period furniture, displays of printing machinery, an old pharmacy, a fascinating collection of 19th- and 20th-century bric-a-brac, and, last but not least, a three-room gallery of impressive modern art by various painters. ✉ *Trg Republike 5, Cakovec* ☎ *040/310–040* 🌐 *www.mmc.hr* 🎫 *€8, includes permanent exhibition of the Museum of Međimurje in the castle and the museum's collections in the fortress.*

**Župna Crkva Svetog Nikole Biskupa i Franjevački Samostan** (*Parish Church of St. Nicolas the Bishop and the Franciscan Monastery*)
**CHURCH** | Čakovec's key ecclesiastical landmark was built between 1707 and 1728 on the site of a wooden monastery that burned down in 1699. The bell tower was added in the 1750s. Inside is a late-Baroque altar decorated with elaborate statues; on the outside is a facade from the turn of the 20th century, when Hungary ruled the region, with reliefs of several great Hungarian kings from ages past. ✉ *Franjevački Trg 1, Cakovec* ☎ *040/312–806* 🌐 *www.facebook.com/zupasvNikolaCakovec.*

## Restaurants

**Međimurski Dvori**
**$$$ | EUROPEAN | FAMILY** | Located in the heart of Međimurje County, in picturesque Lopatinec, 6 km (4 miles) from Čakovec, Međimurski dvori has been known across the region for top gastronomic offerings and friendly professional staff for years. In 2022 the owners swapped out their restaurant for a catering company, but each Sunday, they host a cheerful open-to-the-public Međimurje Meal (Međimurski Obed), a buffet-style lunch with long community tables, available by advance reservation. **Known for:** reservations required for buffet; regional cuisine using locally procured

ingredients; idyllic countryside location in the "Fairy-Tale Forest". 💲 *Average main: €25* ✉ *Vladimira Nazora 29A, Lopatinec, Cakovec* ☎ *098/241–800* 🌐 *medjimurski-dvori.hr* ⏲ *Closed Mon.–Sat. except for private group dining. No dinner Sun.*

**Terbotz** (*Restoran Dvorac*)
**$$$ | EUROPEAN | FAMILY** | In the village of Železna Gora, some 5 km (3 miles) south of Štrigova along a country road to Čakovec, stands one of the area's best restaurants, where you can dine on everything from poultry to pork to wild game to seafood. The restaurant is in a lovely 19th-century country villa with wood-beam ceilings. **Known for:** terrace overlooking the surrounding vineyards; unique Međimurje flavors such as gibanica cake; locally sourced ingredients and wines. 💲 *Average main: €26* ✉ *Železna Gora 113, Štrigova* ☎ *040/857–444* 🌐 *www.terbotz.hr* ⏲ *Closed Mon.*

## Hotels

**Hotel Castellum**
**$ | HOTEL** | A short walk from the bus station and the main square (both of which are less than a mile away), the best hotel in town features a rooftop bar with panoramic views and a wine cellar. **Pros:** on-site gym and parking; modern furnishings and gray wood elements in rooms; good food and drink options on-site. **Cons:** pricier than other spots in the area; along a bland road; a bit impersonal. 💲 *Rooms from: €110* ✉ *Vladimira Nazora 16, Cakovec* ☎ *040/304–200* 🌐 *www.castellum-cakovec.com* *30 rooms* *Free Breakfast.*

# Samobor

*20 km (12½ miles) west of Zagreb.*

That Samobor has been one of the capital's top weekend escapes since before the turn of the 20th century without really being on the way to anywhere else in Croatia testifies to its abundant cultural and natural charms. Close to the Slovenian border, this picturesque medieval town on the eastern slopes of the lushly forested Žumberak Mountains was chartered by the Hungarian-Croatian king Béla IV in 1242. The town and environs are popular with hikers, with trails leading into the hillside right from the center of town. Perched in those hills, just 30 minutes from town on foot, are the ruins of a 13th-century castle, offering sublime views of the town. And what would a visit to Samobor be without a stroll along Gradna, the peaceful stream that runs through town, and its Venice-like canals? After an energetic hike, you may fortify yourself with a glass of locally made *bermet,* a vermouth-like drink whose secret recipe was apparently brought here by French forces during their occupation from 1809 to 1813. Add the traditional pastry called *kremšnita,* a mouthwatering and creamy block of vanilla custard between layers of flaky pastry, and you've got yourself an authentic and tasty Samobor meal.

### GETTING HERE AND AROUND

Samobor is a one-hour bus ride from the central bus station in Zagreb or a 30-minute drive by rental car.

## Sights

**King Tomislav Square** (*Trg Kralja Tomislava*)
**PLAZA/SQUARE** | The look of the city's rectangular main square is largely Baroque and positively lovely, all the more so because some building facades show art nouveau influences. In particular, the pharmacy building at No. 11 has two angels presiding, appropriately, on top. Also overlooking the square is a 17th-century parish church. Enjoy a coffee and a slice of kremšnita at one of the cafés dotting the square. ✉ *Samobor* ☎ *01/336–0044* 🌐 *www.samobor.hr/en/visit.*

Charming Samobor is a popular base for hikers who wish to explore the town's surrounding hills.

**Samobor Museum**

**HISTORY MUSEUM** | Located in a pretty streamside park by the square, this museum tells the story of the town's past. It sits in a manor in which members of the 19th-century Croatian National Revival once gathered and is also the spot where Ferdo Livadić's and Ljudevit Gaj's song "Croatia Has Not Yet Fallen" was first sung (this later became the anthem of the movement). The museum warrants a quick 20-minute walk-through, especially if you're a history buff; it tells the story of Samobor's past chronologically, across two floors, including a geological viewpoint, Roman times, the development of local crafts and the famous Samoborski Fašnik carnival, and 20th-century events. ✉ *Livadićeva 7, Samobor* ☎ *01/336–1014* 🌐 *www.samobor.hr/en/visit* 🎫 *€3.58* 🕓 *Closed Mon.*

## Restaurants

**★ Korak**

**$$$$** | **EUROPEAN** | A 30-minute ride southwest of Samobor's center, this family-run restaurant and winery sitting among the picturesque foothills of the Žumberak Mountains joined Croatia's list of Michelin-starred establishments in 2023. Under chef Bernardo Korak's expert leadership, the elegant modern restaurant offers the best of the surrounding Plešivica region's cuisine in multicourse fixed-price menus with dishes that mix tradition and creativity. **Known for:** on fifth-generation-run family estate with winery tours and tastings; a hot spot, so reserve ahead; ingredients sourced right before cooking (think hand-picked wild plants and fish from the nearby river). $ *Average main: €85* ✉ *Plešivica 34, Jastrebarsko* ☎ *099/276-4204* 🌐 *www.korakwinery.com* 🕓 *Closed Mon. and Tues. No lunch Wed. No dinner Sun.*

**Pri Staroj Vuri**

**$** | **EASTERN EUROPEAN** | **FAMILY** | Small yet ever so cozy, its walls decorated with old clocks and paintings by noted Croatian artists, this lovely old villa a few minutes' walk from the main square is the best place in town to try the area's meaty fare. A wider selection of sausages may be available late in the year, after *kolinje* (the annual sausage-making period, usually in November), when the hogs are butchered and the sausages are smoked. **Known for:** hearty portions of home-cooked dishes; service sometimes inconsistent; location surrounded by green space. $ *Average main: €13* ✉ *Giznik 2, Samobor* ☎ *01/336–0548* 🌐 *www.staravura.pondi.hr* ⏲ *Closed Mon.*

## Coffee and Quick Bites

**U Prolazu**

$ | **CAFÉ** | If you need a dose of sugar to perk you up, try some authentic Samobor kremšnita, which can be tasted at its best at this otherwise small and smoky café with a large outdoor patio. It's one of the original spots in town to make the traditional dessert. **Known for:** doesn't get more central than this; authentic Samobor pastries including, but not limited to, kremšnita; views of the surrounding main square and church. $ *Average main: €6* ✉ *Trg Kralja Tomislava 5, Samobor* ☎ *01/336–6420* 🌐 *www.samobor.hr/en/visit.*

## Hotels

**Hotel Livadić**

$ | **HOTEL** | If you want to spend more than a half-day in Samobor, you could do much worse than this pleasant old-fashioned hotel right on the main square. **Pros:** centrally located with parking; grand interior decor adds old-world vibe; café serves kremšnite. **Cons:** rooms vary in size; café on-site is smoky; some may consider it a bit outdated. $ *Rooms from: €75* ✉ *Trg Kralja Tomislava 1, Samobor* ☎ *01/336–5850* 🌐 *www.hotel-livadic.hr* *21 rooms* *Free Breakfast.*

## Performing Arts

**Samoborski Fašnik**

**CULTURAL FESTIVALS** | By far Samobor's most famous event, this carnival draws thousands of visitors from across the world to town for several days beginning the weekend before Lent (February or March). Guests can take part in or simply enjoy the dazzling sight of the parades, featuring floats and masked revelers. Aside from the one in Rijeka, this is Croatia's most famous carnival. ✉ *Trg Kralja Tomislava 5, Samobor* ☎ *01/336–0044* 🌐 *www.samobor.hr/fasnik.*

## Activities

**Žumberak – Samobor Hills Nature Park**

(*Park prirode Žumberak – Samoborsko gorje*)

**HIKING & WALKING** | Samobor is located in the foothills of the fairy-tale Žumberak Mountains, which stretch along the border with Slovenia and up to the Kupa River's north bank. West of Samobor, Žumberak is a place of small hilltop villages strewn with vineyards, tumbling waterfalls, and towering moss-covered oak, hornbeam, and beech trees. The park covers 342 square km (more than 84,500 acres) and has 350 km (217 miles) of hiking trails. It also has a unique and diverse history as a settling place for various migrant groups, from the Neolithic period to Roman times to the Middle Ages. For a taste of history, try the 4-km-long (2½-mile-long) Trail of Princes (two hours of lightly sloped walking) that will take you to old burial mounds from the Iron Age. Some park highlights are a ruined stone fortress from the 13th century and the 49-foot Vranjak Waterfall, both reachable only by foot. This is also a favored destination among cyclists. Restaurants are available in the foothills, such as Korak for fine dining near Jastrebarsko or the affordable Colombo pizzeria for good Neapolitan pie in Draganić. ✉ *Samobor* ☎ *01/332–7660* 🌐 *www.pp-zumberak-samoborsko-gorje.hr.*

# Karlovac

*40 km (25 miles) southwest of Zagreb.*

Many tourists taste the beer, but few stop by for a taste of the city, though Karlovac is much more than home to one of Croatia's most popular brews, Karlovačko. Founded by the Austrians in 1579 as a fortress intended to ward off Ottoman attacks, Karlovac today is that big dot on the map between Zagreb and the coast. Visitors to the country, more often than not, simply pass it by, but anyone intrigued by how a onetime fortress—still much in evidence—can develop into an urban center will want to stop here for at least a half-day and, perhaps, spend a night on the way to or from the coast. Once you pass through the city's industrial-looking suburbs, an inviting historical center awaits you, one made more romantic because it is wedged between four rivers: the Kupa, the Korana, the Mrežnica, and the Dobra. This location is the source of its nickname, "the city that sits on four rivers." The rivers provide a range of activities, such as kayaking, swimming, and camping, that are likely to draw visitors who love the outdoors for multi-night visits. Karlovac's Renaissance-era urban nucleus is popularly known as the Zvijezda (Star), since its military planners were moved to shape it as a six-pointed star—evidenced in the surrounding moat, which is now a pleasant, if sunken, green space that is even home to a basketball court. Eventually, this center's military nature gave way to civilian life and it took on the Baroque look more visible today. Though the town walls were razed in the 19th century, their shape is still discernible.

### GETTING HERE AND AROUND

If you don't have a rental car, taking a bus from Zagreb is super easy, as Karlovac is along the route of countless buses from the capital. Once there, the best thing is to make a pedestrian beeline to the historical center.

## Sights

**Trg Bana Josipa Jelačića**

**PLAZA/SQUARE** | At the center of this old part of town, accessible by any of several bridges over the moat, is the main square, Trg Bana Josipa Jelačića, one side of which, alas, has a great big empty building with some missing windows. At the center of this otherwise largely barren square is an old well dating to 1869; long filled in, it is ornamented with allegorical imagery. ✉ *Trg Bana Josipa Jelačića, Karlovac* ☎ *047/615-115 for Karlovac Tourist Board* 🌐 *visitkarlovac.hr.*

## Restaurants

★ **Bistro Kastel**

$$ | **EUROPEAN** | Climb the stone stairs onto the spacious terrace or dine inside the softly lit 13th-century manor, one of the most impressive examples of feudal architecture in Croatia. Kastel's offerings reflect its geographic location, representing both the Adriatic Sea and the continental plains with delicious detail. **Known for:** beautiful setting just a seven-minute ride from the center; lovely views of the town; craft beers and good wines. $ *Average main: €22* ✉ *Dubovac Castle, Zagrad Gaj 5, Karlovac* ☎ *047/658–922* 🌐 *www.bistrokastel.com* 🕒 *Closed Mon. and Tues.*

## Hotels

**Hotel Korana Srakovčić**

$$ | **HOTEL** | Deep within a tree-shaded park a few minutes' walk from the Old Town, this boutique hotel overlooks a peaceful stretch of its namesake, the Korana River. **Pros:** spacious rooms, some with balconies; tranquil setting; good restaurant on-site with all-day dining options. **Cons:** somewhat outdated rooms and amenities; pricey for the area; not fully luxurious, despite the four stars. $ *Rooms from: €160* ✉ *Perivoj Josipa Vrbanića 8, Karlovac* ☎ *047/609–090*

🌐 *www.hotelkorana.hr* 🛏 *16 rooms* 🍽 *Free Breakfast.*

## Activities

**Mrežnica River**

**KAYAKING** | The 64-km-long (40-mile-long) Mrežnica River, running south of Karlovac between pastoral villages and a meandering train track, is a lush oasis with dozens of gorgeous waterfalls and light rapids that locals and visitors flock to from mid-spring to early fall. The river is unique for its turquoise color, cleanliness and crystal clarity, and accessibility. Designated areas are rapid-free, and swimmers and kayakers (bring your own) can fairly easily traverse the banks, relax in the waterfalls, and sunbathe on the grassy riverbanks. A good base is Otok Ljubavi (the Island of Love), where you can find a café, grill food such as burgers and ćevapi, and a simple craft beer, Mrežnica Pale Ale, made in nearby Duga Resa. Camping under the stars is also a wonderful option, with the ripples of the river lulling you to sleep. ✉ *Mrežničke Poljice bb* ☎ *098/160–3686 for Otok Ljubavi* 🌐 *www.facebook.com/otokljubavi.*

# Plitvice Lakes National Park

*135 km (84 miles) southwest of Zagreb.*

Triple America's five Great Lakes, shrink them each to manageable size (536 acres, in all), give them a good cleaning until they look strikingly blue, envelop them in lush green forest with steep hillsides and cliffs all around, and link not just two but all of them with a pint-size Niagara Falls. The result? Plitvice Lakes National Park (Nacionalni Park Plitvička Jezera), a UNESCO World Heritage site and Croatia's most-visited inland natural wonder.

### GETTING HERE AND AROUND

The park is on the route of numerous cross-country buses starting from the coast (Zadar, Dubrovnik, Split) or from the capital, Zagreb. After arriving at the park, your feet are the only things you need to work your way around the wonders of this natural miracle.

## Sights

★ **Plitvice Lakes National Park** (*Nacionalni park Plitvička jezera*)

**NATIONAL PARK** | This 8,000-acre park is home to 16 beautiful emerald lakes connected by a series of cascading waterfalls, stretching 8 km (5 miles) through a valley flanked by high forested hills that are home to deer, bears, wolves, wild boar, and the Eurasian lynx. Thousands of years of sedimentation of calcium, magnesium carbonate, algae, and moss have yielded the natural barriers between the lakes. Since the process is ongoing, new barriers, curtains, stalactites, channels, and cascades are constantly forming and the existing ones are always changing. The deposited sedimentation, or tufa, also coats the beds and edges of the lakes, giving them their sparkling azure look.

Today a series of wooden bridges and waterside paths lead through the park. The only downside: because it's so lovely, the trails can get crowded from June through September. That said, there's no litter along the way—a testament to both respectful visitors and a conscientious park staff. There's also no camping, no bushwhacking, no picking plants, and absolutely no swimming. This is a place to look, to spend a day or two, but not to touch. It is, however, well worth the higher summer entrance fee and the lowered fees during the rest of the year. Plitvice Lakes is not just a summer but a year-round spectacle, with blooming flowers in the spring, sunset-color foliage in the fall, and magical-looking frozen waterfalls in the winter.

The park is right on the main highway (E71) from Zagreb to Split, and it's certainly worth the three-hour trip from the capital. There are three entrances just off the main road, about an hour's walk apart, creatively named Entrance 1, Entrance 2, and Auxiliary Entrance Flora. The park's pricey hotels are near Entrance 2, the first entrance you'll encounter if arriving by bus from the coast. However, Entrance 1—the first entrance if you arrive from Zagreb—is typically the start of most one-day excursions, if only because it's within a 20-minute walk of Veliki Slap, the 256-foot-high waterfall. Hiking the entire loop that winds its way around the lakes takes six to eight hours, but other hikes range from two to four hours. All involve a combination of hiking and being ferried across the larger of the park's lakes by national park service boats.

There are cafés near both entrances, but avoid them for anything but coffee, as the sandwiches and strudels don't offer the best value for your money. Instead, buy some of the huge heavenly strudels sold by locals at nearby stands, where great big blocks of homemade cheese, honey, and olive oil are also for sale. Within the lake grounds, there are more than 10 restaurants and bistros offering a mix of local and international cuisine. **TIP→ At the boat landing near Entrance 2, you can rent gorgeous wooden rowboats for €13 per hour (capacity is four people) during the warm season.** ✉ *Plitvicka Jezera* ☎ *053/751–015* 🌐 *www.np-plitvicka-jezera.hr/en* 🎫 *€40 June–Sept.; €23.50 Apr., May, and Oct.; €10 Nov.–Mar.*

**Rastoke**

**TOWN** | A fairy-tale village of water mills and waterfalls, this relatively little-known gem is known as the Mini Plitvice for good reason. Rastoke sits at the intersection of the mighty Korana River and the smaller sparkling Slunjčica. Some 23 waterfalls are nearby, the most famous of which are Buk, Hrvoje, and Vilina Kosa (Fairy's Hair), along with plenty of babbling rapids. The geological makeup of Rastoke's waterfalls is identical to those of Plitvice, just smaller in scale. Legend says this peaceful retreat is home to *vile* (fairies), who love to bathe in the Vilina Kosa waterfall. A handful of restaurants (for the best freshwater fish around, try Ambar in nearby Slunj) and charming rentable apartments and rooms await. There's also a 7½-km (4½-mile) walking trail (one-way). As Croatian writer Ratko Zvrko (1920–1998) implored, writing of Rastoke, "Here you should stay, and further don't be steered! Here, where life into streams is canalized, here, in this roar of wild waters you hear, lies peace for the soul and feast for the eyes!" The village is 105 km (65 miles) southwest of Zagreb and 33 km (21 miles) north of Plitvice Lakes National Park.

## Restaurants

Six restaurants are available around Entrance 2 and two restaurants near Entrance 1, so you should have ample options to appease your appetite before going into the park—unless the food store near Entrance 2 provides enough in the way of staples to fuel your hikes. Two more restaurants can be found deeper in the park (one on the west wing of the Upper Lakes and one northwest of the Lower Lakes, by Parking Lot 3), as well as a café a little further in from Entrance 2. The restaurants offer a variety of regional and international fare at different prices, depending on the establishment. Keep in mind that on-site restaurants take card payments only—no cash.

★ **Lička Kuća** (*Lika House Restaurant*)

**$$$** | **EASTERN EUROPEAN** | **FAMILY** | With its unadorned log walls, wood-beam ceilings, white-curtained windows, lively Croatian folk music playing, and an open kitchen with an open hearth, this is exactly what a restaurant in a great national park should be. Fill up on hearty *lička juha* (a creamy lamb soup with vegetables),

## Did You Know?

Plitvice Lakes is Croatia's most popular national park, but despite seeing 1.2 million visitors a year, there's a wonderful sense of untouched tranquility. That's due to strict rules against camping, picking plants, and swimming in the lakes.

## Bloody Easter

Easter Sunday, March 31, 1991, has gone down in Croatian history as the day Croatia suffered its first fatality—in its war of independence from the former Yugoslavia. The unlikely setting was none other than one of Europe's most visited natural wonders, Plitvice Lakes National Park.

Before the deadly event, Croatian commando units—under the direction of General Josip Lucić, later to become head of the Croatian Armed Forces—were dispatched to Plitvice to restore order. This is because the region had been occupied by Serbian forces led by Milan Martić, who aimed to annex the park to Serbian Krajina. The Croatian commandos were ambushed en route, near the group of hotels at Entrance 2, and one member of the team, Josip Jović, was killed and seven of his fellow soldiers were wounded. As recorded in the annals of Croatian history, nine opposing soldiers were arrested and order was restored, for a time.

The region, which had long been home to both Croats and Serbs, was occupied by Serbian forces for the next four years. The national park became a military encampment, and soldiers threatened to blow up the fragile travertine dams separating the lakes. UNESCO sent missions to prevent war from wreaking havoc on a natural wonder. In the end, with the exception of the park's red-deer population, which fell dramatically during the occupation, the park's natural beauty pulled through intact. Only the built infrastructure was damaged, including the hotels. By 1999, four years after Croatian forces reoccupied the park and painstakingly cleared the area of mines, the last of the three hotels reopened and the park was back in business.

Today a memorial in the park—behind the bus stop at Entrance 2 on the southbound side of the road—marks the life and death of Josip Jović, the first Croatian fatality in what was to be a long and bloody war.

followed by boiled or roasted lamb with vegetables, or suckling pig. **Known for:** proximity to national park; hearty fare, including lamb raised in the mountainous Lika region; seats 270 people (many tourists) but can get busy, so reserve ahead. *$ Average main: €31 ✉ Rastovača 11, Across Entrance 1, Plitvicka Jezera ☎ 053/751–379 ⏲ Closed Tues.*

## Hotels

The main advantage of staying in a rather bland touristy hotel near the park itself is that you'll be right in the center of all the hiking action. The hotels are particularly convenient if you arrive without your own car.

As an alternative, there are lots of private rooms in the immediate vicinity, where doubles go for around €100, a bargain compared to the hotels. Check out the tiny village of Mukinje, about a 15-minute hike south of Entrance 2. A bit farther south is the village of Jezerce, which also has rooms. (Note that the bus does not stop at either Mukinje or Jezerce, but it's a pleasant walk to both.) You can also get a private room in the rather faceless one-road village of Rastovača, just off the main road a few hundred yards north of Entrance 1 (where the bus stops). Practically every one of the village's newish-looking houses has rooms for rent, and they're generally bright, clean, and modern.

A bit farther afield, the village of Rakovica, 12 km (7½ miles) north of the park, usually has more vacancies in high season and is a good option if you have a car. The tourist office in Rakovica (☎ *047/784–450*) can help with bookings. Last but not least, bear in mind that there's no place to store your bags in the park if you arrive by bus and plan to head on to the coast or to Zagreb later in the day—so unless you're ready to cart your bags for hours along the park's steep trails or are traveling light, plan on an overnight stay.

**Hotel Jezero**

**$$** | **HOTEL** | Yards away from other, similarly touristy and basic hotels (the Plitvice and the Bellevue, the Bellevue being the least expensive of the three), this long, three-story, wood-paneled building looks almost like a U.S.-style motel. The rooms are simply furnished and a bit worn but clean, and they offer cheap plastic chairs on the unappealing terraces (not all rooms have terraces). **Pros:** centrally located; the best of the park's three hotel options; decent array of services and amenities. **Cons:** basic, slightly tired-looking rooms; pricey for what it is; some rooms may be smoky. *Rooms from: €200* ✉ *Josipa Jovića 19, Plitvicka Jezera* *Near Entrance 2* ☎ *053/751–500* *np-plitvicka-jezera.hr/en* *224 rooms* *Free Breakfast.*

## Sisak

*75 km (47 miles) southeast of Zagreb.*

Sisak is historically one of the oldest continuously settled places in Europe (since 400 BC), although it's been revealed that human presence in the area goes back even earlier. This unassuming little town was also the site of one of the more important battles in Croatia's history: a 1593 victory against Ottoman forces. More modern history saw the town converted into an industrial hub with life centered around its waterways; Sisak sits at the confluence of the Kupa and the Sava, as well as the Odra and the Kupa rivers.

**Sisak Fortress**

**MILITARY SIGHT** | A bit south of the town center—3 km (2 miles) to be exact, where the rivers Kupa and Sava meet—stands the once-mighty Sisak Fortress (built 1544–50), with one prominent bastion at each point of its triangular form. The fortress has a hugely significant past: it was here, on June 22, 1593, that the Habsburgs, in the company of Croats and Slovenes, pulled off a victory over Ottoman armies, a triumph that figured prominently in halting the Ottoman advance toward Zagreb and into Western Europe. The fortress's interior is closed due to earthquake damage (no reopening date at the time of this writing), but it's worth taking a look at the structure and going for a stroll on the green walkway that surrounds it. ✉ *Obala Tome Bakača Erdoedyja, Sisak* ☎ *091/788–9557* *tzg-sisak.hr.*

## Čigoč

*28 km (17 miles) southeast of Sisak.*

The charming village of Čigoč is officially known as the European Village of Storks because it draws so many of the migrating birds each spring, and a testament to that is its annual Stork Festival, usually held in late June. Several hundred of the birds while away much of the summer here before embarking on their long journey to southern Africa. That said, people live here, too, evidenced by the distinctive wooden houses that are a sight to behold.

Čigoč is also home to the headquarters of the beautiful Lonjsko Polje Nature Park. The UNESCO-listed wetland is one of Europe's largest floodplains, and this protected area is home to diverse flora and fauna. More than 200 species of birds, 40 fish, 10 reptiles, and 15 amphibians make this their home, along with 550 plant species—notably, untouched forests of English oak. This is a place where you can take in the greenery around you as you watch dragonflies (almost 40 dragonfly types live in the park) fly around you and wild boars run through the fields.

## Sights

**Čigoč Information Center**

**VISITOR CENTER** | Located in a traditional wooden Posavina house on the main road through the village center, the information center is the top regional source for all you need to know about storks, the Stork Festival, and nearby Lonjsko Polje Nature Park. Park maps are available for purchase. **TIP→ Ask about the park's educational programs or appealing boat trips; many options are available for an additional price.** *Čigoč 26, Cigoc* *044/715–115* *pp-lonjsko-polje.hr.*

**★ Lonjsko Polje Nature Park**

**NATURE PRESERVE** | One of the largest floodplains in the Danubian basin, this unique ecological and cultural landscape of 20,506 acres along the Sava River was accorded park status in 1990 and is included on UNESCO's roster of World Heritage sites. It has numerous rare and endangered plant and animal species, from white-tailed eagles and saker falcons to otters and the Danube salmon—as well as storks, which are as easy to come by here as in Čigoč. Its 4,858 acres of pastureland are also home to Croatia's highest concentration of indigenous breeds of livestock. Traditional village architecture—in particular, houses made of oak—further contributes to the region's appeal. Three park offices (in Čigoč at Čigoč 26; Repušnica at Fumićeva 184; Krapje at Krapje 16) provide maps and information on where to go and what to see, and also issue park entrance passes. Prices vary with the package; some include boat rides. A car is the easiest way to access the park; if you're driving from Zagreb, exit the motorway at the pretty village of Popovača and take the road to the right through the villages of Potok and Stružec toward Sisak. *Krapje* *044/611–190* *pp-lonjsko-polje.hr* *From €3 for basic ticket (various add-ons available).*

# Jasenovac

*35 km (22 miles) southeast of Čigoč.*

Located where the Sava traces Croatia's long east–west border with Bosnia and Herzegovina until taking a turn into Serbia more than 150 km (93 miles) away, Jasenovac is the site of Croatia's most notorious World War II labor camps. During the war, Croatia was largely a puppet state of Nazi Germany and Fascist Italy. A memorial and museum is now operating on the site.

## Sights

**Memorial Museum Jasenovac**

**HISTORY MUSEUM** | Although the labor camps at Jasenovac were razed after World War II, a memorial park was eventually established at the site, along with a museum featuring photographs and other exhibits related to the memorial. Current estimates are that somewhere between 77,000 and 97,000 people—mostly Serbs, Jews, Roma, and Croatian antifascists—perished at this string of five camps on the banks of the Sava River between 1941 and 1945 from exhaustion, illness, cold weather, and murder. *Ulica Braće Radić 147, Jasenovac* *044/672–319* *www.jusp-jasenovac.hr* *Free.*

Chapter 9



# SLAVONIA

Updated by
Andrea MacDonald

| Sights | Restaurants | Hotels | Shopping | Nightlife |
| --- | --- | --- | --- | --- |
| ★★★☆☆ | ★★☆☆☆ | ★★☆☆☆ | ★☆☆☆☆ | ★☆☆☆☆ |

# WELCOME TO SLAVONIA

## TOP REASONS TO GO

★ **Charming cities:** Osijek, Croatia's fourth largest city, packs a lot of charm into a compact space, including attractive churches and parks, miles of bike lanes, cafés along the Drava River, and Tvrđa, an atmospheric Old Town.

★ **Bird-watching:** Break out your binoculars for a boat ride in serenely beautiful Kopački Rit Nature Park, one of the last great wetlands on the continent.

★ **Age-old traditions:** Discover a land lost in time in the unspoiled Baranja region, with its traditional Pannonian houses, rural restaurants, and extraordinary wine.

★ **Rebirth after war:** The Baroque town of Vukovar is a testament to the destruction wrought by the Homeland War and to the quiet strength of Croatia's rejuvenation.

★ **Wine country:** Cruise the wine roads of Slavonia, visiting 600-year-old cellars in Ilok or the region around Kutjevo that the Romans nicknamed the Golden Valley.

Occupying the northeastern section of Croatia, Slavonia is wedged between Serbia to the east, Hungary to the north, and Bosnia to the south. It is bordered by three major rivers: the Sava, the Drava, and the Danube.

1 **Osijek.** The fun easygoing capital of Slavonia.

2 **The Baranja Region.** An unspoiled area known for its food and wine.

3 **Vukovar.** The site of one of the most tragic battles of the Homeland War.

4 **Ilok.** Castles and wineries perched above the Danube.

5 **Đakovo.** A peaceful town famous for Lipizzaner horses.

6 **The Golden Valley.** A charming wine region.

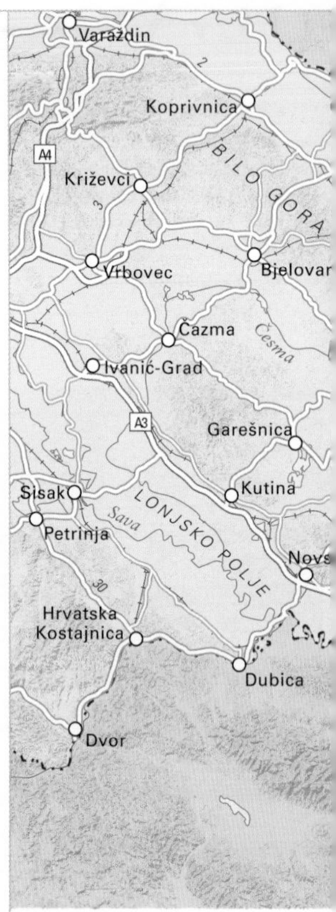

HUNGARY
SERBIA
BOSNIA-HERZEGOVINA
Drava
Danube
Sava
Vuka
Virovitica
Slatina
Donji Miholjac
Beli Manastir
Zmajevac
Karanac
The Baranja Region
Kopački Rit Nature Park
Belišće
Valpovo
Bizovac
Osijek
Aljmaš
Čepin
Tenja
Borovo
Vukovar
Vinkovci
Ilok
Daruvar
The Golden Valley
Papuk Nature Park
Našice
Pakrac
Lipik
Kutjevo
Požega
Đakovo
Okučani
Nova Gradiœka
Slavonski Brod
Županja
0
20 miles
0
20 kilometers

## Somewhere beyond the sea, there is a region called Slavonia. There is no coastline here, which has always meant fewer tourists. What it offers instead is something increasingly rare: unspoiled nature and undiscovered cultural treasures.

As the agricultural breadbasket of Croatia, Slavonia has miles of flat farmland, cornfields, vineyards, flower fields, and, in the right season, towering sunflowers in bloom. It also has centuries-old wine cellars, Baroque towns, art galleries and museums, castles, film and folk festivals, river fish cook-offs, and so much great white wine. There are even sandy beaches along the Danube. One thing is certain: Slavonia will not stay undiscovered for long. But for now, it's all yours. Welcome to the green heart of Croatia.

One of the four historical regions of Croatia, Slavonia has been traversed and inhabited through the ages by more ethnicities than any other region; Croats, Serbs, Hungarians, Germans, Ottomans, and others have all left their mark on its culture. First settled by Slavic tribes in the 7th century and later an integral part of the Hungarian-Croat kingdom, Slavonia experienced a major change of culture with Sultan Suleiman the Magnificent's march toward Hungary and Austria in 1526. For almost 150 years much of the region became an Ottoman stronghold. Osijek and Požega flourished not as part of Christian Europe, but rather as full-fledged mosque-filled Turkish towns. The Turkish retreat in the late 17th century ushered in an era of Austrian influence, and Osijek became the region's economic and cultural capital.

There was a long period of stability and prosperity; Austro-Hungarian and German aristocrats built classical, Baroque, and art nouveau palaces and mansions in Osijek and Vukovar, and Slavonia became a vital transport route for trade between neighboring countries, particularly between Zagreb and Belgrade. The diverse population lived peacefully until the Homeland War in the 1990s, when Slobodan Milošević cited the large Serbian population who lived along the border as an excuse to incorporate the region into Serbia. Fighting was fierce and many lives were lost, and cities such as Osijek and Vukovar were badly damaged (remains of which are still evident physically and culturally); the region wasn't fully reintegrated back into Croatia until 1998.

Today, the Slavonian economy, which is based primarily on agriculture, is the slowest in the country. In recent decades, particularly since Croatia joined the European Union, many Slavonian residents have left to find jobs elsewhere. You'll meet them working all over Croatia, and if you tell them you've visited their hometown you'll give them a very pleasant surprise.

# Planning

## When to Go

The best time to visit Slavonia is spring or early fall, which are considered the high seasons here and conveniently the same months when hundreds of thousands of birds gather at Kopački Rit Nature Park. Late August and September are harvest season, when there are plenty of local agricultural festivals throughout the region. Slavonia can be swelteringly hot in summer (which is actually considered the low season), when many establishments close because everyone has fled to the coast. It gets cold and snowy in the winter, but there are traditional Christmas markets (including the fantastic Advent Market in Osijek), winter festivals, and local mulled wine to keep you warm.

## Getting Here and Around

### AIR

There are direct flights between Osijek and Zagreb, Dubrovnik, Rijeka, Pula, Zadar, and Split on Croatia Airlines, as well as internationally to London and Munich.

**CONTACTS Osijek Airport.** ✉ *Vukovarska 67, Klisa, Osijek* ☎ *031/284–611* 🌐 *osijek-airport.hr.*

### BUS

Public transport in Slavonia is, to put it mildly, difficult. It is infrequent, particularly on weekends and holidays. Come summer, when kids aren't traveling to school, many routes are canceled altogether. If you must use public transport, the bus is more reliable than the train. There are around 10 daily buses between Zagreb and Osijek (4 hours, €15) and a couple of daily buses making the 45-minute trip from Osijek to Vukovar and then onwards to Ilok or to Đakovo an hour away. To reach Kutjevo, take a bus to Požega and transfer to a local bus to Kutjevo. A great resource for comparing routes is 🌐 *getbybus.com.*

**CONTACTS Đakovo Bus Station.** ✉ *Splitska bb, Đakovo* ☎ *060/803–803.* **Osijek Bus Station.** ✉ *Bartola Kašića 70, Osijek* ☎ *060/353–353.* **Vukovar Bus Station.** ✉ *Olajnica BB, Vukovar* ☎ *060/337–799.*

### CAR

Having your own wheels will make your life a whole lot easier in Slavonia, particularly if you want to travel on weekends or visit wineries, nature parks, or small towns that are not served by public transport. Roads are quiet, quick, usually flat, and well-maintained and finding parking is never an issue, making a Slavonian road trip very pleasant. You'll pay around €15 each way on motorway tolls between Zagreb and Osijek.

### TRAIN

Train journeys between Zagreb and Osijek are quick and comfortable, with 12 trains daily (4 hours, €12). Venturing farther afield is a different story, as train services have been reduced in recent years and many stations have fallen into disrepair. Once you actually get on the train, the experience is quite whimsical; it cuts right through the heart of Slavonia, giving you a real sense of the region's sweeping vistas.

**CONTACTS Osijek Train Station.** ✉ *Trg Lavoslava Ružičke 2, Osijek* ☎ *060/333–444.*

## Restaurants

Outside of Osijek, where you're spoiled for choice, there aren't a huge number of restaurants in Slavonia. In many towns, you'll find eating at hotels and wineries is your best (and sometimes only) opportunity to try hearty, spicy, and delicious Slavonian cuisine. Being surrounded by three major rivers, Slavonia's most popular dishes involve river fish, namely carp, pike, catfish, and pike-perch. With paprika-rich Hungary not far away, you'll often see dishes characterized by an unmistakable bright-red zest, most evident in the region's most popular dish: the spicy-hot *fiš paprikaš*, a river-fish stew usually served in a bowl big enough for two. *Perkelt od soma* is another fish stew common in Baranja, often made with sliced catfish and accompanied by homemade noodles, cheese, and bacon.

Meat is a key part of the dining picture as well. Regular menu staples include black Slavonian pig (*crna svinja*), considered one of the highest quality meats due to its diet of acorns from Slavonian oak trees. Another popular dish is *čobanac*, a stew made with game meat bathed in paprika sauce and usually served with spaetzle. But nothing beats the mighty *kulen*, a spicy air-dried sausage similar to chorizo that is Slavonia's most beloved local product, often served on charcuterie boards alongside *čvarci* (pork rinds). Cabbage and cottage cheese are common side dishes, as are pepper, tomato, and cucumber salads straight from the garden. Of course, no trip to Slavonia—Croatia's largest wine-producing area by volume—would be complete without local wine. The region is best known for its whites; look for varieties such as Graševina (known elsewhere as Welschriesling) and Traminac, a type of Gewürztraminer. Red wine lovers should try the delicious Frankovka. Hearty meals, delicious wine, and extremely affordable prices all add up to one certainty: you are going to eat and drink far too much in Slavonia, and you'll love it.

## Hotels

Slavonia might offer fewer accommodation choices than the rest of Croatia, but the best hotels cost less than half of what you'd pay elsewhere. You'll find the more modern hotel options in Osijek, while Ilok offers the chance to sleep in historic wineries with excellent restaurants on-site. In Baranja and Kutjevo, you'll stay in unique rural properties where you can enjoy the countryside, taste homemade products, get to know the locals, and even get your hands dirty helping out at harvest time. You can find great value private rooms and apartments in all towns; Booking.com is the best resource.

⇨ *Restaurant and hotel reviews have been shortened. For full information, visit Fodors.com. Restaurant prices are the average cost of a main course at dinner or, if dinner is not served, at lunch. Hotel prices are the lowest cost of a standard double room in high season.*

### What It Costs in Euros (€)

| $ | $$ | $$$ | $$$$ |
|---|---|---|---|
| **RESTAURANTS** | | | |
| under €15 | €15–€23 | €24–€32 | over €32 |
| **HOTELS** | | | |
| under €150 | €150–€250 | €251–€350 | over €350 |

## Tours

**Tureta Travel**

**SPECIAL-INTEREST TOURS** | This Zagreb-based boutique travel agency runs custom-made private tours around Croatia, including to Slavonia and Baranja. They organize everything based on the client's personal preferences, from transport to accommodation to wine tasting, and they specialize in local, off-the-beaten-track experiences. If you don't have your own transport but want to explore the region, Tureta should be your first call. ☎ *160/116–48* 🌐 *www.tureta-travel.com.*

## Visitor Information

The tourist information offices in Osijek, Vukovar, and Ilok are very helpful, and they can often assist in arranging a private guide to show you around if you'd like one.

**CONTACTS Đakovo Tourist Information.** ✉ *Kralja Tomislava 3, Đakovo* ☎ *031/812–319* 🌐 *visitdakovo.croatia.hr.* **Ilok Tourist Information.** ✉ *Trg Svetog Ivana Kapistrana 5, Ilok* ☎ *032/590–020* 🌐 *turizamilok.hr.* **Osijek Tourist Information.** ✉ *Županijska 2, Osijek* ☎ *031/203–755* 🌐 *www.tzosijek.hr.* **Vukovar Tourist Information.** ✉ *Josipa Jurja Strossmayera 15, Vukovar* ☎ *032/442–889* 🌐 *turizamvukovar.hr.*

# Osijek

*280 km (175 miles) east of Zagreb.*

Croatia's fourth-largest city is an often overlooked cultural treasure and a hive of activity year-round. There are music, food, and sports festivals; historical museums; bustling markets; a thriving café scene; miles of tree-lined streets and bike lanes; beach bars along the river; and no less than 17 parks, making it the greenest city in Croatia. The Drava River runs the length of the city and is a favorite recreational area for residents; you'll see them biking, jogging, or sitting at one of the many riverside terraces with a coffee. Taking a seat beside them is the best way to fully appreciate the local life of Osijek.

In the mid-12th century, Osijek was a prosperous market town in the Hungarian-Croatian kingdom. In 1526 the Turks invaded and subsequently ruled the city for more than 150 years, during which time the city took on a distinctly Ottoman look, as many Islamic places of worship were built as was the famous wooden Suleiman Bridge over the Drava. After several attempts, the bridge was burned down in 1686 for the final time by the Habsburg army and Osijek became a military garrison under the Austrians, who built a walled fortress (present-day Tvrđa) to prevent any further Ottoman invasions. The city thrived economically and culturally during this period; its cathedral, national theater, and many of the prominent buildings along Europska Avenija were built, the tram was introduced in 1884 (and is still in operation), and the city was redesigned in the Baroque style you see today.

Osijek was bombarded during the Homeland War between 1991 and 1992 in what is known as the Battle of Osijek. Some 800 people were killed, two-thirds of the population was displaced, and the majority of those who remained were forced to live in bomb shelters. Most of the damage has since been repaired, but some scars remain in pockmarked building facades. Like Zagreb, which it resembles physically, Osijek today is an easygoing place where locals enjoy a leisurely pace of life. It offers visitors an opportunity to tap into a living and breathing Croatian city and makes a perfect base for explorations farther into Slavonia and Baranja.

### GETTING HERE AND AROUND

Osijek is the easiest place to get to in the region, with regular buses and trains from Zagreb and neighboring countries such as Austria, Serbia, and Hungary. The bus and train stations are both just a short walk from the city center. Osijek also has an international airport with regular flights from Croatia and beyond; the airport is about 20 minutes outside of town and a taxi to the city center costs around €15.

Osijek is very walkable and all the main sights are a short distance from each other. If you're short on time you can hop aboard one of the trams to get around. To get between Gornji Grad and Tvrđa, take Tram No. 1. There are also miles of flat bike lanes, and perhaps the best way

Slavonia
SLOVENIA
HUNGARY
SERBIA
BOSNIA-HERZEGOVINA
Mursko Središće
Čakovec
Mura
Varaždin
Lepoglava
Krapina
Koprivnica
Zabok
Medvednica Nature Park
Križevci
BILO GORA
Drava
Danube
Vrbovec
Bjelovar
ZAGREB
Samobor
Virovitica
Batina Monument
Josic Winery
Zmajevac
Beli Manastir
Karanac
Donji Miholjac
The Baranja Region
Slatina
Čazma
Česma
Velika Gorica
Ivanić-Grad
Žumberak-Samoborko Nature Park
Belišće
Valpovo
Kopački Rit Nature Park
Bizovac
Osijek
Garešnica
Daruvar
The Golden Valley
Papuk Nature Park
Aljmaš
Čepin
Tenja
Karlovac
Kupa
Sisak
Kutina
Našice
Vuka
Petrinja
Sava
LONJSKO POLJE
Pakrac
Lipik
Kutjevačko Vinogorje
Krauthaker
Kutjevo
Duga Resa
Glina
Novska
Požega
Đakovo
Borovo
Vučedol Culture Museum
Vukovar
Spomen Dom Ovčara
Vinkovci
Hrvatska Kostajnica
Okučani
Nova Gradiœka
Slavonski Brod
Ilok
Korana
Dubica
Županja
Plitvice Lakes National Park
Dvor
A1
A2
A3
A4
A5
2
3
6
28
30
34
36
46
51
53
E661
0
20 miles
20 kilometers

to see the city, particularly the riverside, is on two wheels; bikes can be rented from Guesthouse Maksimilian (🌐 *www.maksimilian.hr*).

On the other side of the river, you'll find the zoo, the beach bars around Copacabana, and the road to Baranja. To cross the river without a car, catch a free hourly boat near Kompa restaurant, which will let you off near the Osijek Zoo, or walk across the pedestrian bridge, Pješački Most, one of the most famous symbols of the city.

## Sights

There are three main areas where you'll spend your time in Osijek. **Tvrđa** is the city's atmospheric historical center; while it's a bit sleepy during the day, with just a couple of noteworthy sights, it comes to life at night with bars and terraces filling up the main square.

**Gornji Grad** (Upper Town) is the newer part of town and is the commercial and administrative center, where you will find the cathedral, Hotel Waldinger, and Hotel Osijek, plus many shops and cafés. You can walk between the new and old areas via the riverfront, or take Europska Avenija, a broad avenue lined with late 19th- and early 20th-century neoclassical and art nouveau houses built as private residences.

On the other side of the river from Osijek, you will find quieter walkways, the zoo, Copacabana water park, and a couple of riverside beach bars that make an excellent spot to watch the sun set.

**Arheološki Muzej** (*Archeological Museum*)
**HISTORY MUSEUM** | On Tvrđa's Holy Trinity Square, you'll find the spacious Archeological Museum in the renovated City Guardhouse. It has an impressive range of artifacts from Slavonia through the ages, from the Neolithic Starčevo culture through to Celtic and Roman times. The building itself is modern and airy, with a glass dome over the arcaded courtyard, and the exhibitions are well laid out across several rooms. ✉ *Trg Svetog Trojstva 2, Tvrda* ☎ *031/232–130* 🌐 *www.amo.hr* 🎫 *€3.30* ⏲ *Closed Sun. and Mon.*

**Copacabana**
**WATER PARK** | **FAMILY** | Who says you need the Adriatic to have water fun in Croatia? On the north side of the Drava River, you'll find Copacabana, a complex of outdoor swimming pools, waterslides, mini-golf, and bocce courts. There is also a free sandy beach nearby where you can swim in the river, with a couple of bars for refreshments. It's a great place for the whole family to spend a sunny afternoon or watch the sun set. ✉ *Tvrđavica bb, Osijek* 🎫 *€3* ⏲ *Closed Sept.–July.*

**Crveni Fićo** (*The Red Fićo*)
**MONUMENT** | This unusual monument, located a few blocks away from Tvrđa, commemorates an iconic act of defiance that happened in Osijek in 1991. As Yugoslav army tanks rolled into the city, one man parked his little red Fiat (*fićo*) in the middle of the road in front of them. The man escaped safely, his car was run over by the tank, and it was all captured on television (check out the clip online). The event became a symbol of the strength and resistance of the local people. In this monument, the little red car is rolling over the tank: the victor this time around. ✉ *Kneza Trpimira 4, Gornji Grad.*

★ **Konkatedrala Svetog Petra i Pavla** (*Co-cathedral of Saints Peter and Paul*)
**CHURCH** | This majestic single-nave church is the highlight of Osijek's downtown skyline. At 292 feet tall, its red-brick neo-Gothic steeple is the second-highest structure in Croatia. Built between 1894 and 1898 on the initiative of the famous Đakovo-based bishop Josip Juraj Strossmayer, it has five altars and the walls are painted with colorful frescoes. ✉ *Trg Pape Ivana Pavla II, Gornji Grad* ☎ *031/310–020* 🌐 *svpetaripavao.hr.*

The Co-cathedral of Saints Peter and Paul is the second-highest structure in Croatia.

**Muzej Likovnih Umjetnosti** (*Museum of Fine Arts*)
**ART MUSEUM** | One of the 18th-century mansions along Europska Avenija, formerly belonging to a prominent attorney, is now the home of the Museum of Fine Arts. It focuses on Croatian and Slavonian artists with a permanent collection of paintings, sculptures, and graphic arts. It is well worth a visit, particularly to check out the temporary exhibitions on the ground floor. ✉ *Europska Avenija 9, Gornji Grad* ☎ *031/251–280* 🌐 *www.mlu.hr* 🎫 *€2* 🕐 *Closed Mon.*

**Muzej Slavonije** (*Museum of Slavonia*)
**HISTORY MUSEUM** | One of the largest museums in Croatia, the Museum of Slavonia is located in an imposing Baroque building on Tvrđa's main square. It has myriad objects on display concerning the region's folklore, culture, and natural history, with everything from stuffed animals and old coins to pottery and swords. ✉ *Trg Svetog Trojstva 6, Tvrda* ☎ *031/250–731* 🌐 *www.mso.hr* 🎫 *€2.65* 🕐 *Closed Sun. and Mon.*

**Perivoj Kralja Tomislava** (*King Tomislav Gardens*)
**CITY PARK** | **FAMILY** | With 17 around town, Osijek is known as a city of parks, and this is the largest. The King Tomislav Gardens is a spacious forested oasis that was laid out in the 18th century for Austrian officers to take a breather from life in the citadel. It separates Tvrđa from Gornji Grad and is home to playgrounds and a tennis club. ✉ *Europska avenija 2, Osijek.*

★ **Tvrđa**
**NEIGHBORHOOD** | Now a somewhat sleepy Old Town that always seems to be under construction, this walled fortress has a history dating back to the mid-12th century, when the site was a market town in the Hungarian-Croatian kingdom. It was later occupied by the Ottomans, and finally became a fortified military garrison under the Austrians in the 17th century to try to keep out any further invasions. It has one of the best-preserved ensembles of Baroque buildings in Croatia, with old barracks, churches, and monasteries.

Facing the Drava River, the Water Gate is the only remaining gate in the original fortress wall, most of which was razed in the 1920s. Trg Svetog Trojstva (Holy Trinity Square) is the main square, flanked by the Archaeological Museum and the Museum of Slavonia. In the center is the Votive Pillar of the Holy Trinity, one of Osijek's finest Baroque monuments, erected in 1729–30 by the widow of General Maksimilijan Petraš, who died of the plague in 1728. The café-bars on the square come alive in the evenings as a favorite hangout of the city's student population. ✉ *Tvrđa, Tvrda.*

**Zoo Vrt Osijek** (*Osijek Zoo*)
**ZOO** | **FAMILY** | Croatia's largest zoo is located on the north side of the Drava River in a peaceful location surrounded by parks. There are about 80 animal species spread across 27 acres, including kangaroos, meerkats, lions, chimpanzees, giraffes, and zebras, plus 20 species in the aquarium and terrarium. You can drive across the bridge to get there or take a free *kompa* boat from the city side of the river (it departs across from the zoo outside Kompa restaurant). ✉ *Tvrđavica 1, Gornji Grad* ☎ *031/285–234* 🌐 *www.zoo-osijek.hr* 🎟 *€2.65.*

## Restaurants

★ **Čingi Lingi Čarda**
**$$** | **EASTERN EUROPEAN** | **FAMILY** | Located across the river in Bilje on the outskirts of Kopački Rit, Čingi Lingi is one of Osijek's hottest new restaurants in one of its most historical buildings. Built on the site of a century-old tavern that was the most popular spot in town until it was destroyed during the Homeland War, it has been rebuilt in a rustic-chic style, with a sprawling terrace right on the water, and is once again buzzing with locals. **Known for:** popular spot for local celebrations; traditional local ingredients with sophisticated modern twist; mouth-watering plum cake. [$] *Average main: €15* ✉ *Kralja Zvonimira, Bilje* 🌐 *cingilingi-carda.hr.*

★ **Kompa**
**$** | **EASTERN EUROPEAN** | On the bank of the Drava, just across the river from the Osijek Zoo, family-owned Kompa is a long-standing institution beloved for their traditional dishes. Their homemade sausages are perfectly spicy, the *koljenica* (pig's knuckle) is a firm favorite, and if you are around on a Sunday or holiday, join the locals for a big feast of *teleće pečenje* (roast veal). **Known for:** unique selection of traditional food; riverside location (be prepared for mosquitos); friendly service. [$] *Average main: €12* ✉ *Splavarska 1, Gornji Grad* ☎ *031/375–755* 🌐 *www.restorankompa.hr* 🕒 *Closed Mon.*

**Lumiere**
**$$** | **MEDITERRANEAN** | A sophisticated option in the center of Osijek, Lumiere presents Italian-inspired seasonal dishes that offer a unique take on Slavonian and Croatian ingredients. The menu changes seasonally but favorites include beef and tuna carpaccio, goose pâté, steak with truffle sauce, and an excellent range of homemade desserts. **Known for:** one of most sophisticated restaurants in Slavonia; five-course chef's tasting menu; romantic outdoor terrace. [$] *Average main: €16* ✉ *Šetalište Kardinala Franje Šepera 8, Gornji Grad* ☎ *031/201–088* 🌐 *lumiere.com.hr.*

## Hotels

**Hotel Osijek**
**$** | **HOTEL** | This skyline-dominating glass edifice located right on the riverfront is Slavonia's only luxury hotel; it has a Finnish sauna and Jacuzzi on the top floor with excellent views and a fantastic restaurant, Zimska Luka, on the riverfront that is worth a visit, even if you're not a hotel guest. **Pros:** central riverfront location; great on-site restaurant; rooftop wellness center and spa. **Cons:** large and rather impersonal; many rooms on the

small side; lacking a distinctly Slavonian vibe. $ *Rooms from: €130* ✉ *Šamačka 4, Gornji Grad* ☎ *031/230–333* 🌐 *www.hotelosijek.hr* 147 rooms 🍽 *Free Breakfast.*

**★ Hotel Waldinger**

$ | **HOTEL** | Located in a 19th-century art nouveau building on the main street in Gornji Grad, the Waldinger—named after famous local painter Adolf Waldinger—offers luxury on a cozy scale with an old-world look and feel. **Pros:** old-world luxury; excellent dining at restaurant and café; prime central location. **Cons:** expensive by Slavonian standards; rooms on top floor have small windows; service is a bit indifferent. $ *Rooms from: €120* ✉ *Županijska 8, Gornji Grad* ☎ *031/250–450* 🌐 *waldinger.hr* 16 rooms 🍽 *Free Breakfast.*

**★ Maksimilian**

$ | **B&B/INN** | You'll feel immediately at home amid the soft rich furnishings of this 14-room guesthouse in Tvrđa, a one-of-a-kind accommodation and a great place to base yourself while in Osijek. **Pros:** central location in Tvrđa; very friendly and helpful owners and staff; comfortable, spacious, and beautifully-furnished rooms. **Cons:** some rooms can be noisy; kitchen off-limits for guest use; basic room amenities. $ *Rooms from: €52* ✉ *Franjevačka 12, Tvrda* ☎ *031/497–567* 🌐 *maksimilian.hr* 14 rooms 🍽 *Free Breakfast.*

## Nightlife

Osijek bars and cafés are full day and night with people drinking coffee, eating ice cream, or enjoying a local Osječko beer. The promenade along the river (Zimska Luka) really comes alive on summer weekends with live music across the outdoor terraces. Much of the late-night action among the large student population takes place in Tvrđa. Beware that smoking is still permitted indoors in Croatian bars, so you might want to take a seat on the terrace if cigarettes aren't your thing.

**Gajba**

**BARS** | The first craft beer bar in Croatia, this tiny establishment in the Upper Town is a great place to try Croatian and international craft brews. The staff are serious beer aficionados who also organize the very popular Osijek Craft Beer Festival. ✉ *Sunčana 3, Gornji Grad* 🌐 *www.gajba.hr.*

**Gold by Waldinger**

**BARS** | **FAMILY** | Offering old-world Viennese-style elegance, Gold by Waldinger is one of Osijek's finest café-bars. Located on the main street in Gornji Grad, just across the street from Hotel Waldinger, the terrace is a popular place to people-watch over a cocktail, coffee, ice cream, or incredibly indulgent cake. ✉ *Županijska 15, Gornji Grad* ☎ *031/623–057* 🌐 *gold.waldinger.hr.*

**Merlon**

**BARS** | **FAMILY** | The south end of Tvrđa's main square is lined with café-bars and terraces; Merlon is just around the corner and stands out from the rest with its stylish interior and American-style pub menu, featuring excellent burgers, ribs, and a good selection of veggie burgers. ✉ *Franje Markovića 3, Tvrda* ☎ *031/283–240* 🌐 *merlon.hr.*

## Performing Arts

**Hrvatsko Narodno Kazalište** (*Croatian National Theater*)

**THEATER** | The Croatian National Theater is Osijek's venue for a broad array of Croatian and international plays. The building that has housed the theater since 1907 is an imposing structure whose Venetian-Moorish style renders it the most striking of a string of classical facades along Županijska Ulica. ✉ *Županijska 9, Gornji Grad* ☎ *031/220–700* 🌐 *hnk-osijek.hr.*

## Shopping

Bustling Županijska Street in Gornji Grad is similar to a smaller-scale version of Zagreb's Ilica, with its independent boutiques, shops, and trams. There are also two large shopping malls—Portanova and Avenue Mall—located just outside of Osijek; a bus runs from the city center to both of them.

**★ Green Market**

**MARKET** | This bustling daily market is a super local and authentic place to buy Slavonian delicacies such as cottage cheese, bags of paprika and other spices, elderflower syrup, fresh produce, baked goods, and all manner of smoked meats, including the famous kulen. Around the periphery, there are clothing stalls and a couple of bakeries and cafés, too. The market is held daily from 7 am until around 3 pm. ✉ *Trg Ljudevita Gaja, Gornji Grad.*

# The Baranja Region

*314 km (195 miles) east of Zagreb.*

The bucolic Baranja region, whose name means "Mother of Wine" in Hungarian, begins just across the river from Osijek and stretches to the borders of Hungary and Serbia. It is a flat agricultural land of gently sloping fields, full of farmhouses and quaint villages with only a few thousand residents at most. Life is lived around the Danube, in vineyards and fertile fields, in Pannonian mud houses, and near the swamps of Kopački Rit. There are fish-stew cook-offs, harvest festivals, flower fields, and goulash, and everything is sprinkled with paprika (just one symbol of the strong Hungarian influence here; another is the bilingual street signs). Its celebrated wineries and authentic organic restaurants have earned it top marks in the Croatian culinary world, yet it remains one of the country's least explored corners.

Baranja is compact and its villages are easily explored with a car. It is nearly impossible to get around by public transport so if you don't have a car, organize a day trip from Osijek. If you want to sleep here, the best village to spend the night in is Karanac.

## Sights

**Batina Monument**

**MONUMENT** | High on a hill above the border where Croatia meets Hungary and Serbia is this striking monument, dedicated to the 2,000 members of the Red Army who died in the Battle of Batina, one of the largest battles of World War II in Yugoslavia. It was built in 1946, three years after the battle, by Croatian sculptor Antun Augustinčić. The monument itself—topped by an 89-foot-high obelisk—is quite impressive, but the views of the Danube, forests, and three countries below are the best part of the visit. ✉ *Batina.*

**★ Josić Winery**

**WINERY** | One of the most celebrated wineries and restaurants in Croatia, the progressive Josić Winery, headed by the brilliant Damir Josić in the settlement of Zmajevac, is a must-visit. It is located on a steep deeply-cut road formed by gullies called a *surduk*, which is flanked by wine cellars dug into the hill above called *gatori.* Josić is the best-known but there are other smaller wineries on the same road which can be visited by appointment or during the "wine marathon" that takes place every September. The on-site restaurant, with a romantic indoor setting and lively atmosphere on the terrace, is deservedly popular for its traditional meals, including stews cooked over an open fire at the entrance. Call ahead to arrange a tour of the cellars and a wine tasting; those craving a glass of red wine in this land of whites will be happy to learn that although 50% of its production is Graševina, Josić is renowned for its Cabernet Sauvignon and Cuvée.

⊠ *Planina 194, Zmajevac* ☎ *031/734–410* 🌐 *josic.hr* ⏲ *Closed Mon.* *Reservations recommended.*

**★ Kopački Rit Nature Park**

**NATURE PRESERVE | FAMILY** | One of the largest remaining wetlands along the Danube, Kopački Rit Nature Park is a place of serene beauty. Embracing more than 74,100 acres north of the Drava, the park is covered with immense reed beds; willow, poplar, and oak forests; and crisscrossed by ridges, ponds, shallow lakes, and marshes. More than 300 bird species, hundreds of varieties of plants, and dozens of species of butterflies, mammals, and fish live here; it is also a breeding area for numerous endangered species, including the white-tailed sea eagle, the black stork, and the European otter.

The best times of year to visit are during the spring and autumn bird migrations, when there are often several thousand birds in the park. You can buy tickets at the welcome center, and then a boardwalk walking trail leads to the landing where boat excursions set out into the marshy heart of the park. There are different guided tours available; an early-morning small boat tour is usually your best bet. Call ahead to reserve and bring lots of mosquito repellent.

Another point of interest within the park is Tikveš Castle. Built in the 19th century by the Habsburg family and used as a hunting lodge by various monarchs and politicians over the years, including Tito, it was recently converted into a multimedia exhibition center documenting the history of the park and the region. To reach Kopački Rit from Osijek, cross the river and follow the signs from the municipality of Bilje. Tikveš Castle is a further 11 km (6 miles) away. ⊠ *Mali Sakadaš 1, Kopacevo* ☎ *031/445–445* 🌐 *pp-kopacki-rit.hr* *€19.90 for small boat tour (1 hr); €7.90 for Tikveš Castle* ⏲ *Closed Mon. and Tues.*

## Restaurants

**★ Baranjska Kuća**

**$$ | EASTERN EUROPEAN | FAMILY** | Family-run Baranjska Kuća, located in the village of Karanac, is not only one of Slavonia's best restaurants, but it's also one of the region's must-see sights for its traditional music and decor, lively atmosphere, and interesting ethnographic museum out back. Locals and visitors fill up large wooden tables around the garden, the air fragrant with smoke from outdoor firepits where cooks make čvarci, digging into big bowls of catfish *perkelt*, bean stew, and hearty čobanac with homemade noodles. **Known for:** popularity with locals and visitors; Street of Forgotten Times outdoor ethnographic museum on-site; best place to try traditional Slavonian cuisine. [$] *Average main: €16* ⊠ *Kolodvorska 99, Karanac* ☎ *031/720–180* 🌐 *www.baranjska-kuca.com* ⏲ *Closed Mon.–Wed.*

**★ Kovač Čarda**

**$ | SEAFOOD | FAMILY** | The small settlement of Suza, just over 15 miles from the Hungarian border, is considered the best place in the world to try fiš paprikaš; there are a couple of restaurants where you can try it, and Hungarian-owned Kovač Čarda is as good a place as any. There isn't much else to see in the village and English isn't really spoken, so just come to the restaurant, grab a seat and a bib, and dig in. **Known for:** excellent fiš paprikaš; traditional decor; renowned local institution. [$] *Average main: €12* ⊠ *Maršala Tita 215, Suza* ☎ *031/733–101* 🌐 *kovaccarda.eatbu.com.*

## Hotels

**★ Ivica i Marica**

**$ | B&B/INN | FAMILY** | Just around the corner from Baranjska Kuća in Karanac is this beautifully restored, family-run working farmhouse where you'll stay in rustic rooms with brick walls and heavy oak furniture, each room uniquely decorated and equally homey. **Pros:** large outdoor space with horses and stables; excellent breakfast of local and homemade products; bikes available to explore the surrounding countryside. **Cons:** difficult to reach by public transport; not many amenities within walking distance; rooms can get a little cold. $ *Rooms from: €75* ✉ *Ive Lole Ribara 8A, Karanac* ☎ *091/1373–793* 🌐 *www.ivica-marica.com* 🛏 *25 rooms* 🍴 *Free Breakfast.*

## Shopping

**Asztalos Kermaik**
**CERAMICS** | Located in a renovated steam mill from 1911 and run by artist Daniel Asztalos, this quirky little ceramics shop sells lovely original items such as spice pots, beer mugs, wine glasses, and olive-oil bottles. Asztalos also offers pottery workshops if you want to create your own keepsake. Find it in the settlement of Suza on the road between Karanac and Batina. ✉ *Maršala Tita 96, Suza* ☎ *098/945–5990.*

# Vukovar

*35 km (22 miles) southeast of Osijek.*

There's no doubt that a visit to Vukovar hurts. As you visit the sights, the story of what happened here will slowly unfold, made even sadder by the glimpses of what a sophisticated city this once was. It's a place that holds a tender spot in the hearts of most Croatians, and it will earn a spot in yours, too.

In 1991, Vukovar was a prosperous city. Located at the confluence of the Danube and Vuka rivers, it had a lovely ensemble of Baroque architecture, fine museums, and many restaurants. It was named after the ancient Vučedol culture that inhabited a site 5 km (3 miles) downstream from the present-day city some 5,000 years ago. The area was later the site of a Roman settlement, and by the 11th century a community existed at the town's present location; this settlement became the seat of Vukovo County in the 13th century. After Turkish rule (1526–1687), almost all of Vukovar and its environs were bought by the counts of Eltz, a German family that strongly influenced the development of the town for the next two centuries and whose palace is home to the town museum.

When Yugoslavia started to break apart in 1991 and Croatia declared independence, the JNA (Yugoslav People's Army) and Serb militias began seizing control of areas with a large Serbian population. Vukovar, which at the time had a mixed population of 47% Croatians and 37% Serbians, was steadfastly claimed by both sides. A battle for the city ensued; it was up to lightly armed soldiers of the newly created Croatian National Guard, as well as 1,100 civilian volunteers, to defend it. During the 87-day siege, 12,000 shells and rockets were launched daily in the fiercest European battle since World War II. Those who had not fled Vukovar in the beginning became trapped inside, taking refuge in Cold War–era bomb shelters. On the 18th of November, the defenders of the city, running out of ammunition, numbers, and strength, could hold on no longer. Vukovar fell, and the once-lovely city was reduced to rubble. More than 30,000 Croatian residents were deported, thousands were killed, and thousands more are still missing. Several military and political officials have since been indicted and jailed for war crimes, including those involved in the notorious Vukovar hospital massacre.

In 1998, Vukovar was peacefully reintegrated into Croatia and the slow recovery process began. Even 10 years ago, it would have been unfathomable that a visit here could involve anything other than war. But today there are many other reasons to visit: there are modern shopping malls, cinemas, and 3D street-art installations; the Eltz Castle and the Franciscan Monastery have been rebuilt;

and the ultramodern Vučedol Culture Museum is the first step in a planned archaeological park. Vukovar is also a stop along the Danube bike path network, attracting scores of cycling groups each summer, and its proximity to Ilok has made it a stop on many wine tours and cruises. The center is once again full of busy cafés and bustling markets, and there is a six-day Vukovar Film Festival every August.

Yet the memories are never far away. Next to brand-new structures are the burnt-out frames of old buildings. Walls are still pockmarked, houses remain empty, the population is half of what it was pre-war, and the two ethnic communities remain divided. There is hope in the air, but it's usually not long before a conversation with a local will, inevitably, turn to the past. In a poignant reminder, a tall simple white cross stands at the tip of a narrow causeway overlooking the Danube, with inscriptions in both Cyrillic and Roman letters honoring victims on both sides. With memorials and sites all around town, Vukovar is a living war museum and an important stop on any Slavonian itinerary.

### GETTING HERE AND AROUND

Around five trains and buses make the daily 45-minute journey from Osijek to Vukovar, several of them continuing onward to Ilok. Regular buses and trains also travel between Zagreb and Vukovar, stopping in Vinkovci along the way.

The main sights in Vukovar are spread out over an 8-km (5-mile) stretch of road that runs the length of the city. If you're coming from Osijek, you'll start with the Hospital Museum and end at the Vučedol Culture Museum. Many of the sights are within walking distance of each other in the center of town, but you'll need a car or taxi to reach the Vučedol Culture Museum and the Ovčara Memorial.

## Sights

**Franjevački Samostan i Župa Svetih Filipa i Jakova** (*Franciscan Monastery & Church of Sts. Philip and James*)
**RELIGIOUS BUILDING** | High on a hill southeast of the town center you'll find Vukovar's main ecclesiastical attraction, and one of the largest in Croatia. Construction on the Baroque monastery began in 1723, and it held one of the richest and most valuable libraries in the country, as well as prominent paintings and gold and silver vessels. Both have been restored to their former glory after being ravaged in the war. ✉ *Samostanska 5, Vukovar* ☎ *032/441–381.*

★ **Gradski Muzej Vukovar** (*Vukovar Municipal Museum*)
**HISTORY MUSEUM** | The 18th-century palace Dvorac Eltz has housed the Gradski Muzej Vukovar since 1969. During the siege of Vukovar, the palace was severely damaged and the collection was moved to a Zagreb museum for safekeeping. After decades of reconstruction, the entire museum and all 2,000 of its pieces are once again open for viewing, a positive sign that Vukovar is back in business. Founded in 1946, the museum was originally housed in an old school and then a post office before the palace became its home. It has an excellent range of local archaeological artifacts, from the Vučedol culture that flourished around 3000 BC right up to the siege of Vukovar. ✉ *Županijska 2, Vukovar* ☎ *032/441–270* 🌐 *www.muzej-vukovar.hr* 🎫 *€5.30* ⏲ *Closed Mon.*

★ **Mjesto Sjećanja–Vukovar Bolnica** (*Place of Memory—Vukovar Hospital*)
**MONUMENT** | You'll want to bring a steady set of nerves to this site. During the siege of Vukovar, the top four floors of the hospital were destroyed by consistent bombing, despite being designated as an official safe zone. Staff continued to work in the basement and bomb shelter, helping civilians and soldiers,

The Gradski Muzej Vukovar, the city's municipal museum, is housed in an 18th-century palace.

operating even without running water. After Vukovar fell in 1991, and despite an agreement that the hospital would be safely evacuated, more than 200 people were removed from the hospital by a Serbian militia and brought to Ovčara farm, where they were beaten, tortured, and eventually executed. Others were sent to prisons or refugee camps. Today, the hospital is back in operation while the areas used during that period have been converted into a chilling multimedia museum/memorial. The entrance to the memorial is marked by a giant red cross flag full of holes. ✉ *Županijska 35, Vukovar* ☎ *32/452–111* 🌐 *ob-vukovar.hr* 🎫 *€2.65* 🕐 *Closed weekends.*

★ **Spomen Dom Ovčara** (*Ovčara Memorial*)
**MONUMENT** | On November 20–21, 1991, more than 200 soldiers and civilians were brought from the hospital to this former agricultural hangar, 4 km (2½ miles) outside the city and surrounded by fields of crops, by a Serbian militia. They were beaten, tortured, and eventually executed at another site 1 km (½ mile) away. The mass grave was exhumed in 1996, and 194 bodies were identified; among the dead were men ranging from 16 to 77 years old, one woman, a prominent radio journalist, and a French volunteer. Ovčara Memorial is a somber powerful site; it respectfully pays homage to the victims as well as conveys the horror that took place here. To get to the site, follow signs along the road to Ilok for 6 km (4 miles) past the Memorial Cemetery of Homeland War Victims, the largest mass grave in Europe since World War II—eventually turning right and driving another 4 km (2½ miles) down a country road. ✉ *Ovčara, Vukovar* ☎ *032/512–345.*

★ **Vučedol Culture Museum**
**MUSEUM VILLAGE** | Located 6 km (4 miles) from the center of Vukovar on the road to Ilok is the impressive Vučedol Culture Museum, which celebrates the ancient Vučedol culture that once flourished in the vicinity. Exhibitions include the oldest Indo-European calendar, skulls demonstrating sacrificial practices, and the pit where the famous Vučedol Dove, one

of the symbols of the city, was discovered. This fascinating museum, spread across 19 rooms and built on a slope so that it almost seems to be part of the landscape, is the first step in a planned archaeological park. ⊠ *Vučedol 252, Vukovar* ☎ *032/373–930* ⊕ *vucedol.hr* *€6* ⏲ *Closed Mon.*

★ **Vukovarski Vodotoranj** (*Water Tower*)
**MONUMENT** | Visible from everywhere in Vukovar is its most famous symbol: the water tower. Rising 150 feet into the air, the imposing red-brick structure, built between 1963 and 1968, once had a restaurant at the top with lovely views. Though it had no strategic importance, its sheer size made it a frequent target during the siege; it was hit with artillery more than 600 times which put gaping holes on all sides. But it never crumbled, instead coming to symbolize the strength of Vukovar itself.

A massive renovation project began in 2017, and in 2021, after standing empty for more than 25 years, the water tower finally reopened to the public. You can now visit two levels within the structure; the first features a stirring multimedia exhibit about the siege of Vukovar. The second level is the very top of the tower, where you can walk around outside for 360-degree views of the town, the river, and the surrounding fields. The reopening of the water tower is both an impressive and emotional achievement for Vukovar, made even more impactful by the fact that while the interior has been completely rebuilt, the facade remains unrepaired as a constant testament and reminder of the war's destruction. ⊠ *Bana Josipa Jelačića 3, Vukovar* ⊕ *vukovarskivodotoranj.hr* *€10 for elevator; €8.50 for stairs.*

## Restaurants

### Domestic House Lola

$ | **BISTRO** | A welcome addition to the Vukovar dining scene, Domestic House Lola is a classy affair in a 150-year-old noble family home on Vukovar's pedestrian road. The menu, which changes seasonally, highlights premium ingredients sourced from local family-owned farms with an emphasis on meat such as venison and black pork; try the rolled chicken, stuffed with fresh paprika and locally-produced cow cheese and wrapped in prosciutto. **Known for:** chic restaurant and hotel in historic building; local seasonal ingredients with a modern twist; buzziest spot in town. *Average main: €13* ⊠ *Dr. Franje Tuđmana 7, Vukovar* ☎ *98/934–1312* ⊕ *lola.traveleto.com.*

### Stari Toranj

$ | **EASTERN EUROPEAN** | **FAMILY** | This family restaurant with a small patio and pleasant staff is a local favorite, serving reliably good pizza and a selection of simple traditional meals. It's tucked away in the parking lot beside the old water tower after which it is named. **Known for:** good pizza; very generous portions; traditional Slavonian atmosphere. *Average main: €8* ⊠ *Trg Republike Hrvatske, Vukovar* ☎ *099/732–1255* ⊕ *stari-toranj-restaurant-vukovar.eatbu.hr* *No credit cards.*

## Hotels

### Vila Vanda

$ | **B&B/INN** | The 13 rooms in this pleasant B&B offer a reliable mid-range accommodation choice just a 10-minute walk from the center of Vukovar. **Pros:** spacious rooms with nice balconies; quiet neighborhood; environmentally friendly ethos. **Cons:** slightly far from the center of town; credit cards not accepted; room decor is outdated. *Rooms from: €50* ⊠ *Dalmatinska 3, Vukovar* ☎ *098/896–507* ⊕ *pansion-hotel-vukovar.business.site* *No credit cards* *13 rooms* *Free Breakfast.*

# Ilok

*37 km (22 miles) southeast of Vukovar, 74 km (45 miles) southeast of Osijek.*

Perched high on the western slopes of the Fruška Gora hills above the Danube and built around a medieval fortress, Ilok, Croatia's easternmost town, is one of the loveliest in Slavonia (although it is technically in the region of Syrmia, as the locals will proudly tell you). On a clear day, you can see all the way across the Vojvodina plain to Novi Sad in Serbia just 30 km (18 miles) away.

Ilok has been inhabited since the Neolithic era, but its golden age came in the 15th century when Nicholas of Ilok, the Ban of Croatia and King of Bosnia, built a fortification on a plateau overlooking the river and a castle within, turning Ilok into a fortified royal residence, and began the first construction of wine cellars. The last member of the Iločki family died in 1524; two years later, Ilok was occupied, along with the rest of Slavonia, by the Turks. There are still the remains of a hammam and a Turkish grave in the Old Town from this period, some of the only remaining evidence of Ottoman times in the entire region. After defeating the Turks in 1697, the Habsburgs gave Ilok to the aristocratic Odescalchi family from Italy, who quickly set about rebuilding the town, particularly the castle, in Baroque style. They developed the wine cellars below the castle and began production of the celebrated Traminac wine. There are now more than a dozen other vineyards around town producing award-winning wines, particularly Graševina and Traminac. All can be visited by appointment.

Ilok became part of Yugoslavia in 1918. At the beginning of the war in 1991, it was rapidly surrounded and occupied by Serb forces, sparing it the drawn-out devastation suffered by nearby Vukovar. Ilok was integrated into the Republic of Serbian Krajina and wasn't reintegrated into Croatia until 1998.

Ilok is composed of two parts: the upper half is where the feudal families lived and where today you'll find the city's historical sights and the remains of the fortified walls; the lower half is where the townsfolk traditionally lived and worked beside the Danube.

### GETTING HERE AND AROUND

There are frequent buses between Vukovar and Ilok (45 minutes, €4), many of which start or finish in Osijek; the bus will let you off in the center of the lower town. Ilok is best explored on foot, as most of the main sites, hotels, and wineries are around the center of town; there is a set of steps connecting the upper and lower towns.

## Sights

★ **Muzej Grada Iloka** (*Town Museum of Ilok*)

**HISTORY MUSEUM** | This impressive collection takes you through the ages of Ilok, from the Ottoman era to the Austrian Empire, the wars of the 20th century, right up to a modern art gallery. There are particularly interesting exhibits on the region's Jewish population pre-1945, relics from a 19th-century pharmacy, and an ethnological section on the top floor focusing on Ilok's large Slovak population. The museum is housed in the Odescalchi Castle, an imposing fortified structure overlooking the Danube, which was built on the foundations of the 15th-century castle of Nicholas of Ilok. Legend says that Suleiman the Magnificent once slept in this castle. The rooms themselves are exquisitely designed with period pieces and mood music in keeping with their original function, such as the hunting room and the drawing room. ✉ *Šetalište Oca Mladena Barbarića 5, Ilok* ☎ *032/827–410* 🌐 *www.mgi.hr* 🎫 *€6* 🕓 *Closed Sun. and Mon.*

The town of Ilok is located on the picturesque hills of Fruška Gora, perched above the Danube River.

★ **Stari Podrum** (*Old Cellar*)

**WINERY** | A wine cellar, restaurant, hotel, and history lesson all rolled into one, Stari Podrum is the old cellar of one of Croatia's most renowned wineries, Iločki Podrumi, and a must-visit when in Ilok (even if you're not into drinking wine). The Odescalchi family began producing high-class wines here in the 18th century, including the celebrated Traminac varietal, which was served at the coronation of Queen Elizabeth II. A private tour will take you through the atmospheric cellars, past Slavonian oak barrels to the prestigious archive wines and old bottles, full of dust and cobwebs, that were hidden behind a wall for protection during the Homeland War. You can organize a tour and tasting for around €10. The on-site restaurant serves delicious Slavonian dishes, including melt-in-your-mouth black pork dishes; you can eat inside surrounded by traditional embroidery and heavy wooden furniture or outdoors in the sunny central courtyard. Accommodations can also be arranged in one of 18 spacious and comfortable on-site rooms. ✉ *Šetalište Oca Mladena Barbarića 4, Ilok* ☎ *032/590–088* 🌐 *www.ilocki-podrumi.hr.*

**Župa Svetog Ivana Kapistrana** (*Church of St. John of Capistrano*)

**CHURCH** | This Franciscan church and monastery overlooking the Danube, first constructed in 1349, holds the remains of St. John of Capistrano, a Franciscan friar and Catholic priest. In 1456, at age 70, he led a successful battle against the Ottomans, which earned him the nickname "Soldier Priest." He died three months later in Ilok of the bubonic plague but was said to have performed miracles even on his deathbed. The church—which also holds the remains of Nicholas and Lawrence of Ilok, both of whom made expansions to the monastery complex during their reign—was given a 20th-century neo-Gothic facelift by Hermann Bollé, the same architect who helped design the cathedrals in Đakovo and Zagreb, as well as Zagreb's Mirogoj Cemetery. The tourist information center is next door; if the church is closed, contact them to arrange a visit. ✉ *Trg Svetog Ivana Kapistrana 3, Ilok.*

## Hotels

The best, and only, restaurants in Ilok are located in the hotels, so planning a visit to each of them for either lunch, a wine tasting, dinner, or an overnight stay makes for a nice tour of Ilok.

**Hotel Dunav**
$ | **HOTEL** | **FAMILY** | Located right on the riverbank, this upscale family-run hotel makes a great base for exploring both parts of the town. **Pros:** riverside location; best restaurant in town; peaceful, quiet rooms. **Cons:** feels empty in low season; some distance from wineries; far from the sights in the upper town. *Rooms from: €100* ✉ *Julija Benešića 62, Ilok* ☎ *032/596–500* *www.hoteldunavilok.com* *15 rooms* *Free Breakfast.*

**Principovac Country Estate**
$ | **HOTEL** | Located 1½ km (1 mile) from Ilok in the Baroque summer house of the Odescalchi family, this is an elegant retreat amid miles of rolling vineyards (it's also part of the Iločki Podrumi family). **Pros:** beautifully designed premises; romantic escape; great for walking, biking, tennis, or golf. **Cons:** far from Ilok; no public transport; feels a little secluded. *Rooms from: €110* ✉ *Principovac 1, Ilok* ☎ *032/593–114* *www.ilocki-podrumi.hr* *6 rooms* *Free Breakfast.*

★ **Villa Iva**
$ | **HOTEL** | This peaceful boutique hotel and restaurant is located in the lower part of Ilok, at the base of the steps leading up to the Old Town. **Pros:** nicely decorated and spacious rooms; good on-site restaurant serving pizza and traditional food; sunny central courtyard. **Cons:** not in Old Town; far from main sights; basic amenities. *Rooms from: €60* ✉ *Stjepana Radića 23, Ilok* ☎ *032/591–011* *13 rooms* *Free Breakfast.*

# Đakovo

*38 km (24 miles) southwest of Osijek.*

Đakovo is a peaceful little town, where the din of bicycles and the dribbling of basketballs on a Sunday afternoon outdo the roar of cars. The relatively bustling pedestrian main street is Ivana Pavla II, whose far end has a little parish church that was built rather cleverly from a former 16th-century mosque, one of the few remaining structures left in Slavonia from 150 years of Ottoman rule. The best time to be in town is the last weekend in September, during the annual Đakovački Vezovi (Đakovo Embroidery Festival), which sees a folklore show replete with traditional embroidered costumes, folk dancing and singing, an array of song-and-dance performances, and an all-around party atmosphere—even a show by the famous Lipizzaner horses.

### GETTING HERE AND AROUND

You can get to Đakovo from Osijek by one of several daily trains or buses (40 minutes, €4 one-way). The Đakovo train station is 1 km (½ mile) east of the center of town, at the opposite end of Kralja Tomislava, while the bus station is also about ½ mile from the center of town.

## Sights

**Đakovačka Katedrala** (*Đakovo Cathedral*)
**CHURCH** | Đakovo's centerpiece is its majestic red-brick neo-Gothic cathedral, which towers above the city and is a stunning first sight as you arrive into town. Commissioned by the Bishop of Đakovo, Josip Juraj Strossmayer (1815–1905) and consecrated in 1882 after two decades of construction, the cathedral was called the "most beautiful church between Venice and Constantinople" by Pope John XXIII. ✉ *Trg Strossmayera, Đakovo.*

### State Stud Farm

**FARM/RANCH** | **FAMILY** | The history of the Lipizzaner stud farm dates back to 1506, when one of the bishops kept 90 Arabian horses there. But perhaps the year that really put it on the map was 1972, when Queen Elizabeth II saw the famous Đakovo four-horse team perform at the opening ceremony of the Olympics and insisted on paying them a visit. The story goes that there was no paved road outside the stud farm at the time; by the time the queen arrived to take a carriage ride, one had been built. There are two locations in Đakovo where the prized white Lipizzaners are trained and bred: the Stallion Stable in the center of Đakovo, where a musical show is also held twice per month and plans are in place to build a museum; and Ivandvor, 6 km (4 miles) away, a pasture where the mares and offspring are kept in a peaceful rural setting. It is possible to visit both farms to catch a glimpse of the horses and their stables, and a carriage ride through town can also be arranged. ✉ *Augusta Šenoe 45, Đakovo* ☎ *031/822–535* 🌐 *ergela-djakovo.hr* *€4 for guided tour.*

### Mon Ami

**$** | **EASTERN EUROPEAN** | Located in a big red-brick building around the corner from the Cathedral, this pub-like restaurant specializes in grilled meat and pizza cooked in a giant wood oven. The menu represents good value for money, with its generous portions of hearty traditional Balkan fare. **Known for:** grilled meat; Slavonian breakfasts; long-standing institution. *Average main: €10* ✉ *Luke Botića 12, Đakovo* ☎ *031/821–477.*

### Hotel Đakovo

**$** | **HOTEL** | **FAMILY** | With cheerful rooms, a big restaurant specializing in Slavonian food and wine, and a game room perfect for kids, this is your best hotel option in town. **Pros:** friendly service; nice on-site restaurant; spacious rooms. **Cons:** far from town and public transport; heavily focused on wedding parties; breakfast is disappointing. *Rooms from: €65* ✉ *Nikole Tesle 52, Đakovo* ☎ *031/840–570* 🌐 *www.hotel-djakovo.hr* *25 rooms* *Free Breakfast.*

# The Golden Valley

*150 km (94 miles) southeast of Zagreb, 96 km (60 miles) southwest of Osijek.*

In the center of a fertile vineyard-rich valley in Požega-Slavonia County (one of the smallest in Croatia), lies the area that the ancient Romans knew as Vallis Aurea, or the Golden Valley. Going against Slavonia's reputation as one big, flat agricultural plain, this area is mountainous, with forested hills covered by the vineyards of more than 30 private wineries.

The main town in the area is Požega (pop. 21,000). During the 150-year-long period of Ottoman rule that began in 1537, Požega became central Slavonia's most important administrative and military center. By the 19th century Požega's cultural dynamism had earned it a reputation as the Athens of Slavonia, and in 1847 it became the first city to officially adopt the Croatian language.

Just 23 km (14 miles) northeast of Požega is another small town called Kutjevo. It has a wine-making history dating back to the 13th century, and if there is any place where all of life is dedicated to viticulture, it is here. Nearly all 2,500 residents make a living from wine, and even the main square is named Trg Graševine after Slavonia's signature white wine; indeed, this is an excellent place to try it, as 80% of Croatia's total Graševina production happens here. Kutjevo is a wonderful place to base yourself for a day or two to sample great wine and explore nearby Papuk Nature Park.

### GETTING HERE AND AROUND

There are buses from Osijek to Kutjevo (90 minutes, €11) and to Požega (2 to 3 hours, €12).

## Sights

**Krauthaker**

**WINERY** | If you only visit one winery in the Golden Valley, make it Krauthaker. Vlado Krauthaker was one of the first private wine producers to emerge after the fall of communism, opening his winery in 1992. He is still widely considered one of the best (and most humble) winemakers in the country, producing a dozen varietals including award-winning Chardonnay. The location is lovely, with a terrace overlooking the town, a small pond and bridge, and colorful wine barrels scattered around the premises. Call ahead to arrange a visit. ✉ *Ivana Jambrovića 6, Kutjevo* ☎ *034/315–000* 🌐 *www.krauthaker.hr* 🕓 *By appointment only.*

**Kutjevačko Vinogorje**

**WINERY** | There are 30 different wineries to choose from around Kutjevo; the biggest, and oldest, is Kutjevačko Vinogorje. The story of this winery is the story of Kutjevo itself; its cellars date back to 1232, when the town was founded by Cistercian monks from Hungary. Over the years, it passed into the hands of Ottomans, Jesuits, Habsburgs, and private families, and the stories of each of these eras and the influence they left on Kutjevo are etched chronologically onto the Slavonian oak barrels in the cellar. Ask your guide about the legend of Maria Theresa Habsburg and her dalliances on the circular stone table (where wine tastings are done). Call ahead to reserve an appointment. ✉ *Kralja Tomislava 1, Kutjevo* ☎ *099/379–9822* 🌐 *www.kutjevo.com* 🕓 *By appointment only.*

**Papuk Nature Park**

**NATURE SIGHT** | **FAMILY** | A paradise for hikers, bikers, and nature enthusiasts, Papuk Nature Park was the first geopark in Croatia to be recognized by UNESCO for its geological, biological, and cultural diversity. Within its 336 square km (129 square miles) are beech, oak, and fir forests, fresh rivers, lakes, and waterfalls, along with hiking and biking trails, swimming spots, and a ropes course. There are also archaeological sites from the Sopot and Starčevo cultures (5500–3500 BC), as well as Ružica Grad, an abandoned medieval castle that was built in the 15th century during Hungarian rule; it can be reached by hiking 15 minutes uphill from Lake Orahovica. The lakes and Ružica Grad can be reached in 30 minutes from Kutjevo. Guided tours can be arranged from the visitor center (ask your hotel to call in advance to organize). ✉ *Papuk Nature Park* 🌐 *www.pp-papuk.hr* 🎫 *€3.50.*

**Požega**

**TOWN** | One of the prettiest cities in central Slavonia, Požega is worth visiting for an afternoon. The striking Holy Trinity Square has a 19th-century Franciscan monastery to one side and the massive Bishop's Palace at the other end. There is a plague column (built in memory of the nearly 800 citizens who died from the plague of 1739) in the middle of the square; an inscription explains that the pillar was sculpted by one Gabriel Granici at a cost of 2,000 eggs and 300 forints. He didn't eat the eggs or give them to his relatives; they were used to cement the pillar's marble sand. Tucked away in the corner of the main square is the City Museum, whose collection ranges from regional ethnography, history, and art to archaeology, from prehistoric times to the present day. ✉ *Požega* 🌐 *pozega-tz.hr.*

## Hotels

**★ Sontacchi Boutique Winery Hotel**

**$** | **B&B/INN** | This B&B in the center of Kutjevo is a great mix between a smart boutique hotel and a family-run inn; the Sontaki brothers, Anton and Kruno, will take care of everything you need, including lending you a bike to get around and arranging tastings at local wineries (including their own). **Pros:** excellent breakfast featuring local organic products; small wellness center with sauna and hot tub on-site (extra charge); friendly and helpful owners. **Cons:** some rooms are expensive by Slavonian standards; wellness center facilities not included in price; not many amenities nearby. *Rooms from: €70* ✉ *Trg Graševine 4, Kutjevo, Kutjevo* ☎ *099/512–2312* 🌐 *www.sontacchi-vinarija.hr* *5 rooms* *Free Breakfast.*

Chapter 10



# MONTENEGRO

Updated by
John Bills

| Sights | Restaurants | Hotels | Shopping | Nightlife |
|---|---|---|---|---|
| ★★★☆☆ | ★★★☆☆ | ★★★☆☆ | ★★☆☆☆ | ★☆☆☆☆ |

# WELCOME TO MONTENEGRO

## TOP REASONS TO GO

★ **Beautiful views:** In Kotor, climb to St. John's Fortress, following the medieval walls for postcard views.

★ **Miraculous monasteries:** Ostrog Monastery is one of the most impressive settings in the region, a blinding-white structure built into an almost vertical cliff. The reality is even more magical than one can imagine.

★ **The yachting life:** Charter a yacht for a private sailing trip around the Bay of Kotor.

★ **Floating churches:** Visit Gospa od Škrjela (Our Lady of the Rocks), a lovely church perched on a tiny islet opposite Perast, just outside Kotor.

★ **Mediterranean villages:** Zigzag down the mountain road above Kotor to get a full view of the bay including Kotor, Perast, and the other villages clustered around the sapphire water of this Mediterranean *ria* (a narrow inlet formed by the partial submergence of a river valley).

Of the small diamond-shaped stretch of mountainous terrain that makes up Montenegro, the southwestern face and coastal strip get most of the tourist attention. The most charming sights of this stretch of 100 km (60 miles)—as the crow flies—are at the northern end, though because of the short distances involved, more adventurous visitors can use any of the towns along the coast as a base to visit the inland towns and mountains. The coastline borders Croatia at its northern end and Albania to the south. Onward travel to the better-known towns and islands of Croatia is easily arranged by public transport or hired car, and the less-discovered beaches and ancient sites of Albania are also accessible by regular buses across Montenegro's southern border. The UNESCO World Heritage sites and legendary hospitality of Bosnia and Herzegovina, Kosovo, and Serbia are only a bus journey away.

1 **Kotor.** A historic city tucked into a magnificent bay.

2 **Perast.** A charming bayfront village.

3 **Podgorica.** Montenegro's underrated capital city.

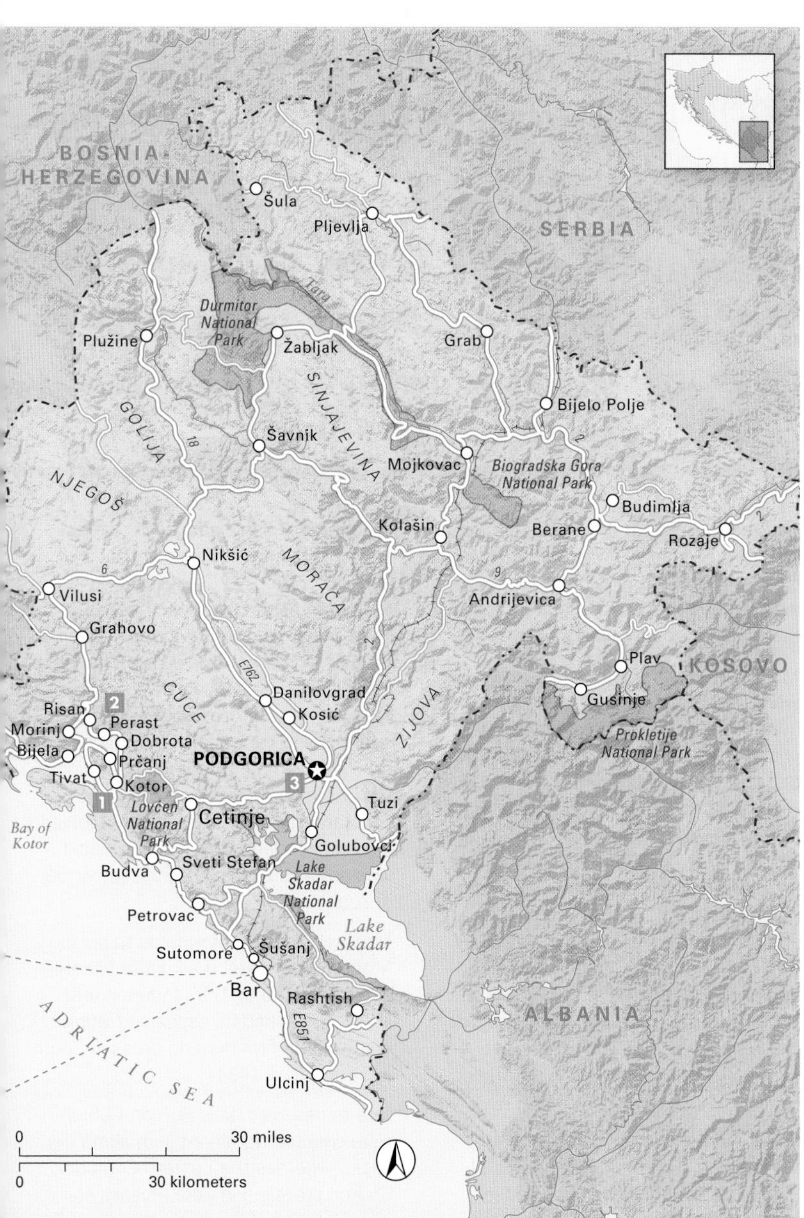
BOSNIA-HERZEGOVINA
SERBIA
KOSOVO
ALBANIA
ADRIATIC SEA
Bay of Kotor
Šula
Pljevlja
Durmitor National Park
Tara
Plužine
Žabljak
Grab
SINJAJEVINA
Bijelo Polje
GOLIJA
Šavnik
Mojkovac
Biogradska Gora National Park
NJEGOŠ
Budimlja
Kolašin
Berane
Rozaje
Nikšić
MORAČA
Andrijevica
Vilusi
Grahovo
Plav
CUCE
Danilovgrad
Gusinje
Risan
Kosić
ZIJOVA
Perast
Morinj
Dobrota
Prokletije National Park
Bijela
Prčanj
PODGORICA
Tivat
Kotor
Lovćen National Park
Cetinje
Tuzi
Golubovci
Budva
Sveti Stefan
Lake Skadar National Park
Petrovac
Lake Skadar
Sutomore
Šušanj
Bar
Rashtish
Ulcinj
E762
E851
18
6
9
2
1
3
0
30 miles
30 kilometers

Officially independent since 2006 but with a long history of fierce self-sustainability, tiny Montenegro (about the size of Connecticut) lies on the Adriatic coast. It is bordered by Croatia, Bosnia and Herzegovina, Serbia, Kosovo, and Albania. The 620,000 people living here call it Crna Gora, which, like Montenegro, means "black mountain"—a reminder of the pine-forested alpine terrain of most of the country.

---

Montenegro's main draw is its beautiful coastline, dotted with delightful Venetian-era fortified towns, home to excellent seafood restaurants, and set against the dramatic mountains of the interior.

Montenegro's first known inhabitants were the Illyrians, who were farmers and hunters, and also worked iron and traded with the ancient Greeks. Urbanization began in the 4th century BC, when the Greeks founded Budva on the coast. In AD 9, the Romans annexed the region into the province of Illyricum (which ran down the Adriatic coast from the Istrian peninsula to Albania), calling it Doclea after the dominant local Illyrian tribe. When the Roman Empire was divided between east and west in AD 395, the fault line passed through Montenegro. Later, this was the dividing line between Eastern Orthodox and Roman Catholic lands.

In the 7th century, the Slavs arrived. They mixed with the descendants of the Romanized Illyrians and lived in the mountains in clans, each ruled by a*župan* (chieftain). Originally pagan, they soon adopted Christianity. In 1077, the pope recognized their independent state of Duklja (the Slavicized version of the Roman name, Doclea) as a kingdom. Later, Duklja became known as Zeta (derived from the old Slavic word for harvest) and kept its freedom by paying off the Byzantine Empire and fighting the Ottoman Turks. Because of the constant threat of Ottoman invasion and fear of rival clans, courage in combat was emphasized as a significant virtue in Zeta.

Meanwhile, most of what is today the Montenegrin coast was under Venetian rule from 1420 to 1797. Independent Montenegro had its capital at Cetinje, home of the first printing press in Southern Europe, in 1494.

Due to ties with Italy, Roman Catholicism was the dominant faith along the coast, whereas the Eastern Orthodox Church prevailed in Zeta. Politics and religion became so intertwined in Zeta that from 1550 to 1696, it was governed by bishops. In 1697, the Petrović-Njegoš family took the helm as prince-bishops. The greatest of their rulers, still loved and revered in Montenegro today, was Petar II Petrović-Njegoš, who organized a 32-man band of traveling magistrates as well as a police force, paid for from a system of taxation that he managed. He was also an epic poet; his work, *The Mountain Wreath,* is considered Montenegro's national poem.

King Nikola I Petrović-Njegoš, who ruled from 1860, was another notable ruler; six of his nine daughters married royal or aristocratic Europeans (including a grand duke of Russia and King Victor Emmanuel III of Italy), which earned him the nickname "the father-in-law of Europe." King Nikola introduced free elementary education, an agricultural college, post and telegraph offices, and freedom of the press. However, the messy end of his reign (which saw him deposed and sent into exile while Montenegro was annexed to Serbia) left a controversial legacy.

During both world wars, Montenegro sided with the Allies. In 1945, it became one of the six constituent republics that made up Yugoslavia, governed along communist lines by President Tito. Yugoslavia was not part of the Soviet Bloc, however, as Tito broke off relations with Stalin in 1948. The country was ruled under Tito's form of communism—far more liberal than that in the former USSR.

During the breakup of Yugoslavia in the 1990s, no fighting took place on Montenegrin soil, though the region suffered economic hardship and political isolation; many civilians were killed by NATO bombing in 1999. When Croatia and Slovenia claimed independence from Yugoslavia in 1991, Montenegro remained loyal to Belgrade. However, by May 2006, when all that remained of Yugoslavia was the so-called Union of Serbia and Montenegro, Montenegro held a referendum. It voted for independence (though it was a close run, with only 55.5% of the votes in favor) and became an independent democratic republic. Today, tourism is the main force behind the economy, and foreign investors keen to cash in on the potential boom are buying up properties fast.

# Planning

## When to Go

May is a lovely time to visit coastal Montenegro, with temperatures running 14°C–22°C (56°F–72°F) but before the busiest crowds of summer. After that, temperatures rise to a peak in August, with an average daily maximum of 29°C (84°F), although hotter temperatures aren't unusual. These are fine days for sun worshippers or anyone willing and able to laze under sunshades and admire the sparkle on the water. Still, if you want to explore the towns where the sun's glare bounces off the white stone, you may prefer to choose a different time of year (or at least plan your sightseeing for early in the day). By September, temperatures are cooling (17°C–26°C [62°F–78°F]) and the crowds in the most famous sights (notably Kotor) are thinning, while the sea is still as warm as in June or July, so this is also a great time to visit. After this, the season is properly over; winter on the coast is a little bleak (temperatures in January run 5°C–12°C [40°F–53°F]), and many businesses shut down.

## Getting Here and Around

### AIR

Several budget airlines fly from Tivat and Podgorica airports to London and other European capitals. Well-served by international airlines, Dubrovnik Airport (Croatia) is a popular alternative gateway to

Montenegro
BOSNIA-HERZEGOVINA
SERBIA
KOSOVO
ALBANIA
CROATIA
Šula
Pljevlja
Tara
Durmitor National Park
Plužine
Žabljak
Grab
SINJAJEVINA
Bijelo Polje
GOLIJA
18
Šavnik
Mojkovac
Biogradska Gora National Park
NJEGOŠ
Kolašin
Budimlja
Berane
Rozaje
2
Nikšić
MORAČA
6
9
Vilusi
Andrijevica
Grahovo
E762
2
Plav
ZIJOVA
CUCE
Danilovgrad
Gusinje
Risan
Kosić
Perast
Morinj
Dobrota
Prokletije National Park
Bijela
Prčanj
Herzeg Novi
Podgorica
Tivat
Kotor
Tuzi
Lovćen National Park
Cetinje
Bay of Kotor
Golubovci
Budvar
Sveti Stefan
Lake Skadar National Park
Petrovac
Lake Skadar
Sutomore
Šušanj
TO ANCONA
Bar
Rashtish
E851
ADRIATIC SEA
Ulcinj
TO BARI
0
30 miles
0
30 kilometers

Montenegro. Still, it's important to note that car-rental agencies may charge extra for taking the vehicle across international borders. Established in 2021 after the post-COVID collapse of Montenegro Airlines, Air Montenegro is now the national carrier.

**AIRPORT CONTACTS Dubrovnik Airport.** ✉ *Čilipi bb, Dubrovnik* ☎ *20/773–100 passenger services* 🌐 *www.airport-dubrovnik.hr.* **Podgorica Airport.** ✉ *Podgorica Airport, Podgorica* ☎ *020/444–244* 🌐 *montenegroairports.com/aerodrom-podgorica.* **Tivat Airport.** ✉ *Tivat Airport* ☎ *032/671–337* 🌐 *montenegroairports.com/aerodrom-tivat.*

### BOAT

Jadrolinija operates daily car ferries year-round to the Montenegrin port of Bar, 38 km (24 miles) south of Budva, from Bari in Italy. The crossing can take anywhere between 8 and 12 hours and costs about €150 per person one-way (in a two-berth cabin with bathroom).

### BUS

Buses are cheap (e.g., €8 for the 2-hour journey from Kotor to Podgorica) and cover practically the entire country. They are generally clean and reliable. Numerous small bus lines operate regularly along the coast between Herceg Novi (in the north) and Ulcinj (in the south), stopping at most towns along the way. For other routes, inquire at the bus station of departure.

**CONTACTS Kotor Bus Station.** ✉ *Put Prvoborca bb, Kotor* ☎ *032/325–126* 🌐 *www.autobuskastanicakotor.me.*

### CAR

Although Montenegro's buses have good service along the coast and can get you to most points in the country, renting a car gives you much more flexibility and makes life easier, especially when visiting the mountains.

Since the Old Town is compact and pedestrian-friendly, you do not need to rent a car in Kotor. It's easy to reach nearby Perast by bus or taxi.

### CRUISE SHIP

Arriving at Kotor from the water via cruise ship is an impressive experience in itself, so be sure to be up on the deck in advance. Your ship will sail up a 28-km-long (18-mile-long) bay (often mistakenly referred to as a fjord), with rugged mountains rising in the background. Cruise ships dock on the quay, immediately in front of Kotor's medieval walled Old Town.

## Restaurants

Along the Montenegrin coast, seafood predominates, with starters including *salata od hobotnice* (octopus salad) and *riblja čorba* (fish soup), followed by risotto dishes—most notably *crni rižot* (black risotto prepared with cuttlefish)—*lignje* (squid), or fresh fish from the Adriatic prepared on a barbecue. The quality is generally excellent, and the prices are slightly lower than in neighboring Croatia, although don't be surprised to see higher prices in Kotor, Perast, and (especially) Sveti Stefan. Note that on restaurant menus, fresh fish is sometimes priced by the kilogram. Inland, cheeses and meat dishes are more common. Cheeses to try include *sir iz ulja* (cheese preserved in olive oil) and *kožji sir* (goat cheese), generally eaten at the beginning of the meal rather than at the end. Popular meat specialties are*pršut* (prosciutto), *Njeguški stek* (steak stuffed with prosciutto and cheese), and *jagnjece pečenje sa ražnja* (whole lamb roasted on a spit).

Montenegrins are also fond of the ubiquitous Balkan *Šopska salata* (a chopped salad of tomato, green peppers, cucumber, onion, olives, and strong white cheese). Regarding local wines, Vranac is the most highly esteemed red and Krstac is a reliable white.

## Hotels

In Montenegro, the best accommodations are the small family-run establishments, many of which are centuries-old stone villas that have been converted into darling boutique hotels full of character and teeming with hospitality. However, many visitors still prefer to rent a private room or apartment, which can be arranged through local tourist information offices and travel agencies. The tourist season runs from Easter to late October and peaks in July and August, when prices rise significantly and it may be challenging to find a place to sleep if you have not booked in advance.

⇨ *Restaurant and hotel reviews have been shortened. For full information, visit Fodors.com. Restaurant prices are the average cost of a main course at dinner or, if dinner is not served, at lunch. Hotel prices are the lowest cost of a standard double room in high season.*

| What It Costs in Euros (€) | | | |
|---|---|---|---|
| **$** | **$$** | **$$$** | **$$$$** |
| **RESTAURANTS** | | | |
| under €15 | €15–€23 | €24–€32 | over €32 |
| **HOTELS** | | | |
| under €150 | €150–€250 | €251–€350 | over €350 |

## Tours

Many private travel agencies offer tours, including hiking in the mountains; rafting on the Tara River; and visits to the towns of the interior, including the gorgeous former capital Cetinje and nearby Lovćen; as well as the other national parks, Lake Skadar (good for bird-watching), Biogradska Gora, and stunning Durmitor. Other companies will offer tours from Montenegro to other countries in the region, including through Prokletije National Park into Kosovo and Albania, or to Dubrovnik and other destinations in Croatia.

## Visitor Information

**CONTACTS National Tourism Organization of Montenegro.** ✉ *Slobode 2, Podgorica* ☎ *08000/1300* 🌐 *www.montenegro.travel.*

# Kotor

*44 km (28 miles) from the border crossing between Croatia and Montenegro.*

Backed by imposing mountains, tiny Kotor lies hidden from the open sea, tucked into the deepest channel of the Boka Kotorska (Bay of Kotor), often mistakenly referred to as Europe's most southerly fjord but actually considered a ria. To many, this town is more charming than its sister UNESCO World Heritage site, Dubrovnik, retaining more authenticity but with fewer tourists and spared the war damage and subsequent rebuilding that has given Dubrovnik something of a Disney feel.

Kotor's medieval Stari Grad (Old Town) is enclosed within well-preserved defensive walls built between the 9th and 18th centuries and is presided over by a proud hilltop fortress. A labyrinth of winding cobbled streets within the walls leads through a series of splendid paved piazzas rimmed by centuries-old stone buildings. The squares are increasingly packed with trendy cafés and chic boutiques, but directions are still given medieval style by reference to the town's landmark churches.

In the Middle Ages, Kotor was an important economic and cultural center with highly regarded schools of stonemasonry and iconography. From 1391 to 1420, it was an independent city-republic, and later it spent periods under Venetian,

Ottoman, Austrian, and French rule. However, the Venetians undoubtedly left the strongest impression on the city's architecture. Since the breakup of Yugoslavia, some 70% of the stone buildings in the romantic Old Town have been snapped up by foreigners. Porto Montenegro, a marina designed to accommodate some of the world's largest superyachts, opened in nearby Tivat in 2011; along the bay are other charming seaside villages, all with better views of the bay than the vista from Kotor itself, where the waterside is often congested with cruise ships and yachts. Try sleepy Muo or the settlement of Prčanj in one direction around the bay or magical Perast and the Roman mosaics of Risan in the other direction.

## GETTING HERE AND AROUND

### AIR

Tivat Airport is 8 km (5 miles) from Kotor. Less convenient is the capital's Podgorica Airport, 90 km (56 miles) inland. Alternatively, some visitors fly in to Dubrovnik (Croatia) and drive 60 km (38 miles) down the coast to Kotor.

### AIRPORTS AND TRANSFERS

Buses run regularly between Tivat Airport and Kotor; inquire at the airport information desks for schedule and fare information. There are frequent buses from Podgorica to Kotor, but you will need to take a taxi from Podgorica Airport to the bus station (approximately €15). You can catch a taxi year-round from both Tivat and Podgorica airports.

### BOAT

During the summer, private taxi-boats operate from Kotor's harbor, taking passengers up the coast to the village of Perast.

## VISITOR INFORMATION

Kotor's tourist information office gives out free maps and information and can help find private accommodations. You'll find the office in a kiosk just outside the Main Town Gate.

**CONTACTS Kotor Tourist Board.** (*Turistička Organizacija Kotora*) ✉ *Stari Grad 315, Kotor* ☎ *032/325–947* 🌐 *kotor.travel.*

## Sights

Kotor's Old Town takes approximately half a day to explore, although don't use that as an excuse to rush. Take your time, and you will be rewarded tenfold. Plan your visit for the morning, when the main sights are open to the public and the afternoon sun has yet to reach peak force.

**Crkva Svetog Luke** (*St. Luke's Church*)
**CHURCH** | Built in 1195, this delightful Romanesque church is the only building in the Old Town to have withstood all five major earthquakes that affected Kotor. Originally a Catholic church, the building later became an Orthodox place of worship. ✉ *Trg Svetog Luke, Kotor.*

**Crkva Svetog Nikole** (*St. Nicholas' Church*)
**CHURCH** | Designed by a Russian architect and constructed in pseudo-Byzantine style between 1902 and 1909, this is Kotor's most important Orthodox church (the Cathedral, by definition, is Catholic). The gold used to gild the spires was a gift from Russia. ✉ *Trg Svetog Luke, Kotor.*

**Glavna Gradska Vrata**
**NOTABLE BUILDING** | The Main Town Gate (also known as the Sea Gate because of its position on the coast), which accesses the Stari Grad via the western facade of the city walls, dates back to the 16th century and comprises Renaissance and Baroque details. Initially, the outer gate bore a relief of the Venetian Lion, but in Tito's time this was replaced by the socialist star and dates, as well as a direct quote recording the liberation of Kotor on November 21, 1944, at the end of World War II. There are two other entrances to the Stari Grad: the Južna vrata (South Gate) and the Sjeverna vrata (North Gate). ✉ *Jadranska Magistrala, Kotor.*

Kotor's Old Town is completely car-free and a designated UNESCO World Heritage Site.

★ **Gradske Zidine** (*Town Walls*)
**HISTORIC SIGHT** | Especially beautiful at night when illuminated, Kotor's well-preserved town walls were built between the 9th and 18th centuries. They measure almost 5 km (3 miles) in length and reach up to 66 feet in height and 52 feet in width. They form a triangular defense system around the Old Town, then rise into the hill behind it to Tvrđava Svetog Ivana (St. John's Fortress), 853 feet above sea level. You can walk up to the fortress along the walls; allow at least one hour to get up and back down, wear good hiking shoes, and remember to bring water. ✉ *Stari Grad* 🎟 *€8.*

★ **Katedrala Svetog Tripuna** (*St. Tryphon's Cathedral*)
**CHURCH** | Undoubtedly Kotor's finest building, the Romanesque cathedral dates back to 1166, though excavation work shows that there was already a smaller church here in the 9th century. Due to damage caused by several disastrous earthquakes, the cathedral has been rebuilt several times—the twin Baroque bell towers were added in the late 17th century. Inside, the most essential feature is the 14th-century Romanesque-Gothic ciborium above the main altar. Also, look out for fragments of 14th-century frescoes, which would once have covered the entire interior. A collection of gold and silver reliquaries, encasing body parts of various saints and crafted by local masters between the 14th and 18th centuries, is on display in the treasury. ✉ *Trg Svetog Tripuna, Kotor* 🎟 *€5 for combined ticket to cathedral and treasury.*

**Pomorski Muzej Crne Gore** (*Montenegrin Maritime Museum*)
**HISTORY MUSEUM | FAMILY** | In the 18th century, tiny Kotor had 400 ships sailing the world's oceans. The Maritime Museum, housed within the 18th-century Baroque Grgurina Palace, traces Montenegro's cultural and economic ties to the sea. The exhibition extends over three floors and includes model ships; paintings of vessels, ship owners, and local naval commanders; navigation equipment; and

uniforms worn by Montenegrin admirals and captains. Audio guides are available in a variety of languages. ✉ *Trg Bokeljske Mornarice 391, Stari Grad* ☎ *032/304–720* 🌐 *museummaritimum.com* 🎫 *€5.*

**Toranj Za Sat** (*Clock Tower*)
**NOTABLE BUILDING** | Built in the 17th century and considered a symbol of Kotor, the Clock Tower stands directly opposite the Main City Gate. In front of the Clock Tower, the Pillar of Shame was used to subject local criminals to public humiliation. ✉ *Trg od Oružja, Stari Grad.*

**Trg od Oružja** (*Square of Arms*)
**PLAZA/SQUARE** | **FAMILY** | The Main Town Gate leads directly into the Square of Arms, Kotor's main square, today a sizable paved space animated by popular open-air cafés. Under Venice, arms were repaired and stored here, hence the name. Notable buildings on the square include the 17th-century Toranj za sat (Clock Tower), the 19th-century Napoleonovo pozorišta (Napoléon Theatre), and the 18th-century Kneževa palata (Duke's Palace), the latter two now forming part of the upmarket Hotel Cattaro. ✉ *Trg od Oružja, Stari Grad.*

★ **Tvrđava Svetog Ivana** (*St. John's Fortress*)
**MILITARY SIGHT** | On the hill behind Kotor, 853 feet above sea level, this fortress is approached via a series of bends and some 1,300 steps. The fantastic view from the top makes the climb worthwhile: the terra-cotta rooftops of the Old Town, the meandering ria, and the pine-clad mountains beyond. On the way up, you will pass the tiny Crkva Gospe od Zdravlja (Church of Our Lady of Health), built in the 16th century to protect Kotor against the plague. Be sure to wear good walking shoes and take plenty of water. The route up starts from behind the east side of the city walls. ✉ *Above Old Town, Kotor.*

## Restaurants

**Galion**
**$$** | **SEAFOOD** | This sophisticated restaurant occupies an old stone building with a glass-and-steel winter terrace extension, serving creative twists on local food. Expect funky modern furniture and chill-out music accompanying a hip and tasty menu. **Known for:** great locale with views of both the Old Town and the sea; the signature mille-feuille cakes; creative takes on traditional dishes. [$] *Average main: €15* ✉ *Šuranj bb, Kotor* ☎ *032/325–054* 🌐 *www.galion.me.*

★ **Konoba Scala Santa**
**$** | **SEAFOOD** | Believed to be the oldest restaurant in Kotor, this rustic eatery is one of the best places in town for lobster, mussels, and fresh fish, such as barbecued *zubatac.* **Known for:** oldest tavern in the Old Town; great Montenegrin seafood dishes; big open fireplace and outdoor dining in the summer. [$] *Average main: €12* ✉ *Trg od Salate, Kotor* ☎ *067/393–458.*

**Marenda Grill House**
**$** | **BARBECUE** | Grill houses and butcher shops go hand-in-hand, making Marenda Grill House a perfectly placed spot just outside Kotor's Old Town. The meat is about as locally sourced as you're going to get, cooked to perfection in a down-to-earth setting. **Known for:** succulent locally sourced meat; popularity with locals; lack of tourists. [$] *Average main: €13* ✉ *Put Prvoboraca 232, Kotor* ☎ *069/340–300.*

**Pržun**
**$$** | **SEAFOOD** | This spot makes a great case as Kotor's most romantic restaurant. Settled in another of the city's hidden squares, Pržun straddles the fine line between private and popular, serving excellent seafood in a professional manner. **Known for:** romantic atmosphere; legendary sea bass; locally crafted beer. [$] *Average main: €19* ✉ *Stari Grad 397, Kotor* ☎ *069/343–061.*

## Hotels

**Hotel Astoria**

$$ | **HOTEL** | In the heart of the Old Town, the quirky Hotel Astoria and its restaurant, housed in a 13th-century town house, is a breath of fresh air amid the blander options elsewhere in the center of Kotor. **Pros:** creative design; central location; good breakfast options. **Cons:** expensive for its category; the huge fleshy murals of Adam and Eve in the public restaurant may not be to everyone's taste; Wi-Fi isn't the best. *Rooms from: €150 ✉ Trg od Pošte, Stari Grad ☎ 032/302–720 🌐 astoriamontenegro.com/astoria-kotor ⇨ 9 rooms 🍴 Free Breakfast.*

**Hotel Cattaro**

$$ | **HOTEL** | This solid old hotel is as magically central as it gets, occupying the 19th-century Napoléon Theatre, the 18th-century Duke's Palace, and other historic buildings on the Old Town's main square. **Pros:** located in Old Town; historic building; great views in all rooms. **Cons:** expensive for the area; slightly lacking in charm; tends to book up. *Rooms from: €170 ✉ Trg od Oružja bb, Stari Grad ☎ 032/311–000 🌐 cattarohotel.com ⇨ 19 rooms 🍴 Free Breakfast.*

**Hotel Monte Cristo**

$$ | **HOTEL** | The family-run Hotel Monte Cristo, housed in a 13th-century building (once the home of the first Bishop of Kotor), offers reasonably priced accommodation in the heart of the Old Town. **Pros:** prime location; great on-site restaurant; very informative staff. **Cons:** its position in the midst of Old Town café life can make it noisy at night; no elevator or step-free access; Wi-Fi is a struggle. *Rooms from: €170 ✉ Stari Grad, Stari Grad ☎ 32/322–458 🌐 www.hotel10.net/hotel-monte-cristo-kotor ⇨ 12 rooms 🍴 Free Breakfast.*

**Hotel Vardar**

$ | **HOTEL** | Described as the only soundproofed place to stay in the Old Town, the Hotel Vardar is centrally located, with some rooms offering a view of the lovely main square where the hotel's restaurant offers a chance for people-watching in the shade of sun umbrellas. **Pros:** Old Town location; soundproofing; stylish bathrooms. **Cons:** even full soundproofing can't guarantee a night free of local bars' music; no twin rooms; breakfast area is in a dark separate restaurant from the terrace. *Rooms from: €130 ✉ Trg od Oružja, Kotor ☎ 032/325–084 🌐 www.hotelvardar.com ⇨ 25 rooms 🍴 Free Breakfast.*

★ **Palazzo Radomiri**

$$ | **HOTEL** | The owners of this family-run boutique hotel were inspired by local sea captains bringing back treasures from around the world. **Pros:** lovely old building; tastefully furnished; great amenities, including outdoor pool and sauna. **Cons:** location outside Kotor; stairs and steps throughout make access difficult; often full in summer. *Rooms from: €180 ✉ Dobrota 221 ✢ 4 km (2 miles) from Kotor ☎ 032/333–172 🌐 www.palazzoradomiri.com ⏲ Closed mid-Oct.–mid-Apr. ⇨ 10 rooms 🍴 Free Breakfast.*

## Shopping

**Green Market**

**MARKET** | Conversation and currency are king at Kotor's daily market, located just outside the main entrance of the city walls (on the main coastal road). It's filled with colorful, local, seasonal produce laid out on marble slabs: think artichokes, asparagus, and cherries in spring; tomatoes, eggplants, and figs in summer, alongside pots of tiny local mountain strawberries. It's also a great place to buy local dried porcini mushrooms. Best and busiest on Saturdays, the market takes place every day. *✉ Gradska Pijaca, Gradska Vrata, Kotor ✢ When facing main entrance from outside the City Walls, market is on the right.*

## Activities

### BEACHES

The small pebble Gradska Plaža (Town Beach), just outside the town walls, is fine for a quick dip after a hot day of sightseeing.

### SAILING

Several charter companies are based in the protected waters of Kotor Bay. Early booking (e.g., by February for the summer) will offer worthwhile discounts, but prices have risen steeply in recent years and are only getting higher. The former military shipyard in Tivat, 5 km (3 miles) away, has been renovated and reopened as Porto Montenegro, a luxury marina able to accommodate some of the world's largest superyachts.

**Montenegro Charter Company**
**SAILING** | With years of yachting experience and intimate knowledge of the country and its waters, Montenegro Charter is an excellent choice for tailored sailing. Seven-day catamaran and sailing yacht trips are available, with prices ranging from €1,700 to €3,400. ✉ *Porto Montenegro Village, Obala bb, Tivat, Podgorica* ☎ *067/201–655* 🌐 *www.montenegrocharter.com.*

# Perast

*15 km (9 miles) from Kotor.*

Tiny Perast is a peaceful bayfront village of stone villas set in gardens filled with fig trees and oleander. Wealthy local sea captains built the town during the 17th and 18th centuries when the area was prosperous enough to have some 100 merchant ships navigating the oceans. Eighteenth-century Russian Tsar Peter the Great so respected Perast's naval skills that he sent his young officers to study at the Perast Maritime Academy.

Today, its main attractions are found in the bay in front of Perast: Sveti Đorđe (St. George) and Gospa od Škrpjela (Our Lady of the Rock), a pair of tiny charming islets, each topped with a church. Perast has no beach, though swimming and sunbathing are possible from the jetties along the waterfront.

Each year on July 22, Perast celebrates the *fasinada,* a local festival honoring the folkloric origins of Our Lady of the Rock, with a ritual procession of boats carrying stones out to the island at sunset. The stones are dropped into the water around the island, protecting it from erosion by the sea for the coming year. The Fasinada Cup sailing regatta is held on the same day.

### GETTING HERE AND AROUND

Perast can be reached by car or bus; it can also be visited on an organized half-day boat trip from Kotor's harbor.

## Sights

Begin your exploration with a look in the Perast Town Museum, then take a taxi-boat from the quayside to visit the island church, Our Lady of the Rock. Head back to town for lunch at one of the area's charming rustic eateries.

**★ The Islands of Gospa od Škrpjela (Our Lady of the Rocks) and Sveti Đorđe (St. George)**
**ISLAND** | St. George is a natural island, but its sibling, Our Lady of the Rocks, is artificial. Folklore says that in 1452, local sailors found an icon depicting the Virgin and Child cast upon a rock jutting up from the water. Taking this as a sign from God, they began placing stones on and around the rock, slowly building an island over it. By 1630 they had erected a church on the new island. The original icon, attributed to the 15th-century local artist Lovro Dobričević, is displayed on the altar. Over the centuries, locals have paid their respects to it by donating silver votive offerings, some 2,500 of which are now on display. The church is also home to more than 60 paintings by local

The island known as Our Lady of the Rocks is man-made but still has more than 350 years of history behind it.

hero Tripo Kokolja, one of the three men honored in Perast's main square.

The other island, home to the Monastery of St. George and dating back to the 12th century, is closed to the public. In the 18th century, the island became a favorite burial place for local sea captains, whose crypts remain today. Though closed to the public, you can snap photos from the shore or from neighboring Our Lady of the Rocks.

To visit Our Lady of the Rocks, hop on a taxi-boat from Perast's waterfront (a 5-minute trip that costs €5 round-trip); there is no shortage of options. ✉ *Bay of Kotor, Perast.*

**Muzej Grada Perasta**

**HISTORY MUSEUM** | In the 17th-century Renaissance-Baroque Bujović Palace, on the water's edge, Muzej Grada Perasta (Perast Town Museum) displays paintings of local sea captains and their ships, plus a horde of objects connected to Perast's maritime past. ✉ *Obala Marka Martinovića bb, Perast* ☎ *069/373–519* 🌐 *muzejikotor.me/en/home/perast-museum* 🎫 *€5; €8 for combined ticket with Roman Mosaics at Risan* 🕘 *Closed Mon.*

**Roman Mosaics at Risan**

**RUINS** | These beautiful mosaics are from a 2nd-century house in a small excavation site that is worth a brief stop if you are in the area. Particularly charming is the mosaic depicting Hypnos, the Roman god of sleep. Tour guides and detailed information panels in many languages are available. ✉ *Risan bb, Risan* ☎ *032/371–233* 🎫 *€5; €8 for combined ticket with Perast City Museum* 🕘 *Closed Mon.*

## Restaurants

**★ Hotel Conte Restaurant**

**$$** | **SEAFOOD** | Widely regarded as one of the best restaurants on the coast, Hotel Conte's gastronomic offerings prove the benefits of culinary education and growth. The chefs have spent time at some of the finest restaurants in Europe, honing their craft and embracing new culinary trends in real time, leading directly to the food on your plate. **Known for:** romantic terrace; extravagant seafood dishes; convivial and professional service. *Average main: €18 Obala Kapetana Marka Martinovića bb, Perast 067/257–387 hotelconte.me.*

**Stari Mlini**

$$ | **MEDITERRANEAN** | This rustic old mill on the Ljuta River, 7 km (4 miles) down the coastal road from Perast, dates back to 1670 and has been run by the current family for more than 40 years. The restaurant offers excellent food, emphasizing fish (you can visit the restaurant's trout ponds set in the attractive grounds). **Known for:** spectacular sea views; excellent local almond cake specialty; location in a historic mill. *Average main: €16 Ljuta bb, Kotor 032/333–555 starimlini.com.*

## Hotels

**★ Hotel Conte**

$ | **HOTEL** | These stone buildings dating from the 15th and 16th centuries have been tastefully converted into well-appointed apartments, some with kitchens and one with a Jacuzzi. **Pros:** lovely old building; tastefully furnished; good breakfast. **Cons:** Muzak in the restaurant not for everyone; steep steps up to some apartments; proximity to church means early morning bells. *Rooms from: €115 Obala Kapitana Marka Martinovića bb, Perast 067/257–387 hotelconte.me 18 rooms Free Breakfast.*

# Podgorica

*90 km (56 miles) east of Perast.*

Montenegro's capital is a square peg in a round hole, but Podgorica deserves more love than it tends to get. The country's best cafés and bars are found here, along with a decent selection of modern hotels and quirky sights. Podgorica also makes an excellent base for exploring Montenegro's most fascinating inland sights, from mausoleums to monasteries.

### GETTING HERE AND AROUND

Podgorica International Airport isn't the busiest airport in Europe, but it has direct connections with many cities, including Belgrade, Istanbul, and Vienna. Podgorica also has a central bus and train station, connecting it with most major stops in the region. The famous rail journey between Belgrade, Serbia and Bar, Montenegro stops in Podgorica.

## Sights

**Njegoš Mausoleum**

**MONUMENT** | Petar II Petrović-Njegoš looms large over Montenegrin history—and not just because of his famously giant frame. The 19th-century titan was a prince, poet, and philosopher largely credited with modernizing Montenegro. It is only fair that his final resting place should be high above the country, in the stunning surroundings of Lovćen National Park. The Njegoš Mausoleum is on Jezerski vrh, the second-highest peak in the Lovćen range, an hour west of Podgorica. Cetinje, Montenegro's royal capital during the Njegoš times, is nearby and deserving of at least a day's exploration. *Jezerski Vrh, Lovćen, Kotor €7.*

**★ Ostrog Monastery**

**RELIGIOUS BUILDING** | Undoubtedly Montenegro's most magical place, Ostrog is peaceful, picturesque, and packed with presence. Located an hour north of Podgorica, the 17th-century Orthodox monastery is built into a vertical cliff above the road to Nikšić and holds the remains of Saint Basil of Ostrog. The complex is divided into upper and lower parts, and walking the almost 3 km (2 miles—uphill, very uphill) between the two is a rite of passage in these parts. The views and history are worth every bead of sweat. Trains run between Podgorica and Ostrog station, from where the long walk begins. The monastery is still an active one, so be sure to be respectful of the monks who live on the property. ✉ *Dabojevići, Podgorica* ☎ *068/800–899* 🌐 *manastirostrog.com* 🎫 *Free, donations encouraged.*

**Stara Varoš**

**NEIGHBORHOOD** | Podgorica's oldest neighborhood is a ticket to a different time before modern technology brought cars and chaos to the city. The clock tower is a central beacon for the Ottoman-era area, while a quaint stone bridge acts as a de facto entrance across the Ribnica River. You'll also find the Natural History Museum of Montenegro, a museum that makes up in curiosity for what it lacks in size. ✉ *Stara Varoš, Podgorica.*

## Restaurants

**Tavern Lanterna**

**$ | EASTERN EUROPEAN** | A longtime staple of Podgorica's traditional dining scene, Tavern Lanterna remains one of the best restaurants in the country. The Old Town location can't be beaten, while the menu touches on Montenegrin classics. **Known for:** good range of veal dishes; traditional decor; extensive liqueur menu. $ *Average main: €12* ✉ *Kralja Nikole 36, Podgorica* ☎ *67/663–163.*

## Hotels

**Boutique Hotel Boscovich**

**$ | HOTEL** | Podgorica has several excellent accommodation options, but the service and standards at Hotel Boscovich help it stand out from the pack. **Pros:** city center location; great range of rooms; friendly staff that can arrange tours. **Cons:** some rooms are pricey; lacks a certain flair; a little loud at night. $ *Rooms from: €110* ✉ *Marka Miljanova 55, Podgorica* ☎ *20/230–722* 🌐 *hotelboscovich.com* *30 rooms* 🍽 *No Meals.*

## Nightlife

**Galerija Café Bar**

**BARS** | Bokeška is the beating heart of Podgorica's café and bar scene, so expect the street to be bustling on most evenings and weekends. There is no shortage of good options, but Galerija is an old favorite, as much for its artistic decor as its range of beverages. DJs ensure the bar is packed on weekends. ✉ *Bokeška 12, Podgorica* ☎ *67/505–311.*

Chapter 11

# SLOVENIA



Updated by
John Bills

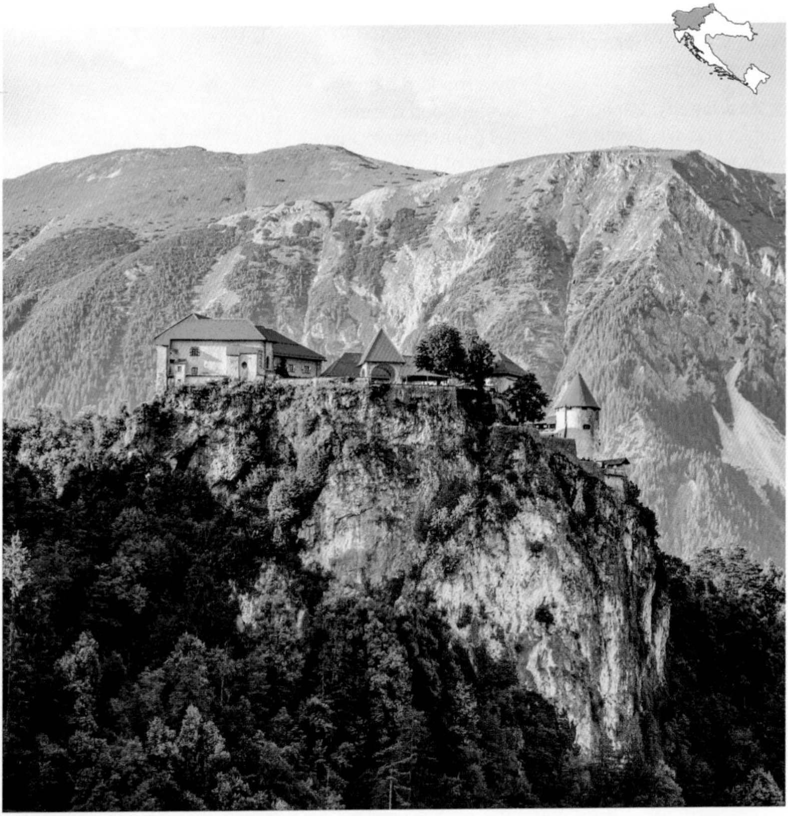

Sights ★★★★☆ | Restaurants ★★★☆☆ | Hotels ★★★☆☆ | Shopping ★★★☆☆ | Nightlife ★★★☆☆

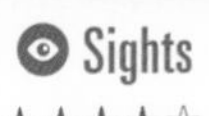

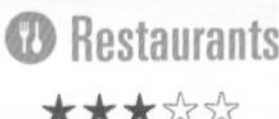

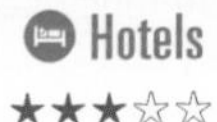

# WELCOME TO SLOVENIA

## TOP REASONS TO GO

★ **Skiing and mountain adventures:** Explore the Julian Alps surrounding Lake Bled or hit the slopes at Kranjska Gora.

★ **Water sports:** Slovenia's small Adriatic coastline is lined with bays, inlets, and tiny secluded beaches while the River Soča offers rafting and canyoning.

★ **An artsy city:** Capital Ljubljana is filled with a wide variety of excellent museums and a tremendously creative population.

★ **Food and drink:** Slovenia is about simple pleasures but this place doesn't skimp on flavor, making it one of Europe's most underrated culinary destinations.

★ **Caving opportunities:** Slovenia's Karst region is filled with some amazing limestone caves.

★ **Lipizzaner horses:** The famed Spanish Riding School stallions in Vienna originally came from a farm in Lipica.

Ljubljana, the capital, takes its place in the country's geographical center, magnetizing entrepreneurs, artists, students, and internationals into making it a funky modern city coated in Habsburg decor. An hour's drive from both the coast and the Alps, Ljubljana is well connected to the rest of the country by a modern highway system and decent rail connections. Just north of Ljubljana, the Julian Alps give way to the mesmerizing lakes of Bled and Bohinj, as well as some excellent skiing and hiking resorts such as Kranjska Gora. To the west of the lakes, the often turquoise yet always stunning river Soča starts its Adriatic-bound flow, yielding sights that must be seen—or better, rafted—to be believed. The Soča offers adventure and excitement in equal measure, raising adrenaline levels with the promise of serenity waiting farther down on the short but memorable Adriatic coast. There, the intact Venetian jewel of Piran holds its own with more renowned cities in Italy and Croatia.

**1 Ljubljana.** Everything great about Europe in one pint-size capital city.

**2 Bled.** One of Europe's most stunning mountain resorts.

**3 Bohinjsko Jezero.** Slovenia's largest lake.

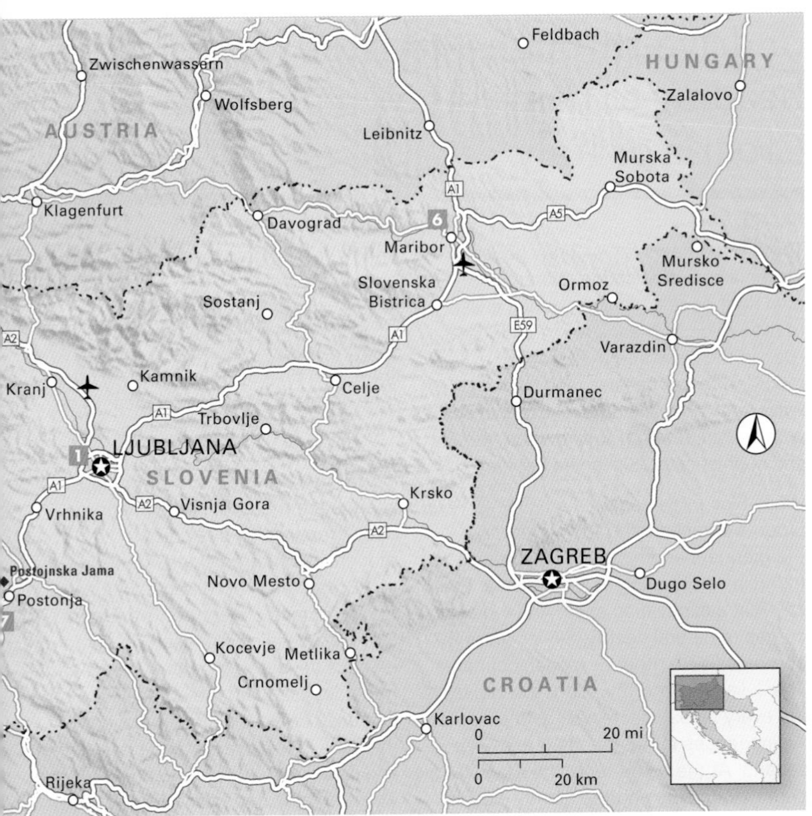


**4 Kranjska Gora.** The country's largest and most beloved ski resort.

**5 Bovec.** The gateway to water activities on the Soča River.

**6 Maribor.** Slovenia's second city and arguably its most underrated

**7 Postojnska Jama and Škocjanske Jame.** Two of Europe's most impressive cave systems.

**8 Lipica.** Where the fabled white Lipizzaner horses were first bred.

**9 Koper.** The onetime capital of the Republic of Venice.

**10 Piran.** The jewel of the Slovenian coast.

Slovenia may be the best-kept secret in Europe. Just half the size of Switzerland, the country is often treated as flyover—or drive-through—territory by travelers heading to better-known places in Croatia or Italy.

That's good news for anyone choosing Slovenia as a destination, either in its own right or as a highlight during a visit to the region. It means fewer crowds—even in the peak summer touring months—fewer hassles, and in many ways, a more relaxed travel experience with a chance to get to know the friendly and sophisticated Slovenian people.

While Slovenia's beautiful artistic monuments and charming towns may lack the grandeur and historical importance found in neighboring Italy or Austria, they still cast a captivating spell. And when it comes to natural beauty, Slovenia easily competes with other European countries. The Julian Alps northwest of the capital are every bit as spectacular as their sister Alpine ranges in Austria, Italy, and Switzerland. At the same time, the magnificent countryside and the quietly elegant charm of Ljubljana await those with the imagination to choose a destination that remains (just) off the beaten path.

## MAJOR REGIONS

**Julian Alps and the Soča Valley.** Northwest of Ljubljana lies an unspoiled region of breathtakingly beautiful mountains, alpine lakes, and fast-running rivers. Much of the region is part of the protected Triglavski narodni park (Triglav National Park), and it's the perfect jumping-off spot for adventure pursuits of all sorts. Excellent skiing, hiking, rafting, biking, and fly-fishing draw people here from around the world.

Each of the major towns and resorts in the region—Bled, Bohinj, Kranjska Gora, and Bovec—offers something a little different. At Bled, the focus is on comfort and excellent facilities, poised against a fairy-tale backdrop of an island church in a green-blue lake. Bohinj's charms are more rustic—a pristine deep-green alpine sea bordered by mountains on three sides. Kranjska Gora and Bovec offer more immediate access to high-octane adventure. The former is Slovenia's leading ski resort. In summer, it opens its lifts to mountain bikers and free-riders seeking the adrenaline rush of a dash down the slopes. Bovec, on the Soča River, offers world-class rafting and canyoning—or gentler floats—down what must be one of the world's most beautiful mountain streams.

These regional centers can be approached individually or, in the summer, by car or bus as part of a large loop running northwest of Ljubljana. Proceed first to Bled and on to Bohinj, then push on farther north to Kranjska Gora, over the impossibly high Vršič Pass, and down to Bovec.

**The Karst Region.** As you move south and west from Ljubljana toward the Adriatic, the breeze feels warmer, the air smells fresher, and the landscape looks less and less like Austria and more and more like Italy.

The word karst, or in Slovenian *Kras*, is a geological and geographic term referring to the giant limestone plateau which stretches roughly from Nova Gorica in the north to well beyond Divača in the south. It is bordered west by the Italian frontier and east by the fertile wine-growing Vipava Valley. Sinkholes, underground tunnels, and streams are standard in the Karst, and the region is also dotted with caves—most notably Postojna and Škocjan, which are jaw-dropping in beauty and size. Slovenia has more than 13,000 caves, but these two are undoubtedly the king and queen of them all.

To most Slovenians, the word "karst" conjures up two things: *pršut* (air-dried ham) and blood-red Teran wine. The two pair beautifully, especially with a plate of cheese and a basket of homemade bread, taken at a traditional *osmica*, a small farmhouse restaurant. Teran is a strong wine made from the refošk grape that you will either love or loathe from the first sip. It takes its name from the *terra rossa*, or red soil, that typifies the Karst.

For visitors, the Karst is ideal for low-key exploration. The gentle terrain and numerous wine roads (look for the sign that reads *vinska cesta*) are perfect for leisurely walks or bike rides. Several wine roads can be found around the town of Komen and along the main road from Komen to Dutovlje. The elegant towns—with their old stone churches and red-tile roofs—are a delight. The Lipica Stud Farm—the original breeding ground of the famed Lipizzaner horses of Vienna's Spanish Riding School—is an excellent base.

**The Adriatic Coast.** A little farther on, Slovenia's tiny piece of the Adriatic coast gives tourists a welcome opportunity to swim and sunbathe. Backed by hills planted with olive groves and vineyards, the small strip is only 47 km (29 miles) long and dominated by the towns of Koper and Piran.

Following centuries of Venetian rule, the coast remains culturally and spiritually connected to Italy, and Italian is still widely spoken. The medieval port of Piran is a gem and a must-see. Its Venetian core is nearly perfectly preserved, while Koper, Slovenia's largest port, is a workaday town that retains a lot of historical charm.

For beachgoers, the best-equipped beach is at Bernadin, between Piran and Portorož. The most unspoiled stretch of the coast is at the Strunjan Nature Reserve—which also has an area reserved for nudists—between Piran and Izola.

Piran and Koper are very different in character, but either can serve as an excellent base, depending on your plan. Choose Koper if you are searching for the bustle of a living city and the busy atmosphere of a working port surrounded by centuries of history. Or pick Piran if you're looking for something quainter, quieter, and more starkly beautiful. Whatever you choose, you can travel easily between the two. Buses make the 45-minute trip at least once an hour in season.

# Planning

## When to Go

The Slovenian countryside is most beautiful in spring and fall, though the best period to visit depends on what you plan to do during your stay. Ljubljana is vibrant the whole year through. Many visitors want to head straight for the coast. Those searching for sea, sun, and all-night parties will find what they're looking for in peak season (July and August), including cultural events, open-air dancing, busy restaurants, and crowded beaches. If you want to avoid the crowds, hit the Adriatic in June or September, when it should be warm enough to swim and more accessible to find a place to put your beach towel.

There are two distinct seasons in the mountains: winter is dedicated to skiing and summer to hiking and biking—some hotels close in November and March to mark a break between the two periods. Conditions for more strenuous walking and biking are optimal in April, May, September, and October.

Lovers of fine food and wine should visit Slovenia during the fall. The grape harvest concludes with the blessing of the season's young wine on St. Martin's Day, preceded by three weeks of festivities. In rural areas, autumn is the time to make provisions for the hard winter ahead: wild mushrooms are gathered, firewood is chopped, and *koline* (sausages and other pork products) are prepared by hand.

## Getting Here and Around

### AIR

There are no direct flights between North America and Slovenia. The Slovenian national carrier, Adria Airways, closed in 2019, but several low-cost airlines, such as easyJet and Wizz Air, serve Ljubljana.

The Ljubljana Airport is at Brnik, 25 km (16 miles) north of the city. Public bus service runs regularly between the airport and Ljubljana's central bus station in the city center. Buses depart from the airport every hour on the hour weekdays and slightly less frequently on weekends. Tickets cost around €4. A private airport shuttle called GoOpti makes the same trip in slightly less time; departures average every 90 minutes or so. Tickets can cost as low as €15, but booking in advance is a must. A taxi costs approximately €40, and the ride takes about 30 minutes.

**CONTACTS GoOpti.** ✉ *Ljubljana* ☎ *1/888–9424* 🌐 *www.goopti.com.* **Ljubljana Airport.** ✉ *Spodnji Brnik* ☎ *04/206–1000* 🌐 *www.lju-airport.si.* **Maribor Airport.** ✉ *Slivnica* ☎ *02/629–1553* 🌐 *www.mbx-airport.si.*

### BUS

International and domestic bus lines and the Ljubljana municipal bus service all operate conveniently from the city's main bus terminal, not far from the city center.

Private coach companies operate to and from Trieste in Italy and Zagreb in Croatia, as well as other European destinations farther afield. Domestic bus service is frequent from the capital to most Slovenian cities and towns. Outside of a car, the bus remains the only practical option to Bled and Bohinj and mountain destinations west and north of the capital. Except during peak travel periods, you can buy your ticket on the bus when you board. Otherwise, purchase tickets a day in advance. Many buses do not run on Sunday.

Hourly buses link Ljubljana to Bled, Bohinj, and Kranjska Gora. The resorts are linked by local buses; their frequency depends on the season. For schedules and fare information, ask at a local tourist information center. Six buses a day connect Kranjska Gora and Bovec during the summer via the jaw-dropping Vršič Pass, and there is one direct bus from Ljubljana to Bovec that takes a little over 4 hours.

Several buses a day connect Ljubljana to Koper and Piran, passing through Postojna and Divača on the way. There is also a daily service connecting the coastal towns to Trieste, Italy.

Within Ljubljana, the municipal bus network is extensive, and service is frequent during weekdays. Service continues but is less frequent on weekends and holidays. Buses on most lines stop running around 11 pm. To ride the bus, you need an Urbana card, which can be purchased from any kiosk and is topped up using the green machines at bus stops. Swipe the card when you get on the bus, and away you go.

**CONTACTS Ljubljana Bus Station.** ✉ *Trg Osvobodilne Fronte 4, Ljubljana* 🌐 *www.ap-ljubljana.si.*

### CAR

The Slovenian border is about a 40-minute drive from both Zagreb and Rijeka and about a 2½-hour drive from Zadar and the northern Dalmatian coast.

You only need a car if you plan to leave Ljubljana; cars are prohibited in the Old Town. However, traveling by car undoubtedly gives you a chance to reach remote areas of the country and will also allow you to appreciate the country's natural beauty. If you're bringing a car into Slovenia, be sure to buy a highway toll sticker, a vignette, at the border. It's required to drive on any highway; fines are steep if caught without one. Short-term stickers are available at most gas stations and post offices. Any rental car hired in Slovenia should already have one.

From Ljubljana, a four-lane highway (E61) runs northwest past Kranj and continues—occasionally reverting to a two-lane highway on some stretches—to the resorts of Bled and Kranjska Gora. Lake Bohinj lies 25 km (16 miles) southwest of Bled along local highway 209. The Vršič Pass, which connects Kranjska Gora and Bovec, is closed during the winter. If you want to go to Idrija, Kobarid, or Bovec from November to April, you will have to approach them via the south.A car is advisable for touring the Karst region. However, parking can be a problem along the coast during summer, when town centers are closed to traffic. And parking in Piran, for example, is restricted to season ticket holders only. The E63 highway connects Ljubljana to the coast, passing through the Karst region en route.

### TAXI

Private taxis operate 24 hours a day. Phone from your hotel or hail one in the street. Drivers are bound by law to display and run a meter.

### TRAIN

Train travel is a pleasant way of getting around Slovenia, which is well-connected to neighboring countries and other European destinations. The Ljubljana train station is just north of the city center. Check the Slovenian Railways website for timetables and to buy tickets. A fantastic weekend option is the IZLETka ticket (€15), which allows unlimited travel on the entire Slovenian network on Saturdays and Sundays. This ticket is a great way to explore several small towns over one weekend.

**CONTACTS Ljubljana Train Station.** ✉ *Trg Osvobodilne Fronte, Ljubljana* ☎ *386/1291–3331* 🌐 *potniski.sz.si.*

## Restaurants

Slovenia's traditional dining institution is the *gostilna,* essentially an inn or tavern but cleaner, warmer, and more inviting than the English translation suggests. These are frequently family-run, especially in the smaller towns and villages, with Mom in the kitchen and Pop out front pouring beers and taking orders. The staff is usually happy to suggest local or regional specialties. Some of the better gostilnas are situated alongside vineyards or farms. In Ljubljana, these are usually on the outskirts of the city. Those in the city center tend to be oriented toward the tourist trade since urban Ljubljaners usually prefer lighter, more modern fare.

Slovenian cuisine is highly regionalized, with offerings quite similar to dishes of neighboring countries and cultures. The Adriatic coast features Italian-influenced grilled fish and pasta, while the inland regions will offer cuisine very similar to that of Austria and Hungary. From the former Yugoslavia (and originally from Turkey), you'll find grilled meats and a popular street food called *burek,* a little pastry pocket stuffed with cheese or meat.

Mealtimes follow the Continental norm for lunch and dinner. Even if a restaurant posts earlier opening times, the kitchen won't usually start operating until noon. Dinners typically start around 7 pm. It can be tough to find a breakfast place, so it's best to take the standard hotel or pension offering of sliced meats and cheeses when available.

Restaurants usually close one day a week; in larger towns like Ljubljana, that's likely to be Sunday. In resort areas that cater to a weekend crowd, Monday is the usual day off. When in doubt, phone ahead.

## Hotels

Don't expect Slovenia to be an inexpensive option; lodging prices are similar to what you see in Western Europe. During peak season (July and August), many hotels—particularly those on the coast—are fully booked. Hotels are generally clean, smartly furnished, and well-run. Establishments built under socialism are often equipped with extras such as saunas and sports facilities but tend to be immense structures lacking in soul. Hotels dating from the turn of the 20th century are more romantic, as are the castle hotels. Over the last few decades, many hotels have been refurbished and upgraded.

Private lodgings are a cheaper alternative to hotels, and the standards are generally excellent. Prices vary depending on region and season. Look for signs proclaiming*sobe* (room to let) or *apartma* (apartments) alongside roads or in towns. Local tourist information centers, or private travel agencies in resorts like Bled or Piran, will often maintain lists of local rooms for rent.

Many hotels will offer better rates for stays of more than three days. Hotel rates frequently include breakfast—usually a mix of bread, cheeses, and cold cuts served buffet-style. Pensions and private rooms may include lunch or dinner—be sure to ask what's included in the price and whether you can opt-out if you choose.

Between April and October, camping is a reasonable alternative. Most campgrounds are small but well-equipped. Camping outside of organized campsites is not permitted.

To experience day-to-day life in the countryside, you should stay on a working farm. Agritourism is rapidly growing in popularity, and at most farms, you can experience an idyllic rural setting, delicious home cooking, plus a warm family welcome. More information is available on the Slovenia tourist board's website.

⇨ *Restaurant and hotel reviews have been shortened. For full information, visit Fodors.com. Restaurant prices are the average cost of a main course at dinner or, if dinner is not served, at lunch. Hotel prices are the lowest cost of a standard double room in high season.*

**WHAT IT COSTS in Euros (€)**

| $ | $$ | $$$ | $$$$ |
|---|---|---|---|
| **RESTAURANTS** | | | |
| under €15 | €15–€23 | €24–€32 | over €32 |
| **HOTELS** | | | |
| under €150 | €150–€250 | €251–€350 | over €350 |

## Visitor Information

Ljubljana's Turistično informacijski center (Tourist Information Center, or TIC) is next to the Triple Bridge on the Old Town side. Open weekdays and Saturdays from 8 to 6 and Sundays from 8 to 3, it's an excellent resource for maps, brochures, advice, and small souvenirs like postcards and T-shirts.

# Ljubljana

Slovenia's small but exceedingly charming capital is enjoying a tourism renaissance. Tourism officials now talk of Ljubljana proudly in the same breath as Prague or Budapest as one of the top urban destinations in Central Europe. That may be enthusiasm and excitement talking as opposed to reality, but there's no denying a sense of excitement as new hotels and restaurants open their doors, and each month seems to bring another admiring article in a prestigious newspaper or magazine abroad. Unfortunately, there is still no nonstop service from the United States.

The compact city center is immediately captivating. Part of the charm is the emerald green Llubljanica River that winds its way slowly through the Old Town, providing a focal point and the perfect backdrop to the cafés and restaurants that line the banks. Partly, too, it's the aesthetic tension between the stately Baroque houses along the river and the white neoclassical, modern, and Secessionist set pieces that dot the streets and bridges everywhere. Meticulously designed pillars, orbs, and obelisks lend the city an element of whimsy, a feeling of good cheer that's immediately infectious. And part of the credit goes to the Ljubljaners themselves, who can be counted on to come out and party in full force on a warm summer evening.

In truth, Ljubljana has always viewed itself as something special. Even when it was part of the former Yugoslavia, the city was considered a center of alternative music and arts. This was especially true during the 1980s, when it became the center of the Yugoslav punk movement. The band Laibach, noted for mocking nationalist sentiments, was the musical wing of the absurdist conceptual-art group Neue Slowenische Kunst (NSK), earning Ljubljana a reputation for pushing creative boundaries.

The romantic heart of the Old Town dates back centuries. The earliest settlement was founded by the Romans and called Emona. Much of it was destroyed by the Huns under Attila, though a section of the walls and a complex of foundations—complete with mosaics—can still be seen today. In the 12th century, a new settlement, Laibach, was built on the right bank of the river below Castle Hill by the dukes of Carniola. In 1335, the Habsburgs gained control of the region and constructed the existing castle fortification system.

The 17th century saw a period of Baroque building, strongly influenced by currents in Austria and Italy. Walk along the cobblestones of the Mestni trg (Town Square) and the Stari trg (Old Square) to see Ljubljana at its best, from the colored Baroque town houses with their steeply pitched tile roofs to Francesco Robba's delightful *Fountain of the Three Carniolan Rivers*.

For a brief period, from 1809 to 1813, Ljubljana was the capital of Napoléon's Illyrian Provinces. In 1849, once again under the Habsburgs, Ljubljana was linked to Vienna and Trieste by rail. The city developed into a significant center of commerce, industry, and culture, and the opera house, national theater, national museum, and the first hotels came into existence.

In 1895 much of the city was devastated by an earthquake. The following reconstruction work was carried out in a striking Viennese Secessionist style. Many of the stately four-story buildings that line Miklošičeva, such as the Grand Hotel Union, date from this period.

After World War I, with the birth of the Kingdom of Serbs, Croats, and Slovenes, Ljubljana became the administrative center of Slovenia. Various national cultural institutes were founded, and the University of Ljubljana opened in 1919. If you have been to Prague, you will already

Ljubljana has a picturesque Old Town bisected by the Ljubljanica River canal.

have seen some of the work of Jože Plečnik (1872–1957). Born in Ljubljana, Plečnik studied architecture in Vienna under Otto Wagner, then went on to lecture at the Prague School of Applied Arts and served as the chief architect for the renovation of Prague Castle. Plečnik added many decorative touches to the city's parks, squares, and bridges. Some of his finest projects include the Triple Bridge, the open-air market on Vodnik Square, and the plans for the Križanke Summer Theater.

The city's years as part of Yugoslavia, under the leadership of Josip Broz Tito, saw increased industrialization. The population of Ljubljana tripled, and vast factory complexes, high-rise apartments, and modern office buildings extended into the suburbs.

## PLANNING YOUR TIME

For short stays of two to three days, base yourself in Ljubljana. Spend at least one day taking in the attractions of the capital and the other day or two on day trips, such as to the Postojna or Škocjan Caves. If you have one other day to spend, you might consider dividing your time between Ljubljana and a town like Koper on the Adriatic coast.

## GETTING HERE AND AROUND

Central Ljubljana is tiny and compact. You'll find yourself walking from place to place. Take taxis or city buses if you need to cover more ground. Taxis are ample and affordable, and the city bus route is extensive.

## TOURS

For a private guided tour of the city, contact the Tourist Information Centre Ljubljana. Tours must be arranged in advance and are offered in several languages.

**Tourist Information Centre Ljubljana**
**VISITOR CENTER** | The central tourist information office provides a broad range of guided tours of the city, covering everything from castle tours to extensive journeys through Plečnik's Ljubljana. Book in advance in their office or on the website. The departure point is in front

of the Town Hall. ✉ *Adamič-Lundrovo Nabrežje 2, Ljubljana* ☎ *1/306–1215* 🌐 *www.visitljubljana.com* 🎫 *Tours from €13.*

## Sights

Much of Ljubljana's architecture from the period between the two World Wars is the work of Jože Plečnik (1872–1957). Born in Ljubljana, Plečnik studied architecture in Vienna under Otto Wagner and was an essential member of the Viennese Secessionist School. Plečnik added many decorative touches to the city's parks, squares, and bridges. Some of his finest projects include the Triple Bridge, the open-air market on Vodnik Square, the University Library, and the plans for the Križanke Summer Theater. Although Plečnik survived World War II, he fell out of favor with government officials because his Roman Catholicism conflicted with the ideologies of the socialist state under Tito. Be on the lookout for his masterpieces. The city center is concentrated within a small area, so you can cover all the sights on foot.

### Cankarjevo Nabrežje

**NEIGHBORHOOD | FAMILY** | An idyllic way to while away a day, Ljubljana's riverside is packed with cafés and restaurants that are perfect for people-watching. Prices have skyrocketed recently, but you're paying for location and atmosphere above all else. ✉ *Between Tromostovje and Čevljarski most, Ljubljana.*

### Cathedral of St. Nicholas

**CHURCH | FAMILY** | This proud Baroque cathedral overlooking the daily market on Vodnikov trg is dedicated to St. Nicholas, the patron saint of fishermen and boatmen who created a powerful guild in medieval Ljubljana. The building took place between 1701 and 1708 under the Italian architect Andrea Pozzo, who modeled it after the church of Il Gesù in Rome. The magnificent frescoes on the ceiling of the nave are by the Lombard painter Giulio Quaglio and depict the transfiguration of St. Nicholas and the persecution of Christians under Diocletian and Nero. In honor of Pope John Paul II's visit in 1996, bronze doors were added to the church. The main entrance tells the story of Christianity in Slovenia, whereas the side door shows the history of the Ljubljana diocese. ✉ *Dolničarjeva 1, Ljubljana* ☎ *01/234–2690* 🌐 *zupnija-lj-stolnica.rkc.si* 🎫 *Free.*

### ★ City Museum of Ljubljana

**HISTORY MUSEUM | FAMILY** | Situated in the grand Auersperg Palace, this museum's beautifully designed exhibits trace the city's history from pre-Roman times through the Austrian domination, the World Wars, the Tito years, and finally, the establishment of independent Slovenia. In the basement, you can walk on a piece of the ancient Roman road or see a cross-sectioned excavation that shows the burning of Emona by Attila the Hun through a black charred stratum. If you're interested, you can arrange for a museum guide to take you to other ancient Roman sites around the city. The city museum also houses the world's oldest wooden wheel, dating from 4000 BC. ✉ *Gosposka 15, Ljubljana* ☎ *01/241–2500* 🌐 *mgml.si* 🎫 *€6* 🕒 *Closed Mon.*

### Dragon Bridge

**BRIDGE** | Four fire-breathing winged dragons crown the corners of this locally cherished concrete-and-iron structure. The dragons refer to the mythological origins of the city when Jason, returning home from winning the Golden Fleece, killed a monster in a swamp on the present site of Ljubljana. It's undoubtedly one of the most photographed attractions in a city full of photogenic spots. ✉ *Resljeva Cesta 2, Ljubljana.*

### ★ Franciscan Church (*Frančiškanska cerkev*)

**CHURCH** | Its color may now garner more attention than its history, but Ljubljana's famous Pink Church has plenty of stories waiting within. A High Baroque beauty

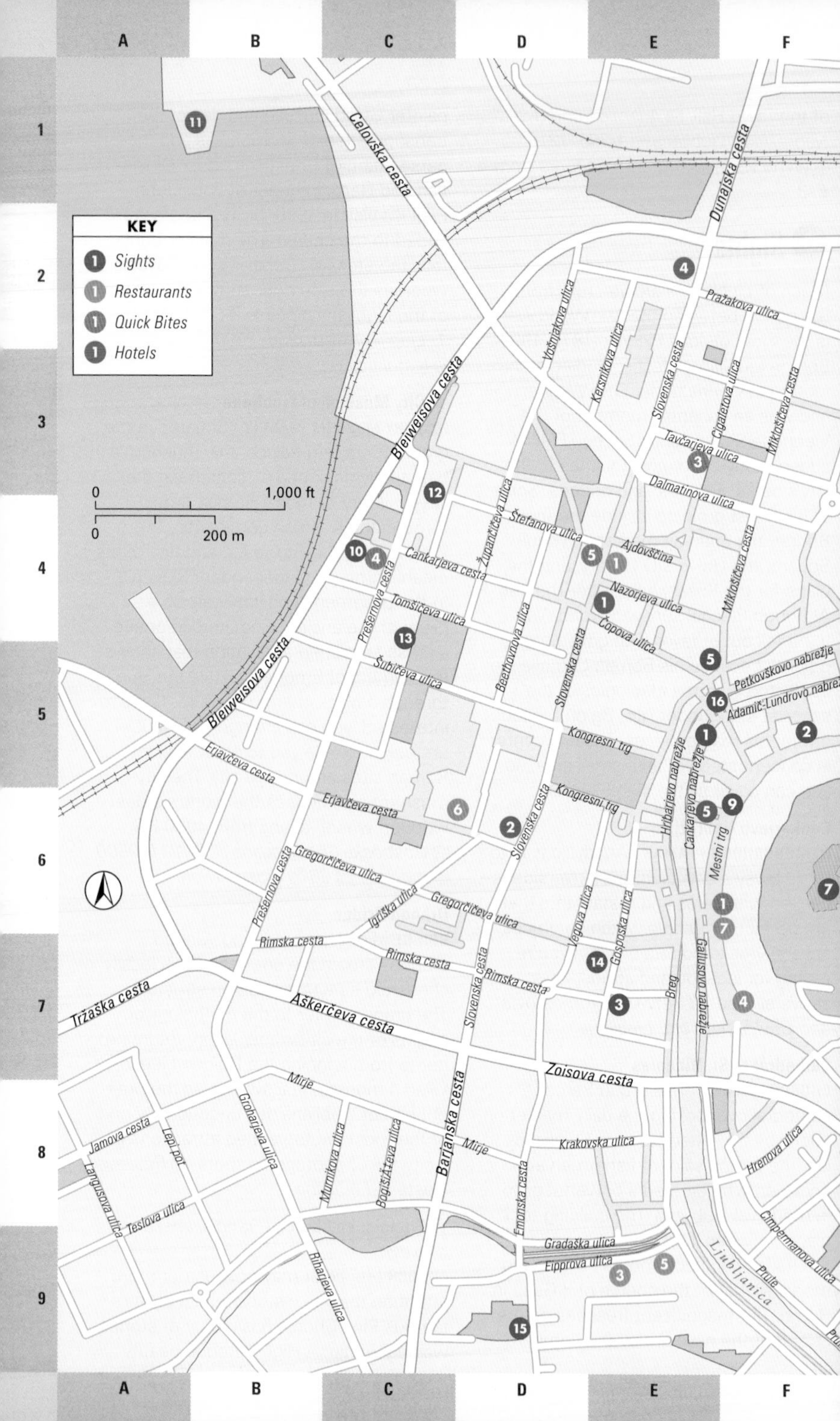

A
B
C
D
E
F
1
2
3
4
5
6
7
8
9
KEY
Sights
Restaurants
Quick Bites
Hotels
0
1,000 ft
0
200 m
Celovška cesta
Dunajska cesta
Pražakova ulica
Vošnjakova ulica
Kersnikova ulica
Slovenska cesta
Cigaletova ulica
Miklošičeva cesta
Tavčarjeva ulica
Dalmatinova ulica
Bleiweisova cesta
Štefanova ulica
Župančičeva ulica
Ajdovščina
Cankarjeva cesta
Nazorjeva ulica
Prešernova cesta
Tomšičeva ulica
Beethovnova ulica
Čopova ulica
Petkovškovo nabrežje
Adamič-Lundrovo nabrežje
Šubičeva ulica
Kongresni trg
Erjavčeva cesta
Hribarjevo nabrežje
Cankarjevo nabrežje
Mestni trg
Gregorčičeva ulica
Igriška ulica
Vegova ulica
Gosposka ulica
Rimska cesta
Gallusovo nabrežje
Breg
Tržaška cesta
Aškerčeva cesta
Zoisova cesta
Mirje
Jamova cesta
Lepi pot
Groharjeva ulica
Murnikova ulica
Bogišiĉeva ulica
Barjanska cesta
Krakovska ulica
Emonska cesta
Hrenova ulica
Langusova ulica
Teslova ulica
Gradaška ulica
Eipprova ulica
Rihaijeva ulica
Cimpermanova ulica
Ljubljanica
Prule

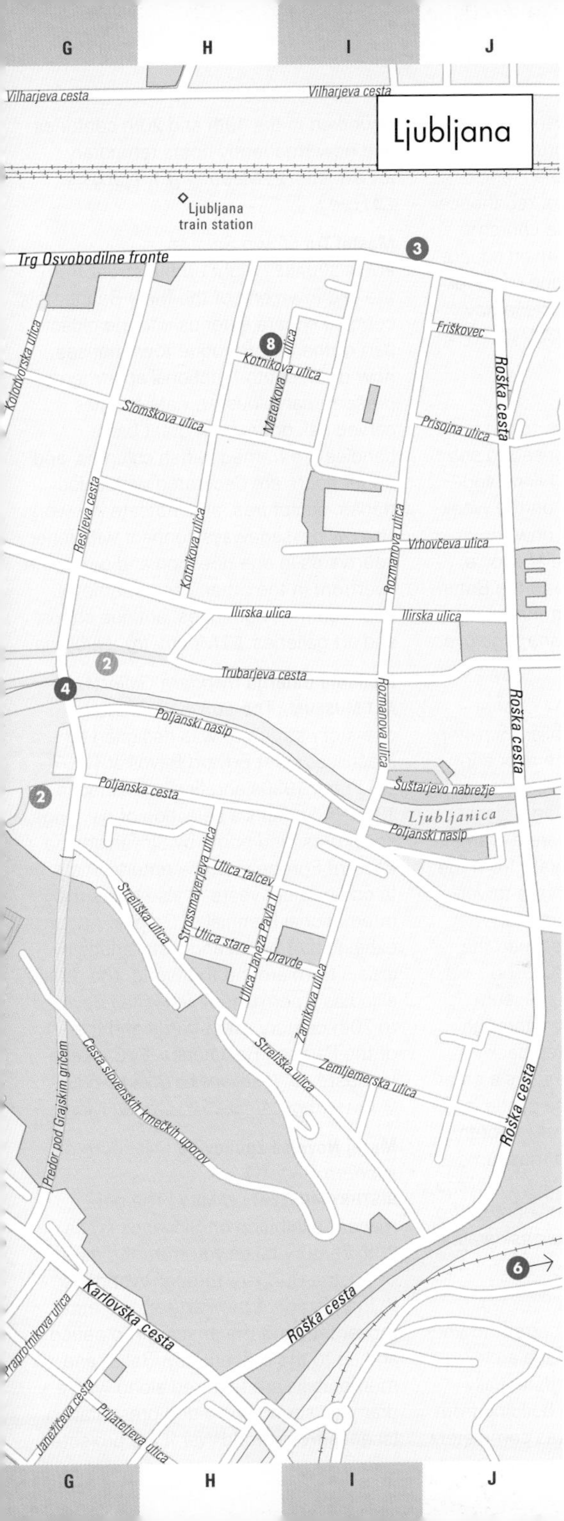

# Ljubljana

## Sights



## Restaurants



## Quick Bites



## Hotels

built in the middle of the 17th century, the church flourished a century later under the watchful eye of the Franciscans, who decided to paint it red (hence the faded pink of today). The church's prime location on the city's main square makes it a prominent meeting point for people of all ages today. ✉ *Prešernov trg 4, Ljubljana* ☎ *01/242–9300* 🌐 *www.franciskani.si.*

**Golovec Hill**
**TRAIL | FAMILY** | Slovenes love to get out and about, so don't be surprised to see whole families packing the hiking and biking trails around the city on the weekend. Less than a mile from downtown Ljubljana, Golovec is a popular choice, with the path starting close to the Botanical Garden. The views from the top are fantastic. ✉ *Golovec, Ljubljana* 🌐 *golovectrails.com.*

★ **Ljubljanski Grad** (*Ljubljana Castle*)
**CASTLE/PALACE | FAMILY** | Ljubljana's hilltop castle affords views over the river and the Old Town's terra-cotta rooftops, spires, and green cupolas. On a clear day, the distant Julian Alps are a dramatic backdrop. The castle walls date from the early 16th century, although the tower was added in the mid-19th century. Architect Jože Plečnik landscaped the surrounding park in the 1930s. The castle also houses a virtual museum showcasing Slovenian history through digital technology. Take a step back through time and do the tour; it's a great introduction to Ljubljana. The castle is also home to the Museum of Puppetry, one of the most underrated museums in the city. ✉ *Grajska Planota 1, Ljubljana* ✥ *Študentovska, uphill from Vodnikov Trg* ☎ *01/306–4293* 🌐 *www.ljubljanskigrad.si* 🎫 *€16 (including funicular).*

**Magistrat** (*Town Hall*)
**GOVERNMENT BUILDING** | The current town hall is the work of the Ljubliana architect Gregor Maček, who substantially renovated the 1484 original building from 1717 to 1719. The interior was completely reworked in the 19th and 20th centuries and now frequently hosts temporary art exhibits. ✉ *Mestni Trg 1, Ljubljana* 🎫 *Free.*

**Mestni Trg** (*Town Square*)
**PLAZA/SQUARE** | Right up the street from the Old Town end of the Triple Bridge, this cobbled square extends into the oldest part of the city. Baroque town houses, now divided into functional apartments, present marvelously ornate facades: carved oak doors with great brass handles are framed within columns, and upper floors are decorated with balustrades, sculptures, and intricate ironwork. Narrow passageways connect with inner courtyards in one direction and run to the riverfront in the other. The street-level floors contain boutiques, antique shops, and art galleries. ✉ *Mestni trg, Ljubljana.*

**Moderna Galerija** (*Modern Gallery*)
**ART MUSEUM** | The strikingly modern one-story structure was designed by Plečnik student Edvard Ravnikar (1907–93) in the 1930s and finally finished in 1948. It contains a selection of paintings, sculptures, and prints by Slovenian and Eastern European 20th-century artists. In odd-number years, it also hosts the International Biennial of Graphic Art, an exhibition of prints and installations by artists from around the world. The gallery also has a permanent collection devoted to 20th-century avant-garde and the art of the Partisan Resistance. ✉ *Cankarjeva Cesta 15, Ljubljana* ☎ *01/241–6834* 🌐 *www.mg-lj.si* 🎫 *€5* 🕘 *Closed Mon.*

**Muzej Novejše Zgodovine** (*Museum of Modern History*)
**HISTORY MUSEUM | FAMILY** | The permanent exhibition on Slovenes in the 20th century takes you from the days of Austria-Hungary through World War II, the victory of the Partisan liberation movement and the ensuing Tito period, and up to the present day. Relics and memorabilia are featured along with a dramatic sound-and-video presentation (scenes from World War II are projected

on the walls and ceiling, accompanied by thundering gunfire, screams, and singing). You'll find the museum in a pink-and-white Baroque villa in Tivoli Park. ✉ *Celovška Cesta 23, Ljubljana* ☎ *01/300–9611* 🌐 *www.muzej-nz.si* 🎫 *€6; free 1st Sun. every month* 🕒 *Closed Mon.*

**Narodna Galerija** (*National Gallery*)
**ART MUSEUM | FAMILY** | This massive building houses an extensive collection of Slovenian art from the 13th through the early 20th century and a smaller but impressive collection of European paintings. It also houses the original of Francesco Robba's *Fountain of the Three Carniolan Rivers.* ✉ *Prešernova Cesta 24, Ljubljana* ☎ *01/241–5418* 🌐 *www.ng-slo.si* 🎫 *€8* 🕒 *Closed Mon.*

**Narodni Muzej** (*National Museum*)
**HISTORY MUSEUM** | The National Museum—home to more than 400,000 archaeological artifacts, rare books, historical documents, and artworks from the prehistoric era through modern times—is not to be missed. The centerpiece here is a bronze urn from the late 5th or 6th century BC known as the Vače Situla. Discovered in Vače, Slovenia, it is a striking example of Illyrian artistry and is decorated with friezes depicting a procession of men, horses, and chariots. Extensive collections of classic artworks from Western and Northern Europe, Russia, and Japan complement the already impressive exhibit of Yugoslav pieces. ✉ *Muzejska 1, Ljubljana* ☎ *01/241–4400* 🌐 *www.nms.si* 🎫 *€8; €10 when combined with Natural History Museum.*

**National and University Library**
**LIBRARY** | Built from 1936 to 1941, the National Library is architect Jože Plečnik's secular masterpiece. The external facades present a modernist version of an Italian Renaissance palazzo, using brick, stone, and even archaeological remains from excavations around Ljubljana. However, these are not arranged in registers as in a traditional palazzo but instead are scattered haphazardly over the entire exterior, creating a dynamic and three-dimensional look that makes the massive building seem light and airy. Inside is a beautiful, colonnaded black marble staircase and a reading room with huge windows at either end to let in light. Plečnik also designed the austere furniture in the reading room. Don't miss the beautiful horse-head door handles on the main entrance. ✉ *Turjaška 1, Ljubljana* ☎ *01/200–1194* 🌐 *www.nuk.uni-lj.si* 🎫 *€5 for reading room* 🕒 *Closed Sun.*

**Plečnik's House**
**HISTORIC HOME** | Architecture enthusiasts will enjoy a visit to architect Jože Plečnik's house, which is home to his preserved studio, living quarters, and garden. A strange combination of refined aestheticism and severe, almost monastic, asceticism permeates the residence of the man who played a large part in transforming Ljubljana between the two World Wars. Exploring the house itself is only possible on one of the hourly tours, but the gardens and exhibition are accessible with a ticket. ✉ *Karunova 4, Ljubljana* ☎ *01/241–2506* 🌐 *mgml.si/en/plecnik-house* 🎫 *€8* 🕒 *Closed Mon.*

**Tromostovje** (*Triple Bridge*)
**BRIDGE** | This striking structure spans the river Ljubljanica from Prešernov trg to the Old Town. The three bridges started as a single span, and in 1931, the two graceful outer arched bridges, designed by Plečnik, were added. ✉ *Ljubljana.*

## Restaurants

Don't let the secret out, but Ljubljana is quietly becoming one of Europe's most engaging gastronomic experiences. The surrounding hills supply the capital with first-class meat and game, dairy produce, fruit, and vegetables. At Ljubljana's more modern restaurants, the menus may verge on nouvelle cuisine, featuring imaginative and beautifully presented dishes. The portions, however, are almost always more ample than their counterparts in

Ljubljana Castle overlooks the Old Town and the river.

other countries. Complement your meal with a bottle of good Slovenian wine; the server can help you choose an appropriate one.

### Barbarella Juicebar

$ | **VEGETARIAN** | Here you'll find brilliant plant-based cuisine that is perfect for breakfast, brunch, lunch, or dinner, made from locally-sourced ingredients. Smoothies, soups, sandwiches, and rice bowls dominate the menu, but don't be surprised to see something out of the ordinary here. **Known for:** filling rice bowls; organic ingredients; colorful dishes. *Average main: €8 Slovenska Cesta 38, Ljubljana 01/320–0705 www.barbarella.si Closed Sun.*

### Čompa

$$$ | **SLOVENIAN** | Wonderful smells waft from the kitchen of this affordable little eatery, which is an absolute must-visit for meat-lovers. With homemade beer to complement the savory menu, exposed stone interiors, and sturdy wooden tables, this cozy eatery makes for a welcome break. **Known for:** the best steak in town; grill-fried bread; romantic atmosphere. *Average main: €25 Trubarjeva Cesta 40, Ljubljana 040/799–334 Closed Sun. and Mon.*

### Dežela Okusov

$$ | **SLOVENIAN** | Meat everything reigns supreme at this charming cuts-fueled bistro on Eipprova. Dežela Okusov is pub grub at an impeccably high standard: stacks of grilled and smoked meats mesh perfectly with any of Slovenia's impressive roster of craft beers. **Known for:** sumptuous smoked meat dishes; house-roasted coffee; lovely terrace. *Average main: €15 Eipprova 11, Ljubljana 01/283–9288 dezela-okusov.si.*

### ★ Druga Violina

$ | **SLOVENIAN** | **FAMILY** | The gorgeous Stari trg location and a hearty menu filled with Slovenian classics would be enough to justify a festive lunch at Druga Violina. Still, there is more to this spot than initially meets the eye: the restaurant doubles as an initiative to help people with disabilities in the region, a talented group of people who help grow the ingredients on a nearby farm and work as the waitstaff in the restaurant itself. **Known for:** fresh locally grown produce; traditional Slovenian food; socially aware outlook. *Average main: €12 Stari Trg 21, Ljubljana 82/052–506 Closed Sun.*

**Manna**

$$ | **SLOVENIAN** | **FAMILY** | Expect exceptional food and service at this pleasant well-known eatery just three minutes from the city center. Every dish on the menu is sure to please, and there's an excellent wine list. **Known for:** lots of outdoor seating; must-try manna strudel; central location. *Average main: €18 Eipprova 1A, Ljubljana 031/529–974 www.restavracija-manna.si Closed Mon.*

**★ Pizzeria Parma**

$ | **PIZZA** | **FAMILY** | Every major city in the region is flooded with pizzerias these days, but only one gets to wear the crown of the oldest pizzeria in Eastern Europe. That honor falls to delightful Parma, a small pizzeria that opened in 1974 and still serves excellent pies today (from the same oven, no less). **Known for:** community favorite; delicious blueberry juice; oldest pizzeria in Eastern Europe. *Average main: €8 Trg Republike 2, Ljubljana 01/426–8222 www.facebook.com/PicerijaPARMA Closed Sun.*

**Valvas'or**

$$ | **EUROPEAN** | An ode to modern design and inventive tastes, Valvas'or will first woo you with their stylish remodel of an old arched tavern and then amaze you with little pleasures like a sorbet between courses. Between ample and excellently prepared dishes, take note of the gold-perforated metal wall that details the city plan of Ljubljana. **Known for:** food to match the beautiful atmosphere; tasting menus available; professional waitstaff. *Average main: €19 Stari Trg 7, Ljubljana 01/425–0455 valvasor.net Closed Sun.*

## Coffee and Quick Bites

The coffee revolution that has swept through Europe has made it to the Slovenian capital. There has never been a better time to enjoy a cup of hot coffee in Ljubljana, with a great selection of cafés on the riverside and farther afield.

**★ Cafetino**

$ | **CAFÉ** | **FAMILY** | A longtime favorite with coffee lovers across Ljubljana, Cafetino is a friendly place to stop for that all-important first cup of the day. The interior is tiny and getting a seat can be difficult, so it's best to stroll up early. **Known for:** picturesque location; conversation-filled setting; wide range of coffee beans. *Average main: €3 Stari Trg 5, Ljubljana 04/222–950 www.cafetino.si Closed Sun.*

**Čokl**

$ | **CAFÉ** | Ljubljana's caffeine mecca, Čokl is a postage-stamp-size café that serves up the best coffee in the city—at least according to those in the know. The terrace is a lovely spot to spend an afternoon, especially considering the interior's size. **Known for:** impressive coffee expertise; teeny-tiny interior; Ljubljana's best espresso. *Average main: €2 Krekov Trg 8, Ljubljana 03/078–9173.*

**Kava Bar Tam Tam**

$ | **CAFÉ** | **FAMILY** | A hugely personable café, Tam Tam is focused on flavor while refusing to skimp on extras, serving snacks along with its coffees, beers, and wines. It has a tranquil authentic atmosphere and an outstanding selection of beverages. **Known for:** great coffee; modernist vibes; serene parkside setting. *Average main: €2 Cigaletova ulica 3, Ljubljana 040/566–044 www.facebook.com/KavaBarTamTam Closed Sun.*

**Kavarna Moderna**

$ | **CAFÉ** | Located in the basement of the Museum of Modern Art, Kavarna Moderna is an excellent place to reflect on the creativity upstairs or to enjoy a quality cup of coffee. An obvious hangout for Ljubljana's artistic types, the café also serves up some delicious breakfast and brunch options. **Known for:** digital-nomad-friendly atmosphere; wide range of bites; cool art gallery vibes. *Average main: €2 Cankarjeva Cesta 15, Ljubljana 041/336–927 www.kavarnamoderna.si Closed Mon.*

**Nebotičnik**

$ | **CAFÉ** | This spot still stands out in Ljubljana, so imagine how imposing it was in the 1930s. This city center structure was Europe's tallest residential building when constructed, and the top floor today is given over to a stylish café with the best views in town. **Known for:** Slovenia's first skyscraper; great coffees and cakes; gorgeous views of the city and castle. *Average main: €3 Štefanova 1, Ljubljana 05/907–0395 www.neboticnik.si.*

## Hotels

Hotel rates in Ljubljana continue to creep towards Western European numbers with each passing year. The standards here are usually high, but rooms, even in older historic hotels, tend to be modern and somewhat lacking in charm. You can get good deals in the summer through private accommodations or university dorms. Ask about these options at the tourist information kiosk in the town center.

**Best Western Premier Hotel Slon**

$$ | **HOTEL** | Close to the city's historic center, this high-rise hotel stands on the site of a famous 16th-century inn and maintains an atmosphere of traditional hospitality. **Pros:** great buffet breakfast; comfortable beds; centrally located. **Cons:** not very personable; decor is outdated; street noise is loud in some rooms. *Rooms from: €150 Slovenska Cesta 34, Ljubljana 01/470–1100 www.hotelslon.com 170 rooms Free Breakfast.*

**★ Cubo**

$$ | **HOTEL** | In addition to its central position next to the National Drama Theater and a mere five-minute walk from the Old Town, this top-rated hotel also boasts excellent service, boutique design, and an excellent restaurant. **Pros:** central location; excellent staff; stylish boutique decor. **Cons:** busy lobby; some rooms feel small; on the more expensive side. *Rooms from: €175 Slovenska Cesta 15, Ljubljana 01/425–6000 www.hotelcubo.com 26 rooms Free Breakfast.*

**Hostel Celica**

$ | **HOTEL** | Celica, which translates to "a cell", is just that: a reconstructed prison that has become one of the most fascinating hostels in the region. **Pros:** energetic and involved staff; fascinating venue setup; fun and convenient location. **Cons:** small bag lockers; inconsistent opening times for café; very basic breakfast. *Rooms from: €35 Metelkova 8, Ljubljana 01/230–9700 www.hostelcelica.com 20 rooms, from double en-suite cells to 12-bed dorms Free Breakfast.*

**Intercontinental Ljubljana**

$$ | **HOTEL** | The arrival of this glass behemoth in the heart of Ljubljana brought mixed emotions from locals, but the class and professionalism offered at the Intercontinental still continue to attract attention and admiration from travelers. **Pros:** city center location; five-star luxury; gorgeous views from rooms. **Cons:** close to main road; modern building feels out of place; not that much of a local feel. *Rooms from: €250 Slovenska Cesta 59, Ljubljana 059/128–000 www.ihg.com/intercontinental/hotels/gb/en/ljubljana/ljuha/hoteldetail 165 rooms Free Breakfast.*

**Vander Urbani**

**$$ | HOTEL** | Arguably the most central hotel in Ljubljana, Vander Urbani was born of architectural creativity; several 18th-century town houses in the old city form this trendy hotel right beneath the Ljubljana castle. **Pros:** stylish design; ideal location; beautiful pool with a fantastic view. **Cons:** some flats feel cramped, though they've done their best to utilize space; hotel might feel like a nightclub to some; breakfast area gets a little too crowded. *Rooms from: €190 ✉ Krojaška 6–8, Ljubljana ☎ 01/200–9000 🌐 www.vanderhotel.com 20 rooms 🍽 Free Breakfast.*

## Nightlife

### BARS

**Godec Rock Pub**

**PUBS** | An intimate rock-music-friendly pub just outside the city center, Godec is a brilliant option for anyone looking for good beer and music, thanks to its classic tunes and a beer list covering Slovenia and beyond. Godec is a favorite with locals, making it a tremendous option for anyone looking for something a little more Ljubljanan. *✉ Knezova 3, Ljubljana ☎ 040/592–359 🌐 www.facebook.com/godecrockpub.*

**★ Klub Daktari**

**BARS** | With its hodgepodge of furniture and an undeniable artistic streak running through the walls, Daktari is a veritable Ljubljana institution. A wide range of patrons regularly enjoys the packed schedule of events here or simply an evening of drinks and discussion from early morning until late at night. You won't find a more eclectic crowd anywhere else in the city, in a more diverse environment. Daktari is Ljubljana at its best, with excellent cold beer and hot coffee. *✉ Krekov Trg 7, Ljubljana ☎ 05/905–5538 🌐 www.instagram.com/klubdaktari.*

**★ Pritličje**

**BARS** | With two fingers on the country's cultural pulse, Pritličje is ground zero for all things social in Ljubljana. The cooler-than-cool vibe is more than just aesthetics at this people-friendly bar with open doors and open minds. Located directly next to the Town Hall, Pritličje is a beacon of positivity all night long. *✉ Mestni Trg 2, Ljubljana ☎ 08/058–742 🌐 www.pritlicje.si.*

**Zorica**

**BARS** | This spot is a magnet for younger crowds looking for quality craft beer and colorful cocktails in seriously stylish surroundings. Its location above iconic club K4 doesn't hurt either. *✉ Kersnikova 4, Ljubljana ☎ 051/343–860.*

### MUSIC

**Cirkus Klub**

**DANCE CLUBS** | A mature and eclectic clubbing scene congregates in this former movie theater turned nightclub near the city center. Considered one of the top nightlife venues in the capital, Cirkus attracts DJs and bands that bring dance, R&B, hip-hop, house, pop, and rock to its multiple floors. It's open Wednesday, Friday, and Saturday. *✉ Trg Mladinskih Delovnih Brigad 7, Ljubljana ☎ 051/631–631 🌐 www.facebook.com/cirkus.klub.*

**★ Kino Šiška**

**LIVE MUSIC** | A significant player in Ljubljana nightlife since forever, Kino Šiška continues to be the capital's best source of live entertainment and partying. The schedule is as packed as Ljubljana schedules get, and the whole place is dripping in modern cool. *✉ Trg Prekomorskih Brigad 3, Ljubljana ☎ 01/500–3000 🌐 www.kinosiska.si/en.*

**Metelkova**

**LIVE MUSIC** | Formerly an army barracks, Metelkova has been transformed into a multipurpose venue for shows and happenings. Today, it is the center of the Slovenian alternative culture scene, full of street art, unique galleries, and music of every genre in its various clubs. Check the website for schedules of openings and performances. ✉ *Metelkova ulica, Ljubljana* 🌐 *www.metelkovamesto.org.*

## Performing Arts

### ANNUAL EVENTS

**Ljubljana Festival**

**ARTS FESTIVALS** | The Ljubljana Festival is held annually across the city from June to August. Music, theater, and dance performances attract acclaimed artists from all over the world. Check the website for schedules and reservations. ✉ *Trg Francoske Revolucije 1–2, Ljubljana* ☎ *01/241–6000* 🌐 *ljubljanafestival.si.*

### CLASSICAL MUSIC

Ljubljana has plenty of events for classical-music lovers. The season, which runs from September through June, includes weekly concerts by the Slovenian Philharmonic Orchestra and the RTV Slovenia Orchestra, as well as performances by guest soloists, chamber musicians, and foreign symphony orchestras.

**Slovenska Filharmonija** (*Slovenian Philharmonic*)

**CONCERTS** | The 19th-century performance hall houses concerts by the Slovenian Philharmonic. This hall was built in 1891 for one of the oldest music societies in the world, established in 1701. Haydn, Brahms, Beethoven, and Paganini were honorary orchestra members, and Mahler was the resident conductor for the 1881–82 season. Check the website for a schedule of performances and to make reservations. ✉ *Kongresni Trg 10, Ljubljana* ☎ *01/241–0800* 🌐 *filharmonija.si.*

### THEATER, DANCE, AND OPERA

Ljubljana has a long tradition of experimental and alternative theater, frequently incorporating dance. Contemporary dance plays by the internationally recognized choreographers Matjaž Farič and Iztok Kovač and performances by the dance troupes Betontanc and EN-KNAP are ideal for those who don't understand Slovenian.

**SNG Opera in Balet** (*Slovene National Opera & Ballet Theater*)

**OPERA** | **FAMILY** | This Neo-Renaissance palace, with an ornate facade topped by a symbolic sculpture group, was erected in 1892. When visiting ballet and opera companies visit Ljubljana, they perform here. The opera house fell into disrepair during the Yugoslav years but has been carefully and lovingly restored since Slovenian independence. From September through June, the SNG Opera in Balet stages productions ranging in style from classical to modern and alternative. ✉ *Župančičeva 1, Ljubljana* ☎ *01/241–5900* 🌐 *www.opera.si.*

## Shopping

**★ Antikvariat Alef**

**BOOKS** | Books on anything and everything, from languages to love and beyond, can be found at this family-run bookshop. It's the perfect place to pick up a new book and have a charming chat in the process. ✉ *Hribarjevo Nabrežje 13, Ljubljana* ☎ *070/396–371* 🌐 *www.antikvariatalef.si.*

**Ljubljana Flea Market**

**MARKET** | **FAMILY** | Held on the Breg Embankment each Sunday morning, the Ljubljana Flea Market offers a good selection of antiques and memorabilia. ✉ *Breg Embankment, Ljubljana.*

**Piranske Soline**

**OTHER SPECIALTY STORE** | **FAMILY** | Beloved worldwide, the salt harvested at the Sečovlje Salina Nature Park is available in various shapes and sizes at this friendly shop on Mestni trg. ✉ *Mestni Trg 8, Ljubljana* ☎ *01/425–0190* 🌐 *www.soline.si.*

**Trgovina IKA**

**SOUVENIRS** | **FAMILY** | Ljubljana has plenty of options for buying souvenirs, but the creative style of those on offer at Trgovina IKA makes it stand out from the pack. ✉ *Ciril-Metodov Trg 13, Ljubljana* ☎ *01/232–1743* 🌐 *www.trgovinaika.si.*

# Bled

*50 km (31 miles) northwest of Ljubljana.*

Bled is among the most magnificently situated mountain resorts in Europe. The healing powers of its thermal springs were known during the 17th century, and the aristocracy arrived in the early 19th century to bask in Bled's tranquil alpine setting. Even today—when Bled can swell to overflowing in the high season of July and August—it retains something of the refined feel of a fin de siècle spa town.

Recent years have brought many improvements to Bled's tourist facilities to cope with the ever-increasing number of visitors. Resorts and wellness centers, arguably the country's best golf course, and a clutch of adventure-oriented travel agencies mean there is now much more to do than simply stroll the banks of the lake. Bled is also an excellent base for hikes into the eastern half of Triglav National Park.

## VISITOR INFORMATION

**CONTACTS Bled Tourist Information.** ✉ *Cesta Svobode 10, Bled* ☎ *04/574–1122* 🌐 *www.bled.si.*

## Sights

★ **Blejski Grad** (*Bled Castle*)
**CASTLE/PALACE | FAMILY** | The stately Bled Castle perches above the lake on the summit of a steep cliff against a backdrop of the Julian Alps and Triglav Peak. You can climb up to the castle for fine views of the lake, the resort, and the surrounding countryside. An exhibition traces the castle's development through the centuries, with archeological artifacts and period furniture on display, but the view steals the show. ✉ *Grajska Cesta 61, Bled* ☎ *04/572–9770* 🌐 *www.blejski-grad.si/en* 🎫 *€15.*

★ **Blejsko Jezero** (*Lake Bled*)
**BODY OF WATER | FAMILY** | Bled's famed lake is nestled within a rim of mountains and surrounded by forests, with a castle on one side and a promenade beneath stately chestnut trees on the other. Horse-drawn carriages clip-clop along the promenade while swans glide on the water, creating the ultimate romantic scene. On a minuscule island in the middle of the lake, the lovely Cerkov svetega Martina (St. Martin's Pilgrimage Church) stands within a circle of trees. Take a ride over to the island on a *pletna,* a traditional covered boat. ✉ *Bled.*

**Čebelarski Muzej** (*Beekeeping Museum*)
**OTHER MUSEUM | FAMILY** | Radovljica is an adorable town not far from Bled, and its intriguing Čebelarski muzej (Beekeeping Museum) may well be its cultural highlight. Located within the 17th-century Town Hall in the town center, the museum explores the humble bee through various interactive exhibitions. The museum also houses its own hive, a buzzing colony of some 5,000 bees, working away behind the safety of a glass cabinet. ✉ *Linhartov Trg 1, Radovljica* ☎ *04/532–0520* 🎫 *€3* ⏲ *Closed Mon.*

**Soteska Vintgar** (*Vintgar Gorge*)
**CANYON | FAMILY** | This gorge was cut between precipitous cliffs by the clear Radovna River, which flows down numerous waterfalls and through pools and rapids. The marked gorge trail leads over bridges, wooden walkways, and gullies. It was discovered almost by accident in 1891 by a photographer and local mayor, but the authorities quickly recognized its potential. By 1893 it was open to the public, and this stunning 1.6-km (1-mile) gorge of natural beauty has been stealing hearts ever since. The vertical walls of the Hom and Boršt hills create a real sense of drama. If you are heading to Triglav National Park from Bled, this is the most exciting (and beautiful) way to do

In the middle of Lake Bled, you'll find a small island with the charming St. Martin's Pilgrimage Church located on it.

it. ✉ *Zgornje Gorje, Podhom 80, Bled* ✣ *5 km (3 miles) northwest of Bled* 🌐 *vintgar.si.*

## Restaurants

**Cafe Belvedere**

**$$ | CAFÉ | FAMILY** | Once a waiting hall for those hoping for an audience with the king (and designed by Plečnik, no less), Cafe Belvedere is now a gorgeous café offering the most exquisite views of Bled. The prices reflect that (expect to pay upwards of €2.60 for an espresso), but finding a better view of the beauty below is downright impossible. **Known for:** important history; gorgeous vistas; pricey coffees. $ *Average main: €15* ✉ *Cesta Svobode 18, Bled* ☎ *04/575–3721* 🌐 *brdo.si/objekti/posestvo-vile-bled* ⏲ *Closed weekdays.*

**Gostilna pri Planincu**

**$ | SLOVENIAN | FAMILY** | With large portions at modest prices, this friendly spot is busy year-round. Rowdy farmers take advantage of the cheap beer at the front bar, and everyone loves the menu "for people who work all day": roast chicken and fries, steak and mushrooms, black pudding, and turnips. **Known for:** big helpings of local pub food; sweet walnut štruklji for dessert; cheap beer. $ *Average main: €14* ✉ *Grajska Cesta 8, Bled* ☎ *04/574–1613* 🌐 *www.pri-planincu.com.*

**Julijana**

**$$$$ | SLOVENIAN** | If you are a celebrity looking for a bite to eat in Bled, Julijana is where you will likely end up. This restaurant is the top of the region's gastronomic scene, a high-class experience that combines incredible food with equally stunning views of the lake and the castle. **Known for:** world-class tasting menu; stunning views; quality over quantity. $ *Average main: €70* ✉ *Cesta Svobode 12, Bled* ☎ *04/579–1000* 🌐 *www.sava-hotels-resorts.com/en/sava-hoteli-bled/gastronomy/the-julijana-restaurant* ⏲ *Closed Sun.–Thurs.*

**1906**

**$$$$ | SLOVENIAN** | Meticulously prepared meals, perfectly paired wine, and homemade ice cream are all offered at a premium price for these parts. However, the setting and experience make that excellent value for your money. **Known for:** elegant yet down-to-earth atmosphere; impressive views; organized events like cooking classes. *Average main: €40 Kolodvorska Cesta 33, Bled 04/575–2610 www.hoteltriglavbled.si.*

## Hotels

**Garden Village Bled**

$$ | **ALL-INCLUSIVE** | **FAMILY** | This collection of unique lodging options (including a family-size tree house) offers innovative new ways to accommodate travelers looking for a downright luxurious retreat that takes them back to nature. **Pros:** wellness offer includes massage and sauna; sophisticated dining on premises; bikes for rent. **Cons:** some tent locations better than others; no a/c in treehouse; Wi-Fi can be iffy in certain spots. *Rooms from: €250 Cesta Gorenjskega Odreda 16, Bled 041/606–257 www.gardenvillagebled.com Closed Nov.–Apr. 24 rooms Free Breakfast.*

**Vila Bled**

$$ | **HOTEL** | Late Yugoslav president Tito was the gracious host to numerous 20th-century politicians at this former royal residence amid 13 acres of gardens overlooking the lake. **Pros:** unforgettable lake views; old-school elegance; fascinating history. **Cons:** rooms can seem a bit dated if you're not a fan of retro style; on the expensive side; hard to get to without private transport. *Rooms from: €200 Cesta Svobode 26, Bled 04/575–3710 brdo.si/objekti/vila-bled 31 rooms Free Breakfast.*

**Vila Prešeren**

$$ | **B&B/INN** | This tastefully renovated 19th-century lakeside villa—named after Slovenia's foremost poet, who was a frequent guest—is a step away from many of the Alpine accommodations in the area and feels more intimate than some of the lodgings near the town center. **Pros:** lakeside location; bold furnishings; romantic ambience. **Cons:** restaurant is popular with tour buses; reception is located in the restaurant and staff are usually busy; nearby church bells seem to ring constantly. *Rooms from: €170 Veslaška Promenada 14, Bled 04/575–2510 vilapreseren.com/en/home 8 rooms Free Breakfast.*

## Activities

During summer, the lake becomes a family playground, with swimming, rowing, sailing, and windsurfing. The main swimming area lies below the castle along the northern shore. In the winter, you can ski day and night on Straža Hill, immediately above the town, thanks to floodlighting. Just 10 km (6 miles) west of Bled, a larger ski area, Zatrnik, has 7 km (4½ miles) of alpine trails. For information on winter and summer sports, contact Bled's tourist information center or one of the many private travel and activity agencies around town.

**Royal Bled Golf**

**GOLF** | The gorgeous King's Course (18 holes) and Lake's Course (9 holes) are run by Royal Bled. Clubs, caddies, and carts are available for rent; the club also provides instruction and sanctions golf events. *Kidričeva Cesta 10C, Bled 04/537–7711 www.royalbled.com King's Course: €220, caddy €150, golf cart €50; Lake's Course: €65, caddy €55, golf cart €25 King's Course: 18 holes, 6666 yards, par 72; Lake's Course: 9 holes, 3089 yards, par 36.*

**3glav Adventures**

**HIKING & WALKING** | **FAMILY** | This company puts together hiking and rafting outings and, for thrill-seekers, organizes more extreme activities like parachuting and paragliding. *Ljubljanska Cesta 1, Bled 041/683–184 www.3glav.com.*

# Bohinjsko Jezero

*29 km (18 miles) southeast of Bled.*

When talking to locals about Lake Bled, don't be surprised to hear them say they prefer Bohinj. Lake Bohinj, the largest permanent lake in Slovenia, sits within Triglav National Park and is a popular spot for swimming, boating, and other water sports. It's a refreshing tranquil alternative to its more famous sibling.

### VISITOR INFORMATION

**CONTACTS Bohinj Tourist Information.** ✉ *Ribčev Laz 48, Bohinjsko Jezero* ☎ *04/574–6010* 🌐 *www.bohinj.si.*

## Sights

**★ Bohinjsko Jezero**

**BODY OF WATER | FAMILY |** Lake Bohinj is the quieter, wilder, and prettier sister of Bled and lies entirely within the Triglav National Park. The entire length of the north shore is rugged and accessible only by foot. At an altitude of 1,715 feet, the lake is surrounded on three sides by the steep walls of the Julian Alps. The altitude means the temperature of the water—even in August—rarely rises above a brisk but still swimmable 74°F. The small village of Ribčev Laz, on the eastern end of the lake, functions as the de facto town center, where you'll find a grocery store, post office, currency exchange, an ATM, and the tourist information center. On the western shore lies the remote village of Ukanc, anchored by the Hotel Zlatorog, a campsite, and a few small shops. Just to the north and east of Ribčev Laz are the tiny hamlets of Stara Fužina, Studor, and Srednja Vas. ✉ *Triglav National Park, Bohinjsko Jezero.*

**Mt. Vogel**

**MOUNTAIN |** At the west end of Lake Bohinj (near Ukanc), a cable car leads up Mt. Vogel to a height of 5,035 feet. You have spectacular views of the Julian Alps massif and the Bohinj valley and lake from here. From the cable-car base, the road continues 5 km (3 miles) beyond the lake to the point where the Savica River makes a tremendous leap over a 194-foot waterfall. The cable car runs every half hour from 8 am to 6 pm. A round-trip ticket costs €28. ✉ *Žičnice Vogel Bohinj, Ukanc 6, Bohinjsko Jezero* 🌐 *www.vogel.si.*

**Sveti Janez** (*St. John*)

**CHURCH | FAMILY |** On the eastern bank of Lake Bohinj in Ribčev Laz, you'll find the 15th-century Gothic church of Sveti Janez. The small church has a fine bell tower and contains several notable 15th- and 16th-century frescoes. ✉ *Ribčev Laz, Bohinjsko Jezero.*

**★ Triglav National Park**

**NATIONAL PARK | FAMILY |** Covering some 4% of Slovenia's entire landmass, Triglav National Park is the ideological and spiritual heart of the country. The iconic three peaks of Triglav (the highest point in the country) are found on Slovenia's coat of arms and its flag, placing this dreamland of gorges, caves, waterfalls, rivers, and forests front and center for the nation. Winter sees locals and visitors alike head here in search of skiing and other snow-based activities, while the warmer months are perfect for amateur and experienced climbers and hikers. Mountain huts dot the landscape offering affordable accommodations for those looking to wander the meadows. Slovenia's only national park, Triglav contains everything that makes Slovenian nature magnificent, all within 840 square km (324 square miles) of magic. ✉ *Triglav National Park, Bohinjsko Jezero* ☎ *04/578–0200* 🌐 *www.tnp.si.*

## Restaurants

**Foksner**

**$$ | EUROPEAN | FAMILY |** The days of Bohinj's one-dimensional eating options are over, and the excellent Foksner is leading the charge. The burgers are as good as anywhere else in Slovenia,

Slovenia's only national park, Triglav is one of its most popular camping destinations.

and the beer menu is equally excellent. **Known for:** brilliant burgers; great craft beer; relaxed atmosphere. $ *Average main: €15* ⊠ *Ribčev Laz 42, Bohinjsko Jezero* ☎ 🌐 *www.facebook.com/foksner.*

**Gostilna Danica**

$ | **SLOVENIAN** | **FAMILY** | Don't be deceived by this restaurant's casual appearance at the Danica campsite, as delicious food lies within. Economically priced while still delivering a full plate, a good portion of the menu changes seasonally. **Known for:** cheerful service; distinctively better than most campsite restaurants; full regional wine menu. $ *Average main: €13* ⊠ *Triglavska Cesta 60, Bohinjska Bistrica* ☎ *04/575–1619* 🌐 *tdbohinj.si/gostisce-danica.*

**Štrud'l**

$ | **SLOVENIAN** | **FAMILY** | This spot offers a quaint backdrop for a menu of alluring local food at a reasonable price. The staff is attentive and the atmosphere is warm, as are most of the dishes. **Known for:** foraged mushroom soup with homemade bread; local products for sale; traditional Slovenian mountain delights. $ *Average main: €10* ⊠ *Triglavska Cesta 23, Bohinjska Bistrica* ☎ *041/541–877* 🌐 *www.strudl.si* ⏲ *Closed Tues.*

## Hotels

The Bohinj area is the perfect place to opt for a stay in a private home or pension. The tourist information center in Ribčev Laz maintains an extensive list of options. Pensions are usually priced per person and often include lunch or dinner. Many of the most excellent properties are in the outlying villages of Ukanc, Stara Fužina, and Srednja Vas, so you will need private transportation (bike or car) to get there.

**Alpik Chalets**

$$ | **B&B/INN** | **FAMILY** | Located a stone's throw from Lake Bohinj, the Vogal ski resort contains a handful of restaurants. **Pros:** good for families or groups; self-contained kitchen; shoe- or ski-drying hallway setup. **Cons:** a walk into town; best to organize arrivial and departure times beforehand; kitchen sometimes

lacks basic ingredients. 💲 *Rooms from: €229* ✉ *Ukanc 85, Bohinjsko Jezero* ☎ *05/123–3190* 🌐 *alpik.com* 🛏 *10 rooms* 🍽 *No Meals.*

★ **Bohinj Park ECO Hotel**

$$ | **HOTEL** | **FAMILY** | As the first ecological hotel in Slovenia, Park ECO has won many awards for good reasons. **Pros:** furnishings made from all-natural materials; stunning views; home to an aquapark with pools and waterslides. **Cons:** can get quite crowded; conferences can seemingly take over the hotel; a little on the pricey side of things. 💲 *Rooms from: €150* ✉ *Triglavska Cesta 17, Bohinjsko Jezero* ☎ *08/200–4140* 🌐 *www.bohinj-eco-hotel.si* 🛏 *102 rooms* 🍽 *Free Breakfast.*

**Hotel Gašperin**

$ | **B&B/INN** | Showcasing no notable frills but all of the clean basic amenities, Hotel Gašperin is organized and set up for easy vacationing. **Pros:** good for families or groups; lots of nearby hiking options; beautiful location by the lake. **Cons:** a walk to the nearest restaurant; no cooking facilities in rooms; outside noise can be heard from rooms. 💲 *Rooms from: €110* ✉ *Ribčev Laz 36A, Bohinjsko Jezero* ☎ *041/540–805* 🌐 *www.gasperin-bohinj.com* 🛏 *24 rooms* 🍽 *Free Breakfast.*

**Vila Park**

$$ | **B&B/INN** | A luxurious little A-frame pension sits astride an impossibly gorgeous alpine meadow and just beside the bright-green Savica stream that feeds Lake Bohinj. **Pros:** good for families or groups; lovely location near stream; excellent breakfast. **Cons:** remote from major area sights; walk to nearest restaurant; decor a bit dated. 💲 *Rooms from: €160* ✉ *Ukanc 129, Bohinjsko Jezero* ☎ *04/572–3300* 🌐 *www.vila-park.si* 🛏 *8 rooms* 🍽 *Free Breakfast.*

## Activities

Bohinj is a natural base for exploring the trails of the Triglav National Park. Before heading out, pick up a good trail map from the tourist information center. The cable car to Vogel is an excellent starting point for many walks. Just remember to start early, wear proper hiking boots, take plenty of water, and protect yourself against the sun. Other popular warm-weather pursuits include swimming, biking, rafting, canyoning, and horseback riding. In winter, you can ski at Vogel and Kobla.

**Alpinsport**

**WATER SPORTS** | **FAMILY** | Reach out to Alpinsport to rent mountain bikes and organize rafting, kayaking, hydrospeed (a small board for bodysurfing rapids), and canyoning trips. ✉ *Ribčev Laz 53, Bohinjsko Jezero* ☎ *041/918–803* 🌐 *www.alpinsport.si.*

**Perfect Adventure Choice/PAC Sports**

**WATER SPORTS** | PAC is another local outfitter offering a slew of water sports, including paragliding, caving expeditions, and ice climbing. ✉ *Ribčev Laz 60, Bohinjsko Jezero* ☎ *040/864–202* 🌐 *en.pac.si.*

**Ranč Mrcina**

**HORSEBACK RIDING** | **FAMILY** | This company organizes horseback rides in and around Bohinj and the Triglav National Park to suit all skill levels. ✉ *Studor, Bohinjsko Jezero* ☎ *041/790–297* 🌐 *ranc-mrcina.com.*

# Kranjska Gora

*39 km (24 miles) northwest of Bled, 85 km (53 miles) from Ljubljana.*

Kranjska Gora is the country's largest ski resort, set amid Slovenia's highest and most dramatic peaks. In summer, the area attracts hiking and mountaineering enthusiasts. It's a pleasant town in any season. The resorts spread along the perimeter, leaving the surprisingly charming core intact.

### VISITOR INFORMATION

**CONTACTS Kranjska Gora Tourist Information.** ✉ *Kolodvorska 1C, Kranjska Gora* ☎ *04/580–9440* 🌐 *kranjska-gora.si.*

## Sights

### Dom Trenta

**VISITOR CENTER | FAMILY** | You'll find the Triglav National Park Information Center at Dom Trenta in Trenta. Here, you can watch a presentation about the history and geography of the region and tour the small museum. It's also a good access point to the 20-km (12-mile) Soča Trail that winds along the river's banks. The center is open from the end of April through to the end of October, daily from 10 to 6. ✉ *Na Logu v Trenti, Trenta* ☎ *05/388–9330* 🌐 *www.tnp.si* ⏱ *Closed Nov.–Apr.*

### ★ Vršič Pass

**SCENIC DRIVE** | From Kranjska Gora, head south over the breathtaking Vršič Pass, some 5,253 feet above sea level. You'll then descend into the beautiful Soča Valley, winding through the foothills to the west of Triglav Peak and passing truly magnificent scenery. From Trenta, continue west for about 20 km (12 miles) to reach the mountain adventure resort of Bovec. The Vršič Pass isn't for the faint of heart—every hairpin turn is fraught with danger—but roads in Slovenia don't come much more exhilarating than this. The truly brave should make the journey via bus from Kranjska Gora. The pass closes when the weather is particularly bad in winter.

## Restaurants

### Bar Pristavec

**$ | ECLECTIC** | This cute laid-back place is just off the main square, and it's perfect for a morning coffee and a light roll or sandwich. It is a splendid spot for a little bit of morning people-watching with your espresso. **Known for:** early morning conversation; pet-friendly policies; quick bites. [$] *Average main: €5* ✉ *Borovška Cesta 77, Kranjska Gora* ☎ *04/588–2111* ▭ *No credit cards.*

### Gostilna pri Martinu

**$ | SLOVENIAN** | This traditional Slovene gostilna is known for its homely good cooking. Try the homemade sausages or a local favorite, *telečja obara* (veal stew). **Known for:** local wedding receptions and large parties; traditional cooking; homemade sausages. [$] *Average main: €13* ✉ *Borovška Cesta 61, Kranjska Gora* ☎ *04/582–0300* 🌐 *www.julijana.info/sl/gostilna-pri-martinu.*

### Hotel Lipa

**$$ | SLOVENIAN** | This pension is primarily a hotel but also has a decent restaurant. The pizza is undoubtedly worth the money, but if you're in the mood for local food, opt for the **Known for:** idylic mountain setting; classic Slovenian fare; elegant dining room. [$] *Average main: €17* ✉ *Koroška 14, Kranjska Gora* ☎ *45/820–000* 🌐 *www.hotel-lipa.si* ⏱ *Closed Mon.*

### ★ Slaščičarna Kala

**$ | SLOVENIAN** | Tucked away near the bus station, this little patisserie is easy to miss yet worth every effort to find. Specializing in homemade ice cream and desserts from the Prekmurje region, this charming café will tempt you and keep you coming back for more. **Known for:** homemade ice cream and cakes; kremšnita (typical Balkan pastry); good coffee. [$] *Average main: €3* ✉ *Koroška 13B, Kranjska Gora* ☎ *04/588–5544* 🌐 *so-be-kala.si* ▭ *No credit cards.*

## Hotels

### Kronau Chalet Resort

**$$$ | RESORT | FAMILY** | Considered one of the best mountain lodges in Slovenia and situated near the famed Kranjska Gora World Cup giant slalom slopes, this a truly relaxing place to stay. **Pros:** paradise for skiers; tastefully decorated; eco-friendly policies. **Cons:** no coffeemakers in rooms; best to arrange arrival and departure beforehand; a little pricey. [$] *Rooms from: €282* ✉ *Bezje 19–24, Kranjska Gora*

51/356–179 www.kronau.si 6 chalets (36 beds) No Meals.

### ★ Skipass Hotel

**$$ | HOTEL | FAMILY** | Family-run and family-friendly, this small hotel of eight spacious rooms and two deluxe suites is affordable yet generous and accommodates guests with indulgent details such as heated bathroom floors and great breakfasts. **Pros:** excellent restaurant; good location; community feel. **Cons:** must book amply in advance; decor is not exceptional; no free parking. *Rooms from: €205 Koroška 14C, Kranjska Gora 04/582–1000 www.skipasshotel.si 10 rooms Free Breakfast.*

## Activities

Skiing is the number-one sport in Kranjska Gora, and Kranjska Gora is the number-one skiing spot in Slovenia. There are more than 30 km (19 miles) of downhill runs, 20 ski lifts, and 40 km (25 miles) of groomed cross-country trails open during the winter ski season, which typically runs from mid-December through mid-March. During summer, from late May through mid-September, mountain biking is huge, and you'll find plenty of places to rent bikes, as well as 12 marked trails covering 150 km (93 miles) to take you through scented pine forests and spectacular alpine scenery. An unused railway track tracing the south edge of the Karavanke Alps brings hikers and bikers to the village of Jesenice, about 20 km (12 miles) away. The Kranjska Gora Bike Park is oriented more toward experienced free-riders and thrill-seekers—those who like to take their bikes to the top of the hill and careen back down. There are also numerous hiking trails; you can pick up an excellent local trail map from the tourist information center or at kiosks around town.

### Fun Bike Park Kranjska Gora

**BIKING** | This company rents full- and front-suspension mountain bikes for use along downhill mountain and forest trails. The emphasis here is on fast adrenaline-filled rides. *Borovška Cesta 107, Kranjska Gora 04/580–9400 www.bike-park.si.*

### Intersport Bernik

**SKIING & SNOWBOARDING** | A full-service sports-equipment rental center, Intersport Bernik rents skis and mountain bikes in their respective seasons. It is located close to the ski center. *Borovška Cesta 88A, Kranjska Gora 04/588–4783 www.intersport-bernik.com.*

### Kranjska Gora Recreational Ski Center

**SKIING & SNOWBOARDING** | This center runs the lifts and is the primary place for skiing information. The website lists prices in English and has a live webcam so you can see the conditions on the mountain. *Borovška Cesta 103A, Kranjska Gora 04/580–9400 kranjska-gora.si.*

# Maribor

*130 km (81 miles) northwest of Ljubljana.*

Slovenia is consistently in the running for Europe's most underrated country, and it is a decidedly Slovene quirk that its second-largest city is its most underrated destination. Located in the country's east, Maribor doesn't jump off the page like Bled, Piran, or the capital Ljubljana, but there is plenty to love in its mazy streets and energetic atmosphere. The surrounding countryside certainly helps, and you'll find many of Slovenia's best wineries in these parts. Much of the goods cultivated in its greenery find their way into the town's bars and restaurants, making Maribor a must for anyone searching for Slovenia's most delicious destination. The Drava River cuts the town in two, and the views from its bridges are fabulous. The riverside Lent district is the city's beating heart, and its main event is the oldest still-growing vine in the world. Maribor is that kind of place;

unassuming, overlooked, and absolutely marvelous.

## Sights

**The Old Vine**

**OTHER ATTRACTION** | Maribor is best known for its miraculous Old Vine, an over-400-year-old vine that still produces grapes today. The Old Vine House tells the story of the vine and Maribor's rich grape-producing history. You rarely get to visit a plant with its own museum. Sampling the fruit of this icon is a must, whether in the museum or one of the many restaurants around Maribor. ✉ *Vojašniška 8, Maribor* 🌐 *oldestvinemuseum.si* 🎫 *€8* 🕐 *Closed Mon.*

**Ptujski Grad** (*Ptuj Castle*)

**CASTLE/PALACE** | The centerpiece of Slovenia's oldest town, Ptujski Grad stands atop a steep hill in the center of Ptuj. Planned around a Baroque courtyard, the castle houses a museum that contains musical instruments, an armory, 15th-century church paintings, and period furniture. The views from the castle are sublime, and there is a café for those looking to refresh themselves in a gorgeous setting. Ptuj is a beautiful little town 30 km (19 miles) south of Maribor and well worth a visit. ✉ *Grajska Raven, Na Gradu 1, Ptuj* ☎ *02/748–0360* 🌐 *pmpo.si* 🎫 *€2.*

## Restaurants

**HiKoFi**

**$ | CAFÉ** | Small but perfectly formed, HiKoFi is the best of Maribor's roster of modern coffee shops. The decor bridges the divide between minimalism and homeliness, while various brews are on offer, covering everything from standard flavors to fruity notes and more. **Known for:** international coffee beans; attentive service; tasty pastries. $ *Average main: €4* ✉ *Tyrševa 13, Maribor* ☎ 🌐 *www.hikofi.eu* 🕐 *Closed Sun.*

★ **Isabella**

**$ | SLOVENIAN** | This minimalist bistro on Poštna is as perfect for a romantic dinner as it is for a quiet afternoon coffee or beer, thanks to its focus on local products no matter which menu you are looking at. Poštna is Maribor's best street for eating and drinking, and Isabella might be the best of both. **Known for:** undeniable sophistication; extensive wine list; minimalist decor. $ *Average main: €10* ✉ *Poštna 3, Maribor* ☎ *059/959–450* 🌐 *isabella-maribor.si.*

# Bovec

*35 km (22 miles) south of Kranjska Gora, 124 km (77 miles) from Ljubljana.*

Bovec is a friendly, relaxed, youth-oriented town that owes its modern existence mainly to the adventure tourism the Soča River provides. The center is filled with private travel agencies, all offering a similar array of white-water rafting, kayaking, canoeing, hydrospeeding, and canyoning trips. The Soča—by the time it reaches Bovec—is a world-class river that regularly hosts international rafting events. The leading tour operators are experienced, and the rafting trips are aimed at all experience levels. The river is at its best in spring, swelled by the melting snowcaps, but it is raftable throughout the summer. Even if you don't decide to ride, plan a walk along the Soča's banks—the emerald green or electric blue (depending on the glint of the sun) color of the water is not to be missed.

## Restaurants

**Gostišče Sovdat**

**$$ | SLOVENIAN** | This family-run inn serves grill specialties and pasta entrées. There is attractive garden seating in the back, and the lively bar is known for singalongs toward the end of the day. **Known for:** burgers with homemade fries; fresh fish; good selection of best Slovenian wines. $ *Average main: €17* ✉ *Trg Golobarskih Žrtev 24, Bovec* ☎ *031/567–567* 🌐 *www.gostiscesovdat.com/en* ⊗ *Closed Wed. and Thurs.*

**Pristava Lepena**

**$$ | SLOVENIAN | FAMILY** | Attention to healthy local food and vegetarian cuisine will quickly win over any traveler who has had their fill of pizza or mediocre meat-and-potato dishes. The picnic area is a lovely place to enjoy the primary specialty of local river fish, and the barbecue is set up for children to help prepare their meals over a campfire. **Known for:** log cabins in picturesque setting; great for vegetarians; lots of open space. $ *Average main: €20* ✉ *Lepena 2, Bovec* ☎ *070/661–326* 🌐 *pristava-lepena.com.*

**Hotel Dobra Vila**

**$$ | HOTEL | FAMILY** | Located in a restored early-20th-century telephone exchange building, the Hotel Dobra Vila truly shines. **Pros:** excellent restaurant; many quiet nooks; books everywhere. **Cons:** could feel too remote if planning a long stay; need a car to get most places; formal atmosphere. $ *Rooms from: €160* ✉ *Mala Vas 112, Bovec* ☎ *05/389–6400* 🌐 *dobra-vila-bovec.si* *11 rooms* *Free Breakfast.*

★ **Hotel Sanje Ob Soči**

**$ | HOTEL | FAMILY** | Family-friendly to the point of featuring full-time babysitters and a mini cinema, Hotel Sanje has positioned itself well as a bright, modern, and fully equipped nature lodge for groups or individuals seeking group interaction. **Pros:** stunning views; many services; tremendous breakfast. **Cons:** difficult to find; no coatracks in rooms; inconsistent showers. $ *Rooms from: €129* ✉ *Mala Vas 105A, Bovec* ☎ *05/389–6000* 🌐 *sanjeobsoci.com* *19 rooms* *Free Breakfast.*

★ **Thirsty River Brewing Bar and Rooms**

**BARS** | In addition to the comfortable and affordable accommodations it offers in the heart of Bovec, Thirsty River lives up to its name with some of the best beer in town. The staff is sociable, informative, and friendly, and the range of beers is fantastic. It's the perfect combination of a comfy bed and a refreshing pint. ✉ *Trg Golobarskih Žrtev 46, Bovec* ☎ *040/530–171.*

White-water rafting is not the only game in town. Bovec is an excellent base for leisurely cycling trips or more aggressive mountain-bike climbs. Private bike outfitters or the tourist information center can provide maps and advice. It's also a great base for hiking the western regions of the Triglav National Park. The map *Bovec z Okolico* is available at the tourist information center and kiosks around town; it marks out several good walks and bike trips of varying degrees of difficulty.

**Soča Rafting**

**WHITE-WATER RAFTING** | This is one of the better-known rafting and kayaking outfitters. They are also well connected to the biggest zipline park in Slovenia. Zipping between trees and over canyons is another way to embrace this region's nature on the fly. ✉ *Ledina 2, Bovec* ☎ *041/724–472* 🌐 *www.socarafting.si.*

**Sportmix**

**WHITE-WATER RAFTING** | This company offers excellent adrenaline-inducing activities on the Soča River tributaries. From canyoning to rafting via kayaking, the professional and meticulous Sportmix team will help get your excitement boosted and your blood pumping. ✉ *Trg Golobarskih Žrtev 18, Bovec* ☎ *031/871–991* 🌐 *sportmix.si.*

# Postojnska Jama and Škocjanske Jama

*44 km (27 miles) southwest of Ljubljana.*

The so-called "Queen of Caves", Postojnska Jama has been wowing visitors since it was discovered in 1818, ahead of a visit by the first Emperor of Austria-Hungary. One of the country's most visited tourist attractions (along with nearby Škocjanske Jama), the caves are home to the famous *olm*, the delightfully monikered "human fish," a species of amphibians who live in total darkness.

## Sights

**Postojnska Jama** (*Postojna Cave*)
**CAVE | FAMILY** | This is one of the largest networks of caves in the world, with 23 km (14 miles) of underground passageways. A miniature train takes you through the first 7 km (4½ miles) to reveal a succession of well-lighted rock formations. This strange underground world is home to the snake-like "human fish," on view in an aquarium in the Great Hall. Eyeless and colorless because of countless millennia of life in total darkness, these amphibians can live for up to 60 years. Temperatures average 8°C (46°F) year-round, so bring a sweater, even in summer. Tours leave every hour on the hour from May through October, six times a day in April, and three times a day from November to March. ✉ *Jamska Cesta 30, Postojna* ☎ *05/700–0100* 🌐 *www.postojnska-jama.eu* 🎫 *€29.50.*

★ **Škocjan Jama** (*Škocjanske Caves*)
**CAVE | FAMILY** | The 11 interconnected chambers that compose the Škocjan Jama stretch for almost 6 km (about 4 miles) through a dramatic subterranean landscape so unique that UNESCO has named them a World Heritage Site. The 90-minute walking tour of the two chilly main chambers—the Silent Cave and the Murmuring Cave—is otherworldly as winds swirl around the dripstone sculptures, massive sinkholes, and stalactites and stalagmites that resemble the horns of a mythical creature. The highlight is Europe's most extensive cave hall: a gorge 479 feet high, 404 feet wide, and 984 feet long, spanned by a narrow bridge lighted with footlights. Far below, the brilliant jade waters of the Reka River rush by on their underground journey. The view is nothing short of mesmerizing. ✉ *Škocjan 2, Divaca* ☎ *05/708–2110* 🌐 *www.park-skocjanske-jame.si/en* 🎫 *€22.*

# Lipica

*5 km (3 miles) west of Divača, 80 km (50 miles) southeast of Ljubljana.*

Lipica is best known as the home of the Kobilarna Lipica, the Lipica Stud Farm, where the fabled white Lipizzaner horses were first bred. The horse farm is still the primary reason most people come here, though the area has developed into a modern sports complex, with two hotels, a popular casino, an indoor pool, tennis courts, and an excellent 9-hole golf course. It makes a pleasant hassle-free base for exploring the nearby Škocjan Caves and Karst region. The horses, the large areas of green, and the facilities of the Hotel Maestoso—including a pool—are all great for families with children.

## Sights

**Kobilarna Lipica** (*Lipica Stud Farm*)
**FARM/RANCH | FAMILY** | Founded in 1580 by Austrian archduke Karl II, the Kobilarna Lipica was where the white Lipizzaners—the majestic horses of the famed Spanish Riding School in Vienna—originated. Today, the farm no longer sends its horses to Vienna; instead, it breeds them for its own performances and riding instruction. The impressive stables and grounds are open to the public. Riding classes are available, but lessons are

geared toward experienced riders and must be booked in advance. ⊠ *Lipica 5, Sežana* ☎ *05/739–1708* 🌐 *www.lipica.org* *€18.*

## Restaurants

**Gostilna Prunk**

$ | **SLOVENIAN** | Cavernous dining rooms and excellently prepared dishes provide an authentic ambience at Gostilna Prunk, a delightful surprise in the backwoods of Slovenia. The menu is simple and meat-centric (the family-owned butcher shop is attached) but enhanced by fresh ingredients and well-chosen spices—the homemade dessert plum cake pairs well with the homemade *šlivovitz* (a plum-based stiff brandy). **Known for:** family-owned butcher shop attached; traditional Slovenian cuisine and experience; reasonable prices. [$] *Average main: €12* ⊠ *Lokev 166 b, Lokev* ☎ *05/767–1102* 🌐 *www.mesarija-prunk.si* ⏲ *Closed Mon.*

# Koper

*50 km (31 miles) southwest of Lipica, 105 km (65 miles) southwest of Ljubljana.*

Today a port town surrounded by industrial suburbs, Koper is criminally underrated by visitors and locals alike. The Republic of Venice made Koper the regional capital during the 15th and 16th centuries, and the magnificent architecture of the Old Town bears witness to the spirit of those times.

The most important buildings are clustered around Titov trg, the central town square. Here stands the Cathedral, with its fine Venetian Gothic facade and bell tower dating back to 1664. Across the square, the splendid Praetor's Palace—formerly the seat of the Venetian Grand Council—combines Gothic and Renaissance styles. From the west side of Titov trg, narrow cobbled Kidričeva brings you down to the seafront.

### VISITOR INFORMATION

**CONTACTS Koper Tourist Information.** ⊠ *Titov Trg 3, Koper* ☎ *05/664–6403* 🌐 *www.koper.si.*

## Sights

**Hrastovlje Church of the Holy Trinity**

**CHURCH** | Hidden behind the 16th-century defensive walls of this small town is the tiny Romanesque Cerkev sveti Trojice (Church of the Holy Trinity). The interior is decorated with a remarkable series of frescoes, including the bizarre *Dance Macabre,* completed in 1490. The church is locked, but if you ask in the village, the locals will gladly open it for you. Alternatively, you can make arrangements to visit at the tourism booth in Koper beforehand. From Koper, take the main road toward Ljubljana, then follow the signs for Hrastovlje, 22 km (14 miles) from Koper. ⊠ *Črni Kal, Koper.*

## Restaurants

**Istrska Klet Slavček**

$ | **MEDITERRANEAN** | **FAMILY** | Creating a homey atmosphere in the center of town isn't the most straightforward task, but Istrska Klet Slavček more than pulls it off. Everything Istrian is embraced on the menu, highlighted by a tremendous seafood selection straight from the port to your plate. **Known for:** local seafood specialties; traditional Istrian atmosphere; family-friendly feel. [$] *Average main: €13* ⊠ *Župančičeva 39, Koper* ☎ *5/627–6229* 🌐 *www.facebook.com/istrskakletslavcek.*

## Nightlife

★ **Bar Cameral**

**BARS** | **FAMILY** | Just about as down-to-earth as you could find on the coast, this homage to all things independent serves delicious coffees and teas by day and an excellent range of Slovenian craft beers

Piran is the most popular spot on Slovenia's Adriatic coast.

by night. Cafés in Koper can lean on the uncreative side of things, but Cameral stands out from the pack. ✉ *Čevljarska 14, Koper* 🌐 *www.facebook.com/bar.cameral.*

# Piran

*19 km (12 miles) east of Koper, 126 km (78 miles) southeast of Ljubljana.*

The Slovenian coast's most popular spot, the medieval walled Venetian town of Piran stands compact on a small peninsula, capped by a neo-Gothic lighthouse and presided over by a hilltop Romanesque cathedral. Narrow, winding, cobbled streets lead to the main square, Trg Tartini, which in turn opens out onto a charming harbor. Historically, Piran's wealth was based on salt-making. Culturally, the town is known as the birthplace of 17th-century violinist and composer Giuseppe Tartini.

If you are arriving by car, avoid the tiny lanes around the harbor and instead leave the car in the lot outside of town. The lot farthest out has the cheapest long-term rates, and a shuttle bus will then take you into town.

Piran fills to capacity in July and August, so try to arrange accommodation in advance. If you show up without a room, inquire at one of the privately run travel agencies. Along the coast, these are likely to be more helpful than the local tourist-information centers.

### VISITOR INFORMATION

**CONTACTS Piran Tourist Information.** ✉ *Trg Tartini 2, Piran* ☎ *05/673–4440* 🌐 *www.portoroz.si.*

## Sights

**Sergej Mašera Maritime Museum** (*Pomorski Muzej*)
**HISTORY MUSEUM** | **FAMILY** | This museum tells the story of Piran's connection to the sea. On display are a beautiful collection of model ships, sailors' uniforms, and shipping instruments, as well as a fascinating historical section on the

town's changing affiliations over the centuries. ✉ *Cankarjevo Nabrežje 3, Piran* ☎ *05/671–0040* 🌐 *pomorskimuzej.si* 🎫 *€5* ⏲ *Closed Mon.*

## Restaurants

Piran's waterfront is filled with romantic open-air restaurants. The quality of the food and the relatively high prices are mostly uniform. Stroll the walk and see which one appeals. Restaurants with better food at better prices can be found away from the shore, though they will not offer the same charming view.

### Caffe Neptun

$ | **CAFÉ** | **FAMILY** | Not to be confused with the restaurant of the same name, Caffe Neptun is a delightful little café located directly next to the bus station. It's a friendly spot that focuses as much on sustainability and ethics as on good coffee and a warm atmosphere. **Known for:** best coffee on the coast; gorgeous sea views; great selection of beers. $ *Average main: €5* ✉ *Dantejeva 4, Piran* ☎ *05/901–5633* 🌐 *caffeneptun.net.*

### Cafinho

$ | **CAFÉ** | **FAMILY** | The cafés and restaurants on the seafront in Piran are generally one and the same, ticking the same boxes with similar menus and offers. Cafinho stands out through its quality of service and attention to detail, not to mention its popularity with those lucky enough to call Piran home. **Known for:** seafront location; solid craft beer list; classic pub dishes. $ *Average main: €13* ✉ *Prvomajski Trg 3, Piran* ☎ *040/554–410* 🌐 *cafinho-piran.business.site.*

### Gostilna pri Mari

$$ | **SEAFOOD** | **FAMILY** | Leave the crowds of central Piran behind and walk 10 minutes out of town to this mom-and-pop restaurant and its unique fusion of Italian and Slovenian cuisine. You will find top-quality fish offered at a fair price. **Known for:** top-quality fish at a fair price; cozy family-run atmosphere; apartments also available to rent. $ *Average main: €20* ✉ *Dantejeva 17, Piran* ☎ *041/616–488* 🌐 *www.primari-piran.com* ⏲ *Closed Mon. and Tues.*

## Hotels

### Art Hotel Tartini

$$ | **HOTEL** | In a convenient location overlooking Tartini Square is this modern hotel with a historic exterior and a spacious central atrium. **Pros:** central and pleasant location; the cocktail bar has the best view in Piran; very relaxing rooms. **Cons:** rooms are rather dully decorated; expensive for what you get; can be noisy at night. $ *Rooms from: €150* ✉ *Trg Tartini 15, Piran* ☎ *05/671–1000* 🌐 *www.arthoteltartini.com* *46 rooms* 🍽 *Free Breakfast.*

### Hotel Piran

$$ | **HOTEL** | Located on a quiet patch of coastline close to the seaside restaurants, Hotel Piran is the best place to stay for an enchanting sea view. **Pros:** great views; historic atmosphere; next to the public beach. **Cons:** rooms aren't elegantly furnished; air-conditioning in only the more expensive rooms; proximity to square means evening noise. $ *Rooms from: €170* ✉ *Kidričevo Nabrežje 4, Piran* ☎ *05/666–7100* 🌐 *www.hoteli-piran.si* *103 rooms* 🍽 *Free Breakfast.*

### Vila Piranesi

$$ | **B&B/INN** | **FAMILY** | At the center of Piran's Old Town, Vila Piranesi occupies a few floors of a renovated high school and offers well-priced modern apartments with fully functional kitchenettes. **Pros:** good for families and groups; modern but not flashy; brilliant location. **Cons:** no parking; lots of stairs; horrible Wi-Fi. $ *Rooms from: €200* ✉ *Kidričevo Nabrežje 4, Piran* ☎ *040/779–935* 🌐 *www.vilapiranesi.com* *17 rooms* 🍽 *No Meals.*

# Index

## A



## B

## C

## D



## E



## F



## G

# Photo Credits

**Front Cover:** Anita_Bonita/Getty Images [**Descr.**: the small beautiful Podrace beach in Brela through pine trees, Makarska Riviera, Croatia]. **Back cover, from left to right:** Dreamer4787/Shutterstock. Nikpal/iStockphoto. Dreamer4787/iStockphoto. **Spine:** Sergii Figurnyi/Shutterstock. **Interior, from left to right:** Ivica Drusany/Shutterstock (1). Xbrchx/Shutterstock (2-3). **Chapter 1: Experience Croatia:** Xbrchx/Dreamstime (6-7). Anton_Ivanov/Shutterstock (8-9). Alexey Stiop/Shutterstock (9). Dziewul/Dreamstime (9). K13 Art/Shutterstock (10). Veronika Kovalenko/Shutterstock (10). Mpaniti/Shutterstock (10). Zdravko T/Shutterstock (10). Jaz1_483959076/iStockphoto (11). Subodh Agnihotri/iStockphoto (11). DavorLovincic/iStockphoto (12). Parkerphotography/Alamy (12). Visit Rijeka (12). Ilijaaa/Dreamstime (12). Xbrchx/Shutterstock (13). Travelpeter/Dreamstime (14). Ivo-biocina/Croatian National Tourist Board (14). Ilijaaa/Dreamstime (14). RomanBabakin/iStockphoto (14). Xbrchx/Shutterstock (15). Littleaom/Shutterstock (15). Zeleno/iStockphoto (20). Phant/iStockphoto (21). Pag Tourist Board (22). Mark Marcec/Shutterstock (22). Nkooume/Dreamstime (22). Zvonimir Atletic/Shutterstock (23). Ivan Tibor Grujić/Samobor Tourist Board (23). **Chapter 2: Travel Smart:** Daliu80/Dreamstime (51). **Chapter 3: Dubrovnik and Southern Dalmatia:** Cge2010/Shutterstock (53). Ihor Pasternak/Shutterstock (63). Indos82/Dreamstime (66). Birute/iStockphoto (68). RomanBabakin/iStockphoto (71). Rndmst/Dreamstime (74). Xbrchx/Shutterstock (84). Donyanedomam/Dreamstime (89). Stjepan Tafra/Shutterstock (94). Novak.Elcic/Shutterstock (99). **Chapter 4: Split and Central Dalmatia:** Emicristea/iStockphoto (101). Xbrchx/iStockphoto (111). Ilija Ascic/Shutterstock (124). Mail2355/Dreamstime (128). Xbrchx/Dreamstime (134). Xbrchx/iStockphoto (142). Xbrchx/iStockphoto (146). **Chapter 5: Zadar and Northern Dalmatia:** Xbrchx/iStockphoto (151). Borisb17/iStockphoto (159). Steveheap/Dreamstime (163). Mareticd/Dreamstime (168). Ilija Ascic/Shutterstock (170). Happy Window/Shutterstock (177). **Chapter 6: Kvarner Bay and the Northern Adriatic Islands:** Ilijaaa/Dreamstime (179). Iascic/iStockphoto (187). Joppi/Shutterstock (191). Ivica Pavicic/iStockphoto (195). Xbrchx/iStockphoto (198). Mislaw/Shutterstock (203). I love taking photos and i think that is a really great opportunity for me to share them/iStockphoto (204). Sebestyenzoltan/Dreamstime (206). Xbrchx/Dreamstime (211). Deymos/Dreamstime (217). **Chapter 7: Istria:** Xbrchx/Dreamstime (221). Electropower/Dreamstime (231). Xbrchx/Shutterstock (232). Epolischuk/Dreamstime (239). Goran234/Dreamstime (240). Sjankauskas/Dreamstime (249). Xbrchx/Shutterstock (254). Xbrchx/Shutterstock (258). **Chapter 8: Zagreb and Inland Croatia:** Dreamer4787/iStockphoto (265). Paulprescott/Dreamstime (278). Zdravko Troha/iStockphoto (281). Zdravko Troha/iStockphoto (282). Davor Djopar/Shutterstock (294). Mislaw/Shutterstock (299). Erix2005/Dreamstime (301). Ilija Ascic/Shutterstock (307). Rognar/Dreamstime (312-313). **Chapter 9: Slavonia:** Ilijaaa/Dreamstime (317). Tcerovski/Dreamstime (326). Ilija Ascic/Shutterstock (333). Tokar/Shutterstock (336). **Chapter 10: Montenegro:** Olga355/iStockphoto (341). MichałBogacz/iStockphoto (350). Nightman1965/Shutterstock (354). **Chapter 11: Slovenia:** Bhirling/Dreamstime (357). Georgios Tsichlis/Shutterstock (366). S-F/Shutterstock (372). Gasparij/Dreamstime (378). Renedreuse/Dreamstime (381). RAndrei/Shutterstock (389). **About Our Writers:** All photos are courtesy of the writers.

*Every effort has been made to trace the copyright holders, and we apologize in advance for any accidental errors. We would be happy to apply the corrections in the following edition of this publication.

# Fodor's ESSENTIAL CROATIA

**Publisher:** Stephen Horowitz, *General Manager*

**Editorial:** Douglas Stallings, *Editorial Director;* Jill Fergus, Amanda Sadlowski, *Senior Editors;* Brian Eschrich, Alexis Kelly, *Editors;* Angelique Kennedy-Chavannes, Yoojin Shin, *Associate Editors*

**Design:** Tina Malaney, *Director of Design and Production;* Jessica Gonzalez, *Senior Designer;* Jaimee Shaye, *Graphic Design Associate*

**Production:** Jennifer DePrima, *Editorial Production Manager;* Elyse Rozelle, *Senior Production Editor;* Monica White, *Production Editor*

**Maps:** Rebecca Baer, *Senior Map Editor;* David Lindroth, Mark Stroud (Moon Street Cartography), *Cartographers*

**Photography:** Viviane Teles, *Director of Photography;* Namrata Aggarwal, Neha Gupta, Payal Gupta, Ashok Kumar, *Photo Editors;* Jade Rodgers, *Photo Production Intern*

**Business and Operations:** Chuck Hoover, *Chief Marketing Officer;* Robert Ames, *Group General Manager*

**Public Relations and Marketing:** Joe Ewaskiw, *Senior Director of Communications and Public Relations*

**Fodors.com:** Jeremy Tarr, *Editorial Director;* Rachael Levitt, *Managing Editor*

**Technology:** Jon Atkinson, *Executive Director of Technology;* Rudresh Teotia, *Associate Director of Technology;* Alison Lieu, *Project Manager*

**Writers:** John Bills, Andrea MacDonald, Melissa Paul, Lara Rasin

**Editors:** Amanda Sadlowski, Linda Cabasin

**Production Editor:** Jennifer DePrima



3rd Edition

ISBN 978-1-64097-680-1

ISSN 2574-352X



**SPECIAL SALES**

This book is available at special discounts for bulk purchases for sales promotions or premiums. For more information, e-mail SpecialMarkets@fodors.com.

PRINTED IN CHINA

10 9 8 7 6 5 4 3 2 1

# About Our Writers

**John Bills** is an independent author, travel writer, and amateur darts player from the small nation of Wales. The majority of his adult life has been spent traipsing across the former Yugoslavia, writing doe-eyed love letters to everywhere from Belgrade to Bloke. He has written a variety of decidedly non-academic books about the region, covering history, travel, and more, all of which are available at 🌐 *www.johnbills.com*. He updated the Zadar and Northern Dalmatia, Montenegro, and Slovenia chapters this edition.

Within 10 minutes of her first arrival in Croatia **Andrea MacDonald**, mesmerized by the stunning old architecture and gorgeous locals, decided to rip up her return ticket and stay. She has since worked at a hostel in Istria learning the proper way to fold bedsheets, spent two summers guiding boat tours around the Dalmatian islands, and wrote a master's thesis about her travels around this wonderfully surprising country. These days, she divides her time between Croatia and her native Canada, leading tour groups around Europe and searching the rest of the world for a sea as beautiful as the Adriatic. For this edition, she updated the Experience, Travel Smart, Dubrovnik and Southern Dalmatia, and Slavonia chapters.

Raised in Southern California, **Melissa Paul** was born craving adventure and kept traveling east to find it. From the mountains of Arizona to the big cities of New York and Philadelphia, Melissa finally managed to get all the way to Croatia, first landing on the island of Krk before falling in love with the hilltop artist town of Labin in Istria. In the six years she's called Croatia home, Melissa has renovated a 500-year-old stone house, jumped off cliffs into the aqua blue waters of the Adriatic Sea, and learned the benefits of slowing down to enjoy the beauty and simplicity of everyday life in Croatia. For this edition, she updated the Istria and Kvarner Bay chapters.

Born and raised in the United States, **Lara Rasin** is a third-culture kid whose family is originally from Croatia. Growing up, she spent every summer in Croatia, diving for seashells and squid-fishing with her grandfather off the coast of his native Drage in Northern Dalmatia and running through the meadows of her grandmother's native Slavonski Brod in Slavonia. After graduating high school, she decided to pack up her bags and move to Croatia where she has since lived, worked, learned, and written in almost all of its one-of-a-kind regions (between a few international sojourns). So far, Croatia has enriched her with love and friendship, several academic degrees, and, last but certainly not least, an addiction to delicious *štrukli*. She updated the Split and Central Dalmatia and Zagreb and Inland Croatia chapters this edition.